*Hitler Strikes North*

# HITLER STRIKES NORTH

*The Nazi Invasion of Norway and
Denmark, 9 April 1940*

JACK GREENE

AND

ALESSANDRO MASSIGNANI

FRONTLINE BOOKS, LONDON

*This book is dedicated to long-time gaming and history buddies*
*Larry Hoffman, Dana Lombardy and Harry Rowland*

*and to the memory of Giovanni Ingellis*

*Hitler Strikes North: The Nazi Invasion of Norway and Denmark, 9 April 1940*
This edition published in 2013 by Frontline Books,
an imprint of Pen & Sword Books Ltd,
47 Church Street, Barnsley, S. Yorkshire, S70 2AS
www.frontline-books.com

Copyright © Jack Greene and Alessandro Massignani, 2013

The right of Jack Greene and Alessandro Massignani to be identified as the authors of this
work has been asserted by them in accordance with the Copyright, Designs and Patents
Act 1988.

ISBN: 978-1-84832-661-3

CIP data records for this title are available from the British Library

For more information on our books, please visit
www.frontline-books.com, email info@frontline-books.com
or write to us at the above address.

Printed and bound by CPI Group (UK) Ltd, Croydon, CR0 4YY [TBC]

Typeset in 10/12.4 point Minion Pro by JCS Publishing Services Ltd,
www.jcs-publishing.co.uk

# Contents

# Maps and Illustrations

## Plates

1 The Norwegian minelayer *Olav Tryggvason* (Author's collection)
2 The elderly armoured coast defence ship *Eidsvoll* (Author's collection)
3 The destroyer HMS *Glowworm* (IWM: HW83)
4 One of the German 'K' class light cruisers (Author's collection)
5 A British Skua dive-bomber (Dave Isby collection)
6 The German pocket-battleship *Lützow* (Author's collection)
7 The *Bruno Heinemann*, a typical German destroyer (Author's collection)
8 The German torpedo-boat *Albatros* (Author's collection)
9 An S-boat used by the Germans for the invasion of southern Norway (Dave Isby collection)
10 One of the three 283mm guns at Fort Oscarsborg (Author's collection)
11 Side view of one of Fort Oscarsborg's gun emplacements (Author's collection)
12 Head-on view of one of the 283mm Krupp guns at Fort Oscarsborg (Author's collection)
13 Close-up of the torpedo rack at Fort Oscarsborg (Author's collection)
14 The torpedo rack in the raised position (Author's collection)

# Introduction

> History is not a schoolmistress ... She is a prison matron who punishes for unlearned lessons.
>
> Russian historian Vasily Klyutchevsky[1]

This book is a combat history of one of the most important battles of the twentieth century. The focus is the events leading up to the invasion of the Nordic nations of Norway and Denmark and the critical events on and immediately after 9 April. These actions merit close study and have lessons to teach us today. For the people of Denmark and Norway, 9 April was the equivalent of Pearl Harbor. It also mirrors 11 September 2001 to the people of the USA. After the war the Norwegian public vowed 'Never another 9 April'.[2]

It is also an excellent example of where deterrence failed. It was unsuccessful because the military deterrence employed was grossly inadequate and both nations made poor choices leading up to 9 April. Norway and Denmark had witnessed what happened to Belgium in the First World War. Belgium had been fought over, mostly occupied and suffered tremendous loss of life and treasure.[3] The political leadership of Norway and Denmark wanted to avoid *at any cost* such a fate for their small nations when the Second World War broke out and so their final bill would be invasion and occupation. It sharply contrasted with what both nations had successfully done to avoid invasion in the First World War and what the Swiss did in both wars. The leaders looked at Belgium's fate, and partly wrapped up in their political worldview, they drew the wrong conclusions.

This book aims to reconstruct the battles and reconcile the various sources to give a clear and accurate picture of what took place leading up to and in the decisive opening of the campaign. The operations in Norway and Denmark were crucial in four ways. First, it assured Germany a steady supply of high-quality iron ore to fuel its war industries. This was in addition to the timber, foodstuffs and other products of Denmark and Norway provided to the German war effort. This was to be a modern era resource war. To forestall any Allied attempt to keep that key resource, iron ore, from Germany's war machine, Hitler fought it as a *preventive* war. Be it Soviet oil or Swedish iron ore, the desire to keep key assets available to one side or to deny another side vital resources directed much of the events in 1939–40. Wars for a commodity, be it ore, oil, food or water, have become more common and will continue to be so in the twenty-first century.

Second, it allowed Germany's navy and air force bases to range far out into the North Atlantic and Norwegian Seas. This ability imposed a heavy price tag on

Allied convoys both in the Atlantic and those journeying to the Soviet Union via the White Sea.

Third, the Allied disaster in Norway would lead to the collapse of the Chamberlain government in Great Britain on 10 May, to be replaced by Winston Churchill as Prime Minister, who would prove a resourceful and successful war leader.

Finally, it tied down important German war resources and men in defending this far-flung German outpost whose future was incorporation into the Greater Reich. There were 7 divisions alone deployed in Norway at the end of the war along with naval, coastal artillery, police, and air personnel, representing a total of 372,000 men effectively lost to the German war effort.[4]

The campaign's most important impact is one that echoes down the corridors of history well into this century and beyond. It was the first full-scale '*joint*' campaign, one that as the twenty-first century unfolds will occur many times. Eric Grove's definition is, '[Joint warfare] emanates from forces drawn from all three Services, both sea and land based, supported by national and commercial resources, exercising influence over the sea, land and air environments.'[5] James S. Corum has written that joint operations are 'more complicated than operations run by a single service . . . Command and control of large forces, a difficult enough task in even the simplest operation, is again complicated when three services are involved in the fighting [as they] have incompatible communications and very different priorities on transmitting information and collecting intelligence data.'[6] Sam Tangredi wrote, 'The artificial separation of military operations into the domains of land, air, sea (and now space and cyberspace), each presumably dominated by a particular service, no longer makes strategic sense.'[7] As Geirr Haarr has written on the campaign, 'For the first time ever, air force, army and navy operated intimately together with interlinked tasks and objectives.'[8] It was this campaign that established on an operational level what could occur with an inferior navy using the sea to *land* forces in a potentially overwhelmingly hostile environment and had a great impact at the strategic level on the course of the war. Coloured as it was with strategic surprise on a grand scale, it warrants close analysis.

The German conduct of this campaign would prove to be brilliant and serves as a template for conducting joint operations, while the Allies would discover their shortcomings in this new combat environment. In the modern age the joint campaign has added space and cyber-warfare to the formula, but the Norwegian campaign remains an important lesson in understanding modern combat.

As the first 'joint' land-sea-air campaign and the use of 'Vertical Envelopment' one can learn certain lessons that apply today. While there had been some minor co-ordination of the various military arms in amphibious operations in China by Japan, or some of the small colonial campaigns, nothing had been attempted before on a national scale like this operation. Such a campaign is more complex by nature as a joint campaign requires various services to *co-ordinate* their efforts by extraordinary efforts at communicating. For example, in the 1939 Polish campaign the

Luftwaffe bombed forward elements of the German army on many occasions. By the time of the Norway campaign this issue had been largely resolved.[9]

The focus here is primarily on the role of Norway, as the attack on Denmark met virtually no resistance. Denmark was a convenient stepping stone to Norway. Denmark is treated as a separate subject in Chapter 7, but both nations are discussed where their actions are intertwined.

Was the battle for Norway over by the middle of April 1940? Though the fighting would continue until early June, the decisive phase of this campaign took place in the detailed preparations for the invasion and in the days immediately following. The defeat in Norway in many ways was achieved on 9 April 1940 by the capture of *every* major coastal city and most of the key bases. The positive results of the new combination of elements in this type of operation lay in the seizure of every major airbase, especially the modern fields at Ålborg in Denmark, Fornebu at Oslo and Sola at Stavanger. For Norway, this was an invasion from the sea that once underway was virtually impossible to defeat. Hitler would later comment, 'the destruction of the enemy's landing is the sole decisive factor in the whole conduct of the war . . '.[10] George Patton noted on the eve of the invasion of Sicily, 'In landing operations, retreat is impossible.'[11] It was on these strategic beachheads that the German invasion needed to be defeated and it simply was not.

The only other hope for the Allies would be a rapid, strong and co-ordinated effort to support the Norwegians, and as will be seen, this did not take place. This Allied failure and the German overland link-up with their isolated garrison in Trondheim resulted in the battle being concluded in southern and central Norway – and that meant the campaign had been won. The bulk of the Norwegian population was here and as May dawned the world would see the Allies had withdrawn and the last fighting remnants of Norwegian troops surrendering in south and central Norway.

Intelligence played a crucial role. From the gathering of details about weather, tides and troop dispositions, it expanded to gaining intelligence on enemy actions. The volume of intelligence was quite substantial and is discussed several times in this book. Numerous reports of heavy shipping traffic first gathering in and then exiting from German Baltic ports was not properly interpreted, as it *should have*, at the top levels of Allied and neutral governments. The multiple failures of Allied intelligence were truly monumental and breathtaking. Surprise was almost total. Much like 11 September 2001, there was *too* much background detail and this prevented recognition of the pertinent information.

Additionally, Norway and the Allies grievously breached a fundamental rule of intelligence in 1939–40. Never assume what the enemy may or may not do – what the enemy is *capable of doing* should be one of the pillars of a nation's defence policy.[12]

The campaign was also heavily coloured by the prewar policies of Denmark and Norway, and this is often overlooked. The Great Depression racked both nations leaving them with unemployment rates hovering near 20 per cent. This would lead in part to chronic underfunding of the military and an anaemic equipment purchasing policy. In turn, both nations, led largely by leftist coalition governments during the 1920s and 1930s, feared an army-led 'White' revolution, while in Norway the army feared a 'Red' revolution. These twin fears would feed a military unpreparedness and political decision-making process that would leave Norway weak in the face of Nazi aggression. Then as the invasion unfolded the officers of the Norwegian army and navy would have to make vital decisions quickly in an environment where often dozens or even thousands of civilians literally filled the streets inter-mixed with advancing German soldiers. This had to be carried out with little or no guidance from political and military superiors, and as a consequence their indecision or bad decisions were often pronounced. The lessons the Norwegians learned on 9 April significantly influenced their postwar actions.

This invasion will be examined at five levels. To conquer a country you need to occupy it, the old boots on the ground concept. So the first element of the Norwegian campaign is the planning to get those boots on the ground to allow for the ensuing campaign to conquer Denmark and Norway. This would be followed by exploitation of the assault and the reaction to the invasion by the Norwegians and the Allies.

The leading element, and the second dimension of this three-dimensional campaign, was the air force, primarily the German Luftwaffe. Early in this new war many lessons were to be learned and relearned with this relatively new arm.

The navy is the third dimension in this campaign, and is divided it into three components. The 'blue-water' or 'power-projection' of naval forces was an element in the campaign and also a success for Germany. Germany had to transport its army over the open seas to Norway with its naval forces facing overwhelming Allied naval forces. After the campaign both its surface and subsurface navy would, by using Norwegian bases, be able to project into the Atlantic power that threatened Britain and to a lesser degree the Soviet Union. It was also a dimension that had its main strength on the surface, but also had a subsurface element, and marginally utilised ship-borne aircraft.

The fourth level and the second naval component would include much of the German naval movement, and later Allied, that would be in the 'green-water' or 'coastal defence' zone of the waters of Norway and Denmark – now best known as 'littoral' waters. Many of the Allied successes with submarines would be achieved in these waters. It is a harbinger of the future that similar waters may bring successes to many of the small diesel submarines being built today with the Air Independent Propulsion (AIP) systems that make them difficult to track, and capable of lying on the shallow ocean bottom waiting to strike. Today, on the surface are small stealth warships of high speed capable of striking with gun, torpedo or missile, such as the modern Norwegian *Skjold*[13] and the new American Littoral Combat Ships. When fighting close to an enemy shore, distances are shorter, reaction times are much faster and the 'fog of war' can be quite thick. The operational tempo of battle is rapid. The gun plays a key role here, as well as mines and torpedoes.[14]

The final naval component of general naval activity would be 'brown-water' or 'inland waterways'. Fjord naval actions would transpire and the ability of German naval forces to aid the German army with naval transport in fjords would play an important role. It is also in these waters, along with the green-water, that naval guerrilla actions took place and will most likely take place in the future.[15]

The planning and implementation of the audacious German plan was one of trying to win immediately and completely. It was an early version of the 'shock and awe' tactics that were employed somewhat successfully in the Iraq War of 2003. In Denmark it succeeded in conquering a country in a matter of 3 hours. In Norway it almost succeeded in 24 hours but would lead to a bitter struggle lasting over several weeks.

* * *

There have been some excellent recent additions to the bibliography of the Norwegian campaigns. Retired from the RN, Graham Rhys-Jones has written the helpful and insightful *Churchill and the Norway Campaign* (2008). This contributes much to the literature on Norway. Retired American colonel of Norwegian descent Henrik O. Lunde's *Hitler's Pre-emptive War: The Battle for Norway, 1940* (2009) is also a valuable addition. Working in the relevant languages, he has focused on the Narvik portion of the campaign and is particularly good on the capture of Narvik and the role of Norwegian Colonel Sundlo during this action.

The definitive naval study of this campaign is the mammoth and well-illustrated two-volume work from Geirr Haarr, *The German Invasion of Norway: April 1940* (2009) and its companion, *The Battle for Norway: April–June 1940* (2010). Brilliant and rich in detail, these books from an amateur historian are outstanding. For any one who wants greater detail than is offered here, these books are worthy of attention.

It has been suggested that the Norwegians have produced more books on the invasion and occupation of their country per capita then any nation during the war. While difficult to prove, there is certainly a plethora of Norwegian histories of the fighting, some written and published as early as 1940.[16]

* * *

We would like to thank Andrew Smith, whom, as always, has been a comrade in arms on our writing journeys, joining us in April 2004 as we toured Denmark's and Norway's battlefields. He was truly our 'Chief-of-Staff' in helping to organise much of our trip.

Also of great help throughout this project has been Geirr Haarr. Dave Isby and Keith Jacobs kindly lent us some important articles. Thanks to Major Jurgen Koll and his helpful staff at the Copenhagen Citadel and to Sverre J. Svendsen, curator at Nordmøre Museum, Kristiansund and Kurt Monsen and his now defunct sponsorship of the Norway in World War II forum on the net. Also of great value is both http://nuav.rforum.biz/ and http://hem.fyristorg.com/robertm/norge/ norway_reference.html. Also helpful was Gert Laursen and his website http:// www.navalhistory.dk/indexUS.htm and also Søren Nørby who contributed much on the Danish navy.

Professor Paolo Ferrari (Undine University), Larry Hoffman, Mark C. Jones, Harry Rowland, Professor Spencer Tucker and Professor Alessandro Fontana di Valsalina (Trieste University) were kind enough to read the manuscript and offer useful suggestions. Vincent P. O'Hara read some of the manuscript and was most helpful.

Dr Leo Niehorster and his incredible order-of-battle site must be mentioned, http://niehorster.orbat.com/500_eto/_40-04_scandinavia.html. Websites featuring interesting photographs are http://www.mil.no/sjo/start/fakta/historie/dagfordag/ apr/#6, http://www.festningsverk.no/index.htm and http://krigsbilder.net/copper mine/index.php.

A special thanks to Lieutenant Colonel (ret.) Arvid Carlsen, the curator at Oscarsborg Fortress and Museum for his great help. At one point, after much correspondence and enthusiasm, it was Jon 'Silver Fox' Selfoss who gained us entrance to the Kvem Museum, which is usually closed in April. Tore Eggan was helpful in supplying photographs and explanations, as was Henrik Lundbak of the Museum of Danish Resistance, 1940–45. Arild Bergstrøm, Simon Orchard, Susan Cross and Wayne 'Three is Tops' Lidbeck were were kind enough to clear up some points.

As always, Carolyn Mueller and the fine staff at the Los Osos Library along with the staff of Dr Friedrich Tessmann at the provincial library in Bolzano went the extra step in obtaining materials for this book.

Jack Greene
Paso Robles, California

Alessandro Massignani
Valdagno, Vicenza

All times are Danish/Norwegian time zones and are an hour earlier than Berlin time.

## Warship Abbreviations

Norwegian and Danish descriptions of warships are used. Most Norwegian warship types were smaller than the contemporaries built by the major powers.

| | |
|---|---|
| **AUX** | Auxiliary |
| **BB** | Battleship[17] |
| **BC** | Battlecruiser |
| **CA** | Heavy Cruiser |
| **CL** | Light Cruiser |
| **DD** | Destroyer |
| **TB** | Torpedo-boat |

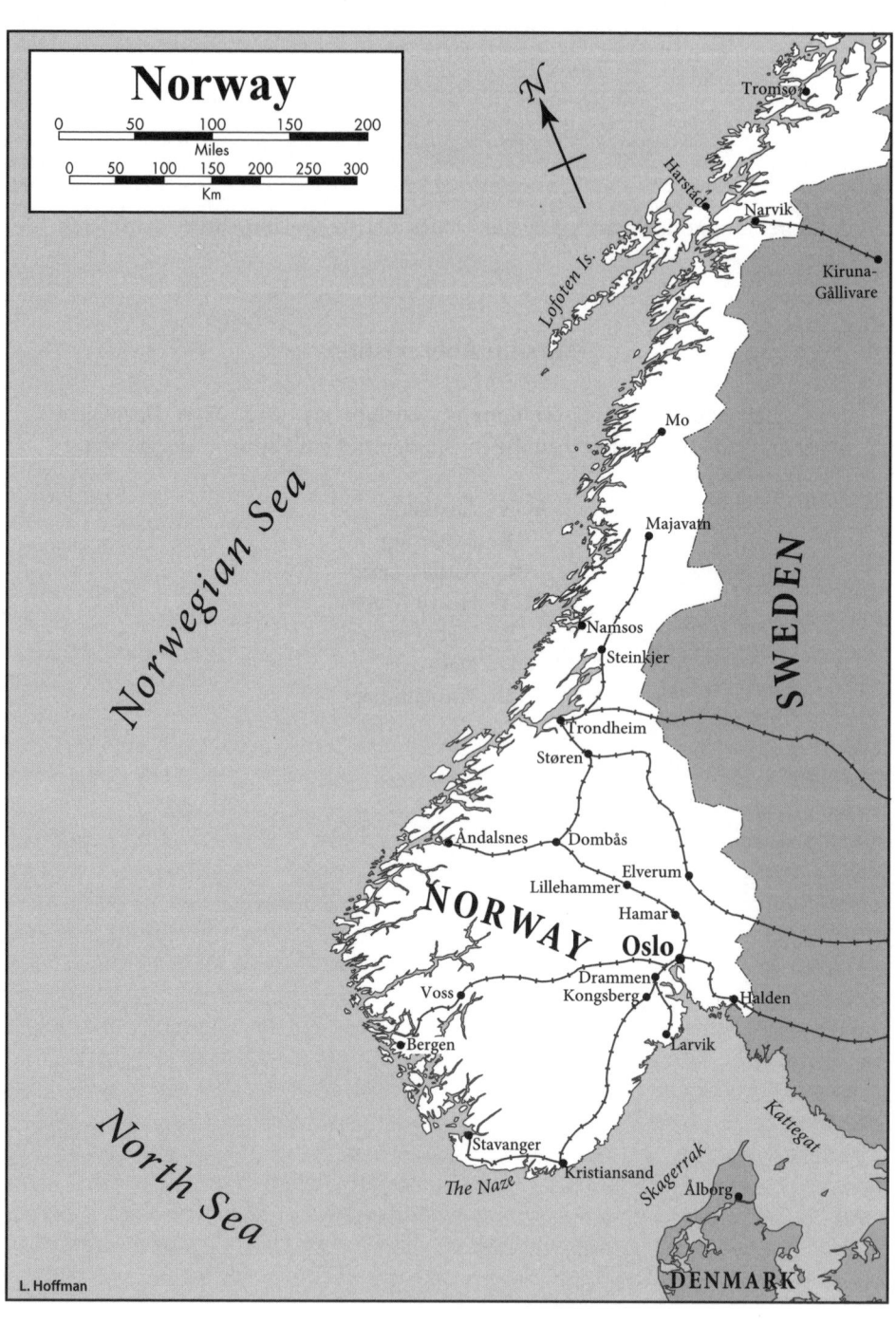

# Norway

| | | | | |
|---|---|---|---|---|
| 0 | 50 | 100 | 150 | 200 |

Miles

| | | | | | |
|---|---|---|---|---|---|
| 0 | 50 | 100 | 150 | 200 | 250 | 300 |

Km

N

Tromsø

Harstad

Narvik

Kiruna-Gällivare

Lofoten Is.

Mo

Norwegian Sea

Majavatn

SWEDEN

Namsos

Steinkjer

Trondheim

Støren

Åndalsnes

Dombås

Elverum

Lillehammer

**NORWAY**

Hamar

**Oslo**

Voss

Drammen

Kongsberg

Halden

Bergen

Larvik

Stavanger

Kattegat

The Naze

Kristiansand

Skagerrak

Ålborg

North Sea

L. Hoffman

**DENMARK**

# CHAPTER 1

# *The Setting*

Churchill and Hitler put their trust in bold and unconventional operations and, because of their inadequate defence policies, the Northern countries provided for outsiders open and tempting doors for such actions.

W. M. Carlgren[1]

On 9 April 1940 Germany invaded Norway and Denmark. The German navy led this invasion, the only major amphibious operation that it would conduct in the Second World War and the first major 'joint operation' carried out in the history of the world. Its success would be a model for all joint operations that would follow into the twenty-first century.

Germany invaded primarily to protect the high-quality iron ore coming from Swedish mines, much of it transported in the winter months from the northern Norwegian ice-free port of Narvik. This resource was vital in producing the steel needed for Germany's war machine. Without it, Germany would have had to severely reduce its war production. The loss of Narvik would also cut off the smaller amount of iron ore exported to the Allies. Speeding north on the night of April 8–9, in the teeth of a violent storm, 10 destroyers of Warship Group 1 carried 2,000 troops charged with securing Narvik.

This mission was the longest of eleven missions for the German navy that night fielded against Norway and Denmark, in addition to independent German army and air force (Luftwaffe) operations. Commodore Friedrich Bonte, commander of all German destroyers, led Warship Group 1. He flew his flag on the destroyer *Wilhelm Heidkamp*. Also in the *Heidkamp* was Major General Eduard Dietl, commander of the 3rd Mountain Division.

The 3rd Mountain Division was the German army's only veteran unit in the initial invasion forces. It had seen some minor action in the Polish campaign of 1939. But this force represented only a stripped down Alpine regiment, with elements of mountain engineers and mountain signals battalions. Also boarding the destroyers were a few German marine coast defence personnel, some Luftwaffe AA personnel and several naval communication staffers. Some of these men would be lost overboard in the heaving seas and most arrived very seasick. Valuable military equipment that was not properly lashed down was also damaged or lost in the gale-force winds and seas battering the German destroyers.

Warship Group 1 reached the more southern point of Lofoten Islands off Narvik at about 23:00 on 8 April and entered the Vestfjord – the outer approach to Narvik. By midnight the force was well inside the fjord where the waters were calmer, a welcome relief to the many thoroughly seasick mountain troops.

At 03:20 on 9 April, the Norwegian patrol vessel *Kelt* reported that nine German destroyers, travelling at high speed, had passed through Vestfjord and entered the Ofot Fjord. The tenth German destroyer was straggling behind, but the German destroyers were all in Norwegian territory, steaming for the port of Narvik.

What had brought Germany, Norway and Denmark and the Allies to this point so early in the Second World War?

* * *

In 1940 Norway was a constitutional monarchy led by King Haakon VII, king since independence in 1905, with a population of some 2,964,000. It is a long, narrow country – Oslo is closer to Paris than it is to Norway's own North Cape. Bounded in the far north by a short border with Finland, Norway shares most of its border to the east with the more populous Sweden. To its south lies the Skagerrak and Denmark, while to the west are the Norwegian and North Seas. Until the eve of the Second World War, when the Soviet Union came to pose a real threat in the light of the 1939–40 Russo-Finnish War, Norway had prepared its chief military defences against Sweden.

The physical nature of Norway is important when discussing the coming campaign. Norway is a long, narrow country with the majority of its population located in the south in relatively small centres. Very mountainous with little cover, half of the land is at an elevation greater than 2,000ft. There is only one major river, the Glomma River that roughly parallels the Swedish border and empties into the Kattegat near the Swedish border. It played a very minor role in the campaign. While Norway had a vibrant maritime industry, including robust sea communications, it had inadequate and slow land connections. Only 3 per cent of Norway was under cultivation. With trees present at lower elevations, most of the Norwegian valleys held only small homes and villages.[2]

The Norwegian interior is quite mountainous with several peaks 5,000 to 6,000ft, with large glaciers. There is a large uplifted interior plateau with a depression around the Trondheim area. This plateau has many deep-cut valleys from water and glacier activity and numerous mountains. This extends toward the west where it falls into the sea. The average elevation of Norway is 1,500ft. Because Norway lies so far north, the tree line is at an altitude of 3,000 to 4,000ft.

There are three major cities in Norway. The capital and largest city is Oslo, followed by Bergen and Norway's second largest economic engine, the ancient capital of Trondheim.[3] The latter two cities were linked by rail to Oslo. Outside of Oslo most roads were narrow and unpaved.[4] The Oslo region was the heart of the nation and its primary farming and industrial centre. It was also the hub of all the railways and roads that were the transportation network for both Norway and for communications with Sweden. Trondheim lies in the centre of Norway, but north of it are sparsely populated and even more rugged lands.

Norway operated a small armaments complex centred in the town of Kongsberg, a few miles west of Oslo. Norway also manufactured and assembled some warplanes at Kjeller airfield, north-east of Oslo, and built small warships at Horten in the lower Oslofjord.

Stavanger in the south was an important city with a small seaplane base. Sola, 8 miles to the south-east, was a relatively large and modern civilian airfield that also operated military aircraft and had the distinction of being the nearest continental airbase to the vital British naval base of Scapa Flow in the Orkney Islands. Sola would be an important strategic position during the campaign.

Isolated far to the north was Narvik, set deep inside a fjord and with a population of about 10,000 people. The outer fjord was known as the Vestfjord and was protected from the west by the Lofoten Islands. Narvik was the railhead for the shipment of high-quality iron ore from Sweden during the winter months when the Baltic was frozen. Narvik's ore was shipped almost entirely within territorial waters through 'The Leads' to the hungry German war factories. The Leads is a series of numerous islands that allow ships to travel almost totally between the coastline and islands the length of Norway's western coast and importantly in wartime remain within territorial limits. This coastal route contains upwards of 150,000 rocky islands of various sizes jutting out of the sea. The British knew German merchant ships used this safe route and as one British author of that time correctly put it, 'German war vessels also had, we claimed, used that route.'[5]

The invasion of Norway came about because of this iron ore. Sweden and Germany in the course of the early part of the Second World War made a series of quota adjustments, primarily in the flow of ore from Baltic ports, which is often missed in many studies on this war. In the full course of the war Germany received significant amounts of the iron ore that was needed for its war machine from Sweden.[6]

North of Narvik lie minor ports, small coastal fishing villages and many islands, while in the Finnmark region that borders Finland there is a significant Finnish minority. At the time of the German invasion, Norway had its strongest force, the 6th Field Brigade, consisting of four mobilised infantry battalions and supporting units, located in the far north to guard against a Soviet incursion. This force had been deployed in response to the Soviet-Finnish 'Winter War' that had just concluded in March 1940.

In April Scandinavia is cold, dark and, as one moves west to east from the relatively milder coastal areas, temperatures drop and snow becomes heavier. The winter of 1939–40 was one of the coldest on record. During the campaign there was anywhere from a 6in to 3ft of snow on the ground, with more in the higher elevations and away from the coast. One British veteran of the campaign considered one March in Norway worse than when he served in Somalia, Ethiopia and Burma.[7] Thaw in central Norway does not begin until May, and lingers into June in the north. Vegetation changes to a more Arctic variety as one proceeds inland and north.

Between Trondheim and Oslo there are two major land routes, essentially long river valleys allowing north to south movement and this would shape the course of the fighting in Norway. One is the Gudbrandsdalen (or Gudbrandsdal) and the other to the northeast is Østerdalen. Both are areas of uplift, narrow valleys and difficult terrain, though the latter is more open and the valleys are not as steep. The Gudbrandsdalen goes from Dombås via Lillehammer to Oslo, while Østerdalen is from Røros through Elverum to Oslo and lies closer to the Swedish frontier. Both routes also contained the strategic railway connecting Oslo with Trondheim, rejoining together at Støren just outside Trondheim. The reader may refer to the map of Norway (see p. xvi) and the two rail lines to understand where the two important inland valleys are. Farming was a carried on in these valleys but was not extensive.[8]

This central part of Norway would define the fighting withdrawal that first the Norwegians, later joined by the British, would undertake during the month of April. In this war there were no wide fronts; instead, narrow valleys created powerful defensive positions at choke points into and out of these areas. Destroyed bridges, explosive-induced landslides and felled trees lying across the rough roads were a part of the landscape that April in those two valleys. This resulted in having only small numbers of troops at any point in combat and this, in turn, would keep the overall losses relatively light during three months of almost continuous skirmishing punctuated with some heavy fighting.

These same mountains create numerous and deep fjords, Norway's distinguishing coastal feature. Oslofjord leads to Oslo and has gentler slopes than the fjords of the west coast. The remaining fjords, with the exception of Trondheim because of the depression in which it is set, tend to be sharp, high and with deep waters. North of Bergen is Sognefjord, 136 miles long and up to 4,290ft deep, the largest and deepest. Although naval mines are one of the important defensive weapons employed by a weaker naval power, they were not extensively used in this campaign. Norway had an extensive stock of them but they were not placed until after war broke out. They are essentially shallow water weapons and the depth of the fjords made them difficult to mine.

In September 1939, Norway had the fourth largest merchant fleet in the world, including many modern tankers that would prove vital in the coming war years. In mid-November, Norway had chartered its largest merchant ships to Great Britain, which while financially rewarding had angered Germany. Britain also received substantial shipments of iron ore and nitrates from Norway and Sweden.

Norway also supplied domestically produced iron ore (only about one-tenth of Swedish production and not of high quality), wood pulp, fish (especially herring) and whale oil to Germany. Beginning in 1936 Germany had increased the importation of these items to stockpile them in the event of war. By establishing a benchmark for the importation of these items, the increase would be viewed when the war came as 'normal trade' and therefore technically could not be interfered with by the Allies in a blockade. Norway was also a producer of aluminum made from bauxite from Yugoslavia, as well as some minor amounts of other important minerals.[9]

But it was the Swedish iron ore shipped through the Norwegian port of Narvik that was the issue driving Germany and the Allies towards war over Norway.

\* \* \*

Early in the war the Allies wanted to hurt Germany's war economy on two fronts. One was to try to deprive it of oil, primarily from the Romanian fields, and the other was to cut or completely curtail the supply of Swedish iron ore. One of Britain's first actions with the outbreak of war was to prepare for coming to the aid of Norway if it was invaded, and after the outbreak of the Winter War between Finland and the Soviet Union, plans were developed to aid Finland and secure the Swedish ore fields (and the route through Narvik) at the same time. Cutting off its supply of iron ore was viewed as a potentially powerful blow against Germany's industrial machine.

When it came to the sinews of war both Great Britain and Germany had a benefit of economy of scale. As major powers they had in the interwar period invested in defence to a degree that could not be matched by tiny powers such as Norway. These two great powers possessed communications and intelligence services that dwarfed those of Norway.[10]

As early as a week before the outbreak of war the British Foreign Office was making enquiries about the vital ore trade that Sweden maintained with Germany, part of that trade being the shipments via Narvik in northern Norway. Winston Churchill, who had become First Lord of the Admiralty on 3 September, was urging action against this supply link as early as 19 September, though actual shipments to Germany from Narvik had dropped considerably with the outbreak of war. By December Churchill recommended 'that every effort be made to cut off *all* Germany's supplies of Scandinavian ore by the end of 1940'.[11]

In October 1939 the newly promoted Grand Admiral Erich Raeder, commander of the German navy (Kriegsmarine), forcefully informed German Chancellor Adolf Hitler that Allied interference in the iron-ore trade with Scandinavia could cost Germany between 2,500,000 to 3,500,000 tons a year in iron-ore imports. Raeder would be the primary, but not the only, German leader urging Hitler to invade Norway.[12]

\* \* \*

Norway and Denmark were members of an informal arrangement known as the Oslo States, with Sweden, Finland, the Netherlands, Belgium and Luxembourg. This was in effect a small-state understanding aimed at maintaining neutrality in any war.[13] It had originated on 22 December 1930 as a trade group to battle rising tariffs on trade. Economically this arrangement gave them some clout in Europe and by March 1937 an ineffective attempt was made to increase this beyond just economic co-operation. It also gave them some prewar influence that was greater than their individual strengths, but in the coming conflict an 'understanding' was not of sufficient weight to stop Germany. Greater co-operation, especially between the Nordic states, was discussed and studied but in 1933 Norway and Sweden chose to reject closer defensive arrangements with Denmark.[14] Later, Danish reluctance to rearm seriously would inhibit a Swedish initiative for a Scandinavian entente. These small nations, with their idealism and hopes for peace, came face to face with realpolitik in 1939–40. They did not want to repeat the death, destruction and occupation that Belgium suffered in the First World War. It is ironic that the actions they took to avoid what befell Belgium in the First World War would lead in large part to their being invaded. Their experience in the Second World War was one reason the postwar left-wing governments of Norway and Denmark would quickly join the North Atlantic Treaty Organisation (NATO).

Norway had not been at war since 1814. In the early 1920s and into the early 1930s, Denmark, Norway and Sweden all made substantial cuts in their military as threats from the nearby Soviet Union and Germany receded at the end of the First World War. They eliminated entire army units; they retired warships and did not replace them; and they largely ignored their minuscule and obsolete air forces. All three countries would be mired in the worldwide economic depression of the 1930s and unemployment rates hovered at about 20 per cent and were only declining slowly on the eve of war. In 1938 Norway was still suffering unemployment at a rate of 22 per cent but with the outbreak of war that dropped to 18.3 per cent. Unemployment tended to impact on the old, young, women and rural areas the most significantly. Led by Sweden, their economies were beginning to recover in the last few years before the war.[15]

Diplomatically they were inexperienced and the Great Powers viewed them largely with indifference – except when it came to valuable bases or resources. To co-ordinate policies aimed at strict neutrality, Denmark, Norway, Sweden and Finland agreed in 1934 that their foreign ministers would meet twice a year in one of the four capitals on a rotating basis. These four, along with the soon to be independent Iceland, signed an agreement, the 'Declaration for the purpose of Similar Rules of Neutrality, with Annexes', on 27 May 1938, to adopt comparable neutrality rules and promise not to change any without informing the other signatories.[16]

By 1939 the League of Nations was politically bankrupt, though the Scandinavian states and other small nations had at one time placed great hope in that institution. The fates of China, Ethiopia, Austria, Czechoslovakia and Albania also played heavily on the small nations of Europe – nations that had been sacrificed to aggressor nations.[17]

With the German invasion of Poland on 1 September 1939, France and Britain called on all the small states to rally to their cause and help stop Nazi aggression. The Oslo States ignored this call, though many later regretted not joining with the Allies. In 1941 Norwegian foreign minister Dr Halvdan Koht explained the reason behind the Scandinavian decision to remain neutral:

There were, however, very powerful reasons for the small nations of Europe to resist the enticement to plunge into a general war, even for such high ideals. They might have the deepest sympathy with Great Britain and France, not to mention unhappy Poland, as the stout defenders of national independence and international security . . . [but] they had learnt to be suspicious about the kind of considerations that were apt to influence the acts of all Great Powers.

Later developments have proved in the most brilliant way the unwavering firmness of the British peoples in keeping up their fight, even against great odds, for the cause of liberty and justice.[18]

On the outbreak of war Scandinavian goals were to remain neutral, avoid pressure from the British, Germans and the Soviets, and develop a degree of Nordic co-operation. The invasion of Finland by the Soviet Union on 30 November immediately called all of this into question. Sweden sent the most volunteers to aid the Finns (alongside volunteers from other nations). Some of these Nordic volunteers from Norway and Sweden were officers. Norway mobilised its 6th Field Brigade along its border with the Soviet Union.

Norway and Denmark endeavoured not to be drawn into the conflict. As will be seen, both nations would take some limited steps to defend their sovereignty, but both were unsuccessful and would suffer invasion and occupation.

CHAPTER 2

# Iron Ore and Casus Belli

If the mines of Lapland had ceased working, the blast furnaces of the Ruhr would have shut down too.

Rolf Karlbom[1]

The immediate cause of the attack on Norway by Germany, using Denmark as a stepping stone to support the main effort, was the perceived Allied threat to Swedish iron-ore supplies shipped to Germany. On 2 November 1934 Admiral Erich Raeder had a conversation with Hitler and *Generalfeldmarschall* (Field Marshal) Hermann Göring, commander of the Luftwaffe, in which Hitler said that an expansion of the German navy was required to 'protect the iron ore shipments from Scandinavia.'[2]

If Germany was deprived of vital industrial materials by a naval blockade combined with military action as in the First World War, German factories could be starved of resources. The two vital raw materials for Germany's war machine were oil and iron ore. Oil involved Romania and the Soviet Union but iron ore meant Sweden.

The initial British and French perception of winning the war with Germany revolved around raw materials. German émigré industrialist Fritz Thyssen reported early in the war to the French Intelligence Service that, 'Cut off the iron ore route and you will see that Hitler will be obliged to capitulate.'[3] Hitler's fear of losing Swedish iron ore was to become an important factor in strategic decision-making for both sides in the opening months of the war.

There were iron-ore deposits in central Sweden west of Stockholm, but these mines had only limited reserves and their production rate and the quality of the ore was average. Some of the best and largest fields in the world were the Kiruna-Gällivare fields located in northern Sweden – about halfway between the Norwegian border and the Baltic coast of Sweden. The iron ore was very pure and had been mined extensively for decades. The ore's purity reduced production costs by 10 per cent. During the summer, ore trade in the protected waters of the Baltic Sea was relatively easy. Most was shipped from the Swedish port of Luleå near Kiruna-Gällivare. About one-fifth of Sweden's total iron-ore trade with Germany passed through the southern Swedish port of Oxelösund, which could operate year round depending on ice conditions. Costs were exorbitant to transport ore by land south to Oxelösund and what was shipped came from smaller, less-valuable nearby ore fields. The importance of Narvik grew during the winter, when much of the Baltic was frozen. With the deep cold of the 1939–40 winter, however, even Oxelösund was closed.[4]

In winter, therefore, the bulk of the high-grade ore had to be transported across Norway to the port of Narvik on the most northerly railway in the world. Completed in 1902, this line connected Narvik with the Kiruna-Gällivare fields as well as the Swedish port of Luleå. The ore was then shipped by sea south through The Leads to Germany. Stopping this trade would be a significant blow to the German war industries, but not as severe as is sometimes portrayed. In the autumn of 1939 the British Ministry of Economic Warfare determined that Germany had 2 million tons of iron ore on hand and required 750,000 tons a month to run its war factories. Still, cutting off the Swedish ore could be an important step forward for the Allies early in the war.[5]

In 1938 Germany had imported a total of 22 million tons of ore, of which about 9 million tons came from Sweden. In addition, Norway supplied 1 to 2 million tons of poorer quality iron ore. From Narvik by sea to Germany flowed 5 million tons of ore in 1937 and 4.8 million in 1938. In 1940 Germany expected to ship via Narvik (and a much smaller amount from Kirkenes farther north) 1.2 million tons of iron ore and 350,000 tons of additional minerals. Before the war Germany had absorbed Austria and Czechoslovakia's iron-ore production into her economy. Additionally, on the eve and in the opening months of the war German domestic iron-ore production increased substantially. But Germany's expanding war industry demanded more iron ore than ever before.[6]

Hitler was aware that Norway could not defend Narvik and its winter ore route from an enemy attack, and he thought that any nations allied against Germany would eventually strike at the homeland by denying this necessary supply route. Further, Hitler was concerned that the Swedish ore mines might be seized or destroyed by the Allies. In a conference with Hitler on 30 December 1939, Raeder offered the opinion that 'serious resistance in Norway, and probably also Sweden, is not to be expected'.[7]

This view was based in part on the pacifist leanings of these countries in the interwar period. From this point forward Raeder was fixed in the belief that the Allies would occupy Norway. The War Diary of the German Naval War Staff noted on 13 January 1940, 'The Chief of the Naval Staff [Raeder] is still firmly convinced that England intends to occupy Norway in the near future in order to cut off completely all exports from the Norwegian-Swedish area to Germany and to prevent the latter from making use of Norwegian bases.'[8] Intelligence reports speculated that at a minimum the Allies would take military action against Narvik and at a maximum against all Norway and Sweden. In the event, the German memorandum delivered to the Norwegian government on the morning of 9 April was clear: '[E]ven if the Royal Norwegian Government desired to take counter-measures, the German Government is convinced that the Norwegian military forces would not suffice to oppose the English and French action successfully.'[9]

For its part, the Norwegian government in 1939 recognised a different threat than the one it had faced in 1914. In the First World War it feared being caught up in a military clash between German and British sea power. One lesson supposedly learned from the war was that the British navy provided a deterrent against German sea power and therefore offered *de facto* protection for Norway.[10] At the start of the Second World War, in the view of Norwegian Foreign Minister Dr Halvdan Koht, economic violations of Norway's neutrality were now the greatest threat, chiefly in the form of a blockade that would interfere with Norway's large merchant fleet and trade in general.[11]

Norway's planned response to this threat was to practise strict neutrality and attempt to be impartial in enforcing that position. International neutrality as a recognised national condition requires a neutral nation not to aid in an armed expedition of another power at war or to allow belligerent warships to operate in its territorial waters. It does allow for trade, but if under blockade regulations, the trade with a belligerent state may not increase, but must maintain the prewar status quo. To be maintained, neutrality must be enforced, yet militarily weak Norway lacked the will to do so. Norway even failed to fully mobilise what inadequate forces it had to act as a deterrent. In its internal orders to the armed forces as part of its Neutrality Watch it was stated that if Norwegian neutrality was violated by a 'considerable superiority of force' it was not required to resist the violation.[12]

The British government was stronger than the French government in coun-selling caution with regard to Norwegian neutrality at their joint Allied council meetings as 1939 moved into 1940. Germany, however, would try to portray itself as defending Norwegian and Danish sovereignty as it ended up robbing both of them of their independence. Both the Allies and Germany faced the most 'contro-versial of all questions: was Norway *determined* to use what little she had in an all out effort to defend her neutrality against both sides?'[13]

* * *

In October 1939 at the Naval Staff Conference, the Chief-of-Staff of the *Oberkommando* (overall command) of the Kriegsmarine, Grand Admiral Raeder detailed three possible naval strategies in the war. Raeder was a veteran of the First World War and had served for part of the war as Vice Admiral Franz Hipper's Chief-of-Staff. Hipper, as commander of the German Scouting Force, had given Raeder important experience as this force saw most of the limited surface naval combat that took place, including being in action at the 1916 Battle of Jutland. Before the war he had been involved in the Imperial German navy's 'propaganda' department.[14] In the interwar period he had moved steadily up through the ranks and was placed in command of the German navy in 1928.

During the interwar years the Reichsmarine, the navy of the Weimar Republic, was known disparagingly as the 'Lilliput Kriegsmarine'. The Reichsmarine was barely able to deal with the defence of the vitally important Baltic Sea, considered only a secondary theatre. Nevertheless, the experiences of First World War at sea had entered the strategic debate and the planning for future strategy. The naval giant in German history is Grand Admiral Alfred Tirpitz who had been the naval architect of the powerful German navy before the First World War. Though largely bankrupt by the end of that disastrous war for Germany, his vision carried on in the ranks of the officer corps. In German thinking the Tirpitz strategic concept that a great power needs a great navy had remained alive.[15]

With war looming Raeder's three options were: to commit all of the country's offensive capability on land and air operations at the expense of naval operations; '*Belagerungskrieg*', or siege war, directed against Great Britain; or delay offensive operations and stay on the defensive. The second was the option he supported and would be adopted.[16]

Such an operation would involve air assets supporting surface and subsurface naval elements. Being able to operate from Norway would facilitate this campaign. On 9 October the commander of the German U-boat force, Rear Admiral Karl Dönitz, advised Raeder that Trondheim would make an ideal submarine base. (In the course of the war it would indeed become a valuable base for U-boat operations, though the as yet unconquered French bases would prove more valuable.)[17]

There were other incidents that drew Hitler's attention to Norway. Several involved the use of supply ships to refuel and replenish German surface (and later subsurface) naval warships operating against Allied merchant ships. But the earliest indicator of Allied notice was intelligence from Vice Admiral Canaris' Abwehr.[18]

One of Abwehr's earliest successes was to note in late September 1939 the Allied interest in cutting off Germany from Swedish iron ore. This was reported directly by Canaris to Admiral Raeder and Vice Admiral Rolf Carls and concerned a possible British military attack on Scandinavia.[19] Admiral Carls was commander of the *Marineoberkommando Nord*, or northern naval command, which included Norwegian waters. This intelligence probably came from a British War Cabinet meeting on 19 September at which Churchill had discussed the possibility of intervention in Norway. Admiral Alfred Saalwächter, who would command 'Naval Group West', would later say on German intelligence coups, 'Churchill is a German agent too!'[20]

On 10 October 1939 Raeder informed Hitler of the intelligence gathered from the British Cabinet meeting and proposed to Hitler that obtaining a submarine base on the Norwegian coast at Trondheim, with the help of the Russian pressure, would improve the German strategic position. Hitler was 'completely surprised' by Raeder's proposed 'assault' on Norway,[21] but told Raeder that he would consider the idea. In the coming months this seed would sprout. In the course of the next few weeks Raeder would become a driving force for the invasion of Norway, something he would later deny after the war at the Nuremberg Trials.[22]

\* \* \*

The concept of a German invasion of Norway and Denmark goes back to the First World War. Lieutenant Commander, later Vice Admiral, Wolfgang Wegener of the German navy advocated the invasion of Denmark in 1915 to permit the German fleet easier access to the Atlantic. He circulated a paper to this effect in the spring of that year, and this also recommended action against Norway to block supplies from reaching Imperial Russia via the White Sea.

Beginning in August 1916 the German navy began planning for war with Denmark. Admiral Prince Albert Heinrich, Admiral Henning von Holtzendorff and Vice Admiral Reinhard Scheer prepared 'Case J', the invasion of Denmark, which was formally adopted in May 1917. During 1916 and 1917, 'Case N' was prepared for the occupation of Norway.[23] The German army, however, strongly opposed such an invasion and both plans were abandoned.[24]

Wegener refined his thinking in *Seestrategie des Weltkreig* (Naval Strategy of the World War) published in 1929. Wegener was concerned with the problems raised during the First World War when the Imperial German navy's surface fleet played only a minor role in the war effort and had been unable to prevent the Allied blockade that led to great suffering in Germany. Wegener's book outlined an invasion of Denmark and Norway (and/or France) to resolve these issues. From naval bases in these countries, Germany could more easily attack British maritime supply lines, conduct a distant blockade of Britain, hinder or even break the Allied blockade of Germany and force a British surrender. By fighting a war limited to bases in the North and Baltic Seas, Wegener did not believe Germany could bring about a decisive result in a war with Great Britain. Wegener's views were known in professional naval circles in Germany and also in other nations, including Norway, Sweden, the Soviet Union and the USA; an Argentine edition of the book appeared in 1939. Nor did they pass unnoticed by the British Admiralty, but only in April 1939 on the brink of war.[25]

While the young officers were enthusiastic about Wegener's views, the German navy's leadership reacted negatively. Senior officers viewed Wegener as being critical of the German navy and his proposal for gaining more distant bases in France, Norway or Iceland, without giving a preference until 1941, was dismissed as unfeasible. Raeder privately called Wegener's thesis a 'potboiler', while Captain, later Admiral, Hermann Boehm commented that Wegener was 'daydreaming'.[26]

In December 1939, Wegener's son, Lieutenant Commander Edward Wegener, published an essay that again suggested seizing naval bases in Norway. He repeated and updated his father's arguments. Raeder suppressed this essay. Edward Wegener would serve on the *Admiral Hipper* during the assault on Norway.[27]

Nonetheless, the Wegener book was said to be Hitler's naval bible.[28] His naval aide, Captain Karl-Jesco von Puttkamer, had given it to him in the winter of 1938–9 and the Führer was very impressed by Wegener's arguments. The ultimate deficiency for the Nazi surface navy was its small size and inability to concentrate its most powerful units into a uniform strike force and instead would be defeated in detail in the course of the war. The invasion of Norway, while a strategic and naval success, would see much of its available strength eroded in the conflict, before newer and more powerful naval units were completed.[29]

Though Raeder appeared later to be 'the father of the Norway idea', in the 1938 manoeuvres he rejected this option as too ambitious.[30] But while openly criticising Wegener's ideas, Raeder used them in his strategic analysis, as the detailed study of Carl-Axel Gemzell demonstrates.[31] The two men clearly differed on the rationale for military action against Norway. The key difference was that Raeder favoured seizing Norway mainly to protect Germany's Swedish iron-ore supply and secondarily to develop naval bases to attack British lines of communication. The latter, the threat of northern German naval bases, was a fear the British had. The 10th Baron Strabolgi, later Labour Party Whip, said in 1940 that Germans in Narvik meant, 'they outflank our naval defence lines in the North Sea and Atlantic'.[32] Wegener's strategy of seizing bases in the Atlantic (including on the French coast) ignored such defensive concerns. As Commander Kenneth P. Hansen, writing in the *Naval War College Review*, put it, Raeder 'would actually seek permission to [invade Norway] only when convinced that Norwegian neutrality could not be relied upon to secure the iron ore supply – not in order to provoke a decisive battle, from which, Wegener assumed, the critical commodities would flow as a consequence of victory'.[33]

When the operation was carried out, Wegener thought the victory to be incomplete because Iceland and the Faeroe Islands should also have been occupied to enhance the German naval strategic position. After the successful campaign, sale of Wegener's book, which had been blocked by Raeder, was resumed in 1941 and it sold well.[34]

Then followed a series of maritime incidents and the outbreak of the Russo-Finnish Winter War.

\* \* \*

The American freighter *City of Flint* became the first American ship captured by the Germans when the pocket battleship *Deutschland* seized it on 9 October 1939, and declared its cargo contraband. The neutral *City of Flint* was carrying lubricating oil from the USA to Great Britain. A German prize crew was placed on it, along with prisoners from two other captured ships, and it was ordered to Germany. In the process of returning indirectly to Germany, Neutrality Laws were violated, the most grievous being laws that required that a belligerent ship could not make landfall if it was carrying prisoners or if it was armed (Norway allowed guns on board to be dismantled). The Norwegian government denied to the American ambassador in Oslo that they knew the location of the *Flint*.[35] The *Flint* was ordered not to stop at any Norwegian port, but on 3 November it stopped at Haugesund between Bergen and Stavanger. The Norwegians seized the *Flint* for having anchored 'without legal cause and contrary to Norwegian neutrality laws'. The American crew ably seconded the Norwegians in their seizure and helped to intern its German prize crew.[36]

The *Flint* steamed to Bergen where the vessel was given an anchorage of honour and its crew was sent packages of welcome supplies. The story of the *Flint's* seizure and release was wired around the world, but especially throughout Europe and to the USA. A local banquet for the American captain was also arranged. Hitler and the German government were displeased with the turn of events. They began to conclude that Norway was incapable of physically defending its neutrality and that it leaned toward the Allies in its neutrality. With regard to ideology, the Norwegian Labour Party dominated government tilted towards the Allies and rejected the idea of entering the war on Germany's side.[37]

On 30 November the Soviet Union invaded Finland. This sent a shock wave through the Nordic nations, primarily Norway and Sweden, which reverberated on to London and Paris. The firm Finnish resistance to the Soviet invasion would be inspiring that winter during the 'Phoney War'.

Strong anti-communist feeling in both Britain and France fuelled a desire to attack the Soviet Union and help Finland. Later, this also presented an opportunity for the Allies to seize the Swedish ore fields.

During the Soviet Winter War with Finland, both the British and the French would unofficially send war supplies as well as volunteers to Finland.[38] The Nordic nations, primarily Sweden but also Norway, would send some men and supplies to help the Finns.

The next incident involved the *Westerwald*. Part of a class of six ships, the *Westerwald* and its soon to be more famous sister ship the *Altmark* were 22,500-ton German supply ships resembling modern tankers, which had been built specifically for duty with the German navy to facilitate commerce raiding. They were designed with a maximum speed of 20.9 knots – speedy for a tanker. The ships carried all sorts of war supplies in addition to fuel, including 11in shells, torpedoes and victuals for German warships operating in the Atlantic Ocean. They were armed with three 150mm (5.9in) and four 20mm anti-aircraft guns and carried one plane with a catapult. Laid down in 1937 under the German naval budget, they had been secretly built and were not identified in naval annuals of the period. They had a complement of 133 naval ratings – not civilians – and their weapons could be concealed so as to allow for illegal 'innocent passage'.[39]

The *Westerwald* was returning from operations in the Atlantic when on 16 November it entered Norwegian coastal waters near Trondheim. Its captain, Peter Grau, was under orders not to allow his ship to be searched. Grau became upset when a Norwegian officer from a small patrol ship boarded him. The Norwegian naval officer was allowed to search the forward ship's section where he noted and asked about the racks for 150mm shells. Norwegian naval aircraft also closed to take photographs.

After some diplomatic wrangling, and with the *City of Flint* incident still fresh, Foreign Minister Koht allowed the *Westerwald* to continue on in contravention of the standing Norwegian naval orders for searches of neutral ships in defence zones near its major naval ports. The *Westerwald* arrived safely back in Germany where it would be renamed the *Nordmark*. The Norwegian navy saw the release of the *Westerwald* as a failure to defend Norwegian sovereignty and the event had the effect of lowering the navy's morale.[40]

Next a possible breach of neutrality occurred on the German side in December 1939, when the *U-38* torpedoed two British merchant ships and one British-chartered Greek merchant ship transporting iron ore near the Norwegian coast. On 14 November, the *U-38* left Wilhelmshaven under the command of Kapitänleutnant Heinrich Liebe for operations in Norway. On 3 December, the U-boat received orders to operate in the Vestfjord area near Narvik but outside the 3-mile limit of Norwegian territorial waters. On 7 December, the U-boat sank the British 4,460-ton *Thomas Walton*, on the 11th the Greek 4,708-ton *Garoufalia* and on the 13th the British 4,101-ton *Deptford*. The British believed all three ships had been sunk in Norwegian waters. After returning to base on 16 December, Captain Liebe reported heavy shipping activity off the Norwegian coast, sailing without proper escorts and that no British warships had been sighted.[41]

On 15 December the British lodged an official protest claiming that the three transports had been sunk inside Norwegian waters. Subsequent investigations by Norway could not determine if the freighters were in or only near their territorial waters, or whether mines or torpedoes had sunk the ships. Some authors believe that the *U-38* was operating inside the 3-mile limit and that at least one of the three merchant ships had been. Some consider this to be key event leading to the invasion of Norway, and, they suggest, Churchill wanted to use these losses as an excuse to seize Narvik.[42]

These unfolding events would culminate with the *Altmark* affair which decisively altered Hitler's view of Norwegian neutrality. The *Altmark* had been given secret orders to be prepared to put to sea in August 1939 and to rendezvous covertly with the German pocket battleship *Admiral Graf Spee* in the Atlantic. The *Altmark* was under the command of Captain Heinrich Dau. After several meetings with the *Graf Spee* to take on prisoners, and refuelling the battleship nine times, the *Altmark* had on board 299 British prisoners[43] from sunken merchant ships. Following the loss of the *Graf Spee* by scuttling on 17 December after the Battle of the River Plate, the *Altmark* was discovered by the Allies to be at sea. After hiding in the vast South Atlantic for several days, Captain Dau decided to return to Germany.[44]

Heading north, the disguised *Altmark* (it was renamed and repainted several times) entered Norwegian waters on 13 February north of Trondheim and was sighted by the Norwegians on the 14th. The *Altmark* was slowly steaming south towards Germany and home. According to international law, the ship could not be considered engaged in 'innocent passage' as it was known that the *Altmark* had supported the *Graf Spee* in the Atlantic; likewise, the prisoners on board should have been released when the ship entered Norwegian waters. It did dismount its AA guns to conform to neutrality rules.[45]

During three superficial searches by the Norwegians they noted to Rear Admiral Carston Tank-Nielsen, commanding the 2nd Norwegian Sea Defence District, that the ship did not carry prisoners. A month previously Tank-Nielsen had read an Oslo newspaper article that stated the *Altmark* was carrying up to 400 prisoners.[46] He issued a memorandum to the ships in his command, though not all of them received it. More importantly, when the *Altmark* entered his jurisdiction he wanted a thorough search. So he steamed out to meet her and sent his Chief-of-Staff on board. The Chief-of-Staff reported back that prisoners were likely on board. This was in part from the prisoners banging on pipes and trying to be heard during his inspection.

Tank-Nielsen decided to let the *Altmark* proceed south but informed Oslo of the situation. The commander in chief of the Norwegian navy, Rear Admiral Henry E. Diesen, was contacted. Hardly a war commander, Diesen had gained his position largely by obeying the requests of Norway's political leaders.[47] With the Norwegian government, including Foreign Minister Koht, aware that illegally held prisoners were almost certainly aboard, Diesen ordered Tank-Nielsen to 'Let the vessel pass in her capacity as a State ship. Escort.' in the hopes of avoiding any diplomatic uproar.[48]

The Norwegians, in the hope of gaining a political pass, would later deny that they were aware that prisoners were present on the *Altmark* and this would be their 'official' position for years – a classic example of political hypocrisy.[49]

Unfortunately for this plan, an Allied spy, one of a net of coast watchers run by both the British and the French, had spotted the *Altmark* near Bergen and alerted the British: '*Altmark* steaming two miles off Norwegian coast north of Bergen.' Nearby was the British light cruiser *Arethusa*, attached to Captain Philip Vian's 4th Destroyer Flotilla of five destroyers with the flagship *Cossack*. A Royal Air Force search plane was the first to locate the *Altmark,* under Norwegian escort. Part of the destroyer flotilla, split in half to join in the search, located the *Altmark* south of Egersund near the tiny Jøssing Fjord. The *Altmark* had been brought to bay. First the destroyers *Intrepid* and *Ivanhoe* tried to board the *Altmark* and the *Intrepid* actually fired a salvo over the bow of the *Altmark*, with at least one shell landing on Norwegian soil. This first attempt failed.

Constantly in touch with the British naval command, Vian now received from Churchill a set of very clear orders:

> Unless Norwegian torpedo-boat undertakes to convoy *Altmark* to Bergen with a joint Anglo-Norwegian guard on board, and a joint escort, you should board the *Altmark*, liberate her prisoners, and take possession of the ship pending further instructions. If Norwegian torpedo-boat interferes, you should warn her to stand off. If she fires upon you, you should not reply unless attack is serious, in which case you should defend yourself, using no more force than is necessary, and ceasing fire when she desists.[50]

The Norwegian escort that changed as the day advanced ended up with the commander of the 94-ton torpedo-boat *Kjell* in command of the escort. He had not read the memorandum put out by Tank-Nielsen and actually thought no prisoners were on board. Vian received two messages from Captain Dau. The first was defiant, but the second said that Dau would transfer the prisoners to Vian in German boats. This message was ignored – possibly in British eyes because the time for diplomacy was over.[51] Vian now charged ahead with forty-five men ready to board wearing steel helmets and armed with rifles and pistols. The destroyer

*Cossack* shined a searchlight to find its quarry. This was not to be a cutting-out operation with boats, but a ship-to-ship boarding reminiscent of the age of fighting sail. The escorting Norwegian ships did not interfere with the British attack, merely protesting and asking the British to leave their waters.

Soon three officers and thirty men of the boarding party were away and gained the enemy ship's deck. In the ensuing one-sided gunfight eight Germans were killed (one by jumping or falling into the icy waters) and ten were wounded. Dau deliberately grounded the ship but scuttling attempts by the Germans failed.

Then, after a pause, the 299 prisoners were freed with the stirring shout of: 'Are there any Englishmen down there?' This was answered with a loud 'YES!'

'Then come up. The Navy's here.'[52] The joy can only be imagined for the prisoners, who thought their next stop was a German prison camp. Two days later *The Times* of London would declare a 'DASHING rescue'. British announcements at the time stressed a real battle, while in reality German resistance was negligible.[53]

The Germans may not have returned fire, though one British sailor was wounded, possibly by friendly gunfire. Hitler would later say, 'No resistance, no British losses.'[54] One German ore ship blundered into the British covering force that early morning and was forced to scuttle. The *Altmark* would return to Germany on 28 March with the assistance of a German tug. Dau was relieved of command and was posted to shore duty co-ordinating German warship supply efforts.

German propaganda machines churned out pamphlets on the incident in English, French and other languages. The British were referred to as 'pirates' and 'murderers'.[55]

The Norwegian government protested to the British, but with little effect and tried to reassure the German government in turn. However, the event weighed in Germany's war calculations. What would Britain and the Allies do next? Adam R. A. Claasen would later write, 'The "*Altmark* outrage" as Hitler would later describe it, showed the British had no intention of observing Norwegian neutrality.'[56] The threat of Allied invasion, the vital iron ore required for the German war machine and the inability of the Norwegians to offer any resistance heavily influenced Hitler's decision to proceed with the invasion. The German naval attaché in Norway, Lieutenant Commander Richard Schreiber, later met with Admiral Diesen and rather bluntly pointed out 'his utter failure to comprehend the attitude of the commanders of the two Norwegian torpedo boats, who could have furnished proof, despite the odds against them, that they could not only talk assurances about neutrality but also die a hero's death for neutrality'.[57]

A fortnight later Hitler declared that an occupation of Norway 'should prevent British encroachment in Scandinavia and the Baltic; further it should guarantee our ore base in Sweden and give our Navy and Air Force a wider start-line against Britain'.[58]

The Allied reaction was interesting. France had been advocating some sort of action in Norway against the Swedish iron ore as a way to provoke Germany to attack Norway. This would open the door for the Allies to intervene where they might be able to hurt Germany's war industry. It also fitted with their strategy of engaging Germany somewhere other than in France. Churchill felt that the *Altmark* affair showed that Norway's policy of neutrality was bankrupt and that now was the time to lay mines in The Leads. Up until his adroit conduct of the *Altmark* affair Churchill had been a minority voice within the British Cabinet. That Norway could not defend its neutrality, as Hitler had noted, was also brought home to Churchill and his supporters. Chamberlain said that the Norwegians 'have put themselves hopelessly in the wrong'. The forces for Allied intervention had seen their position strengthened.[59]

Norwegian Foreign Minister Koht would later argue during the war that the *Altmark* affair had little lasting influence on events.[60] Koht also tried to defend his decisions in a diplomatic note of 21 February, in which he claimed that carrying prisoners was not in violation of Neutrality Laws and the British seizure of the *Altmark* had been illegal. He pointed out that during the Crimean War a British prize ship with Russian prisoners aboard had entered San Francisco Bay and the prisoners had not been forcibly released. The international law aspects of this case are open to argument and various positions have been defended that usually support whatever course the particular government takes at any particular time.[61] Certainly Norway could not claim any moral high ground in this poorly handled affair. Issuing 'protests', while taking no further action, would pave the way for invasion for Norway in the coming months.

One prescient Norwegian army officer who would fight on the day of the invasion, Captain Hans L'Orange, noted, 'A single shot at this point might have spared the country from the catastrophe of war. Our conduct made plain to the entire world that we were unable – or unwilling – to fulfill our obligations as a neutral state.' This was an absolutely vital point. If Norway had returned fire, or had earlier forced the release of the British prisoners, and employed a firm hand, the invasion of Norway would most likely not have occurred. A successful deterrent must have teeth and the *will* to bite. Early and decisive action, even if wielded by a feeble arm, can have an impact much greater and much wider then the actual blow.[62]

\* \* \*

Another factor in Hitler's decision to invade Norway involved the Norwegian fascist party, the *Nasjonal Samling* (National Unity, known by its initials NS) led by Major Vidkun Quisling. Quisling's role and the role of the NS will be more fully discussed in Chapter 4.

While the German invasion of Norway and Denmark was largely predicated on strategy, there was in play an element of German Nazi racial ideology. Alfred Rosenberg, who was head of foreign policy for the Nazi Party, had a fundamental role here. There was a substantial difference between his department and the German Foreign Ministry under Joachim von Ribbentrop. Rosenberg's office had more to do with the Nazi philosophy while the latter was a traditional foreign ministry. Each summer Rosenberg sponsored a meeting at Lübeck of right-wing parties from various Nordic nations. Quisling attended in the summer of 1939 and met with Rosenberg before and during the event.

As a displaced German from Estonia who had fled from Tallin to Germany in 1917, Rosenberg envisioned all the Scandinavian countries, 'the Nordic Community' as he put it, as part of a greater Germany bloc. He supported the small National Socialist parties of Scandinavia – in particular Quisling and the NS. Rosenberg and Admiral Raeder were the strongest German government supporters of Quisling and were instrumental in arranging his first meeting with Hitler on 14 December 1939.[63] Quisling along with a small group of supporters had arrived in Berlin on 10 December. Quisling and Albert Hagelin, his second-in-command, met with Alfred Rosenberg the next day. Later that day, at Rosenberg's suggestion, the two Norwegians met with Grand Admiral Erich Raeder. Raeder and Rosenberg agreed to arrange a meeting with Hitler.

They arranged a meeting on 14 December with Hitler, with a follow-up meeting with the Führer on 18 December. Hans Wilhelm Scheidt, one of Rosenberg's officials, who would play an important role in Oslo on 9 April 1940, attended the meetings. Also present was the Norwegian Baltic trader and businessman Albert Viljam Hagelin, Quisling's most important supporter. Scheidt had met both men earlier in January 1939.

During his discussions with the German leaders, Quisling mixed fact with fiction as to the situation in Norway, strongly suggesting that the 'English Party' was close to increasing support for the Allies. Quisling's German was poor and he relied upon Hagelin to do much of the translation from Norwegian. Hagelin was able to embellish the influence of Quisling and the Norwegian NS party. For example, 100,000 followers became 200,000 in the translation. There were several of these overstatements during the talks.[64] Quisling argued that German intervention with the support of the NS would bring about the 'liberation' of Norway and an alliance with Germany.[65]

Having discussed his intentions, Quisling asked Hitler directly, 'Herr Reich Chancellor, have I understood you correctly that you will help us?' To this Hitler replied, 'Yes, I will.'[66]

Quisling and Hagelin left Hitler worried about possible Allied occupation of Norway and halting of the key iron-ore trade, and with the impression that Quisling and his supporters were stronger then they actually were. As a result of these meetings Hitler ordered preparations for an invasion of Norway or possible support for Quisling's party to stage a coup against the Norwegian government. Hitler directed Major General Alfred Jodl, the chief of Keitel's operations staff, to undertake a small study on the possible occupation of Norway. This would be known initially as '*Studie Nord*' ('North Study').[67]

The idea of a Quisling-led coup received both attention and resources. The NS received in installments some 200,000DM in gold from the German National Socialist Party (NSDAP). This money was mainly used to fuel the propaganda machine of Quisling's party. Foreign financial support for dissident movements is not uncommon. The old adage of 'follow the money' has a great deal of truth to it. However, the Germans quickly came to the conclusion that idea of a NS coup was as a non-starter when Quisling's political weakness became obvious. By 20 January 1940 a possible Quisling-led coup had also been shelved; it was dead by the time of the *Altmark* affair. But it did bring about the involvement of the German navy in the fate of Quisling and the NS. Quisling's strongest supporters at Hitler's court would remain Raeder and Rosenberg. In the end, Quisling's value for the German military was mainly for the intelligence he could gather.[68]

Rosenberg's governmental department had won a round against the German Foreign Ministry. The ministry and the German ambassador to Norway, Dr Curt Bräuer, strongly argued at the time, and later, against working with Quisling, correctly viewing him as weak and ineffective.[69] For Raeder the goal of having Atlantic naval bases in Norway was quickly becoming a reality. He had discussed this idea with Hitler in the past, and now Hitler was taking a real interest in the project.

Over the coming weeks Quisling and other members of the NS were in contact with Germany and repeated warnings of a possible Allied attack and occupation. Direct German financial support, with the source of this money hidden from both public view and the majority of NS membership, now became of great help. These funds allowed Quisling to increase the print run of the *Fritt Folk* (Free People), the NS national newspaper, to 25,000 copies, with many copies targeted at the Norwegian officer corps.[70] The influx of cash also allowed for improvement both in terms of size and equipment at party offices. After the *Altmark* affair, the NS also supplied Germany with sailing information and news items related to Norwegian coastal waters. This relationship continued right up to the invasion.[71]

Hitler did not dwell too deeply on Norway and its role in the Nordic Community. But he did foresee a role in the postwar period for Norway, where that nation would be part of a greater German community and the major source of hydroelectric power for northern Europe. Finally, the left-wing governments in Denmark, Norway and Sweden were by definition enemies to the Nazi government – and were viewed by Hitler as such.[72] The German Foreign Ministry took a decidedly different view on the matter. Ribbentrop strongly argued in Berlin that Great Britain would never directly attack Norway.

At the time of the invasion and afterwards during the occupation, Germany would attempt to paint a picture that it had sent troops, planes and ships to 'protect' Denmark and Norway from Allied occupation. Germany would point to the Allied mining of Norwegian waters and planned Allied landings in Norway – landings that likely would have resulted in some limited combat between the Norwegians and the Allies – to support this claim. In any event, it would be the Germans who drew up and successfully executed the elaborate invasion plans known as '*Weserübung*'. '*Weserübung*' is literally 'Weser (River) Exercise', the Weser being a river in northern Germany. There would be a '*Nord*' (north or Norway) and '*Süd*' (South or Denmark) component to this coming invasion.[73]

# CHAPTER 3

# *Rivals*

Norway . . . was thus squeezed and threatened by both belligerents.

Nils Ørvik[1]

With the outbreak of war the export of Swedish mined iron ore from Narvik to Germany plummeted and the Allies were aware of this. Below is a table showing monthly figures for ore imported from Narvik:

| | |
|---|---|
| September 1939 | 70,418 tons |
| October | 16,286 tons |
| November | 75,383 tons |
| December | 96,948 tons |
| January 1940 | 290,232 tons |
| February | 99,391 tons |
| March | 113,957 tons |
| Total: | 762,612 tons |

This seven-month total was far less than the 4.8 million tons shipped in 1938. But shipments were on the upswing since the Allies had not immediately and forcibly cut off German shipping in Norwegian waters.[2]

Britain was pleased with the initial massive reduction in ore shipments. In a 29 September 1939 memo to the First Sea Lord Admiral Sir Dudley Pound, Winston Churchill noted:

> It must be understood that an adequate supply of Swedish iron ore is vital to Germany, and the interception or prevention of these Narvik supplies during the winter months, i.e., from October to the end of April, will greatly reduce her power of resistance. For the first three weeks of the war no iron-ore ships left Narvik owing to the reluctance of crews to sail and other causes outside our control. Should this satisfactory state of affairs continue, no special action would be demanded from the Admiralty. Furthermore, negotiations are proceeding with the Swedish Government which in themselves may effectively reduce the supplies of Scandinavian ore to Germany. Should however the supplies from Narvik to Germany start moving again, more drastic action will be needed.[3]

Sweden was under pressure from several quarters. By invading Finland the Soviets had turned Sweden's gaze to the East. Earlier, Germany had also looked to the East, concerned with the threat of the Soviet Union, and in June 1939 had dispatched Chief-of-Staff, General Franz Halder, to meet with the Chief-of-Staff of the Finnish Army. However, with the non-aggression pact between Germany and the Soviet Union, Germany could focus on the war in the West.[4]

But Sweden still had to respond to Germany and the Allies. Early in the war Sweden recommended reducing its iron-ore exports to Germany to 7 million tons a year. Needless to say, this proposal was met with German hostility. Germany was also angry with Swedish press attacks on the Reich. To placate the Germans, Sweden chose not to reduce its ore shipments and did implement some minimal press censorship.[5]

Germany had considered invading Sweden to seize control of the ore but was aware that the Swedes had planted explosives in the mines and that a major portion of the mobilised Neutrality Watch of the Swedish army was deployed to defend them. Additionally, the mines in the far north, volumetrically the largest and with the best ore, were furthest from Germany and would therefore be the most difficult to seize. Germany understood that Sweden had devoted relatively large sums of money in the 1930s to build up its defences.[6] In any event, Hitler rejected an invasion of Sweden, though Sweden continued to consider it a possibility.

Britain and France posed other concerns. From the beginning of the war, the British had tried to intercept the ore trade, but outside of Norway's waters. However, on more than one occasion, British warships penetrated Norwegian territorial waters in pursuit of German merchant ships and were warned off by Norwegian warships.[7] Britain now began to consider the mining of Norwegian waters to force German ships into international waters where they could be easily captured. Churchill even entertained clandestine sabotage against Swedish ports on the south-central coast with large stockpiles of iron ore heading for Germany. Churchill was of the opinion that 'with our command of the seas there is no reason why French and British troops should not meet German invaders on Scandinavian soil. At any rate, we can certainly take and hold whatever islands and suitable points on the Norwegian coast we choose.'[8]

With the Soviet invasion of Finland, the question of the iron-ore mines in Sweden already brought to the attention of the political leaders gained greater importance. France especially was committed to intervention in Finland, both to appear to the world as a strong power waging war against tyranny and also to keep the war away from France. On three occasions between December and the March armistice, the Allied governments proposed to Sweden and Norway that they be allowed to pass through those countries to come to the aid of Finland. Sweden, correctly, interpreted the request as a ploy to gain control of their rich northern iron-ore fields.[9]

On 27 December 1939 the Allies presented the first of the three notes to Norway and Sweden. In its reply of 4 January 1940, the Swedish government agreed to the possibility of allowing the passage of supply and civilian technicians but it opposed the transit of troops. A second similar Allied note was sent on

6 January.[10] The second note received a similar response and on 17 January the Swedish prime minister declared publicly that no Allied troops would be permitted to enter Finland via Sweden. By the end of January these plans to enter Finland via Norway and Sweden, along with one calling for the seizure of Petsamo, a key Finnish nickel port, were set to one side for the moment.[11]

The planned advance through Norway and Sweden was surely a pipe dream. Nevertheless, at a meeting on 5 February 1940, the Allied Supreme War Council in Paris decided to proceed. Forces were allotted to what would have amounted to an invasion of Norway. Geirr Haarr has pointed out that, 'The ultimate goal for the Allied planners was the Norwegian west coast and the Swedish iron ore, not aid to Finland.'[12] Narvik and Trondheim were to be occupied by the British 42nd and 44th Divisions, a Polish brigade, a French Alpine brigade and two French Foreign Legion battalions. These forces were then to march towards Finland via Sweden, and along the way seize the Swedish Kiruna-Gållivare ore centre. Churchill proposed flying out two infantry companies as representative of what was to follow; the ever-cautious Chief of the Imperial General Staff, General Sir Edmund Ironside, countered that Britain had the capability to fly out only forty men to Finland.[13] On 2 March the Allies made a formal request to Sweden and Norway to allow the passage of troops. A proposed date for the attack was set as 20 March.[14]

Norway and Sweden consulted before replying. Sweden stated that in the event of an attack through their country by the Allies, Germany should be expected to intervene and that Sweden would fight any attempt to land *any* foreign troops on its soil. Colouring the Swedish response was information that had been leaked to their government by French Premier Édouard Daladier. He had let it be known through diplomatic back channels that the Finnish operation was to be part of a larger Allied offensive against the Soviet Union which would include air attacks against the Baku oilfields – certainly information that did anything but reassure the Swedish government.[15]

Norway's leaders decided to 'be satisfied with a protest' and the government did not issue any orders to the troops at Narvik or elsewhere in the north to resist by force an Allied landing. This must be understood in the context of Foreign Minister Halvdan Koht not wanting to be drawn into a war 'on the wrong side if we cannot avoid being drawn into the fight'.[16] Koht and the Norwegian government were intent on staying out of the war if possible, but under virtually all circumstances to not fight the Allies. The Norwegian government did not want to 'have her land made the battleground for the troops of the Great Powers'. The Norwegian government would go to almost any length to avoid playing the role of Belgium in this war.[17]

During 11–12 March, both Norway and Sweden replied to the Allies third note that they would not allow the transit of Allied troops across their countries to fight in Finland.[18]

\* \* \*

On 5 March, Albert Viljam Hagelin, a Norwegian trader and NS member with much of his business being conducted with Germany, had reported the Allies' intentions to Alfred Rosenberg at the Foreign Policy Office of the Nazi Party. The next day the Abwehr gave Hitler similar intelligence.[19] Hagelin was a successful businessman married to a German wife. This work with Germany provided a convenient cover for frequent visits by and discussions with German officials over the coming weeks. In early 1940 the Norwegian navy retained Hagelin to conclude an agreement to buy Ju87 Stuka dive-bombers from Germany. Hagelin later also passed on the false but not baseless idea that Norway's government would not resist a German invasion. Rosenberg forwarded this information to Hitler. After serving as Vidkun Quisling's second-in-command for most of the war, Hagelin would be tried as a traitor and executed in 1946.

Earlier, on 4 March, Hitler also ordered emergency operations to be prepared in the event of Allied attacks, code-named '*Minimalfall*', which would entail quickly sending troops to Norway and Sweden to fight an invading Allied force. Now Hitler accelerated planning to invade Norway so it could be undertaken by 15 March. The plan was to be ready by 10 March. The troops earmarked for this operation were placed on standby until 14 March and ship transport was to be ready on 26 March.[20]

* * *

The French were the more forceful of the two major Allied powers in pressing for intervention in Scandinavia, in part due to the realisation by the British that actions against Narvik would likely see the end of iron-ore shipments from that port to Britain. After the more aggressive Paul Reynaud replaced Daladier as premier on 21 March, the French government urged for intervention even more forcibly. This was due in part to British reluctance to intervene as quickly and as aggressively as the French wanted to in Norway, as well as Daladier being tainted by his failure to support Finland more fully in its resistance to the Soviet Union. Only the Moscow Peace Treaty between the Soviet Union and Finland on 12 March had finally prevented this operation from being undertaken.[21]

One day before the Winter War treaty with the Soviet Union was concluded, Finland asked Norway and Sweden to consider a defensive alliance. Both nations quickly replied in the affirmative and this note was published in all three capitals on 14 March. The Soviets, realising that the alliance was directed at them, protested and any thought of such an arrangement quickly died as the Soviet Union was so much more powerful and threatening than a possible Nordic alliance could withstand.[22]

One advantage that Norway gained from the Winter War was that upwards of 725 of its nationals including some officers had assisted the Finns in fighting the Soviets. Norway had also given Finland twelve 75mm artillery pieces with ammunition and equipment. During the fighting in Finland, the Norwegian military had gathered intelligence on the use of Molotov cocktails and grenades to stop enemy armour, as well as other military information.[23]

\* \* \*

The signing of the Moscow Treaty ending the Winter War was hastily followed by one of the Allies most ill-conceived half-measures of the war – Operation 'Wilfred'. Churchill had been advocating some kind of action against the ore trade but with the signing of the peace treaty the justification for sending troops to assist Finland and seizing Sweden's northern ore mines in the process was no longer valid. Instead, one of the reasons the Allied governments opted for 'Wilfred' was that their action was in response to German submarine attacks and the illegal sinking of neutral and Allied merchant ships.[24]

'Wilfred' called for three separate naval forces to mine Norwegian waters in three distant spots off the west coast of Norway, consequently forcing German merchant traffic into international waters. It was anticipated that such action would precipitate Germany to land troops in southern Norway. The Allies also contemplated but ultimately rejected a plan to land troops *before* the Germans arrived in Norway as a preventative war action.

This proposed landing operation was known as Plan R4. The 24th Scots Guards Brigade would land at Narvik and simultaneously the bulk of four Territorial battalions would land at Bergen and Stavanger with supporting troops such as Signals units.[25] At Stavanger, one battalion was detailed to Sola airfield and one to the town and harbour. If the landing at Stavanger was threatened, the force was to destroy Sola and then withdraw. These units were stripped of non-essential elements for the initial landing effort.

Trondheim was to receive only one additional battalion two days after the other actions. In the original concept, with the Allies landing before any German troops, if the Norwegians had firmly resisted, the landings would be recalled. If just scattered and reflexive Norwegian resistance resulted, the Allies would push on to their objectives. The Allies allocated up to 100,000 British and 50,000 French and other Allied troops to fill out the entire operation over a period of several weeks. There were to be two Gladiator fighter squadrons with two bomber and two army air co-operation squadrons for the operation, while four squadrons of heavy bombers operating from Britain would offer additional support. Other Allied air support would be from aircraft carriers.

The planners realised that Norwegian resistance could make the success of the operation problematical and they could not be certain of Norway's response. In fact, on 15 March, Norwegian Foreign Minister Koht had argued for issuing written protests and diplomatic notes in the event of possible Allied landings, but to offer no resistance. Whether Norway would have offered serious resistance in the face of Allied landings is not known. While the Norwegians wanted no part of the war, their resistance to Allied landings would probably have been sporadic and driven by local conditions. The Allies in their planning expected some military resistance.[26]

This formula had failure written all over it. The potential for failure lay in three key areas. First, the allocated airpower was ridiculously inadequate, especially as Germany had 500 combat aircraft readying for a strike against Norway and Denmark. Additionally, the British 'air co-operation squadrons' had only a rudimentary grasp of the concept of army–RAF co-operation in combat. That lesson would be driven home during the Battle of France and would lead to a fundamental reform in this area.

Secondly, the initial army landing was designed for friendly occupation, not an opposed landing. The Territorial battalions dedicated to this operation were poorly trained and equipped second-line troops. In the fighting with the Germans during the invasion the Territorial battalions would prove to be weak.

Finally, the Allies did not realise the scope and size of the approaching German hammer blow. Its strength was simply not fathomed – especially the massive use of German airpower.[27]

The military landing part of R4 was not to take place unless and until Germany violated Norwegian neutrality. In the invasion, this force standing by, ready to intervene, would receive new orders which, as will be demonstrated, would lead to failure.

Originally 'Wilfred' was to take place in conjunction with Operation 'Royal Marine', the mining of Rhine river waters with small fluvial mines to be followed eleven days later by mines air-dropped into German canals. These mines would disrupt ship traffic and sink vessels as well as damaging bridges and other structures on the river. The French vetoed the mining operation because they feared German retaliatory bombing against their undefended war-production factories. It would not be until the summer of 1940 that the French would have adequate anti-aircraft defences.[28]

The British and French governments committed to 'Wilfred' on 28 March, the French deciding on 30 March not to allow Operation 'Royal Marine' to commence for at least three more months. On 29 March the Commander-in-Chief of the Allied armies, French Commander-in-Chief General Maurice Gamelin, informed General Ironside of the need to 'prepare everything for a lightning occupation of the Norwegian ports'.[29] It is noteworthy that on several occasions, such as Gamelin's actions here, rapid action was demanded. Yet in many of the Allied moves, speed would be lacking, or when it was applied, it would be poorly executed with important men and equipment left behind or absent. This would stand in stark contrast to the German effort.

* * *

One minor but potentially embarrassing incident took place at this time. The German naval attaché, Lieutenant Commander Richard Schreiber, reported (incorrectly as it was later discovered) that sixty British warships and transports were off the Norwegian coast near Stavanger. Germany sent two U-boats to investigate, and one, the *U-21*, ran aground in Norwegian waters on 27 March. Instead of lying and saying he had engine problems, the U-boat commander said he was off course, so his crew and submarine were interned. Both were released when the Germans later occupied Kristiansand, though the U-boat would afterward only be used for training purposes.[30]

\* \* \*

On 9 March Raeder had made the point to Hitler that 'the Norwegians will not make the decision to fire quickly enough, if they decide to do so at all'. It was this reasoning that would ultimately drive the Germans. They could not trust the Norwegians to defend their nation and keep Germany supplied with iron ore and Raeder was still convinced that it was only a matter of time before the Allies seized part or all of Norway.[31] Raeder also pointed out to Hitler in March that the occupation of Norway by Germany would allow it to put additional diplomatic pressure on Sweden to obtain what Germany wanted.[32]

Germany did have some direct intelligence of the Allied planning for operations in Scandinavia, and were certainly aware of the possibility of an Allied invasion of Norway. The Allied preparations for a landing in Scandinavia in response to the Winter War had been reported to Germany.[33] In March a French naval commander investigating landing sites in Norway had approached Colonel Konrad Sundlo, an NS member and garrison commander at Narvik, and outlined Allied plans to seize Kirkenes, Sola, Stavanger and Trondheim with 'motorised' troops. Sundlo reported this to the NS leadership and Hagelin reported it to Rosenberg on 20 March. Hagelin met with Admiral Erich Raeder on 26 March and told him that in Norwegian naval circles it was expected that Britain would soon take control of Norwegian waters. He also said that the Norwegians expected Britain to try to seize and operate airfields in southern Norway.[34]

The German leadership was aware of some of the Allied preparations for Plan 'R4' from their agents and supplemented this with information gained from partial deciphering of British signals. They viewed their planning for an invasion of Norway as a response to the Allied initiative and as a preventative war.[35] Foreign Minister Joachim von Ribbentrop exploited the intelligence on 9 April at a press conference during which he noted key elements of the Allied plans and further that 'the German Government has for some time had information that English and French military and naval staff officers were present in all parts of Norway to decide upon and prepare landing-places and to make plans for the advance to the south'.[36] But the unsophisticated Allied planning paled in comparison to the German joint blitzkrieg about to be unleashed upon Norway.

As early as 27 March the French public (and later the British) saw news reports indicating possible action in Norwegian waters between the Allies and Germany.[37] With the goading of the more aggressive French Premier Paul Reynaud, the Allies determined to move forward with 'Wilfred' and 'R4', hoping that the 'Germans [would] retaliate and thus extend the war to Scandinavia'.[38] As it has been seen, they did drop the plan to land troops at the Norwegian ports and on 8 April 1940 authorised only the coastal mining operations. Troop landings were to wait upon events but agents for gaining Norwegian co-operation were landed on the Norwegian coast, including at Stavanger.[39]

Finnish telephone lines to their British and French legations ran through Germany and were regularly tapped. While the Finns were aware of this, they still had to discuss items that Germany quickly learned of. Thus a discussion on 12 March about Allied intervention plans was known immediately by Germany.[40] On 30 March German cryptographers had intercepted a Romanian legation signal that indicated the British were planning some sort of action against Norway. Germany later intercepted a Swiss cable that indicated both Germany and Britain intended to invade.[41] The German Abwehr had tapped Paul Reynaud's private telephone exchange and was able to supply Hitler on the eve of the invasion the full text of the 28 March Allied resolution to mine Norwegian waters which strengthened Hitler's resolve to move forward with the German assault.[42] This was such an open secret that in 1 April 1940 issue of *Time* magazine it was freely mentioned that the Allies had intended to land 100,000 troops in northern Norway to advance across northern Sweden to aid Finland.[43]

On the eve of the action, British Foreign Secretary Lord Edward Halifax stated, 'it was difficult to disregard the psychological importance of taking action at the present time'.[44] Norway and Sweden were informed on 5 April that the mining would take place on the 8th.

This was not the only Allied activity.[45] Britain's Secret Intelligence Service, Section D, had become involved in Scandinavia in 1938. Section D was established to carry out covert actions against Axis enemies. The recruitment of A. F. Rickman, a failed import/export businessman, was the first part of a plan to sabotage Swedish ore production. Section D recruited men and women with a variety of backgrounds to expand the group, including a British Navy Reserve yachtsman who had been involved in clandestine surveying along Norway's coast before the war. One covert operation involved sending hundreds of pounds of explosives secretly to the British military attaché in Stockholm. This part of the operation was successfully completed in January 1940. There were also plans afoot to attack the shipping facility at Oxelösund. Due largely to the amateur nature of the Section D recruits and Rickman's inability to recognise when he was being tailed by the Swedish secret police, most of the group were arrested without accomplishing anything of note. The British also discussed sending agents as 'volunteers' to fight in Finland who would try to disrupt iron-ore trade from the Swedish ports of Luleå and Oxelösund. This plan did not come to fruition.[46] The establishment in April 1940 of the 'Norwegian Relief Fund' would follow; the Fund was a front organisation for future clandestine operations in Scandinavia.[47]

'[D]uring the winter of 1939–40,' notes historian T. K. Derry, 'it [was] clear that the existence of the route through The Leads and its use for an essential German war import gave the Allies strong reasons for putting Norway in the forefront of their strategical calculations'.[48] But Allied operations and plans were poorly thought out, hesitant and ultimately would fail when the far more mature German operation swung into action.

Hitler was now intent on securing Norway. In the introduction to his 1 March 1940 war directive he stated:

The development of the situation in Scandinavia necessitates the commencement of preparations for the occupation of Denmark and Norway by formations of the armed forces. This would anticipate English action against Scandinavia and the Baltic, secure our supplies of iron ore from Sweden, and provide the Kriegsmarine and the Luftwaffe with the expanded bases for operations against England.[49]

The Germans and the Allies were primed and ready for intervention. How would Norway respond to this challenge?

## CHAPTER 4

# Norwegian Defence Preparations

And then he'll leave home for a rain of steel,
'Till last he hangs torn on barbed wire will,
Decaying for Hitler's Aryan call,
That is what a man's for – after all . . .

I didn't surmise it – now too late it is
My sentence is just: The verdict's no miss
My faith was in riches, my faith was in peace
In labour, fellowship, and love's fragrant kiss
Yet those who won't die on the battlefield,
Their heads for the axe-man, will certainly yield

I cry in the darkness – if only you knew
There is but one thing – that is right to do
Shield yourself, while your hands still are yearning,
Save your offspring – Europe is burning.

Arnulf Øverland, 'Dare Not to Sleep', 1936[1]

Like most nations, Norway suffered from the Great Depression, and its successive mostly anti-militaristic governments presided over a reduction in defence spending without fully understanding the changing international situation of the 1930s. The average Norwegian argued, 'We want no foreign policy'; they wished to be left alone.[2] An invasion of Norway by Germany was simply not on their radar screen. What had Norway done in the interwar years to defend itself? The short answer is: not enough.

The country had instituted universal conscription in part as a result of the national crisis that bloodlessly achieved Norway's independence from Sweden in 1905. Historically Norway's military preparations were then, and in part would continue to be, against Sweden and the long border they shared. After the First World War, conscription called for 144 days of training when first called to duty, though this was never fully implemented. By 1935 the number of training days had fallen to sixty days for infantry, seventy-two days for the other arms. Furthermore, not all those who were eligible were called up for training – there were many exemptions granted. In 1930 the number of full-time officers was cut by over 60 per cent. Norway's Military Academy (*Krigsskolen*) averaged about ten graduates a year in the 1920s and in 1929 did not graduate one officer.[3] One student of the 1940 campaign summed it up: 'the permanent cadre was too small, the training of recruits too short, and the provision of equipment for the mobilized forces inadequate'.[4] Colonel Otto Ruge, inspector of infantry and later general and commander of the army, noted that the training expenses for the average Norwegian soldier were the lowest in Scandinavia, and about half of Denmark's.[5]

In March 1935 a minority Labour government came to power in Norway and it believed in disarmament (in 1933 it had presented a programme to abolish the navy altogether), but would end up leading a modest rearmament programme. Nils Ørvik has written, 'The party had placed a great deal of faith in the League of Nations. Shortly after Norway had joined the League of Nations it came to be widely believed that the system of collective security would be sufficient to preserve a general peace, and consequently national armies no longer were needed.'[6] By keeping the military, especially the army, small, they could control costs, and if war threatened, they could increase spending on defence. In the event, too little would be done. This government would remain in power until the 1940 invasion.

By 1940 the Labour Party leader, Johan Nygaardsvold, had led the Norwegian coalition government for almost five years, with Halvden Koht as his foreign minister. Koht ran Norway's foreign policy leading up to war. He was very secretive and would be heavily criticised after the war for his conduct of foreign affairs. Carl J. Hambro, a conservative Jew and former journalist, was president of the parliament and head of its Foreign Affairs Committee. A highly effective leader, Hambro would take vital decisions in the early hours of the war. Young Colonel Birger Ljungberg was appointed Minister of Defence just three-and-half months before the German invasion. One reason for him being chosen was that he was known not to have any political opinions or aspirations. He replaced Christian Fredrik Monsen, who had led the ministry since 1936 and been a communist at one point in his political career and written anti-military pamphlets arguing that the only role for the Norwegian army was to oppress the working class.[7] Ljungberg was a 'safe' choice and was viewed not as a policy maker, but as an administrator to carry out day-to-day operations.

The Labour Party government was understandably concerned that the military harboured leaders opposed to their policies and that they might spawn some Nazi-style leader. Labour Party leaders initially wanted to disarm the military and simply establish a national guard, such as in modern-day Costa Rica with 'people's' officers and men. Elements in the cabinet argued, as did their contemporaries in Denmark, but as will be seen without as much success, that resistance to an invasion by any major power would be pointless. This argument held that Norway was too weak and small to be defended by a military. The example of Belgium in the First World War was used. Some Norwegians claimed Belgium should have not resisted the German invasion because of its ultimate cost in blood and treasure. For many their slogan was 'Not a single shot should be fired'.[8] However, as world events developed many members of the Labour leadership changed their tune, though after so many years of anti-military drumbeating it would take time to convert the rank and file.

Support for additional defence outlays and preparation for possible war came from many corners. In November 1936 following the outbreak of the Spanish Civil War Nygaardsvold's government began a modest $900,000 increase in defence spending, while the military wanted $9,000,000 more a year to make up for deficiencies. Much of the initial budget increase funded land-communication improvements, primarily to the road network in the far north near the border with the Soviet Union. By 1941–2 one of the roads in this network was to be completed to the border. In addition, conscription was now applied to the entire population. Infantry training was increased to seventy-two days a year and the number of exemptions was reduced. In 1937 the government passed an additional $4.7 million extraordinary expenditure to be spread over three years.[9] In 1938, as part of a six-year rearmament plan, initial army recruit training was increased to eighty-four days, and a sizeable spending increase was added to the budget in 1940. The defence budget represented about 11.5 per cent of the total budget. It was too little, too late.[10]

King Haakon VII had read *Mein Kampf* in 1935 and this only heightened his desire to strengthen the military. While technically the head of the military, he had no real political or military power as it was at the say of the Norwegian cabinet. He could not translate his concern into meaningful and substantial political action. What he and his son, the Crown Prince, did do was to increase their visits to military facilities and encourage local volunteer rifle clubs (*Skytterlag*). The Norwegian army for decades had encouraged rifle clubs as a way to bolster their military strength. The king also went to a weekly meeting of the 'Military Club' attended mostly by senior officers and made a point of going to the Monday meeting on 8 April in the midst of crisis so has to not upset the public by breaking with the routine. This was in the immediate aftermath of the Allied mining of Norwegian waters, on the eve of the German invasion.[11]

The popular leftist poet Arnulf Øverland was another catalyst. In 1936 a newspaper published his stirring poem 'Dare Not to Sleep', which subsequently appeared in his collected works, a bestseller in Norway in 1937. Øverland was typical of some on the left who had been roused to defend their nation. After the German occupation he would continue his outspokenness and would spend time in prison because of his views and actions.[12]

Also predicting Nazi aggression was the communist Leon Trotsky, who arrived in Norway as an exile in 1935. In December 1935, Trotsky would prophetically say, 'The day is near when the Nazis will drive you from your country.'[13] The following year the Norwegian government ordered Trotsky out of the country, yielding to pressure from the Soviet Union and from Vidkun Quisling. He would continue his exile in Mexico before his eventual assassination.

With the outbreak of the Second World War, Norway saw increased civilian and government activity. Not only did foreign diplomatic staffs (and the number of spies) grow, but also refugees began to arrive from the carnage to the south including large numbers of American tourists enquiring about a return to the USA.[14] By February 1940 rumours had spilled forth from Berlin that an invasion was possible.[15] On 28 March William L. Shirer broadcast from Berlin about the possibility of war with Scandinavian countries. There were many other intelligence titbits and rumours leading up to the actual invasion.[16] Numerous off-course German planes landed in Denmark and Norway as part of the reconnaissance for the invasion. High-altitude German reconnaissance aeroplanes flew overhead. Though agents were present in both nations and information was gleaned, there was no major German intelligence effort. German lack of information, especially in regards to Norway, would become evident.[17]

\* \* \*

Major Quisling played a prominent role in the German plans. A brilliant man, thought by those close to him to be a genius, Quisling had graduated first in his class from the *Krigsskolen*. He worked closely with Norway's first delegate to the League of Nations, Fridtjof Nansen, famous for his Arctic explorations. In the early 1920s Nansen helped bring famine relief to the postwar Soviet Union and arranged for the reparation of almost 500,000 prisoners from the First World War. In these activities, for which he was credited with saving many lives, Quisling was his second-in-command. Quisling's involvement helped bring him to the attention of his fellow countrymen. In 1923 Nansen played a key role in lending stature to the international effort to force Mussolini to back down from his seizure of the Greek island of Corfu and forcing its evacuation by the Italians.[18]

This was the era of the 'Red Menace' and the Communist International. Norway's conservatives viewed the Soviet Union, with some accuracy, as funding and heavily influencing leftist political 'social-democratic' parties such as the Norwegian Labour Party.

In the spring of 1931 the Agrarian Party (moderate-conservative) formed a new coalition government and Quisling was chosen to be the Minister of Defence, largely because of the knowledge of the Soviet Union he displayed in his 1930 book *Russia and Ourselves*. (The book also shows his anti-Semitic side, which was to grow in the coming years.[19]) The appointment gave Quisling a national stage. He made good use of it, following a somewhat comic-opera attempt on his life. The so-called 'Pepper Affair' was the first time a Norwegian cabinet member had suffered a physical attack. Quisling claimed that 'something' – pepper – was thrown in his eyes, he was knocked unconscious for 'some time', suffered a mild concussion, but was not seriously injured. But some in the press mocked him over this 'assault' and questions over the actual event have never been resolved.

Quisling also secretly set up the mechanism to enable the Minister of Defence to launch the army against an 'internal enemy', i.e., a communist or socialist 'coup'. Members of the existing army who were considered 'reliable' were recruited for this special force. The force was never used. Of course, this was precisely what the Labour government feared from the right: was the Norwegian army a danger to

Norwegian democracy? The political left in Norway in the 1920s and 1930s feared a right-wing coup and did not have to look far with the European examples of Italy, Greece and Spain among others.[20] Quisling was forced out in February 1933 and on 13 May he was instrumental in establishing the fascist *Nasjonal Samling*, or National Unity Party (NS).[21]

The NS had roots in both Italy's fascist and Germany's Nazi parties. By August 1935 the NS had grown to have 127 local party branches and held a number of local seats, mostly in eastern Norway. The party received 2.2 per cent of the vote in 1933, but in the 1936 election that support had eroded to 1.8 per cent after which it lost even more party members. Quisling and his party co-operated with the Danish and Swedish Nazi-style parties on the eve of the war. Quisling attended international rallies sponsored by Germany and Italy in the prewar years, including the 1934 'International Fascists Convention' in Montreux, where he was elected to the Central Committee.[22] But importantly the NS never reached the critical mass that Hitler had achieved with the National Socialist party in Germany and it remained a tiny thread in the political fabric of Norwegian politics.

In 1934 the NS adopted the Nazi salute. Quisling also created a small brown shirt contingent[23] called the *Hird* (King's Bodyguard), with upwards of 500 men and its own national flag. The party adopted the leader or *Führer* principle ('*Fører*' in Norwegian). In 1936 Quisling established a small SS-style personal bodyguard called the 'NS *Kamporganisasjon*'. Beginning in 1935, he demanded the 'return' of Greenland to Norway based on Norway's discovery and settlement of the island during the Middle Ages. At his second meeting with Hitler on 18 December 1939, Quisling delivered a memorandum that outlined the 'return' to Norway of Greenland, Iceland and the Faroe Islands.[24]

As the NS became more openly National Socialist in nature, including a strong anti-Semitic line, the party lost further support. A third of its membership abandoned the party between the summers of 1935 and 1936, including many of its best leaders. The German ambassador reported to Berlin that the NS was 'finished politically'.[25] Quisling's biographer Hans Dahl later wrote, 'The Quisling moment in Norwegian public opinion seemed to have passed.'[26]

Despite its small numbers nationally, the NS was prominently represented among the officer corps of the Norwegian army. Of sixteen regimental commanders, three were members of the party. Two additional members were in the higher command, and the proportion in the junior officer ranks may have been as high as or higher than 20 per cent. As David G. Thompson points out, 'One tends to assume that members of the NS were pro-German, which generally was true; yet they were also Norwegian **nationalists** [emphasis in the original].' It is telling that after the *fall* of Norway 1,150 Norwegian officers joined or renewed their membership of the NS.[27] Clearly most Norwegian officers, including members of the NS, resisted the invasion. The Germans, at least at Trondheim, wrote later after the invasion that the younger Norwegian officers supported fascism.[28] The Germans also would later claim that Norwegian armed resistance was greater than from the British.

But clearly by 1940 Quisling as a leader in Norwegian society was long past his prime and his party was moribund. His traitorous involvement with the Nazi government had begun in 1939 when the Abwehr arranged for Quisling to visit Germany. Quisling, desperate for money, became a paid propaganda agent for Germany. During that June visit he met Alfred Rosenberg, who became a firm supporter of Quisling, as his beliefs fitted nicely with Rosenberg's racial ideology. Quisling received the equivalent of RM100,000 in pounds sterling upon signing up and a monthly stipend after that. Quisling provided Rosenberg with the information he *wanted* to hear – that the Allies threatened Norway and that the current leadership of Norway's official government was preparing the way for Allied intervention. Quisling's party had the answer, a NS government. In December 1939 Quisling helped persuade Hitler to begin planning for an invasion of Norway.[29]

\* \* \*

Writing in exile in 1940, Foreign Minister Koht spelled out the position of the Labour government. Triggered by the failure of the League of Nations during the Italo-Ethiopian War that ended in 1936, the Norwegian government,

> In the course of the following years the Government in close co-operation with all the parties of the Storting, obtained increased credits for defence purposes . . . . Most of the various defence preparations came too late. So severely had the military budgets been cut down during the preceding years that a strong system of defence could not be re-established in a hurry. It was impossible to rebuild a navy in a couple of years and an air force could not be improvised. It may also be said, from later experience, that the task was not taken up with the necessary energy and speed. Nobody liked to spend so much money and thus to add so heavily to the economic burdens of the people for the sake of such hateful thing as rearmament. The taxes and the national debt were already extremely high for a country so comparatively poor, and the recent years of economic crisis had left too much undone for the betterment of the condition of the nation.[30]

It is ironic that one of Europe's most anti-fascist governments would fail to prepare its nation for war.

Norwegian military preparations were woefully inadequate in nearly all areas. As far as the nation's naval defences were concerned, Norway was divided into three Sea Defence Districts known as *Sjøforsvarsdistrikt*. The most southern district was the 1st *Sjøforsvarsdistrikt*. Its key naval bases and immediate surrounding waters were designated as a special *Krigshavn*, or 'War Harbour', from which foreign warships were strictly excluded without special authorisation. Entry without permission did allow the commander to open fire on the intruder without prior authorisation. In the invasion Norwegian commanders would

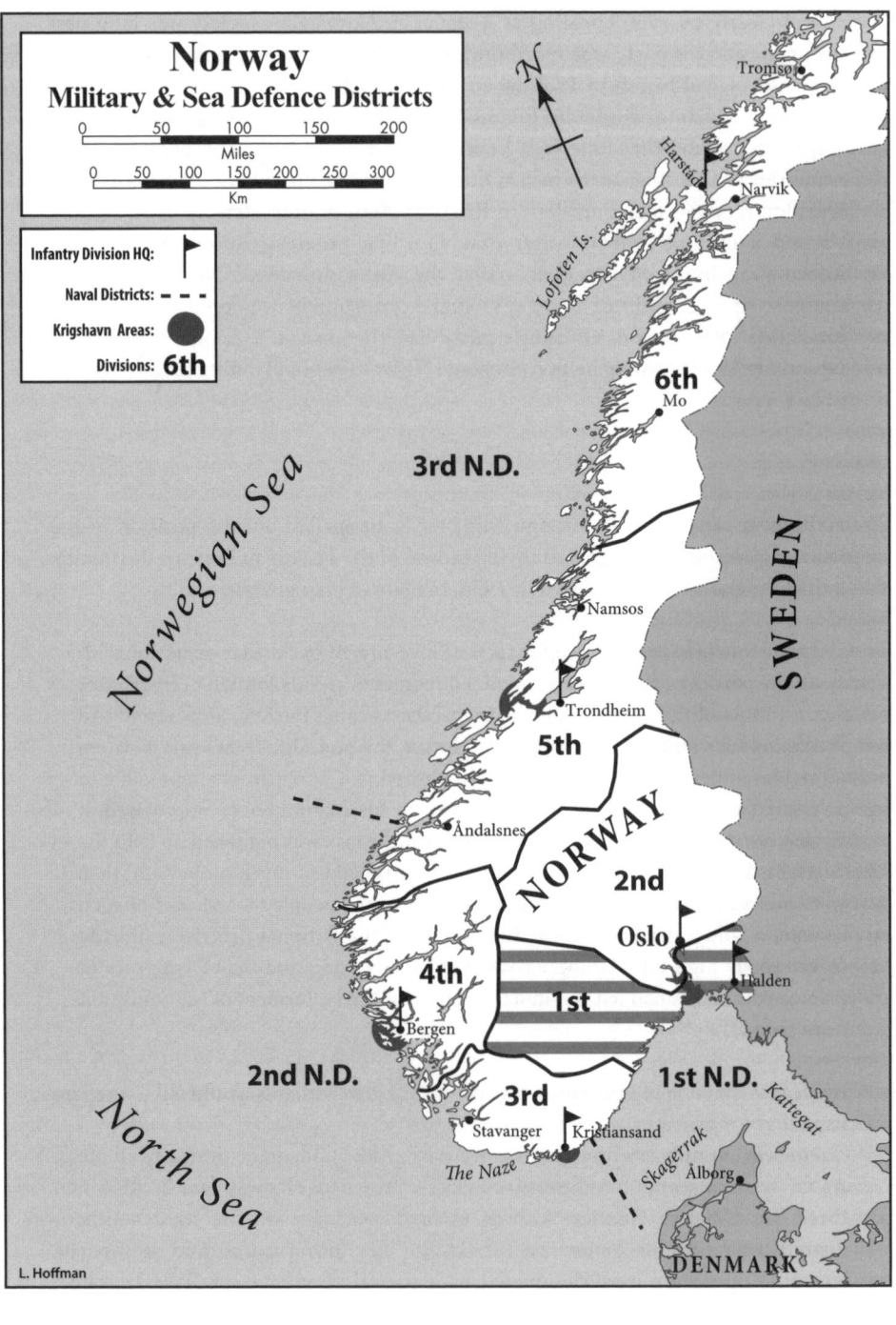

## Norway
### Military & Sea Defence Districts

0    50    100    150    200
Miles

0   50   100   150   200   250   300
Km

Infantry Division HQ:

Naval Districts: - - -

Krigshavn Areas:

Divisions: **6th**

Tromsø

Harstad

Narvik

*Lofoten Is.*

**6th**
Mo

**3rd N.D.**

*Norwegian Sea*

Namsos

Trondheim

**5th**

Åndalsnes

**NORWAY**

**2nd**

Oslo

Halden

**4th**

Bergen

**1st**

**2nd N.D.**

**3rd**

Stavanger

Kristiansand

**1st N.D.**

*Kattegat*

The Naze

*Skagerrak*

Ålborg

**SWEDEN**

*North Sea*

**DENMARK**

L. Hoffman

react in a mixed manner. Placed over this grid were the six divisional districts of the army, which did not directly relate to the Sea Defence Districts, though Norway's population centres, all on the coast, played a fundamental role in army mobilisation. Co-ordination between the army and naval districts was limited.

Rear Admiral Henry Diesen was commander of the Norwegian navy. He had been appointed in 1938 in part due to his political reliability. One officer said, 'We regarded [Diesen] as a Labour Party man, not particularly competent . . .'.[31]

The navy relied heavily on a torpedo and mine doctrine supplemented with old but powerful coast defence batteries, while warship naval gunfire was a distant third element. In the course of the invasion and largely due to the nature of the surprise only one land-based torpedo battery and one ship launched three torpedoes between them.

This was classic a naval defence choice made by a smaller, weaker power. The Germans called it *Kleinkreig*, and it is almost a guerilla-warfare-goes-to-sea approach to naval defence. Its roots go back to the French *Jeune Ecole* (literally 'Young School') of the nineteenth century. It was less expensive to field a force of torpedo-armed warships, sea mines, small armoured coast defence ships and coast defences than to build large battleships, which was clearly beyond the budget of a country like Norway.[32]

The two active small armoured coastal defence ships of the Norwegian navy were stationed at Narvik. The *Norge* and *Eidsvold* were British-built sister ships launched in 1900 but still considered very seaworthy. They were 3,645 tons and armed with two 8.2in guns mounted in single turrets fore and aft. Well armoured, they carried a secondary armament of six 5.9in guns. Their major interwar upgrade had been the addition of some anti-aircraft (AA) guns. Two older near sister ships lay decommissioned at Horten.

The Norwegians also operated a small force of nine submarines. The *A2–A4* had been launched in 1913, the *B1–B6* between 1922 and 1929. The latter six had a standard displacement of 420 tons, took 1 minute to submerge, and could dive to a depth of a mere 50m. Most of these small submarines were posted in southern Norway in the 1st *Sjøforsvarsdistrik*. Unfortunately, they had been poorly maintained in the interwar period and they performed badly in the opening hours of the war. This was a major failure on the part of the Norwegian government in preparing for defending its homeland. If Norway had fielded a properly maintained and vigorous submarine force the losses to the Germans would have been much greater and the deterrent they would have represented might have stopped the invasion from occurring in the first place.[33]

Norway possessed a handful of modern small surface warships. There were three modern 'destroyers' of the *Sleipner* class (and one recently completed near sister the *Odin*) but they displaced only 708 tons at full load. They were armed with three 102mm guns for a main armament (only two for the *Sleipner*) and two torpedoes (four on the *Gyller*). One contemporary British writer referred to them at the time as 'modern miniature destroyers'.[34] A large modern minelayer, the *Olav Tryggvason*, rounded out the modern warships.

The navy had a permanent standing force of about 800 men. For the Neutrality Watch ordered on 5 September, about 5,200 seamen of the Norwegian navy were mobilised. However, to limit costs, coast defence positions were only partially manned and ships did not necessarily have their full complements.[35] The watch was deployed to enforce the country's neutrality along more than 1,600 miles of island-strewn coastline, which could not be adequately covered by the few warships available. There were sixty-three mostly small warships available, of which twenty-five were aged and very small torpedo-boats. Most were very old, only nineteen having been launched after 1918. One warship had been built in 1860. This included three pre-First World War 'destroyers' of the *Snøgg* class. The navy requisitioned and armed approximately fifty additional small vessels for use as patrol craft. Many of the older and requisitioned warships lacked radios.[36]

Horten Naval Shipyard, in outer Oslofjord, had built three destroyers in the late 1930s along with other small warships. Horten also had taken the original Whitehead torpedo from the late nineteenth century, modified it and by the 1920s was producing them in small numbers.

In September 1939 Norway's coastal defences were theoretically at 33 per cent of full personnel complement and many but not all of their gun and torpedo crews were deployed. The army supplied garrisons for these sites but these personnel were not, for the most part, called up and in position. Only six companies of *landvern*, or older reserve troops, had been called up to garrison coast defence batteries. In October four of these companies were sent home and not replaced. The remaining two companies were mostly concentrated in the Oslo fjord area.[37] Thus Oscarsborg Fortress on an island in the narrows near Oslo had enough sailors to man only two of three main battery guns and achieved that by splitting one gun crew into two. The commander there would later employ secretaries, drivers and cooks to man the fort's magazine. A single platoon of army troops guarded the actual fortress from a land attack. No minefields were deployed in any Norwegian waters, though minelayers were on standby with mines ready for deployment if so ordered. Norway did possess a substantial number of mines as mine warfare in her littoral waters had been part of Norway's defensive strategy since before independence. Stavanger and Narvik had no coastal defence batteries at all. In 1940 Narvik had coastal defence battery positions under construction, but guns were not mounted and crews not present.[38]

Suggestively, a Norwegian General Staff report from 1913–14 pointed out that Kristiansand was potentially the port most vulnerable to a German attack, as it was near to Germany and lacked the coastal defence works that Oslo enjoyed. The report also noted that Narvik lacked coast defences.[39]

Norwegian military doctrine held that Germany could not attack Norway west-north-west of Stavanger because of the British navy. The small size of the German navy and presumed British mastery of the North Sea allowed the government to think that the danger of German units landing on Norwegian shores was exaggerated. Admiral Diesen argued that with the Royal Navy in command of the sea, such landings could hardly be implemented and then maintained. In a January 1939 newspaper article, Diesen said, 'in my opinion this scare is highly exaggerated'.[40]

As for the land forces, in 1939 the Norwegian army had mobilised 4 battalions and 6 militia companies, later expanding mobilisation to 7,000 soldiers. Of these, the 4,800 men of the 6th Brigade were deployed in the north near the Soviet border. Both naval and army aviation arms and all anti-aircraft units were also mobilised. In addition to these units were the six divisional schools for officers, NCOs (non-commissioned officers) and specialists. Each had approximately 120 soldiers – the equivalent of a small company – and in the coming campaign this very weak component would be counted upon in the attempt to throw the German invasion back. The rank of sergeant in 1933 was essentially abolished which was a political decision. In any typical year there were thirty-five sergeants in the entire service. At the end of a year of training they were either placed in reserve or offered officer candidate school.[41]

The Norwegian army was armed with a Krag-Jørgensen rifle, designed in the 1890s and manufactured at Kongsberg, just west of Oslo. During the German invasion at least one arsenal, Gjøvik, which lies between Oslo and Lillehammer, issued a number of obsolete Remington 1888/1891 rifles that the Krag had replaced. The beleaguered country requested 20,000 rifles with ammunition, but the Allies were only able to supply 1,000 rifles.[42]

The army's main field piece was the older and worn out 75mm model/01. The model number indicates it was from 1901. More than 100 of these German-built guns were still in service. During the winter of 1939/40 at least twelve were modified to be truck-towed, but were also deployed by being carried in the back of open trucks or *en portee*. This gun was utilised as an anti-tank (AT) weapon but lacked the armour-piercing shells to make it more effective in this role. The majority of Norwegian artillery, as was German, was horse-drawn.

There were several models of a 75mm mountain gun, the first, produced in 1911, could be broken into six parts for hauling over difficult terrain. A new 1939 model had just been introduced and a very few were available at the time of the invasion. A few older 65mm mountain guns were deployed outside Bergen during the fighting. Ammunition for the field and mountain artillery had improved in the prewar years.

There were limited numbers of additional artillery pieces of varying age and condition scattered at depots, coastal battery positions and forts throughout the nation. Heavy and medium fortress artillery dated mostly from the 1890s and was foreign built. These guns had been reasonably maintained, as the fighting at Oslo and Bergen would prove, but many of the fuses were old and did not function properly. The guns themselves would sometimes malfunction after a few rounds due to age and lack of proper maintenance.[43]

Anti-aircraft guns were very scarce. There were approximately eighteen 40mm Bofors and sixteen Norwegian-designed 75mm Model/32s. There were twenty-six other mostly older AA artillery pieces available in September 1939. Most of these guns were deployed around major cities and hydroelectric plants, while four 40mm Bofors were deployed at the Oslo fjord fortification complex. The large firm of Norsk Hydro purchased ten of the Bofors in order to defend its facilities and the guns were manned by employees.[44] There were four 76mm AA guns at Kjeller airfield outside Oslo – otherwise only machine-guns were deployed with hand weapons at the other airfields.

Norway did not have any guns specifically designed as AT guns. Funds had been allocated in 1938 for the production at Kongsberg of 20mm AT guns but the weapons were not completed in April 1940. Weapons for sale from foreign nations had been examined and an order for sixteen 37mm AT guns with 2,000 rounds of ammunition for each gun had been placed with Germany. Ironically, delivery of these was to have been in April 1940 and would have been predominantly deployed when they arrived to the far north facing the Soviet Union. The 1940 Norwegian *Handbok for Soldaten* has a nice picture of the 37mm AT gun they were to receive.[45]

Major General Kristian Laake was the overall commander of the Norwegian army and had been since 1931. His headquarters was at Akershus Fortress in Oslo near the harbour wharves. The starving of army resources over the years had added to a defeatist attitude among many of the officers including Laake. They knew they were working with under-trained and poorly equipped troops. The sudden and overwhelming attack by a relatively modern force like Germany would have a psychological weight all its own.

One final element that needs to be noted is the age of the Norwegian commanders who had never seen action. Take, for example, the commanders in the Oslo area. The two admirals were 65 and 64, the army commander Laake was 65, the commander of the 1st Division was 61, the commander of the 2nd Division was 60 and the commander of the navy's air force was a mere 50. They had been through a career of routine that culminated in a nightmare on an early Tuesday morning in April 1940.[46] While some elderly officers fought bravely, the weight of routine and age influenced their decisions during the initial invasion. The vigour of youth, and not the torpor of old age, was what Norway needed that day.

* * *

The Norwegian army was divided into six divisions (*divisjon*) that were the District Commands (*Distrikt Kommando*). These were geographically based and their size was predicated on the population upon which they could draw. Below are the divisions, location of headquarters and personnel strengths when fully mobilised.

| Division | No. of regiments | Headquarters | No. of men |
|---|---|---|---|
| 1st | three | Halden | 14,000 |
| 2nd | three | Oslo | 15,700 |
| 3rd | two | Kristiansand | 7,700 |
| 4th | two | Bergen | 10,000 |
| 5th | three | Trondheim | 16,500 |
| 6th | three | Harstad | 15,700 |
| | | | 79,600 |

With full mobilisation the Norwegian army would number 119,000, which included militia, border and fortress troops.[47] Approximately 56,000 would make up the field army. Full mobilisation would have taken twelve to fourteen days.[48] A total significantly less than 50 per cent of the Norwegian army mobilised when war came. Possibly as few as 30,000 Norwegian troops were in the field at any one time during the campaign including untrained volunteers who simply showed up at depots.

The 1st, 2nd and 5th Divisions were the only divisions to have a full artillery regiment made up of two light battalions and one heavy battalion. The other three divisions had a single mountain artillery battalion assigned to them. Generally Norwegian artillery represented one-third of the complement of a comparable major European nation.

The king was technically the supreme commander, under him was Laake, the Commanding General, and Laake's staff was the General Staff of the army. Once war broke out it would transform itself into the *Hærens ØverKommando* (HOK) and shed some of its officers to other commands.[49]

Estimates of available Norwegian army troops on the day of the invasion vary. According to some sources the total strength of the army on 8 April 1940 was 13,000 men.[50] German estimates, certainly too high, indicate that at the beginning of 1940 there were 40,000 men with the colours, but this number included the border militia. The usual strength of the Norwegian army was 8,000 in winter and 16,000 in summer.[51] But at the beginning of April the more correct estimates were of 25,050 men, including 4,350 of the border militia. The exact number will most likely never be known.[52]

In 1933 there had been another 'reform' of the Norwegian army that further reduced its capability and budget. The army would call it the 'Bankruptcy Ordinance'. The number of NCOs and middle-level officers was greatly reduced. The number of active duty captains in 1933 went from 260 to 121, while active duty majors took a dramatic cut from seventy-three in 1927 to thirty-five. The number of major generals remained at seven, one for each division and Laake. The divisions and regiments became administrative organisations and each division now fielded a mixed brigade with a core of four battalions. This was known as the 'field brigade' and had about 5,000 men each.[53] As they mobilised, the remaining battalions and miscellaneous troops (fortress, administrative, etc.) were to be directly subordinate to Army Headquarters. This reform was not fully implemented, or fully understood by the politicians, and led to confusion at the time of the German invasion. This hollowing out of the Norwegian army combined with limited training resulted in General Laake in 1932 noting to the government that the resulting 'reforms' of 1933 would allow for a Neutrality Watch but *not* an army capable of defending the nation without additional training and full mobilisation.[54]

Nations require practice for mobilisation to be effective, something the financially and ideologically challenged Norwegian government failed adequately to do. As Professor David G. Thompson has pointed out, 'by 1932, none of the divisional or regimental commanders had ever actually commanded assembled units of that size in maneuvers.[55]

The procedure in place was to mobilise each field brigade at dispersed depots, and the guns, ammunition and firing pins were not kept together. This was a legacy of the fear of a 'red' revolution by the Norwegian army's leadership. Though this practice was ended in 1938–9, the required changes were by no means fully implemented. This would result in chaotic conditions at several mobilisation centres in 1940.[56]

In the actual invasion only a handful of units were at full strength or able to mobilise fully. In turn there was much confusion. For example, one man arrived at Bergen to join an available military unit but since his unit was stationed in Stavanger he was told to proceed there, effectively putting him out of the fight. This situation was repeated throughout the nation as the invasion began. Because of the nature of Norwegian mobilisation, as will be seen in Chapter 8, others were turned away when they arrived at their correct depots too early. Many of the mobilisation assembly areas were near the Swedish border, while the rest were near or in population centres such as Bergen or Oslo, a reflection of the historical context around which Norway planned its defence. The country was not prepared for an asymmetrical assault from Germany. With the rapid German capture of the Norwegian population centres the assembly depots in these cities were quickly lost – and often utilised by the occupying Germans to their benefit.

Each division was almost unique in design due to the different requirements expected of each. For example, the 2nd Division was given substantial fortress garrison units for both land and sea fortifications in excess of the other five divisions. All divisions had special units to guard depots and important sites. The 1st Division was mobilising on *both* sides of Oslofjord, and that meant that the division was effectively split when the Germans captured Oslofjord in the first two days of the war.[57]

The 3rd and 4th Divisions, while technically 'binary', i.e., two regimental strength divisions, did not follow the Italian model adopted in the late 1930s. Instead, the number of local conscripts limited the size of the units, a structure dating back to before the First World War. Many of the men in the west and south saw duty with the navy instead of the army, further reducing the available manpower pool and that triggered the binary design.

A mobilised infantry field brigade consisted of four infantry battalions, a bicycle company, an artillery battalion made up of two or three horse-drawn batteries, a pioneer company, a communication company and support services. Each infantry battalion was made up of three rifle companies with six light machine-guns in each company and at full strength numbered about 850 officers and men. The battalion had a heavy weapons company with two to four Colt 7.92mm heavy machine-guns and only two 81mm mortars. Norway had neither anti-tank guns nor new hand grenades (in the event, the Norwegians would utilise the Molotov cocktail).[58] The bicycle company with each infantry regiment was known as a '*hjulrytterkompani*' – bicycles in good weather, ski troops in snow. The regular infantry was not necessarily ski-equipped or ski-capable, but many Norwegians were familiar with skiing and the use of snowshoes. None of the Norwegian divisions were uniform in their attached artillery batteries. A field brigade was supposed to have a minimum of two batteries, but this did vary. The disruption of the Norwegian mobilisation made this more problematic.[59]

The Guard, or '*Hans Majestet Konges Garde*' (HMKG), was an independent battalion with three companies in Oslo with a fourth, the training company, at Fort Terningmoen, located near Elverum, north-east of Oslo. They wore a distinctive black uniform.[60] There were two other independent battalions mobilised and serving in the far north, the 'Alta' and 'Varanger' battalions.

The three cavalry regiments were theoretically made up of two or three company sized horse squadrons, a machine-gun squadron, a bicycle company, a motorised machine-gun squadron and a mortar section. In reality, all three were unique in design. Each regiment consisted of one or two horse-mounted squadron(s) and one squadron either in the process of being motorised or more likely utilising bicycles. A machine-gun unit was present.[61] Cavalrymen were trained for horses in warm weather and to act as ski troops in winter.

It should be noted here that the bulk of the Norwegian army was *not* trained for winter combat, though their clothing was excellent and April 1940, for much of Norway, was still under winter conditions, in one of the hardest winters on record. In April 1940 in central Norway there was 2–3ft of snow off road, and slush on the roads in the day that refroze overnight.

There had been some talk about creating a mechanised unit. Several articles in professional journals espoused their use, while other articles stressed the superiority of anti-tank guns.[62] In 1936, the Norwegians did purchase the very inexpensive chassis of a 4.5-ton Landsverk L-120 tank of Swedish manufacture and mounted iron plate and a machine-gun on it. The L-120 even in Swedish service did not go into production as it was an obsolete design replete with problems and it is doubtful whether the Norwegians would have utilised this design for a larger purchase. The 'tank' toured the nation and had some colourful names attached to it, such as 'King's Tank', 'Norway's Tank' and the 'Nation's Tank'.[63]

The Norwegians also studied the use of armoured cars. They built at least two simple armoured cars converted from trucks and along with their tank deployed them in manoeuvres in 1938 and 1939. After deliberation they favoured the Swedish L-185.[64] This vehicle and the L-120 were considered for a 'mechanised' cavalry regiment in the 1938 rearmament plan, but the cost had led the government to reject this proposal and they probably would have chosen some other light tank. The regiment would have consisted of a reconnaissance company made up of motorcycles and L-185s, a light tank squadron equipped, two horse squadrons, a motorised machine-gun squadron and a mortar section. Like the Italian '*Celere*' divisions, the mix of horses with motorised units was a stopgap measure, which as with '*Celere*' divisions would most likely have proven ineffective.[65] Norway did employ limited motorisation of its troops and had some motorised units by 1940, mostly artillery. The cavalry was due to be fully motorised, followed by the HMKG battalion. The Germans captured the tank and armoured cars at the Gardermoen army depot outside Oslo.[66]

The Norwegian army was ill prepared for modern war. Foreign Minister Koht wrote shortly after the invasion that, 'In no respect was Norway a military nation. In case of war she would not be able to send any expeditionary forces abroad. She would have her hands full trying to defend her own frontiers. No other policy was open to her but that of neutrality.'[67] The Inspector General of the cavalry in 1938 posed the question, 'In a war, we are going to encounter enemy tanks; is that the first time the Army will ever get to see any?'[68] In 1940 the new *Handbok for Soldaten* contained detailed information on how to engage enemy tanks and aircraft and so sported the appearance of a modern approach, but the army lacked tanks and had a mere handful of aircraft.[69] The frontispiece shows a Norwegian soldier with the new steel helmet, similar in appearance to that of the Danish army, but it had been introduced into service in very limited numbers, with some going to the HMKG. There were some British steel helmets from the First World War that had been purchased after the war as well. But the vast majority of Norwegian soldiers would fight in a cloth kepi reminiscent of those worn by pre-First World War French troops that offered no protection against bullets or shrapnel. There was also a general lack of equipment such as tents, stoves, radios, mortars and more. Ammunition stocks, based on ten days of combat, were woefully inadequate. There were too few army troops stationed at airbases. No matter the number of insightful professional discussions about preparation for a modern war, when war came Norway had neither the tanks, armoured cars, AT guns, AA guns, grenades nor even the steel helmets necessary to fight one.

\* \* \*

The condition of Norway's air forces was even worse. However, with the outbreak of war both the army and navy air forces were almost fully mobilised. Beginning in 1916, there had been a movement to unify the army and navy air forces into a new third branch, but both services, especially at the insistence of the navy, kept their own air element. Many of the aircraft were liaison and training aircraft, and obsolescent at best.[70]

The Norwegian air force (*Hærens Flygevåpen*), under the command of Colonel Thomas Gulliksen, had its main strength, the 1st Air Battalion, stationed at Oslo with planes distributed between the Fornebu and Kjeller airfields and with a bomber detachment at Sola. At Værnes (Trondheim) there was a small base with nine obsolete Fokker C.V. biplane light bombers, and at Bardufoss in the far north was an airfield with six Fokker C.V. bombers.[71]

Norway's most modern operational aircraft were eleven Gladiator biplane fighters based at Fornebu, of which only seven were in service. There were six more on order. Between the three airfields at Oslo and Sola (Stavanger), Norway had twenty-four Fokker C.V and at Sola four of the new Italian Caproni 310s bombers (one was unavailable on 9 April). Trainers and other aircraft were at most of the bases, with Kjeller having an air school. In all, the Norwegian army air force had about eighty aircraft, of which sixty-six were operational on the day of the invasion. The majority (about forty) consisted of the Dutch twin-seat Fokker C.V., first built in 1924.[72]

The lack of preparedness of Norway's air services was only too apparent once the fighting began. As the three operational Caproni 310s were loading bombs in preparation for bombing the Bergen area, the air crews realised that, because of peacetime spending restrictions, they had never actually practised bombing with live bombs.[73]

Norway had on order a significant amount of new army aircraft and nineteen modern Curtiss Hawk P-36 monoplane fighters had arrived, seven of which had been assembled at Kjeller but were not operational. Norway had on order sixty P-36s and thirty-six single-engine Northrup-Douglas 8A scout (or light) bombers. In addition twelve Caproni 312bis twin-engine light bombers and some German training aircraft were on order.

Norway's naval air force (*Marinens Flygevåpen*) was smaller and its aircraft were generally older. Most of the naval air arm's aircraft were at Horten, with additional aircraft at Kristiansand, Flatøen (Bergen), Hafrsfjord (Stavanger), Hitra (Trondheim) and several were stationed in the far north.

The navy had in service 14 MF11s (*Marinens Flyvebaatfabrikk*), a home-built three-seat double-wing floatplane intended for reconnaissance, bombing and torpedo attack. First entered into service in 1932, it had a single 575hp engine, a maximum speed of 150mph and a ceiling of only 16,000ft. For such a poor plane, it served effectively throughout the campaign and was later even employed by the Luftwaffe.[74] Still in service were a few earlier two-seater training biplanes, the MF10. The navy also had six modern He115 floatplanes with twelve on order, one Ju52, and six Douglas DT-2B/C torpedo-bombers, first designed in 1922. There were also a small number of specialty and school aircraft. Of all its aircraft, the navy had twenty-three ready for action, while seventeen others were non-operational.

For anti-submarine duties Norway had on order twenty-four Northrup N-3 single-engine reconnaissance aircraft, at the time the world's fastest floatplane. The Norwegian navy was also negotiating a munitions order from Germany that included thirty-six Junker Ju87 Stuka dive-bombers.[75]

Already before the invasion Norway had been paying the price for possessing the world's fourth largest merchant fleet of 1,960 ships. Since the start of the war Norway had lost 54 ships of 120,000 gross tons and approximately 600 sailors and passengers. Approximately half of these losses were due to German mines. A diplomatic note of protest on these losses, many in violation of international law, was delivered to Berlin on 1 April 1940.[76] It would be one of the last, futile protests from a neutral nation about to be swept into war.

\* \* \*

In early 1940 Norway remained a nation at peace. In Oslo prices had risen due to wartime shortages but as one war correspondent noted, 'the young Norwegians seemed to be having a good time and the beer cellar of the Grand Hotel was crowded with finely built young men and with girls who maintained the Scandinavian standards for schoolgirl complexions and good looks'.[77]

There had been warnings to the government. Some professional articles had discussed the need to stop an invading enemy on the beaches. In a 1938 memo to the Commander-in-Chief of the army, Colonel Ruge had noted that Germany might attack without any warning from Norwegian or other intelligence services.[78] Army Captain Øivinn Øi had published an article in 1939 warning that Germany might seek 'to gain a base to break an English blockade and a base for air operations against the British isles'.[79]

The Norwegian intelligence service was inadequate, consisting of some staff officers with little formal training whose main sources of information were diplomatic cables and information passed along from the Swedish and Danish military services. This lesson was learned and since the war both Norwegian and Danish intelligence services have been greatly expanded and number hundreds of personnel.[80] The lack of good intelligence was compounded by the lack of interdepartmental co-ordination. As Olav Riste has pointed out, at the interdepartmental level 'even imagination does not help: in Norway in 1940 there was no trace of any organized consultation or coordination among the various offices, staffs or ministries which shared the responsibility for alerting the nation to the danger of war'. Simply put, there was no governmental apparatus to analyze and make decisions with the information at hand.[81]

If Norway had been mobilised or better prepared, Hitler might not have ordered the invasion. Ruge would later write,

> If we had been reasonably prepared, our starting position during the first days would have been quite different from what it was. The Germans would have been stopped or thrown back into the sea. We would have gained time; the Allies would have gained time; and they would have had a Norwegian Army to work with instead of the small bands of freedom fighters which were all I could offer them.[82]

This failure to understand the potential of a joint assault, combined with a failure to mobilise in 1939, would result in Norway's defeat and occupation. It was a failure of imagination, one shared by the Allies, while the Germans had the vision to create the bold stroke that would bring them success.

# CHAPTER 5

# *Nazi Planning*

A few hours later the most brilliant piece of strategy had resulted in the country falling into the hands of an enemy. Whatever verdict civilization will place upon the aggression, it will be conceded that for sheer brilliance of execution, it had no parallel in history.

James Tevnan and Terence Horsley[1]

The 14 and 18 December 1939 meetings between Hitler and Vidkun Quisling triggered the start of German military planning for an invasion of Norway. Perhaps more than the interviews with Quisling, it was Raeder's plea on 12 December about the danger to the German war economy posed by the potential of Allied help to Finland through Scandinavia that convinced Hitler to order a study on the invasion.

But direct German military action involved some difficult issues. By 9 March 1940, with plans and preparations well advanced, Raeder told Hitler that this bold plan would fly in the face of naval strategy and was 'contrary to all principles in the theory of naval warfare [and] could be carried out by us only if we had naval supremacy. We do *not* have this; on the contrary, we are carrying out this operation in the face of the vastly superior British Fleet.' This was true.[2]

Hitler took a very personal interest in this project, and exerted tight control over this clandestine operation within the government. Secrecy was necessary to allow for the strategic and tactical surprise that would be required at the time of the attack. It was also Hitler's intention to have his personal stamp on this plan as a warlord leading his nation in battle.[3]

Colonel General Wilhelm Keitel was ordered to assemble a staff devoted to the study of the Norway, and later address the Denmark, 'problem'[4] Keitel headed up the *Oberkommando der Wehrmacht* (OKW, or military high command). He instructed Major General Alfred Jodl, the chief of Keitel's operations staff, to carry out the study. On 13 December, Jodl instructed Captain Schenk von Sternberg of the land defence section (*Landesverteidigung*) to submit an initial report on the matter, which was delivered in 24 hours.

After Hitler's instructions to the OKW, Keitel and Jodl began to work with the three services and ordered the Abwehr to gather information and maps on the two countries. The project would be known as *Studie Nord*, or North Study. It was immediately recognised that the German estimate of the Norwegian armed forces was inadequate. It was not until November 1939 that systematic intelligence activity had begun regarding the Scandinavian countries. However, intelligence requirements were met quickly in the coming weeks.[5]

The Luftwaffe prepared to counter the British command of the sea. It assembled a working staff code-named 'Oyster' under the direction of Colonel General Erhard Milch, state secretary for the Luftwaffe, to conduct a small separate study of the subject.[6]

On 23 January, the OKW requested that the initial military planning begun under *Studie Nord* be transformed to *Gruppe Krancke*,[7] or Krancke study group, led by Captain Theodor Krancke, commander of the pocket battleship *Admiral Scheer*. Kriegsmarine officers prepared the initial detailed planning. On 5 February, the group joined the OKW and began a full-scale work-up of the operation.

Captain Krancke represented the Kriegsmarine; Lieutenant Colonel Walter von Tippelskirch represented the German army; the Luftwaffe, after some delay, sent Colonel Robert Knauss, who had been a manager for Lufthansa before joining the Luftwaffe in 1935. Major Karl Strecker represented the Abwehr. The group was to report to Colonel General Walter Warlimont, deputy to General Jodl – an indication of Hitler's direct interest in this project. The code-name appeared in a letter sent by Keitel to the three military branches on 27 January in which Hitler displayed his intention to go ahead with the operational planning but utilising a limited circle of personnel of the OKW. The document prepared by Keitel divided Operation *Weserübung* into *Nord* for the occupation of Norway and *Süd* for Denmark. *Wesertag* ('day of Weserexercise') was established as 9 April 1940; *Weserzeit* ('Wesertime') would be 04:15. Denmark was included because of pressure from the Luftwaffe to secure adequate airfields closer to Norway instead of relying on the more distant ones located in northern Germany.[8]

From the start, the 'planners saw that the operation depended largely on the element of surprise and that the best way to achieve this was by an overwhelming aerial assault on the first day. It was a visionary concept.'[9] One of the group's recommendations was not accepted and that was to make General Albert Kesselring the overall commander. He was an army colonel until 1933 when he transferred to the Luftwaffe and learned to fly. This gave him a rich mix of experience for a joint campaign, but the Luftwaffe would not release him.[10] This internal dispute shows, as one scholar has noted, 'that even a totalitarian regime requires a high degree of voluntary consensus among participants, and that any government – monolithic or democratic – operates through broad consent to goals and purposes rather than through centralized coerced compliance alone.'[11] This is an important point often overlooked in modern wars. Military and political planners, especially in a democracy, should assume from the start that a dictatorship that they are planning a military operation against is *not* monolithic in the make-up of its political and military leadership. A planning tool from the start must be to create rifts and splits within the enemy's leadership.

Thus the world's first joint campaign would not have a unified commander. Instead, each German military service provided liaison officers who worked closely with each other in the planning and execution of the operation. That this inter-service group worked well together is a reflection of the men involved. Nevertheless, the top leadership of the German army was unhappy with this plan. The army's main objections were twofold. First, not all preparations could be concealed from the Allies and therefore, secondly, the Allies would be ready to destroy the German navy when it put to sea. The two top German generals, Field Marshal Walter Brauchitsch and Chief-of-Staff General Franz Halder, flatly refused to work on the planning for this operation. Halder wrote, 'About this question [*Weserübung*] not one word was exchanged between the Führer and the High Command of the Army. This must be affirmed for the history of the war.'[12]

In part because of this opposition, Hitler turned to his so-called 'Nazi generals' in preparing the invasion. These included Generals Wilhelm Keitel, Alfred Jodl and Walter Warlimont. Their first loyalties were to Hitler.[13]

Hitler was the driving force behind the invasion once he decided to make the attempt. On 1 March 1940, he signed the document calling for the occupation of Denmark and Norway. On 3 March, the operation was given priority over the invasion of France. The Germans thinking was that they were in a race with the Allies to land troops in Norway successfully. On 5 March, the detailed operational orders for the attack were in hand and approved by Hitler.[14]

Hitler had contemplated a similar operation to invade Sweden as early as 1934. That plan had called for the Kriegsmarine to land detachments of troops at various key Swedish coastal positions under the umbrella of the Luftwaffe supported by the German navy. Hitler even discussed the idea of claiming no 'hostile intentions', that Germany would be protecting Sweden from the Soviet Union and/or Great Britain. With typical modesty, he said that, 'it will be a daring, but interesting undertaking, never before attempted in the history of the world'.[15] Hitler wrote to Mussolini on 18 April 1940 that he had 'decided not to listen in the most difficult hours to so-called common sense but instead to the force of honor, to the sense of duty, and finally to my own heart'. He compared his invasion of Norway to Mussolini's 1935 'action in Abyssinia under the English cannon'.[16]

To command the operation Hitler chose Colonel General Nikolaus von Falkenhorst, who was in command of the XXI Corps. Born on 17 January 1886, Falkenhorst's command would be designated the XXI Army Group. His main claim to the position as commander lay in the fact that as captain in the spring of 1918 he had served as chief general staff officer with the German General Staff in Finland when Germany had planned an intervention in Finland. He had some limited experience with naval transport to Finland and so understood the need to co-ordinate two, and now three, services.[17] Falkenhorst was formally appointed *Wehrmachtbefehlshaber Norwegen*, or Commander of Armed Forces, Norway, on 21 February.[18]

When Hitler first asked Falkenhorst if he wanted the command, Falkenhorst went out for a walk to think it over. 'I went to town and bought a *Baedeker*, a travel guide, in order to find out just what Norway was like. I didn't have any idea, and I had to find out what all the harbours were, how many inhabitants there were, and just what kind of a country it was. I had no idea about the whole thing.' In uniform, he had gone to the book market and to disguise his intentions, 'dug deep in his own pockets' and bought several travel guides of various countries, including the one he wanted on Norway. He reported back that afternoon to Hitler, outlined his concept, was offered the command and accepted the position.[19]

Falkenhorst reported directly to Hitler, thus circumventing the regular army chain of command. It was obviously unusual for a German corps commander to organise an operation as important as the invasion of Norway, but it also helped ensure secrecy, especially since the formal military command of the German army opposed this attack.[20] After being tapped to command *Weserübung*, Falkenhorst joined the Krancke study group along with his Alsace-born Chief-of-Staff, Colonel Erich Buschenhagen, and a few other select members of his corps staff.[21]

There was a seamless transition in the planning for the operation. Having determined that it was a vital stepping stone to Norway, primarily for its twin airfields at Ålborg in northern Jutland, the team added Denmark to the plan. One of the twin airfields there met modern standards and was the most important of the two. The Krancke staff study for the invasion of Norway had foreseen the need to use Danish bases, especially these two airfields, but had hoped to apply diplomatic pressure to Denmark to secure their use. It was only after Falkenhorst took over that military action replaced diplomacy in the planning. Thus *Weserübung Süd* was born, a development that was communicated to Keitel and Jodl on 28 February. By this time, Falkenhorst had established strong links with the different military branches. At the height of preparations Hitler met with Falkenhorst daily for updates on the progress of the planning.[22]

Norway was divided into two naval commands. The overall Kriegsmarine commander was Admiral Hermann Boehm. Boehm chose Admiral Alfred Saalwächter to command Norway's 'Naval Group West' (*Marinegruppenkommando West*) and Admiral Rolf Carls for 'Naval Group East'. Luftwaffe forces were placed under the command of Lieutenant General Hans Geisler. A naval aviator in the First World War, Geissler stressed training for air attacks against enemy warships. Falkenhorst's orders to non-army units would go through the Kriegsmarine and Luftwaffe command structures.

Falkenhorst's initial plan included the seizure of the cities of Tromsø, Narvik, Trondheim, Bergen, Stavanger, Kristiansand and Oslo. The very distant Tromsø, over 150 miles north of Narvik, was later dropped. Falkenhorst included detailed measures for taking charge of civil administration, including the control of key communication centres, as well as radio, cable and telephone exchanges. The plan also made provision for an army band to play in front of the royal residence to help persuade the King of Norway not to resist. Regimental bands would accompany several of the main invasion forces.

From the start the campaign plan was innovative. Krancke sought to employ the 7th Airborne and the 22nd Air-Landing Divisions. But with duties already assigned to them for the upcoming assault on France, Belgium and the Netherlands, the divisions were not available.[23] If they had been, the additional force would have made the operation easier. The Luftwaffe eventually delegated a paratroop battalion of five companies to occupy the two airports with concrete runways at Sola near Stavanger and Fornebu at Oslo and for operations in Denmark. The naval element at Oslo was supposed to first pass the forts in the fjord and arrive in the inner Oslo harbour at 04:15. The paratroops would later drop at Fornebu and at Sola near Stavanger. A total of four platoons would be used at Ålborg's two undefended airfields in northern Denmark and some minor installations in the Danish islands, impacting on communications and transportation. Field Marshal Hermann Göring, informed of the operation for the first time on 5 March and that the Luftwaffe was expected to act in a joint command under Falkenhorst, was furious, going as far as making a personal attack on Keitel. It would be Göring who would force each of the three services to have their own chain of command. In the after action report in October 1940, one of the recommendations was that any future combined operation similar to *Weserübung* should use a unified command structure. It is ironic that such a common-sense approach would continue to be debated worldwide among officers in the following decades.[24]

\* \* \*

Germany's plan was to snuff out Norway and Denmark overnight. It would be a *coup de main* on a national scale. Denmark, with its lack of an adequate Neutrality Watch and its general military weakness, lay open to an easy attack. The Danish Colonel Ivan Carstensen had noted in 1937, 'From the German point of view, we do actually invite occupation.'[25] Norway was clearly the more difficult objective.

Intelligence played a key role, especially in light of the fact that Germany had a decided lack of intelligence about Denmark and Norway. A manual entitled *Orientierungsheft Norwegen* (Orientation for Norway) was the best initial source available to the Germans. It had been published in 1907 shortly after Norway became an independent nation. Germany had very little information on the Norwegian army and its dispositions. On the coastal fortifications there 'was not even a usable map'.[26] Nevertheless, preparations for the assault now proceeded rapidly.

The Abwehr had agents in the major German–Norwegian shipping lines and large fishing and fish-processing firms. Some were recruited from about 4,000 Germans who lived and worked in Norway. These agents, utilising a code based on common statistics and numbers employed in the fishing and shipping industries, supplied much important intelligence concerning weather conditions for German warships, freighters and aircraft. Curiously, the German plan made no provision for fog or overcast in April in Norway, a common occurrence at that time of year and one that would have an effect on the attack, most notably at Kristiansand and in the flight of vital aircraft formations.[27]

In late January the Abwehr had assigned Lieutenant Colonel Erich Pruck to head a team of Abwehr officers for the operation, and by 30 January it had begun arriving in Oslo. Pruck operated under the cover name of Ernst Pohl. The team's assignment was to discover '(a) strength, disposition and operational objectives of the Norwegian armed forces; and (b) condition of harbor installations in Oslo, Kristiansand, Stavanger, Bergen, Trondheim and Narvik with a view to landing troops.'[28] The 'Abwehr Outstation Oslo' performed excellently. In a short time it had noted troop dispositions, coastal defences, Norwegian military bases and had created usable maps.

Pruck repeatedly warned Admiral Canaris, the head of Abwehr, that an Allied attack could occur at any time. His reports in March were particularly forceful, referring to the increasing number of 'volunteers' from France and Britain trying to cross Norway to join the Finns in their war with the Soviet Union. Pruck had also noted the return of the British fleet to Scapa Flow from more distant ports in Scotland. After the sinking of the battleship *Royal Oak* there, the base defences at Scapa Flow had been improved. In addition, British troops with transports were identified gathering in Scottish bases. He also stated that the Norwegians would defend themselves and that the guns and torpedoes mounted at their bases could be quite effective.[29]

The Norwegians were aware of the increase in the German legation staff (there had been no German military attaché in Norway until October 1939); British and French embassy staffs were also expanding. Norway ordered Pruck and one other high-ranking Abwehr officer out of the county – to occur after 9 April.[30]

The Abwehr also employed the German trawler *Theseus* to navigate Norwegian waters and make regular radio reports. The Abwehr's Hamburg station and the *Theseus* made 'observations' in Norwegian territorial waters for some weeks.[31] Operation Theseus employed a simple Abwehr code and this was the first code the British broke in the war. A report on the ship's activities was made to the British naval staff on 30 March, but no action was taken as it was thought best not to molest the *Theseus* due to the great cryptanalytical value of its messages. The Admiralty incorrectly assumed the ship was there to gain information about possible British minelaying operations and missed the real significance of the ship's activities. In many ways Field Marshal Brauchitsch and General Halder were correct in their initial concerns – the Allies should have scented out this approaching blow from the dark.[32]

Usually the German navy kept disciplined radio silence, especially the surface ships. Britain gleaned little from its radio traffic. But Luftwaffe pilots used their radios frequently. It was not long before the code-breakers at Bletchley Park began to break the Luftwaffe code introduced on 9 April for use in the invasion.[33]

The Kriegsmarine signal intelligence service had broken some of the British naval codes and, combined with air reconnaissance, British naval movements in the North and Norwegian Seas were fairly well understood by the Germans.[34]

Beginning on 13 March, German naval intelligence began to notice heavy British submarine radio traffic and concluded that upwards of fifteen Allied submarines were operating off southern Norway. On 15 March it was determined that the submarines had been ordered to 'stand down', most likely due to the end of the Winter War. On 26 March Raeder had informed Hitler that the British might mine Norwegian waters to get a German reaction, thus providing the Allies with an excuse to land troops in Norway.[35] According to German intelligence, the British were primarily interested in Stavanger, Bergen, Kristiansand and possibly Trondheim.[36] British radio traffic increased again in early April, suggesting to the Germans that some operation was afoot. Even so, the actual minelaying by the British on 8 April would come as a complete surprise to the Germans.[37]

Admiral Canaris visited Norway on 31 March and was in Oslo under an alias. His visit had three functions. One was to sort out issues between Abwehr officers and the naval attaché Lieutenant Commander Richard Schreiber in Oslo. This he was unable to complete as Pruck was absent from Oslo at the time.[38] Secondly, Canaris wanted to get an update on the situation, and thirdly, let his people know the state of *Weserübung*. He also met with Ambassador Bräuer but did not divulge details of the impending invasion to him. Canaris evidently also met with some Norwegian citizens. Why he did so is unclear, although the timing of his visit suggests it was related to the impending invasion.[39]

Canaris plays a murky and only partially understood role in these events. He would later be implicated in various anti-Hitler actions, but there is no evidence that he betrayed information about Germany's invasion to the Norwegian authorities. He did plant Lieutenant Commander Franz Liedig of the Abwehr on Falkenhorst's planning staff, allowing him access to information on the preparations for the invasion. Liedig made several pre-April 1940 visits to Denmark as part of the planning for *Weserübung*. Canaris apparently believed that the Allies understood the approaching invasion plans and would 'stage a show of strength which would deter the Führer from hopelessly risking the weak German navy in the North Sea'.[40] Liedig, along with Abwehr Colonel (later Major General) Hans Oster, were anti-Hitler conspirators and were at this time working together to undermine Hitler's position in Germany.

Schreiber played an important role in the run-up to the invasion. He not only used his diplomatic immunity and contacts to help send intelligence back to Germany, but he also played up the possibility of unilateral intervention by Great Britain. He supplied information to the Abwehr and was close to Admiral Raeder.[41] Also acting as intelligence conduits were members of the German Foreign Ministry and Rosenberg's Foreign Policy Office of the Nazi Party. Their members were able to send information back to Germany through their own ministry communication systems.

Denmark also received attention from the Abwehr. Lieutenant General of the Luftwaffe Leonhard Kaupisch, who would command the XXXI Corps in its attack against Denmark, noted, 'The documentation on Denmark and the Danish forces was very useful but on certain points it had to be supplemented',[42] for which purpose the Abwehr had 'a whole network of confidential agents' in Denmark.[43] Many were Germans who by the stroke of history were Danish citizens, while some Danes also helped. At the end of the war Denmark identified sixteen such traitors. His Chief-of-Staff was Major General Kurt Himer. At the outbreak of war he had been stationed in Warsaw and witnessed the initial Luftwaffe airstrikes around Warsaw and this gave him a unique perspective on the upcoming operations.

Air reconnaissance played an important role. The Luftwaffe had a reconnaissance group made up of high-altitude multi-engine aircraft that posed as airliners and flew over Norway, Sweden and Denmark on the eve of war to collect air photographs of the targets. This group was known in German circles as the Reconnaissance Squadron Rowehl. Led by Colonel Theodor Rowehl, for most work it utilised pressurised He111s flying at 32,000ft. Narvik received two overflights before the outbreak of war by a longer range aircraft, the Focke Wulf Condor.[44]

When war planning began in earnest, the Luftwaffe sent many additional planes out on missions, primarily to photograph military installations in key cities. However, while they mapped out Norwegian military installations well, they could not accurately determine the exact strength of several of these installations. During the fighting the Germans, with absolute command of the skies, would be well served by their air reconnaissance.[45]

Denmark and Norway were aware of the German overflights and also of overflights by Great Britain. Protests were lodged with both governments but with little result. Neither country tried to halt these high-altitude overflights because they were not viewed as directly hostile. The Norwegians had orders to shoot down foreign warplanes but only if they were actually bombing or strafing. Air-raid drills, primarily at Oslo, were conducted leading up to the outbreak of war.[46]

German security regarding the operation was excellent, despite the fact that by March the limited circle of officers in the know was ever widening. It was later recalled, 'every officer was bound to [secrecy] by shaking hands. The orders and regulations were only drawn up by officers, one of whom undertook the typing work and the preparation of dispatches.'[47] The actual German troops involved in the operations, especially those bound for Denmark, were convinced they were part of a large-scale practice manoeuvre in the Hamburg region.

The final German intelligence action involved German army officer Lieutenant Colonel Hartwig Pohlman. Pohlman had been intimately involved in the planning for the invasion since its early days. He travelled by train to Copenhagen and then went on to Oslo, where he arrived on the morning of 8 April. He hid his role by using the cover of being an anonymous escort to the legation councillor. Pohlman handed Ambassador Bräuer the sealed demands Bräuer was to deliver to the Norwegian government. That night Pohlman ordered the German air attaché to meet the approaching German aircraft at Fornebu airfield. Pohlman would help co-ordinate the German forces landing at Oslo.[48]

Bräuer was occupied on 8 April with numerous phone calls and meetings concerning the British minelaying along the Norwegian coast. As the afternoon wore on, he began receiving messages and enquiries about German soldiers and sailors coming ashore from three ships sinking off Norway's coast.[49] He was not informed of the impending attack until 23:00.

Norway and Denmark had had earlier indications that something was afoot. Threats of invasion of Norway went back as far as Christmas 1939. At that time the Norwegian navy had been ordered to conduct coastal patrols and Christmas leave for its sailors was cancelled. Again in February alarms were raised which did not, however, result in any attack.[50] Swedish intelligence had reports in late March that something was being planned, but much of the intelligence only made sense after the event. Then, as will be shown, on the eve of the invasion, Sweden would have important intelligence, but realising that Sweden was not the target, failed to pass along much of this information to Norway or Denmark.

* * *

Germany had only limited forces available for the invasion. The army staff understandably gave priority to the need for maximum forces to be mustered against the Allies in the coming attack in the Low Countries and France. A total of six divisions were allocated for the Norwegian operation. In addition, two divisions were assigned for Denmark, one of those earmarked for police duties with the second guarding the coast against any Allied response.[51]

The German forces sent to Norway were not the country's finest. Only two divisions were at full strength for their TO&E: the binary (two regiments only) 3rd Mountain Division and the 69th Infantry Division (triangular or three regiments). One recalls Secretary of Defense Donald Rumsfeld, who said, 'as you know, you go to war with the Army you have. They're not the Army you might want or wish to have at a later time.'[52] These German infantry divisions were lacking their armoured car reconnaissance elements so they relied on bicycle troops, which usually included some motorcycles, and most were short of their full artillery complement.

The German order of battle for Norway consisted of the expanded XXI Army Corps, known as Gruppe XXI under the command of General Falkenhorst. There were three divisions in the first wave: the 3rd Mountain Division (two regiments), the 69th Infantry Division and the 163rd Infantry Division; two in the second wave: the 181st Infantry Division and the 196th Infantry Division. The sixth division, the newly-formed 214th, would be part of a third wave assigned to Norway and was to arrive in the Oslo region eight days after the inital invasion. As a reserve unit, and also due to its being almost fully equipped, including all its artillery, on 14 April its orders called for it to move to relieve German forces between Kristiansand and Stavanger.[53]

The invasion of Denmark was the responsibility of the XXXI Army Corps, consisting of 170th Infantry Division, the 198th Infantry Division and the 11th Motorised Infantry Brigade, plus elements of the Hermann Göring Regiment (a Luftwaffe motorised ground unit). These two infantry divisions would have one regiment each with only two instead of the usual three battalions. Both invasion forces included *Panzer-Abteilung z.b.V40*, or 40th Special Armour Battalion, for an armoured element, four companies of paratroops (a fifth company would later be added for an operational drop during the fighting) and other miscellaneous elements, including Luftwaffe heavy flak units.

By the end of the first day of the invasion the plans called for 4,000 troops to have been flown into Norway and 8,850 to have landed from the sea. As it worked out, this target would be almost completely met.

Falkenhorst had requested three mountain divisions but he was only given one. The choice of the well-trained 3rd Mountain Division is interesting. Like the 2nd Mountain Division, it had only two not three regiments. At this time only the 1st had three regiments. So, though technically a binary division, it was not formally designed as one. Future German mountain divisions often were made up of only two infantry regiments, which like the Italian concept, on paper at least, gave the units a larger amount of artillery capable of supporting fewer men – though with the Germans the additional artillery support was more likely to be a reality.

The 3rd Mountain Division was predominantly Austrian in background (both regiments had been raised there). It had seen some light action in the Polish campaign. It also carried lighter equipment for its role as a mountain division. Smaller lighter artillery was very typical. The weapons were designed so they could be broken down and manhandled through difficult and mountainous terrain.[54] This and other lightweight equipment made it easier to transport the division over long distances by ship or plane. The equipment was winterised and designed for combat at high elevations. The Japanese in the early 1941–2 invasions of Allied territory in the Far East often employed mountain artillery units in their attack forces for the same reason – firepower delivered lightly.[55]

The bulk of German force for the Norwegian campaign was made up of the standard infantry division. The typical infantry division had three regiments.[56] They were well armed with both rifles and machine-guns. A regiment of artillery with a total of forty-eight guns was theoretically attached, but only the 3rd Mountain, the 69th and the 214th Infantry Divisions had their full artillery complement. Several were short of one of their three assigned batteries per artillery battalion. It was indicative of the level of preparedness that each of the infantry divisions was formed in 1939 and with several seeing their third regiment added only toward the end of 1939. Only one infantry division (the 69th) had its full complement of vehicles (and the armoured cars were older cars armed only with machine-guns), and all had more horse-drawn transport than earlier divisions. Horse transport was important for German infantry units for both battle transport and bringing guns to the front line as well as for supply and support transport. (Many photographs of the campaign show horse-drawn supply wagons, bridging equipment and gun limbers as well as horses carrying supplies.[57]) More armour and motorised transport was sent from Denmark in the days immediately after the invasion as well as locally requisitioned equipment.[58] Initially the 69th and 214th had been kitted out with captured Czech equipment, but this was replaced by German equipment before the invasion at the insistence of Lieutenant General Fritz Fromm, Commander of the Replacement Army. This wise move was made in order to achieve uniformity, which would make it easier to supply parts.

The standard German infantry division that accounted for the vast bulk of the invasion force was better equipped than any Norwegian infantry division, but for the most part neither army was fully up to strength, and with little combat experience at the enlisted man level. Some German officers and NCOs had had a degree of combat experience in Poland, while the higher command levels had fought in the First World War. Training was intensive leading up to the invasion. It included long marches with a heavy amount of ammunition to make the soldiers fit to carry heavy weapons without means of transport, and to be able to disembark from assault boats carrying all their equipment. Moreover, the troops received training in fighting in urban areas and the occupation of buildings.[59] During the training of the army troops nicknames were used for the objectives (German city names substituted for Norwegian ones). But the training did not meet the rigorous standards set by Falkenhorst. Falkenhorst and the German command staff viewed air-transport and mountain-warfare training, quite important for the Norwegian terrain during winter and spring, as inadequate.[60]

On 6 April, when troops began to embark, there were speeches from the officers, but little fanfare. The troops speculated that they were bound for Scotland. Once at sea on 8 April, the true destination was posted and information about Norway was distributed.[61]

There were two cutting-edge technologies and units that would make key contributions to the rapid victory about to unfold. They were noted and recommended by the original Krancke study group. The paratroops, supported by units that could be airlifted in, was one of these essential elements. The other was the *Panzer* tank.

The 1st Battalion of the 1st *Fallschirmjäger* Regiment under the command of Captain Erich Walther was earmarked for *Weserübung*. These were the paratroops. The battalion consisted of four rifle companies and a headquarters company unit. Each company was made up of three platoons of three squads each. The headquarters company was flown by transports to Ålborg on 9 April and later that day flew on to Fornebu at Oslo and was landed at the airfield after it had been seized.

The Ju52 tri-motor transport was a key to victory in both Denmark and Norway. It was the workhorse of the German air-transport service, though it was not the best aircraft. The jump door and the unusual aerodynamics of the aircraft necessitated that the paratroops be between 5ft 2in and 5ft 10in. At the time of the invasion because of the many new plane crews, only about half of the crews could fly their Ju52s on instruments alone, which in the heavy April weather would lead to accidents and losses.

The paratroopers were required to have all weapons, other than pistols and hand grenades, placed in canisters to be dropped separately from them, which meant that when they landed the troops were virtually defenseless. A platoon of forty to fifty men had fourteen canisters assigned to them, each weighing up to 260lb when loaded. German parachute design, owing in large part to the Ju52's aerodynamics, forced the paratroopers to have a 'hard' chute opening – which is why the men could not carry a rifle or other large gun as the sudden force of the chute opening would cause the weapon to fly into their face. Nor could they manipulate the chute for landing; once out of the plane they were unable to control where they descended.[62] Standard issue for the German paratroops was a pistol with two full magazines and a rimless steel helmet. The standard weapon was the MP 38 sub-machine-gun using a non-standard 9mm round instead of the German infantry 7.92mm round. The men were also issued in their rations a glucose-based energy tablet and an amphetamine-type drug, 'Pervitin'.[63] The pharmaceutical company Temmler had introduced the drug in Germany in 1938. In 1940 the German military ordered 35 million tablets.[64]

The second important decision made by the Krancke study group was the request for inclusion of a tank battalion. This battalion was cobbled together from training areas and numbered about forty tanks. It was known as *Panzer-Abteilung z.b.V40*. Most of the tanks were the small 6-ton PzKw Is and 8.9-ton PzKw IIs (see Chapter 7). The Germans chose the small light tanks from their inventory for their armoured force in Norway and Denmark because they had to transport them by sea to Norway and potentially to the Danish islands, and the concept of economy of force suggested that this would be all that was required against the weak Danish and Norwegian defences. Also three prototype tanks that never went into full production were included. These were the larger Neubau PzKw IV tanks. They would have an impact much greater than their capability because of their large size. When first landed in Oslo in early April, a point was made to parade them through the centre as they were so impressively large even though they were a lightly armoured 1935–6 failed design. At 18 tons, the Neubau PzKw IV had a 37mm and a 75mm gun carried in a shared turret and three machine-guns. Each had a six-man crew. A total of five had been built but only the last three were equipped with armour plate. After one tank was lost at Kvam on 26 April it was replaced with one of the unarmoured prototypes.[65]

In addition to the tanks, the invasion force had one company of armoured cars (thirty-six) attached.[66] Also attached were the 11th Motorised Rifle Brigade and the Kluge detachment (part of the Luftwaffe motorised Hermann Göring Regiment). Parts of all these units would be transferred to Norway before the end of the fighting.

There were also six companies of motorised artillery, four armed with 105mm and two with 150mm guns, attached to the army. The Luftwaffe brought in several units of 88mm anti-aircraft/anti-tank guns and other equipment for airfield defence. Much of the heavy equipment was brought in by sea, while the men and some of the equipment were flown in. The headquarters also had radio units, couriers and mapping units for the campaign.

Also later airlifted in to Stavanger, Bergen and Mandel (about halfway between Stavanger and Kristiansand on the coast) were three Freya radar sets, primarily for alerting the Germans to incoming Allied aircraft. This was accomplished early in the campaign.[67]

The Luftwaffe would use 533 Ju52 transport aircraft, plus 13 modified as seaplanes and 20 other transport aircraft, part of a total of 1,168 planes of the X *Fliegerkorps* under Lieutenant General Hans Geisler.[68] Additional planes brought the total closer to 1,200 aircraft. Most were quickly transferred south to prepare for the planned attack on France in May. The transport planes were under the command of Lieutenant Colonel Carl von Gablenz, who had been a senior manager at Lufthansa and was skilled at directing the heavy logistical traffic created by the 500-plus transports shuttling between Germany and Norway, with occasional stops at the Ålborg airfields in Denmark.

The heart of the German aerial offensive was built around three Wings (*Geschwader*). These were the 4th, 26th and 30th, each made up of a command squadron and three combat squadrons. The first two regiments deployed the He111, while the 30th had Ju88s, both modern twin-engined bombers. Each squadron contained varying numbers of aircraft, from a low of thirteen to a high of thirty-six, while each command squadron consisted of five or six aircraft. For example, the 4th Regiment had six command squadron aircraft, two squadrons of thirty-six He111s each, and a third squadron made up of seventeen He111s and twenty Ju88s.

The He111 would be the bomber in most operations, while the Ju88 had a greater range and was faster. Also deployed to the campaign were seventy-seven short-ranged Ju87 Stuka dive-bombers.[69] These aircraft flew along the army front as it moved north out of Oslo and had a psychological impact on the Allied forces that counted almost as much as their typical payload of about 1,000lb. When within range they were used against Allied naval assets.

The main German fighter in this campaign was the twin-engine Me110. While considered one of Germany's less successful designs in the war, it did mount a powerful armament of five machine-guns (four firing forward) and two 20mm cannon. It had a range of about 700 miles, much greater than the Me109 with a range of just 440 miles. There were sixty-four Me110s and thirty-eight Me109s assigned to the campaign. The Me109 was a much superior fighter to any Royal Navy fighter, primarily the Sea Gladiator or Skua, but in reality there were very few Me109s encountered in this campaign as the Me110 had the required range and the Me109 did not.

Fleshing out the Luftwaffe were older bombers and seaplanes. The two German naval commands also had Luftwaffe units assigned to them. Naval Command West had a squadron of He111s and a squadron of Do18 seaplanes. Naval Command East had a squadron of old twin-engine Do17s and three flights of mostly single-engine floatplanes.

Most of the losses in the invasion wave were incurred in the air-transport section while many Ju52s were transporting troops, fuel and supplies to Denmark and Norway. These losses were a result of a combination of enemy action, the poor weather and flying long distances, often over water.

Air transport of troops and supplies had been carried out in the Italo-Ethiopian War of 1935–6 and had played a vital role in the Spanish Civil War of 1936–9. In the latter, air transport was a key to victory for the Nationalists when thousands of troops were flown in from Spanish Morocco at the start of the fighting.[70] The Japanese in their fighting with the Chinese had employed limited combined air-land-sea operations. It had also been seen as recently as April 1939 during the Italian seizure of Albania.[71] There had also been some minor combined operations in the Polish campaign. But nothing at anywhere near this scale had ever been attempted before.

The Luftwaffe was slow to develop the torpedo-plane. In 1918 the German naval air arm had 1,500 machines, 16,000 men skilled in the use of aerial torpedoes and a special torpedo-bomber. The Kriegsmarine developed two torpedo-plane designs before the war, but the Luftwaffe did not develop the use of torpedoes in the prewar period and it would not employ torpedoes until 1942. Ironically, the first German air-dropped torpedoes were based on a Norwegian torpedo purchased for illegal experiments by the Reichsmarine before Hitler came to power.[72]

The Luftwaffe was also slow to develop four-engine long-range bombers to hit distant targets on land and at sea. Work in this area had begun under the Luftwaffe's first Chief of the General Staff, General Walter Wever, but after his death in an air accident in June 1936 the programme was deferred as Göring wanted numbers over size of aircraft. The greatest success of the Treaty of Versailles was most likely the emasculation of the German air force in the interwar period. Because of it Germany was unable to fully develop the air weapons of modern war. The period between 1919 and 1933 when Germany was forbidden an air force, even though some research and development took place clandestinely, would prove to be a powerful brake on the full evolution of the Luftwaffe. Though the most powerful air force on the planet in 1940, it was essentially a tactical force and never developed fully as a strategic striking force, and had little interest in building up naval aviation.[73]

* * *

The main method to transport the army to Norway, and especially its heavy equipment, was the German navy and merchant marine. Admiral Raeder saw the naval campaign has having three elements: first, approaching the invasion ports; next, entering the ports and seizing the objectives; and finally, returning to Germany.[74]

Important landing areas had their own Warship Group (*Kriegsschiffsgruppe*) assigned to them and there would be a total of eleven Warship Groups. The Kriegsmarine carried many of the first and most important troops to land. A total of seven landing points were selected in Norway, from the north to south: Narvik, Trondheim, Bergen, Egersund, Kristiansand, Arendal and Oslo. Denmark had seven landing spots: Copenhagen, Middelfahrt, Esbjerg, Tyboron, Korsør, Gedser and Nyborg. Some of the Warship Groups were detailed two or more landing places to seize. Six days were required for the transport ships to reach their targets in Norway, while three days were necessary for the warships to reach their objectives. Distances to Norway ranged from the 340 miles between Kiel and Arendal to 1,240 miles between Cuxhaven and Narvik. Distances to

Denmark were much shorter. The ships could be recalled and the operation still cancelled until the third day after sailing. Based on a navy study, it was decided that simultaneous arrival at the targets by the navy groups was of vital importance for the success of the operation. As Earl F. Ziemke has noted, 'The Norwegian Campaign constituted the major point in the German Navy's exploitation of its surface forces.'[75]

Below is a breakdown for the initial onslaught. Note that Stavanger did not have a warship group designated for it, but instead was to be occupied by two battalions of the 69th Infantry division to be brought in by air and landed at nearby Sola airfield after paratroops had seized it. This operation would be carried out successfully. Additionally, the port of Åndalsnes near Trondheim was to be seized by Warship Group 2 (Trondheim), but when the *Lützow* had to be reassigned to Warship Group 5 (Oslo) due to machinery problems with its 400 mountain troops on board with supplies the port was dropped.[76]

| Group | No of troops; Unit | Destination |
|---|---|---|
| Warship Group 1 | 2,000; 3rd Mountain | Narvik |
| Warship Group 2 | 1,700; 3rd Mountain | Trondheim |
| Warship Group 3 | 1,900; 69th | Bergen |
| Warship Group 4 | 1,100; 163rd | Kristiansand;Arendal |
| Warship Group 5 | 1,550; 163rd and | |
| | 400; 3rd Mountain | Oslo |
| Warship Group 6 | 150; 163rd | Egersund |
| Warship Group 7 | 1,990; 198th | Korsør; Nyborg (Dn.) |
| Warship Group 8 | 1,000; 198th | Copenhagen (Dn.) |
| Warship Group 9 | 400; 170th | Middelfart (Dn.) |
| Warship Group 10 | no troops | Esbjerg (Dn.) |
| Warship Group 11 | no troops | Tyborøn (Dn.) |

Dn = Denmark

A German army unit based at Warnemünde (the port of Rostock) would capture the Danish town of Gedser by using the local ferry.

Also landing with these warship groups were miscellaneous naval and air units. The naval units were primarily to man the coastal defence batteries and to establish radio communications, while the Luftwaffe elements were largely for mounting air operations and communications. For example, the force carried on Warship Group 1 consisted of 1,900 men of the 3rd Mountain Division, a company of coastal defence naval infantry or marines,[77] an element of naval radio/signals personnel and minor elements of a Luftwaffe AA battalion. Within the 1,900 men of the 3rd Mountain Division were the advanced party of the divisional command and the regimental command of the 139th Mountain Regiment under the command of Colonel A. Windisch. This force had the longest distance to travel.[78]

The German naval force was primarily a modern navy, but it was small and some of the warships did have problems. The battleships *Scharnhorst* and

*Gneisenau* were the largest warships available to them. Really battlecruisers, they were powerful and fast, but the ships' primary 11.1in (283mm) gun[79] was a lighter weapon than that carried on any British capital ship. Fully loaded, they displaced 37,000 tons but could steam at 30 knots. Well armoured for medium-ranged actions, they were vulnerable to heavy guns firing at long range with their plunging fire. They had been designed to counter French battlecruisers of the *Dunkerque* class and for Atlantic Ocean operations.[80] Vice Admiral Günther Lütjens had command with his flag in the *Gneisenau*.

The German battleships were armed with three triple turrets housing the 11in guns, two forward and one aft. Maximum gun range was over 26 miles, impractical without the support of spotter aircraft. Secondary batteries were twelve 5.9in guns mounted in four double and four single turrets, with six on a broadside. Following German practice, AA armament was separate from secondary guns. The AA armament consisted of a mix of fourteen 4.1in, sixteen 37mm and ten 20mm guns, creating a powerful anti-aircraft platform, a role all capital ships would play in the Second World War.[81]

The German pocket battleship *Lützow* participated in the invasion as part of Warship Group 5. (The ship had been recently renamed and given a new rating as a heavy cruiser, but we will refer to it as a pocket battleship.) The *Lützow* was armed with six 11in guns in triple turrets fore and aft. It also carried eight single-mounted 5.9in guns, a heavy AA battery and above-water torpedo tubes. When new its top speed was about 28 knots, but after seven years of service was slower now. It was well armoured and considerably over the Treaty of Versailles limit of 10,000 tons.

The German heavy cruisers *Admiral Hipper* and *Blücher* were the most modern heavy cruisers in 1940. These handsome ships had been designed for operations in the Atlantic, so were capable of relatively long-range operations. They had been designed to fight the French *Algérie* heavy cruiser or run from a *Dunkerque* battlecruiser. They carried eight 8in guns in four turrets (two fore and two aft), with a secondary armament of twelve 4.1in guns. For so-called Treaty cruisers, named after the Washington Treaty of 1922, they were fairly well armoured, being superior to any British heavy cruiser. This superiority was due both to their recent construction and being grossly over the Washington Treaty weight of 10,000 tons for cruisers, coming in at a hefty 14,050 tons.

German light cruisers were not particularly inspired designs. Five of the six in service in 1940 participated in the campaign. All but one had their three triple turrets arranged with one forward and two aft, so they could bring heavier fire while retreating than attacking. This turret configuration would present a problem in the attack at Kristiansand. The one exception to this configuration was the oldest, the *Emden*, which was part of the force attacking Oslo. *Emden*'s gun arrangement was of the First World War era design with single gun mounts distributed up and down the ship. All five of these ships had been laid down in the 1920s and were small, unexceptional warships, especially when compared to larger and more modern Allied light cruisers.

At the time of the attack, Germany had two classes of very similar destroyers. They were large and armed with five 5.1in guns in separate turrets. Originally designed to fight Soviet, Polish and French destroyers, all of which tended to be large, they were speedy and had good endurance, but were temperamental and prone to engineering and stability problems. The destroyers had a bow design that was not suited for rough Atlantic seas, even after post-construction modifications. There were fifteen destroyers available for the Norway operation; five of the six of the latest class joined the attack on Narvik. The destroyers had fairly effective AA armament for the day, with two pairs of 37mm medium-range guns capable of an effectual eighty rounds per minute. There were six 20mm single-mounted guns similar in capability to the Swiss-designed Oerlikon available for close-in combat. Crews numbered between 313 and 315 men. Fourteen sailed and one destroyer was kept in Germany in reserve.[82]

German submarines had a role to play as well. Rear Admiral Karl Dönitz, based at Kiel, dispatched eight submarine task forces numbered 1–6, 8 and 9. The lull in U-boat activity had been noted, and the dispatch to sea and activity of the U-boats was public knowledge and was reported in the press.[83] The smaller submarines patrolled closer to Germany and off southern Norway, while the larger and newer boats operated to the north and off the British Isles.

If range is not an issue, smaller submarines are superior for operating in littoral waters for several reasons. One obvious advantage is that a smaller submarine can better manoeuvre in shallower and more restricted waters than a larger one. Additionally, the sound transmission for sonar detection is more problematical. Littoral waters often translate into irregular sea bottoms, and the impact of wind, waves, water temperature, currents, tides and freshwater, brackish waters and the varying salinity of coastal waters all combine to make submarine detection more difficult.[84]

The first submarines left port on 31 March, the last heading out on 6 April. They were instructed to open their orders at sea on 6 April as part of Operation *Hartsmuth*.

The U-boats were deployed as follows:

| Group number | No. of U-boats | Operating off |
|---|---|---|
| 1 | 5 | Narvik |
| 2 | 2 | Trondheim |
| 3 | 5 | Bergen |
| 4 | 2 | Stavanger |
| 5 | 6 | NE of Shetland Islands |
| 6 | 5 | Scotland |
| 8 | 4 | Egersund |
| 9 | 2 | SE of Shetland Islands |

(A planned group 7 was abandoned.)

Unfortunately for the Germans there would be technical difficulties with their torpedoes which held Allied losses to a minimum. Germany fielded two torpedoes in this campaign. By far the predominant one carried on all surface warships as well as submarines was the G7a. It was a conventional powered wet-heater compressed-air torpedo similar to British, French and Norwegian models. This 21in torpedo carried a warhead of 660lb, was almost 24ft long and if set at its high speed could travel 6,500yd.[85] It used a magnetic detonator that allowed the torpedo to detonate under a ship without actually striking the target. The submarines also carried the G7e, an electrically-powered torpedo that used two batteries. It had a very short range of 5,400yd at 30 knots but had the advantage of leaving a much less noticeable wake than the G7a. Ever since the beginning of the war the German submarine commanders, who fired by far the bulk of torpedoes, had reported numerous times that the torpedoes were defective.

There were three issues. First, the magnetic detonators were very sensitive to their environment. The stronger magnetic field in the far northern latitudes of Norway simply exacerbated the problem and resulted in either on the surface or deeper torpedo runs when set, resulting in torpedoes running under targets and not exploding. Additionally, some torpedoes exploded short of the target. The magnetic detonators on the G7a had been modified with a switch that allowed them to be set for percussion detonation only. This was the dominant problem in German torpedoes.

Secondly, the standard detonator had been 'improved' since the First World War so that if the torpedo struck its target at an angle rather than head on it would fail to explode. Few torpedoes strike the target at a precise 90-degree angle, so there were many duds, but the few hits that resulted in explosions simply deepened the mystery as to why the other torpedoes failed to explode.

Thirdly, there was a problem with percussion detonation in that the depth of the torpedo had to be correctly maintained as it travelled towards its target. The depth-setting device was faulty in the German torpedoes, and the less salty water of Norway's fjords, fed as they were by numerous freshwater streams, also had an effect.[86] This resulted in torpedoes travelling deeper than programmed. So torpedoes set for shallow or medium depth would pass under the intended victim. During the German destroyer actions at Narvik on 9 April, a German merchant-ship captain reported to the captain of the German destroyer *Bernd von Arnim* that a torpedo passed *under* his ship. The torpedo had been set for 2m and the merchant ship drew 7m.[87] The essence of these problems can be traced to the practice of testing only new torpedoes and the maintenance of shipboard torpedoes being lax.[88]

Sending sailors into combat with weapons that only worked occasionally was simply criminal.

The Germans later said that their submarines attacked the British battleship *Warspite*, which played a prominent role early in the campaign, four times. There were also fourteen attacks on battleships or cruisers, ten on destroyers and ten on transports. According to Dönitz, only one of these attacks, against a transport, was successful.[89] This is not correct as there were other ships sunk by the Germans. The *U-4* sank the British submarine *Thistle* on 10 April; and the *U-13* sank one transport and damaged a tanker. There were four other Allied freighters lost in April in these northern waters to other U-boats. The *Thistle* was the only Allied warship lost to torpedoes. Even so, the ratio of successful attacks to the number of torpedoes fired was very low. Approximately twenty attacks should have been successful if the torpedoes had functioned correctly.[90] That the torpedoes were ineffective most of the time was incredibly fortunate for the Allies.[91] To add insult to injury, four U-boats would be lost. Off the Shetlands the destroyer *Hero* sank the *U-50* on 10 April, while the submarine *Porpoise* off southern Norway sank *U-1* on 16 April. The other two losses will be discussed later.[92]

The problem with the torpedoes used by German warships would manifest itself especially in the fighting at and near Narvik.

\* \* \*

The failure to maintain let alone expand the military in a timely fashion would cost Norway and Denmark occupation by Germany. To state the case of Denmark in August 1914, the army had been partially mobilised and key fortresses around Copenhagen and elsewhere had been manned throughout the war. The Danish navy of 6,000 men had also been mobilised and the Kattegat mined. These actions were certainly a deterrent during the war. But by 1940 such thorough preparations were a thing of the past.

This defeat would generate recriminations and rumours that grew out of this failure. Richard Petrow notes in his study *The Bitter Years*:

> The Scandinavian countries could not have been defeated merely by stronger German forces, better German strategy, or more daring German battlefield tactics; something else must have been involved, something secret, sinister, and shameful. The explanations promulgated in the immediate aftermath of the invasion, and repeated consistently during the war years, took account of these hidden factors by crediting the success of German arms to German treachery, sabotage, and espionage, aided and abetted by the German Fifth Column, that unseen force of spies, rumormongers, collaborators, and traitors believed to have been operating within Denmark and Norway.[93]

There were instances where a fifth column was of help to the Germans, most notably the followers of Quisling, but in reality this fifth column was a shadow of the popular perception. Carl J. Hambro, President of the Norwegian parliament, had an insight into German operations that is still relevant today. He noted in 1941, 'the most dangerous Fifth Column is to be found behind the bars of diplomatic immunity; every German embassy is a potential center of Fifth Column mobilization; every German consulate is an armory, a danger spot, the privileged stable of a Trojan horse'.[94]

On 5 April 1940, the German Embassy in Oslo, with Ambassador Bräuer acting as host, issued a formal invitation to the Norwegian Foreign Office to watch what the Germans called a 'peace' film. Most bureau chiefs attended in formal attire. Foreign Minister Halvdan Koht, Commanding General Laake and Mrs Harriman, the American ambassador, also attended. The film was *Baptism of Fire*, which depicted the bombing and destruction in Poland and of Warsaw in particular. The screening was intended to intimidate the Norwegians not to resist German occupation. The wife of one Norwegian official recalled that the 'Norwegian guests sat in stunned, deathly silence, riveted to their chairs for more than an hour.'[95]

* * *

German plans had been ready for execution since 20 March but due to the cold winter there was too much ice in the southern Baltic to undertake the operation.[96] Wanting to take advantage of the maximum darkness caused by the new moon, 7 April was the first date Raeder proposed. On 1 April, Hitler held another 5-hour meeting regarding the invasion planning. In attendance were the commanders of Gruppe XXI, the air force and navy commanders, and the commander of XXXI Corps for the Denmark invasion. Hitler discussed with them their thoughts, orders and expectations of Falkenhorst's plan. Every landing commander gave Hitler a report. After several questions, Hitler gave his approval to all of the operational details and called *Weserübung* not only 'audacious' but also 'the most impudent operation of the new military history'.[97] The next day Hitler set the commencement of the invasion for 04:15 (05:15 Berlin time) on 9 April and the final orders were issued.

The German plan for invading Norway was brilliant. In the days before the attack innocent merchant ships were to steal north with fuel, supplies and troops – but only a few ships at a time so as not to cause a suspicious spike in the normal flow of merchant traffic. In addition, troops moved from their bases to the invasion embarkation ports and borders. Warships with the longest journeys began to leave the North Sea ports of Cuxhaven, Wilhelmshaven and Bremerhaven on 6 April. Units departing for Oslo and south Norway departed from the Baltic, especially follow-up echelons of merchant ships filled with troops and supplies, many from the port of Stettin. This staggered departure resulted in a long snake of ships off the Norwegian coast or in The Leads.

Was this some sort of exercise – the Germans had released information that they were practising river crossings in northern Germany? Or was this an operation about to be mounted against Scotland? No one knew for sure. The first merchant ships with fuel and war materials departed on 3 April through The Leads and then up towards Narvik. Captains of all the invasion warships were ordered to pretend, on entering Norwegian ports, that they were British.[98]

The Tanker Group (*Tankerstaffel*) consisted of eight tankers. One, the 11,776-ton *Jan Wellem*, a converted whaler, departed from the small port of Sapadnaia just outside of Murmansk, and headed south bound for Narvik, while the departure of others from German ports depended on how far each ship had to travel.[99] From Germany one tanker was dispatched to Narvik, two to Trondheim, one to Bergen, one to Stavanger and two to Oslo. Some were exceedingly small, such as the 322-ton tanker *Belt*, bound for Bergen. Each carried fuel for the warship's return voyage, which was vital in the case of Narvik as the German destroyers did not carry enough fuel to return. The tankers also carried aviation fuel.

The next group, the *Ausfuhr-Staffel* or Export Group, also with staggered sailing over a span of several days, consisted of seven ships with a total of 51,800 tons. Some carried troops, but most heavy equipment, including horses, which was not carried by the warships. They were to arrive as close to the invasion time on 9 April as possible. Three were bound for Narvik, three for Trondheim and one for Stavanger. Only two made it to their destinations.

The largest and final group was called the Sea Transport Group (*Seetransport-staffeln*) and was bound mostly for southern ports. It was made up of two groups totalling twenty-six ships. But also attached to this group were three Luftwaffe ships that do not appear in most rosters, the *Bernhard von Tschirschky*, the *Hans Rolshoven* and the *Karl Meyer*. The first two were assigned to Bergen and the third to Kristiansand, and later Stavanger. They were small (displacing between 960 and 1,351 tons) seaplane tenders armed with 37mm and 20mm AA guns with a top speed of 20–21.5 knots. One Abwehr ship had been dispatched to Oslo before the invasion.[100]

On 5 April fifteen merchant ships displacing 72,000 tons, in dock in Stettin since 12 March, began departing that place. They were carrying 3,761 men, 672 horses and 1,377 vehicles including horse-drawn wagons. Also on board were 6,000 tons of war materiel. On 7 April eleven more merchant ships sailed totalling 53,000 tons and carrying 8,449 men, 969 horses, 1,283 vehicles and 2,170 tons of equipment.

Troops boarding warships arrived by rail at five cordoned-off harbours in the early evening of 6 April and kept indoors. Those on merchant ships were ordered to stay below and where possible boarding was done at night. All loading was complete by midnight.[101]

In spite of the need for secrecy, the Danish, Norwegian, Swedish, USA and Allied governments had received some information about this coming operation – some of it accurate, some not. But there was very little reaction by these governments. They discounted reports of troop concentrations in German ports and heavy activity by the German navy.[102]

French Admiral Jean Darlan reported on 30 March to French Premier Paul Reynaud that the Germans had been gathering shipping and had the capability of launching an attack against the Nordic nations. He wanted shipping to be allocated to the French expeditionary force so they could sail with one week's notice to Norway.[103]

On 2 April foreign correspondents in Berlin had heard rumours of some action underway. William L. Shirer wrote in his diary on that day of German troop concentrations at Baltic ports and he noted a German broadcast that night that stated, 'Germany is now waiting to see what the Allies intend to do in stopping shipments of Swedish iron ore down the Norwegian coast to the Reich.' Shirer raised the question that points out the German audacity – 'But what can Germany do against the British Navy?'[104]

On 2 April the Swedish ambassador called at the German Foreign Ministry and asked point-blank about German troops and merchant shipping gathering at Stettin.[105] This concentration of shipping would be widely reported over the next few days from many sources, and even in an 4 April edition of the British newspaper the *Daily Telegraph*.[106]

German Colonel Oster, who worked under Admiral Canaris at Abwehr, informed a Dutch attaché in Berlin, Colonel G. J. Sas, of the intended attack on Norway and Denmark and said that it might include Sweden. The Danish naval attaché was then notified but the Danish government ignored this information.[107]

On 4 April Major Hans Lunding of the Danish army stationed near the German border also made a report of increased troop concentrations near the border. Lunding even had a final warning that the attack would begin at 04:00 on 8 April. The Danish army command tried to get the government to mobilise but it refused.[108]

Swedish information to the Norwegian ambassador in Berlin convinced the ambassador to send a letter to Foreign Minister Koht, which arrived on 3 April, warning of a possible *Allied* attack. The Norwegian Foreign Ministry acknowledged the message but saw no reason to be concerned.[109]

The invasion began at 04:15 local time on Tuesday, 9 April 1940.

## CHAPTER 6

# Opening Moves and Painful Collisions

The British action against [Norway] was not deemed critical to the Allied war effort, as shown in the halfhearted manner in which it came into being. . . . The Germans, on the other hand, carried out *Weserübung* resolutely, being determined to execute the invasion quickly and thoroughly. The OKW realized from the start that *Weserübung* had to be completed rapidly, with the Allies, Denmark, and Norway being taken entirely by surprise. Total secrecy was therefore maintained.

Oddvar K. Hoidal[1]

In late March the deputy chief of the British Naval Staff, Rear Admiral Thomas 'Tom Thumb' Phillips, suspecting the Germans were planning some sort of landing in southern Scandinavia, approached both Winston Churchill and First Sea Lord Admiral Sir Dudley Pound and recommended the military be ready for land operations. What followed was a tumble of reports – some vital, others irrelevant – flowing in over the next few days from many and varied sources. The failure to discern a pattern among the reports helped doom Norway.

On 30 March it was reported that German troop leave had been cancelled and operations by German destroyers in the North Sea had ceased. On 3 April, British military intelligence warned of troops and shipping concentrating in German ports and that they were capable of launching an attack.[2]

In the first week of April Christopher Morris, one of the ULTRA code-breakers at Bletchley Park, decrypted some messages issued to German troopships heading for Bergen to 'report their positions'. ULTRA intelligence was the code-word adopted in 1940 for information that came from the British Government and Cypher School at Bletchley Park. This was a cryptanalytical section of the Admiralty that was breaking and reading some German codes. This intelligence was duly sent on to the Admiralty, where it was discounted. The term for ignoring such information is the 'Incredulity Factor'.[3] That a direct indication to the Allies of an impending operation was ignored is not surprising at this stage of the war. History is replete with such errors of intelligence – from Operation *Barbarossa* to Pearl Harbor to 11 September 2001. As one historian has noted, 'the Admiralty still saw no reason to pay attention to a bunch of professors who presumed to tell them how navies operated'.[4] ULTRA's value had still not been recognised.

In early April, the RAF Photo Reconnaissance Unit brought back the first excellent views of Kiel harbour. The photo analysts noted the presence of a great amount of shipping being loaded, but without a previous benchmark, the analysts failed to make the proper interpretation.[5] On 2 April, the British ambassador to Sweden reported to London that 200,000 tons of shipping had concentrated at two vital German Baltic ports, Stettin and Swinemünde, and that troops were embarking.[6] The Copenhagen-based British ambassador received at least two reports from the American ambassador telling of troops being readied at Kiel to steam to Narvik. The British ambassador sent the first report to London at 00:25 on 6 April. The American ambassador reported information received from a 'well-placed source' that Hitler had given 'definite orders to send one division in ten ships moving unostentatiously at night to land at Narvik on 8 April occupying Jutland on the same day, but leaving Sweden [alone].'[7] The Admiralty had expected a reaction to the proposed British minelaying (Operation 'Wilfred'), but not now, not before the event actually took place.

This information percolated further up the British government hierarchy to Prime Minister Neville Chamberlain. The assistant private secretary to the prime minister, John Colville, wrote in his diary on 6 April, 'From Denmark comes a rumour that the Germans are proposing to invade Norway on Monday and to land troops at Narvik.'[8]

Britain had reports on 4 April of two large German warships being readied at Wilhelmshaven. Air reconnaissance had revealed on the night of 6–7 April that there was a great amount of activity on wharves and roads along the German coast from Lübeck to Hamburg. Later that day warships were seen heading north by British Coastal Command aircraft. This sighting resulted in the cancellation of the Allied minelaying near Åndalsnes, in the expectation of combat should the German warships attempt a breakout into the Atlantic. Minelaying continued further north off Bodø, south of and near Narvik.

The British were concerned about a possible German sortie into the North Sea or into the Atlantic, or attacks against British minelaying operations. The Allied leadership did not think that a full-scale invasion of Norway was about to take place. One 7 April report of such a possible attack concluded that, 'All these reports are of doubtful value.'[9] Ultimately the British became convinced this activity was a breakout into the Atlantic of the large German warships, something they had seen before. They could not conceive that the unfolding German operation was a massive projection of blue-water power by a markedly inferior naval power. At the 3 April meeting of the War Cabinet Churchill had stated, 'he personally doubted' that the Germans would attack in Scandinavia. As one British historian wrote, '[the German] objectives were so audacious that the British strategists failed to grasp what the movements meant'.[10] Or as the American journalist William L. Shirer put it, 'One can only conclude that the British navy was caught napping.'[11]

In Sweden, similar intelligence about the increase in German ship traffic led Swedish Commander-in-Chief Lieutenant General Olof Thörnell to request additional mobilisation of forces in southern Sweden. His request was denied.[12] The Swedes held a parliamentary Foreign Policy Committee meeting on 6 April to discuss the Allied note of 5 April about the mining about to take place in

Norwegian waters. During the meeting, Foreign Minister Christian Günther was asked about this increased ship traffic. He said it was 'new' but he was not sure if it was 'disturbing'.[13]

What the intelligence services were not taking into account were German *capabilities*, and this was a critical failure. What was *anticipated* from Germany's actions was accepted as the truth, what Germany was capable of was not understood or simply ignored. As the American ambassador Florence J. Harriman would later write, 'Hindsight we all seem to have. But it is fantastic that none of the things which happened in the week preceding the fatal daybreak of April 9th awakened us to danger. A hundred incidents should have prepared us.'[14]

During this same time frame, a possible threat from the Allies was being reported from Germany to Sweden. Chief-of-Staff of the Kriegsmarine for Grand Admiral Erich Raeder, Erich Schulte-Mönting, had told Swedish officials beginning in late March that Germany feared Allied intervention in Norway at any time, particularly against Narvik and the ore trade, to be followed by the seizure of air and naval bases in the south.

Germany had practised tight radio-message control in the lead-up to the attack. 'Not only did the Germans maintain maximum radio silence until first contact with the Norwegian and British elements,' observes one historian, 'they also benefited from B-Dienst's excellent radio intercept and its ability to read some 80 percent of the Royal Navy's ciphers.'[15] B-Dienst (Beobachtungsdienst) was the most important German naval code-breaking section and was very helpful in locating where British warships were stationed. This capability allowed German naval units to avoid contact with the stronger British fleet in the first hours of the invasion. A radio intercept team from B-Dienst was on board the *Gneisenau* during the operation.[16]

During the afternoon of 7 April, General Falkenhorst arrived at the Hotel Esplanade in Hamburg, his command post, also shared by the X Air Corps for easy inter-service communication.[17] General Franz Halder noted in his diary on 8 April that radio silence in Great Britain suggested the 'British fleet is putting to sea'.[18]

Weather conditions in the North and Norwegian Seas at the time were poor. Rain, low clouds, fog and generally miserable conditions with very rough seas were on the agenda for 8–9 April.

\* \* \*

As we have seen, there had been extensive Allied planning for a reaction to 'Wilfred' and the need to counter any German move, probably with troops – the reaction force known as Plan R4. The initial forces consisted of three battalions of the 146th, two of the 148th and three battalions of the 24th Scots Guards Infantry Brigades, all of these units were standing ready though the entire commands were not detailed for the operation. Like the German units, they were stripped of some of their elements for this seaborne operation. These British troops were to quickly have additional British and French reinforcements. On 7 April the first battalion of 24th Scots Guards bound for Narvik boarded a transport in the Clyde, while a battalion bound for Trondheim was already on board. At Rosyth the bulk of four battalions were on board four British cruisers with orders to occupy Stavanger and Bergen with two each. The ground units were lightly equipped and only limited RAF elements would go to Narvik with none going to the south of Norway.[19]

Some of the German naval forces were now about to be discovered. Two German squadrons had left port and were steaming north. Warship Group 2 consisted of the *Admiral Hipper* with four destroyers carrying 1,700 men bound for Trondheim. They had joined Warship Group 1 at Wilhelmshaven, which consisted of 2,000 troops on 10 destroyers bound for Narvik. The battleships *Scharnhorst* and *Gneisenau*, whose presence confused the British into believing a breakout into the Atlantic was under way, were to play an important role.[20] The commander of the Home Fleet, largely based at Scapa Flow, Admiral Sir Charles Forbes, had been appointed in April 1938 and was second only to the First Sea Lord Admiral Pound. His Chief-of-Staff was Rear Admiral Edward King. Forbes would be the commander at sea who would orchestrate in part the Allied naval response to the German invasion. His actions during the coming fighting would earn him among the lower deck, and possibly mistakenly, the name of 'Wrong-Way-Charlie'. Some of his changes in course and plans was in part due to interference primarily from Admiral Pound at the Admiralty. At 08:48 on 7 April British air reconnaissance spotted a German cruiser and two destroyers in the North Sea heading north. By 11:50 Admiral Forbes had this report in hand, later amplified by a report indicating that the force consisted of a German light cruiser and six destroyers with land-based air cover. In fact, the reconnaissance had sighted the heavy cruiser *Hipper* and its escort. The British navy acted on this report and an air strike was mounted against the German force.[21]

This air strike, launched at 10:45, consisted of a total of eighteen Blenheim IV bombers, followed by twenty-four Wellington bombers; due to overcast conditions the latter could not attack. Instead of the cruiser with six destroyers they expected to find, twelve of the Blenheims attacked the *Scharnhorst* and *Gneisenau* and fifteen other warships, resulting only in a near miss on the *Hipper* and a destroyer. One RAF report gave the force as one *Scharnhorst*-class battleship, two cruisers and ten destroyers. Another report identified a battleship, a pocket battleship, three light cruisers and twelve destroyers. Forbes signalled the fleet accordingly. In the commotion, another report had the Germans heading *back* toward Germany and this further confused an already puzzling situation.[22]

The Home Fleet now quickly readied for possible action against the assumed German sortie into the Atlantic. At 14:20, Admiral Forbes received a report of a possible planned German attack on Narvik, relayed through diplomatic contacts. The report of the air attack on the German ships at sea in the North Sea reached Forbes at 17:27.[23] Heavy ships began to steam out of Scapa Flow at 20:15 that same evening. Troops were quickly taken off the four cruisers that had been standing by for a possible landing in Norway and in the ensuing confusion their equipment was left in a disorganised way. This 'confusion' would later seriously affect the initial landing of British troops countering the German invasion.[24]

Admiral Forbes put to sea from Scapa Flow with the battleships *Rodney* (flag) and *Valiant* and the battlecruiser *Repulse* with two cruisers and ten destroyers. The French light cruiser *Émile Bertin* and two French destroyers, *Maillé-Brézé* and *Tartu*,[25] had just arrived that afternoon under the command of Rear Admiral Edmond Derrien. They left to join Forbes but lost their way during the night and returned to Scapa. Later the French steamed out to sea and the three ships would join Forbes. Other forces would shortly put to sea and join Forbes too, while still other forces were detached, altering the size of his force.

Forbes would fight a confused campaign well into 9 April because neither Forbes nor the Admiralty realised what Germany was accomplishing under their noses – an invasion of Norway and not a breakout into the Atlantic. This in spite of a 14:00 report on 8 April of numerous German naval forces passing through the Danish channels and having the Admiralty ask Forbes to address a possible German landing at Stavanger and/or Bergen.[26]

Commanding the German warships at sea was Vice Admiral Günther Lütjens with his flag on the *Gneisenau*. German intelligence supplied to Lütjens by the middle of the 8th made him aware that British cruiser forces were at sea, but he was still unaware that the British battle fleet had sailed. Lütjens knew that the British were aware of his run to the north, and he had increased speed in the course of the day to gain cover of the worsening weather front.[27]

With the German fleet steaming north, the friction of combat was about to impact on the campaign. As the German navy headed north, it had facing it a powerful British fleet. Vice Admiral W. J. 'Jock' Whitworth was in command of the battlecruisers *Renown* and *Repulse,* which during these initial Norway operations seldom operated together. Admiral Forbes liked to team a battlecruiser with one or two of the older battleships to give more flexibility to the much slower British battleships faced with the newer and faster German warships. Whitworth showed some panache and aggressive leadership with these two old and under-armoured warships.[28]

Whitworth was at sea safeguarding the 'Wilfred' minelaying operation with the *Renown* as his flagship and four destroyers as the covering force. The minelaying force was made up of three squadrons. Force WS, consisting of a minelayer and four destroyers, was the most southerly force and with indications of a German naval operation, its mining operation was cancelled and Force WS was withdrawn. The minelayer would retire to port and the four escorting destroyers were ordered to refuel and join Admiral Forbes' force.

As a feint, Force WB with two destroyers approached Norwegian waters near the island port of Kristiansund, near and just north of Bergen. They 'laid' a fake minefield, and were approached by the Norwegian destroyer *Sleipner*. In the ensuing negotiations the British destroyers decided to withdraw and would let the *Sleipner* warn off merchant ships from the alleged minefield.[29] The only minefield placed was by Force WV, which consisted of four minelaying destroyers of the

20th Destroyer Flotilla – the *Esk, Icarus, Impulsive* and *Ivanhoe*. These destroyers were modified to each drop sixty magnetic mines. Each mine was placed at a depth of 120ft.[30] This was probably the first wartime use of the British M Mk I mine. Operations had been planned for the early morning hours of 8 April to avoid contact with Norwegian forces that might actively resist British mining in their home waters.[31]

Covering Force WV were four additional 'H' class destroyers commanded by Captain B. A. W. Warburton-Lee. Force WV successfully laid their mines in the early dawn off Bodø in the relatively sheltered waters of Vestfjord. Norwegian political reaction would be a note demanding their removal and that Norway would do so within 48 hours if the British did not. The Norwegians believed that mines had been placed in three areas, which were, or had been, patrolled by British warships.[32]

A later German claim that they were rushing to the aid of Norway upon learning of British mining operations was recognised for what it was: a lie. On 9 April in the House of Commons, Prime Minister Neville Chamberlain would say of the German claim that 'their invasion of Norway was a reprisal for the action of the Allies in Norwegian territorial waters ... will, of course, deceive no one. So elaborate an operation, involving simultaneous landings at a number of ports by troops accompanied by naval forces, requires planning long in advance'.[33] Lie that it was, the claim of 'reprisal against British mining' would be utilised as a propaganda device by Germany throughout the war.[34] The Germans also uncovered evidence of Operation R4 but at the time the Allies denied its existence.[35] Still, as the contemporary reporter William L. Shirer put it, 'Obviously the action was long prepared and longer planned and certainly put into operation *before* the British mined Norwegian territorial waters the day before yesterday'.[36]

* * *

The British and their allies headed out to sea to confront the Germans with a powerful but aging fleet. In 1940 the battleship was still the dominant force at sea. Its eclipse by the aircraft carrier was fast approaching, but had not yet arrived. This campaign would establish the importance of aircraft in modern naval combat. The largest warship ever sunk by aircraft at this point in history was shortly to take place when the 8,120-ton German light cruiser *Königsberg* would be sunk by an air attack at Bergen. Although Vice Admiral Lionel 'Nutty' Wells, in command of aircraft carriers, was on duty and one or two carriers were normally attached to the Home Fleet, during the initial invasion the British had no carriers available. The *Furious* had been refitting at Clyde but was speeding up the west coast of Scotland and had no fighters on board but was accompanied by the modernised battleship *Warspite*.[37]

No British battleship or battlecruiser was newer than the *Rodney*, a 1920s' design based on lessons learned from the Battle of Jutland.[38] However, the biggest obstacle facing the British was the inferior speed of their capital ships. Their

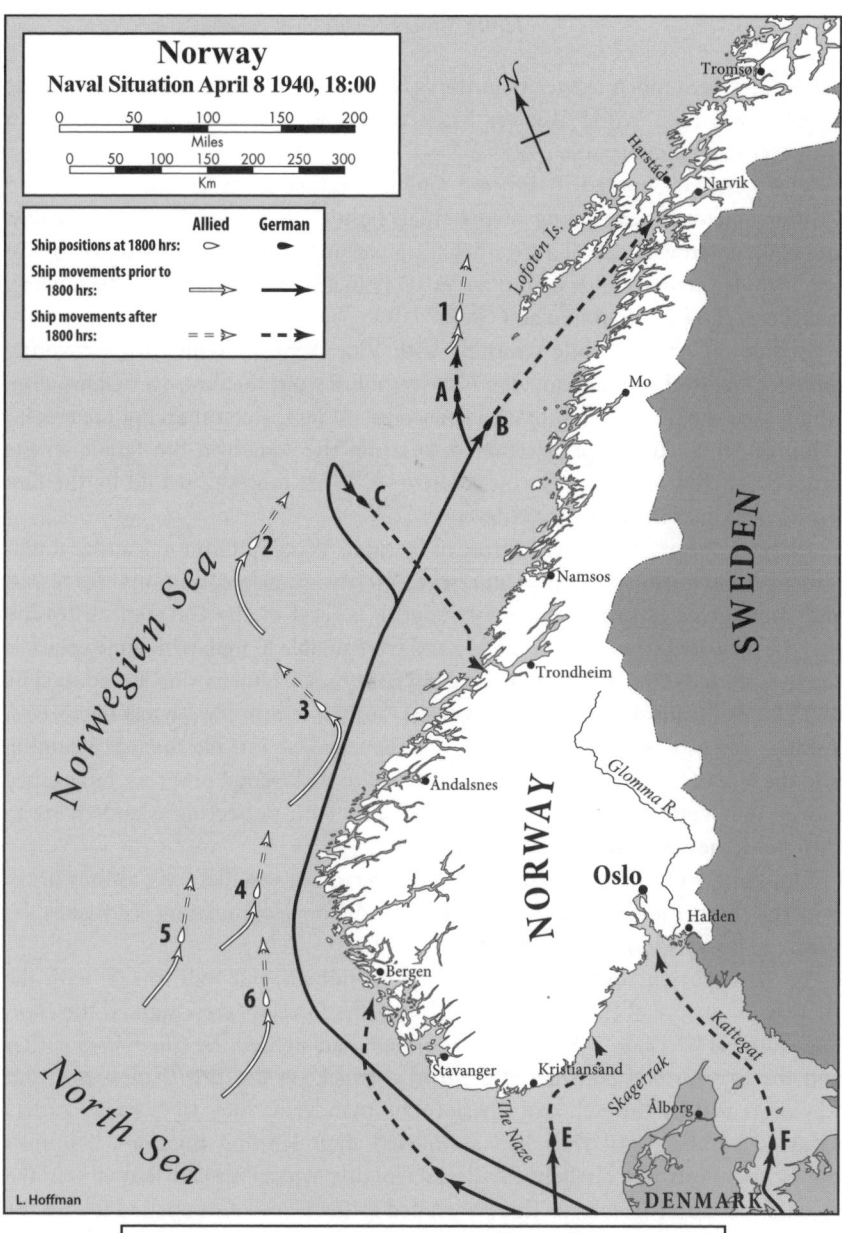

# Norway
## Naval Situation April 8 1940, 18:00

| | | Miles |
|---|---|---|
| 0 | 50 | 100 | 150 | 200 |

| | | Km |
|---|---|---|
| 0 | 50 | 100 | 150 | 200 | 250 | 300 |

|  | Allied | German |
|---|---|---|
| Ship positions at 1800 hrs: | | |
| Ship movements prior to 1800 hrs: | | |
| Ship movements after 1800 hrs: | | |

Tromsø

Harstad

Narvik

Lofoten Is.

1

A

B

Mo

C

2

Namsos

Norwegian Sea

Trondheim

3

Åndalsnes

Glomma R.

NORWAY

SWEDEN

Oslo

Halden

4

5

Bergen

6

Stavanger

Kristiansand

The Naze

Skagerrak

Ålborg

Kattegat

E

F

North Sea

DENMARK

L. Hoffman

## Allied Warships

1 **BB** *Renown*
  14 DD

2 **BB** *Repulse*
  **CL** *Penelope*
  4 DD

3 **BB** *Rodney*
  **BB** *Valiant*
  **CL** *Sheffield*
  10 DD

4 **CL** *Emile Bertin*
  2 DD

5 **CL** *Manchester*
  **CL** *Southampton*
  5 DD

6 **CL** *Galatea*
  **CL** *Arethusa*
  4 DD

## German Warships

A **BB** *Gneisenau*
  **BB** *Scharnhorst*

B 10 DD

C **CA** *Hipper*
  4 DD

D **CL** *Köln*
  **CL** *Königsberg*
  2 Aux
  2 TB

E **CL** *Karlsruhe*
  1 Aux
  3 TB

F **BB** *Lützow*
  **CA** *Blücher*
  **CL** *Emden*
  3 TB

battleships were much slower than the *Scharnhorst* and *Gneisenau* and even the Royal Navy's First World War-era battlecruisers were 2 to 4 knots slower than their German counterparts.

Vice Admiral George F. B. Edward-Collins steamed from Rosyth with the 2nd Cruiser Squadron, consisting of the small light cruisers *Arethusa* and *Galatea* and eight destroyers cobbled together from various convoys, following Forbes to sea. Included under Polish Commander W. Francki were the large modern Polish destroyers *Blyskawica*, *Burza* and *Grom*.

Earlier, on April 6 while steaming with Vice Admiral Whitworth's covering force for 'Wilfred', a man had been lost overboard from the destroyer *Glowworm*, which turned back to pick him up. *Glowworm*, under the command of Lieutenant Commander G. B. Roope, attempted to rejoin the squadron but failed. In the process, its crew sighted a German destroyer. What followed would be the first surface action of the battle for Norway.[39]

Early on 7 April the united forces of German Warship Groups 1 and 2 under Lütjens were steaming north. Under ever-increasing gale conditions (force 7–8 and some gusts hitting hurricane strength), several of the German destroyers became detached from the main body and were unable to make the same speed as the heavier warships. With the increasing heavy seas, Lütjens was forced to slow to 22 knots for his destroyers. Nonetheless, at least ten men were lost overboard, lashings came loose and equipment was damaged or lost overboard. Steaming into the face of the storm, the destroyers failed to make good progress, but as they moved into Vestfjord the storm weakened and, with protecting islands lying to their west, they proceeded toward Narvik.[40]

One danger of a heavy storm in the Norwegian Sea was that seas, as they break over the ships, hit cold metal and often freeze. The accumulating ice makes the ships top heavy and they lose stability.[41]

In these stormy conditions directly off Trondheim but well to sea, with the *Glowworm* unsure of the location of Whitworth's force, its crew sighted the *Hans Lüdemann* at 07:15 on 7 April. The *Lüdemann* had sighted the *Glowworm* earlier and the captain had considered a surprise attack on the British destroyer but was overruled by the onboard division commander as they were under orders to avoid combat until they had completed their landing missions. But now the British destroyer challenged the *Lüdemann*, which replied that it was the Swedish destroyer *Göteborg*. This ploy failed as the *Glowworm* opened fire on the *Lüdemann* with two salvoes that fell short. The *Lüdemann* succeeded in breaking off the action.[42]

At 08:02 the *Bernd von Arnim* sighted the *Glowworm* 7,000yd away on its beam heading in an opposite direction. The *Arnim* opened fire at 08:22, when the range had dropped to 6,000yd. The *Glowworm* returned fire and fighting became general between the two destroyers.

The *Paul Jacobi* and *Hans Lüdemann* were nearby and radioed the action back to the main group. Meanwhile, the *Glowworm* reported that it was in action. The *Arnim* claimed three hits on the *Glowworm*. The fire from the British destroyer was accurate, but no hits were registered. Nonetheless, the *Arnim* was forced to increase speed, make smoke and attempt to disengage, also having received a message from the division commander to break off the action. While attempting to escape, the *Arnim* lost two men overboard and had its engines damaged to the extent that 27 knots was now its top speed. The ship's B gun was put out of action and it sustained other damage to its superstructure, all because of the rough seas.

The fighting conditions were horrific. At one point, the *Jacobi* heeled 55 degrees and five of its boilers were flooded. In addition, five men were swept overboard, though later, through brilliant seamanship, they were pulled safely from the freezing seas.

The *Hipper*, commanded by Captain Helmuth Heye,[43] was detached by Lütjens to assist the German destroyers. Heye immediately ordered all the army personnel below decks. At 08:50 the *Hipper* sighted a destroyer off the port bow. Then a second destroyer, the *Glowworm*, was sighted to starboard. The *Glowworm* made the standard British signal asking the *Hipper* to identify herself, thinking the approaching heavy cruiser to be British due to its high foremast. The last signal received from the *Glowworm* was at 08:55 saying that it was engaged with a German force.[44]

Messages to the Admiralty had the *Glowworm* reporting at 08:30 sighting and engaging an enemy destroyer. It then reported a heavier force before contact was lost.

Both A and B turrets of the *Hipper* opened fire at 08:59 at about 9,200yd. The range quickly dropped as the *Glowworm* returned fire. It was probably hit on the third salvo which damaged the bridge and severed communications with the engine room. With the rapidly decreasing range it was becoming difficult to depress the *Hipper*'s guns by the fifth salvo (at one point a turret ceased operating altogether) and when it fired it was at a deliberate rate – no rapid fire here – due to the weather conditions and rapid range change.

The *Glowworm* now fired several torpedoes, which missed. It then made smoke and disappeared behind it. As the *Hipper* closed, it continued to fire, adding fire from the heavy AA 4.1in secondary armament and later even the 37mm AA guns. Numerous hits were scored on the *Glowworm*'s bridge, guns and superstructure. The *Hipper* received only a minor hit on the starboard bow.[45]

By 09:07 the *Glowworm* was hidden from view, and for the first time the *Hipper* used its radar to locate the British destroyer. At 09:10 the *Glowworm* emerged from the smoke at close range, launching some additional torpedoes that the *Hipper* avoided. The *Hipper* now began firing its light AA battery of 20mm guns at 800yd, forcing the *Glowworm*'s crew to seek cover as shells peppered the deck.

In the action the *Glowworm* had expended all its torpedoes.[46] As the *Hipper* closed on the smokescreen, it presented its bow to avoid British torpedoes. The *Glowworm*, possibly not able to steer due to damage to its rudder, now rammed the *Hipper*. As a consequence, 40m of the *Hipper* was ripped open but the heavier ship drove the *Glowworm* down. The *Glowworm*'s boilers exploded and it quickly

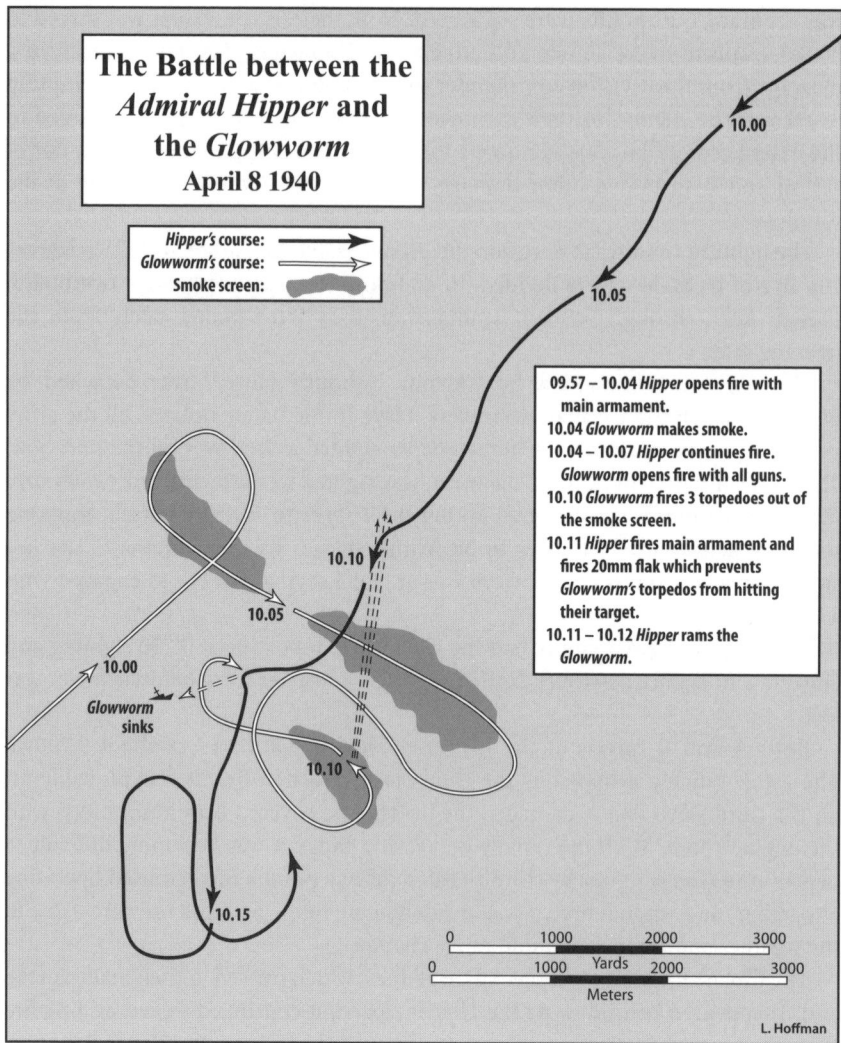

**The Battle between the *Admiral Hipper* and the *Glowworm***
**April 8 1940**

Hipper's course:
Glowworm's course:
Smoke screen:

10.00

10.05

10.00

09.57 – 10.04 *Hipper* opens fire with main armament.
10.04 *Glowworm* makes smoke.
10.04 – 10.07 *Hipper* continues fire. *Glowworm* opens fire with all guns.
10.10 *Glowworm* fires 3 torpedoes out of the smoke screen.
10.11 *Hipper* fires main armament and fires 20mm flak which prevents *Glowworm's* torpedos from hitting their target.
10.11 – 10.12 *Hipper* rams the *Glowworm*.

10.10

10.05

10.00

*Glowworm* sinks

10.10

10.15

0        1000        2000        3000
0        1000   Yards   2000        3000
Meters

L. Hoffman

sank. The *Hipper* took on 528 tons of water, some from having to counter-flood to reduce her four-degree list. *Hipper* lost one man overboard who drowned.

The *Glowworm* lost 112 men with only 40 saved, two of whom later died of wounds. German army troops helped in the rescue effort. Roope was climbing up the side of the *Hipper* when his cold-numbed fingers failed him and he dropped back into the sea and was lost. The *Hipper* was still able to maintain a good speed but would undergo five weeks of repair upon its return to Germany.[47]

There are several lessons that can be drawn from this opening engagement. One is that the manoeuvres of the *Hipper* were driven by the threat of the *Glowworm*'s torpedoes. The *Hipper*'s captain constantly closed bow-on so as to not expose his ship broadside to the *Glowworm*. Secondly, the terrible weather forced a close action and introduced the element of surprise, unusual in the modern electronic era, except in coastal waters strewn with islands and/or in terrible weather conditions. Finally, rapid-fire light armament played an unexpected role, clearing the *Glowworm's* deck of exposed personnel and driving them below. At the end of the war Lieutenant Commander Roope's bravery was recognised with the award of a posthumous Victoria Cross.

Four hours after the *Glowworm* sighted the first German destroyer the German transport *Rio de Janeiro* would be lost as a result of an Allied submarine attack. When the *Rio de Janeiro* was sunk and rescued German soldiers were identified as being on board, this information was ignored because, in part, the Admiralty was still not thinking of an invasion – they were 'target fixated' and failed to see the 'big picture' – and besides, it was only one ship.[48]

Upon receiving the *Glowworm's* message, Admiral Forbes detached the battlecruiser *Repulse*, the light cruiser *Penelope* and four large destroyers to attempt to locate the Germans and support the *Glowworm*. Proceeding north from the main fleet, they steamed towards the area where the *Glowworm* had last been reported.

Further to the north, Admiral Whitworth, with the battlecruiser *Renown* and supporting warships, had to make an important determination: where were the Germans heading? The last signal from the *Glowworm* had been that the *Hipper* was steaming *south*. To add to the confusion it was also identified as a battlecruiser by air reconnaissance and heading west. Whitworth had received Admiralty messages indicating a likely breakout into the Atlantic and the possibility of an attack on Narvik. So he made a list of potential courses of action. First, the Germans were returning to Germany; second, they were planning a descent upon Iceland (a rather odd conclusion to draw unless it was based on the discovery that day of German troops on the sinking *Rio de Janeiro*); third, they were heading for Murmansk and the White Sea to refuel and conduct future, as yet undetermined, operations; or fourth, they were set to attack Narvik.

Whitworth concluded that the Germans could not be steaming at a steady speed greater than 25 knots (in fact, the German destroyers were trying to maintain 22 knots in the teeth of the storm). Whitworth decided to steam north, with the intent to sweep south in the morning with his destroyers spread out in a screen, each warship within sight of the next ship on either side, almost like a line of beaters in a big-game hunt. This tactic dated back to the age of sail and would disappear with the growth of air power.[49]

The large 'Town' class light cruiser *Birmingham* was supposed to join Whitworth, but was short of fuel. Whitworth ordered it and a destroyer to return to Scapa Flow and the two would miss the approaching battle with Lütjens.

Immediately after the action with the *Glowworm*, the Trondheim-bound Warship Group 2 reformed and headed towards the port. It was spotted at about 14:00 by a British Sunderland flying boat. The *Hipper* opened fire on the plane, damaging it and forcing it to head home.[50] But its crew did report to Forbes the presence of a battlecruiser, two cruisers and two destroyers. While not accurate, the message did give an indication to Forbes that a major German naval force was off Trondheim. Unfortunately, at the moment of sighting, Warship Group 2 was steaming west to run out the clock before racing for Trondheim in accordance with the strict German timetable. The British assumed the German force was heading for a breakout into the Atlantic and the Admiralty and Forbes responded accordingly. The Admiralty made the decision that this was to be a naval response to a naval sortie. This decision was a key event in the chain of events that would lead to the Allied defeat and the fall of Norway. While it is impossible to know what would have transpired, clearly cruisers with supporting destroyers with British battalions of combat-ready troops arriving off of Narvik, Bergen and Stavanger on the heels of the invasion and later off Trondheim would have had an impact on the campaign. Such an action would have received limited Norwegian support and encouraged their resistance. At Bergen, if this had been fully supported by British destroyers attempting to enter the inner harbour of Bergen, German losses would certainly have been higher.[51]

Vice Admiral J. H. D. Cunningham[52] now sortied from Rosyth, after landing in a confused hurry the troops and equipment on board for Operation R4. The orders at 11:00 were 'All troops disembark at the double'.[53] He had the heavy cruisers *Devonshire*, *Berwick* and *York*, and the light cruiser *Glasgow,* along with six destroyers.[54] Admiral Forbes was surprised (as was Chamberlain at a meeting of the Cabinet that morning) that the troops had been removed as he thought the developing situation suggested the need for implementation of Operation R4. If plans had been followed two battalions would have arrived at Stavanger shortly before the German paratroop drop and just after the arrival of German warships off Bergen. The impact of this would have been incalculable.[55] In addition, the British navy's superiority over the German, while massive, was not monumental. By ordering warships from the Clyde to sea, the British navy removed any possible escort for the 24th Scots Guards originally allocated for occupying Narvik. Even if the British decided to send those troops they could not without first assembling a new escort.[56]

With no reports of the enemy, Forbes now ordered the *Repulse* group to continue north to reinforce Admiral Whitworth's command and unite the two battlecruisers into a single force. The battlecruisers would link up on the afternoon of 9 April after Whitworth's lone battlecruiser and accompanying destroyers engaged the two German battlecruisers. Forbes wanted to form a scouting line at night with the cruisers. The Admiralty intervened and forced Cunningham and Vice Admiral Edward-Collins to close with Forbes so as not to be engaged and defeated in detail by the Germans. A scouting British cruiser just missed German Warship Group 3 steaming for Bergen.[57] The result was that all the German naval forces arrived safely off their ports. Not too surprisingly, Winston Churchill who was in charge at the Admiralty would after the war write, 'Looking back on this affair, I consider that the Admiralty kept too close a control upon the Commander-in-Chief . . .'[58]

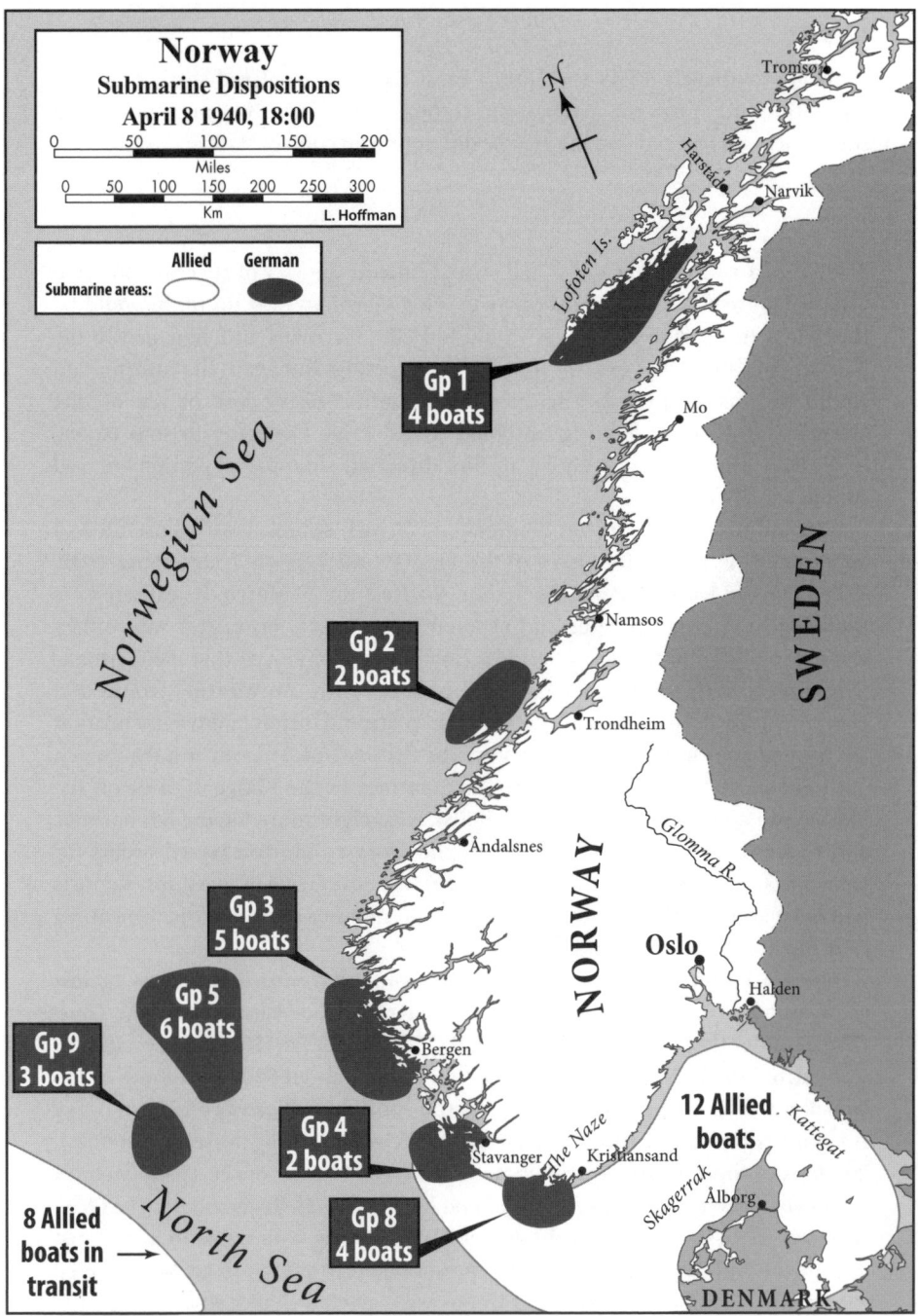

**Norway**
**Submarine Dispositions**
**April 8 1940, 18:00**

0   50   100   150   200
Miles
0   50   100   150   200   250   300
Km                                      L. Hoffman

Allied          German
Submarine areas:  ◯          ⬭

Tromsø

Harstad

Narvik

*Lofoten Is.*

Gp 1
4 boats

Mo

SWEDEN

Norwegian Sea

Gp 2
2 boats

Namsos

Trondheim

Åndalsnes

NORWAY

*Glomma R.*

Gp 3
5 boats

Gp 5
6 boats

Oslo

Halden

Gp 9
3 boats

Bergen

12 Allied
boats

*Kattegat*

Gp 4
2 boats

Stavanger  *The Naze*  Kristiansand

Skagerrak

Ålborg

8 Allied
boats in →
transit

*North Sea*

Gp 8
4 boats

DENMARK

Meanwhile, the wayward destroyer *Erich Giese* had been steaming north by itself when it sighted, on an opposite course in the mist and heavy seas, a British destroyer. It was the *Hero* on patrol. Its crew was not aware until after the war of their close encounter.[59]

At approximately 15:45 the *Hostile* most likely encountered the Trondheim force. Thinking it was the *Renown* and company, the *Hostile* began to close but a snow flurry intervened and the *Hostile* did not make contact.[60]

\* \* \*

The Allied surface forces so far had scored little in the way of success and there was still a great deal of confusion as to what Germany was up to. It would be the Allied submarine effort that would hurt the Germans and signalled to the Norwegians and Allies exactly what was transpiring. But again the information would be misinterpreted. The subs would inflict heavy loss of life on the Germans and as the fighting unfolded would force Germany to ship troops to Norway almost exclusively by air and direct all shipping of equipment and supplies solely to Oslo.

Vice Admiral Max Horton commanded British submarines. Churchill had appointed this submariner hero of the First World War on 7 December 1939. When Horton learned about Operation 'Wilfred' on 29 March, he gathered his available submarine captains and ordered them to sea, no matter where they were at in regard to their rest periods. Horton was convinced that the Germans would react with surface warships and possibly with transporting troops and equipment. By 8 April, the new date set for 'Wilfred', Horton had twenty boats at sea, posted at or near station. They were the British 2nd, 3rd, 6th and the French 10th Submarine Flotillas. There were submarines in the Kattegat, three off the Norwegian coast and six in the North Sea, with eight more having left harbour and proceeding east towards Denmark and Norway. Horton issued orders for transports to be sunk, not limiting his targets to just German warships. Reports had been flowing into Horton that an unusual number of transports were at sea heading north under neutral flags.[61]

It was a Polish submarine, however, that would have the first success against the Germans. The sinking of the *Rio de Janeiro* by the Polish submarine *Orzel* (Eagle) under the command of Lieutenant Commander Jan Grudzinski on its fifth war patrol near Kristiansand took place on 8 April, about 500 miles south of the *Glowworm* action. The *Rio de Janeiro* was transporting to Norway 4 105mm heavy AA guns, 6 20mm AA guns, 73 horses, 71 vehicles (including horse-drawn ones), 292 tons of food, aviation fuel, ammunition and 313 men of the 159th Infantry Regiment, Luftwaffe Flak Regiment 13 and Luftwaffe Flak Regiment 33. The *Orzel* surfaced about 1,300yd from the *Rio* at 11:03, forcing it to come to a stop just outside the Norwegian 10-mile limit, a prescribed restriction placed on the Allied submarines. The German crew and troops were given a chance to abandon ship. Then, after a torpedo fired at 11:45 missed the transport, a second hit the stopped German ship, while a third broke the *Rio*'s keel and sank it. As a result, 19 sailors, 164 soldiers and all the horses perished.[62]

The Norwegian destroyer *Odin* participated in the rescue, along with civilian craft, of 183 German survivors, including soldiers in combat gear, and took them to

Kristiansand. Several said they were on their way to Bergen to protect Norway from the Allies. The local police chief tried to inform the Norwegian naval authorities of the presence of these German troops bound for Bergen, but he was not believed. Both Danish and Norwegian officials were made aware of this.[63] The commander of the 3rd Norwegian Division at Kristiansand announced at 17:15 that evening that approximately 100 men had been saved, along with another 20 injured and 22 dead. Norwegian naval commander Rear Admiral Henry Diesen in Oslo simply refused to believe the story that these German soldiers were bound for Bergen, though reports to him included information that the *Rio* also carried Luftwaffe equipment. As Geirr Haarr would write, 'Nobody reacted and no precautions were taken.'[64] This news was known at the British Admiralty in the first hours of the afternoon and carried by the Reuters News Agency Oslo office at 20:30 on 8 April.[65]

The sinking of the *Rio de Janeiro* brought an end to the 10-mile limit restrictions on the British submarine service. After complaining to the Admiralty, Horton finally received permission to attack all transports off Norway if northward bound, regardless of whether or not they were sailing in Norwegian territorial waters. This order was issued on the afternoon of 9 April.[66]

One of Horton's submarines had sighted the two German battlecruisers steaming off the Swedish coast before turning toward the North Sea and their sortie north. It was not able to attack the battlecruisers, but it did radio a report of the sighting. A second British submarine off the Skaw fired a salvo of torpedoes, but the battlecruisers increased speed and the torpedoes missed. This submarine also reported the presence of the German ships to the Admiralty. A third submarine, on patrol directly in the entrance of the Øresund Sound, had withdrawn to recharge its batteries just as Warship Group 5 steamed through on its passage toward Oslo. Another, the *Sunfish*, sighted Group 5 and notified Admiral Horton of their course towards Norway's south coast.[67]

After the contact by the *Sunfish*, Horton did direct two submarines to operate off Larvik, a port on the southwest side of Oslofjord. He had wanted to place submarines off Horten, the Norwegian naval base at the head of Oslofjord, but for political reasons he had been refused, another example of a political decision that would cost the Allies dearly.[68]

Meanwhile, the submarine *Trident* sank another freighter, the *Posidonia*, at 13:30 off Oslo fjord near Larvik. Its captain was taken aboard the submarine, while the crew made it to shore and arrived by train in Oslo on the night of 8 April.[69] The same submarine missed the *Lützow* with ten torpedoes fired at the very long range of 7,500yd (over 4 miles) at 19:06 later that evening off Skagen.[70] The *Lützow* was a recent addition to Warship Group 5. Due to engine problems, it could not enter the Atlantic after landing troops at Trondheim, so had to be reassigned. It carried 50 Luftwaffe personnel, 400 men of a reduced battalion of the 3rd Mountain Division and 23 tons of supplies and equipment. The *Trident*'s attack on it was the only one on Warship Group 5. The German transport *Kreta*, bound for Kristiansand, was also attacked and reported lost, but survived by entering Norwegian territorial waters only to be later sunk in Oslofjord in May.[71]

Confusing news of these events was raising alarms in Norway and a large number of Norwegians assembled in the main public square in Oslo. Still, the British had not drawn the obvious conclusion: that something other than the breakout of two German battlecruisers was under way. Raeder's deception was succeeding.

* * *

Finally the Norwegians reacted. Admiral Diesen issued orders to 'douse all lights forthwith' at about 22:00.[72] All manned buoys and searchlights were to be extinguished to make passage up and down the coast more difficult. But there proved not to be enough time to extinguish most of the automatic searchlights, or many manned ones north of Bergen, before the German forces had reached their destinations. Even so, the navigating by the Germans, lashed as they were by the storms, and with only a very occasional light or landmark (including a small island that one of the destroyers almost ran aground on) was truly a tour de force. Shortly after that Diesen requested the army to send garrison troops to coast batteries at Bergen and Trondheim on the 9th.

Meanwhile, steaming south at 13 knots was the battlecruiser *Renown* with nine destroyers astern. After heading north to the Lofoten Islands, they were now steaming south as planned to cover the Vestfjord. Of the nine destroyers, four were minelayers and were armed with only two 4.7in guns each and carried no torpedoes. The flagship *Gneisenau* and the *Scharnhorst* were now headed out to sea to draw off the British, while the Trondheim and Narvik forces proceeded on their respective ways.

On 9 April at 03:49 gunnery radar on the *Gneisenau* picked up the *Renown* at the range of 15 miles and shortly after visual identification at 03:59, Admiral Lütjens was informed. The *Gneisenau*, after the initial radar contact, radioed the alarm to the *Scharnhorst*, which had been unaware of the danger. Lütjens waited for visual confirmation before opening fire.[73] When the Germans first made visual contact at about 12 miles, they thought they were facing a powerful *Nelson* class battleship.[74] The *Renown* first spotted one German warship at 03:37, shortly followed by a second sighting, as they were silhouetted in the early dawn light. The *Renown* increased speed first to 15 knots and then to 20 knots and began a pursuit on a roughly parallel course. The Germans successfully drew the British forces away from Narvik, justifying the presence of Germany's heaviest warships in the invasion.

The *Scharnhorst* class battleship was the first German postwar effort at building a modern capital ship. The design was originally conceived as an answer to the French *Dunkerque* class battlecruiser being built in the mid-1930s, but because of restrictions due in part to treaty provisions and some to the lack of expertise in building capital ships, the result was not satisfactory. In the rough seas at the time of the invasion the main guns did not work well because of flooding, a problem made worse by the seasickness suffered by some gunnery ratings during the action.

The battlecruiser *Renown*'s top speed was 29 knots and it was armed with six 15in guns in three turrets, two forward and one aft. It had been reconstructed

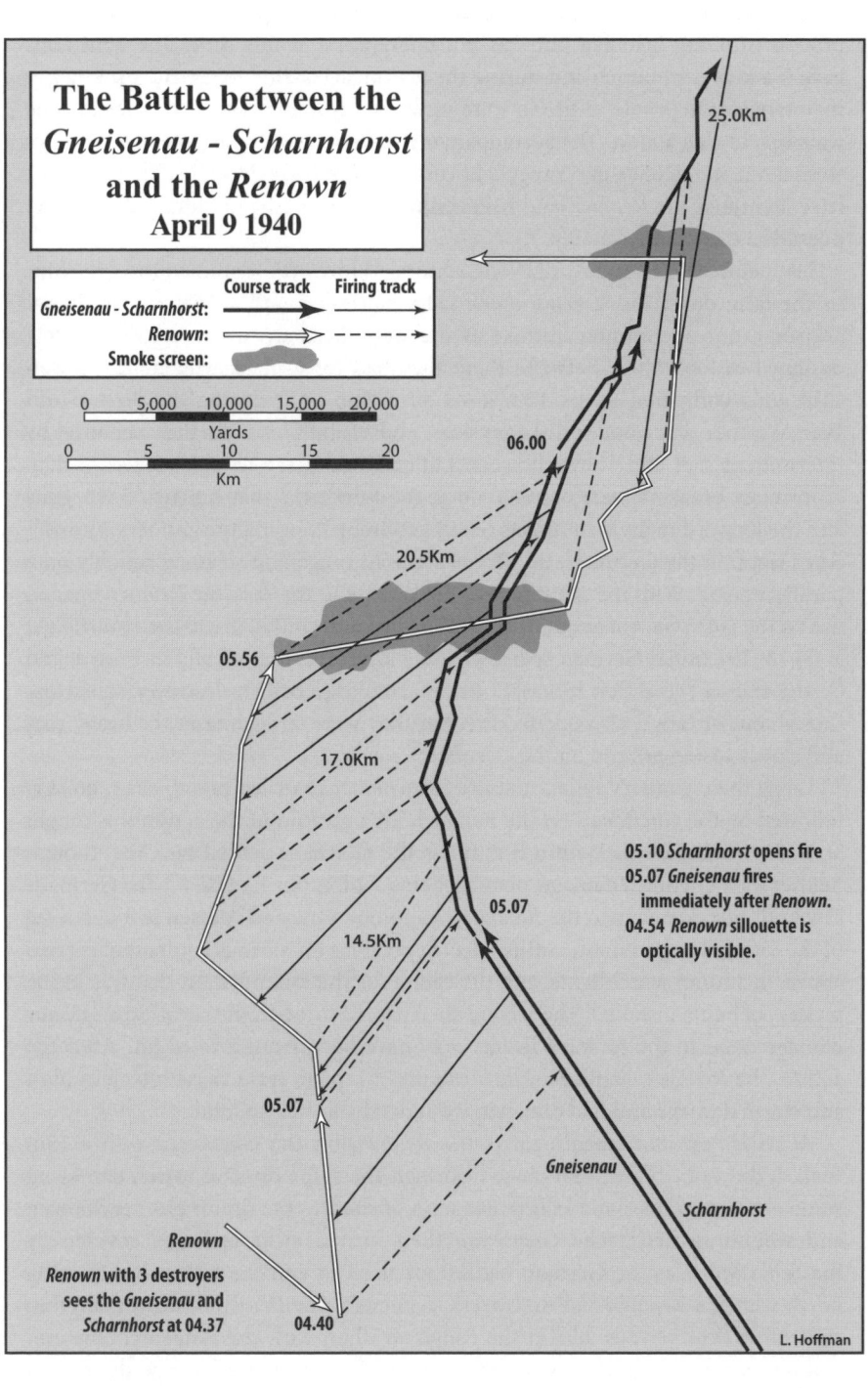

**The Battle between the**
*Gneisenau - Scharnhorst*
**and the *Renown***
April 9 1940

| | Course track | Firing track |
|---|---|---|
| *Gneisenau - Scharnhorst*: | | |
| *Renown*: | | |
| Smoke screen: | | |

0    5,000    10,000    15,000    20,000
Yards
0         5         10        15        20
Km

25.0Km

06.00

20.5Km

05.56

17.0Km

05.10 *Scharnhorst* opens fire
05.07 *Gneisenau* fires
immediately after *Renown*.
04.54 *Renown* sillouette is
optically visible.

05.07

14.5Km

05.07

*Gneisenau*

*Scharnhorst*

*Renown*

*Renown* with 3 destroyers
sees the *Gneisenau* and
*Scharnhorst* at 04.37

04.40

L. Hoffman

in the early 1920s, receiving some additional armour plate. Radar was in the process of being installed but was not operational at this time. The 15in guns gave it a powerful punch and during the action, according to German sources, it maintained a high rate of fire in spite of the sea conditions and the speed of the warships in this action. The accompanying destroyers were of potential help but were never in effective gun range and certainly not torpedo range. The Germans later identified the *Renown* and believed they faced it, the battleship *Nelson* and possibly a third large warship.[75]

Just before 04:00 on 9 April, Vice Admiral Whitworth identified the two ships in the false dawn[76] as a *Scharnhorst* class battleship and a *Hipper* class heavy cruiser, a not uncommon mistake as the large German ships were deliberately designed to look alike. Between them they had for a main armament eighteen 11in guns compared to six 15in guns on a ship built during the First World War. Weather was poor with heavy seas, and visibility was further impaired by intermittent hail and snow showers. Lütjens' war diary would later state that, 'Enormous breakers were coming along the forecastle' that put two 5.9in guns and the forward main 11in turrets out of action by flooding the gunnery rooms.[77] After sighting the Germans, the *Renown* closed range and steamed roughly on a parallel course. With the advantage of the sunrise to the east, the *Renown* opened fire on the *Gneisenau* at about 04:05 at 18,600yd and shifted fire to the *Scharnhorst* at 04:13. The initial German speed was 15.5 knots but it gradually increased, and by the end of the action it was 27 knots. The large British destroyer squadron, though out of range, also opened fire, but they were straggling in the heavy seas and slowly losing ground on the Germans.

Using their gunnery radar, first the *Scharnhorst* returned fire at 04:11, quickly followed by the *Gneisenau* on the *Renown*. This portion of the action was fought at 14,000 to 16,000yd. Within 5 minutes the Germans scored two hits, though neither shell did much damage, possibly being high explosive (HE).[78] The Germans saw both hits. Damage to the *Renown* was minor. One shell passed through a leg of the forward tripod mast, cutting electrical cables for various equipment carried above, including searchlights, and the cables for the radar system that was in the process of being installed. The second shell passed through the stern. Some minor damage done to the forward funnel may have been from a third hit. After the action, the *Renown* would require a month of repairs from these hits, gun blast and storm damage and had one man wounded by a shell splinter.

At 04:25, on its sixteenth salvo, the *Renown* hit the *Gneisenau* with a 15in shell. It did not explode, but passed through the ship's director tower, damaging some electrical cables and killing five men, including the senior gunnery officer, and wounding two.[79] The *Gneisenau* then turned away and was covered by the *Scharnhorst* as the German battleships tried to end the action by steaming north with the *Renown* and destroyers in pursuit. The British destroyers fired in controlled slow salvoes, but in the rough weather, with the range extreme and getting longer, the gunfire was ineffective. Perhaps this gunfire was the reason Lütjens reported that his force was engaged with two battleships.[80]

The *Gneisenau* increased speed and the German force withdrew as quickly as it could when it realised that numerous British destroyers were present. The *Scharnhorst* covered the withdrawal by crossing the *Gneisenau's* stern and laying down smoke. While steaming west and north, the forward turrets of the *Gneisenau* were out of action due to the heavy seas. The British continued to fire from 04:19 to 04:56 and two 4.5in shells hit the *Gneisenau*. One hit was more serious as it effectively disabled the stern 11in turret by damaging the rangefinder and causing flooding from the heavy seas. The second hit was minor.

What followed was a stern chase into heavy seas, resulting in additional damage to the capital ships, with the British destroyers falling further and further behind. One problem for the British, chasing as the *Renown* was, resulted from hot steam entering the forward turrets each time the gun breeches were opened after firing and seawater hitting the hot gun tube. By 06:00 all firing had ceased; during the last hour of the action no hits were scored. The Germans were last sighted by the *Renown* at 06:15. German casualties were eight dead and two wounded.[81]

The *Scharnhorst* was ineffective in this action due in part to malfunctioning radar. While under fire it practised 'salvo chasing' to throw off the *Renown's* fire and was not hit.[82] During the action its gun turrets and engine room were damaged by the heavy seas and severe weather, that would reduce its top speed to 25 knots for its later return to Germany. The spotter aircraft of both battlecruisers were damaged from gun blast and shell fragments.

The British battlecruiser had expended 230 15in shells and 1,065 4.5in shells. The *Gneisenau* expended 44 HE and 10 armour-piercing 11in shells and 10 5.9in shells, while the *Scharnhorst* fired 195 armour-piercing 11in shells and 91 5.9in shells in the action.

An officer on the British destroyer *Hardy* later wrote, 'Like a beaten dog she [*Scharnhorst*] ran for cover. The snowstorm hid her in time.'[83] Admiral Whitworth would later write to his friend and fellow vice admiral A. B. Cunningham of later Mediterranean fame that, 'somehow it never occurred to me that they would not wish to fight'.[84]

The *Renown* and her force now turned towards Narvik. Whitworth was of the opinion that British land forces would shortly be landing there and he could support that with his force.[85]

One footnote to all of this was that two Allied convoys were at sea bound for Norway. In an unusual step, the convoy captain of his own accord ordered the convoy to return to Britain. In the end, the Germans captured or sank thirteen merchant ships from these two convoys.[86]

By this time Admiral Forbes thought some sort of naval operation could be mounted against Bergen. As early as 06:20 on 9 April he was requesting information from the Admiralty on what it knew about Bergen's status. This enquiry would later bring about an air–sea action. That morning, with the invasion in full swing, Secretary Colville noted in his diary, 'Meanwhile most of our fleet is busy chasing German ships towards the North Pole.'[87]

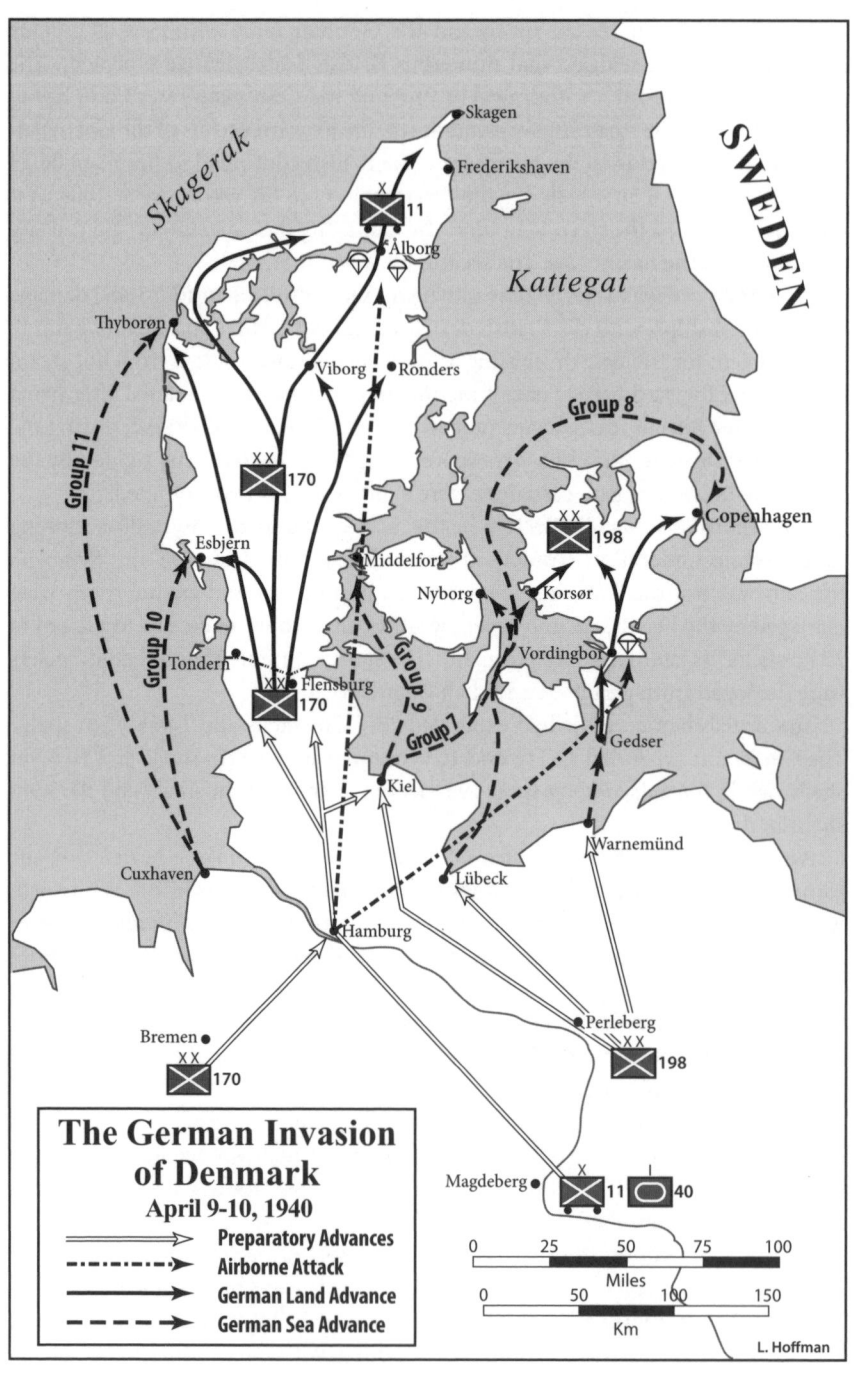

**The German Invasion
of Denmark**
April 9-10, 1940

Preparatory Advances
Airborne Attack
German Land Advance
German Sea Advance

L. Hoffman

# CHAPTER 7

# *The Fall of Denmark*

Churchill and Hitler put their trust in bold and unconventional operations and, because of their inadequate defence policies, the Northern countries provided for outsiders open and tempting doors for such actions.

W. M. Carlgren[1]

Almost 70 per cent of the land area of Denmark consists of Jutland, an almost flat peninsula protruding from Germany between the Baltic and North Seas. The rest is made up of approximately 500 islands, of which 100 are inhabited. The capital and chief naval base, København (Copenhagen),[2] is on the largest island, Sjælland (Zealand). The other major island lying between Sjælland and Jutland is Fyn. Denmark has 4,500 miles of mostly low and sandy coastline.[3] The second major Danish naval base of Århus is on Jutland on the Baltic side. To the north, at the end of the lengthy Lim Fjord, is Ålborg, where two airfields were located. The more important of the two was just two years old in 1940 and would handle the bulk of the air traffic out of this hub over the coming weeks.

To the west of Jutland lies the North Sea. The wide channel directly to the north of Denmark and separating it from Norway is the Skagerrak. To the north-east, broken by the Danish islands, is the narrower channel, the Kattegat, with Sweden lying to the north-east. The division between the two countries is a narrow peninsula known as the Skagen at the tip of Denmark jutting out into the channel. Beyond the Danish islands to the east is the Baltic. Between Sweden and Denmark lies the narrow Øresund Sound (often just called the Sound), while in Danish territorial waters are two additional passageways known as the Great and the Little Belts. To the south lies Germany.

Flat Denmark has many small lakes, and the highest point is only 500ft above sea level in the rolling hills near Århus in eastern Jutland, but unlike the Netherlands, Denmark is not at or below sea level. In contrast to mountainous Norway, blow up a road with dynamite or lay a tree across it and in Denmark one can simply drive or march through the adjoining flat field. In Norway you are likely either to be climbing or descending a steep, or even vertical, rock face.

The island of Sjælland is the heart of the kingdom, home to Copenhagen and several important towns. Sjælland lies 3 miles from Sweden at its narrowest point, and 11 miles from Fyn. It is 2,636 square miles in area and its highest point is some hills that are a mere 350ft in elevation.

Denmark also counted as a possession the island of Iceland, which would achieve its independence during the war, vast but empty Greenland and the strategic Faeroe Islands. All three would play important roles in the Second World War.

* * *

Denmark was dominated in the late 1920s and throughout the 1930s by a coalition government led by the Social Democrats and the leftist Radical Party. The Radicals, in particular, exercised a strong hold on foreign policy. On the eve of the war, Radical Party member Peter R. Munch was foreign minister of Denmark, and Thorvald Stauning of the Social Democrats was the Prime Minister.[4] Munch had been minister of defence during the First World War and was named the chairman of the Defence Commission in 1919. This commission reported back in May 1922 and saw its recommendations implemented that August. These reduced the size of the army; in 1932 it was further reduced from three divisions to two. Policy held that the Danish military would act to prevent accidental border incursions, 'but not to engage in a battle for the country's existence'.[5]

Denmark was the most imperiled of the Nordic nations, sharing as it did a common and difficult to defend border with Germany offering little in the way of any natural barriers. Winston Churchill had summed up the Danish predicament quite well in January 1940, 'The others [Nordic countries] have a ditch across which they can feed the tiger, but Denmark is so terribly close to Germany that it would be impossible to bring aid . . . Denmark has a treaty with Germany, but I have not the slightest doubt that the Germans will swarm over Denmark when it suits them.'[6] And later on 11 February at a luncheon he said that Denmark 'sooner or later it would be taken by Germany'.[7]

But the contrast between Denmark's role in the First World War and the Second World War is striking. In 1914, the Danish army mobilised some 58,000 troops and kept them in the field for the duration of the war. In 1939, a mere 15,000 troops were on Neutrality Watch, and of these 7,840 had been conscripted just two months before the invasion. By April 1940 the number of available troops was much smaller, owing to leave and illness. In August 1914 key fortresses around Copenhagen were manned and remained so throughout the war. Due to military laxness, in 1940 many military installations were not occupied for seven months of the year. Denmark was still a relatively easy nation for Germany to invade in the First World War but by fully mobilising it did provide some deterrent to Germany's potential for invading.

In the Second World War Denmark's independence was at the sufferance of Germany and its powerful army. Denmark could not keep Germany from occupying it, as its army was too small, no major power that Denmark might ally with could come to Denmark's aid in a timely fashion and the other Nordic powers were too weak to offer meaningful help.[8] Still, there is no question that a spirited defence might have deterred invasion and certainly would have delayed Germany's exploitation of Denmark in its fight for Norway.

In 1935 the small Nordic states witnessed the failure of the League of Nations to act during the Ethiopian crisis. They also saw the signing of the Anglo-German Naval Agreement, which allowed for German naval rearmament in violation of the limits set by the Treaty of Versailles. Great Britain had unilaterally pursued this treaty as a way ultimately to *limit* German naval growth, but in the end this policy failed. The Anglo-German Naval Agreement permitted Germany to construct warships far more numerous and powerful than the Scandinavian powers could afford to construct or purchase. The net effect of the subsequent German navy construction was to turn the Baltic into a *Mare Germanicum*. During the Second World War maintaining control of the Baltic was one of the German navy's most important goals.[9]

In 1937 and 1938, Germany, Denmark and Sweden arrived at an arrangement for shipping entering the three Danish Straits to the Baltic. In the First World War, Germany had wanted the three main sea lanes into the Baltic, the Sound and the Great and Little Belts to be mined. This had now changed. Germany now demanded free passage for German warships and aircraft in wartime through the Sound. First Sweden, then Denmark agreed. By 1938, Denmark had agreed on the same plan for the two Belts, even though the Little Belt was no wider than a river in places, which meant that German aircraft would be flying over Danish land as well as its territorial waters.[10]

In the spring of 1939, Denmark concluded a ten-year Treaty of Friendship, a non-aggression pact, with Nazi Germany. On the eve of the signing on 31 May, Munch affirmed that the main goal of Danish foreign policy in the event of war was to minimise its impact on the Danish people.[11]

During and immediately after the Winter War there had been talk of a defensive pact between Finland, Sweden and Norway, but this had been essentially vetoed by the Soviet Union. These Nordic powers recognised that Denmark could not be a party to this and had not pursued Danish participation.[12]

Munch had developed a bizarre political theory called 'Neo-Neutralism'. He believed that nations should not become involved in war even if they were to be occupied. Money usually spent on defence was to be spent on social welfare programmes and consensus building within Denmark so that even if Germany (or some other nation) occupied the country, it would remain a nation and live on. This was not a recent brainstorm but a policy he had advocated during the First World War, arguing that Denmark could not defend itself if Germany attacked it.[13]

In addition, the leftist government of Denmark had a traditional fear of any 'White Army' of anti-labour reactionary forces, a fear the military represented to them, and, as we have seen, mirrored in Norwegian politics. Additionally, foreign minister Munch had embraced disarmament for Denmark as a viable policy.[14] These Danish political actions during the run-up to the war made effective resistance on 9 April 1940 impossible.

Denmark had a tiny and somewhat splintered Nazi-style party, the *National-socialistiske Arbejderparti,* known by the initials DNSAP. It was led by Frits

Clausen, a medical doctor who had served with the German army on the Eastern Front in the First World War. In the 1939 election the party had garnered only 31,000 votes, a tiny 1.8 per cent of the total. There were some 30,000 German nationals living in Denmark and from time to time Germany would make some diplomatic noise over their presence. There was some fear in Denmark that other right-wing elements would support a Nazi-style government but these were all very minor threats to the Danish state. When the actual invasion occurred many of the minority Germans openly supported the German invasion, some appearing outside of their homes with rifles and some acting as guards.[15]

Denmark's failure to prepare adequate defences led to rumours and recriminations about the existence of a fifth column beyond Danish-Germans helping to undermine the country. There were instances of subversion, but in reality the fifth column was a straw man. In Denmark, it was quite small.[16]

Joachim Joesten, a German Communist expatriate living in Denmark, would write prophetically in 1938 that Denmark would become a springboard for aerial operations against other states. He also wrote, 'The German invasion of Denmark may take the outside world and perhaps the Danish *people* by surprise, but surely not its *Government*.' (italics in original). Joesten included air operations against Norway as a possibility.[17]

There were other prophets, many with military ties, who spoke about the likelihood of war and occupation. In 1936, army Captain M. L. Lauesen wrote in a Copenhagen newspaper:

> These foreign powers have our full guarantee that we shall be willing and able to assert our neutrality, we shall undoubtedly be faced, at the very outbreak of war, with the fact that a nation which does not hesitate to protect its interests by all the means at its disposal will immediately take over the defense of Denmark's territory. Our country, in other words, will be occupied.[18]

Of the Oslo States, Sweden was probably the one most concerned during the prewar era about the Danish failure to strengthen its defences. The Oslo States comprised Norway, Denmark, Sweden, Finland, the Netherlands, Belgium and Luxembourg and was an informal arrangement seeking to maintain neutrality in the face of war for small states. A provocative editorial entitled 'A Thermopylae without Spartans' had appeared in a conservative Swedish newspaper on 16 December 1936. It noted,

> Without anti-aircraft protection for Copenhagen, the Danish Government would not be able to assert its liberty of action. Considering what that means to the North as a whole and to Sweden in particular, the justness of the demand for such defenses cannot be overemphasized . . . As long as Jutland is undefended, Denmark's helplessness is bound to increase the war risks for all the North.[19]

After the fall of Denmark, the now very unpopular Munch would argue that Denmark was not a conquered nation since it had not resisted. In July 1940 he was replaced as foreign minister.[20] The Danish army never accepted Munch's theories about non-resistance, but starved of money, it could do little to implement its own strategic vision. It argued that Germany could not apply its full force against Denmark, which was true. Therefore, if the Danes could hold the line, reinforcements could arrive to save the nation. The navy essentially accepted the Munch government's view of national defence.

After the war controversy arose over the approach the Danish government had adopted. The result of that national conversation would be the country's early entry into NATO.

* * *

What did Denmark do in the immediate prewar era to prepare militarily? Following a major review in 1937 a new defence act was passed. Some modernisation occurred, and a few orders were issued for newer equipment, but the most significant change was to move most of the army into a reserve force and reduce the number of troops being trained each year. The decision to cut back on the size of the standing army was leavened with a commitment to purchase new aeroplanes, anti-tank guns, anti-aircraft guns, improve the field artillery and to upgrade the navy. The review also called for only the defence of the largest island, Sjælland. Like his foreign minister, Munch, Prime Minister Stauning did not want to re-arm, claiming in 1937, 'Denmark is not the watchdog of Scandinavia.'[21] Later, when asked about rearmament, he said, 'What is the point?'[22] The 1937 increase of over $2 million represented the first increase in defence spending in Denmark since 1909.[23]

The army introduced a new steel helmet and was in the process of introducing a new uniform. The French Schneider 105mm gun began to replace the pre-First World War 75mm Krupp field gun. Some AA equipment was added before the war, but with only two divisions, the army was still very weak. Not being mobilised fully in September 1939 was not courting disaster – it was embracing it.

Denmark had experimented to a limited degree with armour units in the interwar period. In 1917 the Danes had built an armoured car. Starting in the 1920s they had experimented with half-tracks and in 1928 they had purchased a poorly designed Italian Fiat 3000 tank. Later purchased, and still on display in the Arsenal Museum in Copenhagen, was a Vickers Carden Loyd Patrol Tank IV.[24] Experiments continued with some armoured cars, including several from Sweden and at least three Landsverk L-180s were deployed to one of the cavalry regiments but no serious investment was made. The government purchased only a handful of anti-tank guns before the war and a few 20mm AT guns had been clandestinely sold to Finland during the Russo-Finnish War. They did utilise a number of the Danish Nimbus motorcycles, some mounting their 20mm AT gun on a sidecar.[25]

In the late 1930s, a six-year programme for new naval construction was undertaken. The heart of the programme consisted of three, later four, submarines of very modest dimensions and one minelayer. Danish submarines were quite small, with a displacement of only 320 tons.[26] This was a small increase to an already anaemic navy. Several fighters, bombers and other aircraft were also ordered, but they either arrived too late for the war or were still in crates when the invasion took place.

On 1 April 1938 the government took out a loan of over $11 million, with over $4 million of this to be used to speed up the 1937 acquisitions. When war began there was a further increase in spending. The navy was supposed to receive new AA guns and much-needed repairs to older submarines. Finally, in 1940 parliament voted another increase in the face of declining but still staggering unemployment rates (18.4 per cent in 1939), including almost an $8 million increase to purchase small craft, primarily minesweepers, but this programme was too little and too late.[27]

The Danish defence industry was small, but it did have an impact on the national economy and military establishment. The locally produced Madsen machine-gun, though somewhat complicated to operate, was used both in Norway and Denmark.[28] The M89/28 'Finskydninggevaer', or 'precision shooting rifle', was the basic infantry weapon of the Danish army; it had been introduced in 1889 and manufactured in Denmark but was of Norwegian design. By 1940 it was obsolete. Denmark had a small naval construction capability. Copenhagen had a good naval facility with several docks of various sizes.

There had been a clamour by the Danish political opposition and by the press for some form of AA defence of Copenhagen, especially in light of the dramatic bombings during the Spanish Civil War. In the early 1930s the AA defence of the Danish capital consisted of 'a dozen or so antediluvian guns' so the government purchased three batteries of modern 75mm AA guns. This meant that on the eve of war Copenhagen was 'defended by exactly twelve modern anti-aircraft guns and some old junk'. One squadron of fairly modern fighters was stationed nearby.[29]

In contrast, Stockholm, a smaller Nordic city, had fifty modern AA guns in 1938 supported by nearby fighters. Sweden's air force in 1940 consisted of 596 planes, though only 180 were near modern. As in other Scandinavian nations, the increase in the Swedish defence budget did not begin until 1936, almost doubling by 1938. Then in 1939 it increased over fivefold from $58,575,000 to $322,325,000.[30]

After the outbreak of war there were several incidents, mostly involving off-course British aircraft, some of which resulted in accidental bombings, since AA batteries in western Jutland were under orders to fire on any aircraft in their air space. The Danes posted flags on rooftops so planes would see they were over Denmark and not Germany, but they did not place many searchlights or other forms of ground lighting so as not to be accused by the Germans of helping to guide British bombers to their targets.

The toll of war for Denmark also occurred at sea. One-twentieth of the Danish merchant fleet, many small ships carrying on legal trade with Britain, had been sunk or captured by the Germans by March 1940, resulting in 258 dead.[31]

* * *

In April 1940 Denmark had deployed about 9,000 army troops, along with a contingent of frontier guards. The two Danish divisions' TO&E were old-school 'square' divisions made up of four infantry regiments and one regiment of cavalry each. The Sjælland Division had two regiments of artillery, while the Jutland Division had one, with some units, primarily the heavy artillery, being motorised. Each regiment had six horse-drawn 37mm AT guns; 20mm AT guns were also employed. The 37mm at least had a gun shield to protect the crew. The cadres of three regiments of the Jutland Division were deployed on the mainland with the 6th Regiment on the island of Fyn. Although elements of the 3rd Artillery Regiment garrisoned the naval base at Århus, there were *no military units* garrisoning the twin and important airfields at Ålborg in northern Jutland. Up until 9 April, Danish troops were ordered not to dig trenches or build fortifications along the German–Danish border or to place any land mines.

During the summer of 1939, with tensions increasing in Europe, the Danish navy had formed a 'Naval Protection Force' made up of the majority of its active warships. The navy had 4,300 officers and men serving. The coastal defence ship *Niels Iuel* served as flagship, supported by six torpedo-boats (*Glenten* and *Dragen* classes), seven submarines, and several survey ships, minesweepers, patrol-boats and submarine tenders, all based at the port of Århus on the Baltic side of the Jutland Peninsula. However, the *Niels Iuel* would be at Copenhagen and non-operational when the Germans attacked.[32] The other coastal defence ship *Peter Skram* was stationed at Frederikshavn on the north end of Jutland. Additional naval forces included three ice-breakers, five customs cutters and a small naval force of fishery protection vessels near Greenland.

The role that the two old coastal defence ships played, along with the two operational ones in the Norwegian navy, was to be scaled-down old battleships. Their presence was seen as a deterrent against an aggressor nation utilising just small warships or even cruisers. In the event the Germans would counter the two Danish coastal defence ships with their pair of elderly pre-dreadnought battleships in their last active assignment before retirement and with the torpedo against the Norwegian *Norge* and *Eidsvold*.

Five coastal defence positions around Copenhagen were manned by the navy, along with the command centre at Lynetten, part of greater Copenhagen. The battery at the narrows south of Sjælland controlling the long Storstrøm bridge facing the island of Falster was neither manned nor operational.[33]

The Danish air force (*Hærens Flyvertropper*) was divided into two branches – army and navy. The army branch had one squadron of modern Dutch-designed Fokker XXI monoplane fighters[34] based on the mainland, but these were not fully operational at the time of the invasion, while a squadron of obsolescent Gloster Gauntlet IIJs biplane fighters was stationed near Copenhagen. Two small reconnaissance squadrons and one bomber squadron completed the Danish army air force.[35] The Danish naval aviation service (*Søværnets Flyvetjeneste*) consisted of one fighter squadron made up of aircraft dating back to the late 1920s. The Danish naval air force had eleven Heinkel He8 floatplanes at Copenhagen with nine planes based at nearby Avno. Four other aircraft brought the total operational force to twenty-four planes. On order or projected for acquisition for both services were Fokker light bombers, Italian Macchi 200 fighters and British dive-bombers and torpedo-bombers – none of which had arrived by the time of the invasion.

\* \* \*

Denmark fell in less than a day. The Germans crossed the border at 04:15 and the Danish government agreed to Germany's terms at 07:20. It was a *coup de main* on a national scale. Most studies gloss over the 3-hour 'war' for Denmark, but it has important lessons nonetheless. The quick collapse of Denmark produced substantially shortened German supply lines to Norway and allowed additional German forces to be shipped there quickly. Denmark's rapid collapse also created a measure of ill will between Danes and Norwegians that lasted into the postwar period.[36]

There were some further direct warnings of an impending attack in addition to the ones already chronicled. Two warnings from the Danish ambassador in Berlin starting on 4 April 1940 were ignored. On 30 March, a German Abwehr officer and aide to Admiral Wilhelm Canaris, Colonel Hans Oster, who opposed Hitler and was willing to commit treason, had informed the Dutch military attaché to Berlin, Major Gijsbert Jacob Sas, of the impending invasion of Denmark and Norway. Oster wanted to 'humiliate' Hitler by having Allied warships sink German transports filled with troops on their way to assault Norway.[37] Sas was told the invasion would begin within a week and might also include Belgium and the Netherlands, but not Sweden. Sas, in turn, informed his superiors and asked them to pass the information on to Great Britain (it was not relayed), and to the Norwegian vice-consul, Ulrich Stang, and the Danish naval and air attaché, Captain Frits Kjøelsen. The Danish ambassador sent the naval attaché back to Denmark on 4 April with the reports, but to no avail. As far as Denmark's leaders were concerned, this all had an element of 'crying wolf' since Oster had leaked information about the coming date for an attack on the Low Countries and France to Sas on several previous occasions. Unfortunately for his credibility, the start dates had been repeatedly postponed or cancelled after the information had been passed on to the neutrals. The British thought him to be a German agent.[38]

When Danish truck drivers delivering fish to Hamburg reported large numbers of German troops moving towards or already on the Danish border, their warnings, too, were disregarded. Even literally watching the more than 100 German warships and merchant ships at sea in the Kattegat and Skagerrak moving north – certainly an unusual event – was discounted. This was newsworthy enough to be reported in the evening Danish newspapers on 8 April, with even the presence of German troops on board noted.[39]

Early on the morning of 8 April, Danish frontier guards alerted Copenhagen to the increased German activity and recommended mobilisation. Stauning refused, but did allow some minor redeployment, including moving AA batteries to join nearby troops and moving the army closer to the border to support the frontier guards.[40]

The portion of the small Danish army that was mobilised was split between the islands and the mainland. In addition, part of the division based in Jutland was stationed along the southern coast to defend against a British invasion from the North Sea. This deployment was a political statement and was intended to show Germany that Denmark was ready to defend itself for Germany's benefit. The Danish navy was dispersed, with some warships also deployed to defend against Great Britain.[41]

The 2nd Regiment of the Jutland Division, with the major strength of the regular army units, was positioned nearest the border. The 4th Battalion of bicycle troops of the 6th Regiment, which had been sent down to train and had ignored orders to return to base and demobilise, was in place to reinforce the 2nd Regiment. On the night of 8 April, the 5th Battalion of bicycle troops of the 6th Regiment, on the personal initiative of the regimental officer, began to board trains and proceed from Odense on the island of Fyn to the frontier but they arrived too late to help stem the German advance. While mobilisation was not ordered, live ammunition was issued and distributed, and some civilian trucks were requisitioned.[42] As noted, there were no garrison units at Ålborg to protect the two vital airfields there. A small alert force might have stopped cold the German seizure of this vital air bridge. Instead, these fields within hours would become giant aerial parking lots and staging points for the German resupply effort to Norway. This gross oversight was perhaps due to the inexperience of the Danes, who were unprepared for warfare that depended on air power to fly in troops to seize and hold important objectives.

The Danish navy suffered a terrible fate. On 6 April, its naval commander, Vice Admiral Hjalmar Rechnitzer, requested orders to mobilise his forces. The government refused his request. Rechnitzer then sent many of his officers home on leave, as he saw no reason for them to die in a hopeless struggle. He ordered the navy not to fire on German ships unless given specific orders. Nor did the Danish coastal defence guns fire. In at least one case, the guns were packed in grease and could not fire.[43]

Shortly after the invasion four senior naval officers informed Rechnitzer that the naval officers corps no longer had confidence in him. Rechnitzer resigned shortly after.

\* \* \*

The German battalion commander ordered to secure Copenhagen had flown there with Lufthansa on 4 April, identifying himself as a civil servant. He examined the lovely *Langelinie* (Long Canal) quay in the heart of Copenhagen, the proposed landing spot for German troops arriving by sea. He was even approached by a policeman. The next morning he visited the old Citadel (*Kastellet*), a sixteenth-century fortress at the north end of central Copenhagen. There, a Danish sergeant,

> complied with my request in the friendliest manner. To start with, he took me to the corporal's canteen where I drank a glass of beer with him. At the same time he told me something of the citadel, its garrison and its importance. After I had drunk some beers with him he showed me the quarters of the commanders, the military offices, the telephone exchange, the watch-posts and the old gates by the north and south entrances.[44]

The battalion commander flew back to Germany that afternoon.

Major General Kurt Himer, Chief-of-Staff of the XXXI Corps, visited Copenhagen on 7 April, flying there with the secretary of the legation. Himer arrived in the guise of a high-ranking civil servant (with his uniform in the luggage of the accompanying diplomat carrying the German ultimatum to be delivered to the ambassador). The two called on the German ambassador and delivered sealed instructions to be presented to the Danish government when the invasion began. Himer noted that no undue defence precautions had been taken and that a recent wind had rendered the harbour ice-free. The next day, in the company of the Luftwaffe attaché, Himer toured the harbour area and the Citadel. Himer determined the point of attack – the weakest point of the Citadel, the King's Gate, though in the event both gates would be attacked. He also determined there would be room on the *Langelinie* for the key invasion ship carrying a battalion of troops. All of this important information was immediately reported to Germany.[45]

Himer took care of one other problem during his stay. There was a German reserve officer in Copenhagen (there were about 1,500 German nationals in the Danish islands at the time of the invasion) whom he contacted. This individual agreed to be at the quay at 04:00 on 9 April with a borrowed truck and four compatriots who were members of the Nazi Party. The truck would be used to transport the heavy radio equipment on board the invasion ship, the minelayer *Hansestadt Danzig*, to the Citadel in order that radio communication with Germany could be quickly established.

Falkenhorst had originally wanted to have a battalion arrive in marching order with a band playing but Luftwaffe Lieutenant General Leonhard Kaupisch, commanding the XXXI Corps, decided against it. Kaupisch wanted to take prisoner the elements of the Royal Guard Regiment headquartered in Copenhagen. Himer remained in Copenhagen at the time of the attack and was in telephone communication with Corps headquarters and General Kaupisch in Hamburg from 04:00 to 06:00 on 9 April.[46] After the Danish postal officials, noting the unusual heavy telephone traffic, cut the telephone line, Himer switched to the radio, which was by then established at the Citadel.

At 04:00 on 9 April, German ambassador Cecil von Renthe-Finck requested an emergency meeting with Foreign Minister Munch. Von Renthe-Finck told

Munch that mobilisation would be considered 'a hostile act which would entail consequences'. The German government also declared that 'the Reich Government therefore has, beginning today, set in motion certain military operations which will lead to the occupation of strategic points on Danish soil. . . . The Reich Government declares to the Royal Danish Government that Germany has no intention through her measures now or in the future of touching upon the territorial integrity and political independence of the Kingdom of Denmark.'[47] Hitler had ordered his ambassadors to pressure the governments of Denmark and Norway not to resist at the start of the attack, just as Joachim Joesten had predicted in his 1938 book, *Denmark's Day of Doom*.[48] In Denmark the strategy would succeed.[49] In Joesten's scenario planes would then roar over Copenhagen 'dropping thousands of-oh no! not bombs, just leaflets addressed "To the Population!"' The German navy would lead the attack, while 'wave after wave of *Panzerdivisionen* . . . surged over the unprotected Schleswig frontier, thundering along excellent roads into the fertile plains of Jutland . . . in less then one day they will reach the northern point of the peninsula.'[50]

The XXXI Corps that spearheaded the attack did not consist of *Panzer* divisions, only the more pedestrian German 170th and 198th Infantry Divisions with one battalion of the 69th Infantry Division directly attached to the corps headquarters. Both divisions, especially the 198th, were short of a full complement of artillery and were newly raised and were not veterans of the Polish campaign.[51] Accompanying the infantry were three Luftwaffe battalions of AA guns, of mixed 88mm and 20mm calibre and the 11th Motorised Rifle Brigade, consisting of two motorised regiments of two battalions each and three attached armoured car platoons. Also attached was one motorised cavalry company made up primarily of armoured cars along with a battalion of the SS *Totenkopf*[52] which had only recently been formed.[53]

Also attached was the Kluge detachment that was subordinated to the 11th Motorised Rifle Regiment. The Kluge detachment was part of the Luftwaffe motorised Hermann Göring Regiment and included one motorcycle company, the 8th Flak Battery of four platoons each with three 20mm AA guns, three eight-wheeled armoured cars, the first 1st Guard Company for the protection of the Luftwaffe commander and a headquarters unit with an attached signals platoon. Three armoured trains were available after operations on the Danish border ceased and later reinforced the Norwegian invasion.[54] Both forces had some additional units, including the 1st and 2nd companies of the *Panzer-Abteilung z.b.V40* made up mostly of PzKw Is with some command tanks and PzKw IIs tanks.[55]

On 4 April the 170th Infantry Division had been positioned at Bremen[56] and the 198th in the Perleberg–Pritzwalk area, south-east of Hamburg. The 170th contained two foot regiments (three battalions each) and one truck-mounted regiment of two battalions. Both divisions also had a standard 'bicycle' reconnaissance company of trucks, motorcycles and bicycle troops. Normally, there were only three armoured cars attached to an infantry division reconnaissance unit,[57] but for this invasion they were possibly reinforced, especially as the 170th had a truck-mounted regiment. For example, it is known that the von Hassel reconnaissance squadron of the 170th lost four armoured cars and suffered three dead and four wounded in the opening hour of combat.[58] To keep their intended use secret, the troops were not massed near the Danish border, and it was not until 06:00 on 6 April that elements had been moved just south of Kiel, where some troops of the 198th were to board ships in preparation for a seaborne attack, mostly from the Baltic Sea side.[59]

By 06:00 on 7 April, elements of the 170th were staged forward to Flensburg, just on the German side of the border, where Danish intelligence noted the presence of a column of German troops 30–40 miles long. Heavy motor traffic was reported on the German side of the border at 03:30 on 8 April along the newly constructed Nazi autobahn. The two-lane autobahn crisscrossed Germany and allowed for the rapid deployment of German forces, and was the inspiration of the future interstate freeway system of the USA. The 11th Motorised had driven to the German town of Heide, close to the North Sea, about 50 miles from the Danish border. During the last stage to the border, the Kluge detachment drove at night without lights at speeds of 40mph to keep up with the 11th Motorised. The reinforced motorised regiment of the 170th, spearheaded by its reconnaissance company and the 11th Motorised, was to lead the drive up the Jutland Peninsula with a rapid charge on both the North Sea and Baltic sides of Jutland. At the same time, members of the 198th Division moved by rail to Lübeck and Rostock on the Baltic coast to ready themselves for convoy operations and to support the invasion.[60] The German navy, using almost exclusively small warships and even commercial ferries, would move the 198th to its objectives in the Danish islands. This ability to quickly mass, by use of rail and autobahn, gave the Germans an incredible advantage, but the Danish officials had also ignored clear intelligence of what was about to befall them.

The German invasion force contained classic boots-on-the-ground infantry units, with horses for artillery and transport. Two companies of armour and the motorised brigade provided a hint of modernity, along with the truck-mounted regiment of the 170th and its reconnaissance company, and some tank and armoured car units. But this was also a combined-arms operation, with the Kriegsmarine supplying shipping (and firepower if required) and, above all, the uncontested German Luftwaffe.

The small elements of armoured and motorised units leading from the front without artillery support were about to break through in six areas on the Jutland Peninsula. By 06:00 on the 8th, troops for this portion of the operation were putting to sea and the rear elements were being brought forward. The attack began at 04:15 on 9 April, several hours after the first actions in the outer Oslo fjord in Norway. That lag in time should have eliminated the element of surprise, but it did not. Denmark's political and military leadership was completely surprised at the 'total invasion of the country, without any warning'.[61] German troops were detailed to every essential port, airfield and military base in the opening hours of the war.

Paratroopers under the command of Captain Walther Gericke were earmarked for Operation *Weserübung Süd*.[62] Originally Gericke was going to land with his entire company at Ålborg but on 7 April he decided to reduce the landing to just one platoon to allow for an additional paratrooper drop on a Danish island bridge at Storstrøm. The platoon charged with seizing the two large airfields at Ålborg departed Germany at 05:30, well after the opening shots. This platoon, escorted by Me110 fighters, successfully dropped at 07:00 from just four Ju52s.[63] This operation, including landings elsewhere in Denmark, was the first combat use of paratroops. The first German into the city of Ålborg, to secure hotel accommodations for some pilots, hitched a ride into town from a passing Danish travelling salesman. The field was quickly secured and reinforced by a battalion of the 69th Infantry Division flown in by fifty-three Ju52s. Additional Ju52s carrying aviation fuel and ammunition and the headquarters unit for the paratroops soon followed. Later that same day, planes would fly on to Oslo. This leapfrogging tactic enabled a decisive reinforcement of the air bridge created by the paratroops and is a classic example of the use of air-mobile troops.[64] By the evening of the 9th the Ålborg air bridge received more than 100 German aircraft transporting troops and supplies as well as additional combat aircraft.[65]

Gericke shifted his remaining three platoons to seize and hold the Storstrøm bridge connecting Falster with Sjælland, being dropped from nine Ju52s. This change had been made at the last minute and though it was quickly improvised, it was in the end successful. The small island of Masnedø that lay between was the site of an inactive Danish fort with a caretaker garrison of three men. The paratroops rushed the fort and captured it without any losses as the Danes were sleeping. This action secured the bridge on the Sjælland side.[66] The paratroops were quickly relieved by German elements of the 198th Infantry Division, who came across by ferry from Rostock to the Danish town of Gedser on the south side of Falster. There, just as the campaign started, five Abwehr agents had destroyed communications between Gedser and the central town on Falster of Nykøbing. This was one of several small Abwehr detachments that crossed into Denmark on the 8th for special operations to secure important bridges and roads. Earlier, on 30 March a German officer posing as a visitor had taken the ferry to survey the situation at Gedser and had made a full report on 1 April.[67]

Germany had five warship groups prepared for the invasion primarily for the transport of portions of the 198th Infantry Division. These warship groups were made up of obsolescent warships and small support vessels (mostly minesweepers and trawlers), and in the case of Warship Group 7, the relatively powerful but old pre-dreadnought *Schleswig-Holstein*. It, however, went aground while manoeuvring in shallow Danish waters in the presence of a Danish patrol vessel.[68] Warship Groups 7 and 9 departed Kiel, and Group 9 landed troops at the two ports connecting Jutland with Odense. Group 7 landed German elements of one regiment of the 198th Infantry Division to seize Korsør and Nyborg, key stations for the Great Belt ferry system connecting the mainland to the main island of Sjælland. At Nyborg Danish sailors actually helped moor an arriving German torpedo-boat filled with 160 invasion troops. At Korsør the local garrison, trained to prevent a German landing there, was asleep when it was peacefully occupied.[69] Warship Group 8 departed Lübeck for Copenhagen itself. Warship Group 10 left Cuxhaven and landed sailors and naval infantry at the Danish port of Esbjerg, and Group 11 landed sailors and naval infantry on 10 April at Thyborøn on the North Sea coast with neither Group 10 or 11 meeting with any resistance. Thyborøn was at the entrance to Lim Fjord. In support was an additional squadron that included the elderly pre-dreadnought *Schlesien*, which had been positioned to stop either a Danish naval force issuing from Copenhagen or the *Peter Skram* from Frederikshavn.[70]

Approaching Copenhagen was Warship Group 8 consisting of the minelayer *Hansestadt Danzig*, being escorted north by the diminutive and unarmed icebreaker *Stettin* and two picket boats. The latter two remained outside of the port as *Stettin* and the *Hansestadt Danzig* entered the harbour. When two searchlights from the shore lit up the *Stettin,* the *Hansestadt Danzig* trained its searchlights on its own battle flags. The Danish fort's commander, assigned there just four days earlier, ordered a warning shot to be fired across the minelayer's bow, but grease in the gun, most likely due to the harsh winters, prevented a shell from being loaded. The *Hansestadt Danzig* had for a main armament two 88mm AA guns that could be used for direct fire. It was a high-profile (two decks), 2,431-ton converted passenger ship – clearly not a true warship designed with any sort of proper warship construction techniques. If the Danish coastal defence batteries had been in working order and ready to open fire the *Hansestadt Danzig* would have likely been sunk or would have been forced to retire without landing its battalion at the city dock.

The *Hansestadt Danzig* steamed on, while the *Stettin* remained near the fort. The *Hansestadt Danzig* carried one battalion with some bicycle troops attached to the operation and communication specialists to operate the radio and take control of Copenhagen's newspapers and telephone exchange. Also attached were six Abwehr agents, assigned to search for and arrest French and British spies. The Danes did not fire on any German ship that day.[71]

One of the first German morning air actions was an overflight of Copenhagen by twenty-eight He111s, escorted by twenty-six Me110s. The Danes feared that Copenhagen was to be another Guernica or Warsaw, but, as if following Joesten's fictional invasion plan, the planes instead dropped leaflets calling on the Danes not to resist as Denmark and Norway were now part of the Greater German Reich.[72] Other towns in Denmark experienced similar overflights. German orders were accidentally given to bomb Copenhagen but these were withdrawn in the nick of time. Some of the planes landed at Ålborg because they were low on fuel. Later that morning the occupying German troops placed large Nazi flags on the ground for German aircraft to see that various areas were friendly.

These overflights were intended as a show of strength to convince the Danes that if they resisted, their capital and other cities could be bombed with impunity. They certainly had an impact. Erik Day Poulsen, whose mother was 7 years old on the day of the overflights and lived in Ålborg, recalls her telling him,

On the morning of the 9th of April 1940 my grandfather was taking my mother to school . . . . She told me that on the way to school they heard and saw many German bomber planes circling over the city. Leaflets were dropped all over, and in very poor Danish to the civilian population and was told to keep quiet so the German bombers didn't have to do to Danish cities what they had done to Polish cities. My mother remembered how she took a good grip at her father's very large hand and asked what that all meant. My grandfather was a mason and a very large man. My mother was surprised how frightened he became (he never needed to fear anybody). He told her that we were at war but it would be all right. She did not believe him since he also was afraid.[73]

One Danish plane tried to take off and was shot down; its pilot and observer were killed. Most of the planes in the small Danish air force were strafed on the ground. Strafing destroyed a total of eleven Danish planes and damaged an additional fourteen on the ground. Only one German plane was lost in this 'war', and a very few German air crewmen were wounded by AA fire.

German bicycle troops were assigned to take the Citadel. The Citadel was the residence of commander of the Danish army Lieutenant General W. W. Prior, who had left at 04:45 to travel the few blocks to the Royal Palace of Amalienborg, which lay between the *Langelinie* and the Citadel. The Danes at that time used the Citadel primarily for training, though it also had communication and command functions. The two companies attacked Norwegian Gate, and, from the south, the King's Gate. The Norwegian Gate approach was protected from sight by custom sheds that handled the importation of alcohol and tobacco products.[74] As the Germans approached, they utilised a customs truck on rails to haul their equipment forward. Hand grenades were placed under the gate. One went off prematurely killing one German, and the rest demolished the gate allowing the troops to rush into the defenseless fort. The King's Gate was open and the Germans simply walked in; its garrison of nine soldiers did not resist. The radio equipment from the *Hansestadt Danzig* was quickly set up. The Danish Interior Minister and the army Chief-of-Staff were arrested nearby and kept at the Citadel until the surrender.

To the south in the area of the Royal Place and parliament were three guard posts manned by the personal guard of the king. The elderly king, Christian X (older brother of Haakon VII), had been awakened at about 04:00 and told, as he hurriedly dressed, that his guards were being issued live ammunition. Sporadic firing had broken out in Copenhagen by 05:35. About 20 minutes later, the king ordered the Royal Life Guards to resist and by 06:00 all of the Danish forces had received orders. That early morning three Danish infantrymen in the palace area were wounded as the first German troops fell back and began to prepare a stronger assault.[75] The king later visited one of the wounded, who wrote home, 'I was wounded in my leg during the fight. His Majesty came to see me when I was on the stretcher, and fortunately my wound allowed me to lie at attention.'[76]

While the Danish government conferred, occasional rifle shots rang out and German troops approached the palace a second time. In the meantime, the Danish postal service had noted a large volume of phone calls between Copenhagen and Hamburg and cut those lines off. With the king and government unable to escape into exile, the situation appeared hopeless. General Prior was the only voice calling for further resistance. Prior refused to issue the order to surrender. Berlin correspondent William L. Shirer would write of this that, 'Lieutenant General W. W. Prior, the Danish Commander in Chief, who in the next twenty-four hours was to be one of the few in authority to insist on fighting, however hopeless the odds, demanded immediate mobilization. But the complacent [Prime Minister] Stauning would hear none of it.'[77] At 06:35, orders were sent out for all resistance to halt. The Jutland division received these by 07:00 when the Copenhagen radio station started its normal broadcast service. By 07:20 the surrender was accomplished.[78]

* * *

At the Danish border elements of the Brandenburg Battalion, an Abwehr military unit of what is called today 'special forces', took the first action. A group of eleven men helped secure bridges in the border area for the German army and later, as part of Operation *Sanssouci*, waylaid certain Danish individuals and later turned them over to the Gestapo.[79] Securing the bridges of the two rail lines into Denmark allowed three armoured trains to enter the country. Such armoured trains had been used very successfully during the Polish campaign.

Fighting along the border consisted of a series of short actions which witnessed the Danish troops ambushing fast-moving German reconnaissance units made up of armoured cars, trucks, motorcycle troops and tanks. The German advance units for the 170th Division consisted largely of these components; along with its organic truck-towed AT company. The 170th advanced north, along the eastern side of Jutland. The 11th Motorised Brigade led the other main advance with the goal of linking up with Ålborg on the North Sea side of Jutland. As soon as any contact occurred, the Germans deployed and outflanked the Danish position with their superior numbers. Several Danish units surrendered to the rapidly advancing German units after some sharp fighting.[80]

The Kluge detachment on the North Sea side also seized the small airfields at Esbjerg and nearby Oksbøl. During their advance they were covered by Me110s overhead. Defending Esbjerg was a Danish AA battery, which reported firing on the German planes but inflicted no losses and suffered none.[81]

Towards the end of this short morning of war at Tondern and Vordingborg, the Danes surrendered when the Germans informed them that the Danish government had ordered the cessation of hostilities.

Danish units of 20mm and 37mm AT guns were deployed forward, as Danish doctrine required for AT guns. The 20mm was not very effective against the German tanks. Shells from one hit a command PzKw II six times without penetrating its armour.[82] But the gun was effective against advancing armoured cars. A striking 1946 painting by Anna Maria Mehrn depicts one of these skirmishes, the ambush of the German lead reconnaissance force at Hokkerup.[83] German doctrine called for the armoured cars of the reconnaissance units to advance and locate an enemy's AT guns.[84] At Hokkerup thirty Danish motorcyclist troops were deployed at a roadblock, constructed primarily of felled trees and handcarts, and defended with a 20mm AT gun and a light machine-gun. At 05:30, after German planes had passed overhead, the lead armoured car halted at the roadblock. The 20mm AT gun fired three shots, putting the armoured car into a ditch. Two more armoured cars were hit in succession before the Danish gun jammed. It was quickly repaired and a firefight opened as German motorcyclists arrived; soon 100 Germans, supported by several machine-guns and light mortars, surrounded the Danish detachment and forced it to surrender.

One German commander later noted, 'The availability of tanks and armored cars was of greatest importance. They broke in the first Danish defense positions at six points, without the need of artillery.'[85] Rushing forward in a pell-mell advance, the Germans were occasionally stopped, but against such overwhelming numbers the Danes had little choice but to surrender or retreat. One Danish company commander took his command, elements of the 11th Battalion, and ordered it onto a ferry and into Sweden for internment.[86]

In his after-action report, the commander of *Panzer-Abteilung z.b.V40* noted, 'As the experience in Denmark had already shown, one must continuously calculate on the enemy possessing anti-tank weapons',[87] a reference to the Danish 20mm and 37mm AT guns that saw action that morning.[88] The lack of adequate armour for their tanks and armoured cars was brought home to the Germans. They had learned this lesson in the 1939 Polish campaign, and although they had started upgrading by the time they invaded Denmark, there had not been enough time to make significant improvements to their equipment.

By 07:20, it was all over; Denmark had capitulated. The German advance in Jutland was 15–25 miles into the peninsula and almost through the few Danish units deployed there. By that afternoon, the king was taking his customary horse ride through Copenhagen (with German officers and men saluting him as he rode by) and the Danish police had their side arms returned to them. The king issued a proclamation (countersigned by Stauning) entitled 'To the Danish People' and this was placed on placards that very afternoon calling for calm and instructing Danes not to resist the Germans.[89]

Total casualties on the Danish side were sixteen dead: three frontier guards, eleven soldiers and two airmen; twenty-three others were wounded. Approximately twenty to twenty-five Germans were killed and possibly as many as fifty wounded, though the number of dead may have been higher. German losses were deliberately not released because Germany wanted to portray the occupation as peaceful.[90] Germany also lost at least two and probably three or four PzKw Is and about twelve to thirteen armoured cars. A few Danish civilians were killed and wounded. A German tug was lost in a collision and the crew rescued by a Danish torpedo-boat.

Because Denmark fell so quickly and there was immediate resistance in parts of Norway, the German army quickly shifted elements of the 198th Division from Danish occupation duties to prepare for both airlift and embarkation to Norway.[91]

Germany had a set of post-occupation orders already prepared. Regulations for rationing, control of the press and radio and new currency regulations were all immediately put into place.[92]

After the capitulation to Germany, Danish servicemen were 'met with expressions of scorn and derision from civilians' for their lack of resistance in the invasion. Admiral Rechnitzer would write 'My mood is quite black and I feel extremely dejected and heartbroken. It all seems endlessly sad to me.'[93] Demobilisation of the Danish army was completed peacefully by 17–20 April. A few Danish soldiers slipped up to Norway and would join the fight there.[94]

In turn, there was resentment on the part of the military towards the government, an unexpected backlash against government policies that had been in force for over a decade.[95] Another indication that the government was not in touch with the people was that Foreign Minister Munch, on the day of the invasion, actually blamed Great Britain for the German invasion of Denmark. While an understandable thought, a foreign or defence minister must take responsibility for their nation's actions or inactions. He would be forced to resign the following July.[96]

The king at the time of surrender, who was visibly shaking at the start of the interview, would say to German Major General Kurt Himer, 'General, may I, as an old soldier, tell you something? As soldier to soldier? You Germans have done the incredible again. One must admit that it is magnificent work!'[97] Yet the popularity of the king grew after the surrender, in part for his daily ride through Copenhagen during which he never acknowledged the salutes of the German soldiers. On his birthday on 26 September 1940 hundreds of thousands of Danes gathered in the streets and around the palace to salute him.[98]

\* \* \*

The seventeen Faeroe Islands north of Scotland belonging to Denmark were a strategic island group that the Allies wanted to keep out of German hands. On 12 April, the heavy cruiser *Suffolk* embarked two 3.7in howitzers and 250 marines and immediately headed for Thorshaven, the largest city in the islands. The entire island group had a little more than 26,000 inhabitants, descended mostly from Norwegian settlers. The destroyers *Havant* and *Hesperus* carried out anti-submarine patrols in advance of the *Suffolk*.[99] Two trawlers assisted the *Suffolk* in landing the marines, guns and supplies by the late evening of the 12th.[100] The *Suffolk* fortuitously encountered the 12-knot, 6,044-ton German tanker *Skagerrak* just leaving Thorshaven, and sank it on 14 April.

Iceland was also a Danish possession. The British government wanted to forestall any German action against the island. It was occupied by British troops on 10 May 1940, and they immediately commandeered all communications facilities. The USA took over the occupation of Iceland in July 1941. After 9 April, local Greenlanders declared Greenland a self-governing territory and later an agreement was made with the USA that allowed for American troops to occupy key positions.

* * *

Denmark's defence in 1940 was not the determined struggle of 1864 or 1801. The Germans considered the Danes good fighting men and well trained but poorly equipped. One German colonel who was with the advance up Jutland said of the Danes, 'Not smart in appearance perhaps, but they are tough and crack shots.'[101]

The German conclusion was that Denmark had fallen so quickly due to the surprise seizure of vital points; the demonstration of force by the Luftwaffe; diplomatic actions; and the immediate crushing of resistance, mostly on the border near Germany. The complete *coup* element of the campaign is striking – this was a rock thrown at night and striking home.[102]

By the time Germany invaded Denmark on 9 April it was too late for Denmark. For Denmark to have offered any real resistance, and through that have assisted Norway, Denmark's military would have had to have been on a stronger Neutrality Watch. This action might have lent an element of strength to the government. Such a determined mobilisation in September 1939 might have deterred Germany as it faced France and the British Expeditionary Force; at minimum it might have held the Germans from immediately shifting troops north to Norway. Both Denmark and Norway may have believed their declared neutrality would be respected, but with the example of Poland, Finland, the Baltic States and Albania before them, it is clear that they refused to recognise political reality.[103]

After the war the Danes, like the Norwegians, would vow, '*Aldrig mere en 9 April*', or 'Never an April 9 again'.

The contrast between the Danish lack of effort to defend their country and the determined Norwegian resistance was marked.

# CHAPTER 8

# *The Seizure of Oslo*

This stands alone in the history of the world. In the Napoleonic era there was not the occupation of two enemy capital cities within 24 hours.

Italian Foreign Minister Galeazzo Ciano's greetings to
Hitler on the occupation of Oslo and Copenhagen[1]

Within 24 hours of the start of the invasion, Norway would see its principal harbours and cities and most of its few major airfields in German hands. The capture of Oslo was the critical German operation. If the Germans could seize that city quickly and capture most of the government, including the royal family, they could achieve what they had in Denmark – a quick and low-cost victory. All the second and third waves of reinforcements arriving by sea could be safely routed, or rerouted to Oslo, the closest major port to Germany and furthest from Allied interference. Oslo also had the harbour facilities to handle numerous transports. Oslo was also to be the hub of all Norwegian activity in the coming days.

The German effort to seize airbases, ports and naval bases led to the first battles of the campaign. The initial Allied and Norwegian responses were half-hearted, showing the lack of proper preparation and inadequate communication for the lightning strikes waged by Germany.

Even with the survivors from the *Rio de Janeiro* as firm proof that Germany was about to invade, information known by 18:30 on the afternoon of 8 April, Norway put no major naval or army preparations into effect. The Admiralty did not report this information to Admiral Forbes at Scapa Flow until 22:55.[2]

The brilliant 56-year-old Chief-of-Staff (*Generalstabssjef*) Colonel Rasmus Hatledal, who in 1938 had succeeded Colonel Otto Ruge in this position, requested immediate mobilisation but was refused. The chief communications officer of the Norwegian navy did not order an alert until 01:00 on the 9th – after leaving a party. Colonel Otto Ruge, soon to be Commander-in-Chief of the Norwegian army, later wrote, 'No one in this country had imagined a strategic assault of such an extent and executed with such daring along the entire coast from the Oslo fjord to Narvik.'[3] Herman K. Lehmkuhl, a Norwegian official would write in 1944, 'Everything in Norway was not as it should have been when the Germans attacked. The Norwegians were unprepared mentally and militarily.'[4]

The Norwegian government did nothing decisive to defend the nation in those critical hours. It's mantra of not wanting to fire a shot continued to dominate their actions. But as 8 April turned into 9 April, 'rumors and menaces crystallized into facts'.[5]

Reports of British transports loaded with troops bound for Norway to seize its Atlantic ports raised discussions within the Norwegian cabinet about whether to resist such a British move against its imperiled seaports. Dutch Major Gijsbert Jacob Sas, after learning on 3 April from Abwehr Colonel Hans Oster of an impending German attack, had contacted the Norwegian diplomat and Vice-Consul Ulrich Stang in Berlin. When Stang told Sas that *Britain* was about to attack, the incredulous Sas exclaimed, 'What! You mean the British intend to land in your country? Don't you know the Germans will be landing in Norway next Tuesday?' Stang discounted such an assault. When this information was forwarded to the Norwegian Foreign Ministry it was disregarded there as well, in part due to Sas having repeatedly warned of an impending attack from Germany against Belgium and the Netherlands.[6]

Swedish Intelligence was much better informed by early April. Reports on mountain troops in northern Germany, which has no mountains, contained information that they had been issued seasickness pills. This information coupled with the heavy German naval traffic especially passing off their western coast in Øresund Sound and additional diplomatic reports gave the Swedish a picture of some impending action against Denmark and Norway. Additionally, they were made aware that Sweden was *not* targeted. Based on this information, combined with the Oster disclosures, Swedish Ambassador to Germany Arvid Richert would write on 7 April, 'I have the firm impression that far-reaching actions towards Denmark and Norway are to be expected shortly; most likely within days.' On Sunday 7 April the Swedish government ordered the recall of crews to their active warships and to increase their combat capability.[7] The Swedish government did not communicate this information to either Norway or Denmark.[8]

The Danish navy contacted the Norwegian navy with two messages on the afternoon of the 8th informing them of German warships and merchant ships steaming north off the Danish coast. The second message indicated many people on board, 'possibly troops'.[9]

The 69-year-old American ambassador, Florence Jaffray Harriman, appointed to her post in 1937, received reports from Copenhagen on the evening of 8 April detailing the number and types of German warships and merchant ships moving through Danish waters off the Norwegian coast. Similar reports were arriving at many of the embassies.[10]

Vidkun Quisling and the NS played an important role in the opening hours of war. On 3 April Quisling had met in Copenhagen with German intelligence officer Colonel Hans Piekenbrock, head of the espionage division of Abwehr and close friend of its head, Admiral Wilhelm Canaris. The meeting had been arranged at Hitler's personal order.[11] Quisling may have surmised that war was a possibility, but he had been given no formal confirmation that such was the case. German operational plans for the invasion were already moving ahead, ships

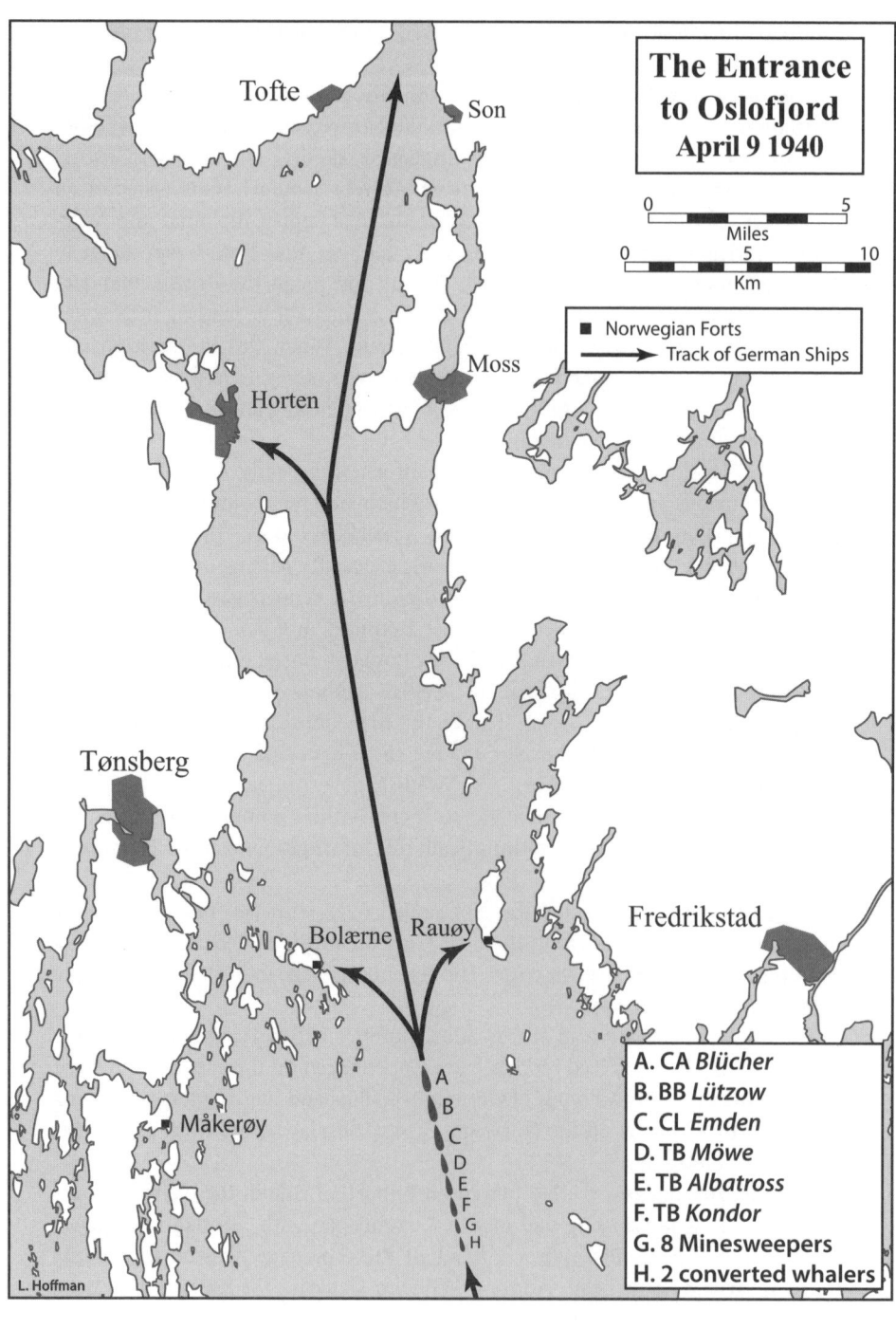

The Entrance
to Oslofjord
April 9 1940

0          5
Miles
0      5      10
Km

■ Norwegian Forts
→ Track of German Ships

Tofte

Son

Moss

Horten

Tønsberg

Fredrikstad

Bolærne    Rauøy

Måkerøy

L. Hoffman

A
B
C
D
E
F
G
H

A. CA *Blücher*
B. BB *Lützow*
C. CL *Emden*
D. TB *Möwe*
E. TB *Albatross*
F. TB *Kondor*
G. 8 Minesweepers
H. 2 converted whalers

were at sea and the war plan was unfolding when Piekenbrock tried to obtain information from Quisling, mostly concerning Norway's military. Specifically he wanted to know if the coastal batteries would open fire on German warships. Quisling answered that they would not, unless the government ordered them to do so. (In the event, some did open fire, and Hitler partially blamed Quisling for this.) Quisling told the German that Oslofjord was not mined and provided some other useful information concerning the air force, readiness and troop strength. Piekenbrock thought that Quisling was evasive but was happy with the interview. Quisling asked if the Germans would be able to seize Narvik if they came to 'protect' Norway from the Allies. Piekenbrock did not answer.[12] While in Denmark, Quisling met with the Danish DNSAP leader, Frits Clausen. Apparently at no point did they discuss any possible invasion of Denmark or Norway.[13] Quisling returned to Oslo on 6 April and met with the NS leadership the next day, but did not discuss with them that he had met with a German intelligence officer.

At this point Germany did not have a specific role for Quisling to play. Germany's goal remained one of coercing the official government led by Prime Minister Johan Nygaardsvold into allowing Germany to 'protect' Norway in much the same way as would occur in Denmark. Quisling now appointed a new role for himself and the NS. On his own initiative, while the invasion was unfolding, Quisling would try to establish a new 'official' Norwegian government.[14]

On 8 April Quisling announced to the NS leadership that with the British mining of Norwegian waters, Norway had been drawn into the war. He had a proclamation distributed throughout Oslo demanding that a new national government be formed with him as its head. When it was clear an invasion was imminent, Quisling left his home, at the insistence of his 'adjutant' Harald Franklin Knudsen. Knudsen was afraid Quisling might be arrested, especially in light of the military action and inflammatory proclamation, and suggested the two stay at a hotel in central Oslo. The Hotel Continental had recently advertised that it had bomb shelters, reason enough for it to have been chosen. Knudsen clandestinely registered there on the evening of 8 April under his name, but Quisling shared the room.[15]

* * *

Oslofjord was a lengthy one guarded by *Oslofjord festning*, or Oslofjord Fortress, part of the 1st *Sjøforsvarsdistrikt*. Fully manned the fortress would have numbered 210 officers and 1,433 men, but only 83 officers and 613 men were on duty on the morning of 9 April. There were two levels of fortifications. The outer defensive position was made up of four small forts – Rauøy, Bolærne, Håøy and Måkerøy – on four separate islands located in the outer Oslofjord. Only the first two would have any impact on the fighting. Rauøy had for a main armament two batteries, each with two 150mm guns. It had one naval officer and fifteen sailors assigned to it, while Bolærne had a garrison of one officer and twenty men. For a main armament it had three 150mm guns and four 120mm guns. (At full strength, the latter would have had 17 officers and 148 men, while the former would have had 23 officers and 210 men.) These were skeleton crews capable of partly manning the main guns, but not able to mount a proper defence in the event of a landing. Both forts had some light AA guns and searchlights and roughly a platoon of Norwegian army troops, but not all the defence positions were manned let alone fully staffed.[16]

The naval anchorage at Tønsberg in the outer roads was garrisoned with nine officers and seventy-three men. It would barely feature in the coming events. Melsomvik, lying south of Norway's main naval base at Horten, had a tiny garrison. Norway's minelayers were stationed there, but on 8–9 April they were at Jersøy, an island located between Tønsberg and the fort at Bolærne.

Horten had an army garrison of 9 officers and 125 men. There were also 130 AA personnel and 15 radio and communication staff. It had four 75mm guns and eighteen machine-guns for AA defence. There were a small number of untrained recent recruits who were excused from duty before the coming action. Several small and mostly old warships were under refit, and there were two improved small *Sleipner* class destroyers under construction. Horten was also the base for the main Norwegian naval aircraft squadron made up of five MF11s, one MF10 and two antediluvian Douglas DT-2B/C torpedo-bombers, with a staff of twenty-six officers and seventy-eight men.[17]

As the fjord narrowed, it came to a bottleneck at the picturesque village seaport of Drøbak. This bottleneck was a narrow channel with fortifications on either side under the command of Colonel Birger Eriksen. From this point on to Oslo was the inner Oslofjord. Kaholmen Island, lying in this narrow channel, had Fort Oscarsborg, a brick and mortar fortress begun in the early 1800s and 'modernised' in the 1890s. This inner fortress system had several positions. One was the torpedo battery at Fort Oscarsborg that would play an important role. Oscarsborg had manned two of its three 283mm guns, supplied by Krupp in the nineteenth century. These gun positions had protected magazines with a concrete and earthen open barbette; the guns were not in armoured turrets, but only gun shields. Four of the positions had 120mm, 150mm or 57mm guns and were not manned, and neither were the two 120mm guns at Håøy. The most important manned and operable coastal battery position other than Oscarsborg was the one opposite, above Drøbak on a low hill, the Kopås battery with its three 150mm guns and two searchlights. Close to the water below Kopås were two manned 57mm guns known as Husvik battery. These were nineteenth-century guns, best known as 'rapid-fire 6-pounders' from the weight of their shell, and were positioned to fire on small ships trying to sweep the minefields (that were never placed). The eastern shore batteries were under the command of Captain Vagn Enger. Enger had augmented his gun crews with about fifty helpful cadets from the local coastal defence artillery school. AA defences were minimal.[18]

At the city of Oslo was the ancient fortress of Akershus. Though it overlooked the inner harbour, it was of little military value being used as a residence for the commander and as a museum. Here, largely for ceremonial occasions, were three companies of the *Hans Majestet Konges Garde* (HMKG), or Royal Guard, totalling 426 soldiers. Later during fighting in central Norway in their distinctive black uniforms they would earn the nickname by the Germans of 'The Black Devils'. The War College and specialist schools for cavalry, engineers and artillery added about 430 more soldiers. Also present near Oslo were four companies – three from the 6th Regiment and one from the 4th Regiment – essentially reserve formations, under the command of two captains.[19]

Outside of Oslo were two airfields. The main Norwegian army and civilian airfield was at Fornebu, which lay next to Oslofjord just to the west of, and clearly visible from, Oslo. Norway's most modern squadron was based there, made up of eleven Gladiator biplane fighters. They formed the *Jagevingen*, or Fighter Wing, of the Norwegian army air force. Of these planes, seven were serviceable on the morning of 9 April. They were much more manoeuvrable then the German Me110 twin-engine fighters they would shortly face. The base was very familiar to the Germans, as Lufthansa had been flying there for several years, and the German air attaché Captain Eberhard Spiller had recently been given a tour of the facility, including the fighters stationed there.[20] At nearby Kjeller airfield, to the east of Oslo, was a secondary airfield with the air school. New aircraft were stored and assembled there. Assembled but inoperable, especially with snow still on the ground as the planes lacked skis, were seven new Curtiss Hawk P36s. A further twelve were in a customs shed in Oslo.[21] That airfield was protected by four 76mm AA guns, twelve machine-guns and eight searchlights.

Warship Group 5 approached Norwegian waters late on 8 April under the command of Rear Admiral Oskar Kummetz. Also aboard his flagship, the new heavy cruiser *Blücher*, was Major General Erwin Engelbrecht, commander of the 163rd Infantry Division, and Major General Wilhelm Süssmann, the commander of the Luftwaffe ground organisation for Norway. Following the *Blücher*[22] was the pocket battleship *Lützow* and the old light cruiser *Emden*. The *Lützow* was to have been operating with Warship Group 2, but machinery problems had caused it to be reassigned to Group 5 with 400 mountain troops, which represented a reduced battalion of the 3rd Mountain Division, and about fifty Luftwaffe ground staff still on board. The mountain troops were the only veteran combat troops in Warship Group 5. There were 2,060 men in this landing force. Also present were the torpedo-boats *Albatros*, *Kondor* and *Möwe*,[23] the 1st R-flotilla with eight minesweepers (R17–R24)[24] and two whalers, the *Rau 7* and *Rau 8*. In addition to the troops and extra food supplies it carried on board, the *Blücher* carried 31 tons of munitions, light field pieces and other weapons. It had orders to land an army detachment at Fornebu airfield after passing the Norwegian forts. After that the bulk of the troops from the three largest ships would be landed in the inner Oslo harbour. Standing by in Germany or at sea were 23 merchant ships carrying 14,000 troops and equipment for Oslo once it had fallen. The *Blücher* was not fully operational at the time of the attack and still had practice ammunition stowed in its magazines. This meant there was not sufficient room for storing the live ammunition the army brought on board, so it was stored topside above the armoured deck and in the torpedo workshop and abaft the forward starboard torpedo tubes.[25] The captain of the *Blücher*'s sister ship, the *Hipper*, steaming with Warship Group 2 towards Trondheim, had made a point to stow all of the live ammunition below the armoured deck.

Wartime propaganda alleged, and it has been repeated many times since, that members of the Gestapo were on board, but a careful review of the troop manifests suggests otherwise.[26] However, the point is really academic. If Gestapo agents were not on the *Blücher* or even in the first wave into Oslo, they would be on the scene shortly, as they had been in Denmark as part of Operation *Sanssouci*.

Rear Admiral Kummetz had issued strict orders for gunfire protocol. Ships were to open fire only if signalled by the flagship and then only if gunfire was heavy. Any Norwegian warning shots were not to be returned. If Norwegian searchlights were illuminated, the warships could use their own searchlights to blind the Norwegian lights, but they were not to open fire.[27]

The Germans were now in the outer defences of Oslofjord as the morning fog began to thicken. The *Blücher* took down its large battle flag to indicate to the Norwegians that this was a 'peaceful' mission. Meanwhile, the crew was ordered to clear the ship for action and prepare for battle.[28]

On the night of 8 April at 22:30 the *Lützow* radio operator picked up a Norwegian order to 'douse all lights forthwith'.[29] This action was intended to extinguish all manned buoy and searchlights to make the passage of the fjord more difficult.

At approximately 23:00 the tiny Norwegian patrol boat *Pol III* with fifteen men and one 76mm gun came upon a wake and followed it. Soon ship's engines were heard and the *Pol III* turned on its searchlight, prompting the German torpedo-boat *Albatros* to close. At 23:10 the coast watch on the island of Færder radioed to Oslo a report of having sighted Warship Group 5. Another patrol boat, the *Farm*, sent a similar message 5 minutes later.

Meanwhile, the *Albatros* closed on the *Pol III* and ordered it not to radio the German's presence, an order that the captain of the *Pol III*, Lieutenant Leif Welding-Olsen, disobeyed. Firing a warning shot, the *Pol III* then either collided or rammed the *Albatros* without causing any significant damage. Two crewmembers either fell onto or boarded the *Albatros* and were captured. The German report states that the *Pol III* rammed the *Albatros*, but virtually all accounts say it was a collision. At 23:10, having recognised German voices on the *Albatros*, Lieutenant Welding-Olsen ordered one white and two red flares fired into the night. The *Albatros* drew off and then fired on the Norwegian boat, quickly disabling it. The *Pol III* had its 76mm gun disabled in the short one-sided firefight. As the crew attempted to abandon ship, Welding-Olsen, his legs shot off and seeing the lifeboat filling and then capsizing, told the crew, 'Don't worry about me. Save yourselves.' and rolled himself overboard into the sea. He was the first Norwegian to die in the war. The crew was taken on board the *Albatros*. The *Pol III* was towed into port by the Norwegians the following day and would be taken over by the Germans on 14 April. The renamed *Pol III* would operate as a German patrol ship during the war and would return to civilian duty after the war. In 1990 it was present at ceremonies commemorating the fiftieth anniversary with two of the original crewmembers.[30]

The Norwegian island battery at Rauøy, after sighting the flares sent up by the *Pol III*, spotted two German ships through the heavy fog. The Norwegians then fired first blank and then five live rounds at the advancing German warships, but the shells fell astern, and with the fog the targets became faint and then disappeared. On board the German ships the rounds were thought to be warning shots only, so they did not return fire. The other outer battery at Bolærne fired one blank warning round as well. Both forts briefly illuminated the distant Germans with their searchlights, and at Rauøy the Germans blinded the searchlight with their own. On board the *Blücher* was Lieutenant K. Johnsen, of Norwegian decent, a propaganda officer. Johnsen later recalled,

> I went on deck to enjoy the entering of Oslo Fjord. Suddenly we were illuminated by land searchlights. A shot was fired on us . . . from that moment I was sure that the Norwegians were not ready to peacefully give up their country. . . . During talks onboard with my comrades I was surprised that they were of a different opinion.[31]

Additionally, Johnsen was surprised that there had not been lifeboat practice as the ships approached Norway.

At about 23:45 Kummetz ordered the German squadron to halt. The *Kondor* was on anti-submarine patrol as the *Blücher* and *Emden* offloaded landing parties onto six of the eight minesweepers. At 02:30 on 9 April the Germans dispatched the torpedo-boats *Albatros* and *Kondor*, with two minesweepers with troops, towards the Norwegian naval base at Horten in the outer waters of Oslofjord. The other four minesweepers steamed towards the two small coastal forts of Rauøy and Bolærne. Later, at 04:00, one of the ships bound for Rauøy stopped at the small port of Engelsviken due to the fog to ask the location of the coastal battery at Rauøy. They had passed just north of it. The manager of the telephone exchange at Engelsviken immediately alerted the garrison at Rauøy at 04:30. The commander urgently requested a company of infantry from the nearby regimental headquarters but was informed no troops were available.[32] Rauøy fired on the German troops when they landed at about 05:30 and actually downed a German aircraft. The garrison, while suffering two dead, would continue to hold the Germans in check until the 08:00 order from Horten caused them to surrender (see below). [33]

The Norwegian government had been following events that foggy night. When the American ambassador called, Foreign Minister Halvden Koht told her, 'Of course, we are sure that they are [Germans].'[34] A report from Bergen just after midnight had confirmed that the ships entering Norwegian waters were German.[35] The air-raid sirens were sounded in Oslo at 00:15 when warships were reported in the fjord.[36]

The inner Norwegian naval fortress had received orders shortly before midnight to go to battle stations.[37] Orders issued soon after to deploy defensive minefields were not carried out due to darkness and a counter order issued by Rear Admiral Diesen's naval headquarters in Oslo. The British naval attaché, retired Rear Admiral Hector Boyes, had visited Admiral Diesen's staff at 01:00 that morning and was informed that no sea mines were deployed at Oslo. Boyes indicated British warships were on their way to Norway and this caused Diesen's staff to issue an order not to lay mines. However, by 03:00 the 1st Minelayer Division at Jersøy was ready to proceed to sea.[38]

The new 370-ton minesweeper *Otra* was ordered to leave Horten at 02:30 and it proceeded to Filtvet, a signal station situated at the head of the narrows. At 04:10 the *Otra* positively identified the warships entering the fjord as Germans. *Otra* was later abandoned by its crew at Filtvet and seized by the Germans on 10 April. Between the action with the *Pol III* and the opening of fire by Oscarsborg at 04:21 the Norwegians were also able to get the three submarines *A2*, *A3* and *A4* based at Teie near Tønsberg into the fjord.

Colonel Eriksen, commander at Oscarborg, knew the approaching warships were not Norwegian since Norway had nothing in its navy the size of the *Blücher*. The standing orders issued well in advance to Eriksen were to fire on any British, French or German warships attempting to enter inner Oslofjord.[39] He had been originally down to take command of the inner fortifications from high atop an adjoining island hill, but decided to command from the main battery instead. This proved to be a wise decision as the fog crept in and the nearby hilltop was completely enveloped.

Eriksen's command was on Neutrality Watch and was severely undermanned. With twenty-eight officers and men and with each gun requiring eleven men to operate, Eriksen elected to man only two of the three 283mm Krupp rifled guns on the island fortress. He commandeered cooks, some reservists who showed up on their own initiative, drivers and secretaries to handle the ammunition supply, but still thought he would only get off two shots at most from the main battery. Manning the hidden torpedo battery were reservists who were very familiar with the turn-of-the-century torpedo racks. The remainder of his command was posted on the eastern shore just past Drøbak towards Oslo. The three 150mm guns at the Kopås battery ably supported those of the main island fortress in the coming action.

Kaholmen is formed of two islands, the north and the south, with the gun fort on the south island and the north island housing a torpedo battery in a hard rock site at sea level. There were two officers and nine seamen manning the torpedo battery. It was armed with torpedo racks, not true torpedo tubes, which were lowered into the water; the timing of the torpedoes could be set and the torpedoes fired from the shore. There were six torpedoes ready for firing. Of these, two were to be fired at each of the first two warships to pass Drøbak, with the remaining torpedoes reserved for one ship each that might follow. A third torpedo was prepared for the *Blücher* but was not fired. There were three other torpedoes available, but these would require loading into the racks.

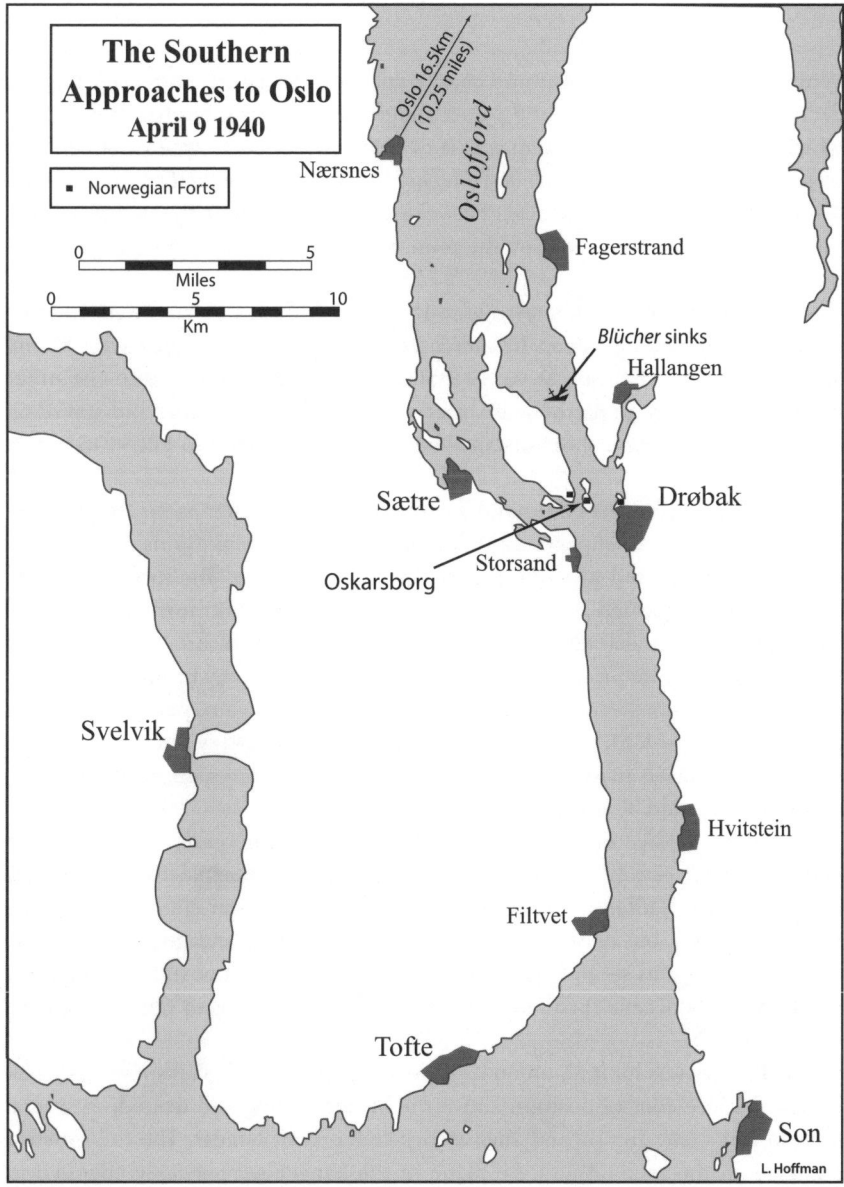

**The Southern Approaches to Oslo April 9 1940**

■ Norwegian Forts

0     5
Miles
0    5    10
Km

Oslo 16.5km (10.25 miles)

*Oslofjord*

Nærsnes

Fagerstrand

*Blücher* sinks

Hallangen

Sætre

Drøbak

Oskarsborg

Storsand

Svelvik

Hvitstein

Filtvet

Tofte

Son

L. Hoffman

In the 1930s the explosive charge in the warheads had been increased. The position had been carved out of granite and was well protected. More importantly it was unknown to the German navy.[40] The Germans were more concerned with electrically-controlled sea mines operated from the fortress. The Norwegians had such mines but had not deployed them.[41]

* * *

With the landing parties away and coastal lights extinguished, Admiral Kummetz decided to slow the advance and pass through the narrows at Drøbak at first light, which would be close to the magic *Weserzeit* time of 04:15 when the landings were scheduled to take place.[42] The *Blücher* led, followed by the *Lützow* and then the *Emden,* with 600yd intervals between the ships. Behind them steamed the torpedo-boat *Möwe* followed by the minesweepers *R18* and *R19.* The speed was only 7 knots.

As Kummetz neared the narrows, only 660yd wide at the narrowest and like most fjords exceedingly deep, he increased speed to 12 knots. The signal station at Filtvet notified Eriksen at 03:38 that warships were passing into the inner fjord. Two Norwegian patrol boats briefly illuminated the *Blücher* and stayed on its starboard side for a short distance before one proceeded to Filtvet to report at about 03:40.[43]

Eriksen prepared his command for the approaching action. In that process he had personally to supervise the loading of the two main guns because one of the officers refused to without a direct order to do so. The torpedo battery commander requested written orders before launching torpedoes at the Germans. Eriksen also chose to ignore his instructions to fire a warning shot first. Somewhere between 04:15 and 04:18 a searchlight again illuminated the *Blücher.* The beam swept from bow to stern and back again, partially blinding the German crew with its intense light, which 'created a very tense atmosphere aboard the cruiser, made worse by a mistiness through which no batteries or other details could be distinguished'.[44]

The *Blücher* was nearing the two looming 283mm guns at Oscarsborg. Nicknamed 'Aron' and 'Moses', each fired a 475lb high-explosive shell.[45] One of the gunners wanted to set the range at 2,000yd. Eriksen countered that the range was closer, but he wanted to hit the superstructure and not the waterline, so ordered the guns set to 1,300yd.[46] The higher hit would not sink the ships but would possibly disable them. Then he ordered the two guns to open fire on the *Blücher* at 04:21.

The *Blücher* was hit high up on its superstructure by both shells. The first shell hit the flak fire-control position above the bridge, killing and wounding several officers and men. The second shell struck the aircraft hangar. The fully-fuelled seaplane on the catapult and the plane in the hangar were quickly engulfed in flames. The third plane had been removed to make room for the army's live ammunition. The ammunition fed the fire and at least one 4.1in gun was disabled.

Eriksen's gunners immediately came under fire from the *Blücher's* light guns and so he ordered his men to take cover behind the ramparts. Eriksen's two guns would not fire in anger again. Eriksen felt he had fulfilled his duty and allowed Oslo, the king and the government the time to take what steps they saw fit.

Seeing the shelling from Oscarsborg, the Kopås battery and Husvik battery opened fire, along with some small arms. The Norwegians hit the now-burning

*Blücher* with numerous 150mm and 57mm shells. The 150mm shell hits were fired from the heights, but since they were not armour-piecing rounds they did not drive deep into the *Blücher*. Nevertheless, due to the short range the shells did penetrate into the immediate interior. This rain of shells disrupted deck operations, increased the number and strength of the fires and inflicted casualties, while these additional hits succeeded in knocking out another 4.1in gun and caused major power failures on board. One of the hits affected the rudder control; the helm was still operable but messages to the engine room to manoeuvre had to be made through a voice tube. The captain ordered full-speed ahead. As the *Blücher* was close to Kaholmen, the ship began to head for the centre of the channel. Norwegian gunfire ended after about 3 minutes of action.

The *Lützow*, following 600yd behind, opened fire with its secondary armament of 5.9in guns, as soon as firing began. It was attempting to bring 'A' turret with its three 11in guns into play when three 150mm shells slammed into the ship. One scored a direct hit on 'A' turret, wounding four sailors and putting the turret out of action. The second shell, coming in at an almost horizontal plane, destroyed the ship's sickbay and a block of toilets, killing two soldiers and wounding several others. Flames were quickly extinguished. The third hit the port aircraft crane, damaging one seaplane, killing four sailors and wounding ten.

Captain August Thiele of the *Lützow*, under fire from small arms and 57mm guns, and with all hell breaking loose on the *Blücher*, ordered the *Lützow* to withdraw, covered by the smoke from the fire in the sick bay on board. The fires were brought under control and a collision with the following *Emden* avoided. Over the next few minutes the *Lützow* restored two of its three guns in its main forward turret but still did not know the fate of the flagship. Clearly, though, the Norwegian batteries were operable and dangerous.

A tiny 107-ton Norwegian merchant ship, *Sørland*, with a six-man crew and a cargo of paper and food, was heading up the fjord toward Oslo when it happened upon the action. The *R18* and *R19* opened fire on it. The ship caught fire, forcing the captain to beach just south of Drøbak. The ship was a total loss and two men were killed in the action. It was the first Norwegian civilian merchant ship lost in the invasion. At the time the Norwegians thought the 2,410-ton German gunnery training vessel *Brummer* had also been lost.[47]

But what was the fate of the *Blücher*? Its captain had ordered full-speed ahead and was gathering way, heading toward the centre of the channel, when the hidden Norwegian torpedo battery came into play. The naval crews manning this battery were long-time reservists and had prepared for this moment for a lifetime. The battery fired two turn-of-the-century but recently overhauled 17.7in Whitehead torpedoes at the *Blücher*.[48] The first one hit amidships, slightly forward; the second one is usually described as having hit amidships, a bit back toward the stern. However, in recent years divers have visited the *Blücher* at the bottom of the fjord at a depth of between 180 and 300ft and determined that the second hit was closer to the stern.[49] Not suspecting torpedoes, the Germans thought Norwegian mines had caused the explosions.

While the damage did not immediately threaten the loss of the *Blücher*, the engine rooms began to flood steadily and the Germans had to anchor the stricken ship to keep from drifting on the shore. The battle to save the ship now began in earnest. Norwegian guns were not firing on it and the Germans finally ceased firing their AA guns. The list of the ship was a not-too-severe 8–12 degrees. Unfortunately for the *Blücher* the fire in the hangar, fed by ammunition from two nearby 4.1in gun positions and the ammunition stored there, had grown into a roaring blaze. Additionally, four 100lb aeroplanes bombs stored in the hangar fed the flames. Another problem was that the fire hoses were run on top of the armoured deck and shrapnel had pierced the hoses making it more difficult to fight the growing fire. The official *Blücher* report noted that where a 4.1in gun used to be 'thick smoke and fierce flames were coming out of the opening. . . . In the vicinity of the aircraft hangar and inside it a conflagration was raging through several decks. In the area of the starboard forward torpedo tube set rifle cartridges were detonating continuously. Great clouds of smoke and steam were rising from the funnel and amidships.'[50] To add to the confusion, naval officers failed to inform the troops of what to do, as army grenades and small-arms ammunition were periodically going off in the spreading fire. The captain ordered the torpedoes on the starboard side to be fired, exploding harmlessly on the rocks, while the port torpedoes were disarmed so as not to contribute to the unfolding disaster.

The captain tried to signal the *Möwe* to approach to aid, but it neither received the message nor could it have passed the Norwegian fortifications with any chance of success. As the fog dissipated, a freshening wind now rose to fan the flames and finally at 05:30, one of the 4.1in magazines exploded. This doomed the *Blücher*. At 06:00 the order to abandon ship was given. Lieutenant Johnsen later said that, 'there was no observable panic, and on the contrary, all soldiers and sailors took this serious situation very calmly.'[51] The *Blücher* sank at about 06:22, approximately 450–550yd from the mainland.

The actual losses on board the *Blücher* have been exaggerated over the years. Sailor and naval officer losses totalled 125, while 1,025 survived. Of the 528 soldiers on board, some 195 died, though the exact figure is in dispute. These numbers are far below the often-cited figure of 1,000 or more.[52] The Norwegians suffered no losses of sailors or soldiers, but three houses in Drøbak were destroyed and two women killed by German AA shells.

In retrospect it was clear that storing the ammunition above the armoured deck was a major error. Crew losses were increased by improper preparation of the ship's boats after the torpedo hits. But Rear Admiral Kummetz's fundamental mistake was in trying to run the forts at half speed. (By contrast, Warship Group 2 ran the gauntlet at Trondheim at high speed.) Had the *Blücher* passed through, even if damaged, and made dockside at Oslo, the campaign would have unfolded much differently. Alternatively, one of the small, more expendable warships in the group could have led the way. That morning General Engelbrecht had urged leading the line with a smaller warship but Kummetz refused, thinking the Norwegians would at most fire warning shots, which is what he thought had been done by the outer forts. Kummetz told Engelbrecht, 'Oscarsborg will never open fire.'[53] The original orders for Warship Group 5 called for the converted whalers *Rau VII* and *Rau VIII* to lead the advance, but they had been detailed to other duties by this time further down the fjord. In a 1948 book in the German Naval Series Vice Admiral Kurt Assmann suggested the *Möwe* for that role.[54] Another possibility, in light of Kummetz ordering speed to be reduced after passing the outer forts, would have been to quickly advance to the inner forts and mount a small-boat attack on both Drøbak and the nearby batteries at Oscarsborg. Kummetz was lucky that neither Norwegian mines nor submarines were properly deployed, something that could have easily added to German losses. The *Blücher* was the largest German warship lost in the campaign.[55]

In our opinion Kummetz should have been relieved of command after the seizure of Oslo. Instead, he would receive the Knight's Cross to his Iron Cross earned in the First World War and further commands, most famously at the 31 December 1942 Battle of the Barents Sea, where again he lost.

Captain Thiele was now in command of the German squadron on the wrong side of the Norwegian defences. He led the squadron to the towns of Son and Moss at the head of the inner fjord. Several hundred troops, meeting no resistance, were landed and given orders to advance up the fjord and capture the Norwegian defences. These were the mountain troops from the *Lützow* and elements of the 163rd Infantry Division. A scratch Norwegian force from the cavalry school was posted between them and Oslo, but with the fall of Oslo they were withdrawn before contact was made with the advancing Germans to the north.

While these events were unfolding, the German expedition to seize the naval base at Horten was under way. At 02:30 that morning, the Germans had dispatched the torpedo-boats *Albatros* and *Kondor* (each with 100 troops on board) with two minesweepers the *R-17* and the *R-27* (each with approximately forty-five troops on board) towards Horten in the outer waters of Oslofjord. The minesweepers were very practical ships. At 682 tons, they were armed with two 4.1in guns, four AA machine-guns and carried depth charges. With a speed of 18 knots and a crew of about 100 men, they were capable of defending themselves and, in this case, delivering troops to a destination.

Norway's main naval base was Horten.[56] Stationed there was 64-year-old Rear Admiral Johannes Smith-Johannsen, commanding the 1st *Sjøforsvarsdistrikt*. Smith-Johannsen was a weak leader and late on 8 April when contacted by the Colonel Eriksen at Oscarsborg, seeking definitive orders, Smith-Johannsen only briefed him on what was unfolding around Norway to that point but refused to issue further orders. This was an abdication of his authority. Eriksen would rise to the occasion, while Smith-Johannsen floundered and failed.[57]

One early initial naval success involved the refitting minelayer *Olav Tryggvason*. Its captain received orders to protect the naval base, and by 02:15 the ship was in position guarding the harbour entrance. The *Olav Tryggvason* was Norway's largest modern warship. Though built as a minelayer, it was seldom used in that capacity between 1936 and 1940, but rather as a slow destroyer. The Labour government had ordered it built, largely to keep the 500 shipbuilders at Horten busy (the smaller Norwegian minelayers were more suitable for minelaying in shallower waters). The *Olav Tryggvason* displaced 1,596 tons, was armed with four 120mm guns, a modest AA armament, four torpedoes and could steam at 23 knots.[58] Also available at Horten was the minesweeper *Rauma* of 370 tons, armed with one 76mm gun, capable of 15 knots and carrying a crew of twenty-five sailors.[59]

When the Germans reached Horten, their commander kept the two torpedo-boats outside the harbour, while the two minesweepers entered the harbour at 4:35 and steamed for the wharf. The *Tryggvason* at first thought the ships were two Norwegian minelayers but when they did not acknowledge its signal, the *Tryggvason* opened fire and quickly sank the *R-17* as it neared the pier. As it sank the depth charges on board exploded, causing additional German losses. The *R-27* exchanged fire with the *Rauma*. Both were damaged and both disengaged. The *R-27* had to retreat from the harbour.[60]

The *Albatros*, trying to navigate through the narrow channel into Horten harbour, now engaged the *Tryggvason* but only with its forward gun. After a few rounds its 4.1in guns malfunctioned. Under accurate Norwegian fire that killed one German sailor, concern for the safety of the troops on board caused the commander of the *Albatros* to withdraw.[61]

Next the Norwegians believed they sighted both the *Emden* and the *Lützow* approaching the harbour entrance.[62] The Germans sent a delegation from the gathered German soldiers now ashore a little before 07:00. As if on cue, twenty-eight He111s passed over Horten, and one was lost as they headed for Bolærne to bomb it. The delegation met with Rear Admiral Smith-Johannsen. It was at this point that the Norwegian army detachment was preparing to counter-attack, but thinking the Germans were surrendering to Smith-Johannsen, they halted their preparations.[63]

The Germans, bluffing well, threatened bombardment from warships just off shore and the Norwegian admiral entered into negotiations for the surrender of Horten. He was allowed to make a phone call to Admiral Diesen, who told him to do what seemed best. Smith-Johannsen decided to surrender his mostly defenceless command with effect from 08:00. By surrendering the Norwegians would avoid the bombing or shelling of Horten. The warships in port were surrendered as well.[64] The battery at Rauøy, still fighting the Germans and holding them off, received the orders from headquarters to cease fire and surrender at 08:00, which they did. German troops would shortly take control of those guns. This was a misunderstanding, never completely sorted out, as to the extent of *what* was surrendered when Smith-Johannsen issued the order.

Elsewhere in the fjord, the 1st Minelaying Division was at sea. Due to the presence of German warships it was decided not to lay mines as the division steamed toward its homeport of Melsomvik. It made port, quietly surrendering to the Germans on 14 April.

The Norwegian had three submarines in the fjord, the *A2*, *A3* and *A4*. They were ordered to sea and departed at 04:00 with orders to attack German ships.

Equipped with badly worn batteries, they could hardly make any speed under water. Two German minesweepers, *R22* and *R23*, discovered the *A2* on 9 April, while proceeding with small forces to attack the battery on Bolærne.[65] The *A2* had been operating at a depth of 80ft when detected. It was depth-charged and forced to the surface, where it surrendered, eventually being towed to Teie. The *A3* and *A4* slowly proceeded into the fjord with German planes constantly overhead. They never received Admiral Diesen's later orders to attack German shipping and then retire to Britain (see below). Instead, they made their way to Tønsberg and were scuttled by their crews on 15 April. The two submarine commanders would be censured for their conduct after the war.[66]

One last drama in the outer roads of Oslofjord needs to be mentioned. With the two German minesweepers already engaged, Bolærne remained in Norwegian hands. At 07:20 on 10 April, Bolærne fired three warning shots at a German transport, which retreated to the south. The *Albatros* and the two whalers, *Rau 7* and *Rau 9*, then approached with troops ready to seize the battery and engaged the little fort at Bolærne. A brief exchange of gunfire at 8,800yd resulted in some of the battery guns malfunctioning, but the Germans drew off. German air power was called into play and the fort was hit several times by bombs. The bombing demoralised the men and after firing approximately sixty-five shells, the guns had all broken down. Their officers, acknowledging the situation, surrendered. The fort was occupied that afternoon by troops from the *Kondor*. The *Albatros,* steaming nearby, ran aground on a hidden reef and was a total loss. The *Rau 7* took the garrison from the fort on board and returning to Horten would also run aground. Eventually that evening it worked its way free and arrived at Horten on 11 April.

The Norwegians continued to resist the Germans in Oslofjord after 9 April. The German navy had not arrived at Oslo, though German troops were ashore at Son and making a tactical advance on Drøbak and Oscarsborg. The strategic seizure of Oslo was not going to come about through naval operations. It was up to the air operations, the third arm of the joint campaign, to achieve the partial *coup de main.*

* * *

The original German invasion plans called for two companies of paratroopers (1st and 2nd companies with headquarters staff, a total of 340 men) to land at Fornebu and capture the base. Fornebu would then act as an air bridge. Shortly after its seizure, two infantry battalions were to arrive there by air, while another two battalions and the heavy equipment for all four battalions arrived by sea in Oslo harbour. The first infantry battalion due to land by plane was to begin arriving 20 minutes behind the paratroops. With the invasion ships stopped at Oscarsborg, the sea assault on Oslo was delayed. The air units were scheduled to drop at about 08:00 – well past *Weserzeit.*

The air transport was commanded by Lieutenant Colonel Karl von Gablenz, who served under X *Fliegerkorps* commanded by Lieutenant General Hans

Geisler. Geisler had firm orders from Air Marshal Göring that if Fornebu was *not* captured by the paratroops, the numerous and vulnerable Ju52s loaded with troops were to turn back. Furthermore, the Me110s would then be lost due to lack of fuel. The Me110s could fly to Oslo from Germany with just 20 minutes of fuel remaining. The plan called for them to clear the skies over Fornebu to allow two companies to parachute in and seize Fornebu. The Me110s were to land on the airfield after its capture. This would have become a one-way trip for them if Fornebu was not quickly captured.[67]

The Norwegian defence force consisted of AA troops and the support services at the base. Located about 10 miles from the centre of Oslo, Fornebu was protected by just seven AA machine-guns, with five set up in shallow foxholes that covered the standing men from the waist down, while the other two were in the open. There was no infantry garrison.

The initial German air-force units over Oslo in the morning were the eight Me110s that had displayed a show of force over the capital. Some Ju52s followed the fighters and then a flight of He111s and several aircraft flew quite low over the capital. One war correspondent wrote, 'Five huge tri-motored bombers, engines wide open, shaved the tops of the buildings across the park. They roared like hungry lions. You could see the German crosses beneath their wings.'[68] For 2 hours that morning planes would be periodically overhead in Oslo and receiving some inaccurate anti-aircraft fire. The attitude of the people of Oslo was to come out and watch this as if it were a show. American correspondent Leland Stow, who was present, would write, 'They simply seemed amazed by the whole performance. They didn't seem to have any idea what one bomb could do.'[69]

Right from the start things began to go wrong. The German ships being fired upon by the outer fjord defences had put Fornebu on alert a little after midnight. Later at 04:21 the gunfire from Oscarsborg could be heard at the airfield.[70] At 05:00 two Norwegian Gladiators were sent up and shortly clashed with a lone Me110. Later two others went up but did not find any targets. By 07:00 five Gladiators were sent up after the sound of many planes approaching was picked up on the 'sonic detector'[71] at Fornebu, followed shortly by two more. The five flew south where they saw smoke from the burning *Blücher*. They then encountered a large number of German aircraft approaching. In the ensuing dogfight five German planes were shot down, including two of the Me110s, with the loss of one Gladiator. The Luftwaffe also lost at least three Ju52s to the weather – planes that collided in mid-air, were shot down or simply disappeared into the fog, ran out of fuel or crashed into the sea.

A total of twenty-nine Ju52s and one communication aircraft approached Oslofjord with paratroops on board. In the heavy conditions, with visibility extremely poor, the commander of the German air group decided to abort the mission and fly back to Ålborg in Denmark and land there. All but three planes had turned back, when the fog began to lift over Oslo and Fornebu. The second wave of fifty-three Ju52s carrying infantry of the 2nd Battalion, 236th Regiment of the 69th Infantry Division was twenty minutes behind the first group.

When this situation report was received in Germany, Geisler ordered the second wave of Ju52s loaded with troops to turn back, and also the escorting Me110s, though the latter were now well past the point of no return. But Lieutenant Colonel von Gablenz, commander of the transport aircraft, refused to issue the order and instead argued with Geisler. Gablenz contended that Ålborg would be unable to handle so many aircraft and all these additional planes landing there would create utter chaos. He urged that the force should be given the chance to succeed. Geisler then finally issued the abort order, but when it was received by the approaching lead Ju52s the commander, Captain Richard Wagner, ignored the order because it had not come from Gablenz, but from the X Fliegerkorps. This was not the proper chain of command and the order was interpreted as a possible fake. The air transports flew on toward Fornebu. The Me110s, without enough fuel, knew they had no choice but to land at Fornebu.

When the six remaining Me110s arrived overhead at about 07:35 there were two Gladiators on the ground being refuelled and rearmed. The weather was clearing as the morning wore on. On the ground, Norwegian Second Lieutenant Armin Skotvedt told his men, 'Now we shall die men! If anybody wants to die first, just don't obey my orders.'[72] The men fired at Me110s and Ju52s with 7.92mm Browning machine-guns. The Me110s strafed the field several times and destroyed the two planes on the ground. The remaining Gladiators, ordered not to land at Fornebu, landed on frozen lakes where most were lost due to thin ice over the next few days – none would see further combat. The Me110s suppressed most of the ground fire from the base save for the south end of the airfield.

As the Me110s circled above the field, short of fuel, and with two having already lost one engine, the first of the air-landing units arrived. Captain Wagner was in the lead plane of the approaching Ju52s. He decided to land and began lining up his aircraft in order to approach the field in a classic landing pattern. The commander of the Me110s thought these were the paratroops. As Wagner's plane came down it was taken under fire; he was killed along with four others. The plane did not land and would fly back to Ålborg, along with most of his force – but not all. The plane directly behind him landed with no losses.

The commander of the Me110s now boldly decided to land on the airstrip to help seize it even as other Ju52s, with troops on board oblivious to the fighting taking place below, were approaching to land. He ordered a plane down. Though not fired upon, it landed badly, overshooting the field, with a lumbering Ju52 also landing at the same moment and barely missing it. The remaining Me110s quickly followed and the five set up in the north-west side of the airfield to provide covering fire from their dismounted and deployed rear machine-guns. Fighting would continue on the ground that morning for 2 hours but the machine-guns of the Norwegians ran low on ammunition and would overheat, while under fire themselves.

Several following planes attempted to land; some succeeded, and some flew off and would return to Ålborg. In the end one crashed, five crash-landed and three were damaged – all as a result of gunfire as they landed. Additionally, there would be collisions and bad landings that would be see a total of fifteen Ju52s written off at Fornebu that day.[73] Several of the landing Ju52s disembarked their infantry, who were unaware of the recent fighting. Others had suffered losses, mostly from AA fire, and over fifty dead and wounded Germans would land in the Ju52s in the first wave.[74] The commander of the Me110s quickly ran over to the troops and had them secure the airfield. Some of the machine-gun positions would continue to fire into approaching Ju52s until their ammunition ran out. By 10:00 many of the Norwegians still left began to abandon the airbase as German aircraft continued to arrive. The Germans did not fire on them while they retreated in the open. Six prisoners from the Norwegian AA unit and service personnel were soon put to work clearing the airfield. The fuel tanks at the airfield were undisturbed and allowed the Germans to immediately begin refuelling operations.[75]

Soon there were 350 infantrymen on the ground. As the weather cleared eighty lost paratroops found their way and quickly flew to Fornebu to reinforce the German troops. The signals unit for the paratroops was on one of the planes that had landed and now signalled the capture of the field. Ålborg picked up the signal and forwarded it to Germany. This signal was also picked up by another German resource that is discussed below.

Back in Germany, the news of the capture of Fornebu was quickly absorbed and reinforcements were ordered to the field, including an infantry company that was scheduled to fly to Sola airfield near Stavanger, but instead was diverted to Fornebu. Planes would straggle in all day. Lieutenant Colonel von Gablenz rushed off to fly up Fornebu to oversee the landing operations. Later, Gablenz told the commander of the Me110s, 'But for your Staffel things might have turned out very differently!'[76]

One of the first Ju52s to arrive was loaded with supplies and carried the base captain of the Me110s. As it approached Norway, the plane had run into several retiring Ju52s that had indicated to the pilot that he should not fly on. Instead of following this advice, the captain called back to his men, 'Get your pistols out! There is fighting in Oslo.'[77] Once on the ground, he quickly organised the surviving Me110s and readied them for additional operations.

The Norwegian command in Oslo learned of the German success and allocated one of the King's Guard companies for a counter-attack. Its departure was delayed due to a lack of transport. Finally obtaining some buses, the company moved out at 09:40, and then took an indirect approach to Fornebu. It was supposed to link up with elements of the 5th Infantry Regiment, but in the confusion failed to find them. While approaching the base, a German column heading for central Oslo easily slipped past the Norwegians. The company returned to Oslo before reaching Fornebu and was captured without having fired a shot. Its commander was a member of the NS; later that day Quisling appointed him to guard the hotel occupied by Quisling's nascent government.[78]

Beginning at 10:30 German forces from Ålborg began to arrive and by midday six companies of the 324th Regiment of the 163rd Infantry Division had landed and were preparing to march on Oslo, led by the regimental band.[79] By that evening eight companies of infantry had arrived by air, bringing in additional support equipment, air-support personnel and additional aviation fuel for future operations.

A representative of Lufthansa, who was also connected to the Abwehr, and the German air attaché Captain Spiller were both on hand to help with the air landings.[80] Lieutenant Colonel Hartwig Pohlman, who had met with Quisling just before the invasion, led the German forces into Oslo that afternoon, some of whom arrived on requisitioned local transport, but with the vast majority on foot. Spiller collected some motorised transport as he waited for the arrival of the remainder of the two companies of *Fallschirmjäger* now returning from Ålborg. On his own initiative later that afternoon and evening, he led some of these troops in the pursuit of the king and the Norwegian government. His pursuit would become known as the 'Spiller Raid'.

At the other airfield, Kjeller, which was more distant from Oslo, nearly all of the planes, mostly trainers, were evacuated to the north. German aircraft bombed Kjeller shortly after making their intimidation flights over Oslo. Kjeller was occupied that day and German aircraft began operations from that field the next day.[81]

\* \* \*

Not all sources agree on what transpired in Oslo from midnight and into the day on 9 April. Some accounts appear to have been constructed to protect the reputation of some official or military leader. What follows is our attempt to reconcile the accounts.

At 23:30 on 8 April, Prime Minister Nygaardsvold was awakened by a telephone call from Minister of Defence Colonel Birger Ljungberg. Colonel Ljungberg had been minister for only three-and-a-half months. He informed Nygaardsvold that unidentified warships had entered the outer Oslofjord. Nygaardsvold asked if the mines had been laid and Ljungberg replied in the negative. Shortly afterwards, another phone call informed the prime minister that the outer fjord forts had fired on the unidentified warships.[82]

It was only after the outer Oslofjord naval defences had made contact with the approaching enemy shortly after midnight that the army ordered Oslo to be blacked out. Air-raid sirens began to sound the alert, adding to the tension. The Norwegian cavalry captain in charge of the air-raid warning system had received a steady stream of reports from Sweden of large formations of planes flying north. They were not attacking Sweden and that only left one other possibility. Now at least some defensive preparations were initiated and a change began to alter the mindset of a people not expecting the war to burst through their front door.[83]

Nygaardsvold called a meeting of the cabinet for 01:30. Phone calls went out, waking most ministers. As one contemporary wrote,

> They all dressed quickly and hurried out into the night. There were no taxis to be had and they had to walk; some of them all the way from the suburbs.

The clouds were low and heavy, and it was pitch dark in the streets.... One of the ministers did not know exactly where in the Government buildings the meeting was being held, and hesitated as he reached the Ministry of Agriculture, where Cabinet conferences were usually held. A young couple emerged from the darkness. 'I believe it is in the Foreign Office,' the man said, 'I saw some people enter the building.'[84]

Foreign Minister Koht hurried through the darkened streets on foot to the government offices, arriving there at 01:30. He felt Oslo was safe with the inner fjord sea defences and did not think the Germans capable of sending sufficient troops by air to seize the capital.[85] The ill 65-year-old commanding general of the Norwegian army, Major General Kristian Laake, though informed of the enemy ships entering Oslofjord (and sighted off Bergen and Stavanger as well), refused at first to believe these reports. He was slow in leaving his country home and proceeded not to the government meeting but to the army headquarters at the Akershus, where Chief-of-Staff Colonel Hatledal was waiting. Hatledal confirmed the report of the 'unknown' warships in outer Oslofjord. Laake hurried on to join the cabinet meeting.[86]

Other government members arrived at the cabinet meeting. The members first debated whether mines should be laid in Norwegian waters. The result was that a few mines would be laid but none in Oslofjord, and far too late for the unfolding invasion. Laake had urged Ljungberg to proceed with the mobilisation for which Chief-of-Staff Hatledal had been advocating since 5 April. This was for the 1st, 2nd, 3rd and 4th Field Brigades – all in southern Norway – but not the 5th in the Trondheim region. Ljungberg raised this idea at the cabinet meeting. However, with the exception of Ljungberg, none of the other government members fully understood *what* mobilisation entailed. The cabinet members were ignorant when it came to their own nation's military. They professed to be unaware of the size of units and their postings anywhere in Norway.[87]

The government directed Ljungberg to order Laake to proceed with 'silent' mobilisation. This required letters to be sent out to those who were to mobilise and they were to assemble on 12 April. Laake, along with the minister of defence, understood this to mean the four field brigades. However, the prime minister and the rest of his cabinet thought that a *general* mobilisation *of the entire army* had been ordered. The decision to mobilise the four field brigades was taken at about 03:00. The 6th Brigade in the far north was already mostly mobilised but this order left out the 5th divisional command with its 5th Field Brigade concentrated near Trondheim and all the ancillary units of all the commands.

This decision was not to be announced on the radio to avoid frightening the populace. Laake had no concept of the speed of modern warfare or what Norway was facing. When Ljungberg told him of Laake's order, Hatledal exclaimed, 'Are you insane?'[88] Hatledal protested to Ljungberg and asked for full mobilisation, which was refused. More fundamentally, this limited mobilisation represented just 5,000 men per brigade. Hatledal, possibly in conjunction with Laake, moved the date requested of 12 April back to the 11th and extended the mobilisation to include the 5th Field Brigade (Trondheim region) and additional troops. In the coming hours soldiers arriving earlier at some depots were actually turned away and told to return on the 11th. But it was all still too little, too late.[89]

The Norwegian General Staff was ordered to leave the exposed Akershus and move to a large hotel in the northern Oslo suburb of Slemdal. The hotel was filled with private guests. Before dawn the General Staff had to move from the hotel when the power went out due to an air-raid warning at 04:30. The writing of the orders for mobilisation would be written at the home of a staff officer on his dining room table. Clearly, the disruptive effect of the German surprise had reached all the way to the top of the Norwegian military.[90]

Laake was also saddled with the issue of the Neutrality Watch and what troops were actually available. By the terms of the 1933 reform of the mobilisation system, a single brigade was fielded for each of the six divisions, thus the division became more of an administrative unit than an actual field unit. In 1939 the government had implemented a further reform of mobilisation rules, mainly to avoid the financial costs of the 1914–18 period, which further reduced the mobilisation of the bulk of the armed services. The new system was aimed at avoiding the great financial strain on the country that a general mobilisation would create, but the advantage of the general mobilisation was that it could be announced over the radio and by every means possible. This would translate into men leaving immediately for their depots to receive their equipment. As has been seen, due to the army's fear of a possible 'Red' revolution, the equipment was *not* necessarily concentrated at one mobilisation centre for the units. This order had been rescinded before the war but not fully implemented.

The new system had been debated, and the politicians had their turn. The majority of politicians, and certainly Prime Minister Nygaardsvold, were not familiar with warfare in general and modern warfare in particular, with its element of speed and the impact of air power. When war began they failed to understand *what* the current system was that was in place or that it had been designed primarily to save money – not to improve military efficiency. As the German attack unfolded they forgot all about the cost-saving restrictions that had been imposed, and seriously thought they had decided upon an immediate and full mobilisation. Only after the war was the system fundamentally changed giving the military standing orders to respond *immediately* to an invasion and have the preparations already in hand for such a response.

Laake apparently also thought that some sort of arrangement had been made by the Nygaardsvold government, about which he had been given no details, to allow Allied warships and transports into Norwegian waters. Why else would orders not be given for the deployment of minefields off key ports and for the mobilisation of all troops?[91] Admiral Diesen, after consulting with Koht and both knowing they faced a full-press attack by Germany, issued an order at 04:20 to all naval commands to fire on German warships but not British warships.[92]

Fortunately, Foreign Minister Koht mentioned to a press correspondent on the morning of the 9th that 'general mobilisation' had been ordered. Shortly after, this news was broadcast on Norwegian radio stations throughout the nation and many Norwegians began heading to their mobilisation depots. The Norwegian navy had by 07:30 been broadcasting a regular radio report announcing, 'that five large German warships and two small ones have forced their way through the outer fortifications of Oslo Fjord'. This also hastened some local Norwegian responses.[93]

Where arms caches were available, Norwegians began arming themselves, while in the occupied cities there was a great deal of confusion. Many Norwegians, under the noses of the occupying Germans, tried to reach mobilisation depots outside of the city centres. The French ambassador, on his way to join the Norwegian government withdrawing to Hamar, noted 'isolated individuals who had learned by chance of the general mobilization order. They were wandering about the countryside with their little suitcase in hand, not knowing where to go, and in most cases they were sent home in the end'.[94] One example of the military bureaucratic muddle is the story told by Sverre J. Svendsen. His father had been in the army in the early 1930s and was at Trondheim on the morning of 9 April. There he reported for duty as the Germans were landing in the town; he was told he had to report to Kristiansand, his official depot, and a 24-hour train ride to the south. Dutifully, he boarded the last train out of Trondheim, but the events of war overtook his journey and he did not mobilise. Similar scenes were repeated throughout the country.[95]

For General Laake reality had not sunk in. At 03:30 Laake remarked, 'A little exercise should do these units no harm.' Later, on the morning of 10 April, Laake would tell the Minister of Justice, 'Given the military situation, we have no other choice than to pursue the negotiations or capitulate unconditionally.'[96]

A second air-raid alert sounded at 04:30 and three or four AA guns began firing. No bombs were dropped on Oslo proper, but later that day an air attack was carried out on the Akershus Fortress, a hilltop AA position and against a nearby island in the harbour. At 05:00 the 2nd Division's commander, Major General Jacob Hvinden-Haug, ordered his headquarters out of Oslo, along with the various military schools – cavalry, cadets, engineers and artillery. Due to an order from the prime minister, discussed below, the AA artillery school candidates remained behind to assist the Oslo AA defences. As a consequence, they would later be placed under German control. Over the next hour Hvinden-Haug also issued orders for the 5th Regiment to deploy immediately in Oslo to defend the city. Elements were ordered to attack Fornebu, but in the end they would only cover Kjeller airfield throughout the morning and then withdrew north.

At 08:10 the weakest of the three King's Guard companies in Oslo, numbering fewer than 100 men, was ordered to make prisoners the survivors from the sinking of the *Blücher*. The men moved quickly down the fjord and at about noon took control of the main body of prisoners, numbering 920 men. (Others were on small boats and the islands in the fjord.) However, the Germans were allowed to retain their arms, mostly sidearms, and after a march to a nearby town, they were released. The guard returned to Oslo at about 16:00. Rear Admiral Kummetz would take a bus into Oslo that evening as it was now under German control.[97]

\* \* \*

King Haakon VII's aide-de-camp awakened him at 01:30. 'Sire, wake up, we are at war.' Haakon asked, 'With whom?'[98] The king, now in the autumn of his years, would subsequently help rally the nation and continue the fight from exile. The 68-year-old was athletic and had always taken a strong interest in the armed services. His memory and abilities to recall remained excellent. In one meeting with the German ambassador on 10 April, he, for the first time in thirty-five years as king, made a statement on behalf of Norway, which constitutionally he was not allowed to do. It was that he would resist and if the government did not he and his family would abdicate. He would play a key role in seeing that Norway fought on and that its invaluable merchant marine would serve the Allied cause.[99]

The king and government began to receive, as did other naval and military centres up and down the Oslofjord, news of the unfolding tragedy. As German Warship Group 5 advanced towards the capital, Koht commented, 'It was like seeing a drama unfolding itself before us and at the same time participating in it. At short intervals, the telephone went on ringing and bringing news from all parts of Norway.'[100]

One phone call came from a German to the Swedish Legation. The Swede answered the call in German and the caller then asked for instructions for his torpedo-boat lying off Oslofjord. The Swede said there were no orders and at that point the German realised he had the wrong number.[101]

Quisling and Knudsen woke when the AA guns opened fire. Quisling remarked, 'This, I dare say, is the German answer to the mines. Well we might as well wash and shave. If a bomb should be dropped on the hotel, we don't want to look disheveled when they dig us out.'[102] There at the Hotel Continental Quisling would be found with Albert Hagelin by Hans Wilhelm Scheidt from Alfred Rosenberg's office. Quisling claimed he did not know Hagelin had been sleeping on the next floor up.[103] Scheidt met briefly with the three men between 07:00 and 08:00.

Earlier, at around 04:00, Scheidt had joined the German naval attaché Lieutenant Commander Richard Schreiber, and the two had gone to the docks to welcome the German navy. Schreiber was under orders to meet the invaders at the docks and arrange berthing, while the air attaché, Captain Spiller, was to meet the Luftwaffe and the army units being flown in to Fornebu airfield. When the German navy failed to arrive, they went on board the German merchant ship *Widar*[104] in the harbour, less than a mile from the Akershus. The *Widar* is not usually included in lists of German ships invading Norway, as it was part of the Abwehr operation. A 5,972-ton merchant ship built in 1936, it had arrived in Oslo the previous day for the operation with equipment for the invaders. It was one of the very few ships pre-positioned for the invasion. On board was Abwehr agent First Lieutenant Hermann Kempf, who operated a suitcase radio transmitter to help in the Oslo operation. For several hours, beginning at 06:00, Kempf would send well over 200 messages to Falkenhorst's command. This 'observation platform' radioed back to Germany at 07:25 that He111s were over Oslo and being fired upon by the AA. At 08:15, Kempf radioed the sighting of five Ju52s, followed by a series of additional messages noting a few scattered Ju52s overhead. At 08:28 he radioed that no German warship had arrived in the harbour. More importantly, he confirmed that Fornebu airfield had been secured.[105]

Schreiber and Scheidt returned to the Continental, where Scheidt was dropped off to meet with Quisling and Hagelin.[106] Scheidt arranged for a second meeting later that morning. At this meeting, Scheidt, without authority but with the support of the German naval attaché who was also present, suggested that Quisling form a new Norwegian government. After some hesitation, Quisling agreed to do so. This may have been encouraged by both the Germans and the Norwegians as a way to avoid German aerial bombardment, as Hitler was upset over the resistance in Norway in contrast to Denmark.[107]

Quisling then spent the day visiting various governmental offices and issuing orders. He visited the Defence Ministry twice, and spent the most time during the day there. Quisling tried but failed to get the Trondheim and Oslo area forts that were still in Norwegian hands to surrender. Quisling also attempted to have Colonel Hans S. Hiorth, commanding the military at Elverum (and an NS member), arrest the government; Hiorth refused. That evening at 19:32, with Scheidt in his SA uniform bluffing the German guards at the radio station into allowing it, Quisling gave a short radio broadcast to the nation.

In the broadcast Quisling called on Norwegians not to resist the Germans, who were there to protect them from the Allies who had mined Norwegian waters. Since the Nygaardsvold government had fled, he argued that it was his and the NS party's right to form a new government. He announced his cabinet without having informed most of them of their new posts. The lack of support for Quisling and the NS was so pronounced that most of his cabinet appointees declined the positions and in two cases reported for duty to the Norwegian army to fight the Germans. Quisling's broadcast was repeated at 20:00 that evening.

Hitler's Germany recognised Quisling's government – at least for the next few days. Propaganda Minister Joseph Goebbels after meeting with Hitler that night wrote, 'Our middleman Quisling comes to the helm.'[108] Hitler thought that King Haakon would have to recognise Quisling and his government under the circumstances. Over the next few days, Quisling issued several proclamations, calling on Norwegians to lay down their arms and for the small naval vessels still in Oslofjord to cease their attacks on German transports. In the same period members of the King's Guard performed sentry duty in front of the Hotel Continental and elsewhere, and the Oslo press referred to Quisling as 'Prime Minister' and printed his 'official notices'. Quisling's 'government' would exist for just six days.[109]

* * *

Early on the morning of 9 April, with the German naval squadron approaching the inner Oslofjord defences, German ambassador Bräuer met with Foreign Minister Koht to present a memorandum calling on the Norwegian government to accept the Germans as friends and not invaders. Bräuer had been handed his instructions by a Lieutenant Colonel Pohlman at 23:00 the night before. As the day unfolded Bräuer realised that he was working at cross-purposes with Rosenberg and Raeder's people. Bräuer and the German foreign ministry wanted the existing Norwegian government to join with Germany, while Quisling was attempting to overthrow it.

The Norwegians were unsure of Allied support. They had not accepted any earlier Allied guarantees, but assumed that they would receive support if they resisted. Koht spoke with the British ambassador at a little past 02:00, telling him, 'So we are now at war.' The British ambassador suggested the government could remain in Oslo with its 'strong' defences but fortunately for the Allied cause this suggestion was not followed.[110]

By 04:30 Bräuer had finally arranged to meet directly with Koht. They met in the room next to where the government was assembled. The memorandum listed thirteen specific articles requiring Norwegian action. Essentially, they called on Norway to give up all its coastal defences and bases, and hand all its means of communication over to the Germans. The Norwegian military was to co-operate on all these matters.[111] After Bräuer delivered his long list of demands, Koht informed him that he would have to wait for the government to decide what to do, though it would literally take just minutes. Koht did throw in his face a quote by Hitler about Czechoslovakia, 'A nation which bows meekly to an aggressor without offering resistance does not deserve to live.'[112]

When Foreign Minister Koht returned from next door and delivered his answer to Bräuer, that Norway would resist, Bräuer grumbled, 'Then there will be fighting and nothing can save you.' Koht replied, 'The fight is already in progress.'[113]

Discussions took place through the morning and the king was firmly in the camp of resistance. Only one cabinet member advocated outright surrender. The President of the Storting, Curt J. Hambro, shone in this moment of crisis. He would be instrumental in taking practical action to defend the government and Norway from the German invasion.

As the afternoon wore on into the early evening of 9 April, Bräuer telephoned Berlin and got Foreign Minister Joachim von Ribbentrop on the line. Bräuer asked for instructions and in particular advice about how to handle Quisling. Hitler came on the line. Angry over Norwegian resistance, Hitler ordered Bräuer to work with Quisling and to tell King Haakon that the new government was to be led by Quisling.[114] Despite his annoyance, Hitler was pleased with the progress of the campaign. Key positions had been captured and losses had been light. That evening Hitler informed Rosenberg that Quisling could form his government.[115]

April 9th would be known as 'Panic Day', and this panic was not confined just to Oslo. Norwegians reacted in various ways to the invasion. But as the day wore on it would be one of panic for many. Thousands of citizens of Oslo and other cities fled due to rumours of a possible French and British aerial (or naval) bombardment of Oslo and other cities. Overhead over much of Norway were the same German aircraft that had heavily bombed Warsaw in 1939.

There was another unfortunate party that became caught up in the events in Oslo. About one-quarter of the British volunteers who had journeyed to Finland during the Winter War were on a train from Sweden that arrived in Oslo on that day. Abandoning their baggage, most boarded the last train back to Sweden and escaped, but eleven were captured and made prisoner.[116]

In Oslo, Hambro quickly issued orders and took actions to help defend Norway. He later wrote,

> the Germans had started a surprise attack on every strategically important point in Norway. Our army was not mobilized. We were absolutely unprepared to meet the attack. And if the King and the Royal Family, the Government and the Parliament should be taken by surprise, Norway would not only be at the mercy of the Germans but would cease to be a sovereign state with an independent government. The only thing to do was to move out of Oslo.[117]

Hambro had been monitoring events closely and recommended that the king and government quickly retire to Hamar, 80 miles inland. Hamar was an important communication centre and, in the event of disaster, had easy access to the Swedish border. He then notified all 150 members of the Storting, which fortunately had been in session, of the government's move. A special train with about a half-dozen cars was readied to depart at 07:00. Escapees were limited to one suitcase, and some governmental personnel joined the train along with the many members of the Storting. The train left just a few minutes late.

Hambro had already contacted the clerk of the Storting and issued various orders to move by truck the national seals, vital state documents and other important material. Plans for such an emergency had been previously prepared, along with shipping crates, and these aided this rapid action. Staff quickly responded to carry out these tasks. Hambro left for Hamar by taxi, and, shortly afterwards the prime minister departed by car. Hambro would later bitterly write, 'In the case of Norway the Germans under the mask of friendship tried to extinguish the nation in one dark night, silently, murderously, without any declaration of war, without any warning given.'[118]

Four ministers of the government did not depart immediately. Minister of Defence Ljungberg was too involved in the fighting, while others continued to address specific duties important to their departments. Minister of Finance Oscar Torp and Director of the Bank of Norway Nicolai Rygg acted quickly to safeguard the nation's finances. Concerned about the nation's gold reserve (at the time worth $55,000,000), Torp had built a bomb-proof vault at the Bank of Norway's office in Lillehammer, about 150 miles north of Oslo. Plans were in place to ship the gold reserve by truck from Oslo on 10 April. Rygg called ahead to Lillehammer at 06:00 to make them aware of the accelerated schedule. Torp had earlier suggested on 6 April at a cabinet meeting that two battalions be mobilised for the Oslo region due to the international unrest. Clearly he was a good choice for the cabinet position.[119]

The entire gold reserve of 55 tons was packed into crates and barrels. The farsighted Rygg had begun this process in 1938, preparing for the possibility of a threat to Oslo. Rygg enlisted truck drivers from where he could and began the slow loading of each truck. There were twenty-six lightly guarded trucks employed in this operation with the first one departing at 07:00 for the drive to Lillehammer. As the day's events unfolded finding trucks to carry this precious cargo became more difficult. The size of the guard for each truck decreased to a single armed bank employee each. Against a backdrop of refugees and those wanting to fight the Germans joining the exodus out of Oslo, the task was accomplished. The last truck left the city as the first twenty German soldiers arrived at the harbour quays.

Complications followed. As the road passed near Kjeller airbase, then under air attack, stray bombs added to the confusion. Some trucks ran short of fuel and were delayed until they could obtain it. In the end, the gold arrived safely at Lillehammer. The following day the regular driver of the Bank of Norway's money truck successfully picked up and drove through German lines to regain Norwegian lines 12,400,000 Kroner (worth just over $2.8 million in 1940). This money had been overlooked while the gold reserve was being moved, but the bank's staff knew that the money would be needed to fight the war against the invader. After withholding approximately 10 per cent for bank operations, the remainder of the cash was turned over to the Norwegian army for the prosecution of the war effort. Vaunted German efficiency failed them this day when it came to the Norwegian money supply. If this money had been seized, the Norwegian war effort in April would have been seriously compromised. The Germans pursued the Norwegian gold as best they could in the coming days to cripple the Norwegian efforts at enhancing the country's war effort and supporting their own. After various adventures the gold safely arrived in North America.

Hambro arrived in Hamar shortly after 08:00. He immediately went to the local police chief, who was unaware of the events sweeping Norway and Denmark. This was in part due to the fact that the radio did not come on the air until 08:00 and as yet there had been no German air activity over Hamar. When Hambro tried to explain this extraordinary meeting of the Storting and the presence of the king and government, the chief could only reply, 'Surely Mr. President, this is not the first of April, this is the ninth!'[120] The prime minister arrived by car at about 10:00.

At the same time General Laake had arrived at the hotel in Slemdal where he expected to find his relocated headquarters from the now-abandoned Akershus. Instead, the headquarters, now reconstituted as the Army Supreme Command (*Hærens ØverKommando* – HOK), had already departed and was heading north to Eidsvoll, where it arrived in the afternoon. There was no one to greet Laake when he arrived at the hotel. He had no vehicle, so he took a tram, tried to hitchhike, walked and finally got a train north. He arrived lacking even his uniform.[121]

The Luftwaffe attack on Kjeller airfield also delayed the train carrying the government north to Hamar. The train stopped and the passengers took shelter in the concrete underground passage between the track and the station. After a while the king ordered the train on; they would have to chance it. Fortunately, the low-flying Luftwaffe ignored the train as it continued north. They arrived at Hamar shortly after 11:00.[122]

At Hamar the hastily convened and still incomplete government went into session with Hambro chairing the meeting at 12:30 with 105 of its members present. Koht gave a detailed presentation of the situation in Norway and noted the acceptance by Denmark of Germany's demands. Koht mentioned again that mobilisation of the four field brigades had been ordered.[123] Hambro now rose and informed the Storting that the necessary administrative staff and seals to keep the government functioning had been removed from Oslo and were present.

Next the prime minister rose to tell the Storting that Oslo was being bombed, the Germans had seized the Oslo Broadcasting Station and that Germans in trucks armed with machine-guns were advancing towards them, though still distant, as he spoke. This was 'Spiller's Raid', which by now had departed Fornebu. Nygaardsvold asked to adjourn this session until 18:00 to allow his cabinet to meet and discuss a course of action. Nygaardsvold also informed the group that the Norwegian radio had announced that the government and Storting were currently at Hamar. This was a classic example of the press announcing something that they should not.[124]

Just before the adjournment of a reasonably upbeat meeting, Nygaardsvold made a statement that illustrated the depth of Norwegian unpreparedness. The prime minister noted that the commander of the AA batteries in Oslo had personally contacted him to say he was neither in communication with General Laake or his staff nor had he been given any orders. What was he to do? The prime minister, who freely admitted he had no knowledge of the military sciences, told him to place himself under the local Oslo commander. This resulted in the AA units at Oslo and three of the four King's Guard companies operating alongside German troops over the next few days. The AA units experienced large numbers of desertions, especially after orders were given to fire on British or French planes. With that, the Storting adjourned, agreeing to meet again that evening.

As the afternoon progressed, 'a steady stream of people had arrived at Hamar from Oslo; including more M.P.s, a large number of civil servants of all ranks, businessmen, officers, journalists, and, of course, diplomats'.[125] American ambassador Harriman arrived in her large Ford saloon car, as well as the French and British delegations, and the town teemed with all sorts of vehicles. Harriman's orders were to 'follow the government' as it retreated north.[126]

That afternoon a clearly shaken Nygaardsvold attempted to resign so as to be able to form a coalition government that included all the parties. The king thought the resignation would send a bad message to the country and Hambro agreed, but perhaps for different reasons. Hambro felt 'the Nygaardsvold Government had to take the responsibility for what had been done and what had been left undone to prepare the nation for this present emergency'.[127]

Hambro's actions in this crisis must be admired and highlight the importance of a key individual taking needed initiative.[128] That afternoon another German demand to surrender was received. While some in the Norwegian government wanted negotiations to be opened, the king, supported by other government members, argued that the Germans could not be trusted and Norway was at war.

By 18:30, 142 members of the Storting were at Hamar, including all three women members. Hambro opened the meeting by recounting events of the invasion. He explained that mobilisation had been ordered and was taking place. It was decided that the Norwegians would hear from Bräuer one more time to see if there was any hope in negotiating with the Germans.

Colonel Ljungberg arrived late, having been caught in the heavy traffic leaving Oslo. As Dik Lehmkuhl would later write, 'Although he had not had time to prepare a report, [Ljungberg] gave a concise summary of the military situation. It was a sad picture. The Germans were just walking in wherever they chose.' All major ports and cities had been captured. The army reported that with the fall of several of the army depots at best only 50 per cent of the troops could be mobilised.[129]

Close to 20:00 Hambro announced that German troops were approaching Hamar. There were no explosives available to blow the bridges between Oslo and Hamar so the decision was made to move the government to Elverum. Thinking the Germans were almost in Hamar, there was a mad rush for the train that quickly pulled out of town with rain falling and its lights off. Nygaardsvold lost his party, which was travelling by car, and had to hail a passing ride.

After arriving in nearby Elverum, the Storting reconvened in a school gym at the end of this long day. The cabinet was increased to include three additional cabinet-level ministers from the other three major parties. After some debate, Nygaardsvold, with Hambro leading the way, passed a motion legalising the actions of the government even though it was not meeting formally in Oslo. This would be the 'Elverum mandate', which would remain in force until the legitimate Norwegian government returned to Norway in 1945.

The minister of justice announced to the gathering that he had ordered the police chief of Oslo to arrest Quisling, but this was not done. Also present, largely by chance, was the forceful Inspector of the Infantry Colonel Ruge who urged vigorous action against the invaders. He told Ljungberg, 'I only want to say one thing, and it is that now, you must not negotiate with the swine.'[130] It was his energy and experience that would see his appointment in the coming days as commander of the Norwegian army.

As for Hambro, he was ordered to Sweden to obtain what military supplies that might be made available. After his arrival, and as a result of German pressure, the Swedish government would essentially block Hambro's efforts to obtain any support or supplies from Sweden. This would stand in sharp contrast to the Swedish support of Germany's military effort in the coming weeks in and around Narvik.[131]

At 22:25 the meeting came to an end. It was to be the last session of the Storting until after the war. It concluded with tears and, for the first time in Storting history, with the members singing two verses of the Norwegian national anthem. Clearly the mood had changed to a fighting mood – its members were '[tired of] being pushed around by the Germans'.[132]

And they had something to cheer about. The Norwegian army had stopped one German advance. Spiller's Raid had been bloodied and turned back. Captain Spiller, accompanied by the *Fallschirmjäger* battalion commander and some headquarter troops, along with part of one company of paratroops, numbering in total over 100 men, had been driving north to capture the government. They had a truck, four buses and a chauffeured embassy car. Spiller sought to seize the king, prime minister and governmental officials so as to decapitate the Norwegian government. If Spiller had succeeded, Norwegian resistance might have been broken. In the afternoon, Spiller begun his chase through the mass of refugees cramming the main road from Oslo to Hamar and beyond. This column covered over 80 miles in a few hours so it was slow going in the night. As they drove, Spiller's troops passed not only civilians, but also Norwegian troops, both in and out of uniform and with some of them armed, proceeding to mobilisation centres. Some Norwegians telephoned ahead to Hamar, and later Elverum, that the Germans were on the way and at least one Norwegian HOK officer, reconnoitring the German advance, was killed when he started to draw his pistol on the Germans. When the Germans entered Hamar they left a detail there to occupy the telephone exchange. As the evening wore on the Germans periodically fired flares into the sky to light their way. But no real opposition was offered to the Germans as they headed north. Later, Foreign Minister Koht attempted to order the troops *not* to fire on the advancing Germans.[133]

Throughout this trying period, Colonel Hatledal was persistent in attempting to get clear government orders to resist but was unable too. He should be applauded for the initiative he showed here.[134] Hatledal, with the help of Colonel Hiorth, tried to organise roadblocks, but the commander of the 2nd Infantry Division, the only division Hatledal could communicate with, failed in this.[135] Hatledal persisted and Major Olav Helset successfully created a roadblock at the head of the long Østerdalen valley with a platoon of the 4th Company of the HMKG, the Royal Guard training unit based at Elverum. The roadblock was 3 miles north-east from the Midtskogen farm, which lay on the main road. Helset set up his roadblock over fairly open and level ground. He had a platoon of the guard with two machine-guns, some troops of the 5th Infantry Regiment which had been training at a nearby rifle range, some industrious local woodsmen who were busily cutting trees to block the roads and members of a local rifle club – a total of just over 100 men.[136]

The trainees were given their first lessons in the use of their machine-guns (one of the two was frozen). They were kept half on duty at the roadblock and the other half practising. The Germans were rushing ahead quickly, continuing to fire flares to light their way. When they arrived at the roadblock, at about 01:30 on the morning of 10 April, Captain Spiller, at the head of the column, loudly demanded that the roadblock be removed. A short time later Spiller was mortally wounded, possibly by two of the rifle-club members who later remarked, 'We got tired of his shouting, and shut his mouth by shooting him!' German accounts have Spiller killed by one of the Norwegian machine-guns.[137]

The action now opened in earnest. It lasted until about 03:00. The German troops exited the buses and attempted to outflank the Norwegian position. At one point when a large nearby barn caught fire, there were Germans on one side letting out farm animals and Norwegians on the other side of the barn doing the same. Fighting in the snow followed and at least three Norwegians were wounded. The Germans suffered two dead and several wounded. Being relatively deep in Norwegian territory and unsure of support, the Germans lost heart and decided to retreat.

After the firefight the retreating German column captured several individuals and small groups of Norwegian troops trudging along the road. These were weak elements of the 2nd Infantry Division and the specialist schools heading north from Oslo. These elements represented artillery, cavalry and infantry units and numbered more than 500 men. Some were motorised. Major General Hvinden-Haug had earlier issued an order stating, 'Should units meet individual vehicles carrying foreign soldiers, combat is to be avoided if at all possible.' The result of this disastrous order would be crippling. As the Germans retired they came across many Norwegian troops not prepared for combat. As a result the retreating German column arrived in Oslo having taken dozens of vehicles, 80 officers, 120 men, 500 rifles, 4 field guns and several machine-guns. One captured officer was the Chief-of-Staff for the 1st Dragoon Regiment. Additional captured Norwegian troops had been told to return home.[138] Earlier in the day American ambassador Harriman had recalled seeing one group of about sixty Norwegians walking towards a mobilisation centre. When asked what they were doing, the reply was, 'We will talk to the Germans and explain everything and it will be all right.'[139]

* * *

The German naval action in Oslofjord was not yet over, and the remaining fortifications there continued to hold out. Rear Admiral Diesen had ordered his remaining forces in Oslofjord to fight the Germans, destroy equipment if resistance was futile and to evacuate to Great Britain if they must. Not all the forces received those orders. But Diesen made a critical decision when he evacuated from Oslo to follow the government so that he would be able to influence their decisions. The trouble with this plan was that it put him out of touch with the naval forces still in action.

One consequence was that neither of the coastal batteries at Måkerøy and Håøy fired a round before they surrendered to the Germans on 14 April, with their guns intact. Måkerøy sighted a convoy of sixteen ships heading for Oslo on 11 April, but held its fire. A similar incident occurred on 14 April. German aircraft flew over both batteries, but failed to bomb them, so a 'truce' was respected.[140]

The German troops had landed in the afternoon at Son and Moss on the east side of Oslofjord, below Drøbak. That afternoon they advanced on Kopås battery.

The Germans began a day-long aerial bombardment of the Oscarsborg complex, both on the Kaholmen islands, as well as the defences on land near Drøbak and elsewhere. In the late morning, twenty-two Ju87s flying from Kiel led the way, then flying on to land at Sola. This again reflected excellent German planning in shuttling these important weapon systems forward to a base from where they could operate against both land and sea objectives.[141]

The _Lützow_ returned about noon. Accompanying it was a small captured Norwegian steamer with a German prize crew. The steamer approached the deadly narrows in an attempt to pass the Norwegian fortifications and discover the fate of the _Blücher_. The _Lützow_ covered this operation and, at a range of 16,000–17,000yd, took Fort Oscarsborg under bombardment with its operable rear turret and three 11in guns that fired some twenty-seven shells. Shortly after passing through the narrows, the captured Norwegian steamer informed Captain Thiele that the _Blücher_ had been sunk. The _Lützow_ and _Emden_ then retired to Horten for the night.

The naval bombardment was followed by attacks through the afternoon from fifty-three He111s. All of these air attacks were filmed and appeared in propaganda films of the era. Eriksen had moved his men indoors and while the air attacks concentrated against Oscarsborg would inflict damage to the fort, no personnel were lost. Early in the day during the air bombardment, communications between Oscarsborg and the mainland were destroyed. At 17:15 Eriksen signalled by lamp to Captain Enger not to fire on German warships unless Eriksen ordered him too. At 18:00 the _Kondor_ and _Möwe_ with some of the minesweepers landed troops at Drøbak without receiving any fire from the Norwegian batteries. At 18:15 Husvik battery reported to Captain Enger that the Germans were occupying it. A German first lieutenant approached under a flag of truce and met with Captain Enger at the Kopås battery. It was occupied by 18:25 and Enger informed Eriksen. As Geirr Haarr has written, 'Some three hundred Norwegians had surrendered to less than fifty Germans.'[142] The _Möwe_ now approached Oscarsborg under a flag of truce and by 18:30 negotiations were opened, first on the ship, and then on the shore. Shortly after, Eriksen promised not to fire on any warships that passed under his guns to rescue survivors from the sunken _Blücher_. Later that night the _Kondor_ and three minesweepers passed Oscarsborg to carry out rescue operations.[143]

Eriksen had last been in communication with his immediate superior, General Hvinden-Haug, in the morning. So Eriksen decided on his own, with his troops somewhat disheartened from the air attacks, and knowing he had delayed the German seaborne prong of their attack on Oslo, to surrender the fortress. A German captain negotiated the terms and the formal surrender was made to Captain Thiele of the _Lützow_. By 09:00 on 10 April a German flag was flying alongside the Norwegian flag over Oscarsborg and the fortress was in German hands.[144]

That morning the _Lützow_, _Emden_, _Mowe_ and several of the minesweepers passed by Oscarsborg, took on pilots, and were at the Oslo city wharves by 10:45. They quickly landed their troops and supplies. The _Emden_ was ordered to remain in the fjord; the two torpedo-boats escorted the *Lützow* beginning its voyage back to Germany that evening. The two torpedo-boats were later detached to assist the sinking *Albatros*. While heading home, the *Lützow*'s radar picked up the surfaced British submarine *Spearfish* and changed course away from it. When the radar image vanished, the captain altered course again for the shortest route to Germany and this allowed the *Spearfish* to intercept and fire six torpedoes at the *Lützow*, scoring a hit in its stern. German torpedo-boats, S-boats and minesweepers, later joined by a Danish tugboat, rushed out to help and bring the *Lützow* safely to port. It finally made Kiel on 14 April. It had suffered fifteen dead from the torpedo explosion.[145]

As German reinforcements from Germany, and shortly from Denmark, poured ashore, Allied submarines were quite active and German propaganda claimed the sinking of sixteen submarines during the operation.[146] The Allies in the early part of the campaign would lose three submarines and have a fourth one captured.

One final act at 17:50 involved a British Short Sunderland, a massive four-engine reconnaissance flying boat, on a mission over Oslo harbour. Two Me110s shot it down.

\* \* \*

The Germans tried to occupy Oslo as peacefully as possible. By 14:30 on the afternoon of 9 April, troops from Fornebu began to arrive in Oslo. One of the first trucks with about twenty soldiers led by a sergeant came to the front of the National Theatre, where mounted police were stationed. At least one older Norwegian woman spat directly into the face of a German soldier, who just wiped it off and smiled. The police leader swung off his horse and shook hands with the German sergeant.[147]

By the end of the day 1,500–2,000 German troops occupied Oslo, a city of 300,000. For several days the Norwegian and German flags flew side by side on government buildings. An American newspaperman captured the moment when more than 20,000 Norwegians watched the main German body from Fornebu march into Oslo that afternoon. Many of the Norwegians were of military age and a Norwegian police-horse guard was at the head of the parade. Norwegian police kept the crowd lines in order. He wrote, 'The only indignant people we met or saw that day were foreigners. The Norwegians of Oslo seemed stunned beyond recovery. All acted curiously, like children suddenly given a chance to see a parade of strange creatures out of prehistoric times – something which had no connection with real life.'[148]

Over the next few days in several Norwegian towns including both Oslo and Trondheim it was not unusual to see Norwegian and German troops conducting joint patrols, sometimes on the opposite sides of the street.[149] There are many instances where the Norwegians were rearmed to handle police services. These services were often performed with band music being played before crowds on the streets and in the parks, courtesy of the German army.[150]

For many this stunned reaction would shortly give way to either panic or resistance. Yet clearly the German strategy of bands playing and singing troops combined with the occupation of key buildings and the telegraph stations kept the vast majority of Oslo's citizens quiescent. This strategy reached its apotheosis on 11 April when thousands of disembarking German soldiers were serenaded, along with the citizens, by roving German soldier choral groups, while a German band played most of the afternoon in the park in front of the parliament building. But the mood of the citizens had changed; Oslo did not want to be occupied by Germany.[151]

On 10 April, the commanding general, Nikolaus von Falkenhorst, and the German naval commander, Admiral Hermann Boehm, arrived by air. Ambassador Bräuer met them, and Falkenhorst established his residence at the Royal Norwegian Automobile Club.

# CHAPTER 9

# Littoral Operations in Action

The Norwegian campaign of 1940 was the first occasion on which all three elements of modern war – sea, land and air – were fully involved. . . . For this reason alone, the campaign has a more lasting importance than that of a small unsuccessful episode of a war fought under conditions unlikely to be repeated.

Major General J. L. Moulton[1]

The seaports of Kristiansand, along with the smaller one at Arendal, were to be occupied by Warship Group 4 under command of Captain Friedrich Rieve. Kristiansand (population of 23,000) was both a secondary naval base and the largest port between Stavanger to the west and Oslo to the east. Arendal was an important telegraph station, with a submarine cable to Britain.[2] The Norwegians had for decades viewed Kristiansand as potentially the most vulnerable port for German seizure because it was relatively close to Germany and, unlike Oslo, lacked substantial defences. In addition, potential British help was distant.

*Kristiansand Festning* was part of the 1st Sea Defence District and under the command of 64-year-old Lieutenant Colonel O. A. Fosby. If fully manned it would have had 148 officers and 1,250 men. On 8 April it only had 55 officers and 385 men on hand, including two infantry companies attached to the fortress. Many of the fortress batteries were not manned. The main fortified position was Fort Odderøya on the rocky heights of an island next to the town and connected to the mainland by a short bridge. It had two 210mm guns protected by a concrete-roofed battery and two twin batteries of 150mm guns which were protected by gun shields. There were four 240mm howitzers, though one was not manned. There were four manned Browning machine-guns available for land defence. There were guns, including four land-facing 75mm field guns, but none of these were manned. Also located there was the 3rd Infantry Division school with 148 students.[3]

In close proximity, to the east of Kristiansand and placed further back in the harbour, was Gleodden battery with three 150mm guns that were manned and two 65mm field guns that were not. Communication between the battery and the fort was by public telephone. In the ensuing action that morning the Gleodden battery to its discredit would not fire a shot and would be captured intact by the Germans. In addition to the fortress garrison there was a half-company of troops, the army garrison for Kristiansand.[4]

Nearby and across the inner fjord from Kristiansand to the north-east was the small airport at Kjevik. The 3rd Infantry Division had prepared obstacles that

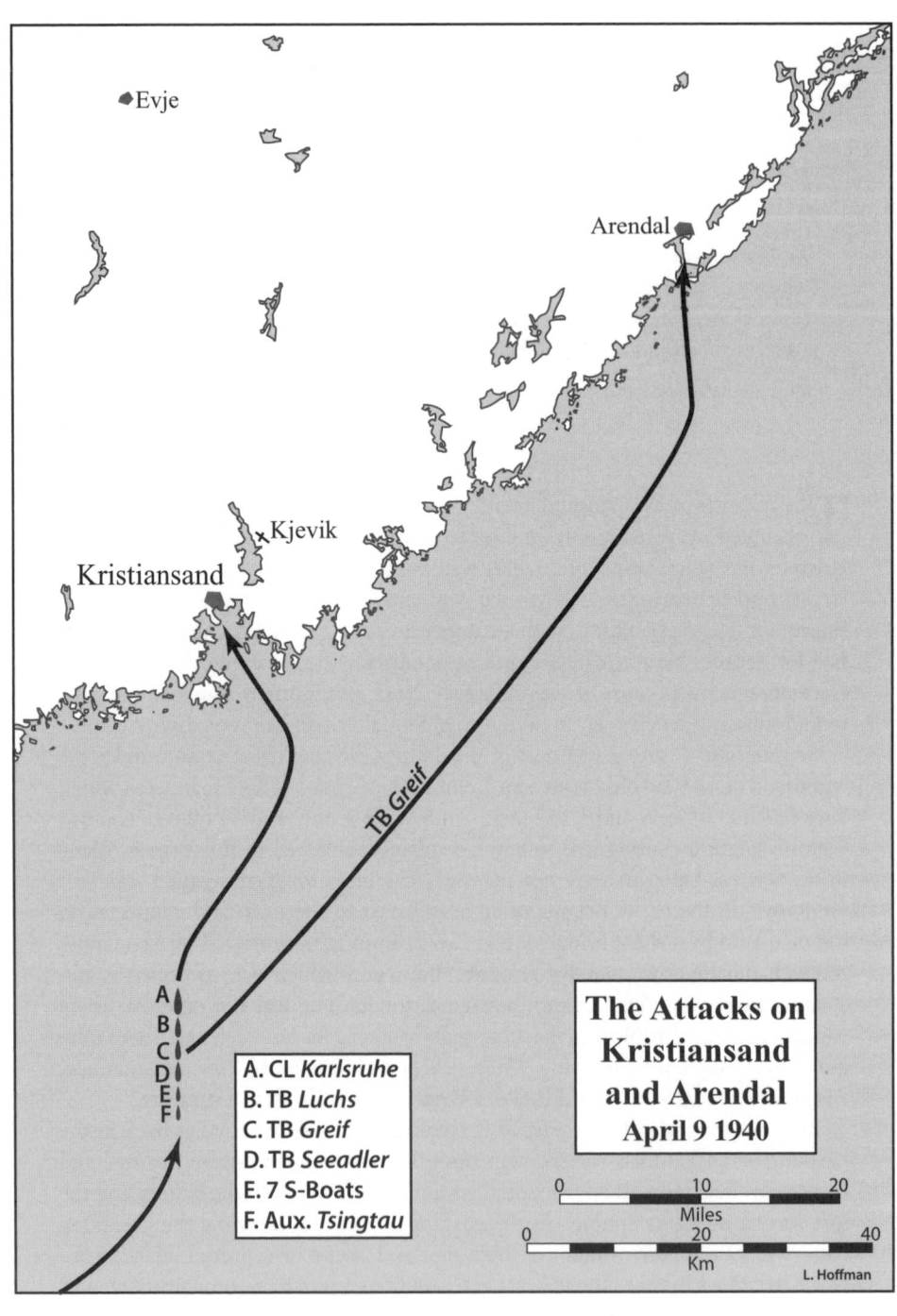

Evje

Arendal

Kjevik

Kristiansand

TB Greif

A
B
C
D
E
F

A. CL *Karlsruhe*
B. TB *Luchs*
C. TB *Greif*
D. TB *Seeadler*
E. 7 S-Boats
F. Aux. *Tsingtau*

**The Attacks on
Kristiansand
and Arendal**
April 9 1940

| 0 | 10 | 20 |
Miles

| 0 | 20 | 40 |
Km

L. Hoffman

could be placed on the airfield in the event of an attack but due to an error the obstacles were too short to block the airfield fully and some inadequate barbed wire was substituted.[5]

The small naval command was under the command of Commodore S. E. Wigers. He had at his disposal two modern but small destroyers, two submarines and six patrol craft. The two destroyers, the *Gyller* and *Odin*, were of the *Sleipner* class. In addition to their three 102mm guns, they both had three AA machine-guns and the former a modern 40mm Bofors and the latter a 20mm Bofors AA gun. One of the destroyers and one patrol craft were guarding the interned German submarine *U-21* in a separate inner harbour opposite the main harbour and wharf area. While there were no Norwegian army aircraft present, there were three navy MF11s and one older MF10 at Kristiansand. Due to the nearby sinking of the *Rio de Janeiro*, Wigers had placed the naval command on alert but neither the small naval patrol craft or the army was informed of this.[6]

In the early morning of 8 April, Warship Group 4 had departed Wesermünde carrying 1,070 men. Rieve's flagship was the light cruiser *Karlsruhe*. Rieve had a good understanding of the Norwegian force he faced and considered it a strong position.[7] He had divided his force into three echelons consisting of the *Karlsruhe*, the large torpedo-boats *Greif, Seeadler, Luchs*, seven S-boats of the 2nd S-boat flotilla (*S-7, S-8, S-17, S30, S-31, S-32* and *S-33*) and the S-boat tender *Tsingtau*. The *Tsingtau*'s speed of 17 knots dictated the top speed of the squadron.

The *Karlsruhe* carried 600 men, the *Tsingtau* 270, while the *Luchs* and *Seeadler* each carried 50. The *Greif*, on special assignment, carried 100. The main force bound for Kristiansand carried were 150 German naval coastal defence artillery troops for manning the captured coastal defence batteries and a small number of motorcycle troops. The *Greif* and *Tsingtau* both carried a total of thirty communication specialists to operate the Norwegian radio, cable and telephone exchanges. On board the *Karlsruhe* were fifty members of 310th Infantry Regiment band. As with all German units in the invasion, the units had been pared down to a degree, so the 500 infantry troops on board the *Karlsruhe* represented three companies at about two-thirds full strength.[8]

At 02:00 on 9 April, in a heavy fog and overcast conditions, with visibility down to 30yd and the temperature hovering just above freezing, the entire squadron concentrated, except the torpedo-boat *Greif*, which proceeded on its detached duty to Arendal. The remaining ships headed towards the entrance of the Kristiansand, arriving at 03:45. The heavy fog forced the squadron, with none of them equipped with radar, to wait before attempting to enter the narrow and shallow waters. As the ships steamed back and forth radio reports of gunfire off Oslo came in.

In the meantime, the Norwegians at Kristiansand had heard the reports that the forts at the outer entrance to Oslo Fjord had opened fire on unknown warships, later identified as German. At 02:30 the Norwegian naval air commander ordered preparations for early morning operations. At 04:45 a report came in of Germans capturing a torpedo-boat at Egersund (see below), lying just to the west. With the fog beginning to clear, a Norwegian naval MF11 aircraft spotted the German force at about 05:00, at a distance of about 1,600yd.[9]

Rieve later reported, 'The fog robbed us of the element of surprise. It was already an hour after *Weserzeit* and past dawn. The Norwegian reconnaissance aircraft would definitely have reported us. In the circumstances I abandoned the plan, which had already been postponed once from 0415, to disembark the army and naval coastal artillery units into six [S-boats] in the inner skerries.'[10]

Lieutenant Colonel Fosby had issued an alarm to the garrison at 05:02; 45 minutes later, the German ships tried to enter the fjord. The *Karlsruhe* was at a disadvantage as it only had one main battery turret forward and Odderøya was situated high up on a bluff. With the cruiser leading, the German squadron entered the harbour in line ahead, essentially limiting their gunnery to the 'A' turret of the flagship. Odderøya had opened an inconsistent fire with the range being about 5,500yd, but landed one near-miss with a 210mm shell just off the bow of the *Karlsruhe* and straddled the ship as it approached the harbour. Rieve had not opened fire until he was taken under fire, but he had difficulty in replying with the narrow waters and the position of Odderøya high on the bluff. This first advance was also discouraged with two false submarine reports and safety concerns for the troops on board and now under fire. He was forced to retire under protection of a smoke screen and called for an airstrike on the battery. Nearby were seven He111s just for this purpose. They flew over the offending battery and bombed it during which one of the magazines blew up and created a great deal of smoke but relatively little damage. The attack was otherwise relatively ineffective, though the bombing did disrupt Norwegian landline communications, and the Germans did chase off two MF11s sent up to bomb the German ships.[11]

The *Karlsruhe* now launched one of its two aircraft, in part to help in gun control, but the radio failed and so was of no help. The plane did make a bombing run on Odderøya but with little result.

A few minutes before 07:00 the German ships made a second attempt to force the entrance, coming from a slightly different direction. The cruiser *Karlsruhe* was able to develop only a limited amount of fire with the forward turret. As the squadron approached the harbour, a merchant ship was spotted. The *Karlsruhe* tried to use it to cover its approach when it was realised that it was the German blockade-runner *Seattle*. The latter thought the approaching warships were British and so steamed away toward the inner harbour. The *Seattle* had left Curaçao on 4 March and passed through the Allied blockade and unwittingly stumbled into a new part of the war. The *Seattle* came under fire from Odderøya and was hit. German bombers also apparently ineffectively attacked it. The *Seattle* was soon on fire and grounded, later drifting into the harbour before sinking on the 13th. The fire from it continued for hours that day. The Norwegians rescued and took prisoner its crew.[12]

The Norwegian defenders at Odderøya again fired on the Germans, forcing them to retreat. The German gunnery during the second run was more effective and some were wounded in the Norwegian batteries. Unfortunately, some of the shells overshot the fort and in the course of the fighting that day the town suffered 13 killed and over 200 buildings damaged. Once more German aircraft of the *Kampfgeschwader* 4 bombed the batteries with little effect. Far from doing any substantial damage, the German bombers were forced higher by the AA guns on the two modern Norwegian destroyers which by now had added to the general pandemonium.

The visibility continued to be rather poor, and a third advance by the torpedo-boats covered by the cruiser was aborted. The fog almost resulted in the *Karlsruhe* going aground at about 09:30. Rieve decided he had to get the troops ashore and loaded what troops he could onto the four most modern S-boats and ordered the two torpedo-boats to lead them in. Rieve followed with the *Karlsruhe* and the *Tsingtau*.

The Norwegians now suffered some confusion as well. When the Germans advanced again, some of the Norwegian defenders thought they were witnessing the arrival of Allied warships. There had been reports identifying the German ships as French, possibly due to some German signal flags being misidentified. Additionally, Allied reconnaissance aircraft had been overhead (and fired on) during the morning and a radio report indicated Allied warships were on their way. Even though the batteries were still capable of operating, they held their fire and the ships had soon slipped under the guns. Fosby may have had his spirit broken by the repeated sea and air attacks. In any case, the German ships entered the port at 11:00, helped by the improved visibility. They rapidly disembarked the infantry battalion (and regimental band) at the south end of the town and columns of troops quickly moved to seize the batteries and the main land entrance into the city. The German naval coastal defence artillery troops had the batteries fully operable by the next day. The fortress radio communication was taken over by German operators and the town was peacefully occupied.

The occupation led to the seizure of two modern small Norwegian destroyers, the *Gyller* and *Odin*, both of which were incorporated into the German navy. They had fired at German planes with their AA armament in the morning but did not offer any resistance to what they thought might be British warships when the harbour was finally forced. Some small Norwegian patrol boats were also captured intact along with two submarines, *B2* and *B5*. The Germans would later operate the *B5*. None of these vessels offered substantial resistance, though the submarines had received information about the action at Oslo that morning.[13] Total Norwegian military casualties were eight dead and just over forty wounded.

The postwar government would later condemn this abject surrender, but no Norwegian officers were convicted of any crimes. Fosby wrote in May 1940 that resistance had become impossible. The naval station commander, Commodore Wigers, had failed to issue orders for his men to fight, and they contributed little to the port's defence. Wigers' conduct is even more bizarre knowing that he and his men had been very much involved in the action that had placed the port at a higher level of alert – the rescue of German soldiers and Luftwaffe AA personnel the day before from the sinking *Rio de Janeiro*. Though no one was punished, the investigation did note that Wigers and the four senior captains acted very passively to the German attack.[14]

The same fog hampered the advance of the *Greif*, which entered Arendal harbour late at 08:20. It succeeded in disembarking the 234th Bicycle Squadron of the 163rd Infantry Division. Arendal was not defended and was captured without a shot fired. The submarine cable connection with Great Britain was seized intact but unknown to the Germans had not been working since Christmas. There were three Norwegian 55-ton torpedo-boats, launched in 1905, based at Arendal, though two were not in port at the time of the attack. The *Jo* was alert and fully operational. Ammunition to the light guns had been issued earlier in the day and the two torpedoes were in operating order. The *Greif* never sighted the *Jo*, about 1,000m off, and the captain of the *Jo* thought about attacking but had no orders to do so and civilians had gathered near the now-docked *Greif*. Shortly after the *Greif* steamed off toward Kristiansand so the *Jo* joined up with the rest of the squadron. It loitered in the area until 17 April among the islands and shore, was strafed and damaged more than once and then was scuttled. The men were sent home and the three commanding officers headed north by land to join the war.[15]

With the fall of Kristiansand, the Germans moved quickly and seized Kjevik airfield, which lay across the bay. Kjevik provided them with an additional landing strip for Luftwaffe operations. By the afternoon a Ju52 had landed there and thirty Me109s were operating from the airfield by 12 April.

As soon as he had established control, the German commander of the 310th Regiment, Major Schröder, began encouraging local citizens to join in the general exodus, which over the next few days would put 20,000 refugees on the roads from the Kristiansand region, clogging them and offering cover for the advancing Germans.[16] The remaining Norwegian troops retreated from Kristiansand and Kjevik inland as elements of the 3rd Norwegian Division attempted to mobilise in the interior at the arms depot town of Evje. The commander of the 3rd, Major General Einar Liljedahl, retreated from Kristiansand with his staff. Liljedahl provided ineffective leadership of the 3rd Division in the coming days.[17]

By 16:00 three German transports had arrived with support staff and the heavy equipment, including the field artillery; a fourth small transport would arrive a few days later.[18] German minesweepers from Warship Group 6 reinforced the German command that afternoon of the 9th. Also arriving was the *Karl Meyer*, a Luftwaffe seaplane support ship. It was later sent to Stavanger, where it arrived on 12 April. A battalion of infantry of the 310th Infantry Regiment arrived by air on 11 April, with the third battalion arriving the next day, also by air.

The three torpedo-boats escorted the *Karlsruhe* at 19:00 on the 9th from Kristiansand to Kiel. The German cruiser, screened by the torpedo-boats, was on a zigzag course when it encountered the submarine HMS *Truant*, which fired four torpedoes at 3,300yd. One torpedo exploded in the engine room, knocking out both engines; the cruiser took on an immediate 12-degree list. Flooding could not be stopped and the cruiser was abandoned at 20:10. However, the ship did not sink immediately and was finally torpedoed twice by one of the escorting torpedo-boats. The German ships attacked the *Truant* with depth charges and damaged the sub, but it managed to escape. Admiral Raeder later condemned the captain of the *Karlsruhe* for not trying to do more to save his ship.[19]

* * *

Meanwhile, fighting was occurring at Stavanger and Egersund. The western port of Stavanger (population 46,000) was a very important objective because of the nearby airport at Sola, which was the most modern in Norway, with a concrete airstrip.[20] It was also less than 300 miles from Great Britain.

The Germans feared Sola would be one of the easiest objectives of a British invasion and wanted to secure it as soon as possible. It was captured by major elements of the 193rd Infantry Regiment of the 69th Infantry Division along with the divisional artillery. Major General Hermann Tittel commanded the 69th Infantry Division, the strongest infantry division participating in the Norwegian invasion. Tittel was charged with securing the points from Egersund to north of Bergen.[21] The German invasion plan called for a strong airlift operation that included ten air-transport groups and four additional squadrons in the first wave, including the two best-trained anti-shipping squadrons in the Luftwaffe.

South of Stavanger was the Egersund cable landing station and potential port for counter-landing for the Allies in Norway's 1st Sea Defence District. At its wharf was the small antediluvian 84-ton torpedo-boat the *Skarv*, built in 1907. The local Norwegian army commander had ordered a platoon of infantry to the port on 8 April and it had arrived. Both Norwegian commands had been ordered to prepare for possible action.

Germany had delegated Warship Group 6 of four minesweepers under the command of Lieutenant Commander Kurt Thoma to take this tiny port. Its ships carried the divisional scouting squadron of bicycle troops and a communications unit to operate the cable station. It had departed Cuxhaven on 7 April. Only two of the four minesweepers, *M1* and *M9*, of Warship Group 6 arrived off the port, without incident at 04:15. Entering the harbour, their presence fooled the few sentries who failed to identify the Germans until it was too late. Without a shot being fired, they captured the *Skarv*, the recently arrived army garrison and the cable station. The missing two minesweepers arrived later, disembarked their troops and by 05:57 all four minesweepers were steaming toward Kristiansand.[22]

Stavanger was also easily captured, despite what British Chief of the Imperial General Staff Edmund Ironside had claimed to the War Cabinet in late February – that it would be impossible for Germany to seize Stavanger by an air-landing operation. With its population of 40,000 people and with many trained as soldiers, he said, 'even very small forces could successfully resist an airborne invasion of this nature'.[23]

The Norwegians had a small army contingent in the vicinity of Stavanger. The Norwegians had posted at the end of March the *Jagerbataljonen* ('Ranger' or literally 'hunter' battalion) on detached duty from the 1st Infantry Division to Stavanger. It

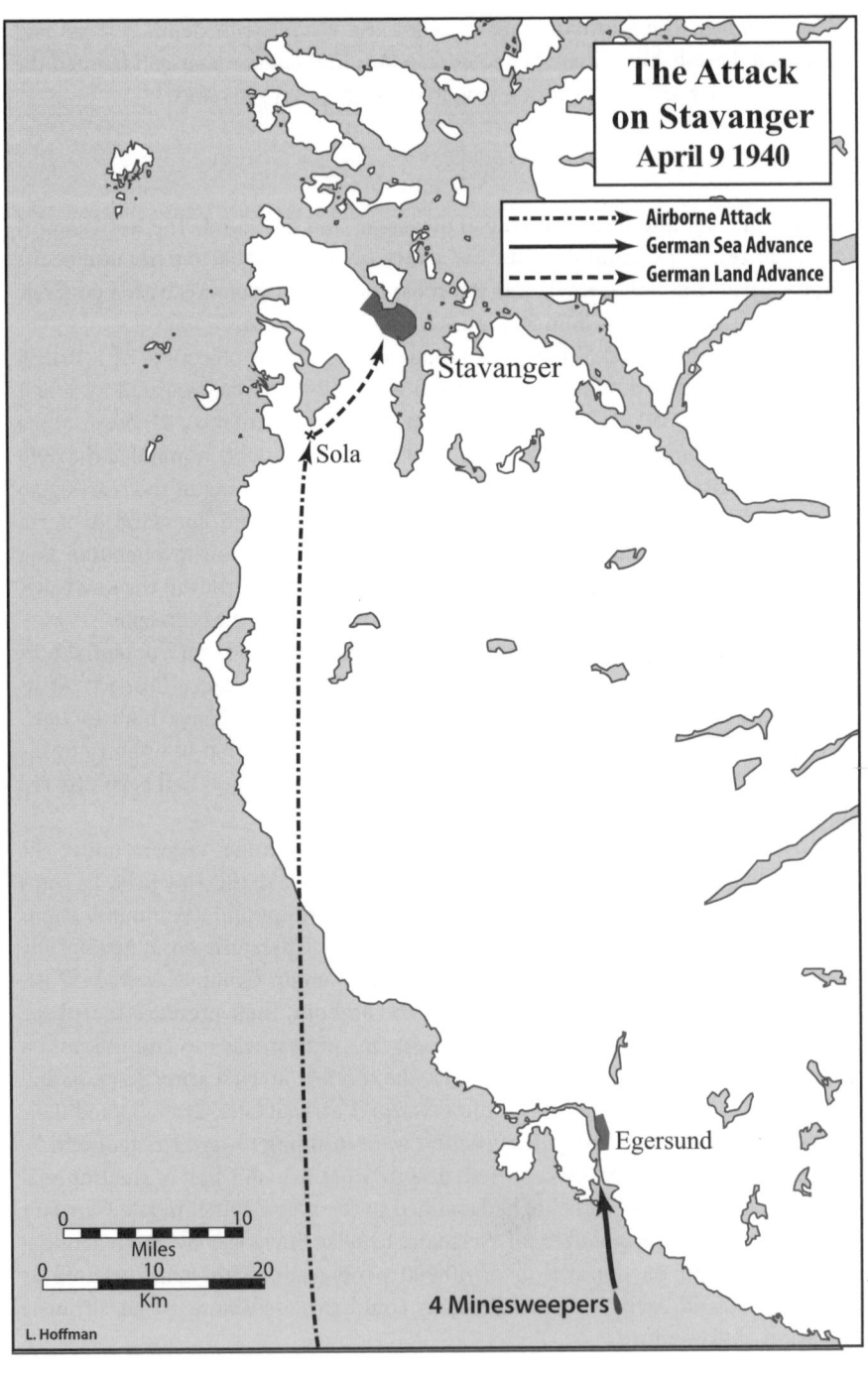

The Attack
on Stavanger
April 9 1940

- - · - - · → Airborne Attack
——————→ German Sea Advance
- - - - - - → German Land Advance

Stavanger

Sola

Egersund

4 Minesweepers

0        10
Miles
0     10      20
Km

L. Hoffman

was posted between Stavanger and Sola and rotated two under-strength platoons to Sola, guarded by one concrete pillbox. A second pillbox was unfinished. Some unprotected minor guns and machine-guns also covered the airfield. Fighting in Finland had demonstrated the need for combat engineer companies to construct obstructions on airfields and transportation lines, but Norway had no such units ready at the time of the attack. Some inadequate obstructions, privately funded by a local businessman, had been prepared for Sola airfield.[24]

Minor elements of a battalion of the Norwegian 8th Regiment under the command of Colonel Gunnar Spørck were in the greater Stavanger area. Stavanger had no coastal defences. At Sola was a small army air detachment of six Fokker C.V.s biplanes, a 1924 design. The biplane carried a crew of two and was a combination reconnaissance and light bomber (200kg bomb load). Also present were three Caproni Ca310s bombers and some small training aircraft. The Caproni was one of Norway's most modern light bombers and was highly regarded by the Norwegians. Of the Caproni it was said, 'that the choice was also based on the possibility of a deal with the Italians, where they supplied the aircraft in exchange for dried cod'. Thus they quickly acquired the nickname 'dried cod bomber'. The crews of the planes had only dropped practice bombs before the invasion.[25]

Near Stavanger was the small naval air station at Hafrsfjord with two MF11s and one He115. Hafrsfjord was also home to a modern small destroyer, the *Æger*[26] and a small elderly destroyer, the *Draug*, both part of the 2nd Sea Defence District. With the British mining operation Captain Nils Larsen Bruun of the *Æger* was convinced war was possible in the near future and on 8 April had brought his ship up to full readiness. Though he was not sure whom he might be fighting, his prudence would bear fruit.

The German plan called for a paradrop on Sola airfield to take place at 08:00. The 3rd Company of German paratroops on board twelve Ju52s was to be escorted by eight Me110s, with eight He111s in support. But due to the heavy fog, the Me110 commander ordered his planes to turn back to Ålborg. Only four of the eight followed that order. Two of the remaining four collided in air and were lost, while the final two arrived over Sola airfield. The four at Ålborg would transfer to Norway in the next day or two. One Ju52 also turned back due to the overcast conditions,[27] but the remaining eleven droned on carrying their company, under the command of First Lieutenant Otto von Brandis.

The Norwegian army air command had been on alert and in the early morning sent up two planes. They sighted two German ships. One of the planes landed, was armed with four small bombs and took off, when it was ordered from the ground not to attack and returned to base.[28] The three operational Caproni bombers and the six Fokkers were readying for take off when the two Me110s came in to strafe, quickly followed by eight He111s. One Caproni was knocked out, while the other Norwegian planes successfully took off and scattered to various landing strips.[29]

The drop of just over 130 *Fallschirmjäger* now followed. The fog had been thick, but as the planes approached it cleared at about 33ft over the waves. Brandis ordered the planes to climb to 400ft for the drop. The commander of the Ju52s later recalled, 'Our speed had to be low to keep the paratroops close together. And to fly at only 400ft above an enemy with his finger on the trigger is not exactly good life insurance.'[30]

There was mixed Norwegian resistance but the two Me110s again strafed the field and, as at Fornebu, landed on aviation fumes to continue the fight. Operating their machine-guns while landed, they accidentally mistook the paratroops for Norwegians and wounded some.

The Norwegians troops fought, but some ran, and all were in a state of surprise at this sudden attack. A Norwegian soldier, R. G. Johansen, manned the pillbox and with his machine-gun killed or wounded several Germans before a concerted effort by the Germans captured it. One of the Caproni bombers returned to bomb the German aircraft already on the airfield, but the pilot dropped the bombs without removing the safety pins, so the attack was ineffective. This essentially ended resistance at the airfield after 31 minutes. German losses were three dead and ten wounded, while Norwegian losses were three wounded and eighty captured. Approximately forty Norwegians ran or escaped from the action.

The Germans immediately removed the barbed wire barriers that were being used to block the runways and the airfield was ready to receive reinforcements. The 1st and 2nd Battalions of the 193rd Infantry Regiment (69th Division) charged with the occupation of Sola and Stavanger began to arrive by air.[31] Planes were fuelled and sent off to keep the airfield clear.

As soon as enough infantry had arrived a detachment was dispatched to Stavanger, with the Norwegian Lieutenant who had commanded the defence at Sola marched in the front at gunpoint. The town fell without a shot.

The Germans had a special plan for the naval and seaplane base at Hafrsfjord. Twelve He-59 biplanes, a 1930 design for a torpedo-bomber, were obsolete by this time but were utilised to carry about forty troops. Arriving by air and landing at the base, the soldiers quickly seized it also without firing a shot and with everything intact.[32]

The German plan called for an immediate reinforcement by sea with four coastal defence guns, 88mm AA guns, ammunition, aviation fuel and other provisions for the two airlifted battalions. The transport ship *Roda*, of 6,800 tons, had been ordered to Stavanger with those supplies. The *Roda* arrived in outer Stavanger on 8 April and requested customs clearance. The captain had placed coal over the hatches so when the customs officer arrived on board he could not examine the hold. However, the ship was riding too high in the water to be carrying a full load of coke, as the bill of lading indicated, which led the Norwegian customs official to notify the destroyer *Æger* of his difficulty in examining the *Roda*. With reports coming in of gunfire off Oslo, Captain Bruun of the *Æger* sent an armed boarding party over to the *Roda*. The German captain still would not co-operate. Brunn lost his patience and early on the morning of 9 April ordered the crew of the *Roda* off the ship and shelled the vessel until it sank.[33]

Later that day the *Æger* opened AA fire on German aircraft sighted overhead. Shortly after, about ten Ju87s came on the scene, a portion of twenty-one that had been searching for the British fleet but had turned back because of lack of fuel. At close to 08:30 during the ensuing attack a 250kg bomb hit just aft of the *Æger*'s smokestack. It penetrated into the bowels of the ship and knocked out the two engine rooms, killing eight and wounding ten. The *Æger* was abandoned and drifted close to shore before sinking. The Stukas then landed at Sola to prepare for operations on 10 April.

The little *Draug* had its own adventure. It intercepted the German transport *Main* as the latter steamed north of Stavanger off Haugesund on its way to Trondheim. The *Main* was carrying equipment for the German force destined for that port. Like the *Roda*, it had blocked its hatches with coal. When the *Draug* sent a boarding party over early on the morning of 9 April, they also were denied access to the hold. The *Draug*'s captain, Thore Horve, radioed to Bergen, but he was informed that the commander there could not issue orders as the Germans had occupied the port.

An MF11 landed nearby and, in conversation with the pilot, Horve realised that Stavanger was also occupied. Forcing the *Main* to accompany him, Horve decided to steam to Britain. As they headed out into the ocean from The Leads, they came under attack by the Luftwaffe. The *Draug*, lacking any AA armament, simply tried dodging the falling bombs, and was lucky not to be hit. The *Main* was also attacked and the German captain ordered the ship to be scuttled; one German died during this process. Horve lent assistance to the crew and then ordered several 76mm rounds fired into the waterline of the *Main*, sinking it. Heading west, now carrying sixty-seven Germans on board, Horve met three British destroyers and eventually arrived in the Shetland Islands. Later, several of its crewmembers served as liaison to Allied forces operating in Norway. After the war Horve was promoted to rear admiral.

By the afternoon the Germans were in complete control of the airport and the harbour and this was fully reported to Germany by 14:00. Three transports arrived and with the help of Norwegian stevedores began unloading. The Luftwaffe seaplane tender *Karl Meyer* was originally ordered to Kristiansand and arrived there on the 10th but was then redirected to Stavanger, arriving on 12 April. It would support reconnaissance operations from Hafrsfjord.[34]

The seizure of Stavanger and Sola was an important success and assured the possession of a modern airfield which would be transformed into an effective base for a later airlift to Trondheim.[35] The quick action allowed the HQ of the X Fliegerkorps to divert to Fornebu the incoming reinforcements transported by Ju52 consisting of the 3rd battalion of the 324th Infantry Regiment (69th Division).[36] The 193rd Infantry Regiment's third battalion arrived by air on 10 April.

\* \* \*

Warship Group 3 led the attack on Bergen under the command of Scouting Forces' Rear Admiral Hubert Schmundt. It consisted of the light cruisers *Köln* and *Königsberg*, the gunnery training ship *Bremse,* the S-boat tender *Carl Peters,* the torpedo-boats *Leopard* and *Wolf* and five S-boats of the 1st Motor Torpedo-Boat Flotilla. The *Carl Peters,* with a top sustained speed of only 18 knots, limited the progress of the entire squadron but was particularly valuable because of the powerful radio it carried. Schmundt's orders were to occupy Bergen, which with its approximately 100,000 inhabitants was the most important Norwegian port facing the Atlantic.[37]

The squadron was transporting two battalions of the 159th Infantry Regiment and the 69th Infantry Division headquarters, two companies of the 169th Engineer Battalion of the 69th Infantry Division and two 'companies' of naval coastal defence artillery (about 100 marines), some regimental artillery personnel and some Luftwaffe AA personnel. The naval coastal defence artillery troops were to man the captured Norwegian coastal batteries. This force totalled 1,900 men, including the regimental band, and had embarked from three separate German ports. The commanding general of the 69th, Major General Hermann Tittel, and his staff were on board the *Köln.* An additional company of the 159th Infantry Regiment was to be flown in by seaplanes, with later flights bringing in the rest of that battalion of the 159th. On board the *Carl Peters* were Vice Admiral Otto von Schrader, who would be the Kriegsmarine commander for the west coast of Norway (*Admiral der Norwegischen Westküste*), and his staff. Once in port, he would make the *Peters* his temporary command post.[38]

The nearness of Bergen to Scapa Flow made Schmundt believe that his objective was the most dangerous. He thought British attacks would be concentrated against Bergen with other lesser strikes on Trondheim and Narvik. He wanted to improve the odds by including the sister-ship to his flagship, the *Karlsruhe,* and by detaching the *Bremse* and *Carl Peters* to the Kristiansand force because of their slower speed. That deployment would have given him a more uniform squadron with three light cruisers of the same class. As a contingency plan Schmundt arranged with the German army commander to carry non-essential men on the *Bremse* and *Carl Peters*, which could be sent to Oslo if needed. In the event, the Kristiansand force benefited from the heavier armament of the *Karlsruhe.*[39] Schmundt elected to not have two separate convoys, one slow and one fast, because as a united though slower force they would have a better AA defence against potential British air attack. They sailed in three groups just before midnight on 7 April. The three separate groups rendezvoused in the North Sea as they approached Norway after the fog had partially dissipated.

They proceeded north with the two cruisers in line abreast in the van. Schmundt had received reports during the day of enemy cruisers supported by numerous destroyers being nearby. This was part of Vice Admiral Edward-Collins' 2nd Cruiser Squadron made up of the small light cruisers *Galatea* and *Arethusa* but supported by fifteen destroyers, which, as has been seen, the Admiralty ordered to close Admiral Forbes' force in fear of being defeated in detail and out of support range of the larger British warships. An encounter by these two enemies would have most likely resulted in the Bergen force being at minimum delayed, and possibly severely punished, especially with the two German cruisers crowded with troops.[40]

After several submarine alarms off Stavanger and passing during the night within about 70 miles of the British 2nd Cruiser Squadron, Schmundt turned east in the rain and mist to enter Kors Fjord just past midnight, 9 April.

Two rather unique 'trawlers' also met with this force off Bergen. These were the armed trawlers *Schiff 9* (formerly the *Alteland*) and *Schiff 18* (formerly the *Koblenz*) and, in the German service, were known as *U-Falle* or Q-ships. Outwardly they appeared to be simple North Sea trawlers, but in reality they were armed warships. The 940-ton *Schiff 9*, completed in 1931, had a speed of 12 knots and was commissioned into Kriegsmarine service in November 1939. The *Schiff 18* was about 820 tons, had been completed in 1930 and also had a speed of 12 knots. She entered naval service in December 1939. Well hidden under false decks, the ships each carried one 88mm AA gun, a 37mm AA gun and a few depth charges. They were outfitted with sonar, had two fixed bow torpedo tubes and were capable of minesweeping. Their AA guns could be used for direct fire on sea and land targets.[41] The two trawlers joined the German squadron and acted as minesweepers as the ships neared Bergen harbour proper. They covered the vanguard and protected the flagship, though at a maximum speed of only 12 knots.

The *Bergen Festning* had six weak forts on the approaches to Bergen harbour and two strong forts at the immediate harbour narrows, Kvarven to the west and the smaller Hellen on the east shore of the harbour.[42] Kvarven was armed with three 210mm Krupp guns built in the late nineteenth century that could deliver plunging fire from the hilltop on an approaching warship. The traverse of the guns allowed a target moving at a good rate of speed to be under fire for no more than 2 to 3 minutes. The fort also contained three 240mm howitzers (they were not manned) and two searchlights. It had a torpedo battery similar to the one at Oslo. However, it was partially manned and in any case the four torpedoes present were missing important components and could not have been fired. To have a vital weapon that was inoperable is inexcusable.

Hellen was armed with three older French 210mm guns and one searchlight. Nearby Sandviksfjell battery was armed with two 240mm howitzers and two 65mm guns but the battery was not manned. Both Hellen and Sandviksfjell had some light AA machine-guns and these gun positions had protected magazines. The guns themselves were protected by a concrete and earthen open barbette, not in armoured turrets, although gun shields protected the crews.

Each of the six outer forts contained two smaller guns and one searchlight and were to guard the outer approaches to Bergen. The entrance to Bergen has many islands and several channels that approach the two main inner harboor entrances. In the Bergen area there were six fixed 75mm AA guns. The guns had been manufactured in the early 1920s and had followed the design of the First World War 'balloon-busting' long-range AA gun. There were three 120mm guns that had been transferred to Bergen that winter from Kongsvinger Fortress, now in reserve status, near the Swedish border, but they had not been installed as well as three 150mm guns originally earmarked for Narvik.[43] If fully manned,

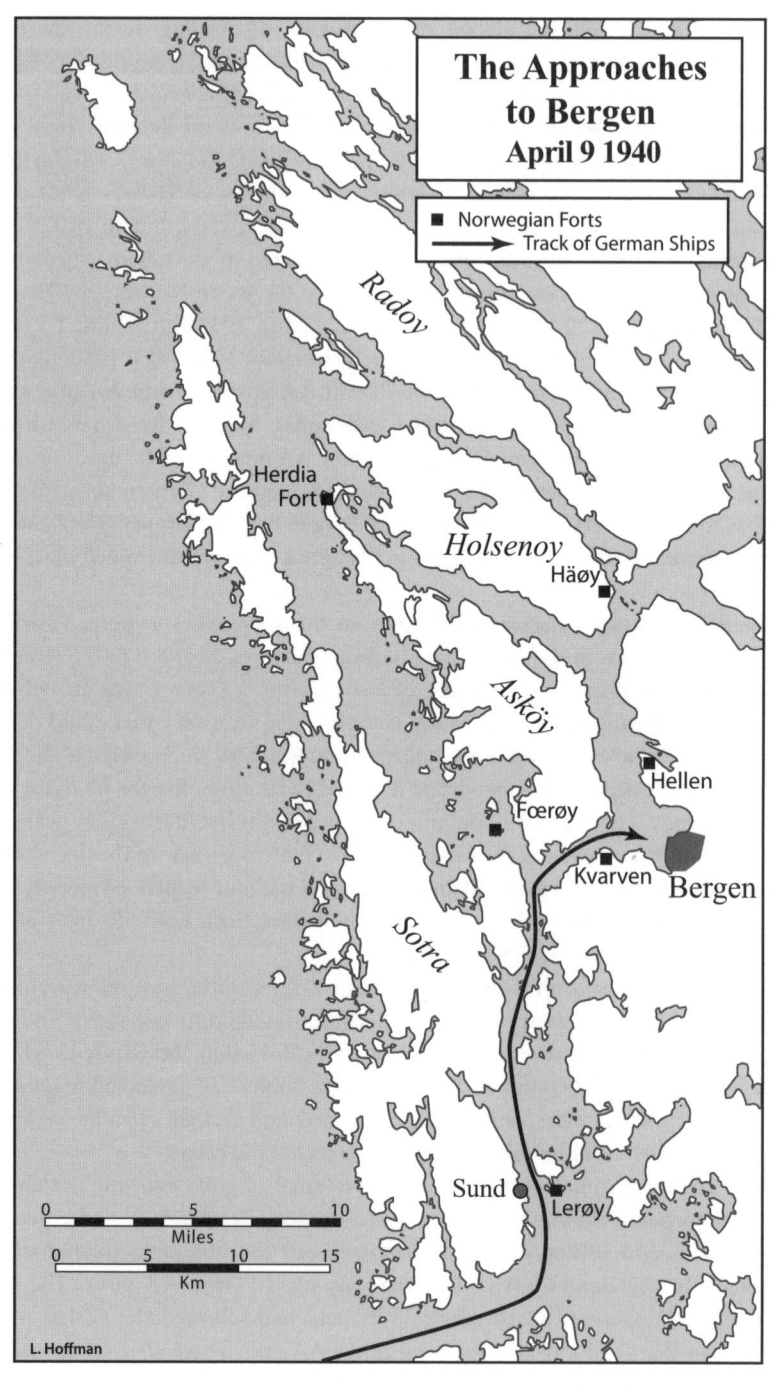

The Approaches
to Bergen
April 9 1940

■ Norwegian Forts
→ Track of German Ships

Radøy

Herdia
Fort■

Holsenoy

Häøy■

Askøy

Hellen■

Fœrøy■

Kvarven■   Bergen

Sotra

Sund●  Lerøy■

0      5      10
Miles
0      5      10      15
Km

L. Hoffman

the *Bergen Festning* garrison would have held 221 officers and 1,738 men. On 8 April there were 33 officers and 529 men on duty. Of that number Kvarven had the bulk, 33 officers and 279 men, while 9 officers and 83 men manned Hellen. Their average age was 40. There was no town garrison but at Ulven Barracks, later a Nazi concentration camp, there was one battalion numbering 775 men of the Norwegian 9th Infantry Regiment. It was 14 miles south of central Bergen.[44]

Rear Admiral Carston Tank-Nielsen, commanding the 2nd Norwegian Sea Defence District based out of Bergen had at his immediate command the submarine *B6*, the destroyer *Garm*, three old torpedo-boats, four minelayers, two minesweepers and several small patrol craft. His command 'was relatively alert' with numerous requests for merchant ship inspections and ship escorts in these waters. The sheer volume of reports made it difficult to identify the intelligence needed to make an informed decision about what was happening. But Tank-Nielsen was determined to fight the approaching German invaders.[45]

Unlike Captain Hellmuth Heye at Trondheim, Schmundt proceeded up the sea passage at slow speed, in part because of the low speed of the *Bremse* and *Carl Peters*. The Norwegians had extinguished the coastal lights as the alarm spread at the presence of foreign warships in this rocky and island-strewn fjord and this also slowed the progress of the squadron.

There was no incident when the *Köln* replied to a Norwegian red flare saying it was the AA cruiser HMS *Cairo* at just past 01:00. This was from the Norwegian patrol ship *Manger*.[46]

At 02:14 the Lerøy Fort just to the south of Bergen reported unknown ships moving up the fjord. The *Königsberg* signalled to the fort, 'English warships *en route* for short stay in Bergen.'[47] But the fort commander noted that the Germans had entered Norwegian protected waters, part of the *Krigshavn*. So, after firing a warning shot he opened fire on the tail of the German squadron with fifteen small 65mm rounds. Even with one near-miss peppering the *Schiff 9*, the Germans did not think the Norwegians were in earnest.[48]

The *Köln* gave the same reply when it encountered the Norwegian torpedo-boat *Sæl*. It retired in the narrow waters and while manned and ready, did not fire. Also that morning the destroyer *Garm*, sister ship to the *Draug*, blundered into the German squadron. The four-funnelled *Garm* trained torpedo tubes on the *Königsberg*, but drew off without firing. The captain claimed he was fired on by the Germans but there is no record of the Germans even sighting the *Garm*.[49]

Tank-Nielsen, however, had by now received a report of gunfire in outer Oslo Fjord and ordered his forces into action. He also alerted Trondheim, which was within his district, and at 02:30 asked for troops from Major General William Steffens commanding the local 4th Infantry Division. The general readily agreed to send a battalion, but the nearest troops were 14 miles away. Steffens and his Chief-of-Staff were preparing by 04:30 to leave Bergen, since it was about to be attacked, by moving to the small town of Nestun, between Ulven and Bergen, on the railway line. Ultimately, it was a fallback position to the other important army depot at Voss, some 70 miles by road in the hinterland. It was the home of the Norwegian 10th Infantry Regiment. In the end the entire defence effort would prove to be an uncoordinated affair. To avoid capture, Tank-Nielsen decided to join Steffens at Nestun at about the same time and left behind most of the port naval staff including his Chief-of-Staff. The two commanders would arrive at Voss at 09:00.[50] In retrospect, Tank-Nielsen should have taken most of the staff with him.

The submarine *B6*, potentially a deadly weapon, proceeded out into the fjord, submerged, and beyond sighting merchant ships in the greater harbour, saw no action and later drew off. It would shortly after withdraw up the Sogne Fjord.[51] The 53-year-old ex-'Rendel' gunboat, now minelayer, *Tyr* laid a minefield that the Germans crossed entering the outer harbour, but failed to detonate it, apparently needing additional time to arm. The *Tyr* drew off as the Germans approached and failed to recognise what the *Tyr* was doing. On the evening of 10 April the *Schiff 9* hit one and sank.[52]

Lieutenant Pettersen, the captain of the torpedo-boat *Storm*, fired the only torpedo by a Norwegian warship in all of Norway that day. The torpedo, like the mine, is a great equaliser in littoral waters, especially for an inferior navy. This day, with the sole exception at Oslo, neither weapon would be of much use to the Norwegians. At 02:20 he fired the *Storm*'s bow torpedo at about 1,300yd as the *Köln* neared Fort Lerøy. No explosion was heard, and Admiral Schmundt apparently was not aware they had been attacked. The intended target was in the middle of the line, possibly the *Carl Peters*. The damaged torpedo was later recovered; it may have hit with the detonator malfunctioning. Alerted by the flash from the torpedo discharge, two S-boats sped after the *Storm*, which escaped by passing through some narrow waters into which the Germans were afraid to follow. The S-boats returned to the squadron to fulfill their orders.[53] The *Storm* stayed in position to ambush any more German ships that approached but none came that morning.

As the Germans approached Bergen the Norwegian naval air force mounted a dawn patrol of one He115 and one MF11. The MF11 was airborne at 03:52 and returned after an hour, the pilot reporting that he had sighted German ships approaching Bergen but was unable to attack due to darkness and poor visibility. The He115 rose at 04:10 under the command of Lieutenant Hans Andreas Bugge, who reported making two attacks and dropping bombs from about 6,000ft on two ships with no result. He later dropped his last bomb, possibly on the *Garm*, but it also missed. Flak drove him off and he landed at Flatøy. Only the *Köln* reported any attacks. Both planes were flown to safety by the end of the day.[54]

The German squadron, now slowing to 7 knots and with the fog increasing, disembarked some troops near Kvarven at 03:30. The *Königsberg* lingered to offload additional troops to capture the known land-based torpedo battery. This offloading and ferrying of troops to land was accomplished with ship's boats, the two trawlers and S-boats. The Germans were aware of the state of readiness of the Kvarven guns and the existence of the torpedo battery but claimed to have limited intelligence on other coastal batteries and especially of the position of the Norwegian gunnery observation posts.[55]

By now Schmundt was convinced that the Norwegians were aware of the impending attack and pushed on, though with some confusion among the Germans, with his flagship and the two torpedo-boats straight through the inner harbour narrows under the guns of the Kvarven battery. It would take between 10 and 12 minutes to traverse the channel that the coastal defence batteries covered. The battery tried to operate its searchlights in the early morning drizzle and fog-filled harbour, but one was controlled by the now blacked-out town power plant (Tank-Nielsen had ordered this), and the auxiliary power was not working. The other searchlight projected a poor light on the scene below. Kvarven hesitated to fire at first due to the presence of two innocent merchant ships trying to pass through ahead of the Germans. The Hellen battery joined Kvarven, but its fire was ineffective. In the confusion, the flagship, without firing a shot at the Norwegians, slipped by unscathed with the two torpedo-boats. These three ships had received two salvoes each from Kvarven, aimed so poorly that the Germans thought they were warning shots across the bow. Some of the Norwegian shells were faulty and there were misfires and temporary jamming of the guns during the firing.

One final obstacle remained. As the German ships began to pass the forts and the sound of gunfire reverberated in the harbour, the old 84-ton torpedo-boat *Brand* lay stationed near Kvarven. The *Brand* was late in leaving port that early morning and since Tank-Nielsen had just been informed that the Kvarven torpedo battery was not ready, he ordered the *Brand* to take up station there as a substitute. It trained two torpedo tubes on the *Köln* at a range of 750–1,100yd range, but the captain did not fire out of fear of disobeying orders – the long period of peace had a numbing effect on Norwegian officers this day. If he had fired, the massed German gunfire would have immediately blown his ship out of the water. Later that morning the *Brand* moored at the city pier and would be captured intact by the Germans.[56] The German ships quickly moved into the inner harbour, the *Köln* landing troops by ship's boats and the *Leopard* and the *Wolf* at the main quay.

Next the *Bremse* and *Carl Peters* attempted to run the gauntlet, but they were not so lucky. The *Bremse* was hit three times, and one hit was devastating. It penetrated the stern and exploded inside where it killed four and wounded fourteen, and made *Bremse*'s return to Germany without repairs questionable. The *Peters*, witnessing the *Bremse* in distress, fell back and was hit once on its mast with a shell that did not explode but wounded some of the soldiers it was carrying. She would not enter the harbour until the fireworks were all over.[57]

Finally, at just past 04:30, the *Königsberg* headed away from the protective rocky shore where it had been landing troops to act as fire support for the main landing. *Königsberg* worked its speed up to 22 knots as it approached the narrow entrance. As soon as *Königsberg* was sighted, the now thoroughly roused garrison placed their one operating searchlight on it and opened fire at 04:43. The first two shots missed. The German captain thought they were warning shots and did not return fire. Instead, he signalled 'Stop Firing! British ship! Good friend!' The next round hit the *Königsberg* on the starboard bow and exploded, opening a hole in its starboard side. The splinters pierced the bulkheads to its oil bunkers, as well as a boiler and a generator room. Fire and flooding resulted, the latter putting out the former. Casualties from this hit were burn cases.

The second hit was on the superstructure and damaged two 37mm mounts, killing and wounding twenty of *Königsberg*'s crew. A third hit quickly followed in the same area, which started a fire in the forward mess. *Königsberg* returned fire and disabled one of Kvarven's guns, and shortly after Kvarven's other two guns malfunctioned. Steaming as best it could, the ship ran the gauntlet and anchored near the *Köln*.

Now Hellen battery rejoined the fray and began shooting at the two light cruisers in the crowded Bergen harbour. Both light cruisers fired on the battery. Shortly after, He111s of the 9th Squadron of the KG4 arrived over Bergen. The He111s had flown all the way from Germany after refuelling on one of the North Sea islands off Germany's coast.[58] After dropping leaflets on Bergen, they attacked Hellen. The battery ceased firing, again from malfunctioning guns. One plane was shot down and one member of its crew of five survived and was taken prisoner by the Norwegians. Later Hellen reopened fire but soon halted due to malfunctioning guns and reports of the presence of a friendly torpedo-boat (the *Brand*).

The German troops were now well advanced in moving up the hill that Kvarven is situated on. There was some fighting around Kvarven but the fort surrendered at 06:20. A total of eight Norwegians died, one from friendly fire, and eighteen were wounded. They killed ten Germans and wounded seventeen. The German naval coastal defence artillery unit brought along specifically for this task immediately manned the battery.

While the aircraft attacked the batteries, the German ships completed landing of the troops in the Bergen harbour, facing very light resistance. The troops from the *Carl Peters* now rushed the fort at Hellen, while more troops headed for Kvarven from the harbour side to link up with the previously landed troops on the other side of the fort. By 11:00 the Wehrmacht was in control of Bergen and began to receive some reinforcements via three seaplanes (a fourth crashed with loss of life). The town castle, known as *Bergenhus* and more a number of old stone buildings then a true castle, would become the temporary headquarters for General Tittel and the German army.[59] Troop reinforcements with seaplanes proved difficult. The seaplanes were unfit for a long-distant flight without radar or experienced navigators for central Norway from Germany and the transport of the bulk of a battalion of the 159th Infantry Regiment to Bergen by seaplane was aborted because of the thick fog.

The Germans radioed at 15:15 that the city and the harbour were under control and the fortifications were prepared for defence.

In the days before the inavasion, three German merchant ships had been sent from Germany to bring troops and heavy equipment to the initial landing force. As has been seen, one, the *Rio de Janeiro*, was lost, while a second was redirected to Oslo. The third, the *Marie Leonhardt*, a 10-knot 2,594-ton freighter, arrived safely on 10 April, one day late.

In addition to the standard lists of support ships given in many sources, there were others. The minelayer *Schiff 11*, which had been converted from a small merchant ship, arrived on 9 April, carrying sea mines for Bergen's harbour defence.[60] Deployment of the sea mines began that morning. By 13 April two rows of mines were laid down to block Bergen's north-west entrance, although the *Schiff 111* grounded and suffered keel damage.[61] The *Hans Rolshoven* and *Bernhard von Tschirschky*, two purpose-built Luftwaffe floatplane supply ships that were intended to support the now-aborted seaplane troop, arrived in Bergen harbour on 9 April. As they approached the harbour, the S-boats that had been lingering out at the harbour entrance, acting as both guides and scouts, came out and escorted them into the harbour.[62]

That afternoon the regimental band marched through Bergen, playing music for anyone who would listen. Crowded earlier in the day, by afternoon the streets were largely deserted as refugees poured out of the city. As at Kristiansand, the added chaos on the roads made any Norwegian army counter-attack problematical.[63]

About half of the Norwegian battalion from Ulven, travelling in requisitioned buses and trucks, reached the edge of town by the time the Germans had secured the harbour and the forts. Crowds of civilians were out and the Norwegians were rightly concerned that any additional fighting could lead to civilian losses. One officer commented, 'People were wandering in the streets to see the show, as though it were a maneuver.'[64] The Germans used this situation to infiltrate troops forward to various key positions, taking advantage of the crowds. The troops began to fall back on the mobilisation centre at Voss. Tank-Nielsen under great stress would be on sick leave on 16 April. Admiral Diesen would take direct command for a short period, but gave great leeway to the staff at Voss.[65]

During the day, German prize crews examined the sixty to eighty merchant ships in the harbour and determined their fate. The *Königsberg* was busy offloading supplies to the floatplane support ship *Berhard von Tschierschky*. She also refuelled from her tanks the torpedo-boat *Wolf*. The damage to the *Königsberg* was now reviewed and it was determined that in its condition, and with a relatively raw crew, it would need two days to refit for the return to Germany, though at a reduced speed.

German orders called for any single-engine plane to be assumed as friendly. This would later aid a successful dive-bombing attack by British Skuas on the light cruiser tied up at the main harbour quay.[66] There were two British high-level bomber air attacks in the course of the day and these resulted in some near misses but did not damage the German ships. However, the British sighted Schmundt leaving the harbour with his flagship and the two torpedo-boats in the evening, so the German ships slipped into a nearby fjord and stayed there throughout 10 April before successfully returning to Germany.

At Bergen the German operation had succeeded brilliantly. It was a thorough and subtle plan, with little distinguishing touches throughout it. From the squadron stealing its way through the harbour entrance, all on a tight timetable, to the *Schiff 9* and *Schiff 18* joining up to steam ahead of the flagship to reveal potential but nonexistent Norwegian mines; from the punch with 6in guns to take out the enemy batteries, to the reinforcements arriving from air and sea – the plan was incredibly sound. It was an excellent example of both 'economy of force' and concentrating power at the decisive point at the critical moment. And at no point in the attack on Bergen did the enemy outnumber the Germans. Nor was success guaranteed. The Norwegians did have some military assets and many of their officers were skilled at the tasks for which they had trained for decades. However, the element of surprise, coupled with the Norwegians' hesitancy about what to do and how to respond, carried a great incalculable force directly leading to the German triumph.

* * *

Warship Group 2, commanded by Captain Heye, was now approaching Norway's ancient capital of Trondheim.[67] The group consisted of Heye's flagship, the heavy cruiser *Admiral Hipper*, and four destroyers, the *Friedrich Eckholdt* (carrying the Naval Special Operations Group, the naval headquarters unit, under the command of Captain Wilhelm Hornack), *Bruno Heinemann*, *Theodor Riedel* and the *Paul Jacobi*. Its objective was the capture of Trondheim and the nearby airfield at Værnes. Trondheim was considered Norway's third city with a population of 60,000. Værnes was about 34km from Trondheim.

The main elements on board were 967 troops of the 138th Mountain Regiment of the 3rd Mountain Division under Colonel Wilhelm Weiss, plus 131 naval coastal defence marines, regimental staff, heavy artillerists, Luftwaffe AA personnel, communications staff, divisional engineers, flamethrowers and machine-gunners and the regimental band. Each destroyer was carrying 200 men. The *Hipper* was carrying food for 2,000 men for a month. The absence of the *Lützow* with its battalion of mountain troops, ordered to join Warship Group 5 at Oslo due to mechanical issues, would soon be felt, as they would have allowed for the seizure of undefended Åndalsnes by two of the destroyers.[68] Also bound for Trondheim were the tankers *Moonsund* and *Skagerrak* and the supply ships *Main*, *Levante* and *Sao Paulo*, laden primarily with general supplies, motorised and horse-drawn artillery and motorised AA guns. In the end, only the *Levante* would successfully arrive; a Narvik-bound ship, the *Bärenfels*, was redirected to Trondheim and arrived on 11 April. It would unload a large amount of aviation fuel and other materials before it was sunk on the 14th.

The *Hipper* launched one of its reconnaissance floatplanes, with orders not to over-fly Trondheim and alert the Norwegians. The pilot reported the fjord was clear; only two freighters were steaming to Trondheim, while the sea to the west was free of Allied warships. With fuel running out, the pilot landed at Kristiansund, a port just south of Trondheim, a little before midnight on 8 April. The floatplane was seized by the Norwegians and would operate briefly in the campaign before being flown to Britain.[69] At 23:30 on 8 April Heye entered the outer area of Trondheim Fjord at a relatively high speed with two destroyers ahead, in line abreast with minesweeping gear deployed. The *Hipper* followed, with the two other destroyers on either flank behind it, acting as an anti-submarine escort. Later, as they neared the Norwegian coastal defences, the minesweeping destroyers drew up behind the *Hipper* in a line-ahead formation along with the other two. Directly behind the flagship was the most important destroyer Heye wanted to shepherd in, the *Eckholdt*. Heye had issued orders if heavily fired upon to saturate the enemy coastal defence batteries with maximum gunfire. In the event it was not necessary.[70]

Very wisely, unlike the captain of the *Blücher*, Heye had ordered all army gear and ammunition stowed below deck. While below-deck storage would make it more difficult to unload the ship quickly, it reduced the possibility of collateral damage from army ammunition in the event of a shell hit. As Heye approached the coastal defences, he rang up 25 knots for the squadron and noted that all lighthouses were operating normally.

Trondheim lies on a fjord that reaches deep into Norway and is within a few dozen miles of the Swedish border. It is an important transportation hub for any land movement going north to south, an active port dealing with fish and timber and enjoys a mild climate considering its position so far north.[71] North of it is rugged, narrow and in spring 1940 it was very cold. Ships headed to Trondheim had to pass three coastal batteries that were components of *Agdenes Festning*, namely the forts of Brettingen with two 210mm, three 150mm and three unmanned 65mm guns, along with a searchlight and three AA machine-guns; and Hysnes similarly manned and armed with only two, rather than three, 150mm guns. Both forts were situated at the fjord's entrance on the northern bank, some 30 miles from the city, with Brettingen the most westerly of the two forts. On the southern side, opposite Brettingen, was the third fort, Hambåra, with two 150mm guns, three AA machine-guns and a searchlight, but it was not manned.[72] Further south and opposite the main channel into Trondheim, about 7 miles from Hambåra, was the undefended port of Agdenes. The Norwegian navy used it as an anchorage and operated a radio station there. It lay just south of the main fjord to Trondheim on the Norwegian coast. The Germans believed, based on their intelligence activities and considering this complex was known as *Agdenes Festning*, that there would be a powerful coastal battery present, thought to have eight 240mm guns. There was no such battery present.[73] If fully manned, *Agdenes Festning* would have had 159 officers and 1,318 men. On 8 April there were 48 officers and 293 men on duty. The Trondheim commander ignored the alert issued by Admiral Tank-Nielsen after German Warship Group 3 had been sighted at the outer reaches of Bergen and did not go on alert until 03:00. Only when his own outer patrol vessels reported the presence of German warships did he sound the alarm.[74]

The Norwegian navy was not particularly strong in this area of the country. Trondheim, part of the 2nd Sea Defence Zone, had the modern destroyer *Sleipner* south of the port at Kristiansund. Three ancient torpedo-boats and nine patrol craft were in the general area, along with the minelayer *Frøya*. The garrison of

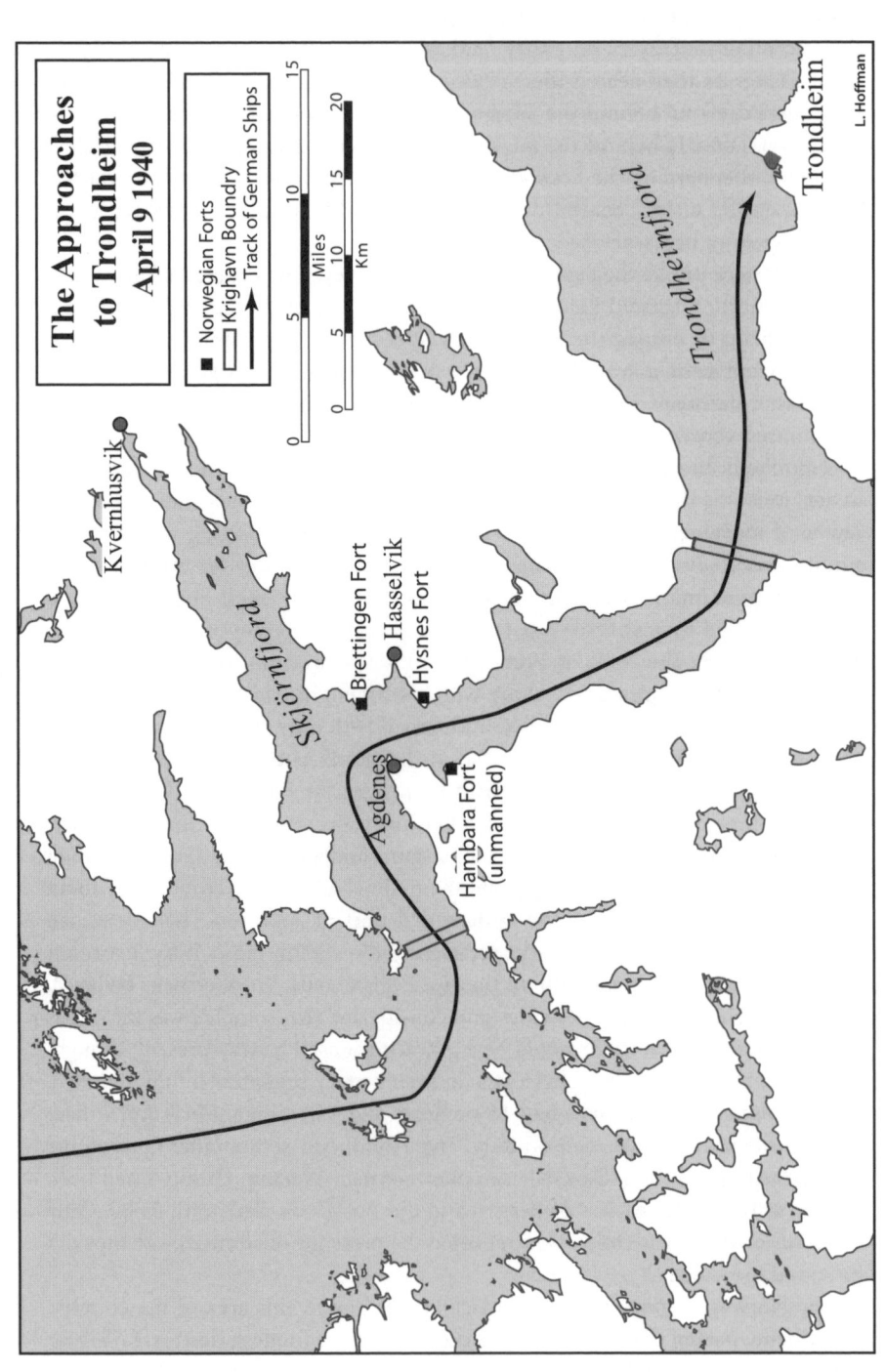

The Approaches
to Trondheim
April 9 1940

■ Norwegian Forts
□ Krighavn Boundry
→ Track of German Ships

Miles
0   5   10   15

Km
0   5   10   15   20

Kvernhusvik

Skjörnfjord

Brettingen Fort
Hasselvik
Hysnes Fort

Agdenes

Hambara Fort
(unmanned)

Trondheimfjord

Trondheim

L. Hoffman

Trondheim was only made up of some divisional staff elements.[75] At Værnes airfield the Norwegian army air force had stationed nine Fokker C.V. light bombers and a lone trainer. The Germans did not consider them much a threat.[76] Near Trondheim there was one Norwegian naval aircraft, a MF11. When the Germans later threatened Værnes, the planes flew north to Fefor airfield near Hamar.[77]

The *Hipper* was sighted entering the outer fjord at 03:04 by the Norwegian patrol ship *Fosen*. The *Hipper* signalled in English that it was the British battleship *Revenge,* that it had permission from the Norwegian government to proceed as it was chasing a German freighter and that it had 'no unfriendly intent'.[78] The *Fosen* signalled the Germans to stop and turned a weak searchlight on them. The Germans thoroughly blinded the *Fosen's* crew with their more powerful searchlight. The *Fosen*, unsure of who they were facing, fired two flares and raised the alarm that unknown warships were entering Norwegian waters. An additional patrol ship amplified the *Fosen's* warning. The Germans were still a few miles from the fort complex guarding Trondheim.

Alhough Trondheim had received some information of German activity elsewhere in the country, the local commander was absent from the two forts on the north side of the fjord. The coastal defences were only partially manned and the local commanders and crews were both sleepy and confused.

Proceeding in line with the *Hipper* leading at 25 knots, the warships were soon passing Brettingen battery, which had begun to go to battle stations at 02:55. The battery fired starshell and switched on its searchlight (thus revealing to the Germans the battery's location), and did open fire though after the line leading *Hipper* had already passed at about 03:12. The Norwegians were unsure of the identity of the warships passing below them but fired on the following destroyers. However, its crew was tired from hauling heavy ammunition from the magazine, some distance away. They only fired two salvoes from the main guns and seven salvoes from the 150mm guns and scored no hits. The *Hipper* returned fire from its two aft turrets resulting in the cutting of the electrical lines powering the searchlights. Dust and smoke from the *Hipper's* gunfire also obscured it from the Norwegian guns, allowing the *Hipper* and the destroyers to proceed up the fjord. This was at about 03:30.

Shortly after, Hysnes battery sighted the Germans but was blinded by their searchlights. In a confused state, the Norwegians did not fire on the passing Germans, who in turn did not fire. The Germans had passed the forts and would reach Trondheim unscathed.

After passing the batteries, Captain Heye detached three destroyers, which proceeded to land troops to capture the coastal batteries of the fjord. The *Paul Jacobi* started to land troops near Agdenes, on the south side of the fjord beyond the active batteries, at 04:00. It was taken under fire by the Hysnes battery and forced to withdraw before landing all the men (only sixty-eight disembarked). That left two light guns and six machine-guns still on board along with 132 men. The two mixed platoons led by a major began the trek over the frozen and rough ground. Though only 2½ miles away, it took the troops 9 hours to reach the three barbed wire lines around the guns at the unmanned but spiked battery at Hambåra. Upon its seizure the Germans transferred to a Norwegian boat and proceeded to the town of Agdenes, arriving there on 10 April, to discover there were neither Norwegian troops nor defences present.

The other two destroyers had gone to the north side of the fjord to land troops to take the two batteries on that side. As dawn broke, the Norwegian batteries could have re-opened fire on those German destroyers, but the local commander choose not to 'provoke' them further.[79] Only after repeated prodding from the local battery commanders were some shots fired on a German destroyer but these missed. The destroyer retired out of range. Later that morning the Norwegian battery fired a warning shot across the bow of the *U-34* running on the surface trying to reach Trondheim. The U-boat promptly submerged.

It took some time for the German company to reach Hysnes, where it mounted a short and hasty assault that resulted in the surrender of the battery at 13:30. This was followed by a German attack on Brettingen, which fell with 192 defenders. About 305 Norwegians were captured in the seizure of the forts, and the guns were prepared for defence against the British. Curiously, the optical sights were still in depots, and it took a couple of days to find them to bring them to the batteries. Total German losses were about twenty-two, while the Norwegians suffered two wounded.[80]

Meanwhile, at Trondheim the *Hipper* and the *Eckholdt* proceeded to the harbour and by 04:25 the Germans had begun to land their troops at the port, meeting no resistance. The remaining two seaplanes of the *Hipper* were launched and one carried out an ineffective bomb run on the Norwegian coastal batteries. They reported the local area was pretty quiet.

The German troops had seized the telephone exchange by 06:30. The troops also took possession of the railway roundhouse. The German regimental commander had a short meeting with the French and the British consuls in the railway station area. Colonel Wilhelm Weiss, commander of the 138th Mountain Regiment of the 3rd Mountain Division, rode in a taxi to the headquarters of the Norwegian 5th Division and found only the deputy commander there. In the course of the day Major General Jacob Laurantzon had concluded he could not defend Trondheim and he left to head for Værnes. The local regimental commander was ordered to remain and peacefully turn over the city to the Germans, which he did. The Germans also made contact with the Trondheim police chief who was assigned twenty German soldiers to help maintain the peace. Later, for a limited time German and Norwegian troops and police actually mounted joint patrols. The Germans captured a total of 30 officers and 320 men Norwegian troops in the greater Trondheim area.[81]

On board the *Hipper* was a contingent of troops with orders to seize Værnes airfield, which was also an armoury for the local 12th Infantry Regiment. Because the planes were fired upon while flying over Værnes airport and training centre, Colonel Weiss hastened to motorise forty men and two small guns with commandeered local vehicles to capture Værnes. He also placed about 260 troops on the destroyer *Heinemann* with some heavy machine-guns to steam to the airfield. The German troops were ready to advance on Værnes by the morning of the 10th. The airport was taken without resistance. General Laurantzon had ordered the Norwegians to withdraw, including Major Hans Holtermann of the Norwegian artillery. Holtermann was determined to do more and in the next few days would help organise one of the great symbols of Norwegian resistance.

Apparently, Laurantzon ordered the retreating Norwegians not to demolish the airfield. The Germans found there a mix of 120 civilians and officers and men and according to the Germans 'the young officers are for us'. General Laurantzon would eventually arrive at Steinkjer that evening. There about 1,000 troops of the 13th Infantry Regiment was beginning to mobilise almost 70km by road to the north of Værnes.

The snow would make the airfield difficult to use for days, and there was a shortage of aviation fuel. Since the Luftwaffe did not have an airfield available to it, twenty-one seaplanes brought troops and supplies to Trondheim during the course of the day. The seaplanes were then ready when needed for reconnaissance work in the coming days. However, the lack of aviation fuel, due to the failure of German supply ships getting through, severely limited their activity.[82]

The Germans had two other duties facing them. They had to prepare the German fleet for its return home and make ready the troops for a possible Allied counter-attack.

The small torpedo-boat *Laks* was captured intact and was under repair. In the course of the day, the captain of the *Laks* made the boat ready for a sneak night attack on the *Hipper*, but she sailed that afternoon so the boat was abandoned to the Germans.[83]

Trondheim was mostly still sleeping when the naval parties took possession of the merchant ships in the harbour. The Germans seized Allied and neutral ships but not those that were American, in order to avoid an incident with the USA. One that escaped was the American *Mormacsea*, which had just taken on board $4,500,00 worth of Swedish government gold for transport to the USA. After some adventures it was able to steam for the USA, leaving Norwegian waters on the 14th and successfully reaching New York harbour.[84]

The process of disembarking troops and equipment took the entire day, while special parties refuelled the German ships in order to allow them to return to Germany with oil taken from the seized merchant ships. There was less fuel than expected, which would have an impact on German actions.

After announcing to the civilian authorities that the German troops had landed in order to protect Norway from the British and that they desired a good relationship with the population, the troops began to expand the bridgeheads. Trondheim was secured and defences were readied for the anticipated Allied retaliation. But it was a beleaguered city, cut off from the main German forces. In the following days the main German goal in Norway would be to link up with Trondheim.

The German troops placed themselves on the defensive, requisitioning vehicles, of which there was a great shortage, and began the task of organising troops and reconnaissance patrols along the road network. The lack of vehicles, artillery and ammunition limited the effectiveness of the Germans. Still, Colonel Weiss was able to radio a report to Falkenhorst that, 'Landing in Trondheim complete. Norwegian division commander ordered no resistance. Good relations with local authorities.'[85]

General Laurantzon's role is controversial in Norwegian history and some histories have turned a blind eye to his actions. A contemporary of his writing in 1940 said of him, 'this old gentleman, feeling the day was lost, was for surrendering.'[86] His office had known at 01:00 on 9 April that the outer forts at Oslo had fired warning shots at unknown warships. He did attempt to get orders from Oslo, but these were never issued to him, and so he did little. That evening, after Quisling's broadcast in Oslo, he ordered his troops not to mobilise or resist the Germans. This would lead directly to the capture virtually intact of the airfield and mobilisation centre at Værnes on the 10th.[87]

Shortly after arriving at Steinkjer he would go on sick leave. At his postwar trial, Laurantzon would argue that the mobilisation orders were only for the 1st to 4th infantry divisions, which was technically correct. He would be sentenced to sixty days in prison for his actions.

The Kriegsmarine ended up retaining two destroyers for defence and requisitioned local Norwegian naval ships as well. One of the destroyers had been slightly damaged below the waterline and was not operational for several days. Both destroyers had some tubes removed and placed as a shore torpedo battery and on two small requisitioned Norwegians vessels. But this took several days and left the Germans vulnerable to a naval assault.[88] Over the coming month some supplies would arrive via U-boats and aircraft. The seizure of local Norwegian horses helped to ease the transportation situation because the horses the Germans brought with them were unfit for the Norwegian climate, while the native horses with their two-wheeled carts 'were successful in the transport of ammunition and supply'. Some local mechanical transport was also requisitioned.[89]

That afternoon German commanders reviewed the naval situation. The *Hipper* had sufficient fuel to reach Germany, but only one destroyer, the *Eckoldt*, had enough fuel to make the journey. This was accomplished only by taking on fuel from two of the remaining destroyers and from merchant ships in the harbour. In addition, four German U-boats had entered the fjord to aid the German defence, though they could contribute little due to their faulty torpedoes.

More importantly, they had secured a key land choke point in central Norway. The Swedish border was a few miles away, and connected by rail. If the Germans could control this point, they effectively cut off northern Norway from the rest of the nation. As Captain B. H. Liddell Hart wrote at the time, 'No reasonable calculation of the Allies ability to drive the Germans out of Norway as a whole can be made until it is seen whether the local situation in the Trondheim zone can be retrieved, and that route of entry for relieving forces reopened.'[90]

\* \* \*

The German actions were not carried out in a vacuum. It was now clear to the British leadership that Germany had launched a full-scale invasion and in the process had seized the ports outlined in Operation R4.[91] The Allied fleet was already mostly at sea and much of it operating nearby. It was now a question of what would they do and how Germany would counter the Allied moves.

The British Home Fleet under Admiral Sir Charles Forbes had begun the morning about 80 miles south-west of Bergen steaming north.[92] At dawn both sides launched scouting aircraft. The British spotted the *Hipper*, the *Köln*, the *Königsberg* (later) and the *Karlsruhe* in their respective Norwegian harbours. The Germans sighted the British near Bergen by 09:00 and were prepared to act against them.

Forbes had begun some aggressive planning. As early as 06:30 he signalled to the Admiralty for information on the Germans in Bergen so he could send in a naval force to engage them. His force consisted by about 09:30 of the quite impressive force of the battleships *Rodney* (flag) and *Valiant;* the heavy cruisers *Devonshire*, *Berwick* and *York;* the French light cruiser *Émile Bertin* and the British light cruisers *Sheffield*, *Galatea*, *Manchester*, *Arethusa*, *Southampton* and *Glasgow;* the French destroyers *Maillé-Brézé* and *Tartu* and the British destroyers *Escapade*, *Electra*, *Griffin*, *Brazen*, *Codrington*, *Jupiter*, *Afridi*, *Gurkha*, *Sikh*, *Mohawk*, *Somali*, *Matabele* and *Mashona*. Forbes detached three Polish destroyers and the destroyer *Tartar* to escort a large Allied convoy just north of Narvik near Hovden. He had lost four destroyers due to a collision and the need to provide an escort.[93]

More importantly, Forbes lacked an aircraft carrier. They were detached to other areas and the only one available, the *Furious*, did not have its fighters. The need was so great it was steaming north with the modernised battleship *Warspite* but was not immediately available for action.

There was some thought of attacking both Trondheim and Bergen. But the First Sea Lord Admiral Sir Dudley Pound at the Admiralty knew that the German battleships were at sea and so he ordered the British at 11:32 not to detach a force against Trondheim, as they did not want to risk being defeated in detail.[94]

The Admiralty did agree with Forbes for his plan to attack Bergen, where by 10:15 the *Köln* was known to be present. The Admiralty told Forbes that he should not assume the coastal batteries were still under Norwegian control.

Vice Admiral Sir Geoffrey Layton was detached with the *Manchester* (flag), *Sheffield*, *Glasgow*, *Southampton*, *Afridi*, *Gurkha*, *Sikh*, *Mohawk*, *Somali*, *Matabele* and the *Mashona,* to be joined by the light cruiser *Aurora* which was in the area, and ordered to attack Bergen. The first four light cruisers were quite modern robust vessels armed with twelve 6in guns in four triple turrets and all were members of the 18th Cruiser Squadron. The *Aurora* was a smaller and older light cruiser and not as big as the *Köln*. The destroyers were large 'Tribal' class ships, each armed with eight 4.7in guns in four twin turrets but only one quadruple torpedo mount. Large and powerful, this class was a successful design built on the eve of the war but having a relative poor AA capability and a smaller torpedo complement then most other British destroyers. The *Afridi*, *Gurkha*, *Sikh* and the *Mohawk* were from the 4th Destroyer Flotilla, while the *Somali*, *Matabele* and the *Mashona* were from the 6th Destroyer Flotilla. They were under the command of the illustrious Captain Philip Vian.

Forbes' plan was for Layton to keep his cruisers at the two main heads of the outer entrance to Bergen, while three destroyers from one flotilla went in from one fjord and the other four into another, and approach Bergen from essentially two different directions. Forbes noted to Layton that he should expect German submarines to be lurking off the entrance, as was indeed the case.[95] It took some time in the heavy seas and with the destroyers limited to 16 knots to get into position. Then at 14:08 came the news that air reconnaissance had spotted *two* German cruisers in Bergen. It was now that the Admiralty intervened again and cancelled the attack.[96] The ships were ordered to keep additional enemy ships and supplies from reaching the ports. The Admiralty and most naval officers thought that cruisers trumped destroyers; the armament of two light cruisers was perceived as too powerful. Admiral Pound kept too close a rein on Layton and should have sent information, not orders. Churchill later admitted his error in allowing this.[97]

To have moved into position and not pulled the trigger on the attack was probably a mistake. It was certainly disappointing to officers ready to deliver the surface attack.[98] The Germans were far from ready for a naval counter-attack and even if the British had suffered greater losses they were in a much better situation to recover from those losses. The Germans were not. A bold stroke at this juncture, as the one at Narvik, soon to be described, would have emboldened the Norwegians in their resistance. Finally, an immediate counter-attack on isolated Trondheim, following on the heels of a strike on Bergen, could have had incalculable benefits. It was an opportunity lost. The Allied force was about to take an aerial beating nonetheless.

The Germans now struck with the Luftwaffe. It had two specially trained *Kampfgeschwader* regiments, the 26th (Lion) and 30th (Eagle). KG26 was made up of He111s and KG30 had the longer range Ju88s. While both were primarily trained for anti-shipping actions, the former specialised in merchant ships and the latter warships.[99]

During the afternoon, Layton and Forbes were attacked several times by forty-one He111s and forty-seven Ju88s. The first attacks were against Layton, who was already retiring on Forbes. His ships suffered damage from near hits and some personnel losses. A 500kg bomb that hit the *Rodney* just penetrated the armoured deck and did little damage, but wounded eighteen. Forbes later noted that a similar hit on the *Furious* would be deadly. The destroyer *Gurkha* was lost. Its captain had become frustrated at not hitting any of the enemy planes with AA fire and had taken his ship out of formation to obtain better results from a different angle and was pounced on and sunk when a bomb opened a 40ft gash on the starboard side and the destroyer caught fire; sixteen men including its captain died. Importantly, some of Forbes' ships had used up 40 per cent of their

AA ammunition. The Germans lost four Ju88s to AA fire and the Lion and Eagle units flew back to base.

Forbes retired to Scapa Flow where he was joined by the *Warspite* and the *Furious*. His force with additions and subtractions now numbered three battleships, one carrier, three cruisers and eighteen destroyers as they busily fuelled and took on ammunition.[100] Forbes was also convinced that his fleet could not operate close to Bergen due to German air power and that he would have to operate further north especially if the *Furious* was present.[101]

By 10 April Stukas and some He111s of the Lion regiment would be operating from Sola.[102] Forbes recalled, 'The scale of air attack that would be developed (later) against our military forces on shore and our naval forces off the Norwegian coast was grievously underestimated when the operations were undertaken.'[103] RAF raids against Bergen were much smaller than the German effort and achieved only one near miss on one German warship.[104]

Additional moves against the Germans in central Norway would have to wait until the Allied army was committed.

# CHAPTER 10

# *Narvik*

We have lost 300 of our comrades at Narvik. They were killed by German aggressors. They died honorably, and may they rest in Peace.

Commodore Per Askim[1]

Narvik from the turn of the century was unlike any other Norwegian fjord seaport. Its role as an iron-ore transfer point gave Narvik a completely different appearance. One British ship captain had written in 1912, 'As we sailed into the bay it suddenly appeared as though we had come across a bit of Newcastle ... it is strange amongst the wonderful scenery to come across furnaces and smoke and all the concomitants of the Black Country'.[2] Cruise ships in the twenty-first century exploring the scenic beauty of Norway's Atlantic coast do not typically put into Narvik because of its unromantic industrial circumstances.

Because Narvik is positioned north of the arctic circle, the weather in the long winter months tends to be cold with frequent blizzards that pile the snow high. Radio communications with distant Oslo and other parts of Norway were often patchy and landlines assumed a greater importance this far north. When the Germans arrived in April the snow was 2m deep. From the end of May to the second half of July, Narvik enjoys the northern summer where the sun never sets, but during winter the sun never rises. Nevertheless, the Gulf Stream influences the area, such that Narvik's fjord, called the Ofot Fjord, never ices. Ofot Fjord is really the Ofot system of fjords. There are several named fjords off Ofot, arranged like fingers on the hand, of various lengths and depths. An almost vertical rock wall nearly 2,000ft high dominates the Ofot and the nearby fjords. In these fjords and inlets are scattered islands and small villages and towns. Nearby and just off the north side of the entrance of Ofot Fjord lies the small port of Harstad on one of the large Lofoten Islands, which played an important role as an Allied base in the coming campaign. It was also the headquarters for the Norwegian 6th Infantry Division. Overlooking Narvik near the Swedish border is the 4,000ft Rombakstøtta, known as Narvik's Matterhorn.

In 1940, there was no road from Narvik to the Swedish border. Instead, a 21-mile single rail line rose from sea level along the Rombaker Fjord, a finger of the Ofot Fjord system. The Rombaker runs the farthest inland toward the Swedish border. The rail line rose 1,600ft to the Bjornfjell pass, where a little village was the last station near the border, then passed over the 150ft-high Norddal bridge and

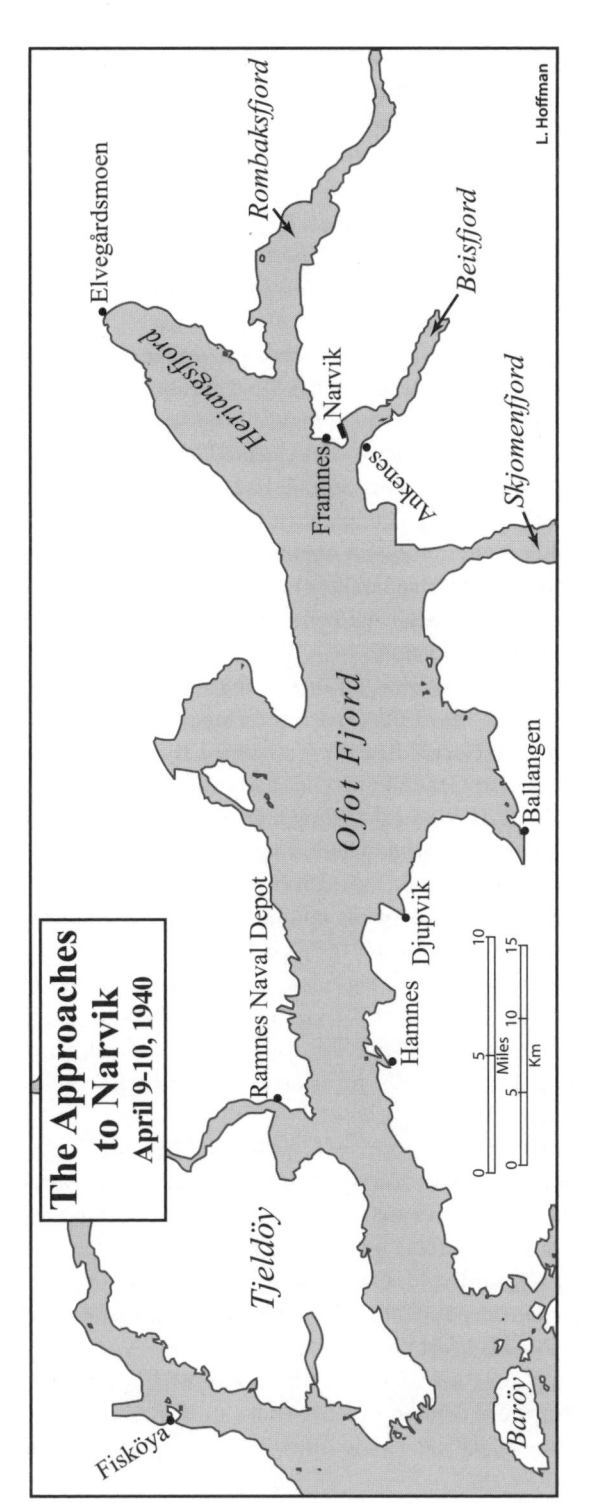

**The Approaches to Narvik**
April 9-10, 1940

Rombaksfjord

Beisfjord

Elvegårdsmoen

Herjangsfjord

Narvik

Framnes

Ankenes

Skjomenfjord

Ofot Fjord

Ballangen

Ramnes Naval Depot

Hamnes  Djupvik

Tjeldöy

Fisköya

Baröy

L. Hoffman

Miles

Km

through twenty-four tunnels into Sweden. Over this rail line came the iron ore vital for the German war machine.

The Narvik region offered other possibilities in the war against Britain. It would be well suited to strikes against Britain's lines of communication. Major General Lothar Rendulic later quoted Hitler's words in appointing him Commander-in-Chief in Norway in 1944, 'The region of Narvik-Tromsø with its hundreds of inlets, cliffs and little fjords is a natural berth for several hundreds of submarines. They can be widely dispersed and hidden so that they offer only little vulnerable targets to the enemy's air force.'[3]

The Norwegian army garrison at Narvik was under the command of Colonel Konrad Sundlo and was attached to the 6th Division. His second-in-command was Major Siguard Omdal. The main focus of the 6th Division's commander and Norway's youngest Major General Carl Gustav Fleischer was even further north near the Soviet frontier. In Narvik Sundlo had one company of the 13th Infantry Regiment, the 6th Engineer Company (minus elements), one 75mm field gun mounted on a railcar,[4] four 40mm AA guns and a battery of machine-guns. A pair of recently completed concrete bunkers built by the army in Narvik on either side of the inner harbour entrance would end up being captured without a shot being fired by troops in either position.

At Elvegårdsmoen, also lying on one of the finger fjords of the Ofot system (Herjangs Fjord), was one of 6th Division's arsenals. Elements of the Norwegian battalion garrisoning Narvik had been stationed there but following reports of German activity Major General Fleischer had ordered it moved to Narvik on the eve of the invasion.[5] After an exhausting 8-mile trek on skis in a snowstorm, the battalion took a ferry to Narvik where it was billeted. Fleischer adroitly ordered additional units forward to Elvegårdsmoen and for his forces immediately to mobilise additional elements of his command (Oslo had radioed to wait until the next day) but they would be too late in arriving to stop the Germans. A motorised artillery detachment was also sent to a prepared position to support army operations in the town of Narvik but would be late in arriving. The 6th Division had six aircraft available but they were stationed close to the border with the Soviet Union. Before the invasion the Germans estimated a total of 1,500 Norwegian troops in the Narvik area.[6]

Colonel Sundlo was a supporter of Quisling and his party. Before the invasion, he had made preparations at Narvik for insurrection and was awaiting Quisling's order to attack.[7] Sundlo had told Quisling, 'I will do nothing for that old soak [the Minister of Commerce], for that pacifist [the Defence Minister] and for that blockhead Nygaardsvold. On the other hand, it can be good and useful to risk your bones for the national uprising.'[8] Sundlo as a soldier did take actions to defend Narvik. But his heart may not have been in it.

Sundlo held a meeting at 02:00 with some of his top officers to discuss troop dispositions but wanted to leave those until first light. He assumed that the Norwegian navy patrols would allow him enough time to alert his mostly sleeping troops.[9]

At the head of Ofot Fjord lay a small underdeveloped naval base at Ramsund. To protect it, the Norwegians had planned to install a battery just up from Ramsund to command the entrance to Ofot Fjord. In 1920, three 150mm guns were delivered but never mounted. They were shipped to Bergen in early 1940. In 1926 Ramsund had been downgraded to an anchorage, thus not requiring coastal defence guns. Opposite Ramnes lay another unfinished battery at Hamnes.[10] In 1940 a patrol craft, the *Torfinn I*, was based out of Ramsund. During 1937–9 there were at least two proposals by the Norwegian army to place stored 105mm and/ or 120mm guns there, but these schemes were never executed. However, both the British and the Germans *believed* there were coastal defence guns in place at these two positions and this intelligence mistake would have an impact on the campaign.[11]

The Norwegian naval detachment at Narvik was under the temporary command of Commodore Per Askim, in the absence of the commander of the 3rd Norwegian Sea Defence District Commodore Leif Hagerup, who was on leave. The headquarters for the 3rd *Sjøforsvarsdistrik* was the more northern town of Tromsø.

The two armoured coastal defence warships (launched in 1900), the *Norge* (flag) and *Eidsvold* (under the command of Captain Odd Isaksen Willoch), had been transferred from Tromsø to Narvik on 29 March. Rear Admiral Henry E. Diesen referred to these two coastal defence ships as 'his old Bathtubs'.[12] On Neutrality Watch, neither warship was anywhere near their full strength of 270 men.[13] Also under Askim's immediate command in Ofot Fjord were the submarines *B-1* and *B-3*, a submarine tender and two patrol craft, the *Kelt* and *Michael Sars*. The port had its own attached fishery protection ship, the *Senja*.[14]

There were several other patrol craft and fishery protection ships stationed in the 3rd Sea Defence District, mostly to the north of Narvik.[15] The local naval air force had three He115s stationed at Tromsø and two MF11s at Vadsø, near the Soviet border.[16]

On the very foggy morning of 8 April at Narvik the two coastal defence ships were anchored by the stern to allow for telephone traffic from ship to shore. The two submarines were also present because their tender was under repair. The patrol craft *Kelt* was on patrol duty at the head of the fjord. At 06:00 when Askim learned of the British minefield laid as part of Operation 'Wilfred', he ordered his ships to raise steam and for the submarines to arm and ready their torpedoes. Askim was concerned that a naval raid against the eleven German merchant ships in Narvik harbour would immediately follow the British minefield operation.[17]

Askim continued to receive reports in the course of the day of numerous German transports in Danish waters as well as German troops moving up to the Danish border. A British Admiralty report received that night stated, 'It is firmly believed that operations against Narvik are intended and that they could arrive at Narvik before midnight.'[18] Askim contacted Diesen's staff at Oslo about this report and the staff there later replied that they thought it was not likely to occur.[19] Askim did receive orders from the Norwegian Naval Staff in Oslo at 18:00 that he was to resist an attack.[20] With that in mind he ordered the submarines to leave Narvik and proceed further up the fjord to remain hidden from view and the *Eidsvold* to take station further up the inner harbour entrance. The *Norge* stayed anchored so as to have access to telephone communications. Askim ordered his two patrol vessels to proceed out into the outer reaches of Ofot Fjord to guard for foreign warships. The two coastal defence ships were ordered to clear decks for action, guns and torpedoes to be readied and steam to be raised in all boilers.

* * *

Speeding north in the dead of night, plunging and swaying in the teeth of a storm, were the ten destroyers of the Warship Group 1 carrying 2,000 troops, whose mission was to make Narvik part of the Third Reich. These destroyers were part of three different flotillas. The 1st Destroyer Flotilla included the *Wilhelm Heidkamp* and the *Georg Thiele*; the 3rd Destroyer Flotilla the *Hans Lüdemann, Hermann Künne, Diether von Roeder* and the *Anton Schmitt*; and the 4th Destroyer Flotilla the *Wolfgang Zenker, Bernd von Arnim, Erich Giese* and the *Erich Koellner*. The commander of all German destroyers, and commanding this naval expedition once Vice Admiral Günther Lütjens detached them from Warship Group 1, was Commodore Friedrich Bonte. He flew his flag on the *Wilhelm Heidkamp*. Also on board was Major General Eduard Dietl, commander of the 3rd Mountain Division.

The ships were carrying elements of the 3rd Mountain Division that were to take control of Narvik and of the rail line to Sweden: the 139th Mountain Regiment commanded by Colonel A. Windisch, one company of the 83rd Mountain Engineer Battalion and elements of the 68th Mountain Signal Battalion. Also on board were 100 men making up a company of coastal defence marines, a few naval radio/signals personnel and elements of the personnel of a Luftwaffe AA battalion.

The very rough voyage, with many of the young men having their first taste of the sea, took its toll. Some men were lost overboard and some of the equipment, including light guns and motorcycles that had been stowed on deck, were also lost in the harsh seas. The ships suffered damage as well, including ship's cutters. Walther Hubatsch, the German historian who would pen the semi-official history of the campaign, later wrote, 'The sea was almost white, the ships enveloped by choppy splashes ... the demand on the ships' hulls were at the highest tolerable point'.[21]

For the initial assault two destroyers were to land troops to capture the non-existent coastal batteries. Three more destroyers, the *Zenker, Koellner* and the *Künne*, with Colonel Windisch in command of the troops were to proceed deep into the Ofot to Elvegårdsmoen where one of the Norwegian 6th Infantry Division's arsenals was located. This was *Gruppe Elvegårdsmoen*. The remaining destroyers, designated *Gruppe Narvik*, were to disembark troops at Narvik. The troops were not only to occupy key installations, hopefully without a fight, but were to hand out leaflets explaining to the locals why they were there.[22]

1. The Norwegian minelayer *Olav Tryggvason* was completed in 1934. It was built in large part to keep the naval yard in work and was employed more as a slow destroyer than as a minelayer. (Author's collection)

2. The elderly armoured coast defence ship *Eidsvoll* in a fjord. Admiral Diesen referred to her and her sister-ship *Norge* as his 'old bathtubs'. (Author's collection)

3. The destroyer HMS *Glowworm* would be lost early in the campaign in a heroic action against the German heavy cruiser *Hipper*. She was laid down in 1934. (IWM: HW83)

4. One of the German 'K' class light cruisers. Two of the three would be sunk in the campaign. (Author's collection)

5. A British Skua dive-bomber. Aircraft of this type sank the German light cruiser *Königsberg* at Bergen. (Dave Isby collection)

6. The German pocket-battleship *Lützow* would be rerouted to Oslo from Trondheim on the eve of the invasion. Originally it was to have proceeded into the Atlantic following the invasion. (Author's collection)

7. The *Bruno Heinemann*, a typical German destroyer of the prewar period. Twenty-two were available at the outbreak of war and ten would be lost at Narvik. (Author's collection)

8. The German torpedo-boat *Albatros* would be lost after accidently grounding in the Oslofjord. (Author's collection)

9. An S-boat used by the Germans for the invasion of southern Norway and later employed in the Norwegian fjords. (Dave Isby collection)

10. One of the three 283mm guns at Fort Oscarsborg. Air Force Lieutenant Colonel (ret.) Arvid Carlsen (L), with Andrew Smith (R) standing between two shells. (Author's collection).

11. Side view of one of Fort Oscarsborg's gun emplacements. One can clearly understand why Colonel Birger Eriksen ordered his gun crews into the bomb shelters when attacked by German aircraft. (Author's collection).

12. Head-on view of one of the 283mm Krupp guns at Fort Oscarsborg. Direct-fire weapons were less effective against the fort than howitzer fire. (Author's collection)

13. Close-up of the torpedo rack at Fort Oscarsborg. The head of the torpedo is in the foreground, it is moved forward onto the rack and lowered into the water for firing. (Author's collection).

14. The torpedo rack in the raised position. (Author's collection).

15. Germans landing from the *Hansestadt Danzig* at the lovely *Langelinie* in Copenhagen harbour. Note the Danish civilians, wondering what is going on. (Aggersbo: The Museum of Danish Resistance, 1940–1945)

16. To counter the threat of the Danish navy, the Germans deployed their remaining pre-dreadnought battleships for the last time. The *Schleswig-Holstein* would run aground during the operation. (Bundesarchiv).

17. Danish soldiers manning one of their 37mm AT guns, wearing their newly-issued steel helmets. The Germans considered the Danes to be good shots. (Royal Arsenal Museum, Copenhagen)

18. This is a German propaganda shot taken of their three Neubau PzKw IV tanks. A failed design, but perfect to scare the Norwegians with their large size, so they were paraded through the streets of Oslo before going to the front. (Tore Eggan collection)

19. The majority of German supplies arrived by sea, primarily at Oslo. (Author's collection)

20. A German hospital ship at Oslo. It arrived after 9 April. (Tore Eggan collection)

21. Small ship transport for both Germans and Norwegians in the green and brown waters of Norway was not unusual. Note the bicycles used by the Norwegians and that many are asleep. (Tore Eggan collection)

22 & 23. These two photographs are of the same German PzKw II tank. Note the German troops making good use of its protection from the accurate Norwegian rifle fire. (Tore Eggan collection).

24. Norwegian infantry column with horse transport in the background, and an officer in the foreground. Note the distinctive hat. (Tore Eggan collection)

25. This is a British Morris-Commercial CS8 telephone line layer most likely captured at the end of the fighting. Note the snow chains. (Tore Eggan collection)

26. German military band marching in downtown Bergen, most likely the day after the invasion. (Author's collection)

27. Another shot of a German horse-drawn battery, after the capture of Bergen. The town was largely deserted at this point. (Author's collection)

28. A Fokker C.V., first introduced in Norwegian service in 1926. This biplane, here equipped with skis, was used for reconnaissance and light transport. (Tore Eggan collection)

29. This shows the destruction wrought by the German Luftwaffe in bombing largely wooden-built Norwegian towns. (Tore Eggan collection).

30. German He111 medium bombers. (Dave Isby Collection).

31. This is one of the 300  bridges demolished by the retreating Norwegians to slow the German advance. (Tore Eggan collection)

32. British prisoners being driven to the rear. Note the typical Norwegian wooden house in the background. (Tore Eggan collection)

German orders called for the troops to be deployed to defend the greater Narvik area, both towards the sea and the Swedish border. This defence perimeter was to include the town of Bardufoss to the north and its small airfield as well as positions along Ofot Fjord. In addition, a detachment was ready to seize the Swedish Kiruna-Gållivare ore fields if required, an extremely unrealistic goal due to the presence of major elements of the Swedish 1st Infantry Division guarding the Swedish border.[23]

Warship Group 1 reached the more southern point of Lofotens at about 23:00 on 8 April and entered the Vestfjord; by midnight they were well inside the fjord where the waters were calmer. The words 'Land in sight!' came as a great relief to the dreadfully seasick *Gebirgsjägers*. In the much calmer water they shortly would be largely recovered from the immediate effects of their seasickness.

At about 03:00 the *Kelt* and the *Sars* both sighted the approaching German warships and signalled their presence to the *Norge*. By 03:20 the patrol vessel *Kelt* definitively reported nine German destroyers, travelling at high speed, had entered the Ofot Fjord. This message would be passed on to the army and to the local naval headquarters at Tromsø.[24] The tenth destroyer, the *Erich Giese*, was straggling about 3 hours behind due to a fuel shortage and compass problems. As the Germans entered Ofot Fjord, they left one destroyer, the *Roeder*, behind on picket duty. Later a German destroyer would return and seize the *Kelt* and *Michael Sars*, firing three rounds over the stern of the latter, and order them to proceed to Narvik, which they did.

Next the Germans detailed the *Lüdemann* and *Schmitt* to drop off some troops to seize the supposed coastal defence batteries at Ramnes and Hamnes.[25] The two companies were instructed to occupy the site, but in order to do so they would have to climb a hillside covered with 2m of snow and attack with flamethrowers. When they arrived on the hills they discovered that there were no guns to capture, only two unoccupied machine-gun blockhouses. At 07:00 the search for the ghost batteries was abandoned and the two companies again boarded ship and steamed for Narvik.[26]

Askim notified the *Eidsvold* of events that were unfolding and ordered the *Norge* to shove off from the dock and load high-explosive shells in its guns. Askim, anticipating enemy torpedoes, ordered his guns to cover the port side, while lifeboats were partly lowered on the starboard side and life jackets distributed.

At 04:15 the *Eidsvold* sighted the lead destroyer of the Narvik group, the *Wilhelm Heidkamp*, with Commodore Bonte and Major General Dietl and staff on board. The *Eidsvold* fired a warning shot and the *Heidkamp* hove to at a distance of about 200yd and dispatched two officers and a signalman to the *Eidsvold*. The Norwegian ship was asked to surrender. The Germans announced that they were there to defend Norway from the Allies. Willoch asked for time to consult with Commodore Askim, and the Germans returned to their launch by *Eidsvold*'s side.

Willoch, ordered by Askim to resist, radioed back, 'I am attacking'. He then recalled the Germans from their launch and informed them that he would fight. As the Germans withdrew, firing a red flare indicating the Norwegians were going to resist, Willoch shouted from the bridge to his crew 'Now we are going to fight, boys'.[27] Manning the guns, the crew was ordered to fire at least twice. Apparently, the guns misfired since no shots were fired. The *Eidsvold* was also ordered, 'Full speed ahead' and began moving towards the *Heidkamp* perhaps with the intention of ramming the German vessel. This old warship had been designed with the ram as a weapon, but ramming is difficult, especially considering the low speed of this old 'bathtub' and the higher speed and manoeuvrability of the German destroyers.[28] The range between the two ships had opened during the negotiations to about 300–500yd.[29] Bonte, in consultation with Dietl, decided to attack, after almost pleading with Dietl, 'Do we have to do this?' Bonte was deeply troubled by this act with the Norwegian ship not firing first. He then fired a salvo of four torpedoes, of which at least two scored hits.[30] Norwegian sources have two torpedoes 'porpoising' and running on the surface, striking the *Eidsvold* armoured belt and doing little critical damage. But the third struck true. The *Eidsvold*'s forward magazine exploded and the vessel quickly sank. Pieces of the ship were later found on land 500–600yd from the water. By 04:37 the *Eidsvold* had settled beneath the waves. Of the 185 men on board, 177 perished, attesting to the tremendous force of the explosion.[31]

Three German destroyers proceeded to Elvegårdsmoen, where there were only two little groups of houses and a wooden pier to land the troops in the face of a strong north wind. The Germans completely surprised the few Norwegian troops remaining, finding and taking supplies (including winter uniforms) that would be very important in their future defence of Narvik. The capturing intact of this depot and others that day would be of great help to the Germans.[32] The destroyers with orders for Narvik now closed on the anchorage, crowded as it was with at least twenty-seven merchant ships.[33]

The *Norge* was still in the harbour but had cast off from the pier. By 04:45 the *Bernd von Arnim* and *Georg Thiele* had slipped into the inner harbour. Through snow and heavy fog the two German destroyers were sighted but before the nationality of the warships could be confirmed, or a shot fired, they had disappeared back into the foul weather. In the crowded harbour they worked themselves around *behind* the *Norge* until they were between it and the shore, and on its starboard side. Their goal remained to land the troops as quickly as possible and as close to *Weserzeit* as dictated to them in their orders.

Now the adversaries sighted each other again. At a range of 700–1,000yd, the *Norge* immediately opened fire on the *Arnim* with its starboard battery, firing off five rounds of 8.2in and seven or eight 5.9in rounds. Due to the poor visibility some shells fell into Narvik. At one point the Norwegian navigating officer shouted, 'No, no, that is not the destroyers. It is only a house on the dock.'[34] The *Arnim* returned fire from its 5in and 37mm guns, scoring several hits. Several of the *Norge*'s crew suffered splinter wounds.[35] The *Norge* moved among the numerous merchant ships, but the *Arnim* found an opening and carefully and with deliberate aim fired off seven torpedoes – two, running on the surface, hit and exploded, sending the *Norge* to its grave; the other five missed or malfunctioned. As it capsized, the *Norge*'s propellers were still slowly turning. Askim would later remark that considering how slow the *Norge* was moving, it spoke poorly of the German torpedo to miss with the other five.[36] The *Norge* lost 105 men; there were 96 survivors.[37] Its gunfire at the German destroyers had been ineffective. The Norwegian losses from these two warships, the *Eidsvold* and the *Norge*, were the largest in a single action on land or sea during the course of the campaign.

Commodore Askim would be hospitalised after the action and escaped on 15 April. Before doing so, Askim assisted, along with some survivors from his two sunken warships, with the organisation of an air-raid warning system utilising Narvik's church bells.[38] He joined up with the Norwegian army on 28 April and left for Britain on 31 May. His evaluation of the conduct of the German troops occupying Narvik was, 'Discipline of Germans excellent. Conduct above criticism.'[39]

All three patrol vessels had been ordered by Askim not to fight the Germans due to their anaemic speed and armament. They were captured intact, but were later lost to British air attacks on Narvik. The submarine *B1* would escape to Britain in June. The *B3* did attempt to attack two German destroyers in the fjord but had to submerge and escape. In the process it started leaking forward. Eventually, it arrived at Tromsø and would later be lost in the evacuation from Norway in June. The submarine tender *Lyngen* would also safely make it to Tromsø.

There were eleven German merchant ships in harbour at the time of the German attack. The captain of one of them, thinking the British were attacking, ran his ship ashore.[40]

* * *

During the landing at Narvik the *Thiele* quickly moved to the pier to disembark its troops and was followed by the arriving *Heidkamp*. Consequently, 600 German soldiers were poised to seize the town in the early dawn at about 05:00.[41] German detachments with machine-guns were detailed to cover central strategic positions such as bridges. The Germans also seized the two main hotels, the railway station, telegraph station and also the city hall, where they unfurled a large Nazi flag.

The garrison in Narvik consisted of 400 men. The night before, it had been reinforced by additional troops from Elvegårdsmoen. They had marched through the cold and the snow and were bivouacked that morning, exhausted and not in good shape for the imminent combat. If one includes the reinforcing troops and support troops, the Norwegian garrison in Narvik numbered almost 800 men. This has led some to argue that Sundlo and the garrison could have put up a spirited defence, but if the Germans had used the overwhelming firepower of their three destroyers, it would have been too much for the Norwegians and the damage and casualties to Narvik and its civilians would most likely have been severe. After the loss of the two old coastal defence ships and the ineffective Norwegian submarines, the Norwegians had no answer for the fifteen 5in guns of the three German destroyers sitting in their harbour – that could be immediately reinforced with additional destroyers if required. Additionally, the destroyers could have augmented the German army troops with armed shore parties.[42]

According to the later declarations of Colonel Sundlo, the commander of Narvik, he was ordered to fire at the Germans but not at the British, should they appear on the scene.[43] The mayor of Narvik had no idea of what was occurring. He later wrote, 'It can't have anything to do with us. Some German ships must have been chased into the fjord by the British.'[44]

Major Omdal attempted, with many officers and men still asleep, to put together a force from the scattered Norwegian units and advance on the Germans now ashore at the city dock with orders to open fire. Sundlo agreed with this decision. As the company-sized force pressed forward, it immediately ran into advancing German troops. Neither side opened fire. As they waited, observing each other, additional German troops began to flank the Norwegians. The Norwegian commander reported back to Sundlo that they could not hold their position if the Germans opened fire, let alone advance to the docks. They also received a new order *not* to open fire.[45]

In another part of the town Captain E. A. Gunderson of the engineering company had been awakened by gunfire while sleeping at a hotel. He came outside and ordered his company to assemble while he began to drive towards the harbour where he was quickly captured. He was taken to Dietl, who was now ashore, and then forced to accompany him.

Dietl continued to play the cards in his hand boldly. He had arrived with several launches containing troops at the dockside where the German consul received him at the pier. In the consul's car and accompanied by a lieutenant, Dietl entered the city followed by a taxi with seven soldiers equipped with a light machine-gun. With the capture of Captain Gunderson he now had him in tow as well. They reached the rail bridge leading to the Framne Peninsula. There, Dietl found Colonel Sundlo along with part of the Norwegian garrison and some of the recently arrived Norwegian troops. During the initial parley Sundlo told the Germans to leave within 30 minutes or they would be fired upon. Dietl explained that the Germans were peacefully occupying Norway and the Norwegian government 'had decided no resistance should be offered'.[46]

Dietl impressed the Norwegians by mentioning the strength of the troops and the naval guns covering them, ready to support his troops; that the Germans had occupied Denmark and that Norway was being occupied as well; and finally that the Norwegian should surrender to avoid a bloodbath. Sundlo asked for half an hour to speak with the commander of the 6th Division, General Fleischer. According to a German account,[47] Dietl refused to grant a delay and insisted upon the immediate surrender of Narvik. However, there was a truce for 30 minutes whereby troops were supposed to remain in place and not move.

Earlier Fleischer had repeatedly ordered Sundlo to resist. The Norwegian major who took Sundlo's call this time told Sundlo he should make the decision as the man on the scene. Sundlo saw and received additional reports of the landing of yet more Germans. He also observed their movement onto some nearby high ground where they were setting up machine-guns positions covering his headquarters building. Local citizens had come out of their homes and were in the midst of all this, with their children. They did not realise the seriousness of what was transpiring and were almost totally unaware of the sinking of the two Norwegian warships and the terrible loss of life. Sundlo now turned to Dietl and said, 'I hand over the town.'[48]

Meanwhile, however, two companies of Norwegian soldiers, under command of Major Omdal, bravely marched out of Narvik towards the Swedish border and later blocked the railway line.[49] Shortly afterwards Sundlo rang up the headquarters in Harstad and told General Fleischer, who was now there, what had occurred. Fleischer angrily relieved Sundlo on the spot and replaced him with Major Omdal as regimental commander.[50]

The result of German bluff, the presence of the German navy and Sundlo's refusal to resist had allowed the key port to fall. In Sundlo's defence, he was outnumbered and had to be concerned with the welfare of the civilians, all under the guns of Germany's trump card at this moment – the three destroyers in the inner harbour capable of putting down an overwhelming amount of firepower. Dietl's conduct could be called into question for not having those destroyers open fire on the retreating Norwegian detachment under Major Omdal. By allowing them to withdraw unmolested, Dietl would have to confront them in the coming days.

The next shoe was now about to drop.

\* \* \*

The Germans had converted the whale factory ship *Jan Wellem* into an oiler, which arrived at about 05:00 on 8 April. The ship had been stopped, boarded and allowed to proceed into the inner harbour by the *Senja*. It was a large whaler (11,776 tons) and had left Soviet waters in the far north to bring fuel oil, food and some equipment for the German destroyers and U-boats assigned for duty at Narvik. It was the only merchant ship to arrive successfully of four 'fifth-column' ships dispatched to support the Germans at Narvik. No other supply ships would arrive as they were either sunk or diverted to other ports. Wartime news reports stating that there were on board 'a swarm of well-armed German regulars' were false.[51] The loss of these additional ships would severely limit the German defence.

By 07:30 on 9 April the *Giese* had finally arrived and headed further up into Ofot Fjord. Meanwhile, the Germans inventoried the merchant ships that lay in the harbour and put watch crews for them in place. Several of the British merchant ships carried small naval guns, and these, along with their ammunition, were seized.[52] One of the first acts of the Germans was to release 200 British merchant sailors held as prisoners on board the destroyers, but others were still being held on board the *Jan Wellem*. The released sailors were told to make themselves scarce until after the action. Among the disarmed and captured Norwegian troops, the

Germans caught a British reporter, Churchill's wife's nephew, Giles Romilly, who was present in Narvik in the days before the invasion. Romilly had visited Sundlo on the 8th after he paid a visit to Commodore Askim. On 24 April he would be flown out of the country to Germany.

As the day wore on more than 1,000 citizens of Narvik tried to leave town. By foot, rail or boat as with all the other towns and cities seized that day, many of the inhabitants became refugees.[53] Yet both the Germans and the Norwegians co-operated to keep Narvik functioning. Within 48 hours a ration board was established, a soup kitchen set up, the hospital, almost overwhelmed with dying and wounded Norwegian sailors, continued to function and many committees were formed. The Red Cross was pressed to its utmost in this man-made disaster. Teachers would be called on to become translators.

There happened to be a shipload of fresh fish in the harbour at the time of the invasion. It could not be kept frozen, so an attempt at salting was made to try to preserve it. Though this attempt was not completely successful, it would allow for fish on the dinner table for the next two months for those who remained in Narvik. However, the off-licence was closed.[54] The city engineer organised the reinforcement of basements for protection and the planting of every available field with crops, mostly potatoes, as food supply was recognised as a critical issue for the town. This pattern was repeated to one degree or another across Norway.

But now the numbers of dead and wounded German sailors were about to increase with a daring attack by British destroyers.

The German squadron had arrived at Narvik with orders to land the troops, seize the objectives, refuel and return to Germany as quickly as possible. These ten represented the single largest squadron of German destroyers in the German navy. Due to the long, fast steaming to the north, their fuel bunkers were close to empty. The Germans had sent two tankers, one of which, the *Jan Wellem*, had safely arrived, and was now crucial for the resupply of the destroyers for their voyage home. The *Wellem* had an inefficient pumping system and could only refuel two destroyers at a time. Bonte refuelled his flagship, the *Heidkamp*, first, followed by the *Zenker* and *Koellner*. Unfortunately, it took 7–8 hours to refuel two destroyers at a time. In addition, the *Arnim* and *Thiele* had both suffered engine damage and would not be ready for immediate departure. Bonte considered ordering the destroyers to sea as soon as they completed refuelling, but was worried that sending them out in pairs might backfire with the British closing in to blockade Narvik. That decision would cost him both his life and the loss of all his ships.

The second tanker, the *Kattegat*, was lost as it neared Narvik on 10 April. Its captain chose not to enter Vestfjord after he received reports about British mines. Instead, the ship waited in Glåmfjord for minesweepers to clear a passage. There, the Norwegian fishery protection ship *Nordkapp* approached and ordered the crew to surrender. The Germans refused and as the warning shots were fired, the captain scuttled his ship; thirty-four Germans were captured and five escaped.[55]

Three German transports carrying equipment had been steaming for Narvik. One, the *Bärenfels*, was successfully diverted to Bergen, arriving there on 10 April.

The British destroyer *Icarus* captured the *Alster* off Bødo that same day with its cargo of motorised transport for 88mm AT/AA guns, 150mm motorised artillery and 20mm AA guns. The equipment was turned over to the Norwegian army, giving the Norwegians some additional motorised transport. The ammunition supply ship *Rauenfels* arrived at the end of the unfolding First Battle of Narvik with disastrous results for it.[56]

The Germans were busily trying to consolidate their positions. General Dietl spoke with Commodore Bonte, who agreed to leave him two destroyers to help defend Narvik since so many of the light field guns had been lost or had not arrived. Dietl had only three mountain field pieces, eighteen machine-guns, plus twenty-seven light and twelve heavy mortars. Two flamethrowers were also available. The troops had twenty days of food on hand but that situation would be partly rectified in the coming days.[57]

By evening confusing reports about the situation in Narvik were being received by both sides. In Germany it was thought that the Norwegians were encircling the Germans. News coming from Britain had Swedish troops expelling the Germans from Narvik. Colonel Weiss at Trondheim radioed and asked General Dietl if such news was correct because of the difficulty in radio communication with Narvik and that this was of great concern at the XXI Army Group headquarters.[58]

Bonte was somewhat secure in his position, even with the lack of Norwegian coastal batteries, because of the three German U-boats in the immediate area. In truth, the U-boats and their faulty torpedoes, along with the very heavy weather, were unable to protect his command. Bonte thought he was so well protected that he offered a berth on board to Dietl, but Dietl declined. Dietl was very involved in activities in and around Narvik. Bonte decided not to try to leave Narvik with any of the refuelled ships until 10 April, a costly decision. Bonte's lack of urgency to depart may have been due in part to simple exhaustion after the harrowing voyage to Narvik in dreadful conditions.

\* \* \*

Captain B. A. W. Warburton-Lee, commanding the British 2nd Destroyer Flotilla, had been placed on detached duty from the battlecruiser *Renown*'s squadron. He received orders at 09:52 on 9 April from Admiral Charles Forbes to proceed to Narvik and make certain no enemy troops landed there.[59] As he threaded his way through the islands towards Narvik, Warburton-Lee questioned some local pilots and citizens (including at least one small boy who gave accurate information that was discounted because of his youth) at Tranøy, just south-west of Narvik in the outer Vestfjord. They informed him that at least one German submarine and six, maybe nine, ships bigger than his destroyers, in two groups, had been seen heading for Narvik. He learned that a U-boat had been seen in Ofot fjord (true) and that the fjord was probably mined (false). He radioed this information to London, where earlier that morning Churchill at the Admiralty had announced that he thought possibly *one* German ship had slipped by the British navy and had arrived at Narvik.[60] The Admiralty now sent orders directly to Warburton-Lee (and forwarded a copy on to Vice Admiral W. J. 'Jock' Whitworth). Warburton-Lee was informed by the Admiralty that 'press reports' indicated a few troops from one ship had landed at Narvik. If he thought it was possible, the flotilla was to capture the (non-existent) coastal batteries at the entrance of Ofot Fjord, as well as Narvik.[61] Warburton-Lee received other reports and orders as he proceeded toward Narvik, wisely ignoring some that would have harmed his mission. Most of the messages came from distant London and the Admiralty, including one suggesting that the Norwegian coastal defence ships *Eidsvold* and *Norge* were now under German operational command. At least the Admiralty did radio that whatever decision Warburton-Lee made, they would support it.[62] Warburton-Lee was now joined by the *Hostile* to flesh out his squadron to five destroyers.[63]

Vice Admiral Whitworth considered, then ordered and then quickly rescinded the reinforcement of Warburton-Lee. Whitworth almost detached the small light cruiser *Penelope* with three large 'Tribal' class destroyers (armed with eight 4.7in guns in four turrets) and one 'K' class destroyer (six 4.7in guns disposed in three turrets). In turn, the Admiralty directly ordered Warburton-Lee to Narvik, thus leaving Whitworth out of the loop. That hampered Whitworth from issuing any additional orders.[64] Whitworth decided that in the heavy weather it would be problematical that they would arrive at dawn to join with Warburton-Lee and might confuse the issue – as it could lead to friendly fire accidents. In turn, such a deployment would leave his two battlecruisers with an inadequate screening force. In the event, the *Penelope* detachment did arrive off the entrance to the fjord at the end of the battle to receive the retreating British flotilla.

Warburton-Lee's flotilla consisted of the flagship *Hardy*, *Hunter*, *Hotspur*, *Havock* and *Hostile* – all of the same class. The *Hardy* was designed as a Destroyer Leader; it was slightly bigger than the other four, carried a larger crew and sported one additional 4.7in gun. The four sister ships were built as part of the 1934 programme (along with the *Hardy*) and each was armed with four 4.7in guns in individual turrets, eight 21in torpedoes in two mounts and could steam at 32 knots with a crew of 145 men. The average age of the crews was about 20 years old. Though given a design speed of 36 knots, in everyday operations they were not able to attain it. The ships' AA batteries and the light guns on board all saw action against the German destroyers.

After some deliberation Warburton-Lee informed the Admiralty and Forbes of his intentions with the signal 'Intending attacking at dawn, high water'.[65] Dawn would give the light in his favour (to the east), while the high water would be insurance against possible mines. After an officers' conference, Warburton-Lee did issue fairly precise orders for the coming action. Just past midnight all ships were to be at action stations. Action was to be opened immediately upon sighting an enemy destroyer or submarine. The ships would approach in a tight quarter-line[66] ahead, allowing for all five warships to train their forward turrets at any enemy sighted ahead. Three destroyers, led by the flagship, were to attack shipping (possibly carrying German troops and equipment according to the Admiralty) and

*Example of quarter-line formation.*

enemy destroyers in Narvik, while one was on scout duty for German destroyers further up Ofot Fjord and one was held in reserve – the latter two if required were detailed to stand by to lay down a smokescreen. Ships were to allocate a platoon-sized landing party from each ship if Narvik was to be occupied.

Warburton-Lee proceeded in thick weather towards Narvik. It was snowing and station keeping was difficult with visibility limited at best to 400yd. There were several near collisions. At least one Norwegian ship, running with full lights, passed *through* the formation during its approach.

The Germans received one report at about 08:22 on 9 April from the *U-51* off Narvik, which had sighted Warburton-Lee's squadron, but as so often in this campaign, the squadron was sighted while steaming away from Narvik, so the report caused Bonte no concern. Later, two other U-boats, directly off the entrance of Ofot fjord, failed to sight the passing British flotilla due to the snowstorm.

German intelligence at this point of the war could decipher about a third of British naval signals, but even with some signals from Warburton-Lee's squadron sent *en clair*, the Germans were as yet unaware of the British approach.[67] The *Diether von Roeder* was guarding the immediate entrance to Ofot Fjord with crews at battle stations, but it was posted there primarily to scout for enemy submarines. At dawn the captain of the *Roeder* decided to retire, even before a relief ship had arrived, leaving the entrance unguarded. The *Roeder* ran parallel with the *Hardy* in the darkness, slowly heading into the harbour at 8 knots. For once the Germans would be the surprised party.

At 03:48, Warburton-Lee slowed to 6 knots to allow a little more of the dawn to illuminate the fjord. The *Roeder* had moved ahead of the British flotilla and was entering inner Narvik harbour when the British flotilla, steaming ever so slowly and now staying close to land, approached the crowded harbour. The ships came in hugging the land on the south because of the British torpedo mechanism, which required the torpedo mounts to be locked in a position perfectly abeam (perpendicular to the ship). British torpedoes were fired in the direction set by the ship itself while German torpedoes could be angled once fired from their tubes. As the British destroyers swung across the harbour, the torpedoes were fired as they bore on various targets. Because of reports that merchant ships might be holding German troops and equipment, they were considered prime targets. In the coming battle many of them would be hit and sunk.

The *Hardy* crept in first, followed by the *Hunter* and the *Havock,* with substantial sea room between them. The other two destroyers were detached, steaming off together with the *Hotspur* to stop any German warships that might approach from the north-western quarter; the *Hostile* remained close by as a reserve. Both were detailed to respond to any gunfire from the non-existent German-occupied coastal batteries.[68] The snow had stopped and visibility was about 1 mile. There were five German destroyers in the crowded harbour, two on either side of the *Jan Wellem* being fuelled (the *Künne* on the inboard and *Lüdemann* closest to the approaching British). The *Roeder* had anchored at the north end of the harbour, farthest away from the approaching British destroyers.

As the *Hardy* edged in, it sighted numerous merchant ships but at about 04:30 its crew spotted the German destroyers, the *Anton Schmitt* and the flagship *Wilhelm Heidkamp* with Commodore Bonte on board asleep. They were anchored about 250 and 500yd south, respectively, from the *Wellem*. They made easy targets, so Warburton-Lee ordered, 'Well, get on with it then'.[69]

The *Hardy* launched three torpedoes. The first one missed the destroyers but hit the bow of a transport. The second hit aft on the flagship and the resulting explosion ignited the after magazine, instantaneously killing Bonte and over seventy other sailors. The third torpedo missed. The British guns opened up but were not very effective. Warburton-Lee ordered 20 knots; four other torpedoes launched by the *Hardy* missed and hit along the harbour edge damaging the ore wharfs, as the torpedo-officer did not anticipate the high speed. She also laid smoke as she exited further lowering the visibility.[70]

Next into the fray came *Hunter.* It fired two salvoes for a total of eight torpedoes, aiming also at the merchant ships as per Warburton-Lee's orders, firing with its guns at the same time. One torpedo hit the *Anton Schmitt* and that hit finally woke the captain who was very soundly asleep. That the flagship had already suffered a tremendous explosion, and the captain of the *Schmitt* was still asleep suggests that lack of sleep had a debilitating effect on the German officers and men.

The last ship in the British line was the *Havock.* As it approached it fired three torpedoes. Of these, two hit two merchant ships, while the third again struck the *Schmitt*, which sank in about a minute with the loss of sixty-three sailors. This hit and the resulting explosion on the *Schmitt* caused the engine-room machinery on the *Künne*, which had just cast off from the *Jan Wellem*, to seize. The *Künne* was not able to move for 45 minutes and when it did, it tied up at Narvik's main pier.

At first most Germans sailors thought they were under air attack. It took a few minutes of the gunfire from the *Hunter* before they realised they it was a surface attack. In the dark, the falling snow and smoke from the explosions, it was difficult for either side to see each other and there was much more firing of guns than hits landed. But in this first run in, the fighting was all in favour of the British. They were untouched by German gunfire.

A German guard on one of the merchant ships that was near the passing *Havock* emptied his revolver at the ship and was machine-gunned for his bravado. The *Havock* was straddled by the gunfire but not hit as it steamed out of the inner harbour. The *Hotspur*, meanwhile, had returned from searching for nearby shore batteries (though it had exchanged small-arms fire with German troops in Narvik) and had laid a smoke screen for the *Hunter* and the *Havock* to pass through as they exited the harbour. The *Hostile* had also returned to the main harbour after noting the absence of shore batteries in the immediate area. It came to a stop and, at 7,000yd and in terrible sighting conditions, opened a deliberate fire on the *Roeder*, which returned fire. The *Hostile* was the better shot and hit the *Roeder* twice, though three torpedoes from the *Hostile* missed.

Each of the three ships had taken about 10 minutes to pass through the harbour and they now assembled outside. Warburton-Lee decided that a second run past the inner harbour entrance was in order. Also, he was thinking there were only six German destroyers present and all of them might very well be accounted for. The British launched the second attack in which they took the *Roeder* under fire and heavily damaged it. In return, the *Roeder* fired off eight torpedoes and several of them ran *under* three of the British destroyers. The faulty German torpedoes, again, carried a heavy price, though they may have been set for too deep a run due to the shallow draft of the smaller British destroyers and their riding high due to the fuel consumption of the past few days.[71]

Fire slackened on both sides as visibility worsened until only three German destroyers were still firing. The *Roeder*, *Künne* and *Lüdemann* would not score a single hit during this part of the action. No British warship had been touched. But reinforcements were on their way. The other German destroyers had reacted when the *Lüdemann* radioed a tardy alarm to the rest of the German command at 05:15. As a result, two approached from the west, having escaped detection when the British had entered Ofot Fjord, while Captain Erich 'Pasha' Bey, commander of the 4th Destroyer Flotilla, approached in quarterline from the east, though not at high speed due to the lack of fuel.

Warburton-Lee had drawn off and held a second conference. Possibly, he thought, all the German destroyers were accounted for. One of his destroyers, the *Hostile,* had a complete complement of torpedoes. It was thought possible (though highly unlikely given the German ground strength) that the British might even put ashore a landing party and recapture Narvik. Certainly this was not the time to retire. So at 06:44 the ships formed line ahead, the *Hardy* followed by the *Havock, Hunter, Hotspur* and the *Hostile,* all steaming at 20 knots. The *Künne* and *Lüdemann* took them under fire as they neared the inner harbour entrance as it was easier seeing *out* of the harbour than *into* it. The *Roeder* was too busy trying to stay afloat to join in. The *Lüdemann* fired four torpedoes, all of which missed, with yet at least another torpedo running under the *Hostile.* The *Hostile* approached the closest and launched four torpedoes into the dark smoky harbour. It took a shell hit as it passed beyond the harbour entrance that caused little damaged.

Bey had just learned from a radio message from the *Lüdemann* that the *Heidkamp* had sunk and Bonte was dead and he was now in command. He opened fire on the British at 7,000yd with the six forward guns from his three destroyers. More importantly in terms of influencing the action, Warburton-Lee, who was one of the first men to sight these three German ships, thought there were four ships approaching and that one was a light cruiser. Doctrine rightly stated that a cruiser was not a warship the British destroyers could take on primarily with gunfire, especially with surprise lost and torpedo complements so low. It was time to steam for home. At this stage of this running gunnery duel there were apparently no other hits scored on either side. British fire was consistently short. Warburton-Lee sent a signal that a cruiser and three new destroyers were present, and at 06:00 Whitworth now ordered the *Penelope* and four destroyers to steam to the head of Ofot Fjord. The *Penelope*'s orders were 'support retirement of 2nd Destroyer Flotilla, counter-attacking enemy force as necessary . . .'.[72] On his own initiative, the commander of the minelaying force detached one of the fully armed British destroyers, the *Greyhound*, which had been covering the force off Vestfjord, to join the *Penelope*'s force.

As the British in line ahead steamed toward the open sea with the three German destroyers in pursuit, the last two German destroyers hove into sight at the head of the British line. The *Thiele* led the way with the *Arnim* following about 1,000yd behind. As they came on they received a signal from Bey. Thinking they were faced with a much larger British force, Bey ordered them to 'break out to the west' since they at least had been fuelled. Captain Max-Eckart Wolff of the *Thiele* decided to ignore the order and instead steamed across the fjord to cross the rapidly approaching British line.

The *Hardy*, making 30 knots, had sighted the approaching German destroyers and its captain at first thought they were reinforcing British light cruisers. But when the German ships began to turn to expose their broadsides, the truth struck home. Crossing the 'T' of the British line allowed the Germans to put all ten of their 5in guns against just two from the bow of the *Hardy*. At 4,500yd the Germans opened fire and on the *Thiele*'s third salvo began scoring hits on the *Hardy*.[73]

Bey's other destroyers had slowed their pursuit as they sighted torpedoes from the *Lüdemann* in front of them and they were taken under fire from the *Germans* in the inner harbour of Narvik. Though no hits were scored, it took some minutes and busy radio signals for the shelling to stop so Bey could continue his pursuit.

At the British van, the five destroyers were now firing on the two German destroyers. Warburton-Lee had just signalled, 'Keep on engaging enemy'.[74] The *Thiele* fired two torpedoes that the *Havock* combed, and the *Hostile* launched torpedoes back. Aimed with the assumption that the German ships were making 20 knots not their actual speed of 27 knots, the torpedoes passed between the two German destroyers.

The *Hardy* was now hit by at least two shells that destroyed the bridge. A contemporary account described the result:

The bridge of H.M.S. *Hardy* was hit and reduced to a shambles. Captain Warburton-Lee was mortally wounded. The only man on the bridge who was not killed or rendered unconscious was the captain's secretary, Paymaster-Lieutenant Stanning, and his left foot was useless ... Realizing that the ship was still steaming fast and without anybody at the helm, Paymaster-Lieutenant Stanning dragged himself to the wheelhouse ... [,] took the wheel himself and steered the ship, looking through a shell-hole.[75]

A furious action was now being fought at 3,000yd range, but with only a minor hit on the *Havock*. The *Hostile* was lagging behind, having closed the harbour as closely as it had on the last run by the harbour entrance. As it passed through the smoke of battle, it sighted the *Thiele* at about 5,000yd and fired its remaining torpedoes, but all missed. The *Hardy*, the ship leading the line, was slowly regaining control as it now sped toward the snow-covered, rocky shore. Paymaster Stanning had managed to begin steering away from the shore when the ship's engines gave out. The *Hardy* coasted ashore and without a boat its crew swam for shore. The wounded captain, being pulled through the icy water, offered encouragement to his crew, 'Swim, lads, swim!' Warburton-Lee would die before reaching shore.[76] Cold and wet, the survivors were taken in by local residents in just a handful of houses – one of which gave refuge to eighty sailors trying to get warm. Many wounded needed medical attention, and shortly some were transported to the nearby hospital. The destroyer *Ivanhoe* would later successfully evacuate most of the crew. For his conduct, Warburton-Lee received the first Victoria Cross of the war.

Wolff now led the two destroyers in a loop to reverse his easterly course and follow the British, staying on their van, and maintaining a heavy fire on them. He thought Bey would pressure the rear of the British line, but Bey was just now safely passing the entrance to Narvik and trying to preserve what little fuel he had left. It was now about 06:05.

Running on parallel courses, with the *Havock* leading the British, both sides began to hit. The *Arnim* took some hits that reduced its speed. The *Thiele* was hit seven times; it lost a gun and suffered flooding.

The British were suffering hits as well. The *Hunter*, second ship in line, was losing speed and was on fire. The *Hostile*, behind it, was having difficulty steering. But the captain of the *Havock*, leading the line, decided to help out the rear by crossing in front of his own line and placing his ship between the British and the *Thiele* and *Arnim*. As it raced down the line, the *Havock* could see the state of the squadron. The captain considered closing the range with the Germans, but several of the *Havock*'s own guns were out of commission. Instead, he closed in behind the *Hostile* to be the new end of the line, and for this daring manoeuvre suffered little more than some splinter damage. Maybe these four could all get home.

The *Thiele* and *Arnim* had been pulling ahead and now Wolff closed the van of the British line. He concentrated gunfire on the lead destroyer, the *Hunter*. Range dropped to 1,700yd and even the 37mm and 20mm AA guns from the German destroyers opened fire. The *Thiele* fired three torpedoes as well and one may have hit near the *Hunter*'s bridge. In any event, the *Hunter* was savaged. It involuntarily swung out of line toward the two German destroyers. Under repeated shell hits, its engines were knocked out, flames shooting skyward forward and the ship came to a stop.

Following behind about 1,000yd back was the *Havock* still moving at close to 30 knots when the *Hunter* was seen stopped ahead. *Havock* was unable to avoid the collision and sliced into the rear of the *Hunter*. The *Hunter* was doomed and would sink in the icy waters with the loss of more than 100 men, though the Germans would make a determined attempt to save those they could after the battle. The two rear ships steamed past their entangled compatriots but as the *Havock* slowly steamed off they turned to cover its withdrawal. The Germans were now about 8,000yd distant. Bey's command was just now coming up and he ordered his flagship, the *Zenker*, to close and investigate the beached *Hardy*. Bey fired on the *Hardy* as even late in the action the crippled ship had fired its last torpedo, which missed. Wolff's *Thiele* and the *Arnim* limped away from the action. Only the *Koellner* followed the retreating British but not too closely. The battle was over by 06:30.

As the British squadron retired it came upon the German ammunition supply ship *Rauenfels* steaming into the fjord. The *Havock* quickly took it under fire and the *Rauenfels* ran ashore where it blew up. Smoke from the explosion reached up 3,000ft into the air. Now the *Penelope* and its destroyers joined the British squadron. The damaged *Hotspur* escorted by the *Hostile* travelled to Skjelfjord in the Lofoten Islands to undergo emergency repairs. Other British ships would be joining it in the future. The report from this relieving squadron noted the presence of five or six large German destroyers and possible 6in gunfire from the shore.[77]

Vice Admiral Whitworth had signalled to London that in Narvik there were a German cruiser, five destroyers and at least one submarine. His goal was to prevent the arrival of any German reinforcements and the destruction of the German force there.

By the end of the naval battle two German destroyers had been sunk, five others had been damaged and eight merchant ships were sunk. The mayor of Narvik saw from his home, 'one German destroyer was afire from stem to stern. Its engines were still operating but it circled aimlessly without direction or plan'.[78] The human losses had been heavy (the number of dead is in parentheses): *Heidkamp* (eighty-one) and *Schmitt* sunk (fifty); *Roeder* hit five times and not seaworthy (thirteen); *Lüdemann* one gun disabled (two); *Künne* (nine); *Thiele* one magazine flooded (thirteen); *Arnim* limited seaworthiness (two); and the other three ships were undamaged and approximately half of their ammunition had been expended.[79]

Of the British ships, the *Hunter* was lost with 108 dead. The *Hardy* was sunk and had lost nineteen dead. The *Hotspur* had suffered twenty dead, while the other two had not suffered any losses. It had certainly been a rough action.

* * *

The Swedes deployed their 1st Division along the rail line from the port of Luleå on the Gulf of Bothnia to the Norwegian border to monitor events going on in Norway. They also mined their northern and central ore fields for demolition in case of attack. In the coming weeks, Germany employed several forms of transport to support its beleaguered garrison at Narvik. These included U-boats and long-range Do26 flying-boats. The Germans also expected limited help by use of the Swedish rail network.[80]

Sweden tried to resist pressure to allow Germany to send troops and supplies to Narvik via Sweden. However, Sweden was intimidated by Germany's strength and actions. Some supplies were smuggled north in Red Cross transports and 'normal' non-military supplies were allowed to pass from Sweden to the Narvik area. About 280 to 300 German soldiers arrived via this route beginning on 19 April, often disguised as Red Cross staff. Among these soldiers were key radio personnel, who helped maintain co-ordination and communication with General Falkenhorst at Oslo. Additionally, ammunition, military equipment and weapons were hidden among the medical and 'non-combatant' materials. Demolition experts were also smuggled in and were used to destroy key sections of the ore railway when the Germans later began their retreat toward the Swedish border. Wounded and unneeded personnel, primarily about 500 German civilian merchant sailors, were sent south from Narvik through Sweden. Among them and travelling illegally was the wounded U-boat Captain Viktor Schültz and the crew of the sunken *U-64*. A bomb from the Swordfish scout plane of the battleship *Warspite* would sink the submarine on the 13th.[81] Until 20 August 1943, more than 2,000,000 German soldiers would transit Sweden to various positions, both in Finland and in Norway.[82] Both this disregard of Swedish neutrality and Sweden's acquiescence created bitterness in Norway that would last into the postwar period.

\* \* \*

At the end of the first full day of battle Denmark had fallen and Norway was reeling. German reinforcements were beginning to pour ashore at Oslo. Smaller numbers of troops were being airlifted throughout Norway. Raeder had seen the first two stages of his naval plan completed. The warships had arrived at their ports, had penetrated the defences and were now readying for the journey or already on their way home to Germany. The first decisive phase of the battle was over and Germany had won. The Germans had lodgements at all the key ports called for in the invasion plan. The question was; could the Allies mount a significant counter-attack?

## CHAPTER 11

# The Aftermath: Allied Reactions and German Exploitation

The ignorance of most members of a pacifist government about elementary military matters can be understood, but the error of the Norwegian government lay in not transferring responsibility for military matters at as early a stage as possible to those competent to act.

Paul M. Hayes[1]

It is now pertinent to examine what the three major players did at this point in the crisis, primarily in southern and central Norway. This is where the bulk of the Norwegian army was located and where it would be destroyed. The focus will be on naval actions that had a direct impact on the land campaign for central Norway.

The initial German plan had been executed with great success. The Norwegians and the Allies were in disarray and fighting the clock as German reinforcements poured into Norway. Under these extremely adverse conditions the Allies would have to decide where to mount a counter-invasion and then to implement it.

The Norwegians had resolved, with some fits and starts over the coming days, to resist the invasion and Colonel Otto Ruge, once in command would attempt to slow the German advance until Allied troops could arrive. Ruge's primary defence would be in the two central valleys that lead out from Oslo towards the west and north-west. The Gudbrandsdalen is on the south-west side, while the Østerdalen is on the north-east side and follows the two rail lines shown on the map of Norway (see p. xvi). Ruge wanted to retain as much territory as he could while requesting that the Allies, in conjunction with local Norwegian forces, recapture Trondheim. The Bergen region was rejected as it is more rugged and it is difficult to advance inland from, lacked a major airfield and was too close to the major German-occupied airbase at Sola.[2]

During these dark, difficult days both sides had to make key decisions in a time-critical environment. As the mayor of Narvik wrote, 'After three days there were six front lines.'[3] Each of these will be addressed in turn.

\* \* \*

Hitler had won. Neither Hitler nor the Allies had realised it at this moment, but the success of the invasion and the resistance to it was so weak and slow that

Germany had secured both Norway and Denmark as assets for the German war machine. Only a sustained and truly massive, co-ordinated and immediate Allied response could have changed the outcome at this point. The Allies were incapable of mounting such an effort.

In Germany by 08:55 on the 9th an extensive report from the headquarters of Army Group XXI had indicated that the invasion from Oslo to Kristiansand was succeeding. The Führer's orders were accomplished. There were some failures, such as the loss of the *Blücher*, the inability to send surface ships to reinforce Narvik, Bergen and Trondheim[4] and the fact that the Norwegian royal family had been allowed to slip away. Moreover, the ammunition situation was difficult in Bergen, Trondheim and Narvik.[5]

That evening at 18:30 an official communiqué was released announcing, 'The occupation of Norway has been carried out according to plan.'[6] Hitler was extremely happy and thought the campaign was over. However, he and Germany would have several crises to face before its final outcome was played out.

The German situation in Trondheim and Narvik had been made worse by the failure of most of the Tanker Group carrying fuel and the Export Group transports carrying men and equipment to arrive successfully at their destinations. This would severely limit the ability of the Germans to exploit their positions from those two ports.[7] However, both ports would receive some air and naval help from Germany.

At Trondheim a few He115s would arrive in the late morning of 9 April, and once the airfield at Værnes was secured, light artillery, five infantry and one pioneer battalion (assault engineers) would be airlifted in over a period of days.[8] The German naval contribution consisted of a disguised trawler, the *Schiff 37*, and six U-boats that were used as transports. The first was sunk and a second trawler, the *Schiff 26*, was later captured bound for Narvik carrying mines, torpedoes, supplies and munitions – both on 26 April. Documents and cipher materials, which were helpful to the staff at Bletchley Park, were found on *Schiff 26*.[9] The employment of U-boats was in part down to the situation in Norway's distant German garrisons but also due to the failure of German torpedo attacks against Allied ships. They would bring in to Trondheim 270 tons of supplies over the next few weeks. Again, this weapons failure influenced the operational actions of Germany.

Both sides at various points in the war would employ submarines as transports. The policy dated back to the First World War when German submarines were used to supply rebel *Senussi* in Italian-occupied Libya and the use of the merchant submarines like *Deutschland*.

Each day that went by allowed the Germans to strengthen the defences at Trondheim. Before any link-up with Oslo, this isolated German command could only utilise the existing Norwegian defences, jury-rig other defences with resources at hand and add to it with what arrived primarily by air. The Luftwaffe was a powerful trump card that could and was called upon by the Germans at Trondheim.[10]

While there was much fighting in store, the German position was extremely good. The war would be decided in south and central Norway. The Norwegian army fielded there was split into largely uncoordinated *ad hoc* units in the process of trying to mobilise with German troops often between the various units. Furthermore, the Germans controlled many of the Norwegian army depots and were about to occupy additional ones.

All major Norwegian communication hubs were in German hands. The spokes reaching out from these hubs, connecting to other hubs, could be exploited for eventual link-ups. The next few days would see German columns issuing forth to pacify the nation and most importantly link up with each other as they defeated the Norwegian army. The main German effort would be from Oslo. The first German goal after seizing Oslo was to clear the Oslofjord region and the immediate east and south-east to the Swedish border and the sea. This quick success would result in the destruction of the mobilising Norwegian 1st Infantry Division. After that was accomplished, the main goal of the German effort would be to link up with Trondheim, Bergen and ultimately Narvik. A lesser effort would be in linking up with Stavanger along the coast and would result in the destruction of the binary (two regiment) Norwegian 3rd Infantry Division.

Barring a strict maritime blockade, seemingly impossible for the Allies to mount in the face of German airpower, equipment and supplies assigned to Norway could continue to pour in by sea to Oslo. The German troops, key supplies and important smaller pieces of equipment would be impossible to stop as most would now be arriving by air in quantities that the Allies did not expect. This was to be a massive airlift, the largest the world had seen to date. The Allies could only bring in their troops and supplies by sea at secondary ports in harsh wintery conditions, often close to German air bases and subject to air attacks. This German advantage would only grow with each passing day.

If the German garrison in Trondheim was relieved, it would be just a matter of time for northern Norway to fall unless the Allies made a supreme effort. After 10 May with the invasion of the Low Countries and France such an already extremely unlikely attempt to send additional Allied forces to northern Norway would be made impossible.

The Allied crisis will be examined first. The British Official historian later wrote,

The ports which the Germans seized on 9th April included each of the four biggest towns in Norway and a clear majority of the principal mobilization centres. In a single swoop they had established themselves at a series of points stretching round the coast from Oslo to Bergen; at Trondheim, 250 miles north of Bergen; and at Narvik, 360 miles north of Trondheim. It is hoped that a separate account ... of the crucial events in and near the capital, followed by a still more cursory note of what happened in other areas from south to north, will not obscure the fact that the simultaneity of the attacks was itself a most important element in achieving the bewilderment of the Norwegian people and the success of the German aims.[11]

Captain B. H. Liddell Hart would write at the time, 'Once the west coast ports were occupied it was obvious that the Norwegians' capacity for sustained resistance was gravely endangered.'[12] Historian Correlli Barnett, after noting that the British had to reassemble a force to land at Narvik, Trondheim and Bergen, as the forces originally allocated for those ports under Plan R4 now lacked for the most part both escort and organisation, has argued that, 'From this moment forward, therefore, the Norwegian campaign was a lost cause, for the initial errors and consequent loss of time, fatal in themselves, were inevitably to lead to half-cock operations hastily mounted with scratch forces.'[13] British historian Sir Llewellyn Woodward later wrote,

> For the British a Scandinavian expedition offered a chance of using the greater mobility given to them by sea power. Unfortunately the project suffered from many of the defects that had caused disaster to British overseas expeditions in the early stages of the previous war. The circumstances in which it had been first put forward quickly changed. It took too little account of enemy counter-moves. It was neither pushed rapidly to execution nor abandoned when the opportunity had passed. From first to last it was an affair of improvisation with insufficient study behind it.[14]

This was a new situation, one that had not been planned for and was certainly unexpected. The most immediate reaction on the part of the British and the French on the 9th was to determine what effort they could mount and where they should strike. This would be coloured by the success the navy would enjoy against the German destroyers now stranded at Narvik.

Initially, the British wanted to rush north to Narvik. The problem with this decision was that it focused on northern Norway, the economic prize, but contradicted previous planning that rightly saw central Norway as the key to victory. As Captain B. H. Liddell Hart wrote at the time, 'If relief was to come while they [the Norwegians] were still holding out, it was clear that it must be quick. . . . If ever there has been a case where audacity is required to counter and retrieve the effects of the invaders' initial audacity, the Norwegian campaign provides it. Time is already slipping away.'[15] Without control of central Norway the Allies could not throw the Germans out. The decision to go to Narvik was made on 9 April. The decision to move into central Norway to retake Trondheim was made on 14 April and by then it was too late.[16] The Allies were hindered by a chaotic chain of command. A proposed plan or directive that involved the French had to go through six gatekeepers to get approval. One commentator has said of the British in 1940 that their 'command structure was not founded on any philosophical or functional principle. The organs of control evolved by adaptation to political pressures and compromises with each other.'[17]

Information was deficient as well. When attacking *southern* Norwegian positions, RAF Bomber Command relied on the 1912 revised edition of Baedeker's, more than likely the same edition Colonel General Nikolaus von

Falkenhorst purchased at a bookstall when considering accepting the position as commander. Topographical information, while available to the Allies, was not properly distributed and the planes operating from the *Furious* had to rely on Admiralty charts of Narvik, which gave no information on contours and mountains. Intelligence was so bad that Chamberlain informed Parliament as late as 16:00 on the 9th that the Germans might have taken Larvik (on the west at the entrance to Oslofjord) and not Narvik.[18]

Information from ULTRA was very limited at this point in the war. Allied intelligence from Bletchley Park was able to read the German army requests for air support beginning on 10 April. But this information, though of immediate operational import, was for the most part ignored by the services that had not yet grasped what this wonderful tool ULTRA was.[19]

This contrasted poorly with the Germans. It caused Admiral Charles Forbes on 15 June, after the loss of the aircraft carrier *Glorious* and two destroyers, to comment to the Admiralty that,

> The enemy reconnoiter Scapa daily if they consider it necessary. Our reconnaissances [*sic*] of the enemy's main bases are few and far between ... It is most galling that the enemy should know just where our ships ... always are, whereas we generally learn where his major forces are when they sink one or more of our ships.[20]

They also had to factor in their disorganised forces. Units had to reform and re-embark before operations could commence. Additionally, the weather was appalling. It was still winter on land once one left the coast and at sea conditions were generally poor.

The several battalions already in place on 8 April, which had been off-loaded from the cruisers and transports they had shipped on, well illustrate the confusion suffered by the British. A British force would later land with field telephones, while the other force landed with the cable – and the generator was left back in Scotland.[21] The battalions had also been designed for unopposed landings and lacked artillery and tanks. Those same troops would end up in Norway, but several days after 9 April, incomplete and missing essential equipment.

On the ground in Norway the Allies would find that radio sets lacked range in the high mountains. This was complicated by the misplaced fear that Quislings had penetrated the civilian telephone service. In many cases in April the Allies would rely on runners to deliver orders and this would lead to poor communications and orders arriving late.[22]

The Germans had another advantage as the Allies tended to inflate overall German troop numbers. These over-estimates occurred for Narvik, Trondheim and Bergen. Major George Fielding Eliot, a war correspondent and prolific military writer of the period, estimated a minimum of 5,000 German troops were present at Trondheim, possibly as many as 8,000 by late April. There were approximately 4,000 present and many were tied down to coastal defence and garrison duty.[23]

Chief of the Imperial General Staff General Sir Edmund Ironside stated in the meeting on 9 April that the troops were not to go ashore at a contested landing site especially in light of German air superiority, as they were not equipped for an opposed landing. This position precluded a direct assault at Narvik, Trondheim or Bergen.[24] Ironside argued that no *ad hoc* force could be simply gathered and thrown ashore. If the Germans had anywhere near 3,000–4,000 troops ashore at Narvik as Churchill indicated at the meeting, then in Ironside's view planning and time was required.[25] As Graham Rhys-Jones has put it, 'orders being drawn up in the War Office reflected the cautious and deliberate approach that Ironside had demanded'.[26]

The disaster of the 1915 Dardanelles campaign in the First World War cast a long shadow over British amphibious operations. No one wanted to repeat that exercise in futility and loss of life, even on a much smaller scale. The idea of putting even a tiny force on the ground from the sea and the disruptive impact it would have had on German operations at Narvik, Stavanger, Bergen or Trondheim was vastly outweighed in the mind of the British command structure by the potential of avoidable casualties. It would seem that an opportunity was lost here. Though still markedly inadequate, especially in terms of airpower, when compared to the German forces an intervention in the central and southern portions of Norway might have resulted in a stronger Norwegian response and better mobilisation. As opposed to Plan R4, this intervention would have been welcomed by Norwegian forces. It by no means meant the Germans could have been turned back, but it offered a better chance than what was done.

Upon returning from sea with the Home Fleet Admiral Forbes signalled several suggestions to the Admiralty. He recommended that the Norwegian ports be blockaded, in conjunction with the mining of Danish and southern Norwegian waters. He wanted the RAF to carry out bombing attacks against the newly acquired Luftwaffe airbases. Forbes argued for additional Allied troops to land and support the Norwegians. He also recommended destroyer sweeps into the Skagerrak during poor weather. All of his points would be implemented to one degree or another.[27]

The Allied effort in Norway would essentially be run from Whitehall. No joint commander for all the services was chosen and it was argued, probably correctly, that there was no single place in Norway that was suitable for a major headquarters. But Norway was a large country and Allied efforts would suffer from poor co-ordination.[28]

The initial Allied effort would involve three well-trained British battalions of the 24th Scots Guards Brigade, a French brigade of alpine troops later to be reinforced and two brigades of partially trained and equipped territorial troops. The 'territorial' units were British reserve units that had been mobilised at the beginning of the war and tended to be second-line troops. They suffered from the added fact that the British had ordered the force doubled in size in 1939 thus diluting an already deficient force.[29]

The attack on Narvik would become known as Operation 'Rupert' and would have for the naval command a hero of the First World War, the 67-year-old Admiral

of the Fleet the Earl of Cork and Orrery. On 12 April Churchill appointed the Earl
of Cork and Orrery as naval Commander-in-Chief of all naval units within 100
miles of Narvik. At the time of his appointment he was not given any written
orders. This move on Narvik siphoned off ships, including the *Warspite*, from the
Home Fleet, as additional units were being transferred to the Mediterranean to
face a soon-belligerent Italy.[30]

One result of the Second Battle of Narvik (discussed below) and its success was
the idea of a direct assault on Trondheim. For the Allies, the plan to seize and hold
Trondheim would become Operation 'Hammer'. The Norwegian government
formally requested such an intervention on 14 April and in Norwegian eyes this
was a key move.

Within the government the chief proponent for this would be an overbearing
and quite forceful Churchill, backed up with public support by another elderly
First World War hero, Admiral of the Fleet Sir Roger Keyes. Churchill wanted
to view the landings at Namsos and Åndalsnes as diversionary and giving heart
to the Norwegians before making a direct naval assault on Trondheim proper.
Churchill envisioned having two aircraft carriers available to put 80 aircraft up
over Trondheim, while the navy and the army went in and landed with 7,000–
8,000 of the best troops available just to the east of Trondheim supported by a
strong surface naval force including battleships. Hammer was to be led by the
navy moving in and landing two Canadian battalions to seize the coastal batteries
guarding the approach to Trondheim, while the 15th Infantry Brigade of well-
trained units landed near the city itself. Churchill wanted to do this as quickly as
possible and thought the proposed naval bombardment of Sola airfield planned
for the 17th by the heavy cruiser *Suffolk* would greatly aid the project.[31]

The Admiralty staff opposed this. They noted a lack of both the most up-to-date
local charts and high-explosive shells for their battleships (armour piercing made
up the vast majority of their ammunition).[32] But the Luftwaffe had little that could
seriously attack a battleship at this point in the war. It had only been a few days earlier that the *Königsberg* had been sunk solely by airpower (see below) and that was
a first. In the end this choice was overruled. Instead, there would be a two-pronged
attack at two smaller ports on each flank of Trondheim. One would be northwards
at Namsos, set for 14 April with the initial landing of some British Marines. The
other strike would to the south of Trondheim at Åndalsnes on 17 April.

The project ended up being delayed, the two landings at Namsos and Åndalsnes
failed to draw off German troops and a new date of 24 April was assigned to it.
Admiral Forbes said that such a direct attack could be accomplished with the
troops in landing craft. Forbes knew full well that at the time there were ten
such craft in Britain. The operation was called off and the 15th Infantry Brigade
ended up reinforcing the drive from Åndalsnes, and later covering the retreat.
The Official British Historian T. K. Derry would write, 'even with relatively small
forces, [we] could have won back the port'. He does suggest that in the face of
German airpower and with the lack of Allied air assets and AA guns they might
have won a pyrrhic victory.[33]

It has been argued that the Allies should have had diverted troops destined to Namsos to Narvik, but Narvik's ability to hold or fall depended on the results of the battle for central Norway and weather conditions that April were terrible. If Trondheim could have been recaptured and held in force, Narvik would have withered, as it was already withering, and fallen like a ripe fruit into the outstretched hands of the Allies. The outcome of the battle for Norway depended on seizing, holding and exploiting out from Trondheim.[34]

While many looked at the First World War operation at Gallipoli as a demonstration of amphibious operations, and thus did not want to repeat that disaster, the Japanese in the 1930s had conducted several successful amphibious operations in China. This was not lost on the Great Powers, and in Britain the 'Inter-Service Training and Development Centre' was established in 1937 to develop an amphibious programme. But this was all in its infancy. The fear of failure coloured Allied thinking for this possible operation.[35]

\* \* \*

As Operation 'Rupert' was taking shape, the Second Battle of Narvik would be fought which would destroy the German naval force there. Additionally, on 11 April the first air attack by carriers in the Second World War took place.

The aircraft carrier *Furious* steamed to the coast near Trondheim with the battleships *Rodney* (flag), *Valiant* and *Warspite*, along with three British cruisers and eighteen destroyers. The *Furious* lacked her fighters for this operation. The plan was to attack the Germans at Trondheim. Already present were four destroyers and a U-boat along with civilian transports. From 90 miles off the coast eighteen Swordfish went in but the depth settings for their torpedoes were not set properly, in part due to poor knowledge of the fjord, and no hits were made.[36]

The British sealed off the fjord entrance to Narvik with a close blockade and set up refuelling and temporary repairs for warships at nearby Skjelfjord. While the Admiralty suggested an early surface attack on the German destroyers at Narvik, the local commander decided to wait for additional reinforcements and to attack on the 12th. This date would later be moved up to the morning of the 13th. There were also reports that Norwegian submarines were in the immediate area which influenced Allied decision-making. They were present but ineffective.

The Germans attempted to airlift vital supplies to Major General Eduard Dietl's command. On 12th it began the first air supply to Dietl's troops and in the evening of the 13 April twelve Ju52 transport aircraft and one special Ju52 carrying signals equipment took off from Fornebu airport to Bardufoss' small airport. Two planes ran short of fuel and were redirected, while one was shot down by British naval anti-aircraft fire. The other Ju52s were compelled to divert to a nearby frozen lake because Bardufoss was still occupied by the Norwegians. One of the aeroplanes hit the ice and broke through, disappearing in the cold water. The others landed on the frozen surface of the lake and disgorged the 2nd Mountain Battery of the 112th regiment, but they were unable to fly back because the weather conditions turned to thaw and they were lost. A heavy cost for four old Skoda 150mm mountain guns with little ammunition that reached the depot of Elvegårdsmoen at about midnight. The radio equipment was unloaded and installed in Elvegårdsmoen and later moved to Narvik.[37]

A further two U-boats were ordered to the area, bringing a total of five operating off Narvik by the 12th but the troubled torpedo armament continued to plague their attacks. Admiral Karl Dönitz, who commanded the German U-boat force, had received enough reports on faulty torpedoes to issue an order on 12 April to the submarines. The impact detonator only was to be used against large enemy ships and the magnetic detonators against destroyers. It would take some time for all the U-boats to comply with the message issued.[38]

As for the German destroyers, the German naval command of Naval Group West ordered Captain Erich 'Pasha' Bey to send fuelled destroyers south, if not back to Germany then to Bergen or other points, but not Trondheim. Trondheim was already taxed with the presence of destroyers. Bey was very hesitant and had to be ordered to sortie with what he could. This was in part due to German B-Dienst radio interceptions that there was a strong British naval force off Narvik. Bey had only two fuelled destroyers ready to depart Narvik by the evening of the 10th. The *Zenker* and *Giese* attempted to run the blockade but they sighted the blockading light cruiser *Penelope* and accompanying destroyers so they fell back into the fjord. To add to Bey's troubles, two destroyers grounded over the coming days and the *Zenker* was one of them. It now could not maintain a speed above 20 knots (though it would exceed that during the battle on the 13th). Superfluous crews from the sunk or heavily damaged destroyers were organised into an armed shore party that performed garrison duties, allowing the mountain troops to operate on the front line. The early capture of the Norwegian arsenal at Elvegårdsmoen would be essential in supplying the hundreds of soon to be marooned German sailors, as it would equip them with warm clothing and fighting equipment.[39]

With each day the British gathered their forces for a decisive blow against the German destroyers. On the 12th the *Furious* launched two air attacks, this time with bombs instead of torpedoes. The first attack killed or wounded twenty-eight on land and two small captured Norwegian patrol craft, the *Senja* and the *Sars*, were also lost. In addition, two planes were shot down to the fully alert German AA crews. The second attack had to be aborted due to worsening weather conditions and one more Swordfish was lost in a landing accident.

Admiral Forbes next had Vice Admiral W. J. Whitworth transfer from the battlecruisers to the *Warspite* with nine destroyers, some being the large 'Tribals'. This would be known as Force B. The light cruiser *Penelope* was originally earmarked to lead the destroyers into Ofot Fjord – the strong tip of the spear, so to speak. But it was damaged from running aground in the shallow waters on the 11th. Whitworth's orders were to launch an attack on 13 April on the remaining German destroyers at Narvik. The Germans were reported as, 'Enemy forces in Narvik consist of one cruiser, five destroyers and one submarine. Troop transports may be expected to arrive through Vest Fjord or through Inner Leads . . .'[40] The Admiralty later raised the German presence to two cruisers. The presence of a cruiser grew out of Captain Warburton-Lee's final report before the destruction of his flagship.[41]

The British decision to reinforce the attacking surface force with the battleship *Warspite* was a dangerous move in case of enemy torpedoes or mines, but the German torpedo was very unreliable and the latter did not exist – but the British were not aware of this. Still, the decision to risk such a large capital unit in littoral waters was hazardous given the known presence of at least one U-boat, though the gamble here would prove successful.[42]

Force B consisted of the *Warspite*, the 'Tribal' class destroyers *Bedouin*, *Cossack*, *Eskimo* and *Punjabi* and five smaller destroyers, the *Forester*, *Foxhound*, *Hero*, *Icarus* and *Kimberley*. *Kimberley* had six 4.7in guns as its main armament with ten torpedoes.[43] The other destroyers were the smaller and older, more traditional British designs with a main armament of four 4.7in guns. Additional forces were in the area, including four destroyers near Skjelfjord.[44]

The Germans had eight destroyers, though with few torpedoes left and several vessels with their ammunition heavily depleted. The *Koellner* was designated to act as a floating battery and most of her fuel was offloaded to other destroyers. The Luftwaffe tried to send twenty-two He111s to attack the British but weather conditions prevented it.

The B-Dienst service had received word of the approach of the British force, with an accurate estimate of the force facing them. Sent at 08:38, Bey received the report by 10:10 on 13 April. He was to expect an attack by the *Repulse* and *Warspite* accompanied by five 'Tribal' class and four additional destroyers in the afternoon. The presence of an aircraft carrier was to be expected. Bey failed to heed this warning promptly and assumed the intelligence was perfectly accurate. He ordered his destroyers to deploy in the afternoon. He should have ordered them to positions immediately and instead was caught flatfooted with the bulk of the available destroyers in Narvik harbour when the British came into sight at the head of the fjord.[45]

Before heading in the *Furious* launched another air raid. Their primary target was the supposed coastal batteries at Ramnes and on the opposite shore from Ramnes. The weather, however, was too thick and the raid was aborted. But later that day nine Swordfish arrived overhead and dive-bombed the Germans. As a result, two were lost and they only sank the requisitioned *Kelt*.

The *Warspite* had earlier launched its Swordfish and received excellent reports including the presence of a U-boat on the surface and later that the disabled German destroyer *Koellner* was being placed in an ambush position. The low cloud level of 3,000ft and the high walls of the fjord made the pilot think it was 'resembling flying in a tunnel'. The Swordfish later successfully bombed the docked *U-64*, sinking it with a loss of eight – the first U-boat in the war sunk by the Fleet Air Arm. After the battle the crew would in a blatant breach of international law return to Germany via Sweden.[46]

The minelaying destroyer *Icarus* was leading the squadron and making use of her bow paravanes to sweep for non-existent mines.[47] This was mostly due to the *U-25* launching an attack late on the 9th off Narvik at two patrolling British destroyers. They had exploded prematurely and the British thought they were electrically-controlled mines operated from the shore.[48]

As the British steamed into the fjord, the surfaced *U-48* signalled the *Eskimo* thinking it was a German destroyer. Realising its error, it quickly dove and later fired a salvo of torpedoes at the passing *Warspite* with no success. There was an element of 'shock and awe' when the large and magnificent-looking *Warspite* was spotted in the channel. As the British headed up the fjord, the still smoldering wreck of the *Rauenfels* grounded on the shore was passed. Next, as the force passed the non-existent batteries at Ramnes, the *U-46* crept up and passed under the destroyer screen, but just before firing at the *Warspite* it grounded. It managed to escape. The *U-48* would later in the day attack two destroyers and the *Warspite* and none of the torpedoes hit and/or functioned properly.[49]

Coming down the fjord was the *Künne* escorting the damaged *Koellner*. A desultory fire was opened by some of the British destroyers on the *Künne* as it withdrew up the fjord. The *Koellner* slipped over to a position near land for ambushing the British. But the alert British attacked first with three 'Tribals' and the *Koellner* never scored a hit as it was pummelled for 8 minutes at ranges of 2,500–3,000m and hit by at least one torpedo. Ablaze in several places and with only one gun left firing, the *Warspite* hove into sight at 3,600yd and silenced her by firing eighteen 15in shells, in addition to 6in shells, of which possibly all hit. The *Warspite*'s 15in shell packed a massive wallop at 1,938lb.[50]

As the *Künne* fell back, zigzagging and laying smoke, no hits were scored and the *Künne* could see German destroyers exiting Narvik and approaching. What followed was a typical Second World War daylight naval action. With ranges being relatively long, dropping to a low of 10,000m and up to 21,000m, no hits were scored. There was little wind that day and with the smoke from the ships and guns, the field of vision became progressively worse. The inaccuracy of the gunfire was not at all unusual during the war. Several daylight naval battles in the Mediterranean resulted in a great deal of ammunition expended and few hits, as also occurred at the Japanese-American naval Battle of the Kormandorski Islands on 27 March 1943. It was difficult to hit a small, fast-moving target at long or even medium range.

With the Germans rapidly running out of ammunition, Bey ordered retirement further up the fjord. The *Giese* had finally raised steam and was leaving Narvik when it suffered an engine casualty and the ship came to a stop. It became engaged with the *Bedouin* and *Punjabi*. All three fired torpedoes and all missed. The *Giese*'s gunfire succeeded in damaging the *Punjabi* and she was forced to withdraw from action with seven dead and fourteen wounded. The *Giese* regained some power, but venturing forth from the inner harbour came under fire from a minimum of five British destroyers and the *Warspite* and was quickly hit and completely wrecked. She would burn into the night before sinking. The British later rescued a German officer from her who during interrogation said there were several U-boats present in the immediate area. This information was quickly forwarded to Admiral Whitworth and influenced his future actions. From the start of operations at Narvik it should have been *assumed* that German U-boats would be in the area. This is a classic example of not recognising what the enemy was *capable* of. But for the lack of effective German torpedoes, Allied ship losses would certainly have been much greater.[51]

Moored at the pier was the damaged *Roeder* with a skeleton crew manning just the two forward turrets. She fired away with her two guns as targets entered her view until the *Cossack* closed, with *Kimberley* supporting, passing through wrecks and remaining shipping at 12 knots, to point-blank range. R.S.V. Sherbrooke was the captain of the *Cossack* and would go on to earn a VC in 1942 at the Battle of the Barents Sea. In the ensuing shoot-out the *Cossack* was damaged and the *Roeder* severely hit. In the end, with ammunition running low, *Roeder* would be hit by at least one 15in shell of the thirty-two fired on her. This move by the two British destroyers, which would leave *Cossack* grounded from the damage, has been criticised as it 'fouled *Warspite*'s range'.[52] At 14:00 Whitworth had ordered *Warspite* to engage shore batteries and the fire from the *Roeder* had been viewed as from a shore battery and not a damaged ship tied to the pier. It is hard to fault a captain for wanting to bring his ship alongside the enemy's but fouling the range of one's powerful flagship is something all good captains should want to avoid.

As Bey fell back with four German destroyers he entered Rombaksfjord – the extreme back of Ofot Fjord. This would be the final position. The fifth remaining destroyer, *Künne*, did not see the Bey's signal and steamed up Herjangsfjord toward Elvegårdsmoen. There, empty of ammunition, it set demolition charges and was also hit by a torpedo from the *Eskimo*. The combination sank it.

Bey and the other four German destroyers realised the end was near. What ammunition was left was transferred to guns that could bear. Scuttling charges were set and as they retreated, the *Lüdemann* released smoking floats to disrupt British gunnery. Two destroyers, the *Zenker* and *Arnim*, steamed for the back of the fjord and began scuttling procedures as they lacked any remaining ammunition. The *Thiele* and *Lüdemann* would try to hold the enemy off for as long as they could. The British approached with three of the smaller destroyers and two 'Tribals'. One, the *Eskimo*, led the way in under the command of Commander John Micklethwait who would later serve in the Mediterranean at the Second Battle of the Sirte. He took the brunt of the German fire, and the *Eskimo* would be hit by literally the last German torpedo launched that would damage but not sink the ship.

It came down to simple mopping up and all the German destroyers were accounted for. None of the original ten would be steaming back to Germany.

The final smoking out of the German destroyers in Rombaksfjord had the *Hero* boarding the deserted *Hans Lüdemann*. On board was a wounded German officer who was taken on board the *Hero* but the *Lüdemann* could not be salvaged and was destroyed. For many years after the war the *Georg Thiele* could be seen at low tide and only in the winter of 2004 did it at last peacefully slide beneath the waves.[53]

Hitler Strikes North

In the immediate aftermath, Admiral Whitworth considered and then rejected putting a landing party ashore at Narvik. The report from the German officer of the presence of several U-boats and the appearance of German bombers over Narvik at 17:55 led him to withdraw. The bombers launched an ineffective attack on an isolated destroyer. Whitworth did signal to the Admiralty at 22:10 that, 'My impression is that enemy forces in Narvik were thoroughly frightened as a result of today's action and the presence of *Warspite* was the chief cause of this. I recommend that the town be occupied without delay by the main landing force.'[54]

Approaching Harstad was the 24th Scots Guards Brigade. There were discussions to divert the brigade to Narvik, especially in light of Whitworth's recommendation, but the decision was made to proceed to Harstad. The military commander would be Major General P. J. Mackesy. Mackesy arrived with a battalion at Scapa Flow on 11 April, and other forces were on his heels. Still, within 48 hours a troop convoy had left the Clyde and was bound for the Narvik region.[55]

The convoy would arrive at Harstad along with the new naval commander, the Earl of Cork and Orrery, who was senior to Admiral Forbes. The Earl had never met Mackesy before and neither had had a chance to co-ordinate beforehand as they had arrived on separate cruisers.[56]

Admiral Dönitz through radio intercepts knew the convoy was bound for Harstad and ordered four U-boats to attack it. As the convoy arrived on the 15th torpedoes were fired at the battleship *Valiant*, the light cruiser *Southampton* and a large liner. All missed or more likely malfunctioned. The *U-49* was lost and while the British rescued most of the crew, they also captured charts showing U-boat dispositions off Norway.

The *U-47* under the command of the very capable Captain Günther Prien was present in the fjord. Prien was famous in the German service for having earlier penetrated Scapa Flow and sinking the battleship *Royal Oak*. That night he silently and stealthy explored the inner fjord, passing up into Bygden fjord, which lies across from Harstad. It was here the British were landing. He suddenly had in front of him 'three large transports, each of 30,000 tons and three more, slightly smaller, escorted by two [light] cruisers'. The transports were stopped, in the process unloading, when Prien attacked, using a mix of contact and a few magnetic detonators. He made two attacks with four torpedoes each and none hit, though one swerved off, hitting the shore and exploding. Prien was fortunate to return to Germany alive and extremely frustrated.[57]

The other German warships had some better results. The *Admiral Hipper* and the destroyer *Friedrich Eckoldt* were prepared to leave Trondheim on the night of 9–10 April. As they proceeded toward the outer fjords, the *U-32* was sighted on the surface by the *Hipper* and fired upon – no damage resulted in this friendly fire incident. This caused Heye to change course and exit a difficult but less-used route. However, as the two ships neared the open seas, conditions were so rough that the destroyer signalled to Heye it could not maintain the required 29 knots Heye wanted to operate at on his return home. So the *Eckoldt* returned to

Trondheim. It would successfully breakout to Germany from Trondheim, along with the *Heinemann*, on 14 April.[58]

The *Hipper* rendezvoused with the returning battleships *Gneisenau* and *Scharnhorst* and steamed for Germany. On the morning of 12 April British aircraft off the Norwegian coast between Kristiansand and Egersund sighted them. The British then launched a series of long-range bomber attacks and suffered heavy losses, in part to newly arrived Me109s based at Kjevik. This modern German fighter was a match for the Allies best fighters, none of which were operating near Norway. The German warships escaped unscathed, while about a dozen British bombers were shot down or damaged and the Germans lost five aircraft. When the ships arrived in Germany they quickly went into port for refitting. Admiral Forbes would later write that the Germans 'had been able to pass all the way from the Lofotens to the Skagerrak without being sighted by any of our air or surface vessels'.[59]

* * *

In the immediate aftermath of the invasion the Norwegian government attempted to organise a defence around Oslo, as well as the rest of the nation. All this was being undertaken in the midst of mobilisation and with many key arsenal depots already under German control. By the 10th German troopships were landing hundreds of men and supplies daily, primarily in Oslo harbour but elsewhere in Norway too.[60] The Luftwaffe was also forwarding troops and light supplies with hundreds of Ju52 transports.

On 10 April the temporary Norwegian capital at Elverum contained the king and most of the Norwegian political and military leadership. The government knew the Spiller Raid had been defeated but remained concerned that the Germans might attempt to seize the government. Elements in the government were still seeking some sort of compromise with the Germans to stop the fighting. That morning Nygaardsvold had asked for and received a representative for talks with the Germans from the three largest political parties. Foreign Minister Halvdan Koht also contacted Inspector General of Infantry Colonel Ruge who was present in Elverum to ask if Norway could still resist and Ruge answered, 'Yes.'

It was against this background that German Ambassador Dr Curt Bräuer requested yet another audience with King Haakon VII, and this was granted. While ceremonial, Haakon was viewed as the head of state. Bräuer had driven from Oslo through roadblocks with a safe-conduct pass. Bräuer wanted to meet with the king alone but the king's German was poor, and after 10 minutes he insisted that Koht join the meeting. Bräuer asked the king to dismiss the current government and appoint Vidkun Quisling as prime minister. Hitler had insisted on the appointment of Quisling and that made the wavering Norwegian cabinet even more likely to reject the German terms. The king said as a constitutional monarch he would present Germany's demands to the government.[61] The king stated that if the government accepted Quisling he, the king, would abdicate and renounce the family line as his successor. The entire discussion was a waste of time for both sides, but does point out that Norway did not want this war thrust upon it and was still seeking some way to end the nightmare. The king later referred with disgust to Bräuer's request for prime minister to be 'that man Quisling.'[62]

Bräuer also said that if these terms were not accepted the fighting would intensify and that it would be the king's fault if that happened. The king said immediately after the meeting to the cabinet, 'He threw the entire responsibility for war on to my shoulders.'[63] Only one minister apparently suggested acceptance to avoid the carnage of war and the same fate suffered by Belgium in the First World War, but the vast majority, fuelled by the king's desire not to appoint a man completely lacking the support of the majority of Norwegians to lead the government, was for fighting the Germans. Koht had the insight to see that accepting the German terms would lead to war with Great Britain and France. If Hitler had not insisted upon Quisling, it is possible that some form of accommodation such as achieved in Denmark might have been an option.[64] But the king and the government stood firm. The new German ultimatum was refused.[65] It was at Elverum that some members of the government and the wife and children of the crown prince crossed into neutral Sweden. For the government members it was to facilitate the war effort from outside of Norway.[66]

With Norwegian resistance now assured, the king and government issued a 'Proclamation to the people of Norway' on the evening of 10 April. Nygaardsvold wrote that Germany had attacked them and called upon the Norwegians to resist. He also stated that his government was the only legal government. This was to disavow any attempt to put Quisling and his rump government into power, or any other one that Germany created. The king added a line, unusual in this constitutional monarchy, at the end of the proclamation. It read, 'I associate myself completely with this appeal which the Government has addressed to the Norwegian people. I am convinced that I have the whole nation with me in the decision which has been taken.'[67]

On 11 April the government was in the village of Nybergsund, when an envoy from Quisling made one last appeal. Shortly after he left the village was heavily bombed by eleven He111s. The Germans thought the General Staff was present with the government and the king with the royal family. Fortunately, most of the Norwegians hid in the woods, which offered protection from the bombs, but one of the buses requisitioned for the government was destroyed, though miraculously no one was killed. After this attack, a visibly shaken Nygaardsvold, a lumberjack by trade, strongly argued to take the entire government into exile in Sweden, and it was in part the argument of the king that stopped this from transpiring.[68] This bombing was most likely on Hitler's direct order, as Bräuer had been directed to find where the king and Norwegian military staff were and to forward that information to General Falkenhorst.[69]

This attack formed part of King Haakon's address to the nation by radio on 13 April 1940:

> Norway has been the victim of a sudden attack from a nation with which we have always had friendly relations. . . . Our position is such, to-day, that I cannot tell you where in Norway I myself, the Crown Prince, and the Government

reside, as the German air force launched a violent attack against us when we had taken refuge in a small undefended and unprotected place.[70]

He deplored the German attacks where 'women and children are being exposed to death and inhuman sufferings'. He went on to say, 'high explosive and incendiary bombs and machine-gun fire were used against the civilian population and ourselves'.[71] This is an example of a long line of usually unsuccessful attempts to chop off the head of leadership. It is difficult because you first must locate your target and than be able to strike quickly and hard enough before the target has moved on. Though it often does fail, it can disrupt enemy operations as well as creating martyrs that can be politically exploited.[72]

The Norwegian government was several days into the war and in the process of utilising the military more fully. But as Koht later wrote, 'the military leaders of Norway had made up their war [plans] upon many different suppositions; but they had never conceived the possibility of what really happened – an attack hitting the country at all places on the coast at once. That was the real surprise: the enemy suddenly appearing at all the separate ports and forts of Norway.'[73] Even though many Norwegians flooded what mobilisation centres were still in Norwegian hands and many volunteers stepped forward, the Norwegian army was not ready for war. Inspector General of Infantry Colonel Ruge had concluded in January 1940, after reviewing the training of troops, that they were not combat ready after their training periods. He suggested a series of reforms but these were by no means fully implemented by the time war swept Norway up. As to their training to fight in a modern war, he had written 'So far, we have not.'[74]

To help rectify this situation the Norwegian government made an important move when it relieved Major General Kristian Laake of command on the evening of 10 April. Laake had been indecisive and the mobilisation had been poorly handled. He had also argued that the government should negotiate with Germany, as the only other recourse was surrender.[75] In retrospect, Laake may have been right. Given the situation, resistance from a strictly military perspective may indeed have been hopeless. As has been suggested, the Germans had already won. The Norwegian army was soon to be outnumbered, lacked equipment, after a few weeks of combat out of ammunition and would see for the most part command after command quickly surrender. But politically and morally *not* to resist was absolutely bankrupt. Norway stared in the face almost certain military defeat, but Norwegians could retain their self-respect in the choice their government made. After the war they would show they had learned from their defeat.

In the meeting where the decision was made, with the Minister of Justice leading the way, both Nygaardsvold and the militarily trained Crown Prince Olav agreed that Laake should be removed – always a delicate decision in the midst of combat. The young and new Minister of Defence Colonel Birger Ljungberg still wanted to retain Laake. That Ruge argued for continued resistance while Laake proposed surrender and had just arrived at the technical retirement age of 65 on 9 April, made the decision easier for all involved.[76]

Colonel Ruge, now Major General Ruge, replaced General Laake late on the evening of 10 April. The 58-year-old Ruge had been Chief-of-Staff until 1938 before becoming Inspector General of Infantry. He was unpopular with some in the military because in 1933 he had accepted army reforms that reduced its strength – the so-called 'Bankruptcy Ordinance'. Ruge at the time recognised that the defence budget was going to be reduced and having been handed lemons made the best lemonade he could. By 1938 his star had fallen in large part due to this lingering resentment and mistrust. Haakon had doubts about him for this reason. But now Ruge was promoted to command for having shown initiative right from the start.

Also soon to be retired was the competent Chief-of-Staff Colonel Rasmus Hatledal on 14 April. Ruge, who was a friend and supporter of Hatledal, insisted he rest as Hatledal suffered from tuberculosis.[77] Ruge would have to replace him.

The Norwegian military was rife with defeatism, born of the sudden German successes, the years of meagre defence budgets and general shock brought about by the nature of modern warfare. This had a great impact on many officers and men. But Ruge, never in direct command of more then a divisional equivalent in the past, in the coming days was positive and resisted the pessimism that sometimes raised its ugly head with his spirit in front of both officers and men.

Ruge stated that southern Norway was lost, but with support, central Norway and the Trondheim district could be retained. Ruge would do what he could in southern Norway but as will be seen, the Oslo region would fall quickly offering little to no resistance. At a meeting at Rena, north of Elverum, Ruge discussed his goals with his staff. He laid out the concept that the Allies would recapture Trondheim and defeat the Germans there. While that was unfolding, he planned to halt the expansion of the Germans from their growing base at Oslo. To do so he attempted to increase the mobilisation of Norwegian forces and to cut off all communication and transport connections from Oslo. The destruction of bridges throughout central Norway would be pronounced over the coming days and as the Norwegian army fell back in the two major central valleys. He also moved his headquarters from Rena to Øyer, about 10 miles north of Lillehammer, which was on the Gudbrandsdalen route.[78] Publicly, he was telling the Norwegian troops, 'Now the time for withdrawing has passed. Stand by and keep together and we shall fight the battle to victory.'[79]

Ruge also formed a cadre of mostly young officers that he used to facilitate his command and to plug the proverbial hole in the line. Known as 'Travelling Officers' and 'Ruge's Commissars', they were given missions to fulfill and sent off to do just that.

Ruge later said of this initial stand, with Germany controlling the cities and many of the radio stations and newspapers, and several of the armouries,

> From Oslo flocked hundreds of men who could not be mobilized there, since the Germans had occupied the city. They rallied around one or another commander and formed a company. They united with other similar groups from other

places and formed a battalion. Some officer assumed command. The accident brought together in the same company infantrymen, artillerymen, sailors, and airmen. By good fortune we even had cars and drivers whom we found, God knows how. These units gradually grew into combat troops. The commissariat was improvised and took care of feeding the small army. The women on the farms cooked and helped the soldiers. We had no medical corps. Thanks to the initiative of energetic doctors it was created from scratch.[80]

One source of skilled volunteers was the local rifle clubs (*Skytterlag*). They would often be given armbands to identify them as soldiers so the Germans would not shoot them as partisans. They gained a reputation (along with many of the Norwegian soldiers) of being quite skilled shots at 600m with the old Krag-Jørgensen rifle.

The Norwegian navy was severely handicapped at this point. The army at least had some depots still under their control. The navy was stripped of every important base except in the far north. Commander-in-Chief Rear Admiral Henry Diesen accepted being placed under Ruge's command. He and his staff then moved inland and by 12 April had established headquarters at a hotel deep in the interior of Norway in the Gudbrandsdalen.[81]

The Norwegian air force was almost non-existent. By the end of 9 April the Norwegian fighter force consisted of one plane.[82] The planes remaining to them were primarily used for reconnaissance and for transporting important individuals in country. By 10 April Germany had complete command of the skies over southern and central Norway. The strength of that grasp would only grow.

* * *

At one point, the German exile and future Chancellor of Germany, Willi Brandt, having fled Oslo arrived at Nybergsund. In his hotel room he found some important government papers that had been left behind in the confusion, and he took charge of these and later delivered them to the Norwegians.[83]

Brandt was in Norway having fled there in 1933 from Germany. He made a living as a journalist. With the attack on Oslo he departed fearing the Gestapo, which wanted to arrest him along with other German émigrés. He had on the night of 8 April addressed a small group of German exiles and told them to expect an attack from Germany, most likely on the 9th, but he had not followed up on that prediction (based on the fast-breaking news of 8 April) in part due to his fiancée being pregnant.[84]

Brandt had an interesting discussion that night with a 'high official' he knew. A few months previously this Norwegian governmental official had argued that one only had to meet halfway with Hitler and things could be worked out in Europe and vis-à-vis Norway. That night, after the initial fighting, that same official said he wished the Treaty of Versailles had been harsher.[85]

* * *

At Oslo the Germans consolidated their position immediately after 9 April. That evening they had one company of paratroopers, one engineer company, one company of marines (reduced) for manning the coastal defence batteries and seven infantry companies.[86] Falkenhorst with his staff was supposed to have taken his post in Oslo on the afternoon of the 9th. It was delayed until 16:00 on the 10th when he arrived at Fornebu, along with Admiral Hermann Boehm and staff who was to command all German naval forces in Norway.

Sea transports arriving from Germany on 10 April and after, with the surrender of Oscarsborg that morning, disgorged troops and equipment at the harbour wharves. The light cruiser *Emden* was ordered to remain in Oslo so its powerful radio could be used for issuing orders.

Original plans called for the dispatch by rail of one battalion of the 163rd Infantry Division to Bergen and one battalion of the 196th Infantry Division to Trondheim. Given the Norwegian resistance, Falkenhorst cancelled that. Falkenhorst would now modify his plans. Instead of the later arriving 181st Infantry Division consolidating the position to the south and east of Oslo, the destruction of the mobilising elements of the Norwegian 1st Infantry Division would take precedence.[87]

By 13 April the bulk of Major General Erwin Engelbrecht's 163rd and Major General Richard Pellengahr's 196th Infantry Divisions were ashore via both air and sea transport. The 163rd had troops and equipment lost when the *Blücher* went down and a regiment was at Kristiansand, while the 196th had lost 400 troops from Allied submarine attacks. However, a regiment each of the 69th and 181st infantry divisions were also at Oslo and they were assigned to the 163rd.[88]

Despite what you may have read elsewhere, the vast majority of these troops were *not* veterans of the Polish campaign. They were older men enlisted into later recruiting wave units of the German army. A number had seen action in the First World War but many were drawn from the manpower pool that came of age between the wars. The officers and NCOs were more likely to have seen some action in either or both wars. But their training and equipment were still greatly superior to the Norwegians now facing them.

With each passing day more and more troops and equipment were arriving at Oslo and these would continue to reinforce these initial two divisions. From this would be formed many *Kampfgruppes* or battlegroups. Battlegroups were *ad hoc* formations, sharing standardised training and usually with a balance of weapons and equipment that could undertake specific military tasks. They made wide use of requisitioned civilian motorised and horse-drawn transport – Norwegian horses were particularly suited to the climate.[89] After several days in Norway these *Kampfgruppes* would usually employ armour if available, artillery, engineers and infantry. They would utilise skis when possible and necessary. The Germans were very adept at their use of battlegroups. The Norwegians would end up deploying 'battlegroups' made up of a conglomerate of miscellaneous formations and men, but they were not part of Norwegian doctrine, but established due to the necessity of fighting with the means at hand.[90]

Falkenhorst had one other ace in his hand – complete air dominance. Hundreds of Ju52s would continue to fly in additional troops and supplies. His bombers and fighters, while primarily concerned with supporting the German garrisons at Stravanger, Bergen, Trondheim and Narvik, would give some help in the German advances to secure the flanks of Oslo. The mere presence of them flying overhead was a heavy intimidating factor for both Norwegian troops and civilians. This was compounded by the ignorance of *what* type of planes were overhead and it would take a few days for the Norwegians to differentiate between bombers and transport aircraft. The German air superiority would be exploited and allowed not only for men and supplies to be shuttled forward, but aircraft spotting for artillery would give the Germans an additional advantage.[91]

Ominously, on 12 April, the Germans in Oslo announced, 'the first saboteurs had been arrested, condemned to death according to international law, and instantly shot'.[92]

On the 12th Falkenhorst ordered his forces 'to break the resistance of Norwegian troops ruthlessly'.[93] He wanted to secure the greater Oslofjord region and so his initial push was to the south and south-east towards the Swedish border, while in addition he prepared for an advance to the north. The swiftness with which he executed the offensive was a vital ingredient in German success.

On 12 April General Pellengahr's 340th and 362nd Infantry Regiments were ordered to Askim, Mysen and Fredrikstad in the south-east corner of Norway, which lies between Oslo and Sweden and is known as the Østfold. Some elements of the 163rd Infantry Division were attached. A detachment was also sent up the Glomma River toward the east and met no opposition. While it did not reach the Swedish border, it acted as a barrier between the Norwegian 1st and 2nd Divisions. Pellengahr's third regiment, the 345th, was ordered north towards the inland valleys of Gudbrandsdalen and the Østerdalen. Pellengahr ordered a three-pronged advance with his other two regiments. It was much colder in the interior then along the fjord at Oslo, but the Germans adapted to it fairly well. There they would attack the bulk of the mobilising Norwegian 1st Infantry Division.[94]

The situation around Oslo for the Norwegians was dire and quickly went from bad to worse. To the immediate north of Oslo were mobilising elements of the Norwegian 2nd Infantry Division. This was under the command of Major General Jacob Hvinden-Haug. He would be the commander of the Norwegian front line until his surrender on 3 May. Until Ruge took firm control of the situation, Hvinden-Haug tried to avoid combat with the Germans and fell back from Oslo. He was somewhat defeatist in his attitude and it is surprising he was not relieved of his command.[95]

Facing the Germans was the Norwegian 1st Infantry Division under the command of Major General Carl Erichsen, with its headquarters near the Swedish border at Halden. The bulk of his division and his headquarters were to the east of Oslofjord, but important elements of his division were located to the west of

Oslofjord. The fjord literally split his command. In the Østfold he also had the bulk of the mobilising 1st Dragoon Regiment and the 1st Artillery Regiment. He had three days mobilising and preparing his troops before the Germans burst upon the division. During that interval he moved his headquarters from Halden to Mysen. By the 12th he had upwards of 3,000 men mostly concentrated near the town of Mysen where an old border fort complex faced Sweden, the two main forts named Trøgstad and Høytorp. A much smaller number of troops were located closer to Oslofjord at Sarpsborg, near Fredrikstad. Sarpsborg also had some older fortifications originally designed for a possible war with Sweden at the turn of the century. But Erichsen was not an inspired commander and he did not possess efficient communications with General Ruge.[96]

Pellengahr had a battalion of the 362nd Regiment move down along Oslofjord toward Moss partially motorised in requisitioned civilian transport. He also utilised the Norwegian railway system linking Oslo to the Swedish border near Halden. They followed the rail line to first Fredrikstad and then on to Sarpsborg, meeting very little resistance and capturing eighty-five Norwegians on the night of 12–13 April. From there, their advance continued south along the railway until it reached the Swedish border before turning north and arriving at Lund on 14 April, at which time all resistance from the Norwegians in this region ceased.

Two reinforced battalions, one from the 362nd Infantry Regiment and the other from the 340th Infantry Regiment, advanced toward Mysen. The 362nd was also partially motorised. The 340th, making up the eastern prong primarily utilising horse and foot transport, passed to the east of the large and long lake Øyeren to arrive near Fort Trøgstad on 13 April. After some minor fighting, the garrison was forced to surrender with 347 men becoming prisoners. Much of the artillery, in addition to other pieces captured at other forts in the course of the campaign, would later be dismantled by the Germans and deployed as coastal defence batteries.

As the centre column approached Mysen it was ambushed at Fossum bridge, just outside Askim. Germans suffered losses from the Norwegians as most of the Germans exited the civilian buses. The Norwegians even had some minor artillery support from Fort Høytorp. Deploying on the night of 13–14 April, the Germans launched a successful attack with their own artillery support, forcing the Norwegians back. Fort Høytorp surrendered on the 14th after suffering one casualty. Even with a Ruge 'Commissar' arriving on the 14th, the rear guard surrendered, numbering 30 officers, 800 men, 96 artillery pieces (many being fortress artillery) and 25 machine-guns.[97]

Resistance in the area between Oslo and the Swedish border had collapsed in just a few days. Høytorp Fort had a 'mobile' battery of eight modern 120mm m/32 howitzers stationed there. Unfortunately, these guns lacked proper ammunition and were worthless. They would be interned in Sweden on 14 April. Another battery of twelve motorised 105mm guns had ten that lacked tyres. Also the military's policy in the 1920s of separating key components of equipment (such as firing pins) and storing them at various arsenals, due to the fear of a Communist

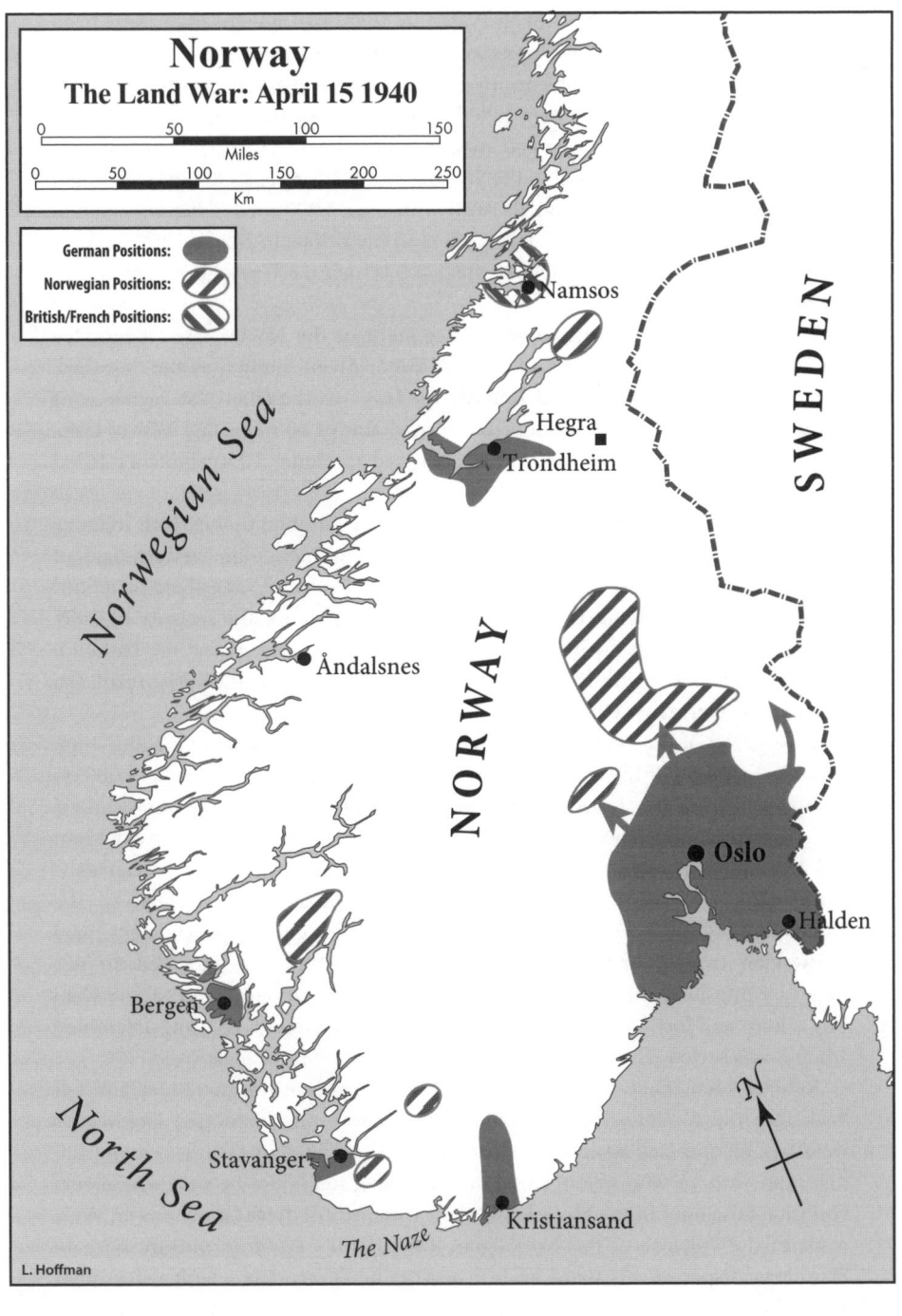

# Norway
## The Land War: April 15 1940

Miles
0    50    100    150

Km
0    50    100    150    200    250

German Positions:
Norwegian Positions:
British/French Positions:

SWEDEN

Norwegian Sea

Namsos

Hegra
Trondheim

Åndalsnes

NORWAY

Oslo

Halden

Bergen

North Sea

Stavanger

The Naze

Kristiansand

N

L. Hoffman

and/or Socialist revolution, though ended in 1938, had not by any means been fully rectified. Thus, not all weapons were readily available for use.

This minor fighting would leave twelve German dead and forty wounded. The Norwegian's lost about 100 men killed. Many Norwegian troops on their own now fled to the Swedish border and crossed over to be interned. The remainder of Erichsen's command marched to the Swedish border and crossed into internment camps with the last arriving on 16 April with over 3,000 men. Erichsen claimed that it was in large part due to 'false orders to his troops to surrender'.[98] In April Sweden would intern a total of 4,610 men, 400 vehicles, 200 machine-guns and 12 artillery pieces.[99]

Two battalions of the 3rd Infantry Regiment of the Norwegian 1st Infantry Division under the command of Colonel Einar Steen, known as the Telemark Regiment, began to mobilise at Kongsberg. This was the chief Norwegian arms manufacturing centre and was located by road almost 60 miles due west of Oslo. It was an early German goal and was assigned to General Engelbrecht's 163rd Division.

The Germans had established themselves with a battalion of the 310th Infantry Regiment (163rd Infantry Division) at Drammen, protecting the western flank of Fornebu airfield and Oslo. Drammen lies between Oslo and Kongsberg on a fjord connected to the Oslofjord. The 163rd was responsible for the security of Oslo. The Germans quickly organised an attacking force by reinforcing the battalion with elements of the 69th Infantry Division and the 307th Infantry Regiment. On 12 April the Germans struck.

A battalion of the 307th and a battalion of the 69th advanced on Kongsberg, with the battalion of the 69th first moving north to capture Hønefoss at 17:00 on 13 April, meeting little resistance. This was a key rail junction for communications with Bergen. The battalion of the 310th pressed on to Kongsberg. The Norwegian 3rd Regiment was just south of Kongsberg at Heistadmoen and the Germans launched a two-column attack which quickly forced the surrender of the Norwegian regiment with the Norwegians not firing a gun. Approximately 1,600 Norwegian troops surrendered, along with equipment that included an AA battery. Kongsberg was captured intact and at the armament factory there were fifty 20mm and forty 40mm AA guns and rifles in the process of being assembled when it was seized. The Norwegian 1st Infantry Division was destroyed.

Reserve Lieutenant Thor Hannevig refused to accept the surrender and fell back into the mountains. After arming his band with abandoned Norwegian weapons, he operated against the Germans. At their height possibly as many 400 men and woman who belonged to the Telemark Regiment or were volunteers continued the fight in the hinterland. Their usual strength was much lower. With news of the collapse of the Norwegian 4th Infantry Division outside Bergen, Hannevig dispersed his band and on 8 May he surrendered with three men, six women auxiliaries and twenty-eight German prisoners. During the war Kongsberg would produce a very limited number of rifles and artillery pieces for the German war effort.[100]

This capitulation by Colonel Steen of the Telemark Regiment was a stain on the Norwegian army. Ruge, from the first questioning Steen's will to resist, had sent one of his 'Commissars' to stiffen resistance but he had arrived too late.[101]

Another German battalion of the 307th headed south from Drammen, bolstered by requisitioned transport, and quickly cleared the western side of Oslofjord, meeting virtually no resistance. By 14 April this force had captured the small coastal defence fort of Måkerøy and had advanced through Larvik to Porsgrunn. Instead of linking up with Kristiansand, the 163rd Infantry Division, leaving garrisons, was now ordered north and would deploy forces on the western flank to keep any Norwegian forces from interfering with the main advance to relieve Trondheim and to link up with Bergen. This change in orders was in part due to the rapid collapse of one of the two regiments of the Norwegian 3rd Infantry Division at Kristiansand.[102]

\* \* \*

The Norwegian situation at Kristiansand was quickly deteriorating. By the end of 9 April Kristiansand and the nearby airport of Kjevik were firmly in German hands and by the 12th two further battalions had been airlifted in. In addition, two transports had safely arrived at the port and were busily unloading supplies and equipment. There they were facing Major General Einar Liljedahl of the Norwegian 3rd Infantry Division commanding a battalion of the 7th Norwegian Infantry and the *hjulrytterkompani* company of the 1st Dragoon Regiment, which had been posted there from Oslo as part of the Neutrality Watch. Behind it at Evje elements of the 7th Infantry Regiment were mobilising with the bulk of forces, which would number almost 2,000 men. Attached to it was a mobilised Neutrality Watch battery of the 2nd Artillery Regiment detached from the Norwegian 2nd Infantry Division. A small force was also posted on the road linking Evje with Arendal. On the roads there were over 20,000 civilian refugees. The other regiment, the 8th Infantry Regiment, of this binary division was mobilising near Stavanger.[103]

The night that Kristiansand had been occupied, German troops headed inland to locate the Norwegian troops and had encountered a Norwegian patrol 7 miles from Kristiansand. Both sides deployed facing each other, but with refugees between them heading north, neither side opened fire.

The German commander ordered a pursuit of retreating Norwegian units into the interior. On the morning of 10 April at the next roadblock, the Germans approached under a white flag to negotiate with the Norwegians. They would declare that they would not open fire on Norwegian troops unless the Norwegians fired first. This peaceful, morale-destroying approach would be repeated several times over the next few days. No gunfire was exchanged and the Norwegians fell back. Over the next two days the Germans advanced as the Norwegians fell back to Hægeland. At one point some of the Norwegian troops panicked, generated by a rumour of German armoured cars approaching (the Germans at this point had neither tanks or armoured cars at Kristiansand). Small numbers of German aeroplanes passed overhead to bomb Evje and this also intimidated the Norwegians.

This would culminate on 13 April with the Norwegian morale in decline (in part for not resisting the German advance to Hægeland), air attacks on Evje and news of the surrender of Kongsberg just to the east. Liljedahl contacted Ruge and asked him for permission to surrender, claiming his men were 'unfit for battle' and that they faced overwhelming numbers. Ruge refused to grant this and ordered Liljedahl to continue fighting. If forced to surrender, he was to order his men to escape into the mountains to continue the fight. Instead, General Liljedahl abandoned his command to Colonel Finn Backer of the 7th Infantry Regiment, and announced he was going to journey to his other regiment, the 8th, in front of Stavanger. Some disheartened Norwegian soldiers directly facing the Germans at this point announced they were ending hostilities.[104]

On the 15th Liljedahl set off for Stavanger and that afternoon Backer surrendered over 2,000 officers and men. Shortly after, a detachment numbering 104 officers and men to the west of Hægeland also surrendered. By 27 April, 241 officers and 2,921 troops had surrendered along with 69 machine-guns and 22 artillery pieces. This was after suffering few casualties and having more than sufficient amounts of ammunition. After the war Liljedahl would be court-martialled and was sentenced to sixty days in prison for his conduct.[105]

The Germans had also requisitioned local transport and sent a column along the coast with the goal of linking up first with Egersund and then Stavanger. It started its journey on 14 April and faced virtually no opposition. The link-up would not take place until 21 April, and when completed would include tanker trucks carrying fuel for the aircraft operating from Sola.

At Stavanger the 8th Infantry Regiment was mobilising under the command of Colonel Gunnar Spørck, who still retained the bulk of the detached *Jagerbataljonen* from the Norwegian 1st Infantry Division. With orders from General Liljedahl telling him to 'act as he considered best',[106] he had decided to not counter-attack immediately. Instead, he withdrew to the south-east and mobilised what he could of his regiment. With the German seizure of Stavanger and Sola, Spørck had lost his mobilisation depot.[107]

On 17 April the German 193rd Infantry Regiment began moving largely by locally requisitioned light sea transport to join the 159th Infantry Regiment fighting at Bergen, a fellow regiment of the 69th Infantry Division. This would largely be completed by the 22nd with little Allied interference. Concurrently, the 355th Infantry Regiment of Major General Max Horn's 214th Infantry Division assumed the occupation of Stavanger from the departing regiment as it arrived by air. This shuttling of forces forward to the fluid front lines of Norway would be a recurring theme over the next weeks of combat. During this time Spørck attempted to move his force toward Kristiansand, but halted that movement upon learning of the surrender of the 7th Infantry Regiment.

As a German column approached Stavanger from Kristiansand, the 214th launched a multi-pronged offensive to the south and east supported by the Luftwaffe operating from Sola. This pinned Sprøck's command against the mountains to the east and he was forced to surrender on 23 April. This surrender of 1,775 men, 104 machine-guns and eight artillery pieces effectively eliminated the Norwegian 3rd Infantry Division. The Germans lost thirty-six killed and seventy wounded in the short campaign against Sporck's command. In retrospect, Spørck should have immediately counter-attacked the Germans with what forces at hand as it is in the initial moments that one is most able to stop an air or sea invasion.[108]

On 16 April the heavy cruiser *Suffolk* was ordered to bombard the Sola airfield near Stavanger, accompanied by four destroyers. Churchill saw this attack as part of his plans for Operation 'Hammer'. This bombardment was going to be Operation 'Duck' and would be in part an attack in support of the landing at Åndalsnes. After steaming at 26 knots across the North Sea, the *Suffolk* arrived off the port on 17 April and there rendezvoused with the submarine *Seal* to find its station. Some minor RAF assets were to assist in this attack, but were for the most part ineffective. *Suffolk* opened up at 20,000yd at 05:13.

It made three runs lasting 48 minutes and fired off 202 8in rounds with difficult-to-discern flares dropped by a RAF Hudson over the target area. It opened first with high-explosive shells to help illuminate the field in the early morning pre-dawn and then switched to armour-piercing shell to break up the concrete airfield. A German Ju88 attacked one of her two Walrus aeroplanes but the Ju88, the two Walruses and the Hudson all returned safely. The damage inflicted was minimal largely due to accuracy and type of ammunition, and it received exaggerated press coverage, where it was reported, 'in a few moments, up in a great bang and blaze went chunks of concrete runways, hangars and transport planes'. Nearby eight floatplanes were destroyed and several damaged but the field itself was largely untouched.[109]

A mix-up and change in withdrawal orders meant that the *Suffolk* did not have adequate fighter protection, in fact none for 6 hours. One RAF intervention was purely accidental. A Blenheim squadron on its way to attack Stavanger saw the *Suffolk* in difficulties and attacked the German Ju88s. They then gained altitude and made an assault on Stavanger. But the *Suffolk* would be under air attack for 6 hours and 47 minutes. A heavy bomb, most likely of 500kg, hit the *Suffolk*, and it was not until 14:15 that friendly escorting aircraft hove into sight – and came under fire from the *Suffolk*. *Suffolk* survived thirty-three separate attacks: eighty-eight bomb splashes were counted and seventeen sailors died. The last 164 miles the *Suffolk* steered with its screws as the steering gear had failed and it arrived back in Britain on the 18th with a top speed of 18 knots, more then 1,500 tons of seawater on board and its quarterdeck awash. The RAF would privately refer to the attack as Operation 'Donald Duck'.

One problem with most warships in 1940 was inadequate AA armament. The British, for example, with the exception of the new 'L' class destroyer with its 4.7in guns capable of being elevating to 50 degrees, all guns were limited to 40 degrees. German destroyers were worse being limited to 30 degrees. This meant that dive-bombers, especially the Ju87, really only needed to fear enemy fighters or close-in weapons – they could ignore in large part the destroyer's main gun armament.

The Bofors 40mm under licence from Sweden and the Swiss-licensed Oerlikon 20mm AA guns were just being introduced into service. Other close-in weapons consisted of too few older 2-pounder pom-pom and other small calibre machine-guns and the like. Norway would be the first test of British and Allied AA defence. The guns would prove to be inadequate.[110]

In mid-April the intense fighting between German aircraft and Allied warships had the Admiralty request that Admiral Forbes reduce AA ammunition expenditure. The navy was running out of ammunition.[111] They were also not operating in range of German airbases after their rough experiences at the hands of the Luftwaffe. One historian later wrote of this in regards to the air–sea battle, 'From first to last, it was air power that shaped the course of the battle for Norway.'[112]

There were some minor Norwegian warships operating in the nearby fjords but by 20 April Germany had captured or destroyed the Norwegian forces. A group of three 55-ton torpedo boats operated for a few days north-east of Arendal among the numerous islands but on 17 April they scuttled themselves near the island of Lyngør near Arendal.

By 15 April the area surrounding Oslo and Kristiansand, and Stavanger by the 23rd, had been subdued and the Norwegian 1st and 3rd Divisions destroyed. With the command of Oslo and surrounding territory, the heart of the nation was controlled by Germany. Before turning to the main German drive from Oslo to relieve Trondheim (and Bergen), it is necessary to examine the situation of those two more distant German enclaves.

* * *

Bergen was viewed by the Germans as less of a beleaguered position than Trondheim was. This was because it was nearer to German-controlled airfields and it proved easier to reinforce and supply from the Stavanger region by small ships.

The most dramatic event after the capture of Bergen was the sinking of the *Königsberg*. British air reconnaissance was aware of her presence there. The *Königsberg* had been damaged in passing the forts. At Scapa Flow's airfield at Hatston there were two squadrons of Skua fighter-bombers from the *Ark Royal*. Flying distance from Scapa to Bergen was 2 hours and the Skua had an official range of 4 hours, 20 minutes. It was argued that the German Me110s fighters operating from Sola would not have time to react and an air attack by the single-engine fighter-bomber would have the element of surprise, which would prove to be true.

With a crew of two, the Skua was first flown in 1937 and was designed as a dive-bomber. Its top speed was a slow 225 miles and was armed with four wing

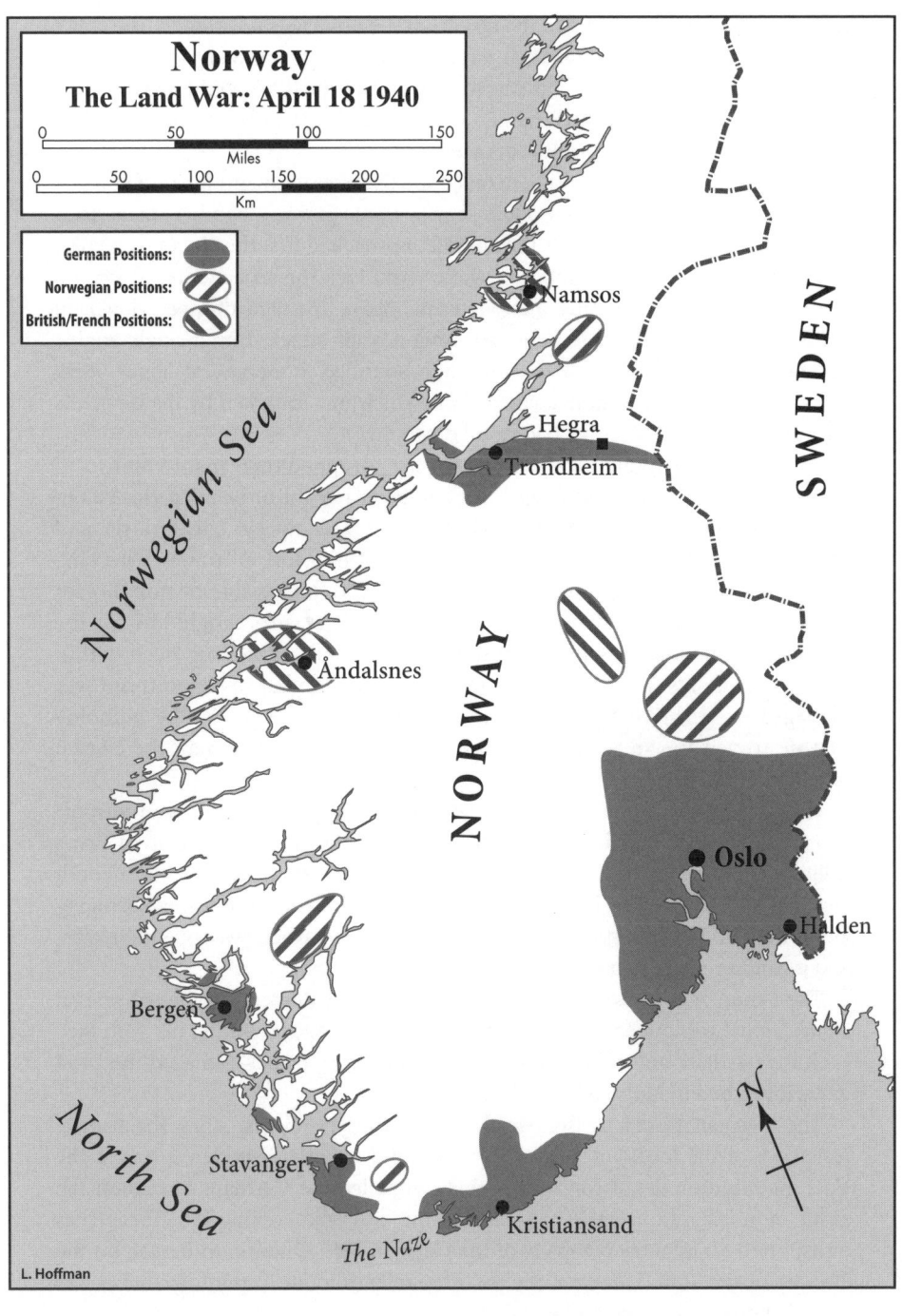

# Norway
## The Land War: April 18 1940

Miles
0     50     100     150

Km
0   50   100   150   200   250

German Positions:
Norwegian Positions:
British/French Positions:

Norwegian Sea

SWEDEN

Namsos

Hegra
Trondheim

NORWAY

Åndalsnes

Oslo

Halden

Bergen

North Sea

Stavanger

The Naze

Kristiansand

N

L. Hoffman

machine-guns and one firing to the rear from the observers position.[113] The crews at this time had lost some of their experienced officers 'on loan' so they could work directly with the RAF. This was to help ensure the RAF would make correct identification of enemy versus friendly warships and better identify ship types. So the two squadrons had some new personnel.[114]

A total of sixteen aircraft were detailed for the operation and took off at 05:00 on 10 April, each carrying one 500lb semi-armour-piercing bomb as their main weapon. Dawn was breaking as the aircraft approached first the Norwegian coast and then Bergen. Through good navigation and luck the sixteen aircraft arrived over the target and one after another went into a dive and dropped down on the *Königsberg* as it lay quiet, not expecting any air attack from a single-engine bomber. There had been an air-raid siren sounded at Bergen at about 06:50 because of a Hudson reconnaissance plane which was mistaken by the Germans for a He111, so the AA crews had stood down.

All the planes, diving though light AA fire, dropped their main bombs and all but one made it back to Scapa. Six bombs either hit or were so close as to rack the *Königsberg*. One of the early hits knocked out electrical power and this made the 88mm AA guns inoperable. The ship lost all power when the boiler rooms flooded and fires broke out that were impossible to stop. Losses were eighteen killed and twenty wounded, which is surprisingly low for the number of hits and was probably due to the bombs exploding deep within the ship. This was the largest warship ever lost in combat to air power. It was damaged from the fort gunfire of the previous day, but it was the bombing that destroyed the ship. The crew would be utilised to help man the coastal defences of Bergen.[115]

In addition, the mines layed earlier by the Norwegian *Tyr* sank the transport *Sao Paulo*, which had been redirected from Trondheim to Bergen to bring military equipment to the Germans. This combined with further losses from both German and Norwegian mines led to the suspension of German ships bringing aid to Bergen. It would not be until the 13th that the harbour was open to traffic, and it would remain dangerous.[116]

The Skuas, now aware they were well in range of Bergen, conducted several attacks, most without as great as success as their first attack. But on the 14th they sank the partially unloaded *Bärenfels*. Later on the 16th they damaged the *U-58* while it berthed in harbour.[117]

The German forces in Bergen also had other problems, since the passive resistance of the local authorities and the build-up of Norwegian forces at the Voss mobilisation depot continued. This compelled the Germans to request the airlift of ammunition which was carried out over the coming days. Seaplanes transported an infantry company of the German 69th Division to Bergen on the evening of the 10th. However, the use of seaplanes to airlift reinforcements was curtailed due to the wear and tear on the aircraft.[118]

The commander of the Norwegian 4th Infantry Division was Major General William Steffens. He had fallen back to the Voss region when Bergen was attacked.

He planned to build up his forces and then recapture Bergen. Over the next few days he mobilised and equipped his forces and fielded a close to complete 4th Field Brigade under the inspired command of Colonel Gudbrand Østbye. Ancillary units made up the remainder of the units at Voss, including volunteers and militia (*landvern*). Other than the 6th in the far north, this would be the only field brigade of the remaining five that the Norwegians mobilised close to plan. The Germans, realising that Steffens' force was too strong, remained largely on the defensive. While they strengthened their defences, they started to shuttle supplies and troops to Bergen and prepare for brown-water operations in the Norwegian fjords combined with an overland advance.[119]

On 18 April Steffens was ordered by Ruge to shift from blocking a German advance from Bergen to stopping the German 163rd Infantry Division from driving from Oslo to Bergen. It would prove to be one of the few successful Norwegian counter-attacks. Led by Colonel Gudbrand Østbye, the bulk of the 4th Field Brigade actually threw the lead elements of the German division back in the Bagn area, with the Germans withdrawing toward Hønefoss on the 20th. In the process the Norwegians took 150 prisoners, quantities of equipment and destroyed two tanks. In the south this was the high-water mark of the Norwegian war effort. Though successful, they were exhausted and running out of supplies. The 163rd was reinforced (using a total of seventeen tanks in the fighting) and began a steady drive against Østbye. On 30 April, in the Fagnes region, the Norwegian colonel was forced to surrender his command of 3,500 men, 4 field pieces, 4 mortars and 85 machine-guns.[120]

Rear Admiral Tank-Nielsen had issued orders for the warships in his command to retire on three interconnected and large fjords to continue action. The largest of the three was the 111-mile long Hardangerfjord and it would be a vital corridor the Germans would exploit in defeating Steffens. Tank-Nielsen would be so exhausted that on 16 April he would on doctor's orders give up his command. Admiral Diesen would take direct command but due to his distance would give great latitude to the local naval staff.

Operating from the port of Uskedal in Hardangerfjord, the Norwegians had two old torpedo-boats, the *Sæl* and *Stegg*, the minelayer *Tyr* and four auxiliaries. A third torpedo-boat, the *Storm*, was lost when it grounded on the 13th. The Germans had requisitioned ships for transporting troops supported by the gunnery training ship *Bremse*, the *Carl Peters*, six S-boats and other craft including one minesweeper, the *M1*. German troop movement utilised towed barges and even towed rowing boats/canoes.[121]

Uskedal lies south of Bergen, along the inner route the Germans were utilising to transport troops up from Stavanger to reinforce Bergen. It was also the head of Hardangerfjord which allowed access deep into Norway to whoever controlled it, including to small ports south of Voss where the Norwegian 4th Infantry Division was assembling.

The Norwegians were able to seize two German merchant ships in the area, converting one to a tender for the naval aircrews and aircraft. By 18 April the

Germans at Bergen were aware of the Norwegian forces and sent in three S-boats to reconnoitre. Of these, two located the *Sæl* and in a spirited encounter sank her.

The Germans now mounted a serious expedition. Led by the *Bremse*, the force consisted of five S-boats, the well-armed converted trawler *Schiff 18* and apparently a requisitioned trawler, *Schiff 221*, which was armed with a 57mm gun. On board were some pioneers, including their three- and seven-man inflatable boats, and infantry. The plan was to land on either side of Uskedal and then advance and capture the small port. They left on the night of the 19th and intended to land under cover of darkness on the morning of the 20th. Uskedal was defended by a handful of Norwegians and had two flatbed trucks with a 65mm gun and a 47mm gun mounted *en portee*.

The *Stegg* was patrolling when it encountered the approaching Germans. It turned back to port to warn the defenders of the approaching Germans. In the ensuing action that lasted until 09:00, Uskedal was captured with thirty prisoners, along with the two flatbeds and the *Tyr* while the *Stegg* was sunk. German losses included several wounded and the two trawlers hit by gunfire and damaged. Many of the Norwegians escaped up the fjord by land.[122]

The Germans would continue to utilise small boats to operate in the fjord and seize additional minor ports and positions in the coming days while facing some Norwegian opposition. By 24 April they had advanced so they were directly south of Voss. By 2 May, well after the Norwegian 4th Infantry Division had abandoned Voss, they had extended their occupation to Odda at the extreme south end of the three-fjord complex. From there, on 5 May, a detachment of German troops utilising skis set out overland to link up with Stavanger.[123]

At Bergen the bulk of the German 159th Infantry Regiment of the 69th Infantry Division was preparing to advance toward Voss. They slowly made their way through the interior, splitting into two columns. One followed the railway line, while another branched off south heading towards Hardangerfjord. On the 22nd, they encountered serious Norwegian resistance. In the ensuing days they continued a slow advance toward Voss ably supported by Luftwaffe bombing. With the Norwegian 4th Field Brigade being used in the east in a counter-attack against the Germans advancing on the Norwegian rear, the Germans were able to advance to the outskirts of Voss by the 25th and capture it. This was accomplished in part due to the argument between two Norwegian officers as to who was in command of the roadblock facing Bergen. They went to see General Steffens when the Germans attacked on the 24th. While there the local Norwegian commander left in control was forced to fall back. At Voss only 300 men were captured, but equipment included 8 field pieces, 25 mortars and 120 machine-guns.[124]

The southern prong had been advancing along the north side of the fjord ably supported by German seapower in control of Hardangerfjord. It now turned inland to arrive on the south flank of Voss on the 26th. With his flank effectively turned, Steffens ordered his command to head north towards Sognefjord, in the hinterland. Seeing no chance for further resistance, he demobilised his command on 30 April, sending his remaining troops home. German troops linked up with troops coming from Oslo on 2 May. The Norwegian 4th Infantry Division was no more.[125]

* * *

Trondheim was more isolated from the rest of the German troops than Bergen had been. Colonel Wilhelm Weiss of the German 3rd Mountain Division was essentially on the defensive until a relieving column from Oslo could reach him.

At the time of the failed air attack on Trondheim by the *Furious* on 11 April two British destroyers from the British fleet were on nearby detached duty. Commander James Clouston had the *Isis* and *Ilex* and they closed the entrance to Trondheim on the morning of the 12th. The German-manned battery at Brettingen took them under fire at 13:20. The destroyers retired undamaged but they reported that the Norwegian batteries were manned. This would be another reason for the Allies to forgo a direct naval attack on Trondheim.[126]

The Germans in Trondheim were receiving troops by air, with a battalion of the 181st Infantry Division arriving quickly. They were renamed 'Group Trondheim' (*Gruppe Drontheim*). After seizing Værnes airfield Weiss wanted to continue the advance to the nearby Swedish border. In the following days, while suffering from the ambushes of *francs-tireurs*, Weiss pushed his *Kampfgruppes* east to the border with Sweden with an improvised armoured train, and south some 40km to the outskirts of Støren where the junction of the two rail lines from Oslo meet. On the outskirts of Støren he called a halt. Weiss lacked the strength to do more. Later, on 27 April, the Germans sent a ski detachment south and west of Støren. The Norwegian blocking force at Støren would hold on against a strengthening German force until 27 April before abandoning the town.[127]

Weiss organised local Norwegian work crews under German direction to increase the capacity of and improve the condition of Værnes and much activity would take place there throughout April. Among the planes using the airfield would be Stuka dive-bombers operating out of there early in April. All this would help greatly in bringing in support to Trondheim and also support the isolated Germans at Narvik as this was the nearest German controlled airfield to them.

In the meantime, Norwegian Major Hans Holtermann, who had escaped when Værnes was captured intact, having few troops available, remembered the old fort of Ingstadkleiva, 8 miles from Værnes near the small town of Hegra. He brought his men there to provide uniforms and weapons. It would become known as the Battle for Fort Hegra. The fall of this fortress would mark the end of the battle for central Norway. Hegra was built on a rocky hill on the road to Sweden in 1907 to defend against a possible Swedish invasion. It was armed with ten large old guns and howitzers and had underground bunkers to fight from. Unfortunately the guns were largely fixed and faced Sweden and could do little against the Germans. The status of Hegra had been downgraded in 1926 but it had an active depot and could supply the roughly 200 men and 1 nurse of this new garrison with supplies, arms and ammunition. Fighting there began on 14 April and they resisted for three weeks, an example of stubbornness in the Norwegian defence of the country. But as a siege this was a minor irritant to the Germans and the fort finally surrendered on 5 May.

Colonel O. B. Getz of the 13th Infantry Regiment would become the *de facto* commander of the 5th Infantry Division and would officially assume that post after Laurantzon's retirement on 'health grounds' on 27 April. He began assembling the 5th Field Brigade at Steinkjer at the back end of Trondheim Fjord. Steinkjer lies on the small Beitstadfjord which is off the main Trondheim Fjord. Steinkjer had an army depot present, but also by forming at the rear of the fjord Getz did not have to fear the German navy's presence commanding the fjord with two destroyers. The back of the fjord was heavily iced-in so for now there was no need to be concerned about their 5.1in guns. He also had a portion of the 3rd Dragoon Regiment, one of Norway's three cavalry regiments, which was mobilising at the time of the invasion for Neutrality Watch at a smaller depot nearby. Part of it was newly transitioned into motorised transport, while other components were still horsed.[128]

To the north of Trondheim lay Namsos and to the south Åndalsnes and by seizing those two secondary ports the Allies could launch a pincer attack on Trondheim. Before the invasion General Falkenhorst had considered Namsos along with Åndalsnes as a possible landing place, but had rejected it with the resources available to him.[129]

* * *

Namsos had the advantage of being relatively close to Steinkjer, where elements of the Norwegian 5th Division were forming at the 13th Infantry Regiment's depot, while Åndalsnes offered a way to link up with the main Norwegian army fighting the Germans advancing from Oslo.

Major General Sir Adrian Carton de Wiart was placed in command of Maurice Force on 14 April. He was unfamiliar with Norway but had earned a VC in the First World War. The order from General Ironside to de Wiart was, 'Capture of Trondheim considered essential'.[130]

The British began to organise two brigades for this operation to be reinforced later. The Namsos force would be constituted with the 146th Brigade. Åndalsnes was to be utilised by Brigadier H. de R. Morgan in command of the 148th Brigade. The French would support the Namsos landing with a demi-brigade of alpine troops.[131] The latter was essentially a reinforced regiment of three battalions with support troops. This was the beginning of Operation 'Maurice'. It would highlight the fact that the Allies, and certainly the British, had learned too little from the Polish campaign and about the speed that the German attacks develop. Ironically, de Wiart had been in Poland on official duty during much of the Polish campaign.[132]

Operation 'Maurice' was a disaster from the start. The town of Namsos, built almost exclusively from wood, would be utterly destroyed in the Luftwaffe bombing before the final evacuation by the Allies on 2 May. The German control of the air would be a crucial reason for why the Allied position was hopeless not even a week into the campaign. Throw in the narrow valleys with dirt roads that by day were muddy or even partly flooded and by night freezing and with snow at the higher elevations, this attempt seemed likely to be doomed from the start.[133]

At the height of the operation, the Norwegians, British and French would muster between them fifteen infantry battalions and nine artillery batteries. But the Norwegian forces were never fully mobilised and the Allies had landed under aerial bombardment. This led to unloading being haphazard and incomplete. Several key equipment parts would end up being separated, in the wrong place and in several cases on transports steaming back to Scotland. When the Germans, now under the command of Major General Woytasch of the German 181st Infantry Division, launched a surprise attack at Steinkjer on 21 April, using airpower combined with landings from German naval forces in Trondheim Fjord to outflank the Norwegians, Colonel Getz was forced to withdraw and the town of Steinkjer was taken on 23 April.[134]

The ice had melted enough in the inner fjord for the Germans to take appropriated local small craft and in conjunction with the destroyer *Jacobi* dominate the Trondheim fjords. Getz had made dispositions in the knowledge that he did not command the local waters and the Germans did. He had no answer to the German main battery guns which with the thaw allowed them to steam to the back of Trondheim Fjord and pass into Beitstadfjord. The Luftwaffe undertook a serious bombing attack on Steinkjer which destroyed most of the town, although with no civilian losses. Again, fires simply burned the largely wooden town down.

The British and the French, realising their position was rapidly deteriorating, especially in light of German airpower, shortly after began withdrawing and instead of handing over equipment to the Norwegians destroyed it. An embittered Getz surrendered his command to the Germans on 4 May. Since 9 April he had lost thirty-seven dead and thirty-two wounded, but he was also almost out of ammunition, claiming he could only fight on for one more day. He now surrendered 2,050 officers and men. Some minor units would continue to fight on in the north to slow the Germans in relieving Narvik.[135]

* * *

By 14 April the German advance to the north and north-west to relieve Bergen and Trondheim was ready to commence. The 196th Infantry Division was personally led by General Pellengahr, who had won his spurs in the artillery. He would spearhead the advance up the two main inland valleys of Norway, while the 163rd Infantry Division operated on the left flank of the German advance.

The Norwegian situation was that the 2nd Infantry Division was assembling north of Oslo on the shores of Lake Myøsa. General Hvinden-Haug established his headquarters at Hamar, while Ruge and his staff were further north at Øyer. Lillehammer is at the north end of this long, thin lake.

Forming at Elverum was Group Hiorth, named after Colonel Hiorth, who was a member of Quisling's NS Party. It consisted of the bulk of two battalions of infantry and some engineers. It was set up to defend the Germans from advancing up the Østerdalen, which parallels the Swedish border in this area. Facing Hiorth was *Kampfgruppe Fischer*, named after Colonel Hermann Fischer of the 340th Infantry Regiment. By 21 April in front of Rena, his force had been reinforced to three battalions, two artillery battalions, one combat engineer battalion with about ten tanks and two motorised companies. By the 24th he would have five PzKw II and fourteen PzKw Is in his command.[136]

Near Hamar, two battalions of the Norwegian 2nd Infantry Division along with elements of the 2nd Artillery Regiment and 2nd Dragoon Regiment were forming up, and together were known as Group Hvinden-Haug. Group Mork, named after Colonel Carl Mork commanding the 6th Infantry Regiment, was mobilising at Hønefoss, north of Kongsberg. Mork was still issuing written protest notes to the Germans as late as 10 April and ordering his troops not to fire on the Germans.[137] Ruge's immediate command would also have the 11th Infantry Regiment mobilising in his rear between Øyer and Trondheim. Ruge's orders on the 15th were, 'our mission in the eastern region is to buy time and hold out until help arrives, so that we then can co-operate with the Allied troops'.[138] None of these units were at full strength, volunteers had joined the commands, units were mixed and battalion strength varied wildly from unit to unit.

Hitler, fearing the Allies had already landed on the Norwegian west coast, ordered a company of 185 paratroops to drop on Dombås. This unit was quickly air-transported up from Germany. Dombås was an important rail junction with one line running to Åndalsnes, while the other continued on to Trondheim. It was also well behind the front lines on 14 April when the drop took place. The drop was to be made from fifteen Ju52s despite the poor conditions. General Falkenhorst felt that since this was a direct order from Hitler he could not delay the operation because of the weather, even for 24 hours. One plane was almost immediately shot down while flying towards the drop zone and over the target there were high winds that scattered the group. Of the planes, five were lost, three landed in Sweden, two at Værnes and five back at Fornebu. In addition, a battalion of the Norwegian 11th Infantry Regiment was forming there at the time and was able to fire on some of the Germans as they were descending. The much-reduced paratroops fought long and hard but by 19 April they had been mopped up by the Norwegians. They had received some supplies that were air-dropped to them, but the Norwegians only grew stronger with each day as the initial battalion was reinforced. The German attack did interrupt rail and road traffic, but it was too small a group to be effective and proper German plans to link up with the detachment were non-existent.

Meanwhile, German reinforcements poured into Oslo. The cutting edge would be the tanks, though the classic use of armour as a force-multiplier in an offensive role became less and less valuable as the war progressed. They were first to see action against the Norwegians on 16 April in the interior as the German columns advanced toward Trondheim.[139]

The Norwegians held out against the initial German advance, and Group Mork actually forced the Germans to fall back near Hønefoss. This was accomplished in large part due to ski-equipped Norwegians. However, it was Mork's command that would be hit with five tanks for the first time in combat. His command ended up in retreat and Mork so mishandled this that Ruge relieved him with Colonel Tor Dahl. Still on the west flank of the Norwegians, this would now be known as Group Dahl.[140]

To the east was the old fort at Kongsvinger. As with so many of the forts, it was designed for the enemy attacking from the east, i.e., Sweden. Additionally, at this point it was more a museum piece than military fortification. A small *ad hoc* force called Company Benckert formed there, named after Gösta Benckert, a Swede who crossed over the border when the fighting broke out with 131 Norwegian and Swedish volunteers. Most of them had just returned from fighting for Finland in the Winter War. The fortress commandant, Major Einar Hoch-Nielsen, refused to issue armaments from the fort's arsenal, claiming that he had not been ordered to release the weapons – but his loyalties were also suspect. Benckert's men broke into to the arsenal to arm themselves. Company Benckert held up a German advance on the 15th, but were dispersed and Kongsvinger was taken on the 16th in the face of a determined German advance. Benckert eventually would end up in Trondheim, later returning to Sweden. Because of this incident the Germans decided to treat foreign volunteers as *francs-tireurs*, subject to immediate execution.[141]

General Pellengahr led the advance in the centre against Group Hvinden-Haug. Arriving at the south end of the lake, Pellengahr sent a column up the west side and then had it advance across the frozen ice to threaten the Norwegian rear. This caused them to withdraw with a small force being cut off and forced to surrender. This would be a very typical German tactic. They would find the enemy front and then flank them by whatever means necessary – skis, climbing, motorised transport – whatever was required.

The other advantage that the Germans enjoyed over the Norwegians was a great number of machine-guns, with a higher rate of fire, and the Norwegians were still without hand grenades. The Germans had tanks, more artillery than the Norwegians and the Luftwaffe.

The failure of the Allies properly to reinforce the Norwegians with trained and plentiful troops was compounded by the dwindling Norwegian supplies. By 21 April the Norwegians in the Gudbrandsdalen were down to 200 mortar rounds and 1,000 rounds of 75mm ammunition. Even if they had been less tardy, it is very doubtful that the British could have supplied 75mm ammunition for the German-made field pieces of the Norwegian army.[142]

This is an important point often not recognised in studies of this campaign. The loss of many of the Norwegian mobilisation depots with the initial invasion by Germany not only took the equipment away from the Norwegian army and where troops were to report, but it also crippled the logistical side of the Norwegian army. Their request for 10,000 rifles from the Allies was because they did not have enough rifles. The expenditure of munitions in the fighting was something that for the most part could not be replaced. Norwegian resistance was fighting the clock on several levels. Not only were additional German troops arriving and the logistical network improving for Germany, but these factors were deteriorating for the Norwegians.

The Germans continued the advance, taking Lillehammer on the 21st. They had advanced 120 miles in eight days. Group Dahl continued to fall back as well, with its morale also in decline. With the fall of Lillehammer, Group Dahl entered the side Gausdalen valley, which due to snowdrifts inhibited movement. Ruge ordered Dahl to break out and Dahl refused. Pellengahr left a holding force there and Dahl, his morale broken, would surrender on 29 April. The approximate number who surrendered was 200 officers, 3,500 men with 7 artillery pieces and 125 machine-guns.[143]

On the eastern side the Germans had *Kampfgruppe Fischer* continuing to push forward with air support overhead. At Rena the Luftwaffe attacked the town and it suffered severely. Group Hiorth retreated from Rena and Colonel Hiorth considered the situation irretrievable. Ruge relieved him of command on the 24th but the Norwegian force in the Østerdalen was finished as an organised fighting force. Some troops continued to resist the Germans, some would be interned in Sweden, while others simply returned to their homes and on the 30th *Kampfgruppe Fischer* linked up with German forces from Trondheim near Støren.

In the Gudbrandsdalen the British troops awaited by Group Hvinden-Haug had arrived from Åndalsnes. What Ruge had hoped for had been accomplished, but he was going to be disappointed.

A large shore party of over 700 British marines and sailors had landed at Åndalsnes on the 17th and greeted Brigadier Morgan's 148th Brigade on the 18th. This would be known as Sickleforce and would end up being under the command of Major General B. G. T. Paget. Åndalsnes was chosen in part as it had a rail depot for a rail line that ran to Dombås. The marines and navy took charge of the port defences and the operation of the base. But the brigade that arrived suffered from the absence of vital items of equipment (e.g., the mortar crews only had smoke rounds) and even part of one battalion. This initial force numbered about 1,000 men. They had been originally allocated to Namsos and so Brigadier Morgan had no background papers for where his command ended up. The dock could only handle one large ship at a time so a portion of Morgan's command arrived at nearby Molde. The small scale of the landing here and at Namsos brought home the need for the Allies to capture Trondheim. They were not off to a good start.[144]

To Morgan's credit, as the German paratroops who had dropped at Dombås were preparing to surrender, he had rapidly shuttled troops by rail to that vital rail juncture. British marines actually lent artillery support against the German paratroops on the 19th.

The question of command came up as the Norwegians assumed the British would fight under their command. The British Imperial General Staff defied that with a direct order to Brigadier Morgan on 20 April not to place himself or his forces under Norwegian command. An agreement with the Allies was arrived at but it did require a meeting between Ruge and Morgan. Ruge had to threaten Morgan that if the 148th Brigade did not fall under General Hvinden-Haug of the Norwegian

2nd Infantry Division, the Norwegians would be forced to cease operations and he, Ruge, would resign. Ruge at one point said to the French military attaché when the argument was going on that 'Norway was not some African colony'. The British had an MI6 agent, Frank Foley, present with Ruge's headquarters. He helped, along with others, to persuade Morgan to accept this logical arrangement. The direct order from the Imperial General Staff was literally pocketed and ignored. London did not learn of this new in-the-field arrangement for several days.[145]

After the campaign, one suggestion for the improvement of future operations was in the matter of liaison. It was recommended that before disembarkation an adequate liaison relationship be adopted with allies. The lack of translators was also noted. In the Norwegian campaign, especially at the start, this was decidedly lacking. The Norwegians were also disappointed in the ability of their British allies, who due to their boots, the cold and the equipment in general, could not venture far from the road in the rough terrain of Norway's interior. Finally, the conduct of primarily British territorial troops towards Norwegian civilians in the matter of looting and harassment of Norwegian women was poor.[146]

Morgan sent troops forward, and in consultation with Ruge, beginning on the 21st a series of actions would be fought in front and then behind Lillehammer. The ill-equipped British troops lacked food, rest and equipment. They had no skis and on the 22nd actually had the brigade headquarters in the rear taken under machine-gun fire from an out-flanking German ski-mounted patrol.[147]

On the 22nd General Pellengahr was operating against the now-joint British–Norwegian front, Group Hvinden-Haug with more troops. He had three battalions of his division,[148] two companies of motorised machine-guns, one artillery battalion (two batteries), two companies of mountain troops, one pioneer company and a detachment of tanks.

Realising that flanking attacks were not needed with the presence of tanks, Pellengahr began making frontal attacks leading with the tanks. The PzKw IIs were quite effective in this campaign as they could fire 20mm high-explosive shells that also set wooden buildings on fire. Working with infantry to give support and pioneers to clear roadblocks, this was an effective team. By using three to five tanks in the lead with one being armed with a gun and not just machine-guns, they could lead the way on the road.[149]

Pellengahr's column also had two of the monster 18-ton Neubau PzKw IVs.[150] Lightly armoured and though a failed design, they had a 37mm and a 75mm gun carried in a shared turret and three machine-guns. Each had a six-man crew. The 75mm gun was particularly effective especially when German artillery was not yet up to the front. One would be knocked out in the fighting at Kvam. Later in the course of the month losses were replaced by a shipment to Norway of additional tanks. Of those lost, the Norwegians destroyed a minimum of seven tanks with explosive charges or Molotov cocktails. In the fighting the Germans used a total of fifty-four tanks, including one replacement 'test model' Neubau PzKw IV, which had only steel and not armour plating. They also had some additional armoured cars present in Norway by mid-April. Colonel Østbye would later write

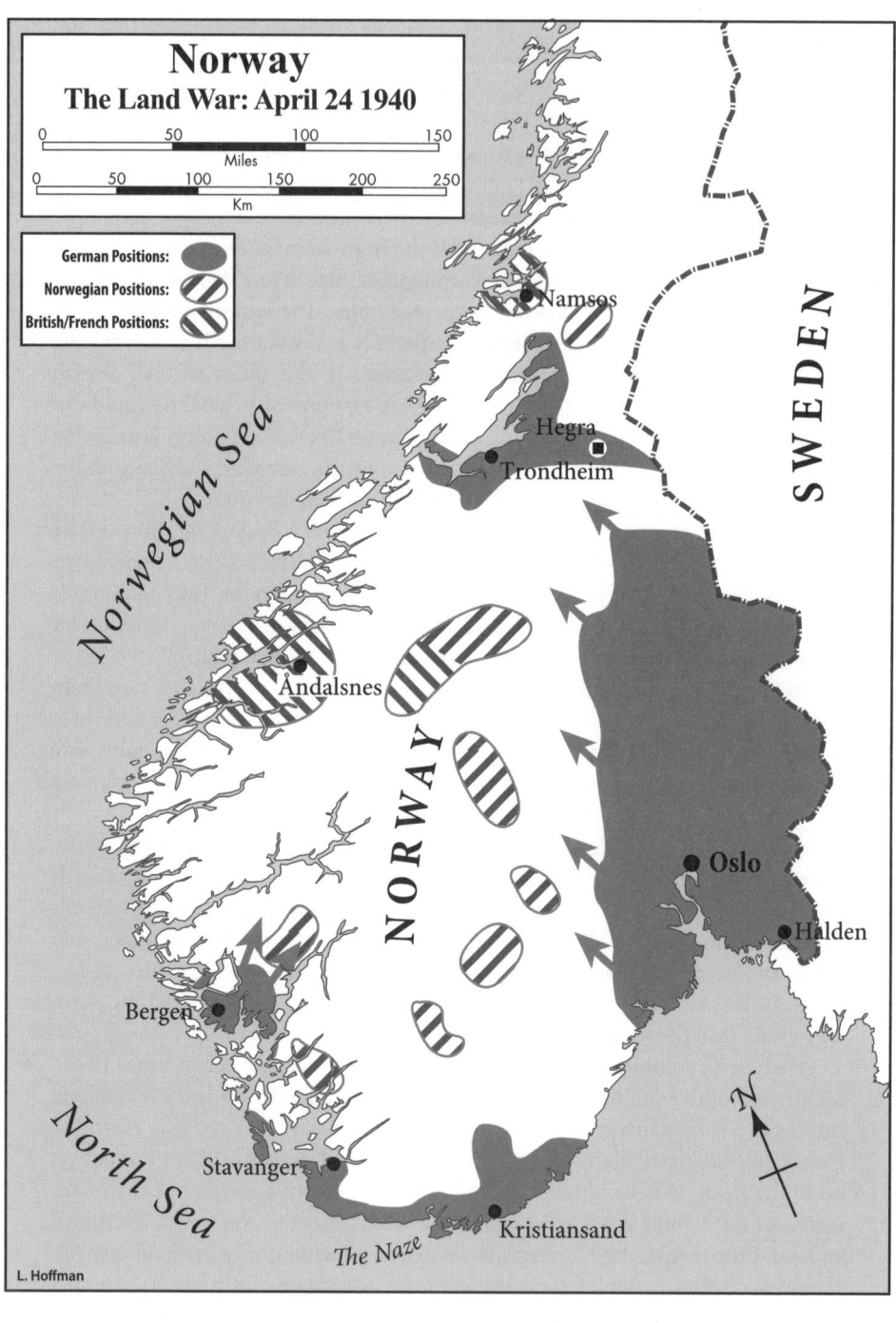

# Norway
## The Land War: April 24 1940

| 0 | 50 | 100 | 150 |

Miles

| 0 | 50 | 100 | 150 | 200 | 250 |

Km

German Positions:
Norwegian Positions:
British/French Positions:

Namsos

Hegra
Trondheim

Norwegian Sea

N O R W A Y

Andalsnes

S W E D E N

Oslo

Halden

Bergen

North Sea

Stavanger

The Naze

Kristiansand

N

L. Hoffman

of the German tanks that they had 'colossal significance for carrying out offensive operations, even in mountainous terrain'.[151]

British anti-tank rifles could penetrate the tanks' armour and later the French lent the British some of their 25mm Hotchkiss AT guns which were used at Kvam. Both were effective against these thin-skinned tanks, but it was too little and too late.

The German advance was rapid and overcame a series of defensive positions. The decisive action took place on 23 April at the village of Tretten. The Germans deployed five tanks combined with 105mm artillery fire and under attack many of the British troops broke and ran. The British had in the meantime landed the 15th Infantry Brigade under the command of Brigadier H. Smyth. This was made up of regular troops and performed better than the territorial troops. They had originally been part of the force Churchill wanted to land at Trondheim in conjunction with Operation 'Hammer'. The enlarged force of Sickleforce was under Major General Paget.

Smyth would be rushed up to the front lines to help hold back the advancing Germans. He was supplied with the French-lent 25mm AT guns. He would make a stand with British regular troops at Kvam on 25–6 April, though he would be wounded and evacuated. The Allies fell back towards Dombås, making another stand there on 30 April. The Luftwaffe had heavily bombed the British rear and on the 28th the decision was made to evacuate central Norway. Paget informed Ruge on the 28th. The British were retiring on Åndalsnes and evacuation. It would be accomplished by 2 May. With the evacuation went the Norwegian government's gold reserves, the king and crown prince, as well as the government and Ruge's staff. Ruge and the king would continue to operate up in the Narvik area before final evacuation to Britain.[152]

Group Hvinden-Haug covered the British withdrawal and surrendered to the Germans on 3 May. Ruge had ordered General Hvinden-Haug first to allow any in his command who chose to leave and head north to continue the resistance, but he ignored Ruge's orders. Instead, on the 3rd he surrendered his entire command of 123 officers and 2,500 men. A large amount of ammunition, machine-guns and field artillery was also captured with their transport.[153]

German tactics were key to the victory in central Norway as well as their numbers. They would field 100,000 troops in Norway and Hitler had just ordered the German 2nd Mountain Division to Norway to help relieve their fellow alpine troops at Narvik.

One effective tactic used by the Germans was the simple rotation of troops. With such a narrow front in the steep mountain valleys, the Germans would post a unit on the front while other units rested in the rear. Then, rotating in a rested unit early in the day, they would be ready at daylight to pressure the Norwegian front line that often was not 'fresh'. This wore down the Norwegians and as the campaign unfolded the Norwegians' morale would drop due to fatigue and the constant retreating in the face of German pressure – one officer recorded Norwegian soldiers sleeping during the noise of combat.[154]

Pellengahr, the artillery-trained commander, later wrote of his employment of artillery, 'The artillery was always placed far forward in the column, so that some of the *Kampfgruppe*'s strongest firepower was immediately available when one encountered the enemy. This prompt response of fire-support and the psychological effect of the shells contributed significantly to breaking the resistance rapidly.'[155] It was usually the German soldier who as dawn broke had scaled the mountains on one or both sides of the valley and would surprise the Norwegians and later British troops by having the high ground. This would almost always lead to the hurried retreat of the Allied forces. What is interesting here is that while the Norwegian army had mountain-trained and ski-trained troops, these formed a minority of the army and the bulk were in the Norwegian 6th Infantry Division posted in the north.[156]

* * *

Narvik's population not only had to feed the additional German troops and sailors, but was also burdened by the merchant seamen from the damaged and sunk merchant ships now littering the waterfront. Over 200 British sailors and 500 German seamen had to be cared for, housed and protected from Allied naval and air attacks.[157]

The supply situation was worsening as a result of the sailors who had survived the sunk destroyers – a further 2,500 men had to be fed, housed and clothed. On 11 April Hitler ordered that long-range Do26 planes be placed under the X Air Corps to help supply Narvik, and at the same time use submarines to bring supplies, while limited help was expected via use of the Swedish rail network.[158] The Swedish government allowed a limited number of Germans in civilian clothes to bring some material aid to Dietl across the border by rail – and to leave Narvik and return to Germany. A lone Do24 seaplane reached Narvik on the evening of the 13th but could bring little to the isolated 3rd Mountain Division.

Another attempt to resupply Narvik commenced on 10 April. Dönitz ordered the submarines *U-61*, *U-26*, *U-29* and *U-43* converted to transport duty and each were capable of loading 40–50 tons of ammunition and equipment. They departed individually north for Narvik between 12 and 16 April. The small *U-61* was diverted to Bergen while the other three would end up being redirected to Trondheim as the situation was too fluid at Narvik for their safe arrival.

These operations were a success, though the *U-32* was almost lost due to aviation fuel fumes in the confined submarine. On her return the *U-26* would get a rare success in sinking a British transport. The unescorted 5,200-ton *Cedarbank* carrying supplies on 21 April was torpedoed and sunk by *U-26* north-west of Bergen. The destroyer *Javelin* later rescued the captain and twenty-nine crewmembers, while fifteen perished.[159]

It was a time of crisis inside the German High Command, pressured also by the fact the British were landing troops at Namsos and Åndalsnes and a landing attempt at Narvik was expected too. Hitler and Keitel were thinking of abandoning

Narvik, giving the order to break out south towards Trondheim. The possibility of bringing out the troops by air from Narvik was taken into account, but Jodl strongly opposed any retreat from Narvik as it was impossible to carry out due to the weather situation and the enemy presence. Since an evacuation via air was impossible, Hitler was prepared to sign an order to allow Dietl's force to cross the border and be interned in Sweden.[160]

However, officers in the OKW Land Defence Office were more optimistic about the situation. They were proven to be correct, especially Lieutenant Colonel Bernhard von Lossberg. The Naval Command was supporting the opinion that after having lost ten good destroyers Narvik should 'be held and defended as long as possible'.[161] Therefore, Dietl was instructed to resist and hold enemy forces at Narvik. Moreover, on the 18th Hitler sent Captain Schenk von Sternberg with a personal message to Dietl, reflecting the orders already issued on 15 April, that is to carry on the defence on the strong mountain position near the rail line. Sternberg would arrive at Narvik on the 22nd.[162]

On the same day the Dietl group was posted under the direct command of OKW and was lucky enough that morale remained high. 'Troops cut off from Germany greeted with delight every time when a German plane appeared in the sky over them.'[163]

Although the support from the air was important, the Germans gathered intelligence on Norwegian military movements from the radio station at Tromsø and from Finland. As late as 18 April, though cut off and with the destroyers sunk, General Franz Halder could still record, after hearing from a staff officer who had flown out of Narvik, that 'morale of troops [remained] good'.[164]

On the 16th the Germans launched the first push to enlarge the bridgehead towards the most important point, the Swedish border. At 03:00 a reinforced company with a ski platoon attacked a Norwegian company and seized the Norddal bridge that was damaged by the retreating defenders and the border station of Bjornfjell. The latter was stubbornly defended, being the last position between the Germans and Sweden. The Germans captured almost sixty Norwegians.[165]

As Dietl explained to von Sternberg at his HQ at Hotel Royal on 22 April, the Norwegian 6th Infantry Division was closing the way north, the British were at sea and at Harstad and finally it would be impossible to retreat south toward Trondheim with the poorly equipped forces of the Narvik Group. To do so would require them to pass icy mountains, frozen lakes and a plateau covered by high snow. The best strategy was to fight for the port and the city as long as possible and then slowly conduct a fighting withdrawal to the Swedish border along the rail line, destroying any facility the British could use to transport the iron ore from the Swedish border to their ships.[166]

Allied strength would continue to increase as additional French and a brigade of Polish troops were committed to the battle for Narvik. Dietl's isolated command would be forced back to the Swedish border and Narvik was retaken. But with the invasion of France and the collapse of the Allied position in the rest of Norway, evacuation of the Allied troops was the only possible outcome.

* * *

Another change in Norway after the initial invasion was the fall of Vidkun Quisling's 'National Government'. While Hitler had supported Quisling as success crowned Germany's endeavors in the opening hours, disquieting news began to filter into Berlin from Oslo. Only the tiny Communist Party joined with Quisling calling for surrender to the German invaders.[167] Quisling gained only very limited support from business and labour, which were mainly concerned with preventing an economic collapse in occupied Norway. Quisling's days were numbered as the self-proclaimed leader of the 'National Government'.

Quisling had, in the view of the German high command, hurt their efforts. First, Ambassador Bräuer never liked Quisling. He believed that Quisling's support in the nation was miniscule and that he malignly influenced Colonel General Nikolaus von Falkenhorst and other generals. Secondly, Hitler and the German high command attributed the loss of the *Blücher* at Oslo to Quisling not supplying all the correct information (the torpedo racks were known about by German intelligence but not through Quisling) and they blamed the loss of the ten German destroyers at Narvik on Quisling. This was because he indicated a coastal defence battery was present and the Germans, as at Bergen and Trondheim and elsewhere, had carried on their ships naval personnel to man those batteries. At Narvik the guns did not exist, just the concrete emplacements. Thirdly, Norwegian resistance was stiffer then they had expected, and they blamed Quisling in part for this. When Quisling made his radio broadcast on the evening of 9 April, it was viewed by the German army as directly leading to a flood of young Norwegian men who headed into the interior to take up the fight.[168] As early as 11 April General Halder knew Quisling was not the right man to be the German-backed puppet leader of Norway.[169] In the planning for the operation there was a note about him where Falkenhorst's staff said, 'Friend of Germany, of no importance, held to be a dreamer of fantasy'.[170]

A report that Hitler received on 11 April from beleaguered Trondheim cut off from the rest of German-occupied Norway said, as Professor Oddvar K. Hoidal has noted, 'the *Wehrmacht* declared that the city's population, which previously had been passive, had become aroused in favor of resistance because of Quisling'.[171] Finally, many Norwegians coalesced around Ambassador Bräuer and the Norwegian Supreme Court, which remained in Oslo, telling the Germans that this was a terrible decision.

Berlin refused to recognise Quisling's government and this was a blow. Only the German navy supported Quisling, while Alfred Rosenberg's meddling in foreign affairs by helping Quisling on 9–12 April was now, with Norwegian resistance, thought to be unhelpful by Hitler. On the 13th, Hitler received Hagelin as the new minister for the economy and food,[172] but already on 11 April he had expressed the view that Quisling had little support. This estimate was very near to that of foreign ministry officials, and Quisling's true position found confirmation after the beginning of the campaign, when the German diplomats reported that

Quisling is having certain difficulties, he is facing in Oslo as well in the country strong refusal to accept him.'[173]

On 15 April an Administrative Council that pledged itself to King Haakon replaced Quisling and his 'National Government'. This situation would not last long as Hitler was unhappy about these developments. He would have Dr Bräuer recalled on 16 April and sacked him. By the 17th negotiations with the Nygaardsvold government were completely terminated. Norway formally declared war on Germany on the 18th. Germany would declare war on Norway shortly after and Norwegian and German flags no longer would fly side-by-side.

By 19 April Hitler would appoint the Nazi stooge Josef Terboven as *Reichskommissar* for Occupied Norwegian Territory and German rule would be imposed on the still-resisting Norway. This was formalised in a 24 April decree by Hitler establishing the soon-to-be-hated Terboven in office. He reported to Hitler, and shared equal but separate power with Falkenhorst as the fighting continued.[174]

Terboven's goal was to maintain order in Norway, gain the co-operation of the Norwegians and aid the German military in completing the conquest of Norway. In his attempt to subjugate Norway, he would utilise many unpleasant means. By September 1940 a puppet government headed by Quisling would be in place.

\* \* \*

Swedish reaction to the invasion was one of trying to maintain strict neutrality but German pressure was immediate. As has been seen, there was some illegal movement of German supplies and key personnel to and from Narvik. The Swedish army quietly increased the active army from 90,000 on 9 April to 320,000 by the end of the month. Many of the new troops were posted to the west coast of Sweden and in the south, opposite occupied Denmark. Swedish troops (unlike during the Winter War) were forbidden to volunteer to help the Norwegians. Sweden wanted to defend strictly her neutrality and guarded the Kiruna mines with the best troops available against the possible attacks from Narvik.[175] Moreover, aeroplanes passing through Swedish air space were shot at.

The British were considering Operation 'Paul', which called for blockading the Swedish ore port of Luleå. In March 1940 a plan to block the port with a merchant ship combined with a bombing attack was examined but the fall of Denmark and southern Norway eliminated that possibility. Sabotage in the form of an almost James Bond attempt was considered as well, though first at the ore port of Oxelösund, a key port for iron ore from central Sweden. All through April there were discussions about some sort of sabotage or even armed movement on Luleå but it was also realised that both the Germans at Narvik and the Swedes would fight and would destroy the railway as the Allies advanced into Sweden. Possible 'accidental' bombing with the Narvik campaign was analysed too and as late as 23–4 May plans were discussed to fly off fifty torpedo-bombers from aircraft carriers, letting them refuel at Narvik and continue on to attack shipping at Luleå. If an attack took place by the Allies, Sweden would have resisted.[176]

* * *

Willi Brandt, who had fled with the Norwegian government on 9 April, was deciding what he would do. For two weeks he helped collect blankets and medical supplies for the retreating Norwegian army.[177]

With Germans closing in he needed to escape from Norway. Paul Gauguin, a grandson of the famous painter and a friend of Brandt, advised him to disguise himself as a Norwegian soldier. He was taken prisoner in an ill-fitting uniform, but with an excellent command of Norwegian, and would later be released in June, along with most other Norwegian soldiers. Brandt visited Oslo and by August 1940 was in Sweden. At first interned, he became a Norwegian citizen (Hitler's Germany had nullified his German nationality in 1938) that same August. Over the coming winter he worked with the Norwegian resistance and entered Norway several times. In 1941 he had published in Sweden *Kriget I Norge*, the story of the three-month war.[178]

* * *

The fighting would continue for weeks, but the die had been cast. The unprepared Norwegians would see their remaining forces in the south-east surrender by early May, while the last forces resisting near Trondheim would surrender by 4–5 May. Admiral Diesen ordered all Norwegian warships left in central Norway to steam for Great Britain or head to northern Norway, which was still resisting. Some escaped but others were scuttled or surrendered to the Germans intact.[179]

The official historian of British grand strategy in the Second World War, J. R. M. Butler, would sum it up with the following:

> It can hardly be denied that the principle of maintaining the aim was flouted: there were far too many changes of plan, and the changed plans did not allow time for corresponding changes to be made in preparations at a lower level. The result was often chaos. Troops were used for purposes for which they had not been designed nor trained nor equipped; ports were found inadequate to maintain the forces assigned to them; ships were not loaded as they should have been and essential gear could not be disembarked in time. Commanders on land, with hardly an exception, felt that there had been a total lack of realistic planning, especially on the administrative side.[180]

Ultimately the events favourable to German attackers compelled the king and the government to retire to the Tromsø area, where the last cabinet in Norway of the Norwegian government took place on 7 June. It was decided that king and government should continue to function in Britain and cease fighting in Norway. The war formally came to an official end in northern Norway on 10 June.

# CHAPTER 12

# *A Tale of When Deterrence Failed*

I approve Hitler's action whole-heartedly. It is a gesture that can have incalculable results, and this is the way to win wars. The democracies have lost the race. I shall give orders to the press and to the Italian people unreservedly to applaud this German action.

Mussolini[1]

It can be argued that the war in Norway was over by midnight of 9 April. The surprise was so complete and the occupying German force so strong that there was little Norway and the Allies could do to retrieve the situation. Both sides were still and would continue to scramble to build their positions – neither side had realised that Germany had essential control of both Nordic nations. The strategic surprise, greater strength, speed, planning and better organisation of the Germans had led to victory.

Simply put, this was a result of the deficient preparation and mobilisation of resources on the part of Norway, combined with the inability and lack of planning to put the resources required into action in a timely manner. This combined with a massive failure to interpret properly and pass on relevant intelligence that could have forewarned and forearmed both the Norwegians and the Allies. The Danes can be excused, as they had essentially given up the option of meaningful resistance well before 9 April.

It is ironic that the fear the Norwegian leftist government had, an understandable and real fear as has been shown, of the Norwegian army leading a coup or violently suppressing the political left would be a vital ingredient in the virtual disarmament of the Norwegian nation in the face of German aggression. In turn, the army dispersing guns, ammunition and other means of resistance out of fear of the left – which only ended on the eve of war – would hamper resistance to Nazi Germany's invasion.

These failures were exploited by the detailed German preparations and brilliant execution of the campaign. A contemporary and relatively neutral source put it in mid-May of 1940, 'Even after discounting Norse innocence, lack of equipment, treachery within, discounting also British amateurishness and unpreparedness, the German campaign was a masterpiece of organization as well as cunning surprise.'[2]

The inability to stop the invasion early was decisive in the outcome of the campaign for Norway. Field Marshal Erwin Rommel later said on the eve of

Operation 'Overlord', 'The enemy must be annihilated before he reaches our main battlefield. We must stop him in the water, destroying all his equipment while it is still afloat!'[3] In Norway, indecision, poor decisions and the failure to counter-attack immediately reinforced disaster on a national scale. The Germans were not going to fail once established in their beachheads.

Excepting the drawn-out recapture of Narvik, really a distant and beleaguered German garrison under siege, the Allies would fail to mount a serious counter-attack to regain lost positions from the Germans during the fighting.

* * *

Probably the single largest result of this campaign for the Axis was that Hitler had designed much of the assault and at times, in spite of his involvement, it was a grand success, without any formal military training at a high level on his part. One must recall he never went to quartermaster school, and neither had he participated in any other high-level military educational programme. In addition, he had never been out of Europe. If it had failed, as many of his conventional thinking generals and admirals thought – and some hoped, this might have been the 'setback' many wanted. Instead, his reputation of a constantly successful 'sleepwalker'[4] was reinforced. A major setback would have possibly kept the war in the West from expanding and perhaps led to the overthrow of Hitler. Instead, and with Germany's success against the Allies in France coming just a few weeks away, Hitler and Germany's powers were strengthened.

Hitler said that he had envisioned a naval attack on Norway during his first interview with Quisling and also acknowledged that 'luck' was certainly on his side in achieving his success. This made him and others think that his future direct interventions in the running of the war would be successful, when many would not be. Had he not been correct earlier in interpreting how the occupation of the Saar, the *Anschluss* and the Munich crisis would play out and result in Germany and Hitler's success? Yet here success would breed failure. Too sure of himself, he would lead Germany to ruin. Hitler's false sense of omnipotence combined with his continued focus on Norway over the coming years can be summed up by his statement concerning Norway, 'Kriegswichtig, Kriegsnotwendig, Kriegsentscheidend' ('Important for the war, a necessity for the war, decisive for the war').[5] After the Norwegian campaign a series of books and magazines appeared in Germany discussing the success of the fighting in some detail. All this tended to reinforce Hitler and the Nazi's Party's hold on Germany.[6]

Germany's victories in Denmark and Norway had some other far-reaching effects. Germany now had flanking naval bases facing the Atlantic that would be helpful in sending air and naval forces against the Allied convoy system. The consolidation of this was evidenced with the visit of Grand Admiral Erich Raeder to Oslo to meet with naval staff and discuss the bringing of Bergen and Trondheim on line as submarine bases while the campaign was still being fought.[7] Trondheim was envisioned as a future major naval base. An additional benefit to Germany was that some in the Allied camp *assumed* Germany could not launch an attack into the Low Countries until the invasion of Norway was wrapped up.[8]

Another gift of the campaign was that the Allies were cut off from Norwegian and Danish supplies, largely timber, iron ore and aluminum, but other commodities such as bacon were now no longer available to the Allies from those nations. The resources of both nations would be exploited in the course of the war by the German war machine. This was an added benefit but not overlooked when the Germans first made the decision to invade.

The single most important positive for the Allies lay in bringing Winston Churchill to power, who would be the war leader Great Britain and the Allies needed to win the war. Between 7 and 8 May the famous 'Norway Debate' took place in the House of Commons. Among many speeches, David Lloyd George made his last important address, calling on Chamberlain to resign. Chamberlain tried to argue in Parliament that Trondheim was no Gallipoli and that the failure in Norway was due to too few friendly airfields and the speed of the Germans in their actions. Two days after the debate the resulting vote supported the government, but showed it was haemorrhaging support – Neville Chamberlain resigned and would be replaced by Winston Churchill.[9]

Another plus for the Allies from the campaign was that the Norwegian merchant fleet, the fourth largest in the world, was firmly in the Allied camp. While the Allies were already utilising much of it, this campaign assured full access to it.

Another major lesson was provided to the British who realised the extent of their command failure as the campaign in Norway unfolded into May and finally June 1940. Their command failures would, in this, the first real campaign of the war for Great Britain, be a wake-up call. They would respond and as a result there would be a better chain of command in future fighting in the war.[10] James S. Corum would say when discussing the revolutionary joint warfare employed in the overwhelming of Denmark and Norway that, 'essentially, the campaign in Norway exemplified a very new way of war-fighting'.[11] The lessons of this operation were not lost on the British regarding the balance of war and remain now relevant as a case study on joint warfare and the operational art.[12]

The campaign also strengthened the hand of those who opposed American isolation from the war. Many of the isolationist Republicans from the mid-west had family ties to Denmark and Norway and they now saw their ancestral homelands occupied. The nomination of Wendell Willkie as the Republican candidate for president in 1940, a man who was not a member of the isolationist wing of the party, was due in part to the German attack.[13]

One of the most interesting lessons of this campaign is that you might love your enemy but they do not love you in return. The failure to have the Aryan Norwegians and Danes embrace their Aryan German brothers was troubling to the Nazi world view. In many ways, Germany invaded Norway and Denmark to 'protect' them. That philosophically they were Aryan and part of the 'bigger' Nazi world vision did *not* make these two small nations change their attitudes. They were attacked and occupied by their so-called Aryan brother and while in terms of occupation this was much milder than say in Yugoslavia or Poland, they still resisted the yoke of Germany. Although collaboration ran deep in both Nordic nations, so did resistance. Grand Admiral Erich Raeder, especially in light of his early advocacy of strong relations with Vidkun Quisling and his political party, would later declare that when he resigned in 1943 the inability of the Norwegians and Germans to become closer was one of the 'main reasons for resigning'.[14]

One point from the war that is seldom noted is that the Germans conducted themselves very well with the Norwegians and Danes, especially during the fighting. German atrocities by troops on the ground were virtually unheard of until after the fighting was over. But there was also an economic boom in Norway and Denmark and the unemployed were put to work, and well paid by Nordic standards, to build numerous fortifications and bases along this part of the Atlantic Wall. During the actual fighting in April and May Norwegians were hired to maintain and repair key facilities including occupied airfields. Many of the Norwegians and Danes who benefitted from this would understandably be punished in the immediate postwar period. This was collaboration with the enemy pure and simple and was viewed as such after the war.[15]

* * *

There were many military lessons learned from this campaign. One scholar has noted that, 'the invasion of Norway was a showcase for joint operations . . . and *Weserübung* was a first for several more inventive employments of tactical means'.[16] Another stated,

> German operational and tactical use of sea and air transportation to deliver forces along 1,200 miles of coastline to seize key points supporting the campaign was a noteworthy achievement for any modern military force. Disregarding secure flanks or a continuous front, the German armed forces ably balanced the competing requirements of force protection and force projection, achieving a rapid decision through multi-axis attacks that leveraged speed, tempo, and mobility to knock out their opponents.[17]

Germany's air transport corps performed splendidly in this operation. As the Norwegian campaign was unravelling, the eminent strategist Captain B. H. Liddell Hart was writing in *Life* magazine that 'The issue of this campaign hangs in the balance and the outcome will be at least one test of the ability of air power to fulfill the bright expectations of the German strategists . . .'.[18] General Jodl stated at the time that the 'Luftwaffe proved to be the decisive factor in the success of the operation'.[19] In April alone they deployed 571 Ju52s and 11 other air transports. They landed men and material for all three services and shipped 29,280 troops, 2,376 tons of war material and 1,178,100 litres of fuel. This was a vital contribution in light of the early naval and merchant-ship losses.[20] Luftwaffe general Ulrich O. E. Kessler summed it up, 'Nothing, in the early stages of World War II, is more illustrative of Air Power and its revolution of the traditional concept of warfare than the invasion of Norway.'[21]

The naval and merchant-ship support of the invasion by Germany was impressive as well. By 15 June 1940 270 ships and 100 trawlers totalling 1,192,000 GRT had moved 107,581 troops, 16,102 horses, 20,339 vehicles (many horse-drawn) and 109,400 tons of supplies. A total of 21 ships with a tonnage of 111,700 were lost, and about 2,000 men on board drowned. Some of the materials were salvaged from these sunken ships.[22]

As the world's first joint campaign, the German after-action report concluded that 'in future operations the three Wehrmacht branches must have one commander with full command authority and a joint personal staff organized towards a fully unified conduct of the campaign'.[23]

Clearly, the Germans had a more unified command than the Allies, who were burdened with armed forces from four nations engaged in action. At the lower and middle levels, co-operation between the German service branches was good but at the top it was filled with deep rivalry. It was noted that 'at the operational level, the Germans showed an excellent understanding of command and control. While the Germans lacked joint support at higher echelons, the component commanders in the operation coordinated actions with each other and never lacked unity of effort'.[24] The Allies never matched this in the campaign.

Both the German and British services suffered from wearing blinkers. They often saw their particular service problems and not those of their sister services. The army, for example, did not understand why the Luftwaffe was off bombing enemy warships when they wanted more close support for their troops. For Britain, as the land campaign continued, the losses that the British navy and the RAF suffered on a day-to-day basis were not fully understood at the time. But the experience in Norway and Crete drove home to the British that they had to dominate the air if they were to mount an amphibious operation.[25] This is a problem that continues into the modern era and may not disappear until all services are united under one umbrella – or inter-service liaisons and exchanges are more heavily promoted.

Germany would never again mount a joint campaign, though they studied possible actions for the invasion of Britain, Malta and Gibraltar. It would be the Allies that would become masters of this type of fighting, especially in the large European invasions from the sea and the island fighting in the Pacific.[26]

For the Allies, the lack of a unified command structure is striking. T. K. Derry would later write that if the command had been unified under one supreme commander, 'the situation would have been quite different'.[27] These lessons remain true to this day, when 'Success in modern warfare depends on joint teamwork. Battles and wars are won by maritime, ground and air forces operating effectively together in support of shared military objectives'.[28] Arthur Marder would write of it, a 'classic example of "divided" counsels, contradictory orders, muddle, and improvisation', or, more succinctly, it was largely 'order, counter-order, disorder'.[29] Lieutenant General Carton de Wiart and Lieutenant General H. R. S. Massy later argued that they received poor intelligence and from distant London came planning that was 'concocted hour to hour'.[30] The 10th Baron Strabolgi MP would write in 1940 that in addressing the failure of British intelligence to ferret out the German plan, 'Our Intelligence Service was inefficient . . . [and] the conclusion that we were caught napping is inescapable'.[31]

It is ironic that war plans developed before the invasion could have made a difference to the Allies if they had been utilised. If the troops standing by on the cruisers for intervention at Trondheim, Bergen and Stavanger had not been offloaded but instead sent straight in, the Allies would have had at least a good chance of local success. As noted in the 3 January 1940 'Report by the Chiefs of Staff' to the Cabinet that these forces by ready for 'instant dispatch' from the moment the British had placed their mines (and they were ready) a success might have been gained.[32] The early recapture of the major cities, excepting Oslo and Kristiansand, might have reversed Norway's fate.

It should also be noted that the Allies, really the British, failed to assault Trondheim directly with naval forces because in part of their fear of the Luftwaffe. As Strabolgi wrote in 1940, 'the *threat* of air attack on our Fleet led to our defeat in the first round of the campaign in Norway'.[33] Actual warship losses inflicted by the German Luftwaffe in the campaign would be relatively small.

That the Allies could have defeated the Germans at Narvik with an early land attack must also not be forgotten. As one scholar has written, 'If the British had directly assaulted Narvik early on as Lord Cork wanted, Dietl's force might have been overwhelmed before it was able to consolidate its hold on the area . . . the quick elimination of Dietl's force would have dramatically changed the strategic situation in the north of Norway'.[34] But the decisive theatre remained central Norway.

By early June, the Norwegian, British, French and Polish troops would recapture Narvik and this would be the first battle won against the German army in the Second World War. But it was at the tail end of the campaign and ultimately did not affect the outcome of the war. It can be argued that isolated Narvik, far to the north, was really of little consequence beyond the destruction of the ore facilities. Norway's fate would be decided by the battle that was being waged to the south – in the heart of Norway.[35]

David Hamer gives a summary of naval lessons learned:

> It could only be regarded as a decisive win for air power, for the Home Fleet had effectively abandoned the whole eastern half of the North Sea to the Luftwaffe. The pre-war belief of the Royal Navy that surface ships would have little to fear from daylight bombing evaporated in the first test. The air-defence deficiencies of the navy – the very inaccurate medium-range gunfire, the inability of destroyers to fire their 4.7-inch guns at attacking dive-bombers, the inadequate numbers of effective close-range guns, the poor performance of the carrier-based fighters and the lack of any efficient fighter-directions arrangements in the carriers – were all starkly revealed.[36]

Admiral Forbes would later say, 'our Fleet Air Arm aircraft are hopelessly outclassed by everything that flies in the air and the sooner we get some different aircraft the better'.[37] Some additional lessons include:

- The importance of co-ordinated leadership and agreed-upon goals.
- The importance of daytime control of the air, and control of enemy air reconnaissance. This would later translate in modern times to control of the air at *all* times.
- The fact that, in wartime, attack can come at any time from any source. (HMS *Glorious* learned that one the hard way.)

The Japanese navy also took away a lesson from the campaign. It reinforced the navy's view that land-based airpower could be relied on to deliver powerful blows against an enemy. This was a course they had already adopted with their long-range 'Nell' and 'Betty' bombers. The power of Allied carrier-borne aircraft really had not received a true audition in the Norwegian campaign.[38]

On 7–8 December 1941 the Japanese would conduct a major joint operation on a grand scale. Timing their attacks, just as the Germans had, they attacked across the Pacific by striking at Pearl Harbor, Malaya, the Dutch East Indies and the Philippines among other places. The Japanese would employ both naval and army paratroop units in their invasion of the Dutch East Indies. And, as in the lead up to the invasion of Denmark and Norway, the Allies failed properly to interpret the intelligence provided to them before attack.[39]

* * *

For the powers involved, relatively speaking Norway sustained the worst losses. As Foreign Minister Halvdan Koht noted, 'Norway has been robbed of her national independence.'[40] Norwegian losses in the field were at least 566 in the army, 283 fallen sailors and 4 pilots, as well as 185 civilians. Some sources increase these numbers to about 2,000 in total. Bombing was particularly destructive in some towns, although civilian casualties were low. The predominantly wooden buildings did not perform well under bombing. Towns severely damaged included Elverum, Åndalsnes, Molde, Nybergsund, Kristiansund, Steinkjer, Namsos and Bødo. Where battles were fought there would be further damage such as at Narvik. Norway had approximately 4,000 buildings totally destroyed, 10,000 damaged and 300 bridges destroyed – many of the latter due to Allied military action in attempting to delay the German advance. The occupation would see higher civilian losses in the war years, primarily because of sailors lost on merchant ships, bringing the total to about 10,000.[41]

The port of Narvik had been heavily damaged and would not resume shipping iron ore south to Germany until January 1941. The volume it would ship would be about half of what it had been in 1938 or 1939, while the percentage of shipping increased dramatically from Luleå and slightly from other Swedish ports.[42]

The Norwegian military suffered terribly in this war. A total of five aircraft escaped to Great Britain along with two destroyers (but only one modern one, the *Sleipner*), a single old submarine and ten miscellaneous craft. Norway would have a little over 1,000 men in its army in exile in July 1940 and by the end of the war that number would grow to almost 4,000. Norway would also have an air force and navy in exile, with aircraft and warships largely supplied by Great Britain to augment its strength.[43]

Germany saw 1,317 men die in battle with another 2,375 lost at sea or declared missing. The wounded numbered 1,604 in the campaign. Allied estimates of German losses were too high. Planes losses totalled 242, while 1 heavy and 2 light cruisers were sunk. Also sunk were ten destroyers, one torpedo-boat, six U-boats and many smaller craft.[44] General Falkenhorst, who had commanded in Norway until 1944 when he retired, was convicted at Nuremburg in 1946 for war crimes committed after the invasion. He was to be shot, but his sentence was commuted and he would be released from prison in 1953. He would live until 1968.

Britain lost 1,869 men dead and wounded, while France and Poland lost 170 men killed. British aircraft losses amounted to eighty-seven. Allied ships lost, not including Norwegian and Danish ships, were one aircraft carrier, two cruisers, nine destroyers and six submarines, along with miscellaneous craft.

One future dramatic act would be the eventual scuttling of the Danish navy. After the fall of Mussolini in Italy, the Danes began street protests. The Germans decided they would have to take over the running of Denmark and not leave it to the collaborationist government. The navy got wind of this and on 29 August 1943 with German troops entering the dockyards the fleet was scuttled, though the Germans seized fourteen vessels. Four Danish warships fled to internment in Sweden.

At the end of the war Norway contained a German garrison of close to 400,000 men (34,000 were from 40 non-German populations). There were also 80,000 prisoners of war in Norwegian camps and 11,000 refugees from 28 different nationalities. About 5,000 Norwegians served in the German army on the Eastern Front.[45]

For Norway and Denmark the German occupation would also lead to trials and executions. In Denmark there would be 13,000 convictions and 46 executions for those who collaborated. In Norway 90,000 were investigated and 46,000 sentences issued with 20,000 mostly NS members being sent to jail and upwards of 30,000 heavy fines and/or loss of civil rights applied as well. Quisling, along with twenty-four others, was executed.

The Norwegian Ministry of Defence made its own investigation in 1945 which led to the removal of 1,000 officers from the rolls. This was followed in 1946 with an additional military commission, which reported in 1947 and resulted in only a minor purge of four officers out of the thirty investigated. Punishment for those convicted was often for a short period of confinement of no longer then sixty days. Local public opinion did force many others to resign their commissions for not adequately resisting in 1940.[46]

Norway punished 1,400 per 100,000, while in Denmark the rate would be 300 per 100,000, making Norway's the highest rate in Western Europe of the occupied nations. Norway would grant amnesty to those still in prisons in 1957.[47]

Both the Danish and Norwegian public strongly supported the movement for 'Never Another April 9th'.[48] One result of this for Norway was the establishment of a commission, which reported in late 1946. It was to look at what diplomatic and military actions it could have taken to avoid being invaded. It concluded with several important recommendations. The Neutrality Watch should have been stronger. Proper co-ordination between the military services and the government was lacking. Based on intelligence, full mobilisation should have been ordered on 5 April and mining of the waters should have been executed much earlier. The commission concluded the conduct of diplomacy leading up to the invasion by Foreign Minister Koht was deplorable.[49]

One sad episode is the ongoing fate of the 10,000–12,000 children born to Norwegian women and fathered by Germans during the occupation. It was not until 2003 that the Norwegian government decided to compensate them for their mistreatment over the decades since the war. Known as Norway's 'whore children' or 'German kids', they have been abused for years and at one point the Norwegian government considered shipping 8,000 of them to Australia.[50]

In Denmark the occupation resulted in the death of 2,350 Danes (550 in concentration camps, many being policemen) and cost 10,000 million Kroner. Another 1,281 sailors died on the 230 merchant ships of 680,000 tons outside of Danish waters when war broke out. Another 8,000 volunteered to fight for the Axis and 3,900 of these traitors died. There were sixteen Danes who were identified as Abwehr agents working for Germany at the time of the invasion. The resistance executed 375 during the course of the war. But this must be put into the perspective that both Denmark and Norway (especially the latter) as a result of being occupied by a nation with a higher standard of living witnessed almost full employment, which raised the economies of both these countries.[51]

Danish Prime Minister Anders Fogh Rasmussen, a recent conservative leader of the Danish government, would state in 2003 that Danish 'co-operation' with Nazi Germany was wrong. This was the first public admission by a Danish leader of the utter failure of the Danish government to defend their nation in the period after September 1939. In 2005 Rasmussen would also apologise for some actions taken by the Danish government to refuse refugees, often Jewish, and their eventual shipping to German concentration camps. The Danes did have a resistance movement and they did successfully smuggle out many Jews to Sweden, but not all their actions, as Rasmussen correctly acknowledged, were a credit to Denmark.[52]

One major outcome of the defeat of Denmark and Norway would be their 1949 decision to enter NATO and during the Cold War to maintain an adequate military. Their mobilised armies were well equipped (including the German-built Leopard tank) and numbered over 100,000 each, their navies sported modern surface warships and small submarines for work in coastal waters, and modern air forces were built around (at the end of the Cold War) F-16 fighters.[53]

After the experiences of 1940, Norway in 1948 developed a special unit to defend key airfields – *Flypasstropp*. Ironically, one of the early components was the German PzKw III tank. The Norwegians also established a protocol whereby garrison units needed no special orders to defend their bases and to mobilise so as not to repeat the mistakes of 9 April 1940. In Norwegian military circles it is known as 'The Poster on the Wall' in the base's main office.[54] The stamp of defeat on these nations in 1940 resulted in important lessons that have continued to be heeded to the present day.

* * *

The role of neutrals is interesting. Sweden, because of Germany's strength, did not practise perfectly strict neutrality. Some men and supplies, as has been seen, were sent to the German troops fighting in Narvik. The Swedes were prepared, if threatened with a German ultimatum, to concede more in the way of help and later would allow German troops to transit Sweden, helping Germany in her war with the Soviet Union. Such pressure on neutrals should be recalled in future actions – that the rules could be bent. A nation under pressure must have the means to defeat or deter an aggressor – and the *will* to resist. Sweden, geographically isolated and with an inferior military, had to consider her weakness and position in making decisions. Sweden could not fight Germany and hope to win with the means available.[55]

The fall of Mussolini on 25 July 1943, coupled with German defeats in the Soviet Union and North Africa, was a trigger that would bring about greater assistance to the Allies from Sweden beginning in August 1943. Also, about 50,000 Norwegians would flee to Sweden during the war and about 15,000 would receive military instruction. These trained troops would enter Norway shortly after the end of the war in May 1945 to liberate their homeland and help maintain order.

* * *

There are important lessons with modern applications that can be learned from the Norwegian operations.

The policy of economy of force has some significant shortcomings. This dictum posits that a minimum of force be employed to achieve the objective. The problem arises when not enough force is employed at the start of an operation. It seems prudent to throw in as much as possible to overwhelm the enemy quickly as opposed to having just enough to succeed in the strategic goal. An excellent modern example of this is the failure in the Iraq War of 2003 to send an overwhelming force to the theatre of action and maintain its presence in a volatile postwar environment.

Another lesson that draws directly on littoral warfare is the need for powers such as Singapore, the Koreas, Iran, Taiwan or China today to operate aggressive offshore patrolling. In addition, there needs to be an element of randomness and unpredictability in it. In today's modern naval environment there have been calls to reconstitute the United States Asiatic Fleet, made up of smaller warships for littoral operations operating from Singapore, Darwin and the Philippines.[56] If Norway had taken that stance, even with its limited resources in April 1940, the approaching German forces might have been encountered before they were directly offshore and a stronger warning could have been given.

In addition, this aggressive patrolling in the modern age should be in four dimensions – electronically in all of its dimensions, in the air, under the sea and on the surface. This would be one way a possible threat could be scouted or even possibly deterred. The European niche in undersea warfare is one reason why its navies with their small diesel and now Air Independent Propulsion (AIP) submarines have an advantage over the American navy. The American submarine capability to work underwater in shallow waters has lagged behind because of the intransigence of naval leadership.

Another aspect of littoral operations is the need for close-in fighting weapons for small and even tiny warships. The success of the attack on the USS *Cole* in 2000 and the French oil tanker *Limburg* in 2002, mirrored by the successes of Italian surface-explosive motor boats in the Second World War, recently saw the British navy inviting bids for 'an automatic 30mm gun with associate tracker or an improved variant of the Phalanx Gatling gun' to deter just such a threat. The American navy has added numerous old-style, 50-calibre machine-guns to many of their naval vessels in the last few years to help counter this threat. Both conventional small-boat attacks and kamikaze speedboat attacks are part of the war on terror that will continue for years to come.[57]

During the Cold War Norway worked on small-boat attacks by its missile boats and was successful in wargames in delivering missiles on target against American aircraft carriers. This threat has been increased with the use of massive numbers of small explosive craft and Unmanned Aerial Vehicles (UAV) in littoral waters. The developments in Iran of this former threat are an obvious example. Supported now by small and difficult to detect AIP submarines and/or mini-subs (and SEAL type forces) makes operating close to an enemy coast more hazardous than in the past.[58]

A danger, one that may be a false danger given that the Nordic powers have built and deployed small modern warships for over a century, is size. It has been argued that the 3,000-ton warship is almost a minimum as a sizeable crew is necessary to handle damage control, a small ship is easier to sink and a warship needs to be fairly large for logistical purposes for potentially distant and sustained deployments.[59] While almost reminiscent of the arguments that Rear Admiral Alfred Thayer Mahan used against the British *Dreadnought* at the beginning of the last century, size does matter. It may be that the USA could learn from Nordic shipbuilding techniques and that a support ship(s) for smaller warships for distant waters is a direction that the USA and Europe should be going in. This would allow a mother ship to operate smaller warships in waters distant from a friendly base.

Certainly there is one aspect to this that cannot be denied. As two scholars have pointed out recently, 'the need for brown-, green- and blue-water navies, each with a specific set of force structure, ship design, and operational doctrine characteristics, will continue to dominate the development of navies and naval policy worldwide. The contention that any of these types of navies will become obsolescent any time soon is surely an ill-conceived notion.'[60]

\* \* \*

Perhaps the most important point learned from this study of the invasion of Denmark and Norway is the lesson in deterrence. Denmark and Norway's handling of the military in the First World War versus the Second World War *is* that lesson. Any power, but especially a small power, nearby a major and possibly aggressive power must maintain an adequate defensive force. Both Norway and Denmark in the First World War maintained a force strong enough to deter Imperial Germany from attacking them, even when conquering both would have offered some important strategic advantages such as better access to the North Sea and the Atlantic.

In the Second World War these two nations did not mobilise forces as robustly and their Neutrality Watch was more one of watching and less of defending their neutrality. The Norwegian mantra of 'Not a single shot should be fired' is one key reason *why* they were invaded.[61] While Norwegian military weakness was not the reason *per se* for the invasion by Germany, it did convince Hitler that Norway was incapable of defending herself against Allied encroachment of her national sovereignty. This contrasts markedly with the way Switzerland handled its Neutrality Watch in both the First and Second World Wars. On both occasions at the outbreak of war Switzerland mobilised over 200,000 troops and this was a vital reason it was not invaded.[62]

The populace largely ignored or was indifferent to foreign policy and even the political leadership of both Nordic nations was focused largely on internal politics. Two individuals, Foreign Ministers Koht and Peter R. Munch, largely dominated foreign policy in their respective nations. They had a major influence on foreign policy and to a lesser degree on defence policies. Even Prime Minster Johan Nygaardsvold was not sure what Koht was promoting as Norwegian foreign policy at any given point. A lack of knowledge of their military policies was also prevalent in the political leadership of both nations before the war and knowledge and understanding of the military would markedly increase in the postwar period. This change was due to 9 April.

Given Norwegian politics in the 1920s and 1930s, Norway should have taken a different course. Norway should have further *reduced* the size of the army and allocated the limited funds to obtaining adequate equipment for the army. To starve any army to the point that it lacks the weapons to defend itself properly is immoral and unethical. In conjunction with a better trained and smaller Norwegian force it should have had a much greater portion on Neutrality Watch.

Also, considering all the intelligence the Norwegian government had on both the Allied and German possible courses of action during the preceding month, to have had the coastal fortifications undermanned, or as was seen in the case of several naval forts at Trondheim, Oslo and elsewhere, unmanned was inexcusable.

One can always make a *political* decision to not fight, but to place your nation at a point where it *cannot choose to fight* is reprehensible and invited invasion. As Bismarck once stated, 'A conquering army on the border will not be stopped by eloquence.'[63] In the Second World War Denmark and Norway simply did not do enough to deter the German invasions. By attempting to avoid the fate of Belgium in the First World War they adopted the wrong policies to avoid becoming part of the Greater Reich.

The Norway campaign has given the modern world the blueprint and template for waging a joint campaign. The principles established in that campaign are with us today and an understanding of those principles point the way forwards for conducting a modern campaign in today's world.

# Chronology Leading Up to War

| | |
|---|---|
| **1929** | Vice Admiral Wolfgang Wegener publishes book advocating the invasion of Norway in a future war with the British Empire. |
| **December 1930** | Norwegian Minister of Defence Vidkun Quisling attempts to make direct contact with the NSDAP but is refused by the Germans. |
| **13 May 1933** | Quisling establishes *Nasjonal Samling*. |
| **2 November 1934** | Newly in power, Adolf Hitler in a meeting with Grand Admiral Erich Raeder and Field Marshal Hermann Göring notes vital need to keep iron ore flowing to Germany from Scandinavia. Also in 1934, Hitler devises concept of invading Sweden, a plan very similar to the one used against Norway. |
| **4 May 1937** | Captain Hellmuth Heye issues 'Study of the Tasks of Conducting a Naval War 1937–8'. Admiral Rolf Carls notes that in such a war it was likely that Denmark would have to be seized. |
| **28 April 1939** | German Foreign Minister Joachim von Ribbentrop offers Norway a non-aggression pact. |
| **17 May** | Norway declines Germany's invitation to sign a non-aggression pact. |
| **31 May** | Non-aggression pact between Denmark and Germany signed. |
| **June** | Norwegian right-wing leader Quisling visits Rosenberg in Berlin. |
| **18 August** | Abwehr issues warning of Norway falling under British influence. |
| **1 September** | King Haakon VII, at the Norwegian government's behest, declares Norway's neutrality with the outbreak of war in Europe. |
| **September** | British Chiefs-of-Staff dismiss as 'impractical' German operations on Norway's western coast. |
| **28 September** | British Admiralty discusses possible action against German ore trade with Narvik. |
| **1 October** | Admiral Rolf Carls advises Admiral Raeder of value of Norway to the German navy. |
| **10 October** | Raeder meets with Hitler and advises him of the value of Norway and danger of possible British occupation. |
| **3 November** | *City of Flint* seized by Norwegians in a Norwegian port from German prize crew and returned to the USA. |
| **30 November** | Soviet Union invades Finland – Winter War commences. |
| **30 November** | British Cabinet discusses closing German trade route with Narvik. |
| **7 December** | The *U-38* sinks the first of three Allied merchant ships possibly within Norwegian territorial waters near Narvik. |

| | |
|---|---|
| **10–18 December** | Quisling meets with Rosenberg, Raeder and has two meetings with Hitler. |
| **12 December** | Raeder notes strongly to Hitler the need to protect the iron-ore supplies from Scandinavia. |
| **14 December** | Hitler orders OKW to study possible invasion of Norway. Initially done as *Studie Nord*. |
| **15 December** | British deliver a note to the Norwegian government claiming German U-boat(s) in Norwegian territorial waters had sunk three merchant ships. |
| **19 December** | Hitler orders General Alfred Jodl to keep the planning for the operation within OKW. |
| **20–21 December** | German naval attaché Richard Schreiber in Oslo reports that Allied preparations and espionage are taking place. |
| **21 December** | Allies deliver a note requesting passage through Sweden and Norway to assist Finland. This would be rejected. |
| **30 December** | Admiral Raeder in a meeting with Hitler again stresses the need to keep Norway out of Allied hands. |
| **31 December** | British Chiefs-of-Staff report favourably on waging a campaign in Scandinavia. Planning for what would later develop into Operation 'R4' begins. |
| **13 January 1940** | A German working staff is established for planning an invasion of Norway to forestall an Allied attack on Norway. |
| **13 January** | Allies make second request to Sweden and Norway for passage through their nations to aid Finland. |
| **20 January** | Idea of a possible Quisling-led coup against the Norwegian government supported and sponsored by Germany is dropped. A German-led invasion is viewed as the only real option available that could lead to success. |
| **27 January** | Hitler names the planning *Weserübung*. *Gruppe Krancke* study group for *Weserübung* ordered, taking over from *Studie Nord*. |
| **28 January** | British Chiefs-of-Staff argue that forces should be ready by 20 March to seize Narvik and have land forces ready to seize Norwegian Atlantic ports. Planning for operation authorised on 7 February. |
| **2 February** | Winston Churchill, in an interview with a Swedish reporter, says he would not be unduly upset if the war spread to Scandinavia. |
| **5 February** | Krancke group holds first meeting. |
| **13 February** | German naval supply ship *Altmark* enters Norwegian territorial waters. |
| **16 February** | Norwegian government has reports of possible Allied planning to seize North Atlantic ports. |
| **16 February** | *Altmark* stormed by sailors from the British destroyer *Cossack* and prisoners on board are released. As a result, eight German sailors are killed or drowned and ten wounded; one British sailor is wounded. |

| | |
|---|---|
| **19 February** | General Jodl proposes to Hitler a larger staff and a commander for *Weserübung*. |
| **20–1 February** | Colonel General Nikolaus von Falkenhorst interviewed by Hitler and appointed commander for *Weserübung* on the 21st. |
| **21 February** | Raeder relays Luftwaffe requirement to Hitler that Denmark must be included for operational purposes. |
| **22 February** | British Chief of the Imperial General Staff Edmund Ironside in London learns that the French legation in Stockholm is spreading news of planned Allied landing in Narvik. |
| **23 February** | Raeder tells Hitler that it would be best to keep Norway neutral in this war but occupation of Norway by the Allies would be intolerable. |
| **23 February** | Finland call on Norway and Sweden to allow foreign troops to cross their countries to help Finland in its fight. |
| **28 February** | Denmark formerly added to the planning for invasion by General Falkenhorst. |
| **1 March** | First operational directive signed by Hitler placing all forces involved under Falkenhorst. |
| **2 March** | Swedish and Norwegian governments informed by the Allies that they intend to aid Finland by crossing their territory. Transit would begin on 20 March. |
| **3 March** | Hitler gives *Weserübung* precedence over planned operations against France and the Low Countries. |
| **4 March** | Hitler orders emergency operations with the code-name *Minimalfall* in the event of Allied attacks on Norway and Sweden. In effect until 14 March. |
| **4 March** | German submarines readied for *Weserübung*. |
| **4 March** | Norway and Sweden reject Allied proposal to transit their countries to aid Finland. |
| **5 March** | Göring informed of *Weserübung*, and 'flies into a rage' because he was out of the loop regarding the planning and requirements from the Luftwaffe for the operation. |
| **5 March** | Finland decides to open negotiations with the Soviet Union. |
| **7 March** | Hitler signs directive for Operation *Weserübung*. |
| **9 March** | Raeder reports to Hitler again that Allied occupation of Norway would be disastrous but *Weserübung* poses a great risk of heavy losses to the Kriegsmarine. |
| **11 March** | Hitler orders measures to be taken in the event of British intervention in Norway. German submarines for planned operations off Narvik and Trondheim are dispatched from Germany. |
| **11–12 March** | Norway and Sweden categorically refuse to allow Allied troops transit rights to Finland. |
| **12 March** | Finland and the Soviet Union cease hostilities with Treaty of Moscow. |

| 12 March | German merchant shipping for invasion assembling at Stettin on the Baltic coast. |
|---|---|
| 18 March | Churchill argues in Cabinet meeting for operations against the German ore trade. |
| 20 March | Norwegian Colonel Konrad Sundlo learns from French of plan to seize Narvik and other Norwegian ports (part of Plan 'R4') and this information is passed on to Rosenberg. |
| 20 March | German planning is complete. Operation awaits implementation orders. |
| 21 March | Édouard Daladier replaced by Paul Reynaud as French premier over failure to help Finland and lethargic Allied war effort. |
| 25 March | German ambassador informs Foreign Minister Halvdan Koht that Germany will protect Norwegian neutrality if Norway cannot. |
| 26 March | Quisling's second-in-command Albert Hagelin reports to Raeder the fear among Norwegian naval officers of British intervention in Norway and the seizing of southern Norwegian airfields. |
| 26 March | Raeder reports to Hitler that all the plans are ready for the invasion and all the ships, both warships and transports, are standing by. He also reports the British are planning to place minefields off Norway. |
| 27 March | German submarine *U-21* runs aground in Norwegian territorial waters and is interned along with its crew. |
| 28 March | Supreme War Council decides to mine Norwegian waters on 5 April. Warning to Norwegian and Swedish governments to be given on 1 April. Reynaud agrees to plan. |
| 28 March | Swedish naval attaché in Berlin informed by German Naval Chief-of-Staff of concern by Germany of Allied landings in Norway. |
| 30 March | French Admiral François Darlan notes in French War Committee that operations on Norwegian coast may cause German shipping assets gathered in the Baltic to be used to invade Norway. Darlan states, 'Recent information reveals that she has gathered material for an expedition against bases in south Norway or Sweden.' French decide not to act at this time, largely due to not wanting to drop fluvial mines in the Rhine on 4 April for fear of German aerial retaliation against vulnerable French war industries. |
| 30 March | British Admiralty informed of German ship operating in Norwegian waters for several weeks using simple Abwehr code radioed to Hamburg. British assume it is present to monitor future British mining operations. It is sending information on conditions before invasion. |
| 31 March | German submarines for rest of Operation *Weserübung* begin leaving port. All would be at sea by 6 April. |

| | |
|---|---|
| **31 March** | Abwehr leader Wilhelm Canaris visits Oslo for undisclosed meeting, primarily with local Abwehr staff. |
| **1 April** | Hitler goes over operation for 5 hours with various unit commanders. |
| **2 April** | Orders issued by Hitler to launch attack on morning of 9 April at 0415 (0515 Berlin time). Foreign newspaper reporters in Berlin hear rumours of planned invasion. |
| **2 April** | Swedish foreign minister asks Germany why it is concentrating so much shipping with troops in Baltic ports. Nothing meaningful is in the German reply. |
| **2 April** | The British ambassador to Sweden reports to Britain that shipping at two vital German Baltic ports, Stettin and Swinemünde, had 200,000 tons of shipping concentrated and troops were on board. |
| **3 April** | British government decides to go ahead with the mining of Norwegian waters. |
| **3 April** | A British MP informs Norwegian ambassador of impending military action against German iron-ore trade in Norwegian waters. Ambassador informs Koht. Koht later states this gave him more concern than the intelligence coming from Germany. |
| **3 April** | First slow German transports and supply ships depart bases, including in the Soviet Union, towards Norway. |
| **3 April** | British War Office gains intelligence of troops concentrating around Rostock and troop transports present in Stetting area. |
| **3 April** | Quisling meets in Copenhagen with German Abwehr Colonel Hans Piekenbrock. |
| **3 April** | Churchill during War Cabinet meeting said, 'he personally doubted' that the Germans would attack in Scandinavia. |
| **4 April** | A German Abwehr officer, Colonel Hans Oster, tips off a Dutch military attaché of impending attack. Warning is ignored. |
| **4 April** | Vice Admiral Max Horton orders twelve submarines, of which one is Polish and two are French, with six more in transit, to waters off Denmark and southern Norway to cover Operation 'Wilfred'. Horton orders that transports be considered primary targets if encountered with German warships. |
| **4 April** | Chamberlain gives speech with famous line that of Hitler, 'One thing is certain, he missed the bus.' |
| **First week of April** | ULTRA information on possible German invasion ignored as too incredible. |
| **5 April** | Norwegian and Swedish governments informed of planned Allied mining operations in Norwegian waters. |
| **5 April** | Based on the political climate and intelligence reports, Norwegian Army Chief-of-Staff Colonel Rasmus Hatledal requests of Norwegian Minister of Defence Birger Ljungberg permission to begin preliminary army mobilisation. Ljungberg refuses to give the order. |

**6 April**    By midnight all German troops, horses and equipment are on board their warships or merchant ships.

**6 April**    German U-boat commanders at sea may open sealed orders.

**6 April**    Army Chief-of-Staff Hatledal again requests permission from Minister of Defence Ljungberg to mobilise at least the four field brigades in southern Norway. Ljungberg again refuses.

**7 April**    Coastal Command reports German cruiser and two destroyers in the North Sea heading north.

**7 April**    With knowledge of German mountain troops present in northern Germany and issued with seasickness pills, the Swedish ambassador to Germany writes he expects action against Denmark and Norway in the immediate future.

**7 April**    German Major General Kurt Himer, Chief-of-Staff of the XXXI Corps, arrives at Copenhagen and remains there until the invasion.

**8 April**    British lay one minefield and act as if they laid two additional ones (one of these cancelled due to German naval activity). Troops stand by for possible intervention but only if Germans attempt to seize ports in Norway. British troops are ordered not to respond to Norwegian fire unless their fire is 'intolerable'. Norwegian naval command focused on British naval mines and does not order proper precautions.

**8 April**    That morning, Army Chief-of-Staff Hatledal again requests Minister of Defence Ljungberg for a mobilisation of at least the four southern military divisions. Ljungberg refuses again, though asks for cost estimates and smaller, less expensive responses. At around noon, Hatledal returns to see Ljungberg, accompanied by Commanding General Kristian Laake, both of whom urged the minimum mobilisation of the four southern field brigades. Ljungberg stated he would discuss it at a general government meeting later that afternoon. At the meeting Ljungberg did not bring the matter up.

**8 April**    At 13:30 Norwegian minelayers in Oslofjord ordered to prepare for minelaying operations.

**8 April**    German Army Lieutenant Colonel Hartwig Pohlman clandestinely arrives in Oslo to facilitate the German invasion.

**8 April**    British destroyer *Glowworm* engages with German naval Group 2 and is sunk. British Navy focuses on possible outbreak of German warships into the Atlantic instead of invasion of Norway.

**8 April**    At 11:45 the Polish submarine *Orzel* off southern Norway sinks the German freighter *Rio de Janeiro*. German survivors tell Norwegian troops they are on their way to Bergen to 'protect' Norway from the British. Norwegian government assumes German troops ignorant of what they were actually ordered to do and simply alert coastal command of incident. At

13:00 the submarine *Trident* sinks German tanker *Posidonia*. British focused on loss of *Glowworm* and do not draw proper conclusions.

**8 April**   Allied submarines ordered to move closer to German ports, away from Norwegian ones.

**8 April**   At 23:15, the German torpedo-boat *Albatros* fires on and disables the Norwegian patrol ship *Pol III* in Oslo Fjord.

**9 April**   04:15 local time invasion of Denmark and Norway formally begins.

# APPENDIX 1

# *Order of Battle – Denmark*[1]

Danish Army, Lieutenant General W. W. Prior commanding. The majority of the army was conscripted, but only a small percentage was inducted each year and training lasted for only a few weeks. In peacetime the Life Guards consisted of two battalions with a third battalion in reserve – all tall volunteers. NOTE: this represents the mobilised army, but this was not the case on 9 April 1940. Only a very small portion of this order of battle was available on that day.

**General Command** (headquarters at Copenhagen)
Air Defence Regiment (minus the 13th and 14th AA Battalion)
Eleven artillery batteries (four horse, four light, three heavy)
Three motorised AA batteries (four guns each)
Engineer Regiment (minus 1st and 2nd Pioneer battalion)
Signal battalion

**Sjaelland Division** (headquarters at Copenhagen)
Life Guards Regiment
1st, 4th and 5th Infantry Regiments
- Four battalions each
  - Five companies each
- (Attached) heavy weapons company
Guards Hussars Regiment (*Garde Hussar Regimentet*)
- Two battalions, each with three squadrons – two horse-mounted and one bicycle[2] but one horse-mounted company was to convert to Swedish supplied armoured cars just before the war
- Attached were one motorcycle squadron and one heavy weapons squadron
1st and 2nd Artillery Regiments
- The 1st consisted of three battalions of twelve guns each. One battalion had motorised 75mm field guns and the other two were of 150mm guns which were scheduled to be motorised that summer. They were the heavy artillery of the Danish army and were attached to the division
- The 2nd had four battalions of three batteries each. Each battalion had two batteries of old Krupp 75mm and one of new French Schneider 105mm howitzers.[3] They were in the process of having the 75mm guns replaced. A battery consisted of four guns
13th AA battalion (three batteries deployed at Copenhagen)
1st Pioneer battalion (four engineer companies)

**Jylland Division** (headquarters at Viborg – northern Jutland)
 2nd, 3rd, 6th, and 7th Infantry Regiments four battalions each
 - The 6th had two battalions of bicycle troops – the 4th and 5th. The former
   had been sent down to the border for training prior to the invasion, while
   the latter began to mobilise on the night of 8 April
 Jylland Dragoon Regiment (two battalions, each with three squadrons – one
   horse mounted and two bicycle, and one with three armoured cars. Six more
   were on order)
 - Attached were one motorcycle squadron and one heavy weapons
   squadron
 *Pioneer Fodfoldsregimentet* or Frontier Guards was attached to the Jutland
   Division and was the best-equipped and most motorised of any Danish
   unit. The two battalions consisted of one mortar and three machine-gun
   companies each.[4]
 3rd Artillery Regiment (equipped similarly as the 2nd Artillery Regiment
   above)
 14th motorised AA battalion of three batteries at Århus
 2nd Pioneer Battalion (two engineer companies and an infantry pioneer unit
   of regimental strength with two battalions having a battalion HQ and four
   companies. Their primary duty was to lay mines on the Danish border)

**Independent forces**
 10th AA Artillery Regiment (three batteries) assigned to Copenhagen
 One battalion of Signal troops attached to the engineer regiment
 Bornholm Guard for the defence of Bornholm Island. One under strength
   regiment, due to leave and lack of funding on 9 April; it had thirty men
   under arms. At full strength:
 - Four battalions of infantry
 - One bicycle squadron
 - Four 75mm guns
 - Heavy weapons company

The Danish army had tested a few armoured vehicles for evaluation purposes
including the Italian Fiat 3000B, French Renault NC2 (NC.31) and British Vickers-
Armstrong Carden-Loyd Patrol Mk.IV of 1931 design. The latter were light tanks
armed with machine-guns and Denmark bought three but they were worn out by
1940. She had ordered eighteen Swedish Landsverk Lynx (L185) armoured cars
but only three had arrived at the time of war and were assigned to the Jutland
Division. One of those three was probably an earlier and similar model, but with
lighter armour, a L181.

Motorcycles were of the Nimbus Model C, built in Copenhagen by Fisker &
Nielsen. Thousands were produced after the war, while approximately 300 were
used in Europe during the war. Denmark had experimented in the 1930s on an
armoured Harley-Davidson (which was too heavy and was a failure) but did arm

some Nimbus motorcycles with a 20mm Madsen machine-gun which could not be used while the motorcycle was in motion.

When fully mobilised there were a reserve division, additional fortress troops and a minor home guard.

## Danish Navy

Commanded by Vice Admiral Hjalmar Rechnitzer

At Frederikshavn and mobilised was the coastal defence ship *Peder Skram* (3,785 tons and launched in 1908). Also torpedo-boats *Dragen*, *Hvalen* and *Laxen* (290 tons and launched in 1929–30)

At Århus was the submarine tender *Henrik Gerner* and submarines *Havfruen*, *Havmanden* and *Havkalen* (320 tons and launched in 1937–8. A fourth would be completed after the invasion)

In Great Belt area there were 180 mines, *Glenten* and *Høgen* torpedo-boats (290 tons and launched in 1933), one minelayer, three minesweepers and five patrol craft

In Little Belt area were 264 mines, one patrol craft and one guardship

In Grønsund area were a few mines and two patrol craft

At Nyborg was the *Ørnen* torpedo-boat (290 tons and launched in 1934)

At Copenhagen was the flagship, the coastal defence ship *Niels Iuel* (4,100 tons and launched in 1918 – refitting). Also submarines *Daphne* and *Dryaden* (308 tons and launched in 1925–6) and *Rota*, *Flora* and *Bellona* (301 tons and launched in 1918–20), two minesweepers and two guardships

Elsewhere, including two patrol ships at Greenland, were seven patrol ships, two minelayers, one seaplane tender and one guardship

The German and Danish order of battles are included as the Allied and Norwegian ones are easily taken from Leo Niehorster's site and from Geirr Haarr's two volumes on the Norwegian campaign. The Danish, due to their short resistance, is difficult to come by and the German army order of battle is usually built upon incorrect assumptions. The Germans were not at full strength when they were committed to the Scandinavian campaign.

# APPENDIX 2

# *Order of Battle – Germany*[1]

The German forces sent to Norway were not Germany's finest. As has been noted, they were later wave divisions only recently raised and with little combat experience. Equipment was often lacking. Only two divisions were at full strength for their TO&E: the binary 3rd Mountain Division and the 69th Infantry Division. The 196th was particularly under-strength for support units. One recalls Secretary of Defense Donald Rumsfeld, who said, 'as you know, you go to war with the Army you have. They're not the Army you might want or wish to have at a later time.'[2] Germany's divisions were missing their armoured car reconnaissance elements, so they relied on bicycle troops and some motorcycles, and most were short their full artillery complement.

A German infantry division in 1940 was based on 3 infantry regiments and 1 artillery regiment, a signals battalion, a recon battalion, an AT battalion, an engineer battalion and miscellaneous support elements. An infantry regiment had 3 battalions and 1 engineer company. Each battalion had 3 infantry companies (2 officers, 21 NCOs and 201 men) and 1 machine-gun company, which was made up of 1 mortar (6 3in mortars) and 3 platoons each with 4 sub-machine-guns, with a total of 77 men. The total strength of an infantry battalion was 820 officers and men. Each infantry company had 16 sub-machine-guns and 12 light machine-guns available; moreover, there were 3 AT rifles and 3 light 50mm mortars present.

The German army was armed with a Mauser 7.92mm rifle, introduced in 1898 but shortened in 1935. It weighed 3.9kg. The infantry had the MP 38 sub-machine-gun available, and also the MP 18 Bergmann. Both would be replaced starting in 1940, but at the time of the invasion they had not. The support weapons of the infantry squad were the MG 13 and MG 34 machine-guns, the latter not completely distributed in 1940. They were both air-cooled and the latter was an excellent weapon both in the light and heavy role.

The artillery regiment was based on 3 artillery battalions, 1 heavy (150mm) and 2 medium battalions (105mm) each made up of 3 batteries of 4 guns each, making a total of 36 guns. Attached to each regiment was 1 artillery engineer company.

The German term pioneers (*pioniere*) means engineers.

# Danish Invasion Force

**XXXI Corps** (one battalion of 69th Infantry Regiment attached)
170th Infantry Division
    401st, 399th and 391st Infantry Regiments
        Three battalions each (one detached from 399th for amphibious operations.
            Remainder of 399th and HQ motorised)
- 240th Reconnaissance Bicycle Company
- 240th motorised AT Company
- 240th Artillery Regiment (2nd battalion short one battery)
- 240th Engineer Battalion
- 240th Signals Battalion

198th Infantry Division
    305st, 308th and 326st Infantry Regiments
        Three battalions each
- 235th Reconnaissance Bicycle Company
- 235th motorised AT Company
- 235th Artillery Regiment (three battalions with two batteries only in each)
- 235th Engineer Battalion (only one company)
- 235th Signals Battalion

11th Motorised Infantry Brigade
    110th and 111th Motorised Infantry Regiments
        Two battalions each
        Each with one motorcycle company
    677th Motorised Artillery Battalion (three batteries of 105mm howitzers)

214th Infantry Division was slated for Norway and stationed furthest from the Danish border of any Geman unit. It would begin moving to Norway on 14 April)
    355st, 367th and 388st Infantry Regiments
        Three battalions each
- 214th Reconnaissance Bicycle Company
- 214th motorised AT Battalion
- 214th Artillery Regiment (full strength)
- 214th Engineer Battalion
- 214th Signals Battalion

# Norwegian Invasion Force

## XXI Army Group
69th Infantry Division
    236th, 193th and 159st Infantry Regiments
    Three battalions each, except 159th with detached third battalion to Danish
      invasion force
- 169th Reconnaissance Battalion
  - 169th Bicycle Company
  - 169th Armoured Car Platoon (three cars)
  - 169th motorised Signals Company
  - Three motorised AT Companies
- 169th Artillery Regiment (full strength)
- 169th Engineer Battalion
- 169th Signals Battalion

163rd Infantry Division
    307th, 310th and 324st Infantry Regiments
    Three battalions each
- 234th Reconnaissance Battalion
  - 234th Bicycle Company
  - 234th motorised Signals Company
  - 234th motorised AT Company
- 234th Artillery Regiment (three battalions with two batteries only in each)
- 234th Engineer Battalion
- 234th Signals Battalion

196th Infantry Division
    340th, 345th and 362nd Infantry Regiments
    Three battalions each
- 233rd Reconnaissance Battalion
  - 233rd Bicycle Company only
- 233rd Artillery Regiment (three battalions with two batteries only in each)
- 233rd Engineer Battalion
- 233rd Signals Battalion

181st Infantry Division
    334th, 349th and 359th Infantry Regiments
    Three battalions each
- 222nd Reconnaissance Battalion
  - 222nd Bicycle Company only
  - 222nd motorised AT Company

- 222nd Artillery Regiment (three battalions with two batteries only in each)
- 222nd Engineer Battalion
- 222nd Signals Battalion

3rd Mountain Division
  138th, 139th Infantry Regiments
  Three battalions each
  - 222nd Reconnaissance Battalion
    - 112th Heavy Mountain Bicycle Company
    - 48th motorised Mountain AT Battalion (two companies)
  - 112th Artillery Regiment (two battalions with two batteries only in each)
  - 83rd Engineer Battalion
  - 68th Signals Battalion

**Attached for duty in both countries**
- Two companies of the 40th zbV armour detachment, 5 PzKw I headquarter tanks, 29 PzKw Is and 10 PzKw IIs. Third company detached to Oslo
- Three armoured trains
- Two batteries of the motorised 729th artillery
- Independent truck unit for carrying equipment
- Communication unit (possibly for the radar to be transported to Norway)
- One armoured car company deployed to Denmark

**Warship Group 1** – destination Narvik, Norway
Commanded by Commodore Friedrich Bonte

1st Destroyer Flotilla: *Wilhelm Heidkamp* and *Georg Thiele*
3rd Destroyer Flotilla: *Hans Lüdemann, Hermann Künne, Diether von Roeder* and *Anton Schmitt*
4th Destroyer Flotilla: *Wolfgang Zenker, Bernd von Arnim, Erich Giese* and *Erich Koellner*
They were carrying 2,000 troops that were the elements of the 3rd Mountain Division: the 139th Mountain Regiment, one company of the 83rd Mountain Engineer Battalion and a platoon of the 68th Mountain Signal Battalion. Also on board were elements making up a company of coastal defence marines, a platoon naval radio/signals personnel and minor elements of a Luftwaffe AA battalion

**Warship Group 2** – destination Trondheim, Norway
Commanded by Captain Heye

*Hipper*:  551 troops of the 138th Mountain Regiment (all or part of five companies of the 3rd Mountain Division)
57 regimental staff
63 battalion staff

18 heavy artillerists
100 Luftwaffe AA personnel
11 men of the regimental band
6 communication duties personnel
34 divisional engineering
60 communication duties personnel

*Riedel*:     104 troops of the 138th Mountain Regiment
14 battalion staff for 2nd Battalion
7 men of the regimental band
25 flamethrower personnel
50 naval coastal defence marines

*Jacobi*:     104 troops of the 138th Mountain Regiment
7 men of the regimental band
34 mortar men of the heavy weapons company
4 flamethrower personnel
51 naval coastal defence marines

*Heinemann*:  104 troops of the 138th Mountain Regiment
27 machine-gunners of the heavy weapons company
69 naval coastal defence marines

*Eckoldt*:    104 troops of the 138th Mountain Regiment
45 battalion staff for 3rd Battalion
21 divisional engineering
30 naval coastal defence marines

**Warship Group 3** – destination Bergen, Norway
Commanded by Rear Admiral Hubert Schmundt

The force consisted of the light cruisers *Köln* (flagship), *Königsberg*, gunnery training ship *Bremse*, S-boat tender *Carl Peters*, the torpedo-boats *Leopard* and *Wolf* and five S-boats of the 1st Motor Torpedo Boat Flotilla.

They carried on board the following troops but we were unable to break down specific ship assignments. The squadron was carrying two battalions of the 159th Infantry Regiment and the 69th Infantry Division headquarters, two companies of the 169th Engineer Battalion of the 69th Infantry Division and two companies of naval coastal defence artillery (about 100 marines). The latter were to man the captured Norwegian coastal batteries. The commanding general of the 69th, Major General Hermann Tittel, with his staff, were on board the *Köln*. This force numbered 1,900 men

**Warship Group 4** – destination Kristiansand and Arendal, Norway
Commanded by Captain Rieve

*Karlsruhe*:  500 men of the 310th Infantry Regiment (163rd Infantry Division)
50 men of the regimental band

|              |                                                           |
|--------------|-----------------------------------------------------------|
|              | 50 naval coastal defence marines                          |
| *Tsingtau*:  | 150 troops of the 310th Infantry Regiment                 |
|              | 100 naval coastal defence marines                         |
|              | 20 men for communication duties                           |
| *Greif*:     | 90 bicycle troops of the 310th Infantry Regiment          |
|              | 10 personnel for communication duties                     |
| *Seeadler*:  | 50 troops of the 310th Infantry Regiment                  |
| *Luchs*:     | 50 troops of the 310th Infantry Regiment[3]               |

**Warship Group 5** – destination Oslo, Norway
Commanded by Rear Admiral Oskar Kummetz

|            |                                                                             |
|------------|-----------------------------------------------------------------------------|
| *Blücher*: | 600 troops being part of two battalions of the 307th Regiment (163rd Infantry Division) |
|            | 12 members of Colonel General Nikolaus von Falkenhorst's advanced staff     |
|            | 50 men of the XXI's Army Group staff                                        |
|            | 50 men of the 163rd Infantry Division staff                                |
|            | 80 men of the regimental band                                              |
|            | 20 postal and telegraph personnel                                          |
|            | 10 propaganda personnel and war correspondents                             |
|            | (total of 822 men)                                                         |
| *Lützow*:  | 400 mountain troops                                                         |
|            | 50 Luftwaffe support staff                                                 |
| *Emden*:   | 460 troops of one battalion of 307th Infantry Regiment                     |
|            | 50 engineer troops                                                         |
|            | 100 naval coastal defence marines                                         |
| *Albatros*:| 100 troops of the 307th Infantry Regiment                                  |
| *Kondor*:  | 100 naval coastal defence marines[4]                                       |

**Warship Group 6** – destination Egersund, Norway
Commanded by Commander Thoma

*Mi*, *M2*, *M9* and *M13* (minesweepers) carrying 150 men of a company of bicycle troops of the 169th Infantry Regiment of the 69th Infantry Division and a platoon of signal corps troops

**Warship Group 7** – destination Korsør and Nyborg, Denmark
Commanded by Captain Kleikamp

*Schleswig-Holstein*; experimental ships *Claus von Bergen* (former torpedo-boat *T190*), *Nautilus* and *Pelikan* (First World War minesweepers); transports *Campinas* and *Cordoba*; two tugs and six trawlers. They were carrying 1,990 men of the 308th and 326th Infantry Regiments of the 198th Infantry Division[5]

**Warship Group 8** – destination Copenhagen, Denmark
Commanded by Commander Schröder

*Hansestadt Danzig, Stettin* and two picket boats. They were carrying 1,000 troops of a battalion of the 308th Infantry Regiment and included a squad of propaganda troops and a squad of propaganda film troops, as well as a bicycle platoon from the 326th Infantry Regiment

**Warship Group 9** – destination Middelfart, Denmark
Commanded by Captain Leisner

*Rugard* (transport), *Arkona*, *Otto Braun* and *M157* (minesweepers), *R6* and *R7* (small motor minesweepers), (*Cressida* and *Silvia* (patrol craft), *UJ107* (subchaser), *Monsum* and *Passat* (tugs). They were carrying 400 troops of the 1st battalion of the 399th Infantry Regiment of the 170th Infantry Division and a platoon of the signal corps

**Warship Group 10** – destination Esbjerg and Nordby, Denmark
Commanded by Captain Ruge

*Königin Luise* (minelayer), minesweepers (12th Minesweeper Division), *M4*, *M20*, *M84*, *M102*, *M1201–M1208*, motor minesweepers (2nd Motor Minesweeper Division), *R25–R32*. No troops carried

**Warship Group 11** – destination Limfjord, Thgyborøn, Denmark
Commanded by Captain Burger

*Von der Gröben* (minesweeping tender), minesweepers (4th Minesweeper Division), *M61*, *M89*, *M84*, *M1102*, *M111*, *M134*, *M136*, motor minesweepers (4th Motor Minesweeper Division), *R33–R40*. No troops carried

# Glossary of Terms

**AA** Anti-aircraft guns.

**Abwehr** The German military intelligence and counter-intelligence organisation. It was designed to serve all three services and included intelligence gathering, sabotage and combating enemy propaganda.

**Air-Landing** Troops air-lifted in to a friendly airbase and not necessarily paratroop trained. Regular infantry were used in the battle with only light equipment brought along.

**AT** Anti-tank guns.

**B-Dienst** Beobachtungs-Dienst (Observation Service) was the German Radio Intelligence Service.

**'Bankruptcy Ordinance'** The nickname given by the Norwegian military to the 1933 defence reforms. It saw the six army divisions turned into administrative elements, the virtual elimination of sergeants and massive reduction in the number of middle-level officers.

**Currency** In 1939 an American dollar was worth 4.4 Norwegian Kroner and 4.5 Danish Kroner.

**Destroyer** Each nation's definition is employed, so Norway had three old destroyers of the *Draug* class in service at the start of the war which displaced 540 tons – no Great Power would call them destroyers in 1940. See torpedo-boat below.

**DNSAP(*Nationalsocial-istiske Arbejderparti)*** The Danish National Socialist Workers Party.

**En portee** Artillery mounted on a truck such as a flatbed, often in an AT role, so creating a jury-rigged motorised artillery piece.

**Fallschirmjäger** German paratroops.

**Festning** Norwegian fortress.

**Fifth Column** During the Spanish Civil War the Nationalists were preparing an attack and the Fascist General in command pointed out to the press his four advancing columns on the city. He indicated that a 'fifth' column was in the city made up of fellow underground Nationalists waiting to help capture the city from the Loyalists. Hence traitors and enemy agents were operating behind the lines to sow dissension and help in taking over the objective.

**Fliegerkorps** A Luftwaffe air corps numbering between 300 and 750 aircraft. Fliegerkorps X would lead the attack on Denmark and Norway.

**Fluvial Mine** A British naval mine designed for use in rivers. They weighed 70lb and had an explosive charge of 25lb of TNT.

**Gebirgsjäger** German Mountain or Alpine Troop.

**Hærens ØverKommando (HOK)** The Norwegian Army Supreme Command activated once war was declared.

**HE** High Explosive.

**Hird** Literally the King's Bodyguard, but the NS organisation that is comparable to the Nazi Brownshirts.

**HMKG (Hans Majestet Konges Garde)** Haakon VII's guard battalion of four companies.

**Hjulrytterkompani** The Norwegian bicycle troops which in winter were converted to ski troops.

**Joint** Joint is defined as employing all military services under a unified command in a campaign in which all services play a vital role.

**Kampfgeschwader** German bomber wing.

**Kriegsschiffsgruppe** Name for German Warship Group. Eleven groups targeted both large and tiny ports in Denmark and Norway.

**Krigshavn** Literally Norwegian 'War Harbour', they are the protected waters within the Norwegian *Sjøforsvarsdistrikt* where enemy warships could be fired upon unless invited. Usually the immediate waters around a key naval or military facility.

**Krigsskolen** Norwegian Military Academy, equivalent of Sandhurst or West Point.

**Littoral** While literally the water between high and low tide on the coast, it has taken on the concept of coastal or green waters. Here littoral combat is treated as the interface between land and sea where forces on, under or over may be in combat.

**Luftflotte** A German Luftwaffe air fleet, of which Germany fielded four at the start of the war.

**MF11** A Norwegian three-seat twin-wing floatplane intended for reconnaissance, bombing and torpedoing. First delivered in 1932, it had a single 575hp engine, a maximum speed of 150mph and a ceiling of only 16,000ft.

**Neutrality Watch** Usually a force of army, navy and air forces that are partially but not fully mobilised to guard a nation's neutrality in an active war zone. This force can take many forms and be more fully mobilised near a border where an active war, or threat of war, is taking place.

**NSDAP** The German National Socialist Party or Nazi Party.

**NS (*Nasjonal Samling*)** The Norwegian Nazi-style party led by Quisling literally translated as National Unity.

**OKW (*Oberkommando der Wehrmacht*)** Armed Forces High Command for army, air force and navy, though dominated by the army.

**Oslo States** An economic grouping first formed on 22 December 1930 of Norway, Denmark, Sweden, Finland, the Netherlands, Belgium and Luxembourg. As the Second World War approached this group tried to develop into a stronger political force to preserve their neutrality but would fail.

**Panzer-Abteilung z.b.V40** The name for the German tank battalion used in the Norwegian campaign. Literally translates as the '40th Special Tank Detachment'.

**Q-ship** A decoy ship, usually a merchant ship, but also small trawlers, utilised to entice submarines to the surface so that they may be attacked with gunfire and torpedoes. The German trawlers carried sonar and depth charges.

**Reichsmarine** The name of the German navy under the Weimar Republic.

**S-boat** German PT boat, small and fast.

**Salvo Chasing** A manoeuvre technique developed in the First World War where a ship steams towards where the last enemy salvo landed, reasoning that the enemy would be correcting the range based on the salvo that had just landed – a simple but often effective manoeuvre.

**Secret Intelligence Service (SIS)** British overseas intelligence or MI6.

**Skerry or Skerries** A rock or rocks that are above water and too small to be inhabited, usually just off the coast.

**Sjøforsvarsdistrikt** Norway was divided into three of these naval districts.

**Sonic Detector** A directional acoustical device based on the ground for detecting aircraft and relative bearing.

**Storting** The Norwegian parliament, sometimes appears as the 'Storthing'.

**The Leads** More formally known as the Inner Leads or the Norwegian Leads, it is a series of islands that allow ships to travel almost totally between the coastline and islands the length of Norway's western coast. The Norwegians call it the 'Skerry-fence'. This allows ships to be in Norwegian territorial waters and thus usually safe from the Allied blockade and with very little exposure to the ocean, and leads to unusually calm waters. In 1918 plans were in place to mine these waters when the war ended. Winston Churchill referred to it as the 'covered way'.

**TO&E** Table of Organisation and Equipment.

**Torpedo-boat** In the interwar period several of the Continental powers built 500–800 ton torpedo-boats which were like destroyer escorts in American service or scaled down destroyers. Norway's had several elderly small (200-ton and smaller) ones.

**Wehrmacht** All three German services. The army is properly 'Heer'.

**Weserübung** Is literally 'Weser (River) Exercise or Operation'. This was the code-name for the invasion on 9 April 1940 of Denmark and Norway. There would be a Nord (north or Norway) and Süd (South or Denmark) component to this.

**Wesertag** The assault day, 9 April.

**Weserzeit** The hour set for the invasion.

## Military Rank Equivalents

| *Norwegian* | *German* | *British* | *USA* |
|---|---|---|---|
| Generalmajor | Generalleutnant | Major General | Major General |
| Brigader | Generalmajor | Brigadier | Brigadier General |
| Oberst | Oberst | Colonel | Colonel |
| Oberstløytnant | Oberstleutnant | Lt. Colonel | Lieutenant Colonel |
| Major | Major | Major | Major |
| Kaptein* | Hauptmann | Captain | Captain |
|  | Rittmeister |  |  |

## Naval equivalents

| Viseadmiral | Viceadmiral | Vice Admiral | Vice Admiral |
|---|---|---|---|
| Kontreadmiral | Konteradmiral | Rear Admiral | Rear Admiral |
| Flaggkommandør** | Kommodore | Commodore | Commodore*** |
| Kommandørkaptein | Kapitän-zur-See | Captain | Captain |
| Kaptein | Fregattenkapitän | Commander | Commander |
| Kapteinløytnant | Korvettenkapitän | Lt. Commander | Lt. Commander |

* Rittmester in cavalry service
** Sometimes shown as Kommandør
*** After April 1943

# Notes

## Introduction

[1] Quoted in, George Sviatov ,'The Kursk's Loss Offers Lessons' U.S. Naval Institute *Proceedings*, 129.6 (2003), p. 71.

[2] David G. Thompson, *The Norwegian Armed Forces and Defense Policy, 1905–1955*, Lampeter, Wales: Edwin Mellen, 2004. pp. 417–18. This still resonates today, as the Prime Minister noted in his speech after the 22 July 2011 massacre in Norway. He said, 'We will carry this with us as we start to shape Norway after 22 July 2011. Our fathers and mothers promised us, "There will never be another 9 April." We say, "There will never be another 22 July."' See http://www.regjeringen.no/en/dep/smk/ aktuelt/taler_og_artikler/statsministeren/ statsminister_jens_stoltenberg/2011/ statsminister-jens-stoltenbergs-tale-pa-. html?id=651840.

[3] The Belgian army lost over 50,000 dead and combined with civilian deaths the total dead was over 120,000. This represented over 1.5 per cent of Belgium's prewar population. In contrast, Norway would suffer 0.3 per cent military and civilian dead in the whole of the Second World War.

[4] While mostly recently raised infantry units, two of the divisions were highly trained mountain divisions.

[5] Eric Grove, 'BR1806, Joint Doctrine and Beyond', in Andrew Dorman et al. (eds), *The Changing Face of Maritime Power*, New York, NY: Palgrave, 2002, p. 59.

[6] James S. Corum, 'Uncharted Waters: Information in the First Modern Joint Campaign – Norway 1940', *The Journal of Strategic Studies*, Vol. 27, No. 2 (June 2004), p. 345.

[7] Sam Tangredi, 'Mistral Deal a Message, nor a Mystery', *Defense News*, 11 July 2011, p. 29.

[8] Geirr H. Haarr, *The Battle for Norway April–June 1940*, Barnsley: Seaforth Publishing, 2010, p. 4.

[9] James S. Corum, *The Luftwaffe: Creating the Operational Air War, 1918–1940*, Lincoln: University of Kansas, 1997, p. 274.

[10] Quote in Stephen E. Ambrose, *D-Day: June 6, 1944, The Climactic Battle of World War II*, New York, NY: Simon & Schuster, 1994, p. 13.

[11] Robert Debs Heinl, *Dictionary of Military and Naval Quotations*, Annapolis: Naval Institute Press, 1966, p. 11.

[12] Elliot Carlson, 'Missing Clues and Cracking Codes in the Pacific War', *Proceedings*, December 2011, pp. 66–71.

[13] http://en.wikipedia.org/wiki/Skjold_class _patrol_boat.

[14] Even in the missile age the gun has not lost its importance, primarily in littoral waters and for shore bombardment. The shell is cheaper, but more importantly a gun crew can react faster than a missile crew in acquiring and firing. Now with shells that can have their direction changed to follow a target, it makes this arm even more important. See Tom Kington, 'Oto Melara Blurs Missile-Munitions Line', *Defense News*, 29 November 2004, p. 13. Also note that the small submarine may play a larger role in littoral actions then sometimes thought. This is particularly so in this modern age of stealth design that is being acquired at a *worldwide* level.

[15] The current fighting in the Nigerian delta region is a modern example.

[16] Colonel O. B. Getz published the uncensored *Fra Krigen I Nord-Trøndelag 1940*, Oslo: H, Aschehough in 1940 in Oslo detailing operations near Trondheim. It was permitted by the Nazi regime since it heavily criticised the poor Allied assistance there.

[17] The German pocket battleship *Lützow* is referred to as a battleship although it was relatively small for a true battleship of the day.

## Chapter 1

[1] W. M. Carlgren, *Swedish Foreign Policy*

*during the Second World War*, New York: St Martin's Press, 1977, p. 59.

[2] Thomas K. Derry, *The Campaign in Norway*, London: HMSO, 1952, p. 1.

[3] Earl F. Ziemke, *The German Northern Theater of Operations, 1940-1945*, Washington DC: Department of the Army Pamphlet, 1959, pp. 26-7.

[4] Ibid.

[5] A. D. Divine, *Firedrake*, New York: E. P. Dutton, 1943, p. 61.

[6] Martin Fritz, *German Steel and Swedish Iron Ore, 1939-1945*, Göteborg: Institute of Economic History of Gothenburg University, 1974, *passim*.

[7] Joseph Kynoch, *Norway 1940: The Forgotten Fiasco*, Shrewsbury: Airlife Publishing, 2002, p. 63.

[8] Major George Fielding Eliot, 'A Fight for the Valleys', LIFE magazine, 6 May 1940, pp. 25-8.

[9] Nils Ørvik, *The Decline of Neutrality, 1914-1941*, London: Frank Cass, 1971, p. 223 and Fritz, *German Steel and Swedish Iron Ore*, p. 34. Germany also imported iron ore from France, Spain and North Africa and some additional sources that would be cut off after September 1939.

[10] Corum, 'Uncharted Waters', p. 346.

[11] J. R. M. Butler, *Grand Strategy*, Vol. II, *September 1939-June 1941*, London: HMSO, 1957.

[12] Ibid. and David Irving, *Hitler's War*, Vol. 1, New York: Viking Press, 1977, pp. 36, 69. Irving has been correctly condemned for some of his later works due to his hard right political comments, but as a historian, he has done some solid research. Hence, he needs to be handled carefully. Some who have read the text think he should not be included at all or have said this comment should be dropped altogether. Instead of putting our collective foot in it, we think it should stand as given and let the reader Google his name and see why the comment is there.

[13] Halvdan Koht, *Norway Neutral and Invaded*, London: Hutchinson & Co., 1941, pp. 22-3.

[14] Denmark approached the other two states in 1933. Hans Kirchoff, 'Denmark, September 1939-April 1940', in Neville Wylie (ed.), *European Neutrals and Non-Belligerents during the Second World War*, Cambridge: Cambridge University Press, 2002, p. 36.

[15] Henrik S. Nissen (ed.), *Scandinavia during the Second World War*, Minneapolis, MN: University of Minnesota, 1983, p. 23.

[16] Karen Larsen, *A History of Norway*, New York, NY: Princeton University Press, 1950, p. 535 and Joachim Joesten, *Denmark's Day of Doom*, London: V. Gollancz Ltd., Left Book Club Edition, 1939, p. 208.

[17] Thomas K. Derry, *A History of Scandinavia*, Minneapolis, MN: University of Minnesota Press, 1979, p. 316 and Koht, *Norway Neutral and Invaded*, pp. 13-15.

[18] Koht, *Norway Neutral and Invaded*, pp. 11-12.

## Chapter 2

[1] Rolf Karlbom, 'Sweden's Iron Ore Exports to Germany, 1933-1944', *The Scandinavian Economic History Review*, Vol. XIII, No. 1, p. 1.

[2] Klaus A. Maier, 'German Strategy', in Klaus A. Maier et al., *Germany and the Second World War*, Vol. II, Oxford: Clarendon Press, 1991, p. 185.

[3] Quoted by Françoise Bédarida, 'France, Britain and the Nordic Countries', *Scandinavian Journal of History*, 2, 1977, p. 14. Thyssen was a Ruhr industrialist who fled Germany and would aid the Allies. He was a strong advocate, probably too strong, of the importance of Swedish iron ore to Germany. He and his wife were turned over to the Germans by Vichy France but he survived the war.

[4] Maier et al., *Germany and the Second World War*, Vol. II, p. 189.

[5] Richard Petrow, *The Bitter Years; The Invasion and Occupation of Denmark and Norway, April 1940-May 1945*, New York, NY: William Morrow & Company, 1974, pp. 12-13. The British figures were not perfectly accurate but it was the data on which they based their wartime decisions. The fall of France would make the issue of iron ore less important, as the French ore fields would be available.

[6] Butler, *Grand Strategy*, Vol. II, September 1939-June 1941, pp. 91-3 and P. Brøyn, 'Den Svenske malmeksort frem til besetnignen av Narvik I 1940', unpublished thesis, University of Oslo, 1964, *passim*.

[7] Ibid., p. 191.

[8] Quote in Major Timothy F. Lindemann,

*Joint Operations Case Study Weserübung Nord: Germany's Invasion of Norway, 1940*, A Research Paper Presented To The Research Department Air Command and Staff College In Partial Fulfillment of the Graduation Requirements of ACSC by Major Timothy F. Lindemann (March 1997), p. 9.

[9] Koht, *Norway Neutral and Invaded*, p. 70.

[10] Olav Riste, 'Intelligence and the "Mindset": The German invasion of Norway in 1940', in *Intelligence and National Security*, No. 4, Vol. 22 (2007), pp. 521–36.

[11] Ørvik, *The Decline of Neutrality*, pp. 220–1.

[12] Quote in James Cable, *Gunboat Diplomacy 1919–1991*, Basingstoke: Palgrave-Macmillan, 1991, p. 22 and Ørvik, *The Decline of Neutrality*, p. 225.

[13] Ørvik, *The Decline of Neutrality*, p. 226.

[14] Keith Bird, *Erich Raeder*, Annapolis, MD: Naval Institute Press, 2006, *passim*.

[15] Jost Dülffer, 'Determinants in German Naval Policy, 1920–1939', in Wilhelm Deist (ed.), *The German Military in the Age of Total War*, Leamington Spa: Berg, 1985, pp. 152–70.

[16] Ziemke, *The German Northern Theater of Operations*, p. 4.

[17] James S. Corum, 'The German Campaign in Norway 1940 as a Joint Operation', *Journal of Strategic Studies*, Vol. 21, No. 4 (December 1998), pp. 50–77 and Geirr H. Haarr, *The German Invasion of Norway: April 1940*, Barnsley: Seaforth Publishing, 2009, p. 1. The war-built, concrete-enclosed submarine pens are still present at Trondheim.

[18] The Abwehr was the German military intelligence and counter-intelligence organisation. Canaris became a full admiral in January 1940.

[19] On intelligence to Raeder see Walther Hubatsch, *Weserübung. Die deutsche Besetzung von Dänemark und Norwegen 1940*, Göttingen: Musterschmidt, 1960, p. 29.

[20] Quote in Heinz Bonatz, *Die deutsche Marine-Funkaufklärung 1914–1945*, Darmstadt: Wehr und Wissen Verlagsgesellschaft, 1970, p. 121 and Heinz Höhne, *Canaris*, New York, NY: Doubleday & Company, 1979, p. 402.

[21] Von Below recalled the event on 10 September 1939 but probably he is referring to 10 October. See Nicolaus von Below, *Als Hitlers Adjoutant*, Mainz: von Hase & Koehler, 1980, p. 213.

[22] Gerhard Weinberg, *A World at War*, Cambridge: Cambridge University Press, 2005, p. 113.

[23] John Lukacs, *The Last European War September 1939–December 1941*, New Haven, CT: Yale University Press, 1976, p. 73 and www.geocities.com/armdury/1914-18.pdf. See Holger H. Herwig, *Luxury Fleet: The Imperial German Navy 1888–1918*, 1st edn, London: George Allen & Unwin, 1980, pp. 168–9, 190–1, Erich Raeder, *My Life*, Annapolis, MD: US Naval Institute, 1960, p. 13 and Hew Strachan, *The First World War*, Vol. 1, Oxford: Oxford University Press, 2001, p. 439.

[24] Rear Admiral M. W. W. P. Consett, with Captain O. H. Daniel, *The Triumph of Unarmed Forces (1914–1918)*, New York, NY: Brentano's, 1923, pp. 95–7.

[25] F. H. Hinsley et al., *British Intelligence in the Second World War*, Vol. I, London: HMSO, 1979, p. 117, Wolfgang Wegener, *Die Seestrategie des Weltkrieges*, Berlin, 1929, *The Naval Strategy of the World War*, introduced by Herwig H. Holger, Annapolis, MD: NIP, 1989, p. xliii, Patrick Salmon (ed.), *Britain and Norway in the Second World War*, London: HMSO, 1995, p. 5 and Willy Brandt, *Kriget I Norge*, Stockholm: Albert Bonniers, 1941, pp. 9–10.

[26] Werner Rahn, *Reichmarine und Landesverteidigung 1919–1928. Konception und Führung der Marine in der Weimarer Republik*, Munich: Bernard & Graefe, 1976, p. 131 and for the rift between Wegener and Raeder see Naval War College: http://www.nwc.navy.mil/press/Review/2005/autumn/art5-a05.htm. For additional debate on Wegener and his ideas see http://www.strategypage.com/militaryforums/335-449.aspx and Henrik O. Lunde, *Hitler's Pre-Emptive War: The Battle for Norway, 1940*, Drexel Hill, PA: Casemate, 2008, p. 46.

[27] George Burns Williams, '*Blitzkrieg and Conquest: Policy Analysis of Military and Political Decisions Preparatory to the German Attack Upon Norway, April 9. 1940*', Princeton, NJ: Yale University Dissertation, 1966, pp. 72–3. This is an invaluable study and has been missed by most scholars of the campaign. A special thanks goes to David Isby for locating this for us.

[28] Derry, *The Campaign in Norway*, p. 17.

[29] Several important warships were never

completed and the growing ability to strike successfully from the air would degrade surface combat naval forces in the course of the war.

[30] Quoted by Herwig Holger in introduction to Wegener, *Die Seestrategie des Weltkrieges*, *The Naval Strategy of the World War*, p. xxxix. Carl-Axel Gemzell, *Organization, Conflict and Innovation: A Study of German Naval Strategic Planning 1888–1940*, Stockholm: Esselte Studium, 1973, pp. 280–1.

[31] Carl-Axel Gemzell, *Raeder, Hitler und Skandinavien. Der Kampf für einen maritimen Operationsplan*, Lund: C. W. K. Gleerup, 1975, p. 277.

[32] Lord Strabolgi, 10th Baron, *Narvik and After*, London: Hutchinson, n.d, p. 19.

[33] Kenneth P. Hansen, *Raeder versus Wegener*, at http://www.nwc.navy.mil/press/Review/2005/autumn/art5-a05.htm.

[34] 'Norway, Sweden and Romania, whose holding as supplying states are of *vital* importance', in 'Comments to the Memorandum of the 15 October 1939 of the German Naval Command', in Michael Salewski, *Die deutsche Seekriegsleitung 1935–1945, Denkschriften und Lagebetrachtungen*, Frankfurt a. M: Bernard & Graefe, 1973, p. 100.

[35] Florence Jaffray Harriman, *Mission to the North*, New York, NY: Lippincott, 1941, p. 230.

[36] Joseph Gainard, *Yankee Skipper*, New York, NY: Frederick A. Stokes, 1940, p. 239.

[37] Harald Høiback, *Command and Control in Military Crisis: Devious Decisions*, London: Frank Cass, 2003, pp. 80–1.

[38] Much of what was sent would arrive late, sometimes without operating manuals or repair kits. The most valuable items were fighter planes and artillery.

[39] Geoffrey Jones, *Under Three Flags*, London: Kimber, 1973, pp. 20–3. One of the class of six was not completed.

[40] Ibid., pp. 38–42 and Thompson, *The Norwegian Armed Forces and Defense Policy*, p. 138.

[41] Quote from *KTB/Skl*, Vol. 4, p. 136 (17 December 1939), *KTB/Skl*, Vol. 4, p. 19 and Franz Kurowski, *An Alle Wölfe: Angriff!*, Wölfersheim-Berstadt: Podzun Pallas, 1986, p. 41ff.

[42] James L. Moulton, *The Norwegian Campaign of 1940: A Study of Warfare in Three Dimensions*, p. 55, Magne Skodvin,

'Norwegian Neutrality and the Question of Credibility', *Scandinavian Journal of History*, 1977, Vol. 2, Nos 1 and 2, pp. 77–8, Thomas Munch-Petersen, *The Strategy of Phoney War: Britain, Sweden and the Iron Ore Question 1939–1940*, Stockholm: Militærhistiska Fœrlaget, 1981, pp. 77–8, and Thompson, *The Norwegian Armed Forces and Defense Policy*, pp. 138–9. Thompson's is an excellent study relying heavily on Norwegian language source material. We give special thanks to Mark C. Jones in locating this source. Moulton is an older but very useful study that also makes great use of Norwegian sources.

[43] Numbers vary up to 303 but 299 prisoners is the total our research indicates.

[44] Our discussion of the *Altmark* affair is based on Petrow, *The Bitter Years*, pp. 18–30, Jones, *Under Three Flags*, pp. 61–71, Stephen W. Roskill, *The War at Sea 1939–1945*, 4 vols, London, 1954–61, Vol. 1, pp. 150–7, Arthur Marder, '"Winston is Back": Churchill at the Admiralty 1939–1940', in *From the Dardanelles to Oran. Studies of the Royal Navy in War and Peace, 1915–1940*, London: Oxford University Press, 1974, pp. 139–40, Winston S. Churchill, *The Gathering Storm*, New York, NY: Houghton Mifflin Co., 1948, pp. 500–3, the very well done Richard Wiggan, *Hunt the Altmark*, London: Robert Hale, 1982, pp. 97–159 and Gerhard Koop and Klaus-Peter Schmolke, *Pocket Battleships of the Deutschland Class*, Annapolis, MD: Naval Institute Press, 2000, pp. 49–50.

[45] Wiggan, *Hunt the Altmark*, p. 98.

[46] Cable, *Gunboat Diplomacy*, p. 16.

[47] Thompson, *The Norwegian Armed Forces and Defense Policy*, p. 101 and Haarr, *The German Invasion of Norway*, pp. 22–3.

[48] Quote in Cable, *Gunboat Diplomacy*, p. 17.

[49] Thompson, *The Norwegian Armed Forces and Defense Policy*, p. 148. This point is missed in most studies relying on English language sources.

[50] Willi Frischauer and Robert Jackson, *The Altmark Affair*, New York: Macmillan Co, 1955, pp. 203 and 218.

[51] Adam R. A. Claasen, *Hitler's Northern War: The Luftwaffe's Ill-Fated Campaign 1940–1945*, Lawrence, KS: University Press of Kansas, 2001, p. 32.

[52] http://216.239.57.104/search?q=cache

:-mVLAxq4H6UJ:www.hmscossack.free
serve.co.uk/download/altmark.doc+firern
+norway+patrol&hl=en is helpful. Jürgen
Rohwer and Gerhard Hummelchen, *Chronology of the War at Sea 1939-1945. The Naval History of World War Two*, 2nd edn, Annapolis, MD: Naval Institute Press, 1992, p. 12 states 303 were freed. Some English language accounts do not note German losses.
[53] Frischauer and Jackson, *The Altmark Affair*, p. 244.
[54] Irving, *Hitler's War*, Vol. 1, p. 90 and quote from Petrow, *The Bitter Years*, p. 31.
[55] One example aimed at the American populace was the English-language pamphlet, Friedrich Frisch, *The Raid on the 'Altmark'*, Berlin: Wilhelm Grave, 1940. At fifty-four pages long, it has a short narrative, pictures and consists largely of international law arguments with verbatim presentation of directives and press releases from the time of the incident.
[56] Claasen, *Hitler's Northern War*, p. 33. This is a solid account.
[57] Derry, *A History of Scandinavia*, p. 334 and quote from Paul M. Hayes, *Quisling*, Bloomington, IN: Indiana University Press, 1972, p. 196.
[58] Quoted in Derry, *A History of Scandinavia*, p. 334.
[59] Quote from Munch-Petersen, *The Strategy of Phoney War*, p. 150. Allied strategy is discussed pp. 150-3. See also Graham Rhys-Jones, *Churchill and the Norway Campaign*, Barnsley: Pen & Sword, 2008, p. 6.
[60] Koht, *Norway Neutral and Invaded*, pp. 46-7.
[61] Frisch, *The Raid on the 'Altmark'*, pp. 12, 17.
[62] Thompson, *The Norwegian Armed Forces and Defense Policy*, pp. 149-50.
[63] Lunde, *Hitler's Pre-emptive War*, p. 52.
[64] Hans Fredrik Dahl, *Quisling: A Study in Treachery*, Cambridge: Cambridge University Press, 1999, p. 152.
[65] Oddvar K. Hoidal, *Quisling*, Oslo: Norwegian University Press, 1989, pp. 340-3.
[66] Quote from ibid., p. 351.
[67] Haarr, *The German Invasion of Norway*, pp. 3-5, Thompson, *The Norwegian Armed Forces and Defense Policy*, p. 147 and Claasen, *Hitler's Northern War*, pp. 14-21. Claasen includes an excellent discussion of Rosenberg and the role of 'Nordic blood'. By

1938 Heinrich Himmler (commander of the SS) was also influencing events and wanted to establish the *Germania* Regiment in the SS with only non-German Nordic members.
[68] Patrick Salmon, 'Norway', in Wylie (ed.), *European Neutrals and Non-Belligerents during the Second World War*, p. 67, Hayes, *Quisling*, pp. 171-2, Hoidal, *Quisling*, pp. 342-50 and Dahl, *Quisling*, pp. 149-51.
[69] A 'turf war' would be fought over the coming weeks between Rosenberg's ministry and the foreign ministry, but at this stage, Rosenberg was in the ascendant.
[70] Hoidal, *Quisling*, pp. 329-30.
[71] Ibid., pp. 193-8.
[72] Williams, *Blitzkrieg and Conquest*, p. 83.
[73] Koht, *Norway Neutral and Invaded*, pp. 52-3.

## Chapter 3

[1] Ørvik, *The Decline of Neutrality*, p. 220.
[2] Brøyn, 'Den Svenske malmeksort frem til besetnignen av Narvik I 1940', p. 88. Special thanks to Geirr Haarr for supplying this data. Note that shipping of iron ore from the Swedish southern ore port of Oxelösund to Germany almost doubled to a total of 519,000 tons in the September–December 1939 period. From Luleå shipping totals in the same period also doubled and saw a total of 1,871,000 tons shipped, although ice in the Baltic ended this in early December. See Fritz, *German Steel and Swedish Iron Ore*, p. 43.
[3] 'Sweden', http://www.spartacus.schoolnet.co.uk/2WWsweden.htm.
[4] Waldemar Erfurth, *Der Finnische Krieg 1941-1944*, Munich: Limes, 1977, p. 21.
[5] Munch-Petersen, *The Strategy of Phoney War*, p. 63. In terms of censorship Sweden would block certain books from publication. Swedish policies changed to being more pro-Allied in July 1943 after the fall of Mussolini.
[6] Paul A. Levine, 'Swedish Neutrality during the Second World War: tactical success or moral compromise?', in Wylie (ed.), *European Neutrals and Non-Belligerents during the Second World War*, p. 318, *Führer Conferences on Naval Affairs 1939-1945*, London: Chatham, 2005, p. 79 and Munch-Petersen, *The Strategy of Phoney War*, *passim*.
[7] Koht, *Norway Neutral and Invaded*, p. 48.
[8] Munch-Petersen, *The Strategy of Phoney War*, pp. 77-9, quote on p. 79.

[9] Jukka Nevakivi, *The Appeal that was Never Made*, Montreal: McGill-Queen's University Press, 1976, pp. 106–7 and Rhys-Jones, *Churchill and the Norway Campaign*, p. 5.

[10] Martti Häikiö, *The Race for Northern Europe, September 1939–June 1940*, in Henrik S. Nissen (ed.), *Scandinavia During the Second World War*, pp. 53–97.

[11] The Anglo-Canadian mining trust Mond Nickel Company was beginning to exploit the nickel mines of Petsamo, therefore the Allies favoured an option of landing volunteers and supplies in the Petsamo peninsula to come to the aid of Finland. The cover for the operation was to be the exiled Polish forces, since Poland had been invaded by the Soviet Union. See H. Peter Krosby, *Finland, Germany and the Soviet Union 1940–1941. The Petsamo Dispute*, Madison: University of Wisconsin, 1968, p. 4ff.

[12] Haarr, *The German Invasion of Norway*, p. 33.

[13] Nevakivi, *The Appeal that was Never Made*, p. 118.

[14] Petrow, *The Bitter Years*, pp. 16–17, Carlgren, *Swedish Foreign Policy during the Second World War*, pp. 48–9 and Höhne, *Canaris*, p. 403.

[15] Nevakivi, *The Appeal that was Never Made*, pp. 108–12. Daladier had earlier passed on information that seemingly was working at cross-purposes to then-stated Allied policies.

[16] German Foreign Office, *Britain's Designs on Norway Full Text of White Book No. 4*, New York, NY: German Library of Information, 1940, p. 61.

[17] Thompson, *The Norwegian Armed Forces and Defense Policy*, p. 146.

[18] Maier et al., *Germany and the Second World War*, Vol. II, p. 201.

[19] Williams, *Blitzkrieg and Conquest*, pp. 378–80.

[20] Nevakivi, *The Appeal that was Never Made*, p. 147.

[21] Carlgren, *Swedish Foreign Policy during the Second World War*, p. 49, Munch-Petersen, *The Strategy of Phoney War*, pp. 190–1 and Nigel de Lee, 'Allied Failure in Norway in 1940', in Gary Sheffield and Geoffrey Till (eds), *The Challenges of High Command*, Basingstoke: Palgrave-Macmillan, 2003, p. 60 and 'Foreign News', *Time* magazine, 1 April 1940, Vol. XXXV, No. 14, pp. 20–3.

[22] Carlgren, *Swedish Foreign Policy during the Second World War*, pp. 54–5.

[23] Thompson, *The Norwegian Armed Forces and Defense Policy*, p. 144.

[24] Monica Curtis (ed.), *Norway and the War*, London: Royal Institute of International Affairs, 1941, pp. 43–4.

[25] An expanded order of battle is in German Foreign Office, *Britain's Designs on Norway*, p. 14.

[26] Williams, *Blitzkrieg and Conquest*, pp. 380–1.

[27] Derry, *The Campaign in Norway*, p. 15, Carlgren, *Swedish Foreign Policy during the Second World War*, p. 56, Moulton, *The Norwegian Campaign of 1940*, p. 58 and Butler, *Grand Strategy*, Vol. II, September 1939–June 1941, p. 123. Several plans were proposed early on going under different code-names. 'Wilfred' was the final one.

[28] Williams, *Blitzkrieg and Conquest*, pp. 654–5 and John Campbell, *Naval Weapons of World War Two*, London: Conway Maritime, 1985, p. 98.

[29] Williams, *Blitzkrieg and Conquest*, p. 655.

[30] Ibid., p. 436.

[31] Charles S. Thomas, *The German Navy in the Nazi Era*, Annapolis: Naval Institute Press, 1990, p. 190.

[32] *Führer Conferences on Naval Affairs 1939–1945*, p. 86 and Maier et al., *Germany and the Second World War*, Vol. II, p. 194.

[33] Hoidal, *Quisling*, p. 360.

[34] Gemzell, *Organization, Conflict and Innovation*, pp. 376–7.

[35] James P. Levy, *The Royal Navy's Home Fleet in World War II*, New York, NY: Palgrave, 2003, p. 48.

[36] Curtis (ed.), *Norway and the War*, p. 63. Ribbentrop also noted Allied plans to seize Swedish northern ore fields. The Allies were also aware of German preparations, but only on 9 April were these fully understood; see Churchill's speech, ibid., pp. 68–71.

[37] Carlgren, *Swedish Foreign Policy during the Second World War*, p. 56 and Munch-Petersen, *The Strategy of Phoney War*, pp. 195–7. As with so many decisions that are 'political' in nature, there was a great amount of back and forth before the final decision was made.

[38] John Colville, *The Fringes of Power: 10 Downing Street Diaries 1939–1945*, London: Sceptre, 1986, p. 90.

[39] Thompson, *The Norwegian Armed Forces and Defense Policy*, p. 206.

[40] Nevakivi, *The Appeal that was Never Made*, p. 93.

[41] Irving, *Hitler's War*, Vol. 1, p. 102 and John H. Waller, *The Unseen War in Europe*, New York, NY: Random House, 1996, p 122.

[42] Walter Schellenberg, *The Labyrinth*, New York, NY: Da Capo, 2000, p. 101.

[43] 'Foreign News', *Time* magazine, 1 April 1940, Vol. XXXV, No. 14, p. 23. This story was carried by other news agencies as well.

[44] Quote in Munch-Petersen, *The Strategy of Phoney War*, p. 197.

[45] Charles Cruickshank, *SOE in Scandinavia*, London: Oxford University Press, 1986, pp. 28–58.

[46] Nevakivi, *The Appeal that was Never Made*, pp. 76–7.

[47] Cruickshank, *SOE in Scandinavia*, p. 39. Cover organisations, which appear on the surface to have the best of intentions, are still in use today, most notoriously for supporting terror operations in the Middle East.

[48] Derry, *The Campaign in Norway*, p. 11.

[49] Quoted in Claasen, *Hitler's Northern War*, p. 21.

## Chapter 4

[1] http://www.dagbladet.no/kultur/2005/06/30/436130.html. To our knowledge, this wonderful poem has never been formally published in English.

*Dare Not to Sleep*

I was awakened one morning, by the
   quaintest of dreams
'twas like a voice, spoken to me
It sounded afar - like an underground
   stream,
I rose and said: Why do you call me?

Dare not to slumber! Dare not to sleep!
Dare not believe, it was merely a dream!
Yore I was judged.
The gallows were built in the court this
   evening,
They'll come for me — 5' in the morning

This dungeon is teeming,
And barracks stand dungeon by dungeon
we lie here, awaiting, in cold cells of stone,

We lie here, we rot, in these murky holes.

We know not ourselves, what does lie ahead
Who will be the next one they'll reach for.
We moan and we shriek: But do you take
   heed?
Is there none among you who'll hearken?

No one can see us,
None know what befalls us.
Yet more:
None will believe - what the day will bring
   us!

And then You defy: This dare not be true!
That men can be utterly evil.
There has to be some one with merits pure
Oh, brother, you still have a great deal to
   learn

They said: You will give your life, if
   commanded
We've given it now, for naught it was
   handed
The world has forgotten, we've all been
   deceived
Dare not to sleep in this hour - this eve.

You oughtn't go to your business hence,
Or think: What's your loss – or what is your
   gain?
You oughtn't attribute your fields and your
   kine,
Nor say you've enough - with all that is
   thine.

You oughn't abide, sitting calm in your
   home
Saying: Dismal it is, poor they are, and alone
You cannot permit it! You dare not, at all.
Accepting that outrage on all else may fall!
I cry with the final gasps of my breath:
You dare not repose, nor stand and forget.

Pardon them not - they know what they do!
They breathe on hate-glows, and evil pursue,
They fancy to slay, they revel with cries,
Their desire is to gloat, when our world is
   at fire!
In blood they are yearning to drown one
   and all!
Don't you believe it? You've heard the call!

You know how infants will soldiers remain,

While dashing through streets, fields,
chanting 'bout pain
Aroused by their mothers' assurance of
glory
They'll shelter their land – and they'll never
worry

You know the fatality of the lies,
that glory and faith and honor abides
You discern the dauntless dreams of a child,
A saber, a banner, he'll flaunt them so wild,

And then they'll leave home for a rainfall
of steel,
'Till last they hang ragged on barbed wire
will,
Decaying for Hitler's Aryan call,
That is what a man's for - after all…

I couldn't imagine – too late now it is
My sentence is just: The verdict's no miss
I believed in prosperity, dreamt about peace
In labor and fellowship; love's fragrant kiss
Yet those who don't die on the battlefield,
Their heads for the axeman, will certainly
yield

I cry in the gloom – if only you'd knew
There is but one thing – befitting to do
Defend yourself, while your hands are still
yearning,
Protect your offspring – Europe is burning.

—

I shook from the chill. To dress, up I rose
Without stars were shining, so far, yet so
close
'twere simply a brilliant ray in the east,
Admonishing warning from the dream that
just ceased

The day that soared up from earths
furthermost strand
Augmenting with blood – and with
firebrand
It grew with terror - like a breath that was lost
It seemed like the starlight – was slain by
the frost.

I weighed: Something is imminent – and
it's dire
Our era is over – Europe's on fire!

[2] Quote from Olav Riste in J. Andenaes,
Olav Riste and Magne Skodvin, *Norway and the Second World War*, Oslo: Johan Grundt Tanum, 1966, p. 9.

[3] Thompson, *The Norwegian Armed Forces and Defense Policy*, p. 59.

[4] Quote in Maurice Harvey, *Scandinavian Misadventure*, Tunbridge Wells: Spellmount, 1990, p. 5. Dahl, *Quisling*, p. 50 and Ørvik, *The Decline of Neutrality*, p. 227.

[5] Olivier Desarzen, *Nachritendienstliche Aspekte der "Weserübung" 1940*, Osnabruck: Biblio, 1988, pp. 113–14, 128–9; see also Claasen, *Hitler's Northern War*, p. 45.

[6] Ørvik, *The Decline of Neutrality*, p. 227.

[7] Thompson, *The Norwegian Armed Forces and Defense Policy*, p. 142. Monsen was ill at the time of his replacement and is one of the notable and powerful Norwegian political leaders of the early twentieth century. He had mellowed somewhat from the anti-militaristic stance he adopted in the 1920s.

[8] Høiback, *Command and Control in Military Crisis*, p. 72, Thompson, *The Norwegian Armed Forces and Defense Policy*, p. 111 and Rolf Hobson and Tom Kristiansen, *Norsk Forsvarshistorie 1905–1940*, Bergen: Eide Forlag, 2001, Vol. 3, p. 46.

[9] Thompson, *The Norwegian Armed Forces and Defense Policy*, pp. 106–9.

[10] Ørvik, *The Decline of Neutrality*, pp. 227–9 and Nissen (ed.), *Scandinavia during the Second World War*, p. 52. Finland devoted about 25 per cent, while Sweden devoted about 17.5 per cent towards defence on the eve of war. A graph of the defence-budget decline and then growth appears in Thompson, *The Norwegian Armed Forces and Defense Policy*, p. 57.

[11] Thompson, *The Norwegian Armed Forces and Defense Policy*, pp. 108–9 and Tim Greve, *Haakon VII of Norway*, London: C. Hurst, 1983, p. 131.

[12] Larsen, *A History of Norway*, p. 534. Also thanks to Geirr Haarr for his insights about this great Norwegian poet.

[13] Quote in David Binder, *The Other German: Willy Brandt's Life & Times*, Washington, DC: New Republic Book Company, 1975, p. 59.

[14] Larsen, *A History of Norway*, p. 539.

[15] William L. Shirer, *Berlin Diary*, New York, NY: Alfred A. Knopf, 1941, p. 291.

[16] Intelligence will be discussed in greater detail in Chapters 5, 6 and 7.

[17] Petrow, *The Bitter Years*, pp. 2–3. See also Harriman, *Mission to the North*, p. 116 on the perception that the vaunted Nazi war machine had been secretly preparing for the invasion of Norway for decades. The reality, as will be shown, was very different.

[18] Larsen, *A History of Norway*, pp. 512–13. One of Norway's new frigates is named after him.

[19] Vidkun Quisling, *Russia and Ourselves*, Metairie, LA: Sons of Liberty Books, 1994, pp. 29–30. Rehabilitation of this traitor by the Black International has been attempted in the postwar decades.

[20] Thompson, *The Norwegian Armed Forces and Defense Policy*, pp. 81–3.

[21] Dahl, *Quisling, passim* and Hoidal, *Quisling*, pp. 80–1 and 88–9. Of the nine cabinet posts, only four were held by members of the Agrarian Party. Quisling was not a member of that party but had campaigned for it in the election. Hoidal's book is the single-best English biography of Quisling.

[22] Hoidal, *Quisling*, pp. 204–5.

[23] The brown shirt was defended not as a copy of the German brown shirt, but as practical 'for work and sport'. See *ibid.*, pp. 169–70.

[24] Dahl, *Quisling*, p. 157 and Oddvar K. Hoidal, 'Vidkun Quisling's Decline as a Political Figure in Prewar Norway 1933–1937', *The Journal of Modern History*, Vol. 43, No. 3 (September 1971), pp. 440–67.

[25] Hoidal, *Quisling*, p. 282. The party newspaper ran an article in 1937 stating that the forged *Protocols of the Wise Men of Zion* was true and usually had some articles attacking Jews.

[26] Quote is Dahl, *Quisling*, p. 109. See also Hoidal, 'Vidkun Quisling's Decline as a Political Figure in Prewar Norway 1933–1937', p. 466. A good discussion of the decline of the NS can be read in Hoidal, *Quisling*, pp. 243–79.

[27] Thompson, *The Norwegian Armed Forces and Defense Policy*, pp. 243–4, quote on p. 243.

[28] Nara T312-982 fr. 9173650, 'Meldung von Detmold: 12.4.40 11.30 Uhr' signed by Colonel Weiss.

[29] Dahl, *Quisling*, pp. 340–1 and Williams, *Blitzkrieg and Conquest*, p. 358.

[30] Koht, *Norway Neutral and Invaded*, pp. 18–19.

[31] Thompson, *The Norwegian Armed Forces and Defense Policy*, p. 101.

[32] Jack Greene and Alessandro Massignani, *Ironclads at War: The Origin and Development of the Armored Warship, 1854–1891*, Conshocken, PA: Combined Publishing, 1998, pp. 190–2.

[33] Having learned the lesson the hard way, Norway has recently begun in 2008 to increase its defence budget as a result of the possible new threats posed by it being resource rich in a rapidly changing world. http://www.regjeringen.no/en/dep/fd/Press-centre/Press-releases/2007/Defence-budget-2008.html?id=484847.

[34] Robert Gardiner (ed.), *Conway's All the World's Fighting Ships 1922–1946*, Annapolis, MD: Naval Institute Press, 1980, p. 379 and Divine, *Firedrake*, p. 61.

[35] Haarr, *The German Invasion of Norway*, p. 15.

[36] Ibid., p. 250. A list of forty-nine can be found in Rolf Scheen, *Norges Sjøkrig*, 2 vols, Bergen: John Griegs, 1947, Vol. 2, pp. 303–7.

[37] Thompson, *The Norwegian Armed Forces and Defense Policy*, p. 163.

[38] Conversation with Lieutenant Colonel (ret.) Arvid Carlsen, curator at Oscarsborg and Haarr, *The German Invasion of Norway*, p. 446.

[39] Thompson, *The Norwegian Armed Forces and Defense Policy*, p. 37.

[40] Quote in Høiback, *Command and Control in Military Crisis*, p. 724. Olav Riste, *Norway's Foreign Relations. A History*, Oslo: Universitetsvorlaget, 2001, p. 140. British leadership held this opinion as well.

[41] Moulton, *The Norwegian Campaign of 1940*, p. 11. On sergeants see http://niehorster.orbat.com/022_norway/_ranks_norway.htm.

[42] Derry, *The Campaign in Norway*, p. 176. The Krag was a front-line weapon in the American army during the Spanish-American War, though the USA used a larger calibre. Thanks to Trond Wikborg on this point.

[43] Thompson, *The Norwegian Armed Forces and Defense Policy*, p. 118 and Haarr, *The German Invasion of Norway*, p. 252.

[44] The notorious German firm of I. G. Farben was a shareholder in the company.

[45] Thompson, *The Norwegian Armed Forces and Defense Policy*, pp. 165–6. Picture in

*Handbok for Soldaten*, Oslo: Merkantile Boks and Akcidenstrykkeri, 1940, p. 21.

[46] Scheen, *Norges Sjøkrig*, Vol. 1, p. 144.

[47] Michael Tamelander and Niklas Zetterling, *9 April: Nazitysklands invasjon av Norge*, Oslo: Spartacus, p. 58.

[48] Ruge gives a figure of 106,000 men but the higher figure may include fortress troops and Ruge's figure is for the field army, see below. Exact head counts are always elusive.

[49] Haarr, *The German Invasion of Norway*, p. 180.

[50] This low figure from Hubatsch, *Weserübung. Die deutsche Besetzung von Dänemark und Norwegen*, p. 41, n. 3.

[51] NARA, T-312-981, fr. 9172807: Gruppe XXI, *Derzeitiger Stand ders norwegischen Heeres*, dated 4 March 1940.

[52] NARA, T-312-981, fr. 9172816: Gruppe XXI, Abt. Ic Nr. 8/40 g.Kdos of the 3 April 1940: *Feindnachrichtenblatt Nr. 2.*

[53] Hobson and Kristiansen, *Norsk Forsvarshistorie*, Vol. 3, pp. 276–7 and Thompson, *The Norwegian Armed Forces and Defense Policy*, p. 87.

[54] Thompson, *The Norwegian Armed Forces and Defense Policy*, pp. 89–91. Thompson includes an interesting chart showing the decline of NCOs and officers from 1909 to 1933.

[55] Quote in ibid., p. 91.

[56] Haarr, *The German Invasion of Norway*, p. 175 and Thompson, *The Norwegian Armed Forces and Defense Policy*, pp. 91–5 and 202.

[57] For the Norwegian order of battle see Tamelander and Zetterling, *9 April: Nazitysklands invasjon av Norge*, p. 57, Hobson and Kristiansen, *Norsk Forsvarshistorie*, Vol. 3, pp. 276–330, http://niehorster.orbat.com/500_eto/_40-04_scandinavia.html, Ronald Tarnstrom, *The Sword of Scandinavia*, Lindsborg, KS: Trogen Books, 1996, pp. 124–47 and the valuable http://hem.fyristorg.com/robertm/norge/norway_reference.html.

[58] There were some grenades left over from the First World War era that were unreliable.

[59] Thanks to Geirr Haarr for clearing up some of details regarding this. See also *Hankbok for Soldaten*, pp. 19, 25–8.

[60] An interesting site on the guard is http://www.festningsverk.no/index.htm. Photographs here show some wearing captured German helmets.

[61] http://hem.fyristorg.com/robertm/norge/norway_reference.html.

[62] Thompson, *The Norwegian Armed Forces and Defense Policy*, p. 115.

[63] http://mailer.fsu.edu/~akirk/tanks/norway/norway.htm. Photographs appear in Hobson and Kristiansen, *Norsk Forsvarshistorie*, Vol. 3, pp. 211, 233.

[64] http://www.wwiivehicles.com/html/sweden/armored_cars/landsverk.html. The L-185 was a Swedish design with a speed of 37mph, was protected by 8.5mm of armor and weighed 9,408lb.

[65] Tarnstrom, *The Sword of Scandinavia*, p. 127. For the '*Celere*' see http://niehorster.orbat.com/019_italy/40_organ/div_celere_40.htm and Jack Greene, *Mare Nostrum*, Watsonville, CA: Typesetting Etc., 1990, pp. 51, 54.

[66] Gardermoen would become Oslo's main airport after the war.

[67] Koht, *Norway Neutral and Invaded*, p. 22.

[68] Quote in Thompson, *The Norwegian Armed Forces and Defense Policy*, p. 116.

[69] *Handbok for Soldaten.*

[70] Thompson, *The Norwegian Armed Forces and Defense Policy*, pp. 114–15.

[71] We rely on Christopher Shores et al., *Fledgling Eagles: The Complete Account of Air Operations During the 'Phoney War' and Norwegian Campaign, 1940*, London: Grub Street, 1991, pp. 219–22 and Helge Mehre, *Flyvåpnene 1 den 2. vergdenskrig*, Lillestrøm, Norway: Aksidenstrykkeriet, pp. 7–8.

[72] http://niehorster.orbat.com/022_norway/no_aaf.htm.

[73] Shores et al., *Fledgling Eagles*, p. 225. Gulliksen would be discredited in the course of the fighting and would be relieved.

[74] Arild Kjæraas, *Høver M.F. 11, Profiles in Norway Nr. 2*, Andebu, Norway: self-published, 2004, *passim*. The author in this new series can be emailed at akjae@online.no.

[75] For the Ju87s see Williams, *Blitzkrieg and Conquest*, pp. 379–80.

[76] Koht, *Norway Neutral and Invaded*, pp. 30–1. A list of the ships lost is in Scheen, *Norges Sjøkrig*, Vol. 1, pp. 35–7.

[77] Quote from Leland Stowe, *No Other Road to Freedom*, New York, NY: Alfred A. Knopf, 1941, p. 84.

[78] Ibid.

[79] Quote from Thompson, *The Norwegian Armed Forces and Defense Policy*, p. 120.

[80] Riste, 'Intelligence and the "Mindset": The German invasion of Norway in 1940', pp. 521–36.

[81] Ibid. and Thompson, *The Norwegian Armed Forces and Defense Policy*, pp. 417–21.

[82] Thompson, *The Norwegian Armed Forces and Defense Policy*, p. 171.

## Chapter 5

[1] James Tevnan and Terence Horsley, *Norway Invaded*, Manchester: Willy Grove Press, n.d., pp. 13–14. This was a Cherry Tree War Special paperback produced in 1940 (May?) and carried the seeds of many of the rumours and future inaccuracies of other more formal histories. It has a far too active fifth column and the Gestapo arrives much sooner in Norway than it would historically. It is a great early example of an 'instant history' produced immediately on the heels of a dramatic event.

[2] *Fuehrer Conferences on Naval Affairs*, p. 86; italics in the original.

[3] Williams, *Blitzkrieg and Conquest*, p. 374 and Corum, 'The German Campaign in Norway 1940 as a Joint Operation', pp. 50–77.

[4] All warnings by Raeder on the possibility of British occupation of Narvik received no attention by the Führer or by other high officers like Jodl, according to Walter Warlimont, *Im Hauptquartier der deutschen Wehrmacht 1939–1945. Grundlagen, Formen, Gestalten*, Frankfurt a. M: B&G, 1962, p. 83. Colonel General Warlimont was serving at the time at the OKW as commander of the land defence section.

[5] Adam Claasen, 'The German Invasion of Norway 1940: The Operational Intelligence Dimension', *Journal of Strategic Studies*, Vol. 27, No. 1 (March 2004), pp. 114–35.

[6] Claasen noted the short life of this staff headed by the Luftwaffe. See his detailed account in Claasen, *Hitler's Northern War*, p. 27.

[7] It was also called *Sonderstab Weserübung*,

[8] NARA, T-312, roll 980, fr. 9172309, Führer's order OKW/WFA Abt. L Nr. 22128/40 g.K.Chefs of 2 April 1940.

[9] Corum, 'The German Campaign in Norway 1940 as a Joint Operation', p. 61.

[10] Ibid., p. 59.

[11] Williams, *Blitzkrieg and Conquest*, p. 4.

[12] Generaloberst Halder, *Kriegstagebuch 1939–1942* 3 Vols., ed. by Hans Adolf Jacobsen, Stuttgart: W. Kohlhammer, 1962–3, Vol. I, 204, entry of 21 February 1940. Halder had been approached in September 1939 by the Chief-of-Staff of the navy about an invasion of Norway and he had stated, 'he rejected such an operation completely'; see Williams, *Blitzkrieg and Conquest*, p. 220.

[13] Allen Welsh Dulles, *Germany's Underground*, Boston, MA: Da Capo Press, 1947, p. 59. In the same breath, Halder also complained of lack of consultation with him; see Hayes, *Quisling*, p. 201.

[14] Hayes, *Quisling*, p. 201 and Irving, *Hitler's War*, Vol. 1, p. 92.

[15] Williams, *Blitzkrieg and Conquest*, p. 79.

[16] Ibid., p. 300.

[17] E. H. Stevens, *Trial of Nikolaus von Falkenhorst*, London: William Hodge, 1949, p. xxiv and Williams, *Blitzkrieg and Conquest*, p. 523.

[18] Ibid., p. 271 and NARA, T-312-980-9172062, War Diary of the Gruppe XXI. Hubatsch, *Weserübung. Die deutsche Besetzung von Dänemark und Norwegen*, pp. 39–40, *Tagebuch General Jodl*, 21 February 1940.

[19] Petrow, *The Bitter Years*, p. 32. Quote in Louis de Jong, *The German Fifth Column in the Second World War*, Chicago, IL: University of Chicago Press, 1956, p. 172, Williams, *Blitzkrieg and Conquest*, p. 525, and http://www.worldwar.nl/battles/Norway.htm. A Baedecker guide would also be used later by the British due to lack of proper prewar planning; see Derry, *The Campaign in Norway*, p. 54.

[20] Chris Mann and Christer Jörgensen, *Hitler's Arctic War*, New York, NY: Thomas Dunne Books, 2002, p. 38.

[21] T312- roll 380, 9172061 and sgg.

[22] Corum, 'The German Campaign in Norway 1940 as a Joint Operation', pp. 50–77, and Williams, *Blitzkrieg and Conquest*, p. 542.

[23] Corum, 'The German Campaign in Norway 1940 as a Joint Operation', p. 61.

[24] See Robert W. Strahan, *Command and Control of the First Modern Campaign: The German Invasion of Denmark and Norway – April, 1940*, Newport, RI: Naval War College, 1998, *passim*; special thanks to Dave Isby for obtaining this document for us.

[25] Quoted in Joesten, *Denmark's Day of Doom*, p. 78.

26 Quote from Walther Hubatsch in Jong, *The German Fifth Column in the Second World War*, p. 173.

27 Schellenberg, *The Labyrinth*, p. 100 and Jong, *The German Fifth Column in the Second World War*, pp. 177–8.

28 Heinz Höhne, *Canaris*, New York: Doubleday, 1979, p. 403, and quote in John H. Waller, *The Unseen War in Europe* New York: Random House, 1996, p. 122.

29 Haarr, *The German Invasion of Norway*, pp. 59–60, Höhne, *Canaris*, p. 403 and quote in Waller, *The Unseen War in Europe*, p. 122.

30 Email from Geirr Haarr, dated 22 March 2005. Several 'businessmen' were also expelled.

31 Email from Andrew Smith, dated 24 March 2005.

32 Hinsley et al., *British Intelligence in the Second World War*, Vol. I, p. 120. Thanks to Andrew Smith for information on this. During April two German trawlers would be captured by the Norwegian navy, one ending up in Norwegian service as the *Honningsvaag*.

33 Quote in Kenneth Macksey, *The Searchers: How Radio Interception Changed the Course of Both World Wars*, London: Cassell, 2003, p. 72.

34 Corum, 'Uncharted Waters', pp. 345–69, this p. 354.

35 Lukacs, *The Last European War*, p. 271.

36 NARA, T-312-981, fr. 9172803: *Die Wehrmacht Norwegens 1937 Oktober – 1940 April*, Anlagenband zur KTB Nr. 1 Anlage 59. 'Their people are already deeply entrenched in Stavanger and Bergen'.

37 Geirr Haarr from email, dated 22 March 2005 and Jak P. Mallmann Showell, *German Naval Code Breakers*, Annapolis, MD: Naval Institute Press, 2003, pp. 47–9. Showell's book is very poorly edited and replete with minor errors of fact. The original publisher was Ian Allen Publishing.

38 Haarr, *The German Invasion of Norway*, pp. 59–60 has the best discussion of this visit, which is usually overlooked by other historians.

39 Hayes, *Quisling*, pp. 203–7 and Haarr, *The German Invasion of Norway*, pp. 59–60. The Canaris archives were destroyed in 1945 and this remains a sad loss for the study of history. In the late 1980s the authors were involved with an Austrian who claimed he had those archives and wanted to sell them to a major American university but we quickly recognised that while he had important historical records, mostly from the First World War, he did not have the rumoured archives.

40 Quote in Williams, *Blitzkrieg and Conquest*, pp. 457–8.

41 Ibid., pp. 244–5.

42 Jong, *The German Fifth Column in the Second World War*, p. 159. Kaupisch was recalled from retirement at the outbreak of war and had been a general in the Luftwaffe. On the 14 April he was made a General of Artillery in the army.

43 Ibid.

44 Corum, 'Uncharted Waters', pp. 345–69 and David Kahn, *Hitler Spies*, New York, NY: Collier Books, 1978, p. 115.

45 Corum, 'Uncharted Waters', pp. 352–3.

46 Williams, *Blitzkrieg and Conquest*, p. 431.

47 http://www.nizkor.org/ftp.py?imt/nca/nca-06//nca-06-3596-ps, 301.

48 *Tagebuch General Jodl*, 5 February 1940; for the period 1 February–26 May 1940 it is printed in IMT, Vol. XXVIII, pp. 397–434 as Document 1809-PS. Pohlman's rank appears differently in various sources.

49 These were invasion ships lost to Allied submarines and are discussed in detail in Chapter 6.

50 Koht, *Norway Neutral and Invaded*, pp. 60–1.

51 Williams, *Blitzkrieg and Conquest*, p. 528.

52 http://www.washingtonpost.com/wp-dyn/articles/A132-2004Dec14.html.

53 Ziemke, *The German Northern Theater of Operations*, p. 19.

54 James Lucas, *Alpine Elite*, London: Jane's Publishing, 1980, pp. 205–52.

55 Largely due to manpower issues and the delivery of artillery support Germany would adopt the two-regiment binary division for many of her secondary army units in the 1943–5 period.

56 Corum, 'The German Campaign in Norway 1940 as a Joint Operation', p. 60.

57 W. J. K. Davies, *The German Army Handbook*, New York, NY: Arco, 1973, pp. 94–5.

58 Email from Leo W. G. Niehorster to David Isby, dated 14 January 2005.

59 NARA, T-312, roll 986, fr. 9412 and ff. 69th Infantry Division 261/40 Erfahrungsbericht of 22 July 1940.

60 Of the infantry only the 69th Division had

been in existence at the time of the Polish campaign but it served in the West.

61 Theodor Broch, *The Mountains Wait*, London: Michael Joseph, 1943, p. 102.

62 Conversation with Robert Riddervold in July 1998. Robert actually clambered around in a Spanish tri-motor based on the Ju52 design to see how difficult it was to move in. Max Schmeling, the famous German boxer, who was over 5ft 10in, had to bail out from the rear door used for loading cargo.

63 Knoll Pharmaceutical also supplied a near equivalent called 'Isophan'.

64 http://amphetamines.com/nazi.html. Roger Edwards, *German Airborne Troops*, Garden City, NY: Doubleday, 1974, *passim*. The Benzedrine drug is a form of 'speed'. Italian frogmen also made use of a similar drug; see Jack Greene and Alessandro Massignani, *The Black Prince and the Sea Devils*, Cambridge, MA: Da Capo Press, 2004, p. 97. A Norwegian related to us that his father had to fire his weapons over the heads of some captured paratroopers to maintain order and it may have been due in part to the prisoners being high on Benzedrine.

65 Thomas L. Jentz, *Panzer Tracts No. 4 Panzerkampfwagen IV*, Darlington, MA: Darlington Productions, 1997, pp. 6–9 and www.achtungpanzer.com/norway.htm. This is misidentified as a V and a VI, but is indeed officially a type IV.

66 Klaus-Jürgen Thies, *Weserübung*, Vol. 2, *Der Zweite Weltkrieg im Kartenbild*, Osnabrück: Biblio Verlag, 1991, bottom.

67 Louis Brown, *A Radar History of World War II*, Philadelphia, PA: Institute of Physics Publishing, 1999, p. 106.

68 Shores et al., *Fledgling Eagles*, pp. 215–16 and Hubatsch, *Weserübung. Die deutsche Besetzung von Dänemark und Norwegen*, p. 407. Shores does not include some air units that were assigned to the Danish invasion and this includes some seaplanes and liaison aircraft. John J. Vasco and Peter D. Cornwell, *Zerstörer*, Norfolk, VA: Jac Publishing, 1995, p. 11 states 571 Ju52s.

69 The term Stuka is a contraction of *Sturzkampfflugzeug*, the German term for dive-bomber.

70 Jack Greene and Alessandro Massignani, *The Naval War in the Mediterranean*, 3rd edn, Barnsley: Frontline Books, 2011, Chapter 2, *passim*. The Spanish started with four

then six of their own planes in transporting troops across the Strait of Gibraltar and were quickly augmented by seventy-two German and fifty-six Italian air transports.

71 http://niehorster.orbat.com/019_italy/39-04-07_albania/sqa_transp.html.

72 Sonke Neitzel, 'Kriegsmarine and Luftwaffe Co-operation in the war against Britain, 1939–1945', *War in History*, Vol. 10, No. 4 (November 2003), pp. 448–62. Early in the war Germany would purchase 300 torpedoes from Italy. Ironically, the Italian design was based on a Norwegian torpedo purchased early in the 1930s.

73 Taylor Telford, *The March of Conquest: The German Victories in Western Europe, 1940*, New York, NY: Simon and Schuster, 1958, pp. 24–5.

74 *Fuehrer Conferences on Naval Affairs*, p. 93.

75 Ziemke, *The German Northern Theater of Operations*, p. 109.

76 Haarr, The *German Invasion of Norway*, p. 74.

77 German naval marines were an odd animal. Most sources list them as a company, though 100 men really would be the equivalent of 2 platoons. Additionally, they were more like USMC Defense Battalions used at such detached places like Wake or Midway Islands. They were not assault troops. They were primarily utilised in this campaign to man coastal defence batteries.

78 See the excellent http://niehorster.orbat. com/500_eto/_40-04_scandinavia.html.

79 We refer to them as 11in.

80 Timothy P. Mulligan, 'Ship-of-the-line or Atlantic Raider', *The Journal of Military History*, Vol. 69, No. 4 (October 2005), pp. 1017, 1039.

81 M. J. Whitley, *German Capital Ships of World War Two*, London: Arms & Armour Press, 1989, pp. 22–35 and Gerhard Koop and Klaus-Peter Schmolke, *Battleships of the Scharnhorst Class*, Annapolis: Naval Institute Press, 1999, pp. 18–22.

82 Erich Gröner, *German Warships 1815–1945*, Vols One and Two, Annapolis, MD: Naval Institute Press, 1990, Vol. 1, pp. 199–202 and M. J. Whitley, *Destroyer!*, London: Arms & Armour Press, 1983, p. 80. In the course of the war there would be many modifications including the removal of a 5.1in gun to allow for more AA weaponry.

[83] 'World War', *Time* magazine, 1 April 1940, Vol. XXXV, No. 14, p. 30.

[84] Milan Vego, 'The Right Submarine for Lurking in the Littorals, *USNI Proceedings* (June, 2010), Vol. 136/6/1.288, pp. 17–18.

[85] If set for 30 knots it could travel 15,300yds, with the third setting being 8,750yds at 40 knots. See Campbell, *Naval Weapons of World War Two*, p. 263.

[86] Haarr, The *German Invasion of Norway*, p. 341.

[87] Peter Dickens, *Narvik: Battles in the Fjords*, Annapolis, MD: Naval Institute Press, 1974, p. 39. This is a solid book from German and British perspectives, but does not cover the Norwegians to any great extent.

[88] Cajus Bekker, *Hitler's Naval War*, Garden City, NY: Doubleday, 1974, pp. 124–30, Whitley, *Destroyer!*, pp. 80–2 and Eberhard Rössler, *The U-Boat*, London: Cassell, 1981, pp. 143–4.

[89] Quoting Dönitz in Moulton, *The Norwegian Campaign of 1940*, p. 118.

[90] Lunde, *Hitler's Pre-Emptive War*, p. 255.

[91] J. Rohwer, *Axis Submarine Successes of World War Two*, Annapolis, MD: Naval Institute, 1999, pp. 17–18.

[92] Rohwer and Hummelchen, *Chronology of the War at Sea*, p. 15.

[93] Petrow, *The Bitter Years*, p. 1.

[94] C. J. Hambro, *I Saw it Happen in Norway*, New York, NY: D. Appleton-Century Co., 1941, p. 4. This Trojan horse is still used today. Money, drugs, bombs and guns have regularly been transported in diplomatic bags in the modern era.

[95] Quote from Stowe, *No Other Road to Freedom*, p. 85. For an excerpt from the film go to http://www.historyguy.com/worldwartwo/world_war_two_video_german_invasion_of_poland.htm. Larsen, *A History of Norway*, p. 540.

[96] Derry, *A History of Scandinavia*, p. 335.

[97] 'NARA, T314-980, 9172300-3: 'Notiz für das Kriegstagebuch', 1.4.1940; *Tagebuch General Jodl*, 31 March 1940.

[98] Irving, *Hitler's War*, Vol. 1, p. 102 and Jong, *The German Fifth Column in the Second World War*, p. 172.

[99] The *Wellem* also carried food and U-boat equipment. Its only difficult time in the operation was clearing the Soviet Union as its departure was announced at the proverbial eleventh hour.

[100] Special thanks to Geirr Haarr and Andrew Smith for clearing up this point.

[101] Williams, *Blitzkrieg and Conquest*, pp. 575–6.

[102] Petrow, *The Bitter Years*, p. 42.

[103] Derry, *The Campaign in Norway*, p. 22.

[104] Shirer, *Berlin Diary*, p. 309.

[105] Williams, *Blitzkrieg and Conquest*, pp. 451–2, 576. Shipping had been gathering since 12 March at Stettin but major troop movements did not begin arriving until 4 April.

[106] Ibid., pp. 452–8. Numerous indications would be ignored, though the Swedish intelligence service seemed to be the best informed in the days before the invasion. They noted that Sweden was not an intended target.

[107] Petrow, *The Bitter Years*, p. 42.

[108] Ibid., pp. 42–3.

[109] Email from Geirr Haarr, dated 24 March 2005.

## Chapter 6

[1] Hoidal, *Quisling*, p. 361.

[2] Munch-Petersen, *The Strategy of Phoney War*, p. 200 and Harvey, *Scandinavian Misadventure*, p. 33.

[3] Macksey, *The Searchers*, p. 77.

[4] Quote in Stephen Budiansk, *Battle of Wits*, New York, NY: Free Press, 2000, p. 140 and also see letter from Viktor Frampton in *Warship International*, Vol. 39, No. 3 (2002), p. 226.

[5] Mallmann-Showell, *German Naval Code Breakers*, p. 49 and Harvey, *Scandinavian Misadventure*, p. 33.

[6] Harvey, *Scandinavian Misadventure*, p. 34.

[7] Hinsley, *British Intelligence in the Second World War*, Vol. I, p. 122.

[8] Colville, *The Fringes of Power*, Vol. 1, p. 111.

[9] Levy, *The Royal Navy's Home Fleet in World War II*, p. 173.

[10] Quoted in ibid., p. 201 and Derry, *A History of Scandinavia*, p. 335.

[11] Shirer, *Berlin Diary*, p. 315.

[12] In April 1941 the General recommended in a report that Sweden should prepare to fight the Soviet Union.

[13] Koht, *Norway Neutral and Invaded*, p. 61 and Carlgren, *Swedish Foreign Policy during the Second World War*, p. 58.

14 Harriman, *Mission to the North*, p. 246.

15 Macksey, *The Searchers*, p. 77.

16 Ibid. and Kahn, *Hitler's Spies*, p. 217.

17 Williams, *Blitzkrieg and Conquest*, p. 575.

18 Charles Burdick and Hans-Adolf Jacobsen (eds), *The Halder War Diary 1939–1942*, Novato, CA: Presidio Press, 1988, p. 114.

19 Munch-Petersen, *The Strategy of Phoney War*, p. 207, German Foreign Office, *Britain's Designs on Norway*, p. 14, Derry, *The Campaign in Norway*, pp. 15–16 and Lunde, *Hitler's Pre-emptive War*, pp. 39–41.

20 Letter from Randall E. Doty in *Warship International*, Vol. 38, No. 3 (2001), pp. 255–6. In 1982 through Quarterdeck Games Jack Greene published NORWAY-1940, a naval game of the invasion of Norway. The victory conditions were fluid – usually the Germans were attempting to breakout into the Atlantic and that caused the Allied player to adopt completely different tactics to win.

21 David Brown (ed.), *Naval Operations of the Campaign in Norway: April–June 1940*, London: Frank Cass, 2000, p. 9 and James Levy, 'Lost Leader: Admiral of the Fleet Sir Charles Forbes and the Second World War', *Mariner's Mirror*, Vol. 88, No. 2, 2002, pp. 186–95. Forbes served on the *Iron Duke* at Jutland and to echo Levy, a biography of the man is yet to be written and should be.

22 Shores et al., *Fledgling Eagles*, p. 217.

23 The delay was due to the planes having to return to base before reporting. A radioed report was not received.

24 Butler, *Grand Strategy*, Vol. II, September 1939–June 1941, pp. 125–7.

25 The *Bertin* was a cruiser-minelayer and usually served as the flagship for destroyer flotillas. It had a main armament of 9 6in guns in triple turrets and carried only very light armour with 200 mines. It was lightly built, being less then 6,000 tons and required strengthening of its hull after construction to allow it to fire salvoes. The two destroyers were early examples of the 'super-destroyers' the French were fond of building. Displacing over 3,000 tons when loaded, they carried five 5.5in guns with a good rate of fire, improved from earlier classes but with a shorter range. Armed with six torpedo tubes, they were rated at 37 knots, though they had not achieved that speed in a decade.

26 David Brown in Salmon (ed.), *Britain and Norway in the Second World War*, p. 29.

27 Haarr, *The German Invasion of Norway*, p. 76.

28 Levy, 'Lost Leader: Admiral of the Fleet Sir Charles Forbes and the Second World War', pp. 186–95.

29 Haarr, *The German Invasion of Norway*, pp. 87–9.

30 Peter C. Smith, *Into the Minefields*, Barnsley: Pen & Sword Maritime, 2005, pp. 118, 136–41 and Edgar J. March, *British Destroyers*, London: Seeley, Service & Co. Ltd, 1966, p. 291.

31 Campbell, *Naval Weapons of World War Two*, pp. 94–6 and Brown (ed.), *Naval Operations of the Campaign in Norway*, p. 8. They were concerned about the intervention of the two elderly Norwegian ironclads.

32 Rohwer and Hummelchen, *Chronology of the War at Sea*, 2nd edn, p. 15 and Curtis (ed.), *Norway and the War*, p. 46.

33 Curtis (ed.), *Norway and the War*, p. 61. It could be argued in this Allied publication appearing in 1941 that it was the British boarding of the *Altmark* that started serious German planning.

34 Kathleen Stokker, *Folklore Fights the Nazis: Humor in Occupied Norway 1949–1945*, Madison, WI: University of Wisconsin Press, 1995, p. 109 has a classic poster printed in Oslo in 1940 by the Germans about the mining incident.

35 'Foreign News', *Time* magazine, 16 May 1940, Vol. XXXV, No. 19, p. 26.

36 Shirer, *Berlin Diary*, pp. 309–11; quote on p. 310.

37 Levy, *The Royal Navy's Home Fleet in World War II*, p. 21.

38 Neil McCart, *Nelson & Rodney*, Liskeard: Maritime Books, 2005, pp. 1–2.

39 The description of this action is based on Gerhard Koop and Klaus-Peter Schmolke, *Heavy Cruisers of the Admiral Hipper Class*, Annapolis, MD: Naval Institute Press, 2001, pp. 42–4, Gerhard Koop and Klaus-Peter Schmolke, *German Destroyers of World War II*, Annapolis, MD: Naval Institute Press, 2003, pp. 53–4, John English, *Amazon to Ivanhoe*, Kendal: World Ship Society, 1993, pp. 96–7, Derry, *The Campaign in Norway*, pp. 29–30, Bernard Ash, *Norway 1940*, London: Cassell, 1964, pp. 37–9, Brown (ed.), *Naval Operations of the Campaign in Norway*, pp. 12–13, March, *British Destroyers*, p. 304, Vincent P. O'Hara, *The German Fleet at*

*War*, Annapolis, MD: Naval Institute Press, 2005, pp. 18–20, Whitley, *Destroyer!*, pp. 119–20 and letter from Randall E. Doty in *Warship International*, Vol. 38, No. 3 (2001), p. 256.

[40] Dickens, *Narvik*, p. 32.

[41] Captain Steinar Amundsen, *Strategic Decisions and Implications of the German Assault on Norway*, Carlisle, PA: US Army War College, 2005, p. 19.

[42] Haarr, *The German Invasion of Norway*, pp. 90–1.

[43] Heye would end the war as a Vice Admiral and would later serve in the postwar German legislature.

[44] Petrow, *The Bitter Years*, p. 54 and Haarr, *The German Invasion of Norway*, pp. 92–3.

[45] The *Hipper* class carried a heavy (4.1in or 105mm) AA battery, a medium AA battery of 37mm guns and a close-in 20mm light AA battery. As in British warships, they were not designed for dual-purpose (DP) but could be utilised as such.

[46] *Glowworm* carried two quintuple mounts. It may have fired several at the *Arnim* and only three at the *Hipper*. Alternatively, the *Glowworm* may have fired all its torpedoes at *Hipper* according to several sources (see Pierre Hervieux, 'The Heavy Cruiser *Admiral Hipper* at War', in *Warship*, Vol. IX, Annapolis, MD: Naval Institute Press, 1985, p. 233) that would suggest it followed torpedo doctrine – email from Vincent P. O'Hara, dated 20 February 2007.

[47] The *Hipper* expended 31 8in, 104 4.1in, 136 37mm and 132 20mm rounds in the action. Moulton claims that the *Hipper* tried to ram, but German accounts deny this. It tried to stay bow-on to avoid British torpedoes and that may have been misinterpreted.

[48] Riste, 'Intelligence and the "Mindset": The German invasion of Norway in 1940', pp. 521–36.

[49] Dickens, *Narvik*, p. 28, David Brown in Salmon (ed.), *Britain and Norway in the Second World War*, pp. 28–9 and Brown (ed.), *Naval Operations of the Campaign in Norway*, pp. 13–14.

[50] Koop and Schmolke in *Hipper Class* report it incorrectly as being shot down.

[51] Rhys-Jones, *Churchill and the Norway Campaign*, p. 33.

[52] He was not related to Admiral A. B. Cunningham of Mediterranean fame.

[53] German Foreign Office, *Britain's Designs on Norway*, p. 33.

[54] The destroyers were the big 'Tribal' class destroyers. They were armed with eight 4.7in guns in four turrets.

[55] Brown (ed.), *Naval Operations of the Campaign in Norway*, p. 17, David Brown in Salmon (ed.), *Britain and Norway in the Second World War*, p. 29 and Haarr, *The German Invasion of Norway*, p. 107.

[56] Correlli Barnett, *Engage the Enemy more Closely*, New York: W. W. Norton, 1991, p. 117.

[57] Derry, *The Campaign in Norway*, p. 31.

[58] Quote in David Brown in Salmon (ed.), *Britain and Norway in the Second World War*, p. 31.

[59] Dickens, *Narvik*, pp. 28–9. Dickens states that the *Hero* was patrolling a dummy minefield but the time sequence suggests it was more likely the 'live' field near Bodø. The *Giese* had compass problems and was steaming more slowly due to storm damage actually holing the ship. It would be 3 hours late arriving at Narvik.

[60] Haarr, *The German Invasion of Norway*, p. 96.

[61] Brown (ed.), *Naval Operations of the Campaign in Norway*, p. 195.

[62] Some sources state that only the two torpedoes were fired.

[63] *Nachrichtendienstliche Aspekte der Weserübung*, p. 100, Michael Alfred Peszke, *Poland's Navy 1918–1945*, New York, NY: Hippocrene, 1999, p. 63, and Tamelander and Zetterling, *9 April: Nazitysklands invasjon av Norge*, p. 69. Admiral Forbes of the Home Fleet was informed 5 minutes before midnight.

[64] Quote in Haarr, *The German Invasion of Norway*, p. 100. Williams, *Blitzkrieg and Conquest*, pp. 497, 579.

[65] Hinsley et al., *British Intelligence in the Second World War*, Vol. I, p. 124 and Haarr, *The German Invasion of Norway*, pp. 97–100. Haarr states that the Admiralty was unaware of the report until the Reuters news report was issued.

[66] W. L. Chalmers, *Max Horton and the Western Approaches*, London: Hodder & Stoughton, 1954, p. 76.

[67] Haarr, *The German Invasion of Norway*, p. 120 and Peter K. H. Mispelkamp, 'Avoidable Loss: The Saga of the *Blücher*', *Northern Mariner*, Vol. 6, No. 3, 1996, pp. 25–38.

[68] Ibid., p. 77. Apparently Horton was intrigued with the name Horten. Horton had operated extensively in the Baltic in the First World War.

[69] Levy, *The Royal Navy's Home Fleet in World War II*, p. 23. The *Posidonia* had been building when the war broke out and was requisitioned by the Kriegsmarine and renamed *Stedingen*. The Norway operation was its only assignment.

[70] Whitley, *German Capital Ships of World War Two*, pp. 118–19.

[71] Hinsley et al., *British Intelligence in the Second World War*, Vol. I, pp. 490–1.

[72] http://hem.fyristorg.com/robertm/norge/history_section.html.

[73] Brown, *A Radar History of World War II*, p. 106.

[74] The *Nelson* and *Rodney* were slow, well armoured and mounted nine 16in guns.

[75] This action is based on Brown (ed.), *Naval Operations of the Campaign in Norway*, pp. 19–21, Derry, *The Campaign in Norway*, p. 32, William H. Garzke Jr and Robert O. Dulin, *Battleships Axis and Neutral in World War II*, Annapolis: Naval Institute Press, 1985, pp. 127–202, Haarr, *The German Invasion of Norway*, pp. 309–14. Koop and Schmolke, *Battleships of the Scharnhorst Class*, pp. 96–102, O'Hara, *The German Fleet at War*, pp. 20–6, Alan Raven and John Roberts, *British Battleships of World War Two*, Annapolis, MD: Naval Institute Press, 1978, p. 344 and Bekker, *Hitler's Naval War*, p. 107. Bekker does not discuss the encounter between the two German battleships and the *Renown*.

[76] Dawn this far north was at 04:25 and light was seen at 03:23.

[77] Quote is in Koop and Schmolke, *Battleships of the Scharnhorst Class*, p. 41. The flooding was due largely to the fact that the back of the turrets were partially open for ejecting shell casings and the seawater cascaded through those openings into the interior of the turrets.

[78] Haarr, *The German Invasion of Norway*, p. 310.

[79] O'Hara, *The German Fleet at War*, gives six killed and nine wounded. Some accounts list two 15in shell hits.

[80] Tevnan and Horsley, *Norway Invaded*, pp. 87–8, Dickens, *Narvik*, p. 35 and Bernd Stegemann in Maier et al., *Germany and the Second World War*, Vol. II, p. 206.

[81] Losses are reported differently from source to source. We use Wolfgang Kähler, *Schlachtschiff Gneisenau*, Herford, Germany: Kohler, 1979, *passim*.

[82] Salvo chasing is seeing where the last enemy shells landed and slightly altering your direction to close to that range, which has one assuming that the next salvo will be corrected to the last position of the target ship.

[83] Tevnan and Horsley, *Norway Invaded*, p. 89.

[84] Quoted in Levy, *The Royal Navy's Home Fleet in World War II*, p. 55.

[85] Haarr, *The German Invasion of Norway*, p. 336.

[86] Brown (ed.), *Naval Operations of the Campaign in Norway*, p. 11.

[87] Colville, *The Fringes of Power*, Vol. 1, pp. 98–9.

## Chapter 7

[1] Carlgren, *Swedish Foreign Policy during the Second World War*, p. 59. There is a classic photograph (p. 60) showing six men sitting below a statue reading newspapers on 9 April, in Gothenburg, Sweden with the headlines reading, 'Germany Attacks Norway', 'Denmark under German Administration', 'Bergen and Trondheim Occupied by German Troops', and 'Denmark Surrenders without Fighting'. Sweden had no contingency war plans for a possible German occupation of Norway and had to prepare such plans at short notice. See Sven-Ake Bengtsson, 'Swedish War Plans', *Europa*, No. 74, p. 10. Sweden did quietly increase its army through mobilisation (though it was not called that) from 90,000 men, mostly located in Lapland, to 320,000 by mid-April throughout the nation. We thank Gert Laursen at gert@milhist.dk for his thoughtful reading of this chapter.

[2] We use the very common Copenhagen for this section.

[3] This section is drawn from the *Encyclopedia Britannica*, 11th edn, New York, NY: the Encyclopedia Britannica Company, 1910, Vol. 8, pp. 23–4 and Vol. 19, pp. 799–802 and Derry, *The Campaign in Norway*, pp. 1–7.

[4] Stauning first served in 1924. He would lead an 'all-parties' government after the surrender of Denmark. He died before his

seventieth birthday in 1942, thinking, as a classical Marxist, that there was no future for Social Democracy in a fascist-dominated Europe. The Radicals dominated foreign affairs and vetoed some of the proposed increases in defence spending in the 1930s.

[5] Kirchoff, 'Denmark, September 1939–April 1940', p. 33.

[6] John Danstrup, *A History of Denmark*, Copenhagen: Wivel, 1948, p. 172. A slightly different rendering is given in a speech by the Danish ambassador to the United States Ulrik Federspiel on 14 November 2003 at the Philadelphia Club, Philadelphia.

[7] German Foreign Office, *Britain's Designs on Norway*, p. 66.

[8] Henrik S. Nissen, 'The Nordic Societies', in Nissen (ed.), *Scandinavia during the Second World War*, p. 9.

[9] Joesten, *Denmark's Day of Doom*, pp. 52–3, Fritz, *German Steel and Swedish Iron Ore*, p. 41 and special thanks to Andrew Smith on this point. Joesten made use of the term '*Mare Germanicum*' for the Baltic, though it has also been used for the North Sea.

[10] Susan Seymour, *Anglo-Danish Relations and Germany 1933–1945*, Gylling, Denmark: Odense University Press, 1982, pp. 67–71.

[11] Ibid., p. 75.

[12] Munch-Petersen, *The Strategy of Phoney War*, pp. 182–3.

[13] Ibid., pp. 33–4, Danstrup, *A History of Denmark*, p. 138 and Joesten, *Denmark's Day of Doom*, pp. 101–4. Munch was a twentieth-century proponent of the 1880 movement known as the *Forsvarsnihilisten*, or Defense Nihilists. This was an anti-war and anti-defence spending movement that sprang up in that period to protest against the high taxes that defence spending entailed under the Conservative government of the day. The members of the movement also argued that after the defeat of 1864 Denmark was incapable of defending itself against any Great Power. Munch conveniently ignored the Danish success of 1914–18, which it had achieved by maintaining neutrality through strength. Later, Stauning and Munch rejected the idea of any sort of Nordic defensive arrangement. See Stauning's important policy declaring speech at Lund, Sweden, on 8 March 1937, in Joesten, *Denmark's Day of Doom*, pp. 215–17. In Norway there were some on the political left that thought

Munch's direction might suit Norway as well, but it never gained the strength of Munch's.

[14] Derry, *A History of Scandinavia*, pp. 325–6.

[15] Jong, *The German Fifth Column in the Second World War*, pp. 160–1.

[16] Hambro, *I saw it happen in Norway*, p. 4, Petrow, *The Bitter Years*, pp. 2–3 and Joesten, *Denmark's Day of Doom*, pp. 61–3, 158–9. One spy ring was broken up on 22 November 1938 and involved German 'correspondents'. Nine Germans and three Danes were arrested for tracking shipping bound from the USSR to Loyalist Spain, as well as British merchant trade in the Baltic. It was also thought to be spying on Danish naval and air operations.

[17] Quote in Joesten, *Denmark's Day of Doom*, p. 82. Joesten would later move to the USA and late in his career would write on the Kennedy assassination.

[18] Ibid., p. 83.

[19] The previous day a member of the Swedish Party, who was also a member of the Riksdag's Committee on National Defence, had written, 'It is of vital interest to Sweden in particular that Denmark should not appear as a *vacuum*, militarily speaking. . . . There can be no question that the security of us all would be seriously impaired if our southern neighbor were to be gobbled up some day by an aggressive Great Power and Denmark's territory then used as a base for all sorts of operations, especially in the air.' (italics in original), quoted in ibid., p. 210.

[20] The Danish government remained in power until 1943 with the Germans as occupiers. Munch would advocate resistance to the Nazi occupiers after he quit his post in the government.

[21] Quoted in William L. Shirer, *The Challenge of Scandinavia*, Boston, MA: Little, Brown and Company, 1955, p. 222.

[22] Quoted in John Roberts, 'Danish Navy', in Robert Gardiner (ed.), *Conway's All the World's Fighting Ships 1922–1946*, Annapolis, MD: Naval Institute Press, 1980, p. 381.

[23] Email from Søren Nørby, dated 13 December 2004.

[24] http://www.milhist.dk/weapons/systemer/koretojer/fp5/fp5_oversigt.htm. Excellent museum on arms literally collected over the centuries.

[25] http://mailer.fsu.edu/~akirk/tanks/denmark/denmark.html gives an excellent

background to Danish prewar armoured forces – but is a bit suspect on its impact. Also see http://www.armyvehicles.dk/lvlynx.htm. Other L-180s were ordered but not delivered at the time of the invasion.

[26] H. G. Thursfield (ed.), *Brassey's Naval Annual 1938*, London: William Clowes, 1938, p. 44.

[27] Email from Søren Nørby, dated 13 December 2004.

[28] Some were sold to South American countries.

[29] Quotation is from Joesten, *Denmark's Day of Doom*, pp. 109–10.

[30] http://en.wikipedia.org/wiki/Swedish_neutrality.

[31] Seymour, *Anglo-Danish Relations and Germany*, p. 140. The Danish merchant marine numbered about 800 ships.

[32] Hans-Henrik Wesche, 'Die dänische Marine während des Zweiten Weltkrieges', in *Marine Rundschau*, LVII (1965), pp. 141–52. The 3,800-ton *Niels Iuel* is often spelled *Neils Juel*. The torpedo-boats were about 300 tons each and armed with two 3.5in or 3in guns and six or eight 18in torpedoes. They did have a respectable AA armament. The *Niels Iuel* had been rebuilt in the interwar period (it was completed in 1918) had carried ten 5.9in guns and a considerable AA armament. The German navy viewed the *Niels Iuel* as the only formidable Danish warship. The *Peter Skram* displaced 3,500 tons and carried two 9.4in guns fore and aft, with four 5.9in and eight 3in guns, along with a modest modernised AA armament.

[33] Much of this is drawn from www.navalhistory.dkAugust 29.htm and Shores et al., *Fledgling Eagles*, p. 223.

[34] A rugged poor man's fighter introduced in 1936, it was armed with four machine-guns and had non-retractable landing gear. Primarily used by the Dutch in the East Indies.

[35] http://home5.inet.tele.dk/gla/9april/9april.html, Shores et al., *Fledgling Eagles*, pp. 222–3, A. E. Goodwin and James D. Parmenter, 'Denmark in World War II', *E.T.O.*, No. 53 (February 1990), pp. 1, 15–22 and Tarnstrom, *The Sword of Scandinavia*, pp. 74, 77. Shores tends to overestimate what was actually available. The Gloster Gauntlet was a biplane that predated the obsolescent Gloster Gladiator biplane fighter deployed by the British in the early part of the war.

[36] The personal resentment towards the Danes by the Norwegians was noted several times (by both Danes and Norwegians) during our visit in 2004 to conduct research for this book, and since then in personal chance meetings with Norwegians. It was a mild but persistent resentment, in part diluted by the intervening years, and despite the understanding that Denmark could have done little in the way of resistance. On this see Palle Lauring, *A History of the Kingdom of Denmark*, Copenhagen: Høst & Søn, 1963, p. 243 and Danstrup, *A History of Denmark*, p. 174. Some Danes (like some Swedes, Finns and Estonians) volunteered in the coming months to help Norway in its fight. The Germans threatened the Danish government that such volunteers would be treated as *francs-tireurs* and face immediate execution. As to ignoring the fall of Denmark, one account, Donald Macintyre's solid *Narvik*, New York, NY: W. W. Norton, 1960, devotes two very short footnotes to the Danish invasion.

[37] Claus Bjørn, 'Denmark', in I. C. B. Dear and M. R. D. Foot (eds), *The Oxford Companion to World War II*, Oxford: Oxford University Press, 1995, p. 293 and Höhne, *Canaris*, pp. 403–12.

[38] Dulles, *Germany's Underground*, p. 59 and Riste, 'Intelligence and the "Mindset": The German invasion of Norway in 1940', *Intelligence and National Security*, pp. 521–36. Stang's reaction will be recounted in Chapter 8.

[39] Goodwin and Parmenter, 'Denmark in World War II', pp. 1, 15–22 and Hubatsch, *Weserübung. Die deutsche Besetzung von Dänemark und Norwegen 1940*, pp. 123–31.

[40] Hubatsch, *Weserübung. Die deutsche Besetzung von Dänemark und Norwegen 1940*, pp. 127–30.

[41] Goodwin and Parmenter, 'Denmark in World War II', pp. 1, 15–22. Also see Kîrchoff, 'Denmark, September 1939–April 1940', p. 46.

[42] Goodwin and Parmenter, 'Denmark in World War II', pp. 1, 15–22 and http://www.geocities.com/armdury/9_4_1940.htm.

[43] Ziemke, *The German Northern Theater of Operations*, p. 60, Goodwin and Parmenter, 'Denmark in World War II', pp. 1, 15–22 and Hubatsch, *Weserübung. Die deutsche Besetzung von Dänemark und Norwegen 1940*, pp. 128–9.

[44] Quote in Jong, *The German Fifth Column in the Second World War*, p. 163.

[45] Ibid.

[46] Petrow, *The Bitter Years*, p. 46. There are two entrances to it, the Norwegian and the King's gates.

[47] 'World War', *Time* magazine, 15 April 1940, Vol. XXXV, No. 16, p. 26.

[48] Joesten, *Denmark's Day of Doom*, pp. 95–6. Leaflet dropping from aircraft first occurred in the 1911–12 Italo-Turkish War and had been used as recently as the Spanish Civil War and the seizure of Albania by Italy in April 1939.

[49] Goodwin and Parmenter, 'Denmark in World War II', pp. 1, 15–22.

[50] Ibid., p. 96.

[51] The 170th was short a battery, while all three of the 198th's artillery battalions were short a battery. With the latter's primary duty capturing islands, the lack of a full complement of artillery was less of a problem. See Thies, *Weserübung*, Vol. 2, *Der Zweite Weltkreig im Kartenbild*, p. 166.

[52] One source has two battalions.

[53] Email from Leo W. G. Niehorster to David Isby, dated 14 January 2005. Niehorster has published much over the years on the German order of battle. This would most likely consist of eighteen to twenty-three armoured cars (AC), but the HQ platoon did have four heavy armoured cars (AC) armed with 20mm guns, with the others all being the smaller lighter models. Normally they would *not* be attached to the HQ company. This is one of the little factoids that drives historians crazy. Most Danish sources indicate that two German AC companies with thirty-six armoured cars each participated in the invasion. There is a reference in Thies, *Weserübung*, Vol. 2, *Der Zweite Weltkreig im Kartenbild*, p. 166, bottom that there was one company of unattached armoured cars. As to German armoured cars there may have been more then the standard three light armoured cars attached to a German infantry division in 1940, usually the older Kfz.15s. Since one of the regiments of the 170th was lorried, it may have had attached a motorised division recon unit of six heavy and seventeen light armoured cars. A motorised armoured car company attached to a motorised division would have twenty-three armoured cars, with three in the headquarters company (mostly set up for signals and radio), and three platoons – one heavy with three Sd.Kfz.231s and three Sd.Kfz.232s. The mixed platoon had four Sd.Kfz.221s and four Sd.Kfz.222s, while the light platoon had six Sd.Kfz.221s. To support the Danish contention, we do have a photograph of two Sd.Kfz.222s on an Oslo dock most likely taken in April. Also, though several photographs taken in Danish towns during the brief fight and following occupation show German tanks and mechanised transport, but only one instance of a disabled newer armoured car – in Kay Søren Nielsen, *Soldaterne den 9. april 1940*, Copenhagen: Forkaget /Wøldike, 1990, *passim* and especially p. 48. The Kluge detachment had three eight-wheeled (heavy) armoured cars with it. We can confirm the presence of at least twenty-one armoured cars and that is one more then the standard order of battle would suggest, plus the attached company of thirty-six. If the divisional ACs were present along with a full reconnaissance company, this would bring the total to sixty-eight ACs. If we had to guess, we would suggest a number closer to fifty were present in Denmark and many were later shipped on to Norway. See John Milsom and Peter Chamberlain, *German Armoured Cars of World War Two*, New York, NY: Charles Scribner's Sons, 1974, pp. 11, 44 and Leo W. G. Niehorster, *Mechanized Army and Waffen SS Units (1st September 1939)*, Vol. 1/I, Hannover 1990, private printing, p. 186.

[54] Attached was a battalion of the *Totenkopf SS*, see http://niehorster.orbat.com/011_germany/40-04_scandinavia/corps_31.html.

[55] This unit was made up of three companies, with the third company having detached one platoon for the invasion of Norway. PanzerKampfwagen I Bs were 6-ton 25mph lightly armoured tanks (originally 13mm at the thickest part) armed with two 7.92mm machine-guns in a turret. PanzerKampfwagen II As, Bs and Cs were 8.9-ton, 25mph tanks with armour at the thickest point being 15mm and armed with a 20mm gun in a turret and one machine-gun. The IIs were effective because of their 20mm HE shells during the fighting in Norway, especially at clearing roadblocks. Only a few had been recently up-armoured after the experience

in the 1939 Polish campaign. See Thomas L. Jentz, *Panzertruppen*, Atglen, PA: Schiffer Military History, 1996, Vol. 1, pp. 110–12.

56 Samuel W. Mitcham Jr, *Hitler's Legions: The German Army Order of Battle World War II*, Briarcliff Manor, NY: Stein and Day, 1985, p. 144.

57 Only the 69th Infantry Division invading Norway had its three armoured cars at the start of this campaign. The other infantry divisions, including the two allocated for the invasion of Denmark, *lacked* their armoured cars.

58 Franz Kurowski, *The History of the Fallschirmpanzerkorps Hermann Göring*, Winnipeg: J. J. Fedorowicz, 1995, pp. 44–8. Kurowski must be handled carefully.

59 Thies, *Weserübung*, Vol. 2, *Der Zweite Weltkreig im Kartenbild*, maps 1 and 2.

60 Ibid., map 3.

61 Kirchoff, 'Denmark, September 1939– April 1940', p. 49.

62 At this time, the fourth platoon was not a heavy weapon unit as it would later become.

63 Vasco and Cornwell, *Zerstörer*, pp. 11–13.

64 Shores et al., *Fledgling Eagles*, p. 227 and Hubatsch, *Weserübung. Die deutsche Besetzung von Dänemark und Norwegen 1940*, p. 93.

65 Shores et al., *Fledgling Eagles*, p. 227.

66 Special thanks goes to Danish naval historian Søren Nørby for clarifying this point. Cajus Bekker, *The Luftwaffe War Diaries*, New York, NY: Ballantine, 1964, pp. 99–101 has an embellished account of the operation.

67 Höhne, *Canaris*, p. 408 and Jong, *The German Fifth Column in the Second World War*, pp. 159–60.

68 The *Schleswig-Holstein* and her sister ship the *Schlesien* were pre-dreadnoughts completed in 1908. This operation would be the last one that they would participate in as active elements. Some interesting pictures of it aground can be found at: http://ww2db.com/photo.php?source=all&color=all&list=search&foreigntype=B&foreigntype_id=93.

69 Lukacs, *The Last European War September*, p. 73 and Jong, *The German Fifth Column in the Second World War*, p. 161.

70 The *Peter Skram* was operational – Hubatsch, *Weserübung. Die deutsche Besetzung von Dänemark und Norwegen 1940*, p. 127.

71 The *Hansestadt Danzig* carried 781 men of the 2nd battalion, 308th regiment (198th division) and attached was a small contingent of radio operators and some naval personnel to handle the management of the port. Also on board were three trucks and 9 tons of ammunition. The radio unit would operate Radio Copenhagen in the early hours and continually broadcast the announcement of Denmark's surrender. Most likely attached was the bicycle company of the 326th regiment of the same division. The *Hansestadt Danzig*, 2,431 gross tons, was built in 1926 and had a good turn of speed at 20 knots. Capable of carrying 360 mines (absent for this operation), the ship had a light armament of two 88mm L/45 guns and four 20mm C/30 AA guns, see Gröner, *German Warships 1815–1945*, Vol. Two, pp. 185–7; a drawing of the *Hansestadt Danzig* is at the top of p. 187.

72 The twenty-six Me110s were the main long-range fighter for this operation. Dr Alfred Price, 'Messerschmitt Bf 110', *International Air Power Review*, Vol. 16 (2005), p. 131.

73 http://www.kilroywashere.org/009-Pages/Eric/Eric.html.

74 Special thanks to Major Jurgen Koll and his helpful staff at the Citadel in explaining the action that day. See also http://www.nizkor.org/ftp.cgi/imt/nca/ftp.py?imt/nca/nca-06/nca-06-3596-ps and Jong, *The German Fifth Column in the Second World War*, pp. 162–7.

75 P. Henningsen, 'Fektningen ved Amalienborg', in Arne Stevns (ed.), *Danmark Niende April*, Oslo: Cammermeyers Boghandel, 1941, pp. 21–2. We located two books, this being one, that were published early in the German occupation with very little (if any) censorship. It points out that German control of the press was not instantaneous. *Niende* means ninth in Norwegian.

76 As quoted in http://www.geocities.com/armdury/9_4_1940.htm. The Queen saw two wounded Danish soldiers and asked her husband, the King, to end the bloodshed. Christian X had intervened at least once before in government actions in August 1914 when he dramatically insisted, by banging on the floor with his sword, that the government agree with Germany to mine the Danish sea passages at Germany's insistence – see Joesten, *Denmark's Day of Doom*, p. 258.

[77] Shirer, *The Challenge of Scandinavia*, p. 224.

[78] Seymour, *Anglo-Danish Relations and Germany*, p. 165 and http://www.nizkor.org/ftp.py?imt/nca/nca-06//nca-06-3596-ps.

[79] Höhne, *Canaris*, p. 408. After May the Brandenburgers would be enlarged to a regiment.

[80] A short video is at http://www.youtube.com/watch?v=o-5Q3mcj-n4&NR=1&feature=endscreen.

[81] Kurowski, *The History of the Fallschirm-panzerkorps Hermann Göring*, p. 44.

[82] Nara Roll T314-836/019. Small-calibre AT units, unless they had powerful German dual-purpose AA/AT 88mm or Italian dual-purpose 90mm AA/AT guns, had to be deployed at close range to be effective.

[83] Anna Mehrn Skraep's painting of the action at Hokkerup can be found at http://www.nomos-dk.dk/skraep/1940-1945.htm and also see http://www.chakoten.dk/dan_army_090440_1a.html.

[84] Milsom and Chamberlain, *German Armoured Cars of World War Two*, p. 11.

[85] Nara Roll T314-836/006.

[86] Goodwin and Parmenter, 'Denmark in World War II', pp. 1, 15–22. It is cited as a battalion in some sources, which is too large. Hubatsch, *Weserübung. Die deutsche Besetzung von Dänemark und Norwegen 1940*, pp. 123–31 states it was a colonel who led these elements and that they thought a war existed between Germany and Sweden.

[87] Quoted in Jentz, *Panzertruppen*, Vol. 1, p. 110.

[88] There are 20mm and 37mm AT guns on display at the Danish Royal Arsenal in Copenhagen located near the Parliament building. One particular 37mm gun was used in action that day and has several bullet holes in its shield. Its left wheel is smashed and bent from a German tank literally running over it – the entire gun crew became casualties. We have seen this particular gun numerous times in sources ranging from books published as soon as the war was over to sites on the Internet.

[89] A similar proclamation in Norway was issued on 9 April but Falkenhorst, not King Haakon VII, signed it.

[90] Danish dead have been reported differently elsewhere, with ten additional air-force dead, but it appears to be only the pilot and observer that died that day. Oddly, an official German figure has never been released to the best of our knowledge and the figures for the Germans may be a total of twenty dead and wounded. Thanks to Geirr Haarr for his comments on this in an email, dated 9 March 2004.

[91] Burdick and Jacobsen (eds), *The Halder War Diary*, p. 114.

[92] Tevnan and Horsley, *Norway Invaded*, pp. 71–2.

[93] Petrow, *The Bitter Years*, p. 50; quoted in Lars Ericson's article 'Denmark's Hour of Destiny', *The Royal Swedish Academy of War Sciences* Journal, No. 4 (2001).

[94] Lunde, *Hitler's Pre-Emptive War*, p. 391.

[95] Petrow, *The Bitter Years*, p. 50 and Kirchoff, 'Denmark, September 1939–April 1940', p. 35. See also report of an unnamed Danish officer who relayed this to the Italian ambassador. The ambassador also reported that neutral observers in Copenhagen considered the attack on Norway and Denmark with the resultant German naval losses as the first big error made by Hitler in the war – Italian Minister in Copenhagen to Foreign Minister Ciano, message of 12 April 1940, in *Documenti Diplomatici Italiani*, 9th Serie, Vol. IV, Rome: Libreria dello Stato, 1960, p. 38.

[96] Kîrchoff, 'Denmark, September 1939–April 1940', p. 46. In 1950–1 there were some press reports that Munch had secretly met with Himmler and other German leaders on 16–17 March to arrange for the occupation of Denmark. As with so many conspiracy theories, this one was false. See Hubatsch, *Weserübung. Die deutsche Besetzung von Dänemark und Norwegen 1940*, p. 130.

[97] Quoted in William L. Shirer, *The Rise and Fall of the Third Reich*, New York, NY: Crest, 1962, p. 923. Himer commented that the king 'appeared inwardly shattered'.

[98] John Oram Thomas, *The Giant-Killers*, London: Michael Joseph, 1975, p. 14.

[99] These were two of six Brazilian-ordered modified 'H' class destroyers requisitioned for the war effort. Their main drawbacks were increased weight and primitive ASW capability.

[100] Brown (ed.), *Naval Operations of the Campaign in Norway*, p. 44.

[101] http://www.chakoten.dk/dan_army_090440_1a.html.

[102] Nara Roll T314 836, Frame 11 and 12: Bericht ueber die Besetzung Daenemark am 9. und 10.4.40 und die dabei gemachten Erfahrungen.

[103] We would like to thank Geirr Haarr, Mark C. Jones, Andrew Smith, Peter Spitzkowsky and John Swift for their comments on this point.

## Chapter 8

[1] *Akten zur Deutschen Auswaertigen Politik 1918–45*, Serie D, Vol. 9, Frankfurt a. M.: Keppler, 1962, p. 101. This is often attributed to Mussolini. It is noted in a letter on 10 April from the German Ambassador Hans Viktor von Mackensen. Mussolini would remark upon learning of the attack on 9 April, 'That is the way to win wars. Whoever gets there first is right', quoted in Macgregor Knox, *Mussolini Unleashed*, Cambridge: Cambridge University Press, 1982, p. 91.

[2] Derry, *The Campaign in Norway*, p. 30. The local commander at Kristiansand would make important military preparations with the survivors from the *Rio* coming ashore at his port. Other commanders would take note of the event while others ignored what it portended.

[3] Quote in Riste, 'Intelligence and the "Mindset": The German invasion of Norway in 1940', pp. 521–36 and Petrow, *The Bitter Years*, p. 43.

[4] Herman K. Lehmkuhl, *Hitler Attacks Norway*, London: The Royal Norwegian Government Information Office, 1945, p. 19.

[5] Quoted in Williams, *Blitzkrieg and Conquest*, p. 494.

[6] Quote from Höhne, *Canaris* p. 407. Also see Riste, 'Intelligence and the 'Mindset': The German invasion of Norway in 1940', pp. 521–36 and clarification in an email from Geirr Haarr, dated 20 February 2007. The conversation occurred at the bar of the Hotel Adlon – in the modern days of hotel surveillance, such as in Las Vegas, this sort of conversation would never take place. The Germans had been murmuring to the Swedish and indirectly to the Norwegians that the Allies were planning landings in Scandinavia as early as late March.

[7] Per Insulander and Curt S. Ohlsson, *Pansarskepp*, Goteborg: C. B. Marinlitteratur, 2001, p. 276.

[8] Haarr, *The German Invasion of Norway*, p. 55.

[9] Lunde, *Hitler's Pre-emptive War*, p. 93.

[10] Harriman, *Mission to the North*, p. 250.

[11] Hoidal, *Quisling*, p. 367.

[12] Dahl, *Quisling*, pp. 166–7.

[13] Ibid., p. 167.

[14] Hayes, *Quisling*, pp. 201–2.

[15] Geirr Haarr assisted us in understanding this situation, email dated 22 August 2004 and Franklin Knudsen, *I was Quisling's Secretary*, London: Britons Publishing Co., 1967, p. 77. Knudsen must be taken with a pinch of salt.

[16] Steen, E. A., *Norges Sjøkrig 1940–1945*, Vols 1–4, Oslo: Gyldendal Norsk, 1956, Vol. 2, pp. 11–13.

[17] Ibid., Vol. 2, p. 10.

[18] Haarr, *The German Invasion of Norway*, p. 130, http://hem.fyristorg.com/robertm/norge/Norw_fortifications.html. This is a very helpful site on the invasion. See also http://en.wikipedia.org/wiki/Oscarsborg_Fortress.

[19] Steen, *Norges Sjøkrig*, Vol. 2, p. 13. The 5th Regiment of the 2nd Infantry Division would send some elements down south under orders in the course of the day. But on the whole, this division would accomplish little.

[20] Cato Guhnfeldt, *Fornebu 9, April*, Oslo: Wings Forlag, 1990, p. 50. This is a lovely over-sized book filled with photographs and information.

[21] The ones at Kjeller would be captured intact and were later transferred to Finland. The nineteen in the shed had some enterprising customs officer smash and cut what he could making them unusable.

[22] Koop and Schmolke, *Heavy Cruisers of the Admiral Hipper Class*, p. 99. The *Blücher* had two of its three aircraft on board, with bombs stored in one hangar and one of the aircraft on its catapult. Early Allied accounts in May had the *Blücher* as the *Gneisenau*. Photographs of its sinking can be viewed at http://www.admiral-hipper-class.dk/links/links.html.

[23] Built shortly after the First World War, they were 924 tons and were known as 'maids of all work'. They were also larger then any Norwegian 'destroyer'. Roger Chesneau, *Conway's All the World's Fighting Ships 1922–1946*, London: Conway Maritime Press, Inc., 1980, p. 37.

24 These were tiny 115-ton minesweepers. They could steam at 21 knots and had two 20mm AA guns.

25 Letter of Robert A. Bellars in *Warship International*, Vol. 45, No. 3, (2009), p. 201.

26 The most obvious of these postwar writings may be the chief source for this myth, Churchill, *The Gathering Storm*, p. 590. His account of the attack on Oslo is poor on details and as with much of Churchill, when discussing the enemy it needs to be checked for possible errors, usually of exaggeration.

27 M. J. Whitley, *German Cruisers of World War Two*, Annapolis, MD: Naval Institute Press, 1985, p. 94.

28 Koop and Schmolke, *Heavy Cruisers of the Admiral Hipper Class*, p. 101.

29 Bekker, *Hitler's Naval War*, p. 107.

30 Much of this section is based on Koht, *Norway Neutral and Invaded*, p. 92, http://www.warsailors.com/homefleet/shipsp.html#pol3, http://www.feldgrau.com/norwegian.html, http://ww2chat.com/norway/1553-pol-iii-valiant-face-overwhelming-odds.html and Haarr, *The German Invasion of Norway*, p. 122. The other final quote from Welding-Olsen is given as, 'I am useless anyhow'. Many accounts incorrectly have the *Pol III* being sunk.

31 NARA, T312-982 Frames 9174065 to 9174070 Blücherbericht 5. 4. 40.

32 Whitley, *German Cruisers of World War Two*, p. 94 and Steen, *Norges Sjøkrig*, Vol. 2, pp. 100–2. The 1st Infantry Regiment was located at Fredrikstad on the mainland about 5 miles from the island battery.

33 Steen, *Norges Sjøkrig*, Vol. 2, pp. 104–5 and Haarr, *The German Invasion of Norway*, p. 160.

34 Harriman, *Mission to the North*, p. 252.

35 Derry, *The Campaign in Norway*, p. 37.

36 Oscar González, *German Paratroopers in Scandinavia*, Atplen, PA: Schiffer Publishing, Ltd, 2009, p. 61.

37 Dik Lehmkuhl, *Journey to London*, London: Hutchinson & Co., 1945, p. 9.

38 http://hem.fyristorg.com/robertm/norge/history_section.html. This is a valuable site, though not recently updated.

39 Conversation with curator Lieutenant Colonel (ret.) Arvid Carlsen at Oscarsborg Fortress, April 2004.

40 The Abwehr had reported it but that report was lost in the workings of the German bureaucracy, Haarr, *The German Invasion of Norway*, p. 131.

41 Jack Greene and Andrew Smith were able to tour this remarkable battery. This well-maintained torpedo battery had existed since the turn of the century and had always been kept in full working order and much thought over the decades had been put to good use in planning how to make use of this hidden weapon. See letter of Robert A. Bellars in *Warship International*, Vol. 45, No. 3, (2009), p. 201, http://www.admiral-hipper-class.dk/bluecher/miscellaneous/oscarsborg_bluecher_wreck_site_today/oscarsborg_bluecher_wreck_site_today.html.

42 Our account is drawn from Haarr, *The German Invasion of Norway*, pp. 131–8, Koop and Schmolke, *Heavy Cruisers of the Admiral Hipper Class*, pp. 102–10, Koop and Schmolke, *Pocket Battleships of the Deutschland Class*, pp. 51–2, Steen, *Norges Sjøkrig*, Vol. 2, pp. 54–64, C. J. Pargeter, *Hipper Class Heavy Cruiser*, Shepperton: Ian Allan, 1982, pp. 38–41. A very well done video of the episode can be found at http://zomobo.net/play.php?id=QF74K7FTW6I.

43 Haarr, *The German Invasion of Norway*, p. 131.

44 Quote in Koop and Schmolke, *Heavy Cruisers of the Admiral Hipper Class*, p. 102. For orders see Høiback, *Command and Control in Military Crisis*, pp. 95, 100.

45 The shells appear to have been HE as per email from Kent Crawford, dated 25 February 2007. If a common shell was fired it would have been heavier, 255kg. Aron is Aaron in the Bible, who was with Moses. The third gun was named Joseph.

46 Haarr, *The German Invasion of Norway*, p. 133. Haarr states the *Blücher* was at 1,040yd distant. German accounts tend to have the range closer (650yd is typical) than it was and Norwegian gunfire heavier than it was and hits more numerous than they were.

47 Email from Geirr Haarr, dated 5 March 2006. The *Brummer* is sometimes incorrectly included in Warship Group 5 on 8–9 April and stated as being sunk early on 9 April, which would lead to some incorrect contemporary news stories and histories extending into the immediate postwar period. The German gunnery training and minelayer *Brummer*, a modern 2,410-ton warship, had been held in reserve and as a command ship in Germany

at the time of the invasion in Wilhelmshaven. The *Brummer* carried 409 troops from the northern Danish port of Frederikshavn to Oslo on 14 April. After arriving at Oslo on the morning of 15 April, it left Oslo that afternoon with an escort of three warships. The *Brummer* was torpedoed in the early evening of the 15th by the submarine *Sterlet*, and after a lengthy attempt to save it sank in 80m of water. In the ensuing counter-attack the *Sterlet* was lost with all hands. Some sources give a higher number of troops, over 800, and this probably represents those on the three escorts that accompanied the *Brummer* to Oslo.

[48] Pargeter's account of the torpedoes is incorrect. The torpedoes were fixed, but in racks, not tubes. Only two were fired and both hit.

[49] The naval museum at Horten has a display showing the two torpedo hits in the classic positions, while a display at the maritime museum in Oslo shows the positions on a model with the *Blücher* in the way we describe.

[50] Koop and Schmolke, *Heavy Cruisers of the Admiral Hipper Class*, p. 103.

[51] NARA, T312-982 Frames 9174065 to 9174070 Blücherbericht 5. 8. 40.

[52] Koop and Schmolke, *Heavy Cruisers of the Admiral Hipper Class*, p. 107.

[53] Quote in Høiback, *Command and Control in Military Crisis*, p. 122.

[54] Kurt Assmann, *The German Campaign in Norway*, London: Naval Staff - Admiralty, 1948, p. 34.

[55] Ibid., pp. 111–12.

[56] Both authors were able to visit this lovely small town south of Oslo on the west side of the fjord. It contains a must-visit naval museum with an excellent staff. Norway's main naval base is now near Bergen.

[57] Høiback, *Command and Control in Military Crisis*, p. 78.

[58] Thompson, *The Norwegian Armed Forces and Defense Policy*, p. 65.

[59] Also present and mothballed in the port were two elderly coastal defence ironclads which would later be activated by the Germans as AA warships.

[60] Thompson, *The Norwegian Armed Forces and Defense Policy*, p. 176 and O'Hara, *The German Fleet at War*, pp. 26–8.

[61] Special thanks to Vincent O'Hara for this.

[62] There is some question as to what was present, but the threat was certainly real. Jean Lassaque, *Guerre Navale en Norvêge*, Aix: Editions du Gerfaut, 2003, p. 69 states the *Emden* was present.

[63] Haarr, *The German Invasion of Norway*, p. 151.

[64] The captured *Olav Tryggvason* would be renamed *Albatros* but shortly after would be renamed the *Brummer*. Three small destroyers similar to the *Sleipner* would be captured intact or almost completed at Horten and Fredrikstad in Oslofjord.

[65] Steen, *Norges Sjøkrig*, Vol. 2, pp. 90–4.

[66] Thompson, *The Norwegian Armed Forces and Defense Policy*, pp. 200–1 and Haarr, *The German Invasion of Norway*, p. 162.

[67] Our account is based on ibid., Bekker, *The Luftwaffe War Diaries*, pp. 102–9, Claasen, *Hitler's Northern War*, pp. 68–9, Guhnfeldt, *Fornebu 9, April, passim*, Shores et al., *Fledgling Eagles*, pp. 230–7, Haarr, *The German Invasion of Norway*, pp. 163–9 and Vasco and Cornwell, *Zerstörer*, pp. 13–15.

[68] Leland Stowe, 'How a Few Thousand Nazis seized Norway', *LIFE* magazine, 6 May 1940, pp. 90–103.

[69] Ibid., pp. 94–5.

[70] González, *German Paratroopers in Scandinavia*, p. 62.

[71] In the pre-radar era the sonic detector was utilised to hear the sound of the approaching engines. The range was limited and obviously a single plane or small force was more difficult to pick up.

[72] Guhnfeldt, *Fornebu 9, April*, p. 3. There are numerous and some very striking photographs from the action in this book.

[73] About seventy Ju52s would be lost in the campaign.

[74] Haarr, *The German Invasion of Norway*, p. 166.

[75] Ibid., pp. 166–9.

[76] Quote in Vasco and Cornwell, *Zerstörer*, p. 15.

[77] Quote in Bekker, *The Luftwaffe War Diaries*, p. 108.

[78] Thompson, *The Norwegian Armed Forces and Defense Policy*, pp. 188–9. The officer was not charged with any crime and the affair suggests lack of vigour and not the act of a traitor.

[79] Franz Kurowski, *Sturz in die Hoelle. Die deutschen Fallschirmjaeger, 1939–1945*, Munich: Heyne, 1986, pp. 27ff.

[80] From the summer of 1938 to the start of the war Spiller had been assistant air attaché in Britain. He was assigned to Oslo in October 1939. His duties included obtaining information for the planning of the invasion from Oslo to Narvik and points in between, see Guhnfeldt, *Fornebu 9, April*, pp. 51–2.

[81] Shores et al., *Fledgling Eagles*, p. 236.

[82] Lehmkuhl, *Journey to London*, p. 9.

[83] Guhnfeldt, *Fornebu 9, April*, p. 511 and Wilhelm Keilhau, *King Haakon VII in the History of Norway*, London: Hereford Times, 1942, p. 54. Norway had a total of sixteen 1932-designed 75mm AA guns of which twelve were at Oslo and the other four at Raufoss, north of Oslo where Norway had her main plant for manufacturing ammunition. Oslo also had two older model 75mm guns AA guns, forty-seven machine-guns and ten searchlights.

[84] Lehmkuhl, *Journey to London*, p. 10.

[85] Haarr, *The German Invasion of Norway*, p. 437.

[86] http://hem.fyristorg.com/robertm/norge/history_section.html.

[87] Email from Jan Egil Fjørtoft, dated 13 January 2004. Based on *Innstillingen fra Undersøkelseskommisjonen av 1945*, a commission at the end of the war that investigated the 9 April invasion and was based on memory and the desire in some cases to protect reputations.

[88] Quote in Thompson, *The Norwegian Armed Forces and Defense Policy*, p. 187, Lunde, *Hitler's Pre-emptive War*, p. 225, Koht, *Norway Neutral and Invaded*, p. 64 and François Kersaudy, *Norway 1940*, London: William Collins Sons, 1990, pp. 67–9.

[89] Høiback, *Command and Control in Military Crisis*, p. 80, Lunde, *Hitler's Pre-emptive War*, p. 225 and Thompson, *The Norwegian Armed Forces and Defense Policy*, p. 89.

[90] Høiback, *Command and Control in Military Crisis*, p. 77.

[91] Williams, *Blitzkrieg and Conquest*, p. 498.

[92] Haarr, *The German Invasion of Norway*, p. 173.

[93] Quote in Stowe, *No Other Road to Freedom*, p. 89.

[94] Kersaudy, *Norway 1940*, quote from pp. 100–1.

[95] Email from Sverre J. Svendsen, dated 23 February 2004. Sverre, who was kind enough to help us in our research, is the curator at the Nordmøre Museum in Kristiansund. The museum has an extensive collection on the terrible bombing of that town by the Germans from 28 April–1 May which was intended to reduce it as a potential Allied port. Although over 790 buildings were burnt out, there was no loss of life as the town had been evacuated.

[96] Both quotes from Kersaudy, *Norway 1940*, pp. 69, 101.

[97] Koop and Schmolke, *Heavy Cruisers of the Admiral Hipper Class*, p. 107.

[98] Quote in Kersaudy, *Norway 1940*, pp. 67–8.

[99] Keilhau, *King Haakon VII in the History of Norway*, passim.

[100] Koht, *Norway Neutral and Invaded*, p. 65.

[101] Ibid., p. 66.

[102] Quote from Knudsen, *I was Quisling's Secretary*, p. 82.

[103] Hoidal, *Quisling*, p. 374 thinks this was unlikely. Quisling was too close to Hagelin to not know where he was.

[104] Hubatsch, *Weserübung: Die Deutsche Besetzung von Dänemark und Norwegen*, p. 89 and *Fuehrer Conferences on Naval Affairs*, p. 92.

[105] Hoidal, *Quisling*, p. 374, Haarr, *The German Invasion of Norway*, p. 181 and Höhne, *Canaris*, p. 408.

[106] Haarr indicates that Scheidt was aware of only Hagelin's presence at this time, but was quickly made aware of Quisling's presence, see Haarr, *The German Invasion of Norway*, pp. 187–8.

[107] Ibid. and Hoidal, *Quisling*, pp. 374–83, which gives the best account of Quisling's movements.

[108] Dahl, *Quisling*, p. 175.

[109] Hoidal, *Quisling*, p. 386 and Knudsen, *I was Quisling's Secretary*, pp. 92, 98. As in Denmark, one can find, without too much difficulty, disturbing period photographs of German and Norwegian troops sharing cigarettes or standing joint guard.

[110] Hoidal, *Quisling*, pp. 74–5. Quote from Derry, *The Campaign in Norway*, p. 37.

[111] Reprinted in Koht, *Norway Neutral and Invaded*, pp. 197–209.

[112] Lehmkuhl, *Journey to London*, p. 12. This is an excellent account of the opening moments of an unforeseen crisis. The quote is sometimes stated as being given on 10 April. Haarr, *The German Invasion of Norway*, p. 177 renders it as 'A people who

submissively give in to a violator, does not deserve to live.'

[113] Koht, *Norway Neutral and Invaded*, p. 76.

[114] Hoidal, *Quisling*, pp. 381–3.

[115] Dahl, *Quisling*, p. 175 states the 10th, but it is 9 April.

[116] Nevakivi, *The Appeal that was Never Made*, p. 178.

[117] Hambro, *I Saw it Happen in Norway*, p. 11. The German strategy of attacking all key points is one that has been repeated many times since in wars from the Hue Offensive in Vietnam and the numerous wars in the Middle East.

[118] Ibid., p. 2.

[119] Hans Christian Adamson and Per Klem, *Blood on the Midnight Sun*, New York, NY: W. W. Norton, 1964, p. 17. This is the best source in English on the journey of the gold reserve. Torp would serve as Prime Minister in the 1950s.

[120] Hambro, *I Saw it Happen in Norway*, p. 15. April Fool's Day is recognised in Norway.

[121] Kersaudy, *Norway 1940*, p. 72 and Haarr, *The German Invasion of Norway*, p. 180.

[122] Keilhau, *King Haakon VII in the History of Norway*, p. 56.

[123] Kersaudy, *Norway 1940*, p. 73.

[124] Lehmkuhl, *Journey to London*, p. 17.

[125] Ibid., p. 18. The British had so many documents to burn that they built a bonfire in the garden and the Oslo Fire Brigade promptly arrived and tried to put the 'fire' out.

[126] Harriman, *Mission to the North*, p. 253.

[127] Quote in Hambro, *I Saw it Happen in Norway*, p. 25 and Haarr, *The German Invasion of Norway*, p. 183.

[128] Koht is very complimentary of Hambro's action, see Koht, *Norway Neutral and Invaded*, pp. 79–80.

[129] Quote in Lehmkuhl, *Journey to London*, pp. 19–20 and Koht, *Norway Neutral and Invaded*, p. 78. Some sources estimate no more then 20 per cent of the Norwegian army was in the field during the campaign at any one point, but we think that figure is a too low. It was well under 50 per cent in any case.

[130] Quote in Thompson, *The Norwegian Armed Forces and Defense Policy*, p. 192.

[131] Haarr, *The Battle for Norway*, p. 25.

[132] Lehmkuhl, *Journey to London*, p. 22, quote from p. 21.

[133] Andreas Hauge, *Kampene I Norge 1940*, 2 vols, Sandefjord: Krigshistorisk Forlag A.S., 1995, pp. 52–8, Haarr, *The German Invasion of Norway*, pp. 185–6, Høiback, *Command and Control in Military Crisis*, p. 84 and Lunde, *Hitler's Pre-emptive War*, pp. 227–8.

[134] Thompson, *The Norwegian Armed Forces and Defense Policy*, p. 192. Captain Oliver Møystad, an NS member and rabid anti-Semite, would participate in the action and is sometimes listed as commanding it.

[135] Thompson, *The Norwegian Armed Forces and Defense Policy*, p. 192.

[136] Ibid., p. 191.

[137] The story is told by Magne Lein, author of *Spioner I eget land*, Norway: 2003, in an email dated 29 December 2004, Kersaudy, *Norway 1940*, p. 80 and González, *German Paratroopers in Scandinavia*, pp. 69–72. Technically, the Germans could have, if captured, shot the shooting club riflemen as illegal combatants. Members of various rifle clubs throughout Norway in the coming days would join army units to fight the Germans and several would be killed.

[138] Thompson, *The Norwegian Armed Forces and Defense Policy*, pp. 192–3. Quote is from p. 192.

[139] Harriman, *Mission to the North*, p. 262.

[140] Ibid., p. 201.

[141] Shores et al., *Fledgling Eagles*, p. 236.

[142] Haarr, *The German Invasion of Norway*, p. 156.

[143] Ibid. and Steen, *Norges Sjøkrig*, Vol. 2, pp. 117–22.

[144] The flags would fly alongside each other until 21 April. After the action Colonel Eriksen would retire to the town of Drøbak. Whenever German officers would see him in town, they made a point of saluting him – a salute he would not return.

[145] Whitley, *German Capital Ships of World War Two*, pp. 120–1.

[146] German Army Command, *Kampf em Norwegen*, Berlin: Zeitgeschichte, 1940, p. 27.

[147] Knudsen, *I was Quisling's Secretary*, p. 85 and Dahl, *Quisling*, p. 173.

[148] Quote in Tevnan and Horsley, *Norway Invaded*, 39 and Strabolgi, *Narvik and After*, pp. 50–1.

[149] Email from Sverre J. Svendsen, dated 23 February 2004. German Army Command, *Kampf em Norwegen*, opposite p. 53 has a

photograph of an armed German soldier with an armed soldier of the HMKG on sentry duty. During the occupation of Denmark this was also true, see Nielsen, *Soldaterne den 9. april 1940*, p. 20 for a contemporary photograph of two armed German soldiers talking with a Danish royal guard officer.

150 http://www.youtube.com/watch?v=H3Ng FAGBhWs&feature=related.

151 Tevnan and Horsley, *Norway Invaded*, pp. 47–8.

**Chapter 9**

1 Moulton, *The Norwegian Campaign of 1940*, p. 11.

2 Scheen, *Norges Sjøkrig*, Vol. 1, p. 237.

3 Steen, *Norges Sjøkrig*, Vol. 2, p. 180.

4 Haarr, *The Battle for Norway*, pp. 198–200 and Thies, *Weserübung*, Vol. 2, *Der Zweite Weltkreig im Kartenbild*, map 35.

5 Thompson, *The Norwegian Armed Forces and Defense Policy*, p. 162. The Norwegian military did have a large quantity of barbed wire in stock.

6 Haarr, *The Battle for Norway*, p. 199.

7 NARA T312 roll 981fr. 9172583-4: 'Feind-nachrichtenblatt Kristiansand'. Anlage 4 to X Fliegerkorps, Ia Br. B. Nr. 10053.

8 Haarr, *The German Invasion of Norway*, p. 440 and Steen, *Norges Sjøkrig*, Vol. 3, p. 199.

9 Steen, *Norges Sjøkrig*, Vol. 3, p. 195.

10 Gerhard Koop and Klaus-Peter Schmolke, *German Light Cruisers of World War II*, Annapolis: Naval Institute Press, 2002, p. 110.

11 Shores et al., *Fledgling Eagles*, p. 228 and Haarr, *The Battle for Norway*, pp. 204--5.

12 A photograph of the *Seattle* burning and ashore taken from the Odderøya battery is in Sverre Steen, *Norges Krig 1940–1945*, 3 vols, Oslo: Gyldendal Norsk Forlag, 1947, Vol. 1, p. 136. The *Seattle* is sometimes listed incorrectly as having a British prize crew on board.

13 Steen, *Norges Sjøkrig*, Vol. 3, p. 228.

14 Thompson, *The Norwegian Armed Forces and Defense Policy*, p. 185.

15 Haarr, *The German Invasion of Norway*, p. 216. Some accounts state 07:50 for entrance by the *Greif*.

16 Ibid., p. 205.

17 Steen, *Norges Sjøkrig*, Vol. 3, p. 247.

18 http://niehorster.orbat.com/011_ger-many/40-04_scandinavia/inf-div_163.html.

19 Koop and Schmolke, *German Light Cruisers of World War II*, pp. 112–13 and Whitley, *German Cruisers of World War Two*, pp. 90–1.

20 NARA T312 roll 981fr. 9172585-6: 'Feind-nachrichtenblatt Stavanger'. Anlage 5 to X Fliegerkorps, Ia Br.

21 It was at full strength for its artillery, and even had its armoured car detachment, unlike any of the other infantry divisions. It had detached one battalion for duty in Denmark which was airlifted into Ålborg. NARA, T-312, roll 986, 69th Infantry Division 110/40: 'Befehl für die Besetzung von Bergen', enclosed to the Erfahrungsbericht of 22 July 1940.

22 Haarr, *The German Invasion of Norway*, pp. 236–9.

23 Quote in Nevakivi, *The Appeal that was Never Made*, p. 107.

24 Thompson, *The Norwegian Armed Forces and Defense Policy*, p. 162 and Haarr, *The German Invasion of Norway*, p. 226.

25 Quote in Arild Kjærass, *Profiles in Norway: Caproni Ca. 310*, Andebu, Norway: self-published, 1999, p. 6.

26 An interesting site, some of which is in English, that discusses the *Æger* can be found at http://home.no.net/ifurre/ww2.htm.

27 NARA, T-312, roll 986, 69th Infantry Division 110/40, 'Befehl für die Besetzung von Bergen', enclosed to the Erfahrungsbe-richt of 22 July 1940.

28 Haarr, *The German Invasion of Norway*, p. 227.

29 Shores et al., *Fledgling Eagles*, p. 238. Five of the Fokker C.V.s successfully flew on to the small airbase Steinsfjorden, north of Oslo.

30 Bekker, *The Luftwaffe War Diaries*, p. 111. Brandis would be killed in action in May 1940 in the Netherlands.

31 Kurowski, *Sturz in die Hölle. Die deutschen Fallschirmjäger*, p. 27ff.

32 Haarr, *The German Invasion of Norway*, pp. 230–1.

33 Ibid., pp. 222–4.

34 Ibid., p. 231.

35 Doug Dildy, *Small Air Forces Observer*, Vol. 13, No. 3, p. 76.

36 NARA, T312, Roll 1647, fr. 539, Meldung of 9 April 1940, 16.00 hour.

37 Our account is based on Thompson, *The Norwegian Armed Forces and Defense Policy*,

pp. 181–3, Moulton, *The Norwegian Cam-paign of 1940*, pp. 87–90, Whitley, *German Cruisers of World War Two*, pp. 82–8, Koop and Schmolke, *German Light Cruisers of World War II*, pp. 81–4.

[38] The admiral of the Norwegian command would initially have three sector admirals reporting to him, one in the South, Schrader in the West and one on the North coast. Later a Polar sector would be added.

[39] Lunde, *Hitler's Pre-emptive War*, p. 115 and Whitley, *German Cruisers of World War Two*, pp. 83–4. Whitley notes the *ad hoc* nature of the invading force. Neither cruiser was fitted to be a flagship, the *Königsberg* had just left the dockyards and had no practice with its guns or torpedoes, and had fifty of its crew down with the flu and other ailments. The *Carl Peters* was still going through its sea trials.

[40] Haarr, *The German Invasion of Norway*, p. 101.

[41] Email from Andrew Smith, dated 30 November 2005. Several of these types of warship would fight in the campaign. One of this type was captured by the British on 26 April 1940.

[42] One of the authors spent an enjoyable afternoon at the Kvarven fort site, which has a view from the hill down on the harbour entrance and is in a park-like setting today.

[43] Haarr, *The German Invasion of Norway*, p. 445. http://hem.fyristorg.com/robertm/norge/norway_reference.html gives four 120mm.

[44] Haarr, *The German Invasion of Norway*, p. 252.

[45] Thompson, *The Norwegian Armed Forces and Defense Policy*, pp. 181–2. Many in the navy thought in 1938 he should have been placed in charge of the navy instead of Admiral Diesen. See Thompson on this point, p. 101.

[46] Haarr, *The German Invasion of Norway*, p. 256.

[47] Signal in Whitley, *German Cruisers of World War Two*, p. 85. Other signals planned for use by the Germans included, 'Going Bergen. Chasing German steamer.' and 'Please repeat last signal.', all in English. All the ships were given British naval identification, so the *Königsberg* became the AA cruiser *Calcutta*, the *Bremse* became the destroyer *Faulknor*, etc.

[48] Haarr, *The German Invasion of Norway*, p. 259.

[49] Ibid., pp. 259, 263–4. The *Garm* would be lost in bombing on 26 April.

[50] Haarr, *The German Invasion of Norway*, p. 265 and Haarr, *The Battle for Norway*, p. 39.

[51] The *B6* would later surrender in early May.

[52] Seven were laid off Lerøy fort and later sixteen in a narrows between the fort and Bergen. Steen, *Norges Krig*, Vol. 1, p. 147 and Haarr, *The German Invasion of Norway*, p. 259. The Rendel gunboat was a small iron gunboat developed in Great Britain by the Armstrong company and named after the designer. Many copies were built and many were exported. They were armed with one heavy gun forward and the first example was built in 1867.

[53] Haarr, *The German Invasion of Norway*, p. 259.

[54] Correspondence with Geirr Haarr and Eric Schwarz. Some accounts give later times for the landing of the He115.

[55] It is interesting to note that there was not a tactical doctrine concerning the landing of troops on an enemy coast. Therefore Schmundt's squadron prepared a draft of a 'Tactical Study' for the coming operation, with several discussions held to co-ordinate land operations with aerial support.

[56] Haarr, *The German Invasion of Norway*, p. 262.

[57] Haarr states that the *Bremse* was not hit on the stern/afterdeck while German sources state it was, see Haarr, *The German Invasion of Norway*, p. 262.

[58] The attacking German aircraft are given variously as four or six planes.

[59] Haarr, *The German Invasion of Norway*, pp. 267–8.

[60] *Hanonia* was her name, flying an Estonian flag, when captured by German U-boat *U-34* in September 1939. In 1940 she could make 6 knots, having been built in 1900. She was armed with 3 AA machine-guns and carried 144 mines. Email from Andrew Smith, dated 10 January 2006.

[61] We could not confirm but it may have been lost the following month after repairs due to a mine. The keel damage certainly put it out of immediate action but it had laid its minefield.

[62] Very helpful emails from Geirr Haarr, dated 7 January 2006 and 19 March 2006, and

Andrew Smith, dated 18 March 2006, have helped to clear up this point. These three additional ships are seldom mentioned. The *Marie Leonhardt* would be lost in May in the Denmark Straits after hitting an iceberg while acting as a blockade-runner. The *Tschirschky* was originally down to steam to Trondheim but instead was ordered to Bergen.

[63] One of the curators at the Bergen Maritime Museum related being on the hill overlooking the harbour when the British bombers attacked the *Königsberg* as his mother was taking him and his two brothers out of Bergen, for fear of a bomb attack on the town.

[64] Quote in Thompson, *The Norwegian Armed Forces and Defense Policy*, p. 183.

[65] Haarr, *The Battle for Norway*, p. 39.

[66] David Hamer, *Bombers versus Battleships*, Annapolis, MD: Naval Institute Press, 1999, p. 59.

[67] The German spelling for Trondheim was Drontheim.

[68] See Steen, *Norges Sjøkrig*, Vol. 3, pp. 189–90 and Haarr, *The German Invasion of Norway*, p. 74. Special thanks to Simon Orchard on this point.

[69] Hubatsch, *Weserübung: Die Deutsche Besetzung von Dänemark und Norwegen 1940*, p. 74.

[70] Our account is based on Haarr, *The German Invasion of Norway*, pp. 290–9, Thompson, *The Norwegian Armed Forces and Defense Policy*, pp. 179–82, Moulton, *The Norwegian Campaign of 1940*, pp. 87–90, Whitley, *German Cruisers of World War Two*, pp. 100–3, Assmann, *The German Campaign in Norway*, pp. 28–9 and Koop and Schmolke, *Heavy Cruisers of the Admiral Hipper Class*, pp. 42–5.

[71] Michael W. Richardson, *Forcible Entry and the German Invasion of Norway, 1940*, Fort Leavenworth, KS: U.S. Army Command and General Staff College, 2001, p. 75.

[72] J. Adams, *The Doomed Expedition. The Campaign in Norway 1940*, London: Leo Cooper, 1989, p. 24 states that it was down to be manned later on the 9th but events overtook it.

[73] Hubatsch, *Weserübung: Die Deutsche Besetzung von Dänemark und Norwegen 1940*, p. 75.

[74] The Norwegian commander would serve sixty days for neglect of duty in 1949.

[75] Thompson, *The Norwegian Armed Forces and Defense Policy*, p. 181.

[76] Nara T312 roll 981, fr. 9172592-3, ‚Feind-nachrichtenblatt Drontheim' Anlage 7 to X Fliegerkorps, Ia Br. B. Nr. 10053.

[77] The trainer would be utilised for communication duties in the rear areas.

[78] Whitley, *German Cruisers of World War Two*, p. 102.

[79] Thompson, *The Norwegian Armed Forces and Defense Policy*, p. 180.

[80] Karl Ruef, *Odysse einer Gebirgsdivision. Die 3. Geb. Div. im Einsatz*, Graz: Stocker, 1976, pp. 24–31. Some sources give one more Norwegian killed.

[81] Richardson, *Forcible Entry and the German Invasion of Norway*, p. 77.

[82] Quote in Nara T312-982 fr. 9173650, 'Meldung von Detmold: 12.4.40 11.30 Uhr' signed by Colonel Weiss and Claasen, *Hitler's Northern War*, p. 73. A sixteenth He115 was shot down by the Norwegians.

[83] Haarr, *The Battle for Norway*, p. 304.

[84] James D. O'Keefe, 'Daring Escape of gold ship Mormacsea', Sea Classics, Vol. 39, No. 11 (November 2006) or http://findar-ticles.com/p/articles/mi_qa4442/is_200611/ai_n17194590/.

[85] Quote in Thompson, *The Norwegian Armed Forces and Defense Policy*, p. 181.

[86] Strabolgi, *Narvik and Afterv*, p. 128.

[87] Thompson, *The Norwegian Armed Forces and Defense Policy*, pp. 198–9.

[88] Haarr, *The Battle for Norway*, p. 303.

[89] NARA, T-312, roll 986, fr. 9441-2, 69th Infantry Division 261/40 Erfahrungsbericht of 22 July 1940.

[90] B. H. Liddell Hart, 'The Prospect in Norway', LIFE magazine, 29 April 1940, pp. 26–7.

[91] Brown (ed.), *Naval Operations of the Campaign in Norway*, pp. 23–4.

[92] Derry, *The Campaign in Norway*, p. 42.

[93] Brown (ed.), *Naval Operations of the Campaign in Norway*, p. 154. Rohwer and Hummelchen, *Chronology of the War at Sea*, 2nd edn, p. 19 does not include *Brazen* or *Arethusa*.

[94] Rhys-Jones, *Churchill and the Norway Campaign*, p. 41.

[95] Derry, *The Campaign in Norway*, p. 42.

[96] Churchill, *The Gathering Storm*, pp. 595–6.

[97] Brown (ed.), *Naval Operations of the Campaign in Norway*, p. 23. Churchill received

the news from Pound as he left a meeting, and reluctantly agreed with Pound's actions. Rhys-Jones, *Churchill and the Norway Campaign*, p. 41 has the cancellation coming at 13:57, which appears to be too early.

[98] Rhys-Jones, *Churchill and the Norway Campaign*, p. 41.

[99] Shores et al., *Fledgling Eagles*, pp. 240–2.

[100] Haarr, *The Battle for Norway*, p. 288.

[101] Dickens, *Narvik* , p. 100.

[102] Hamer, *Bombers versus Battleships*, pp. 57–8, Raven and Roberts, *British Battleships of World War Two*, p. 344, Claasen, *Hitler's Northern War*, p. 76, McCart, *Nelson & Rodney*, p. 69 and John English, *Afridi to Nizam*, Gravesend: World Ship Society, 2001, p. 32.

[103] Quoted in Roskill, *The War At Sea*, Vol. 1, p. 179.

[104] Shores et al., *Fledgling Eagles*, pp. 240–2.

**Chapter 10**

[1] Per Askim, *Office of Chief of Naval Operations, Office of Naval Intelligence*, Translation No. 376 Washington, DC: GPO, 1940, p. 1.

[2] C. C. Lynam, *To Norway & the North Cape in Blue Dragon II*, London: Sidgwick & Jackson, 1913, p. 223.

[3] Lothar Rendulic, *The Importance of the Narvik Region (Northern Norway) for Naval War* (Foreign Study P-127).

[4] Sometimes shown as either two guns or they are 65mm guns.

[5] Lunde, *Hitler's Pre-Emptive War*, p. 145.

[6] Ibid., p. 170 and Alex Buchner, *Narvik. Die Kämpfe der Gruppe Dietl im Frühjahr 1940*, Neckargemünd: Scharnhorst Buchkameradschaft, 1958, p. 21ff.

[7] Quote from Hayes, *Quisling*, pp. 182–3. Sundlo served as a leader in the NS's Hird. He would later work with Quisling after he surrendered his Narvik post. He would be sentenced to prison for life but was not charged with treason, see Petrow, *The Bitter Years*, p. 356.

[8] Email from J. E. Fjörtoft, dated 17 October 2003.

[9] Lunde, *Hitler's Pre-Emptive War*, p. 170.

[10] Sometimes given as Vargfjord or Havnes.

[11] Steen, *Norges Sjøkrig*, Vol. 4, p. 22, Thompson, *The Norwegian Armed Forces and Defense Policy*, p. 164 and email from Andrew Smith, dated 7 July 2006.

[12] Kersaudy, *Norway 1940*, p. 11.

[13] Steen, *Norges Sjøkrig*, Vol. 4, p. 65.

[14] Askim, *Office of Chief of Naval Operations, Office of Naval Intelligence*, Translation No. 376, p. 1 and *passim*. We rely on this report for the actions of the Norwegian naval forces at Narvik. Askim would survive the war and be one of the Norwegian officers to accept the German surrender in May 1945. Also of value is Moulton, *The Norwegian Campaign of 1940*, pp. 80–2, O'Hara, *The German Fleet at War*, pp. 30–1 and Ziemke, *The German Northern Theater of Operations*, *passim*.

[15] Steen, *Norges Sjøkrig*, Vol. 4, pp. 20–4.

[16] Figures from Karl Rommetveit, 'From Mountain Warfare in Winter Conditions to the Allied Recapture of Narvik', in Karl Rommetveit (ed.), *Narvik 1940: Five Nations at War in the High North*, Oslo: Institutt for Forsvarsstudie, 1991, pp. 85–113.

[17] Lunde, *Hitler's Pre-Emptive War*, p. 142 and Haarr, *The German Invasion of Norway*, p. 409. The *Jan Wellem* had arrived that morning.

[18] Quote in Olav Riste, 'Intelligence and the "Mindset": The German invasion of Norway in 1940', pp. 521–36.

[19] Haarr, The *German Invasion of Norway*, p. 320.

[20] Riste, 'Intelligence and the "Mindset": The German invasion of Norway in 1940', pp. 521–36.

[21] Quote in Hubatsch, *Weserübung: Die Deutsche Besetzung von Dänemark und Norwegen 1940*, p. 70. Ruef, *Odysse einer Gebirgsdivision*, pp. 18–19.

[22] Lunde, *Hitler's Pre-Emptive War*, p. 177.

[23] NARA, T312 Roll 980, 9172318, Gruppe XXI Ia 194/40 of 2 April 1940, Anlage E, Operation in Nordnorwegen'.

[24] Haarr, *The German Invasion of Norway*, pp. 321–3.

[25] Maier et al., *Germany and the Second World War*, Vol. II, p. 208.

[26] NARA, T312/983, 9174937-9. 'Wegnahme der Küstenbefestigungen von Narvik', Anlage 1 to 3rd Mountain Division Nr. 50/40.

[27] Quoted in Petrow, *The Bitter Years*, p. 57.

[28] On ramming in the modern era see Greene and Massignani, *Ironclads at War*, pp. 118–21.

[29] Steen, *Norges Sjøkrig*, Vol. 4, p. 69.

[30] Quote in George Paloczi-Horvath, *From Monitor to Missile Boat*, Annapolis, MD: Naval Institute Press, 1996, p. 95.

[31] Letter of Viktor Frampton in *Warship International*, Vol. 41, No. 1 (2004), p. 29 and Haarr, *The German Invasion of Norway*, pp. 324–7. Most accounts have four torpedoes fired and two hitting, though Norwegian accounts usually state three hits. A possible magazine or boiler explosion may account for a third explosion. The number killed is also difficult to determine with 175 often mentioned but 178 appearing in Hobson and Kristiansen, *Norsk Forsvarshistorie*, Vol. 3, p. 308. We give special thanks to Vincent O'Hara for his help on this section.

[32] Lunde, *Hitler's Pre-Emptive War*, p. 184.

[33] Haarr, *The German Invasion of Norway*, pp. 318, 408–9.

[34] Quote in Askim, *Office of Chief of Naval Operations, Office of Naval Intelligence*, Translation No. 376, p. 6.

[35] Haarr, *The German Invasion of Norway*, p. 327 states only machine-gun fire hit the *Norge*.

[36] O'Hara, *The German Fleet at War*, pp. 30–1.

[37] Some accounts give 110 men lost and 89 survivors. See Haarr, *The German Invasion of Norway*, p. 327.

[38] Broch, *The Mountains Wait*, p. 139.

[39] Askim, *Office of Chief of Naval Operations, Office of Naval Intelligence*, Translation No. 376, cover letter.

[40] Jong, *The German Fifth Column in the Second World War*, p. 174.

[41] Whitley, *Destroyer!*, p. 122.

[42] Lunde, *Hitler's Pre-Emptive War*, p. 168.

[43] Petrow, *The Bitter Years*, pp. 58–9 and Gerda-Luise Dietl and Kurt Hermann (ed.), *General Dietl*, Munich: Münchner Buchverlag, 1951, p. 66. Some accounts have this unit not arriving at all.

[44] Broch, *The Mountains Wait*, p. 76. Broch was the mayor of Narvik and his book reads almost like a novel, and is quite revealing of the time and place. General der Flieger Ulrich O. E. Kessler, 'The Role of the "Luftwaffe" and the campaign in Norway', MS # B-485 (supplied by David C. Isby), p. 3.

[45] Lunde, *Hitler's Pre-Emptive War*, p. 173.

[46] Quote in Haarr, *German Invasion of Norway*, p. 329.

[47] Dietl and Hermann (ed.), *General Dietl*, pp. 61–2.

[48] Quote in ibid., p. 59 and Lunde, *Hitler's Pre-Emptive War*, p. 178.

[49] Some sources give this as Major S. Spjeldnær, but it was Omdal's in the retreat from Narvik.

[50] Haarr, *The German Invasion of Norway*, pp. 3228–30.

[51] 'Battle of Narvik', *LIFE* magazine, 22 April 1940, p. 33.

[52] Haarr, *The German Invasion of Norway*, pp. 333–4.

[53] Broch, *The Mountains Wait*, pp. 80–1.

[54] Ibid., p. 85.

[55] O'Hara, *The German Fleet at War*, p. 32. O'Hara and Whitley have a third tanker, the *Skagerrak*, assigned to Narvik, but it was sent to Trondheim and was scuttled on 14 April, failing to arrive there. The *Nordkapp* was a sister ship to the *Senja* and was a purpose-built warship, launched in 1937 with a crew of twenty-two and armed with a single 47mm gun. The design speed was 13.7 knots. The *Kattegat* would be raised and employed during the war.

[56] The Norwegian action of 9 April is simply referred to as the Battle of Narvik Harbour but should properly be known as the First Battle of Narvik. But we will maintain the custom of calling the engagement on 10 April the First Battle of Narvik. We rely on Dickens, *Narvik*, pp. 41–104, Haarr, *The German Invasion*, pp. 317–74, Derry, *The Campaign in Norway*, pp. 43–5, Macintyre, *Narvik*, pp. 77–88, English, *Amazon to Ivanhoe*, pp. 103–13, O'Hara, *The German Fleet at War*, pp. 31–40, Brown (ed.), *Naval Operations of the Campaign in Norway*, pp. 26–9. Captain Dickens' account is excellent.

[57] NARA, T312/986, 9179071, 3. Gebirgsdivision Ia Nr. 241/40 of the 16 April 1940 'Erfahrungsbericht über den Einsatz der Division in Norwegen', 10.

[58] NARA, T312/982, 9173613, Colonel Weiss to General Dietl of 10 April 1940.

[59] Quoted in Levy, *The Royal Navy's Home Fleet in World War II*, p. 57.

[60] Rhys-Jones, *Churchill and the Norway Campaign*, p. 57.

[61] Brown (ed.), *Naval Operations of the Campaign in Norway*, p. 21.

[62] Dickens is particularly good in detailing the decision-making for Warburton-Lee to proceed ahead. The patently absurd concept of the Germans being in control of the two Norwegian coastal defence ships reflects the deficient thinking going on back in London.

No German crew could be acclimatised to a new foreign warship that quickly, a time requirement usually measured in months. To have the Norwegians fighting for the Germans after the events of 9 April defies logic.

63 Derry, *The Campaign in Norway*, p. 43.

64 Haarr, *The German Invasion of Norway*, p. 336. Haarr has some excellent insights into the British decision-making process on this issue.

65 Quote in Macintyre, *Narvik*, p. 78.

66 It is a line abreast, pulled back at a sharp angle, like a flying wedge but with only one side of the wedge.

67 Hinsley et. al., *British Intelligence in the Second World War*, Vol. I, pp. 140–1.

68 Haarr, *The German Invasion of Norway*, p. 339.

69 Quote in Dickens, *Narvik*, p. 61.

70 Haarr, *The German Invasion of Norway*, pp. 340–1.

71 Ibid., p. 341.

72 Quote in Brown (ed.), *Naval Operations of the Campaign in Norway*, p. 29.

73 Haarr, *The German Invasion of Norway*, p. 345.

74 Brown (ed.), *Naval Operations of the Campaign in Norway*, p. 78.

75 Tevnan and Horsley, *Norway Invaded*, p. 82.

76 Ibid., p. 97.

77 Haarr, *The German Invasion of Norway*, p. 352.

78 Broch, *The Mountains Wait*, p. 84.

79 Koop and Schmolke, *German Destroyers of World War II*, pp. 58–9. Some accounts give higher German losses.

80 *KTB/Skl*, Vol. 8, note on 11 April 1940, p. 101.

81 Carlgren, *Swedish Foreign Policy during the Second World War*, p. 64, Munch-Petersen, *The Strategy of Phoney War*, pp. 216, 222, Broch, *The Mountains Wait*, p. 127 and email from Geirr Haarr, dated 22 August 2004.

82 http://www.arcticwar.com/timeline.htm.

## Chapter 11

1 Hayes, *Quisling*, p. 211.

2 Thompson, *The Norwegian Armed Forces and Defense Policy*, p. 211.

3 Broch, *The Mountains Wait*, p. 92.

4 A June operation to relieve Narvik by the Germans involved an air assault on Bardofoss airfield while 6,000 troops with tanks arrived by sea 145 miles north of Narvik. The troops and supplies were to be brought by two fast and large ocean liners. When the campaign ended with the evacuation of northern Norway by the Allies, Hitler immediately proposed using this force to seize Iceland. See Claasen, *Hitler's Northern War*, p. 133.

5 NARA, T312-roll 982.

6 Quote in Williams, *Blitzkrieg and Conquest*, pp. 581–2.

7 Rhys-Jones, *Churchill and the Norway Campaign*, p. 63.

8 Haarr, *The German Invasion of Norway*, pp. 299, 451. A German infantry battalion, if all of it was included in 1940, numbered 820 officers and men. Units being flown in were often sent with some elements left behind.

9 Derry, *The Campaign in Norway*, p. 76, Karl Rommetveit (ed.), *Narvik 1940*, p. 133 and Haarr, *The German Invasion of Norway*, pp. 88–9. *Schiff 37* and *Schiff 26* were small converted trawlers and the *Schiff 26* may have been redirected to Trondheim. Derry indicated captured Norwegian artillery was also being transported. When closed, the *Schiff 37* actually rammed the destroyer *Arrow* before being sunk. Due to looting by the crew the usefulness of the captured codes was not apparent until early May.

10 Strabolgi, *Narvik and After*, pp. 129–30.

11 Derry, *The Campaign in Norway*, p. 35.

12 Liddell Hart, 'The Prospect in Norway', pp. 26–7.

13 Barnett, *Engage the Enemy more Closely*, p. 118.

14 Sir Llewellyn Woodward, *British Foreign Policy in the Second World War*, London: HMSO, 1970, Vol. 1, p. 16.

15 Liddell Hart, 'The Prospect in Norway', pp. 26–7.

16 De Lee, 'Allied Failure in Norway in 1940', p. 64.

17 Ibid., p. 60. Bureaucracies never seem to die. In 2010 the SEALS requested a dog team to be sent to Afghanistan and this had to cross five Rear Admirals' desks before it could be signed off.

18 Derry, *The Campaign in Norway*, p. 66.

19 Budiansk, *Battle of Wits*, p. 141.

20 Roskill, *The War at Sea*, Vol. 1, p. 198.

21 Kynoch, *Norway 1940*, p. 36.

[22] De Lee, 'Allied Failure in Norway in 1940', p. 67.

[23] Fielding Eliot, '*A Fight for the Valleys*', pp. 25–8 and Haarr, *The German Invasion of Norway*, p. 279.

[24] Rhys-Jones, *Churchill and the Norway Campaign*, p. 57.

[25] Ibid.

[26] Ibid., p. 61.

[27] Levy, *The Royal Navy's Home Fleet in World War II*, p. 61. The large and fast French destroyers would make a sweep in late April. They were the best suited for the operation with their high sustainable speed. See K. D. McBride 'Operation Rake, Captain Barthes in the Skagerrak, April 1940', *Mariner's Mirror*, Vol. 85, No. 1, pp. 84–6.

[28] Butler, *Grand Strategy*, Vol. II, September 1939–June 1941, p. 129.

[29] David French, *Raising Churchill's Army: The British Army and the War Against Germany 1919–1945*, Oxford: Oxford University Press, 2000, p. 48.

[30] Levy, *The Royal Navy's Home Fleet in World War II*, p. 59.

[31] Rhys-Jones, *Churchill and the Norway Campaign*, pp. 85–6.

[32] Levy, *The Royal Navy's Home Fleet in World War II*, pp. 61–3.

[33] Lunde, *Hitler's Pre-Emptive War*, pp. 317–19 and Derry, *The Campaign in Norway*, pp. 74–7, quote on p. 77.

[34] See Levy, *The Royal Navy's Home Fleet in World War II*, p. 60 and Barnett, *Engage the Enemy more Closely*, p. 119 on this point.

[35] Moulton, *The Norwegian Campaign of 1940*, p. 32.

[36] Shores et al., *Fledgling Eagles*, p. 253.

[37] Olaf Trapp, *Kämpfe um Narvik. Erlebnisse des Funkers Willy Schadock mit einer Nachrichten Ju-52*, Lemwerder: Stedinger, 2000, pp. 19–37.

[38] Clay Blair, *Hitler's U-Boat War*, New York, NY: Random House, 1996, Vol. 1, p. 150.

[39] Dickens, *Narvik*, pp. 99–101 and Haarr, *The German Invasion of Norway*, pp. 353–5. The *Penelope* would be damaged by rocks on 11 April.

[40] Brown (ed.), *Naval Operations of the Campaign in Norway*, p. 29. The battlecruisers *Renown* and *Repulse* had to return to Scapa Flow to refuel.

[41] Dickens, *Narvik*, p. 98.

[42] Dickens has an interesting discussion of this point, including Churchill's view, ibid., pp. 157–8.

[43] The 'K' class was a large destroyer but with one less twin turret then the 'Tribals'. Along with the similar 'L' class, the 'K' class was an outstanding success. It is the type featured in Sir Noël Coward's film *In Which We Serve*. Some sources incorrectly list it with eight 4.7in guns.

[44] We base our account on Haarr, *The German Invasion of Norway*, pp. 358–74, Dickens, *Narvik*, pp. 112–48, Brown (ed.), *Naval Operations of the Campaign in Norway*, pp. 34–50 and O'Hara, *The German Fleet at War*, pp. 40–54.

[45] Malcom Murfett, *Naval Warfare 1919–1945: an Operational History of the Volatile*, New York, NY: Routledge, 2008, p. 75. Murfett notes that B-Dienst had broken part of the Royal Navy's code to ascertain this.

[46] Quote in V. E. Tarrant, *Battleship Warspite*, Annapolis: Naval Institute Press, 1991, p. 77. Two 100-lb anti-submarine bombs were employed to sink her.

[47] Smith, *Into the Minefields*, p. 141.

[48] Haarr, *The German Invasion of Norway*, p. 352.

[49] Blair, *Hitler's U-Boat War*, Vol. 1, pp. 151–2.

[50] Tarrant, *Battleship Warspite*, p. 80 and Haarr, *The German Invasion of Norway*, pp. 361–2. The gunnery officer claimed *all* hit but it is unlikely.

[51] Quote in Rhys-Jones, *Churchill and the Norway Campaign*, p. 71 and Tarrant, *Battleship Warspite*, p. 83.

[52] Quote in O'Hara, *The German Fleet at War*, p. 50.

[53] Wreck divers have enjoyed Narvik over the years. http://www.ocean-discovery.org/batleofnarvik.htm.

[54] Rhys-Jones, *Churchill and the Norway Campaign*, p. 72.

[55] Mackesy is the father of Piers Mackesy, the excellent British historian, best known for *The War for America 1775–1783* (Harvard University Press, 1964). The general would be faulted in the fighting at Narvik for being unduly cautious.

[56] Stephen W. Roskill, *Churchill and the Admirals*, London: Collins, 1977, p. 103. One of the many failed German U-boat torpedo attacks was against the cruiser *Effingham* carrying the commander.

[57] Blair, *Hitler's U-Boat War*, Vol. 1, pp. 153–4.

[58] Koop and Schmolke, *German Destroyers of World War II*, p. 97.

[59] Quote in Rhys-Jones, *Churchill and the Norway Campaign*, p. 64. Shores et al., *Fledgling Eagles*, pp. 256–8.

[60] NARA, T312, 982, Ktb Gruppe XXI, on 10 April 1940, 10.35.

[61] Keilhau, *King Haakon VII in the History of Norway*, p. 58.

[62] Quote in Greve, *Haakon VII of Norway*, p. 135.

[63] Ibid., p. 134.

[64] Hoidal, *Quisling*, p. 384.

[65] Lehmkuhl, *Journey to London*, p. 12 and Haarr, *The German Invasion of Norway*, p. 177.

[66] Greve, *Haakon VII of Norway*, p. 136.

[67] Koht, *Norway Neutral and Invaded*, pp. 210–11; quote p. 211.

[68] Greve, *Haakon VII of Norway*, p. 136.

[69] Ibid., p. 136. The population in 2000 was 335. See Hoidal, *Quisling*, p. 387 for Hitler's involvement.

[70] Keilhau, *King Haakon VII in the History of Norway*, pp. 59–60.

[71] Quoted in Curtis (ed.), *Norway and the War*, pp. 72–3.

[72] Examples include actions in the Afghanistan and the Iraq Wars. The alleged killing of Colonel Gaddafi's adopted daughter Hana is another example of the propaganda value of a failed attempt, even, as noted in this case, she may have not been killed. See http://www.csmonitor.com/World/Middle-East/2011/0901/Hana-Qaddafi-dictator-s-daughter-survived-Reagan-s-bombs.

[73] Koht, *Norway Neutral and Invaded*, pp. 91–2.

[74] Quote in Thompson, *The Norwegian Armed Forces and Defense Policy*, p. 169.

[75] Ibid., p. 195.

[76] First quote from ibid., p. 86, and second ibid., p. 87 and Kersaudy, *Norway 1940*, pp. 100–7. Laake could have had his term extended until he was 68. Four months earlier Ruge had been considered but was passed over for Ljungberg's position.

[77] Haarr, *The Battle for Norway*, p. 17.

[78] Moulton, *The Norwegian Campaign of 1940*, p. 135.

[79] Quote in '*World War*', *Time* magazine, 6 May 1940, Vol. XXXV, No. 19, p. 22 and

Koht, *Norway Neutral and Invaded*, p. 83.

[80] Willy Brandt, *My Road to Berlin*, Garden City, NY: Doubleday & Company, Inc, 1960, p. 108.

[81] Haarr, *The Battle for Norway*, pp. 18, 39.

[82] Dildy, *Small Air Forces Observer*, Vol. 13, No. 3, p. 77.

[83] Brandt, *My Road to Berlin*, p. 107. Brandt was part of the German movement known as the 'Other Germany'. Other émigrés like him were residents in Scandinavia.

[84] Ibid., p. 99.

[85] Ibid. Brandt's apartment in Oslo would be searched later by the Gestapo as the Nazis had him on their list of people to be detained, see David Binder, *The Other German*, p. 78.

[86] Thies, *Weserübung*, Vol. 2, *Der Zweite Weltkrieg im Kartenbild*, map 17. Moulton gives an incorrect total and it is an error that is repeated in other works.

[87] Lunde, *Hitler's Pre-Emptive War*, p. 233, Haarr, *The Battle for Norway*, p. 3, http://hem.fyristorg.com/robertm/norge/history_section.html and Thies, *Weserübung*, Vol. 2, *Der Zweite Weltkrieg im Kartenbild*, map 55.

[88] Moulton, *The Norwegian Campaign of 1940*, p. 138.

[89] Thompson, *The Norwegian Armed Forces and Defense Policy*, p. 202.

[90] Lunde, *Hitler's Pre-emptive War*, p. 313

[91] Hauge, *Kampene I Norge 1940*, Vol. 1, p. 184.

[92] Brandt, *My Road to Berlin*, p. 108.

[93] Quote in Thompson, *The Norwegian Armed Forces and Defense Policy*, p. 202.

[94] NARA, T312-roll 982.

[95] Thompson, *The Norwegian Armed Forces and Defense Policy*, p. 195.

[96] Ibid., p. 202.

[97] Thies, *Weserübung*, Vol. 2, *Der Zweite Weltkrieg im Kartenbild*, map 25 and Hauge, *Kampene I Norge 1940*, Vol. 2, pp. 76–7, Lunde, *Hitler's Pre-emptive War*, pp. 232–6 and Thompson, *The Norwegian Armed Forces and Defense Policy*, pp. 203–4.

[98] '*World War*', *Time* magazine, 29 April 1940, Vol. XXXV, No. 18, p. 19.

[99] Thompson, *The Norwegian Armed Forces and Defense Policy*, p. 204 and Hubatsch, *Weserübung: Die Deutsche Besetzung von Dänemark und Norwegen 1940*, p. 258.

[100] Hauge, *Kampene I Norge 1940*, Vol. 2, p. 70 and Thompson, *The Norwegian Armed Forces and Defense Policy*, p. 228. Hannevig

received his training in 1915. Lunde confuses Kongsvinger near the Swedish border with Kongsberg. The surrender is sometimes given as 5 May.

[101] Thompson, *The Norwegian Armed Forces and Defense Policy*, p. 204.

[102] Thies, *Weserübung*, Vol. 2, *Der Zweite Weltkreig im Kartenbild*, map 25.

[103] Ibid., map 37.

[104] Lunde, *Hitler's Pre-Emptive War*, pp. 234–5; quote in Petrow, *The Bitter Years*, p. 79.

[105] Thompson, *The Norwegian Armed Forces and Defense Policy*, pp. 204–5 and Moulton, *The Norwegian Campaign of 1940*, pp. 139–43 and Hubatsch, *Weserübung: Die Deutsche Besetzung von Dänemark und Norwegen 1940*, p. 291.

[106] Quote in Haarr, *The German Invasion of Norway*, p. 444.

[107] *Handbok for Soldaten*, p. 10.

[108] Thompson, *The Norwegian Armed Forces and Defense Policy*, p. 206, Haarr, *The German Invasion of Norway*, p. 444 and Thies, *Weserübung*, Vol. 2, *Der Zweite Weltkreig im Kartenbild*, maps 41 and 42.

[109] Quote from 'World War', *Time* magazine, 29 April 1940, Vol. XXXV, No. 18, p. 24. This action based on Brown (ed.), *Naval Operations of the Campaign in Norway*, pp. 64–5, Haarr, *The German Invasion of Norway*, pp. 247–9 and Shores et al., *Fledgling Eagles*, pp. 271–2.

[110] Hamer, *Bombers versus Battleships*, pp. 42–6.

[111] Roskill, *The War at Sea*, Vol. 1, p. 186.

[112] Levy, *The Royal Navy's Home Fleet in World War II*, p. 52.

[113] Enzo Angelucci and Paolo Matricardi, *World War II Airplanes*, 2 vols, Chicago, IL: Rand McNally, 1978, Vol. 1, p. 33.

[114] Richard T. Partridge, *Operation Skua*, Yeovilton: Fleet Air Arm Museum, 1983, p. 50.

[115] This action is drawn from ibid., pp. 50–61 and Haarr, *The German Invasion of Norway*, pp. 273–9.

[116] Haarr, *The German Invasion of Norway*, p. 279.

[117] Ibid., pp. 280–1.

[118] NARA, T312-982, fr. 9173871, 'Bericht über besondere Ereignisse' of 10 April.

[119] Thompson, *The Norwegian Armed Forces and Defense Policy*, p. 211 and Derry, *The Campaign in Norway*, p. 101.

[120] Ibid., pp. 212–13.

[121] Haarr, *The Battle for Norway*, pp. 41–4. Photographs in H. H. Ambrosius, F. Dettmann et al., *Unser Kampf in Norwegen*, Munich: F. Brukmann, 1940, pp. 16–17.

[122] Haarr, *The Battle for Norway*, pp. 44–8 and Thies, *Weserübung*, Vol. 2, *Der Zweite Weltkreig im Kartenbild*, map 45.

[123] Thies, *Weserübung*, Vol. 2, *Der Zweite Weltkreig im Kartenbild*, map 45. For greater detail on these brown-water actions see Haarr, *The Battle for Norway*, pp. 47–50 and for a wartime perspective see Georg von Hase, *Die Kriegsmarine erobert Norwegens Fjorde*, Leipzig: v. Hase & Koehler, 1940.

[124] Thies, *Weserübung*, Vol. 2, *Der Zweite Weltkreig im Kartenbild*, map 45.

[125] Ibid. and Thompson, *The Norwegian Armed Forces and Defense Policy*, p. 211.

[126] Haarr, *The German Invasion of Norway*, p. 306. Clouston would be killed at Dunkirk helping to evacuate Allied troops.

[127] Thies, *Weserübung*, Vol. 2, *Der Zweite Weltkreig im Kartenbild*, map 48.

[128] Haarr, *The Battle for Norway*, p. 103. Later in 1940 Getz would have published in Oslo an account of his campaign: Colonel O. B. Getz, *Fra Krigen I Nord-Trøndelag 1940*, Oslo: H, Aschehough, 1940.

[129] Derry, *The Campaign in Norway*, p. 19. It was dropped when the *Lützow* developed engine problems and had to be reassigned to the Oslo invasion force.

[130] Haarr, *The Battle for Norway*, p. 110.

[131] http://france1940.free.fr/oob/cefs.html.

[132] French, *Raising Churchill's Army*, p. 159 and Haarr, *The Battle for Norway*, p. 109.

[133] Peter Hore, An Unlikely Encounter: Norway 1940', in Peter Hore (ed.), *Seapower Ashore*, London: Chatham, 2001, p. 249.

[134] Moulton, *The Norwegian Campaign of 1940*, pp. 167–75 and Thies, *Weserübung*, Vol. 2, *Der Zweite Weltkreig im Kartenbild*, map 48.

[135] Thompson, *The Norwegian Armed Forces and Defense Policy*, pp. 225–8.

[136] Lunde, *Hitler's Pre-Emptive War*, p. 335 and Jentz, *Panzertruppen*, Vol. 1, p. 110. Fischer would end up commanding the 181st Infantry Division in 1942.

[137] Thompson, *The Norwegian Armed Forces and Defense Policy*, p. 196.

[138] Quote in ibid., p. 207.

[139] Derry, *The Campaign in Norway*, p. 102.

140 Thompson, *The Norwegian Armed Forces and Defense Policy*, p. 209.

141 Ibid.

142 Ibid., p. 213.

143 Thies, *Weserübung*, Vol. 2, *Der Zweite Weltkreig im Kartenbild*, map 29 and Thompson, *The Norwegian Armed Forces and Defense Policy*, p. 225.

144 Derry, *The Campaign in Norway*, pp. 98–9 and Haarr, *The Battle for Norway*, pp. 68–9.

145 Thompson, *The Norwegian Armed Forces and Defense Policy*, pp. 217–18 and de Lee, 'Allied Failure in Norway in 1940', p. 67; quote in Thompson, p. 218. Foley had been in Berlin in the pre-war era and had saved the lives of many German Jews as a passport officer. He was transferred to Oslo in August 1939. MI6 was one of the intelligence branches of British intelligence.

146 Derry, *The Campaign in Norway*, p. 243 and Kynoch, *Norway 1940*, p. 66.

147 Derry, *The Campaign in Norway*, p. 109.

148 The 1st and 2nd battalions of the 345th Infantry Regiment and the 3rd battalion of the 362nd.

149 Jentz, *Panzertruppen*, Vol. 1, pp. 110–15.

150 The third was with *Kampfgruppe Fischer*.

151 Quote in Thompson, *The Norwegian Armed Forces and Defense Policy*, p. 247.

152 Derry, *The Campaign in Norway*, p. 138.

153 Thies, *Weserübung*, Vol. 2, *Der Zweite Weltkreig im Kartenbild*, map 28 and Thompson, *The Norwegian Armed Forces and Defense Policy*, p. 222. The number of men who surrendered is generally agreed upon, but this is not the case for surrendered equipment. For example, Thompson states seventeen artillery pieces including AA guns, while Thies has fifty-seven.

154 Thompson, *The Norwegian Armed Forces and Defense Policy*, pp. 248–9.

155 Ibid., p. 254.

156 Ibid., pp. 254–5.

157 Ibid., p. 110.

158 *KTB/Skl*, Vol. 8, note on 11 April 1940, p. 101.

159 Blair, *Hitler's U-Boat War*, Vol. 1, pp. 148–57.

160 Hubatsch, *Weserübung. Die deutsche Besetzung von Dänemark und Norwegen*, pp. 165–6, KTB/Skl, Vol. 8, annotation of 14 April 1940.

161 *KTB/Skl*, Vol. 8, p. 143.

162 Hubatsch, *Weserübung. Die deutsche Besetzung von Dänemark und Norwegen*, pp. 166–7. The Hitler letter is published in Alex Buchner, *Narvik. Die Kämpfe der Gruppe Dietl im Frühjahr 1940*, Neckargemünd: Scharnhorst Buchkameradschaft, 1958, Anlage 9, p. 199.

163 NARA, T312-986, 3. Gebirgsdivision Ia Nr. 241/40 of 16 April 1940, 'Erfahrungsbericht über den Einsatz der Division in Norwegen', 7.

164 Burdick and Jacobsen (eds), *The Halder War Diary*, p. 122.

165 Buchner, *Narvik*, pp. 45–6 and Tamelander and Zetterlig, *9 April: Nazitysklands invasjon av Norge*, pp. 203–5.

166 Ruef, *Odyssee einer Gebirgsdivision*, pp. 79–83.

167 It garnered even fewer votes then the NS in the last election before the war held in 1936.

168 Hoidal, *Quisling*, pp. 393–5. Quisling, while operating from the Hotel Continental, had at least one verbal confrontation with Major General Erwin Engelbrecht of the 163rd infantry division. Quisling was almost evicted by the German generals, as they needed the room at the Hotel Continental. The discussion is recounted in Jong, *The German Fifth Column in the Second World War*, p. 177.

169 Burdick and Jacobsen (eds), *The Halder War Diary*, p. 117.

170 Jong, *The German Fifth Column in the Second World War*, p. 173.

171 Ibid., p. 393. One report from the Trondheim consul stated that the Norwegians preferred German occupation to a Quisling government, see Jong, pp. 393–4.

172 Andreas Hillgruber (ed.), *Staatsmänner und Diplomaten bei Hitler*, Frankfurt a. M.: B&G, 1970, Vol. II, p. 111ff., Akten zur Deutschen Auswärtigen Politik, Serie D, Vol. IX, 2, Frankfurt a. M., P. Keppler, 1962, pp. 79, 95, 117ff.

173 ADAP, Unsigned Memorandum on 10 April 1940, docs 79, 95.

174 Ibid., pp. 414–16.

175 *KTB/Skl*, Vol. 8, p. 205, 20 April 1940.

176 Ibid., pp. 217–20, 234–6. The Swedish sensed something was afoot by the middle of April and recommendations were made for additional AA batteries to be deployed in the north.

[177] Binder, *The Other German*, pp. 78–9.

[178] http://www.willy-brandt.org/english/biographie/index_flash.htm. Willy Brandt, *Kriget I Norge*, Stockholm: Albert Bonniers, 1941. This is an account of the war from 9 April–9 June 1940.

[179] For example the *Snøgg* and *Troll* surrendered, as did the submarine *B6*.

[180] Butler, *Grand Strategy*, Vol. II, September 1939–June 1941, p. 149.

**Chapter 12**

[1] Malcolm Muggeridge, *Ciano's Diary 1939–1943*, London: William Heinemann, 1947, p. 234.

[2] 'World War', *Time* magazine, 13 May 1940, Vol. XXXV, No. 20, p. 25.

[3] Quote in http://www.secondworldwarhistory.com/ww2-quotes.asp and David Fraser, *Knight's Cross: A Life of Field Marshal Erwin Rommel*, New York, NY: Harper Collins, 1993, p. 463.

[4] Hitler had earned the moniker of 'sleepwalker' from his numerous political and now military successes since coming to power. During his first eight years of power his every action seemed to lead to success.

[5] Quote in Williams, *Blitzkrieg and Conquest*, pp. 506–8.

[6] Von Hase, *Die Kriegsmarine erobert Norwegens Fjorde* and Dr Fritz List with Hans Giese, *Kurs Norwegen*, Berlin: Steiniger, 1940 are just two examples of the German 'instant' publication. The former had an introduction by Erich Raeder and both featured excellent photographs and quality bindings amidst a war economy. The dustjacket of this book is taken from a German-style '*Life*' magazine on the campaign published in 1940.

[7] 'World War', *Time* magazine, 27 May 1940, Vol. XXXV, No. 22, p. 30.

[8] Major Willard Buhl, *Sea-Based Airpower – The Decisive Factor in Expeditionary Operations?*, Quantico, VA: USMC Command and Staff College, 2002, p. 31 and Claasen, *Hitler's Northern War*, p. 250.

[9] 'Foreign News', *Time* magazine, 20 May 1940, Vol. XXXV, No. 21, p. 34.

[10] Buhl, *Sea-Based Airpower*, pp. 27–9.

[11] Corum, 'Uncharted Waters', pp. 345–69.

[12] Richard H. Hooker Jr and Christopher Coglianese, 'Operation Weserübung and the Origins of Joint Warfare', *JFQ* (Summer 1993), pp. 100–11.

[13] Lukacs, *The Last European War*, pp. 74–5. The fall of France during the summer was a larger blow to the already weakened Isolationist wing of the Republican Party.

[14] Quoted in Bird, *Erich Raeder*, p. 148.

[15] Høiback, *Command and Control in Military Crisis*, p. 130.

[16] Amundsen, *Strategic Decisions and Implications of the German Assault on Norway*, p. 17.

[17] Buhl, *Sea-Based Airpower*, p. 27.

[18] Liddell Hart, 'The Prospect in Norway', pp. 26–7.

[19] Quote in Claasen, *Hitler's Northern War*, p. 251.

[20] Hubatsch, *Weserübung. Die deutsche Besetzung von Dänemark und Norwegen 1940*, p. 353.

[21] General der Flieger Ulrich O. E. Kessler, 'The Role of the "Luftwaffe" and the campaign in Norway', MS # B-485 (supplied by David C. Isby), p. 3.

[22] Assmann, *The German Campaign in Norway*, p. 51 and Stegemann in Maier et al., *Germany and the Second World War*, Vol. II, p. 211.

[23] Quote in Corum, 'The German Campaign in Norway 1940 as a Joint Operation', pp. 50–77.

[24] Lieutenant Commander Michael A. Brown, *Naval Operational Art in the Battle for Norway: Success in 1940 and Application in 1995*, Newport, CT: Naval War College, 1995, pp. 11–12.

[25] Hugh McManners, *Forgotten Voices of the Falklands*, St Ives: Ebury Press, 2007, p. 59.

[26] Stegemann in Maier et al., *Germany and the Second World War*, Vol. II, pp. 218–19.

[27] Quote in Buhl, *Sea-Based Airpower*, p. 29.

[28] Quote from 1998 Strategic Defence Review in Keith Hartley, 'The Economics of Joint Forces', in Andrew Dorman et al. (eds), *The Changing Face of Military Power*, p. 201.

[29] Marder, 'Winston is Back', p. 154.

[30] Buhl, *Sea-Based Airpower*, p. 28.

[31] Strabolgi, *Narvik and After*, p. 64.

[32] Quote in Munch-Petersen, *The Strategy of Phoney War*, p. 100.

[33] Strabolgi, *Narvik and After*, p. 186.

[34] Tom Haymes, 'Narvik on the Brink of Victory', *WWII History* (March 2005), p. 90. Major General Mackesy was opposed to a direct attack on Narvik.

[35] Koht, *Norway Neutral and Invaded*, p. 103.

[36] Hamer, *Bombers versus Battleships*, p. 64.

[37] Quoted in Levy, *The Royal Navy's Home Fleet in World War II*, p. 53.

[38] David C. Evans and Mark R. Peattie, *Kaigun*, Annapolis, MD: Naval Institute Press, 1997, p. 497.

[39] Gordon W. Prange with Donald M. Goldstein and Katherine V. Dillon, *Dec. 7, 1941*, New York, NY: McGraw-Hill, 1988, p. 5.

[40] Koht, *Norway Neutral and Invaded*, p. 189.

[41] Lunde, *Hitler's Pre-Emptive War*, pp. 541–3 discusses losses in some detail but cites the much too high losses on the *Blücher*.

[42] Fritz, *German Steel and Swedish Iron Ore*, pp. 66. Iron ore from Luleå in 1939 as a percentage of the entire trade was 27 per cent and rose to 53 per cent in 1940.

[43] http://home.online.no/~gestrom/history/norartxt.htm.

[44] Stegemann in Maier et al., *Germany and the Second World War*, Vol. II, p. 218.

[45] Stevens, *Trial of Nikolaus von Falkenhorst*, p. xxv.

[46] Thompson, *The Norwegian Armed Forces and Defense Policy*, pp. 417–21.

[47] Dahl, *Quisling*, p. 416 and Thompson, *The Norwegian Armed Forces and Defense Policy*, pp. 415–17.

[48] Thompson, *The Norwegian Armed Forces and Defense Policy*, pp. 417–18.

[49] Thompson, *The Norwegian Armed Forces and Defense Policy*, p. 418. Ironically, in 1911 Koht had published his book on Bismarck – *Bismarck Statsmanden*. Clearly he did not learn enough from the research.

[50] Article by Julia Stuart in *The Independent*, dated 12 July 2003. Another aspect to Norway's agony concerns Knut Hamsun, who was Norway's greatest writer after Ibsen, winner in 1920 of the Nobel Prize for Literature, and considered to be Norway's Poet Laureate before 1940. He was a member of the *Nasjonal Samling* which would see him convicted as a war criminal after the war. He also supported Hitler and contributed fifteen articles during the war to German publications. See www.uib.no/elin/elpub/uibmag/grafikk/eng-96/hamsun.htm.

[51] Thomas, *The Giant-Killers*, p. 12 and Jong, *The German Fifth Column in the Second World War*, p. 159.

[52] 'World Briefing' section, *New York Times*, 30 August 2003 and http://www.jcpa.org/phas/phas-vilhjalmsson-f06.htm.

[53] John Chipman, director, *The Military Balance 1999–2000*, London: Oxford University Press, 1999, pp. 51–2, 66–7. While taken from after the fall of the Berlin Wall, the military hardware was ordered during the Cold War. Denmark recently eliminated their submarine force due to the replacement cost.

[54] Email from Jan Egil Fjørtoft, dated 13 January 2004.

[55] Carlgren, *Swedish Foreign Policy during the Second World War*, pp. 64–5. http://www.indianembassy.org/US_Media/2000/march/india_needs_bomb_mar_24_2000.htm.

[56] http://the-diplomat.com/flashpoints-blog/2012/01/17/america%E2%80%99s-new-asiatic-fleet/.

[57] Quote from 'In Brief' in *Defense News*, 19 January 2004, p. 3 and see Greene and Massignani, *The Black Prince and the Sea Devils*, *passim*.

[58] One of the museum staff at Horten participated in one of these successful legendary wargame operations of which we had heard rumour of and mentioned in literature over the years.

[59] Rear Admiral W. J. Holland Jr, Letter in *The Proceedings* (January 2007), pp. 50–4.

[60] Michael Lindberg and Daniel Todd, *Brown-, Green-, and Blue-Water Fleets: The Influence of Geography on Naval Warfare, 1861 to the Present*, Westport, CT: Praeger, 2002, p. 224.

[61] Høiback, *Command and Control in Military Crisis*, p. 72.

[62] http://en.wikipedia.org/wiki/Switzerland_during_the_World_Wars.

[63] http://www.qotd.org/search/search.html?aid=5290.

## Appendix 1

[1] This is largely drawn from Andrew Mollo, *The Armed Forces of World War II*, London: Orbis Publishing Ltd, 1981, pp. 32–5, Goodwin and Parmenter, 'Denmark in World War II', pp. 1, 15–22, Tarnstrom, *The Sword of Scandinavia*, pp. 72–80: www.milhist.dk/organisation/oob1940.html and http://www.navalhistory.dk/English/Webmaster/Webmaster.htm.

[2] Some accounts show a second bicycle squadron.

[3] The Germans wanted to test the French 105mm howitzers upon capture to see where current French technology had taken their artillery.

[4] Many European nations maintain a separate military force deployed on national boundaries, a sort of enhanced equivalent of the US Border Patrol with heavy weapons.

**Appendix 2**

[1] This is largely drawn from Thies, *Weserübungi*, Vol. 2, *Der Zweite Welt-kreig im Kartenbild*, Appendix 1, Mollo, *The Armed Forces of World War II*, pp. 32–5, and http://niehorster.orbat.com/011_germany/40-04_scandinavia/_okw.html, http://www.warandtactics.com/smf/toe-world-war-2-axis/strength-of-german-infantry-divisions-may-1940/?action=printpage.

[2] http://www.washingtonpost.com/wp-dyn/articles/A132-2004Dec14.html.

[3] Steen, *Norges Sjøkrig*, Vol. 3, p. 199.

[4] Steen, *Norges Sjøkrig*, Vol. 2, pp. 25–6.

[5] The *Leuna, Buenos Aires, Entrerios* may have been attached (see Niehorster, but he has *Campinas* as a tug, and it was a transport, and Roger Jordan, *The World's Merchant Fleets – 1939*, Annapolis, MD: Naval Institute Press, 1999, p. 65).

# Bibliography

**Working Tools**

Bird, Keith W., *German Naval History. A Guide to the Literature*, New York, NY: Garland, 1985

**Printed Documents**

ADAP (Akten zur Deutschen Auswärtigen Politik), Serie D, vol. 5
Engel, Major, *Heeresadjutand bei Hitler 1938–1945. Aufzeichnungen des Majors Engel*, a cura di Hildegard von Kotze, Stuttgart: DVA, 1974
*Fuehrer Conferences on Naval Affairs 1939–1945*, London: Chatham, 2005
German Army Command, *Kampf em Norwegen*, Berlin: Zeitgeschichte, 1940
German Foreign Office, *Britain's Designs on Norway Full Text of White Book No. 4*, New York, NY: German Library of Information, 1940
*Handbok for Soldaten*, Oslo: Merkantile Boks & Akcidenstrykkeri, 1940
Hillgruber, Andreas (ed.), *Staatsmänner und Diplomaten bei Hitler*, Frankfurt a. M.: B&G, 1970, Vol. II
*Hitler's Weisungen für die Kriegführung 1939–1945*, ed. Walter Hubatsch, Koblenz: Bernard & Graefe, 1983
KTB/OKW (*Kriegstagebuch des Oberkommandos der Wehrmacht*), Vol. II, ed. Andreas Hillgruber, Munich: B&G, 1982
KTB/Skl (*Kriegstagebuch der Seekriegsleitung 1939–1945*, Vol. 4 (December 1939), Vol. 8 (April 1940), Vol. 9 (May 1940), Vol. 10 (June 1940), Vol. 11 (July 1940), Vol. 15 (November 1940), ed. Werner Rahn and Gerhard Schreiber with Hansjoseph Maierhöfer, Berlin: Mittler & Sohn, 1989
*Lagevorträge des Oberbefehlshabers der Kriegsmarine vor Hitler 1939–1945*, ed. Gerhard Wagner, Munich: Lehmanns, 1972

**Books and Articles**

Adams, J., *The Doomed Expedition. The Campaign in Norway 1940*, London: Leo Cooper, 1989
Adamson, Hans Christian and Klem, Per, *Blood on the Midnight Sun*, New York, NY: W. W. Norton, 1964
*Akten zur Deutschen Auswaertigen Politik 1918–45*, Serie D, Vol. 9, Frankfurt a. M.: Keppler, 1962
Ambrose, Stephen E., *D-Day: June 6, 1944, The Climactic Battle of World War II*, New York, NY: Simon & Schuster, 1994
Ambrosius, H.H., Dettmann, F., Erck, Charles, Georg Graf Engelbert and 'Rear Admiral S. Lützow', *Unser Kampf in Norwegen*, Munich: F. Brukmann, 1940
Amundsen, Captain Steinar, *Strategic Decisions and Implications of the German Assault on Norway*, Carlisle, PA: US Army War College, 2005
Andenaes, J., Riste, Olav and Skodvin, Magne, *Norway and the Second World War*, Oslo: Johan Grundt Tanum, 1966
Angelucci, Enzo and Matricardi, Paolo, *World War II Airplanes*, 2 vols, Chicago, IL: Rand McNally, 1978
Ash, Bernard, *Norway 1940*, London: Cassell, 1964

Askim, Per, *Office of Chief of Naval Operations, Office of Naval Intelligence*, Translation No. 376, Washington, DC: GPO, 1940

Assmann, Kurt, *The German Campaign in Norway*, London: Naval Staff - Admiralty, 1948

Assmann, Kurt, *Deutsche Seestrategie in zwei Weltkriegen*, Heidelberg: Scharnhorst Buchkameradschaft, 1957

Barnett, Correlli, *Engage the Enemy More Closely*, New York: W. W. Norton, 1991

'Battle of Narvik', *LIFE* magazine, 22 April 1940

Bédarida Françoise, 'France, Britain and the Nordic Countries', *Scandinavian Journal of History*, Vol. 2 (1977), pp. 7–27

Below, Nicolaus von, *Als Hitlers Adjoutant*, Mainz: von Hase & Koehler, 1980

Bekker, Cajus, *Angriffshöhe 4000*, Oldenbourg: Stalling, 1964

Bekker, Cajus, *The Luftwaffe War Diaries*, New York, NY: Ballantine, 1964

Bekker, Cajus, *Hitler's Naval War*, Garden City, NY: Doubleday, 1974

Bengtsson, Sven-Ake, 'Swedish War Plans', *Europa*, No. 74, p. 10.

Binder, David, *The Other German: Willy Brandt's Life & Times*, Washington, DC: New Republic Book Company, 1975

Bird, Keith, *Erich Raeder*, Annapolis, MD: Naval Institute Press, 2006

Birnbaum, Friedrich Karl, 'Der Untergang der Blücher am 9. April 1940', *Marine-Rundschau*, LXII, 65, pp. 76–84

Bjørn, Claus, 'Denmark', in I. C. B. Dear and M. R. D. Foot (eds), *The Oxford Companion to World War II*, Oxford: Oxford University Press, 1995, pp. 293–5

Blair, Clay, *Hitler's U-Boat War*, New York, NY: Random House, 1996, Vol. 1

Bonatz, Heinz, *Die deutsche Marine-Funkaufklärung 1914–1945*, Darmstadt: Wehr und Wissen Verlagsgesellschaft, 1970

Brandt, Willy, *Kriget I Norge*, Stockholm: Albert Bonniers, 1941

Brandt, Willy, *My Road to Berlin*, Garden City, NY: Doubleday & Company, Inc, 1960

Broch, Theodor, *The Mountains Wait*, London: Michael Joseph, 1943

Brown, David (ed.), *Naval Operations of the Campaign in Norway: April–June 1940*, London: Frank Cass, 2000

Brown, Louis, *A Radar History of World War II*, Philadelphia, PA: Institute of Physics Publishing, 1999

Brown, Lieutenant Commander Michael A., *Naval Operational Art in the Battle for Norway: Success in 1940 and Application in 1995*, Newport, CT: Naval War College, 1995

Brøyn, P., *Den Svenske malmeksort frem til besetnignen av Narvik I 1940*, unpublished thesis University of Oslo

Buchner Alex, *Narvik. Die Kämpfe der Gruppe Dietl im Frühjahr 1940*, Neckargemünd: Scharnhorst Buchkameradschaft, 1958

Budiansk, Stephen, *Battle of Wits*, New York, NY: Free Press, 2000

Buhl, Major Willard, *Sea-Based Airpower – The Decisive Factor in Expeditionary Operations?* , Quantico, VA: USMC Command and Staff College, 2002

Burdick, Charles and Jacobsen, Hans-Adolf (eds), *The Halder War Diary 1939–1942*, Novato, CA: Presidio Press, 1988

Butler, J. R. M., *Grand Strategy*, Vol. II, *September 1939–June 1941*, London: HMSO, 1957

Cable, James, *Gunboat Diplomacy 1919–1991*, Basingstoke: Palgrave-Macmillan, 1991

Campbell, John, *Naval Weapons of World War Two*, London: Conway Maritime, 1985

Carlgren, W. M., *Swedish Foreign Policy during the Second World War*, New York, NY: St Martin's Press, 1977

Carlson, Elliot, 'Missing Clues and Cracking Codes in the Pacific War', *U.S Naval Institute Proceedings*, December 2011, pp. 66–71

Caroff, *La Campagne de Norvège*, Paris: Service historique de la marine, 1955

Chalmers, W. L., *Max Horton and the Western Approaches*, London: Hodder & Stoughton, 1954

Chesneau, Roger, *Conway's All the World's Fighting Ships 1922–1946*, London: Conway Maritime Press, Inc., 1980

Churchill, Winston S., *The Gathering Storm*, New York, NY: Houghton Mifflin Co., 1948

Claasen, Adam R. A., *Hitler's Northern War: The Luftwaffe's Ill-Fated Campaign 1940–1945*, Lawrence, KA: University Press of Kansas, 2001

Claasen, Adam, 'The German Invasion of Norway 1940: The Operational Intelligence Dimension', *Journal of Strategic Studies*, Vol. 27, No. 1 (March 2004), pp. 114–35

Colville, John, *The Fringes of Power. Downing Street Diaries 1939–1945*, 2 vols, London: Sceptre, 1986

Consett, Rear Admiral M. W. W. P. with Daniel, Captain O. H., *The Triumph of Unarmed Forces (1914–1918)*, New York, NY: Brentano's, 1923

Corum, James S., *The Luftwaffe: Creating the Operational Air War, 1918–1940*, Lincoln: University of Kansas, 1997

Corum, James S., 'The German Campaign in Norway 1940 as a Joint Operation', *Journal of Strategic Studies*, Vol. 21, No. 4 (December 1998), London: Frank Cass, pp. 50–77

Corum, James S., 'Uncharted Waters: Information in the First Modern Joint Campaign – Norway 1940', *The Journal of Strategic Studies*, Vol. 27, No. 2 (June 2004), pp. 345–69

Cruickshank, Charles, *SOE in Scandinavia*, London: Oxford University Press, 1986

Curtis, Monica (ed.), *Norway and the War*, London: Royal Institute of International Affairs, 1941

Dahl, Hans Fredrik, *Quisling: A Study in Treachery*, Cambridge: Cambridge University Press, 1999

Danstrup, John, *A History of Denmark*, Copenhagen: Wivel, 1948

*Das Deutsche Reich und der Zweite Weltkrieg*, Vol. 2, Klaus A. Maier, Horst Rohde, Bernd Stegemann, Hans Umbreit, *Die Errichtung der Hegemonie auf dem europäischen Kontinent*, Stuttgart: DVA, 1979

Davies, W. J. K., *The German Army Handbook*, New York, NY: Arco, 1973

de Lee, Nigel, 'Allied Failure in Norway in 1940', in Gary Sheffield and Geoffrey Till (eds), *The Challenges of High Command*, Basingstoke: Palgrave-Macmillan, 2003

Dear, I. C. B. and Foot, M. R. D. (eds), *The Oxford Companion to World War II*, Oxford: Oxford University Press, 1995

Derry, Thomas K., *The Campaign in Norway*, London: HMSO, 1952

Derry, Thomas K., *A History of Scandinavia*, Minneapolis, MN: University of Minnesota Press, 1979

Dickens, Peter, *Narvik: Battles in the Fjords*, Annapolis, MD: Naval Institute Press, 1974

Dietl, Gerda-Luise and Hermann, Kurt (eds), *General Dietl*, Munich: Münchner Buchverlag, 1951

Dilks, David, 'Great Britain and Scandinavia in the "Phoney War"', *Scandinavian Journal of History*, Vol. 2 (1977), pp. 29–51

Divine, A. D., *Firedrake*, New York, NY: E. P. Dutton, 1943

*Documenti Diplomatici Italiani*, 9th Series, Vol. IV, Rome: Libreria dello Stato, 1960

Dorman, Andrew et al. (eds), *The Changing Face of Maritime Power*, New York, NY: Palgrave, 1999

Dorman, Andrew et al. (eds), *The Changing Face of Military Power*, New York, NY: Palgrave, 2002

Dülffer, Jost, 'Determinants in German Naval Policy, 1920–1939', in Wilhelm Deist (ed.), *The German Military in the Age of Total War*, Leamington Spa: Berg, 1985, pp. 152–70.

Dulles, Allen Welsh, *Germany's Underground*, Boston, MA: Da Capo Press, 1947

Edwards, Roger, *German Airborne Troops*, Garden City, NY: Doubleday, 1974

Eliot, George Fielding, 'A Fight for the Valleys', *Life*, 6 May 1940

*Encyclopedia Britannica*, 11th edn, New York, NY: the Encyclopedia Britannica Company, 1910

English, John, *Amazon to Ivanhoe*, Kendal: World Ship Society, 1993

English, John, *Afridi to Nizam*, Gravesend: World Ship Society, 2001

Ericson, Lars, 'Denmark's Hour of Destiny', *The Royal Swedish Academy of War Sciences Journal*, No. 4 (2001)

Erfurth, Waldemar, *Der Finnische Krieg 1941–1944*, Munich: Limes, 1977

Evans, David C. and Peattie, Mark R., *Kaigun*, Annapolis, MD: Naval Institute Press, 1997

*Français et Britanniques dans la drÛle de guerre*, Actes du Colloque, Paris: CNRS, 1979

Fraser, David, *Knight's Cross: A Life of Field Marshal Erwin Rommel*, New York, NY: Harper Collins, 1993

French, David, *Raising Churchill's Army: The British Army and the War Against Germany 1919-1945*, Oxford: Oxford University Press, 2000

Frisch, Friedrich, *The Raid on the 'Altmark'*, Berlin: Wilhelm Grave, 1940

Frischauer, Willi, and Jackson, Robert, *The Altmark Affair*, New York: Macmillan Co, 1955

Fritz, Martin, *German Steel and Swedish Iron Ore, 1939-1945*, Göteborg: Institute of Economic History of Gothenburg University, 1974

Gainard, Joseph, *Yankee Skipper*, New York, NY: Frederick A. Stokes, 1940

Gardiner, Robert (ed.), *Conway's All the World's Fighting Ships 1922-1946*, Annapolis, MD: Naval Institute Press, 1980

Garzke, William H., Jr and Dulin, Robert O., *Battleships Axis and Neutral in World War II*, Annapolis: Naval Institute Press, 1985

Gehlen, Reinhard, *Der Dienst*, Munich: Droemer, 1971

Gemzell, Carl-Axel, *Organization, Conflict and Innovation: A Study of German Naval Strategic Planning 1888-1940*, Stockholm: Esselte Studium, 1973

Gemzell, Carl-Axel, *Raeder, Hitler und Skandinavien. Der Kampf für einen maritimen Operationsplan*, Lund: C. W. K. Gleerup, 1975

Getz, Colonel O. B., *Fra Krigen I Nord-Trøndelag 1940*, Oslo: H, Aschehough, 1940

Gibbs, N. H., *Grand Strategy*, Vol. I, *Rearmament Policy*, London: HMSO, 1976

González, Oscar, *German Paratroopers in Scandinavia*, Atplen, PA: Schiffer Publishing, Ltd, 2009

Goodwin A. E. and Parmenter, James D., 'Denmark in World War II', *E.T.O.*, No. 53 (February 1990), pp. 15-18

Greene, Jack, *Mare Nostrum*, Watsonville, CA: Typesetting Etc., 1990

Greene, Jack and Massignani, Alessandro, *Ironclads at War: The Origin and Development of the Armored Warship, 1854-1891*, Conshocken, PA: Combined Publishing, 1998

Greene, Jack and Massignani, Alessandro, *The Black Prince and the Sea Devils*, Cambridge, MA: Da Capo Press, 2004

Greve, Tim, *Haakon VII of Norway*, London: C. Hurst, 1983

Gröner, Erich, *German Warships 1815-1945*, Vols One and Two, Annapolis, MD: Naval Institute Press, 1990

Guhnfeldt, Cato, *Fornebu 9, April*, Oslo: Wings Forlag, 1990

Haarr, Geirr H., *The German Invasion of Norway: April 1940*, Barnsley: Seaforth Publishing, 2009

Haarr, Geirr H., *The Battle for Norway: April-June 1940*, Barnsley: Seaforth Publishing, 2010

Häikiö, Martti, *The Race for Northern Europe, September 1939-June 1940*, in Henrik S. Nissen (ed.), *Scandinavia During the Second World War*, Minneapolis, MN: University of Minnesota, 1983, pp. 53-97

Halder, Generaloberst, *Kriegstagebuch 1939-1942* 3 Vols., ed. by Hans Adolf Jacobsen, Stuttgart: W. Kohlhammer, 1962-3

Hambro, C. J., *I Saw it Happen in Norway*, New York, NY: D. Appleton-Century Co., 1941

Hamer, David, *Bombers versus Battleships*, Annapolis, MD: Naval Institute Press, 1999

Harriman, Florence Jaffray, *Mission to the North*, New York, NY: Lippincott, 1941

Hart, B. H. Liddell, 'The Prospect in Norway', *Life* magazine, 29 April 1940, pp. 26-7

Hartley, Keith, 'The Economics of Joint Forces', in Andrew Dorman et al. (eds), *The Changing Face of Military Power*, New York, NY: Palgrave, 2002

Harvey, Maurice, *Scandinavian Misadventure*, Tunbridge Wells: Spellmount, 1990

Hase, Georg von, *Die Kriegsmarine erobert Norwegens Fjorde*, Leipzig: von Hase & Koehler, 1940

Hauge, Andreas, *Kampene I Norge 1940*, 2 vols, Sandefjord: Krigshistorisk Forlag A.S., 1995

Hayes, Paul M., *Quisling*, Bloomington, IN: Indiana University Press, 1972

Haymes, Tom, 'Narvik on the Brink of Victory', *WWII History* (March 2005)

Heinl, Robert Debs, *Dictionary of Military and Naval Quotations*, Annapolis: Naval Institute Press, 1966

Henke, Josef, *England in Hitler's politischem Kalkül 1935-1939*, Boppard am Rhein: Boldt, 1973

Henningsen, P. 'Fektningen ved Amalienborg', in Arne Stevns (ed.), *Danmark Niende April*, Oslo: Cammermeyers Boghandel, 1941

Hervieux, Pierre, 'The Heavy Cruiser *Admiral Hipper* at War', *Warship*, Vol. IX, Annapolis: Naval Institute Press, 1985, pp. 232–9

Herwig, Holger H., *Luxury Fleet: The Imperial German Navy 1888–1918*, 1st edn, London: George Allen & Unwin, 1980

Hillgruber, Andreas, *Der Zweite Weltkrieg 1939–1945*, Stuttgart: Kohlhammer, 1982

Hillgruber, Andreas, *Hitler's Strategie, Politik und Kriegführung*, 1st edn 1964, Koblenz: Bernard & Graefe, 1984

Hinsley, F. H., Thomas, E. E., Ransom, C. F. G., and Knight, R. C., *British Intelligence in the Second World War*, London: HMSO, 1979, Vol. I

Hobson, Rolf and Kristiansen, Tom, *Norsk Forsvarshistorie 1905–1940*, Bergen: Eide Forlag, 2001, Vol. 3

Höhne, Heinz, *Canaris*, New York, NY: Doubleday & Company, 1979

Høiback, Harald, *Command and Control in Military Crisis: Devious Decisions*, London: Frank Cass, 2003

Hoidal, Oddvar K., 'Vidkun Quisling's Decline as a Political Figure in Prewar Norway 1933–1937', *Journal of Modern History*, Vol. 43, No. 3 (September 1971), pp. 440–67

Hoidal, Oddvar K., *Quisling*, Oslo: Norwegian University Press, 1989

Hooker, Richard H., Jr and Coglianese, Christopher, 'Operation Weserübung and the Origins of Joint Warfare', *JFQ* (Summer 1993)

Hore, Peter, *Seapower Ashore*, London: Chatham, 2001

Hubatsch, Walther, *Weserübung. Die deutsche Besetzung von Dänemark und Norwegen 1940*, Göttingen: Musterschmidt, 1960

Insulander, Per and Ohlsson, Curt S., *Pansarskepp*, Goteborg: C. B. Marinlitteratur, 2001

Irving, David, *Hitler's War*, New York, NY: Viking Press, 1977, Vol. 1

Isby, David (ed.), *The Luftwaffe and the War at Sea 1939–1945*, London: Chatham Publishing, 2005

Jäger Jorg, Johannes, 'Sweden's Iron Ore Export to Germany', *Scandinavian History Review*, Vol. 15, Issue 1-2, 1967

Jentz, Thomas L., *Panzertruppen*, Atglen, PA: Schiffer Military History, 1996, Vol. 1

Jentz, Thomas L., *Panzer Tracts No. 4 Panzerkampfwagen IV*, Darlington, MA: Darlington Productions, 1997

Joesten, Joachim, *Denmark's Day of Doom*, London: V. Gollancz ltd., Left Book Club Edition, 1939

Jones, Geoffrey, *Under Three Flags*, London: Kimber, 1973

Jong, Louis de, *The German Fifth Column in the Second World War*, Chicago, IL: University of Chicago Press, 1956

Jordan, Roger, *The World's Merchant Fleets – 1939*, Annapolis, MD: Naval Institute Press, 1999

Kähler, Wolfgang, *Schlachtschiff Gneisenau*, Herford, Germany: Kohler, 1979

Kahn, David, *Hitler Spies*, New York, NY: Collier Books, 1978

Kahn, David, *The Codebreakers*, New York, NY: Scribner, 1996

Karlbom, Rolf, 'Sweden's Iron Ore Exports to Germany, 1933–1944', *Scandinavian Economic History Review*, Vol. XIII, Nos 1 and 2 (1965), pp. 65–93

Keilhau, Wilhelm, *King Haakon VII in the History of Norway*, London: Hereford Times, 1942

Kirchoff, Hans, 'Denmark, September 1939–April 1940', in Neville Wylie (ed.), *European Neutrals and Non-Belligerents during the Second World War*, Cambridge: Cambridge University Press, 2002, pp. 31–52

Kersaudy, François, *Norway 1940*, London: William Collins Sons, 1990

Kjærass, Arild, *Profiles in Norway: Caproni Ca. 310*, Andebu, Norway: self-published, 1999

Kjæraas, Arild, *Høver M.F. 11, Profiles in Norway Nr. 2*, Andebu, Norway: self-published, 2004

Klefos, Brede, *They Came in the Night*, New York, NY: Harian Publications, 1959

Knox, Macgregor, *Mussolini Unleashed*, Cambridge: Cambridge University Press, 1982

Knudsen, Franklin, *I was Quisling's Secretary*, London: Britons Publishing Co., 1967

Koht, Halvdan, *Norway Neutral and Invaded*, London: Hutchinson & Co., 1941

Koop, Gerhard and Schmolke, Klaus-Peter, *Battleships of the Scharnhorst Class*, Annapolis: Naval Institute Press, 1999

Koop, Gerhard and Schmolke, Klaus-Peter, *Pocket Battleships of the Deutschland Class*, Annapolis, MD: Naval Institute Press, 2000

Koop, Gerhard and Schmolke, Klaus-Peter, *Heavy Cruisers of the Admiral Hipper Class*, Annapolis, MD: Naval Institute Press, 2001

Koop, Gerhard and Schmolke, Klaus-Peter, *German Light Cruisers of World War II*, Annapolis: Naval Institute Press, 2002

Koop, Gerhard and Schmolke, Klaus-Peter, *German Destroyers of World War II*, Annapolis, MD: Naval Institute Press, 2003

Krosby, H. Peter, *Finland, Germany and the Soviet Union 1940–1941. The Petsamo Dispute*, Madison: University of Wisconsin, 1968

Kurowski, Franz, *An Alle Wölfe: Angriff!*, Wölfersheim-Berstadt: Podzun Pallas, 1986

Kurowski, Franz, *Sturz in die Hölle. Die deutschen Fallschirmjaeger, 1939–1945*, Munich: Heyne, 1986

Kurowski, Franz, *The History of the Fallschirmpanzerkorps Hermann Göring*, Winnipeg: J. J. Fedorowicz, 1995

Kynoch, Joseph, *Norway 1940: The Forgotten Fiasco*, Shrewsbury: Airlife Publishing, 2002

Langton, Col. Christopher (ed), *The Military Balance 1999–2000*, London: Oxford University Press, 1999

Larsen, Karen, *A History of Norway*, New York, NY: Princeton University Press, 1950

Lassque, Jean, *Guerre Navale en Norvège*, Paris: Gerfaut, 2003

Lauring, Palle, *A History of the Kingdom of Denmark*, Copenhagen: Høst & Søn, 1963

Lehmkuhl, Dik, *Journey to London*, London: Hutchinson & Co., 1945

Lehmkuhl, Herman K., *Hitler Attacks Norway*, London: The Royal Norwegian Government Information Office, 1945

Levine, Paul A. 'Swedish Neutrality during the Second World War: tactical success or moral compromise?', in Neville Wylie (ed.), *European Neutrals and Non-Belligerents during the Second World War*, Cambridge: Cambridge University Press, 2002, pp. 304–30

Levy, James P., 'Lost Leader: Admiral of the Fleet Sir Charles Forbes and the Second World War', *Mariner's Mirror*, Vol. 88, No. 2, 2002, pp. 186–95

Levy, James P., *The Royal Navy's Home Fleet in World War II*, New York, NY: Palgrave, 2003

Lindberg, Michael and Todd, Daniel, *Brown-, Green-, and Blue-Water Fleets: The Influence of Geography on Naval Warfare, 1861 to the Present*, Westport, CT: Praeger, 2002

Lindermann, Major Timothy F., *Joint Operations Case Study Weserübung Nord: Germany's Invasion of Norway, 1940*, A Research Paper Presented To The Research Department Air Command and Staff College In Partial Fulfillment of the Graduation Requirements of ACSC by Major Timothy F. Lindemann, March 1997

List, Dr Fritz with Giese, Hans, *Kurs Norwegen*, Berlin: Steiniger, 1940

Look, Hans-Dietrich, *Quisling, Rosenberg und Terboven. Vorgeschichte und Geschichte der nazionalsozialistische Revolution in*, Stuttgart: Deutsche Verlags-Anstalt, 1970

Lorbeer, Hans-Joachim, *Westmächte gegen die Sowjetunion 1939–1941*, Freiburg i. B.: Rombach, 1975

Lucas, James, *Alpine Elite*, London: Jane's Publishing, 1980

Ludlow, Peter W., 'Scandinavia Between the Great Powers. Attempts at mediation in the First Year of the Second World War', *Historisk Tidskrift*, 1974, pp. 1–58

Lukacs, John, *The Last European War September 1939–December 1941*, New Haven, CT: Yale University Press, 1976

Lunde, Henrik O., *Hitler's Pre-Emptive War: The Battle for Norway, 1940*, Drexel Hill, PA: Casemate, 2009

Lutzhöft, Hans-Jürgen, 'Deutschland und Schweden während des Norwegenfeldzuges (5. April – 10. Juni 1940)', VfZG, 22 (1974), pp. 382–416

Lynam, C. C., *To Norway & the North Cape in Blue Dragon II*, London: Sidgwick & Jackson, 1913

McCart, Neil, *Nelson & Rodney*, Liskeard: Maritime Books, 2005

Macintyre, Donald, *Narvik*, New York, NY: W. W. Norton, 1960

Macksey, Kenneth, *The Searchers: How Radio Interception Changed the Course of Both World Wars*, London: Cassell, 2003

McManners, Hugh, *Forgotten Voices of the Falklands*, St Ives: Ebury Press, 2007

Maier, Klaus A., Rohde, Horst, Stegemann, Bernd, and Umbreit, Hans, *Germany and the Second World War*, Oxford: Clarendon Press, 1991, Vol. II

Mallmann Showell, Jak P., *German Naval Code Breakers*, Annapolis, MD: Naval Institute Press, 2003

Mann, Chris and Jörgensen, Christer, *Hitler's Arctic War*, New York, NY: Thomas Dunne Books, 2002

March, Edgar J., *British Destroyers*, London: Seeley, Service & Co. Ltd, 1966

Marder, Arthur, '"Winston is Back": Churchill at the Admiralty 1939–1940', in *From the Dardanelles to Oran. Studies of the Royal Navy in War and Peace, 1915–1940*, London: Oxford University Press, 1974

Mehre, Helge, *Flyvåpnene 1 den 2. vergdenskrig*, Lillestrøm, Norway: Aksidenstrykkeriet, 1986

Milsom, John and Chamberlain, Peter, *German Armoured Cars of World War Two*, New York, NY: Charles Scribner's Sons, 1974

Milward, Alan S., 'Could Sweden have stopped the Second World War?', *Scandinavian Economic History Review*, 11, Nos 1 and 2 (1967), pp. 127–38

Mitcham Jr, Samuel W., *Hitler's Legions: The German Army Order of Battle World War II*, Briarcliff Manor, NY: Stein and Day, 1985

Mollo, Andrew, *The Armed Forces of World War II*, London: Orbis Publishing Ltd, 1981

Morzik, Fritz, *Die deutschen Transportfliegerkräfte im Zweiten Weltkrieg*, Frankfurt a. M.: Bernard & Graefe Verlag, 1966

Moulton, James L., *The Norwegian Campaign of 1940: A Study of Warfare in Three Dimensions*, London: Eyre & Spottiswoode, 1966

Muggeridge, Malcolm, *Ciano's Diary 1939–1943*, London: William Heinemann, 1947

Mulligan, Timothy P. 'Ship-of-the-line or Atlantic Raider', *The Journal of Military History*, Vol. 69, No. 4 (October 2005), pp. 1013–44.

Munch-Petersen, Thomas, *The Strategy of Phoney War: Britain, Sweden and the Iron Ore Question 1939–1940*, Stockholm: Militærhistiska Fœrlaget, 1981

Murfett, Malcom, *Naval Warfare 1919–1945: an Operational History of the Volatile*, New York, NY: Routledge, 2008

Neitzel, Sonke, 'Kriegsmarine and Luftwaffe Co-operation in the war against Britain, 1939–1945', *War in History*, Vol. 10, No. 4 (November 2003), pp. 448–62

Nevakivi, Jukka, *The Appeal that was Never Made*, Montreal: McGill-Queen's University Press, 1976

Niehorster, Leo W. G., *Mechanized Army and Waffen SS Units (1st September 1939)*, Hannover: private printing, 1990, Vol. 1/I

Nielsen, Kay, Søren, *Soldaterne den 9. april 1940*, Copenhagen: Forkaget /Wøldike, 1990

Nissen, Henrik S. (ed.), *Scandinavia during the Second World War*, Minneapolis, MN: University of Minnesota, 1983

O'Hara, Vincent P., *The German Fleet at War*, Annapolis, MD: Naval Institute Press, 2005

O'Keefe, James D., 'Daring Escape of gold ship Mormacsea' in *Sea Classics*, vol. 39, #11, November 2006 or http://findarticles.com/p/articles/mi_qa4442/is_200611/ai_n17194590/.

Ørvik, Nils, *The Decline of Neutrality 1914–1941*, London: Frank Cass, 1971

Overy, Richard, *War and Economy in the Third Reich*, Oxford: Clarendon Press, 1994

Paloczi-Horvath, George, *From Monitor to Missile Boat*, Annapolis, MD: Naval Institute Press, 1996

Pargeter, C. J., *Hipper Class Heavy Cruiser*, Shepperton: Ian Allan, 1982

Partridge, Richard T., *Operation Skua*, Yeovilton: Fleet Air Arm Museum, 1983

Peszke, Michael Alfred, *Poland's Navy 1918–1945*, New York, NY: Hippocrene, 1999

Petrow, Richard, *The Bitter Years; The Invasion and Occupation of Denmark and Norway, April 1940–May 1945*, New York, NY: William Morrow & Company, 1974

Prange, Gordon W. with Goldstein, Donald M. and Dillon Katherine V., *Dec. 7, 1941*, New York, NY: McGraw-Hill, 1988

Price, Dr Alfred, 'Messerschmitt Bf 110', *International Air Power Review*, Vol. 16 (2005)

Quisling, Vidkun, *Russia and Ourselves*, Metairie, LA: Sons of Liberty Books, 1994

Raeder, Erich, *My Life*, Annapolis, MD: US Naval Institute, 1960

Rahn, Werner, *Reichmarine und Landesverteidigung 1919–1928. Konception und Führung der Marine in der Weimarer Republik*, Munich: Bernard & Graefe, 1976

Raven, Alan and Roberts, John, *British Battleships of World War Two*, Annapolis, MD: Naval Institute Press, 1978

Rhys-Jones, Graham, *Churchill and the Norway Campaign*, Barnsley: Pen & Sword, 2008

Richardson, Michael W., *Forcible Entry and the German Invasion of Norway, 1940*, Fort Leavenworth, KS: US Army Command and General Staff College, 2001

Rickman, A. F., *Swedish Iron Ore*, London: Faber and Faber, 1939

Riste, Olav, 'The Norwegian War Historical Department', in Robin Higham (ed.), *Official Histories. Essays and Bibliographies from around the World*, Manhattan, KS: Kansas State University Library, 1970, pp. 352–5

Riste, Olav, *Norway's Foreign Relations. A History*, Oslo: Universitetsvorlaget, 2001

Riste, Olav, 'Intelligence and the "Mindset": The German invasion of Norway in 1940', *Intelligence and National Security*, No. 4, Vol. 22 (2007), pp. 521–36

Roberts, John, 'Danish Navy', in Robert Gardiner (ed.), *Conway's All the World's Fighting Ships 1922–1946*, Annapolis, MD: Naval Institute Press, 1980, pp. 381–4

Rohwer, J., *Axis Submarine Successes of World War Two*, Annapolis, MD: Naval Institute, 1999

Rohwer, Jürgen and Hummelchen, Gerhard, *Chronology of the War at Sea 1939–1945. The Naval History of World War Two*, 2nd edn, Annapolis, MD: Naval Institute Press, 1992

Rommetveit, Karl, 'From Mountain Warfare in Winter Conditions to the Allied Recapture of Narvik', in Rommetveit, Karl (ed.), *Narvik 1940: Five Nations at War in the High North*, Oslo: Institutt for Forsvarsstudie, 1991

Roskill, Stephen W., *The War at Sea 1939–1945*, 4 vols, London, 1954–61

Roskill, Stephen W., *Churchill and the Admirals*, London: Collins, 1977

Rössler, Eberhard, *The U-Boat*, London: Cassell, 1981

Ruef, Karl, *Odysse einer Gebirgsdivision. Die 3. Geb. Div. im Einsatz*, Graz: Stocker, 1976

Salewski, Michael, *Die deutsche Seekriegsleitung 1935–1945, Denkschriften und Lagebetrachtungen*, Frankfurt a. M.: Bernard & Graefe, 1973

Salmon, Patrick (ed.), *Britain and Norway in the Second World War*, London: HMSO, 1995

Scheen, Rolf, *Norges Sjøkrig*, 2 vols, Bergen: John Griegs, 1947

Schellenberg, Walter, *The Labyrinth*, New York, NY: Da Capo, 2000

Schuur, Heinrich, 'Auftragserteilung und Auftragsdurchführung beim Unternehmen 'Juno' vom 4. Bis 10. Juni 1940', in Heinrich Schuur, Rolf Martens and Wolfgang Koehler, *Führungsprobleme der Marine im Zweiten Weltkrieg*, Freiburg i.B.: Rombach, 1986

Seymour, Susan, *Anglo-Danish Relations and Germany 1933–1945*, Gylling, Denmark: Odense University Press, 1982

Sheffield, Gary and Till, Geoffrey (eds), *The Challenges of High Command*, Basingstoke: Palgrave-Macmillan, 2003

Shirer, William L., *Berlin Diary*, New York, NY: Alfred A. Knopf, 1941

Shirer, William L., *The Challenge of Scandinavia*, Boston, MA: Little, Brown and Company, 1955

Shirer, William L., *The Rise and Fall of the Third Reich*, New York, NY: Crest, 1962

Shores, Christopher, Foreman, John, Ehrengardt, Christian-Jacques, Weiss, Heinrich, and Olsen, Bjorn, *Fledgling Eagles: The Complete Account of Air Operations During the 'Phoney War' and Norwegian Campaign, 1940*, London: Grub Street, 1991

Skodvin, Magne, 'Norwegian Neutrality and the Question of Credibility', *Scandinavian Journal of History*, Vol. 2, Nos 1 and 2 (1977), pp. 123–45

Smith, Peter C., *Into the Minefields*, Barnsley: Pen & Sword Maritime, 2005

Steen, E. A., *Norges Sjøkrig 1940–1945*, Vols 1–4, Oslo: Gyldendal Norsk Forlag, 1956

Steen, Sverre, *Norges Krig 1940–1945*, 3 vols, Oslo: Gyldendal Norsk Forlag, 1947

Stevens, E. H., *Trial of Nikolaus von Falkenhorst*, London: William Hodge, 1949

Stevns, Arne (ed.), *Danmark Niende April*, Oslo: Cammermeyers Boghandel, 1941

Stokker, Kathleen, *Folklore Fights the Nazis: Humor in Occupied Norway 1949–1945*, Madison, WI: University of Wisconsin Press, 1995

Stowe, Leland, 'How a Few Thousand Nazis seized Norway', *Life* magazine, 6 May 1940, pp. 90–103

Stowe, Leland, *No Other Road to Freedom*, New York, NY: Alfred A. Knopf, 1941

Strabolgi, Lord, 10th Baron, *Narvik and After*, London: Hutchinson, n.d.

Strachen, Hew, *The First World War*, Oxford: Oxford University Press, 2001, Vol. 1

Strahan, Robert W., *Command and Control of the First Modern Campaign: The German Invasion of Denmark and Norway – April, 1940*, Newport, CT: Naval War College, 1998

*Tagebuch General Jodl* for 1.2.1940 to 26.5.1940 printed in *Trial of the Major War Criminals - The International Military Tribunal at Nuremberg* (IMT), vol. XXVIII, Nuremberg,1948, pp. 397–434: donloadable from http://www.loc.gov/rr/frd/Military_Law/NT_major-war-criminals.html

Tamelander, Michael and Zetterling, Niklas, *9 April: Nazitysklands invasjon av Norge*, Oslo: Spartacus, 2000

Tarnstrom, Ronald, *The Sword of Scandinavia*, Lindsborg, KA: Trogen Books, 1996

Tarrant, V. E., *Battleship Warspite*, Annapolis: Naval Institute Press, 1991.

Taylor, Telford, *The March of Conquest: The German Victories in Western Europe, 1940*, New York, NY: Simon & Schuster, 1958

Tevnan, James and Horsley, Terence, *Norway Invaded*, Manchester: Willy Grove Press, n.d.

Thies, Klaus-Jürgen, *Weserübung*, Vol. 2, Der Zweite Weltkrieg im Kartenbild, Osnabrück: Biblio Verlag, 1991; a brilliant and not well-known series of war atlases, although they suffer from not displaying terrain

Thomas, Charles S. *The German Navy in the Nazi Era*, Annapolis: Naval Institute Press, 1990

Thomas, John Oram, *The Giant-Killers*, London: Michael Joseph, 1975

Thompson, David G., *The Norwegian Armed Forces and Defense Policy, 1905–1955*, Lampeter, Wales: Edwin Mellen, 2004

Thursfield, H. G. (ed.), *Brassey's Naval Annual 1938*, London: William Clowes, 1938

Trapp, Olaf, *Kämpfe um Narvik. Erlebnisse des Funkers Willy Schadock mit einer Nachrichten Ju-52*, Lemwerder: Stedinger, 2000

Vasco, John J. and Cornwell, Peter D., *Zerstörer*, Norfolk, VA: Jac Publishing, 1995

Vego, Milan, 'The Right Submarine for Lurking in the Littorals, *USNI Proceedings* (June, 2010), Vol. 136/6/1.288

Waller, John H., *The Unseen War in Europe*, New York, NY: Random House, 1996

Warlimont, Walter, *Im Hauptquartier der deutschen Wehrmacht 1939–1945. Grundlagen, Formen, Gestalten*, Frankfurt a. M.: B&G, 1962

Wegener, Wolfgang, *Die Seestrategie des Weltkrieges*, Berlin, 1929,; English edition, *The Naval Strategy of the World War*, introduced by H. Holger Herwig, Annapolis, MD: NIP, 1989

Weinberg, Gerhard, *A World at Arms*, Cambridge: Cambridge University Press, 2005

Wesche, Hans-Henrik, 'Die dänische Marine während des zweiten Weltkrieges', *Marine Rundschau*, LXII (1965), pp. 141–52

Whitley, M. J., *Destroyer!* , London: Arms & Armour Press, 1983

Whitley, M. J., *German Cruisers of World War Two*, Annapolis, MD: Naval Institute Press, 1985

Whitley, M. J., *German Capital Ships of World War Two*, London: Arms & Armour Press, 1989

Wiggan, Richard, *Hunt the Altmark*, London: Robert Hale, 1982

Wiggins, Melanie, *Fatal Ascent: HMS Seal, 1940*, Stroud, Gloucestershire: Spellmount, 2006

Williams, George Burns, '*Blitzkrieg and Conquest: Policy Analysis of Military and Political Decisions Preparatory to the German Attack Upon Norway, April 9. 1940*', Princeton, NJ: Yale University Dissertation, 1966

Woodward, Sir Llewellyn, *British Foreign Policy in the Second World War*, London: HMSO, 1970, Vol. 1

Wylie, Neville (ed.), *European Neutrals and Non-Belligerents during the Second World War*, Cambridge: Cambridge University Press, 2002

Zetterling, Niklas, *9. april. Nazitysklands Invasjon av Norge*, Oslo: Spartacus, 2000

Ziemke Earl F., *The German Northern Theater of Operations, 1940–1945*, Washington DC: Department of the Army Pamphlet, 1959.

## Websites

http://f16.parsimony.net/forum28300/index.htm
http://hem.fyristorg.com/robertm/norge/site-index.html
http://niehorster.orbat.com/500_eto/_40-04_scandinavia.html
http://www.chakoten.dk/dan_army_090440_1a.html
http://www.geocities.com/armdury/9_4_1940.htm
http://www.milhist.dk/besattelsen/9april/9april.html

## Wargames

Narvik (GDW)
Norway '40 (Quarterdeck Games)
Storm Over Scandinavia (GR/D)

# Index